THE NEW OXFORD ANNOTATED APOCRYPHA

New Revised
Standard Version

Fully Revised Fourth Edition

THE NEW OXFORD ANNOTATED APOCRYPHA

New Revised Standard Version

Michael D. Coogan, *Editor*

Marc Z. Brettler, Carol A. Newsom,
and Pheme Perkins, *Associate Editors*

OXFORD
UNIVERSITY PRESS

OXFORD
UNIVERSITY PRESS

Oxford New York
Auckland Cape Town Dar es Salaam Hong Kong Karachi Kuala Lumpur
Madrid Melbourne Mexico City Nairobi New Delhi Shanghai Taipei Toronto

With offices in
Argentina Austria Brazil Chile Czech Republic France Greece Guatemala
Hungary Italy Japan Poland Portugal Singapore South Korea Switzerland
Thailand Turkey Ukraine Vietnam

Published by Oxford University Press, Inc.
198 Madison Avenue, New York, New York 10016

http://www.oup.com/us

Design and typesetting by 2Krogh AS, Denmark.

10   9   8
Printed in the Netherlands

CONTRIBUTORS

Contributor	Book(s)
John R. Bartlett	1 Maccabees
Theodore A. Bergren	2 Esdras
John J. Collins	3 Maccabees
Tamara Cohn Eskenazi	1 Esdras
Matthew Goff	Baruch, Letter of Jeremiah
Lester Grabbe	Wisdom of Solomon
Daniel J. Harrington	Sirach
David Lambert	Prayer of Manasseh
Mary Joan Winn Leith	Greek Esther
Amy-Jill Levine	Additions to Daniel, Tobit
Judith H. Newman	Psalm 151
Daniel R. Schwartz	2 Maccabees
David A. de Silva	4 Maccabees
Lawrence M. Wills	Judith

Michael D. Coogan: *The Geography of the Bible*

Carol A. Newsom: *Introduction to the Apocryphal/Deuterocanonical Books; The Persian and Hellenistic Periods*

CONTENTS

The Apocryphal/Deuterocanonical Books

The Apocryphal/Deuterocanonical Books are listed here in four groupings, as follows:

Maps

ALPHABETICAL LISTING OF THE BOOKS OF THE APOCRYPHA

LIST OF ABBREVIATIONS

The following abbreviations are used for the Apocryphal/Deuterocanonical Books:

In the textual notes to the Apocryphal/Deuterocanonical Books, the following abbreviations are used:

Ant.	Josephus, *Antiquities of the Jews*
Aram	Aramaic
Ch, chs	Chapter, chapters
Cn	Correction; made where the text has suffered in transmission and the versions provide no satisfactory restoration but where the Standard Bible Committee agrees with the judgment of competent scholars as to the most probable reconstruction of the original text.
Gk	Septuagint, Greek version of the Old Testament
Heb	Hebrew of the consonantal Masoretic Text of the Old Testament
Josephus	Flavius Josephus (Jewish historian, about A.D. 37 to about 95)
Macc.	The book(s) of the Maccabees
Ms(s)	Manuscript(s)
MT	The Hebrew of the pointed Masoretic Text of the Old Testament
OL	Old Latin
Q Ms(s)	Manuscript(s) found at Qumran by the Dead Sea
Sam	Samaritan Hebrew text of the Old Testament
Syr	Syriac Version of the Old Testament
Syr H	Syriac Version of Origen's Hexapla
Tg	Targum
Vg	Vulgate, Latin Version of the Old Testament

The following abbreviations of additional ancient works are used in the introductions and annotations to the Apocryphal/Deuterocanonical Books:

		Homer, *Od.*	Homer, *Odyssey*
Ag. Ap.	Josephus, *Against Apion*	HS	Holiness School
Apoc. Bar.	*Apocalypse of Baruch*	Ignatius, *Philad.*	Ignatius, *Epistle to the Philadelphians*
Apoc. Zeph.	*Apocalypse of Zephaniah*		
Aristophanes, *Ran.*	Aristophanes, *Ranae* (Frogs)	Irenaeus, *Adv. Haer.*	Irenaeus, *Adversus omnes Haereses*
Aristotle, *Pol.*	Aristotle, *Politics*	JB	Jerusalem Bible
Aristotle, *Rh.*	Aristotle, *Rhetoric*	Jer. Sot.	Jerusalem Talmud, *Sotah* (see *y. Sot.*)
Aristotle, *Virt.*	Aristotle, *Virtues and Vices*		
2 *Bar.*	2 *Baruch* (another name for the Apocalypse of Baruch)	Josephus, *Ant.*	Josephus, *Jewish Antiquities*
		Josephus, *Ap.*	Josephus, *Against Apion*
b. B. Bat.	Babylonian Talmud, Tractate *Baba Bathra*	Josephus, *J.W.*	Josephus, *Jewish War*
		Jub.	*Jubilees*
b. Ber.	Babylonian Talmud, Tractate *Berakot*	Juvenal, *Sat.*	Juvenal, *Satires*
		KJV	King James Version (1611)
b. Eruv.	Babylonian Talmud, Tractate *Eruvim*	l	liter
b. Git.	Babylonian Talmud, Tractate *Gittin*	*Lam. Rab.*	*Lamentations Rabbah*
b. Meg.	Babylonian Talmud, Tractate *Megillah*	lit.	literally
		LXX	the Septuagint
b. Ned.	Babylonian Talmud, Tractate *Nedarim*	*m. Abot*	*Mishnah Abot*
		m. Avoda Zara	*Mishnah Avoda Zara*
b. San.	Babylonian Talmud, Tractate *Sanhedrin*	*m. Ber.*	*Mishnah Berakot*
		m. Ketub.	*Mishnah Ketubim*
b. Shabb.	Babylonian Talmud, Tractate *Shabbat*	*m. Ned.*	*Mishnah Nedarim*
		m. Ohalot	*Mishnah Ohalot*
b. Yoma	Babylonian Talmud, Tractate *Yoma*	*Midr.*	*Midrash*
CD	Cairo Genizah, Damascus Document	*Midr. Pss.*	*Midrash Psalms*
		Midr. Rab.	*Midrash Rabbah*
Cicero, *Fin.*	Cicero, *De finibus*	*m. Shabb.*	*Misnah Shabbat*
1 *Clem*	1 *Clement* (First Epistle of Clement)	*m. Sot.*	*Mishnah Sotah*
CoS	*The Context of Scripture: Canonical Compositions, Monumental Inscriptions, and Archival Documents from the Ancient World,* 3 vols. (ed. W.W. Hallo; Leiden: Brill, 1997–2002)	NIV	New International Version
		NT	New Testament
		P. Oxy.	*Oxyrhynchus Papyri*
		Philo, *De Conf.Ling.*	Philo, *De Confusione Linguarum*
		Philo, *De spec. leg.*	Philo, *De specialibus Legibus*
		Philo, *Flaccus*	Philo, *Against Flaccus*
Did.	*Didache*	Philo, *Her.*	Philo, *Quis rerum divinarum heres sit*
Dio Chrys., *Or.*	Dio Chrysostom, *Orationes*	Philo, *Leg. all.*	Philo, *Legum allegoriae*
Diod. Sic.	Diodorus of Sicily (*Library of History*)	Philo, *Leg. Gai.*	Philo, *Legatio ad Gaium*
		Philo, *Migr.*	Philo, *De migratione Abrahami*
1 *En.*	1 *Enoch*	Philo, *Opif.*	Philo, *De opificio mundi*
Ep. Arist.	*Letter of Aristeas*	Philo, *Quest. in Gen.*	Philo, *Quaestiones in Genesis*
Euripides, *Tro.*	Euripides, *Trojan Women*	Plato, *Cri.*	Plato, *Crito*
Eusebius, *Hist. eccl.*	Eusebius, *Historia ecclesiastica*	Plato, *Gorg.*	Plato, *Gorgias*
Eusebius, *Praep. Ev.*	Eusebius, *Praeparatio Evangelica*	Plato, *Phaedr.*	Plato, *Phaedrus*
Gen. Rab.	*Genesis Rabbah*	Plato, *Symp.*	Plato, *Symposium*
Gk	Greek	Pliny, *Nat. Hist.*	Pliny, *Naturalis Historia*
Hermas, *Mand.*	*Shepherd of Hermas, Mandate*	Plutarch, *Mor.*	Plutarch, *Moralia*
Hermas, *Sim.*	Shepherd of Hermas, *Similitude*	*Pro Rabirio*	Cicero, *Pro Rabirio Postuma*
Hist.	Herodotus, *Histories*	*Pss. Sol.*	*Psalms of Solomon*

11QTemple	The Temple Scroll from Qumran Cave 11 (11Q19)	*Sifre Num.*	*Sifre Numbers*
		Sib. Or.	*Sibylline Oracles*
1QH	Hodayot (Thanksgiving Hymns) from Qumran Cave 1	Sophocles, *Ant.*	Sophocles, *Antigone*
		Strom.	Clement of Alexandria, *Stromateis*
1QM	Milhamah (War Scroll) from Qumran Cave 1	Tacitus, *Hist.*	Tacitus, *Historiae*
		T. Abr.	*Testament of Abraham*
11QMelch	Melchizedek Scroll from Qumran Cave 11 (11Q13)	*T. Jos.*	*Testament of Joseph*
		T. Jud. (Test. Jud.)	*Testament of Judah*
1QpHab	Pesher to Habakkuk from Qumran Cave 1	*T. Levi*	*Testament of Levi*
		T. Moses	*Testament of Moses*
11QPs^a	The Psalms^a Scroll from Qumran Cave 11 (11Q5)	*T. Naph.*	*Testament of Naphtali*
		T. Reuben	*Testament of Reuben*
1QS	Rule of the Community (Serek Hayahad) from Qumran Cave 1	*T. Sol.*	*Testament of Solomon*
		Tg. Ps-.J.	*Targum Pseudo-Jonathan*
Quintilian, *Inst.*	*Institutio Oratoria*	*Tr. Eruv.*	Babylonian Talmud, *Tractate Eruvim* (see *b. Eruv.*)
REB	REVISED ENGLISH BIBLE		
RSV	REVISED STANDARD VERSION	*y.*	Jerusalem Talmud
Seder Olam R.	*Seder Olam Rabbah*	*y. Sot.*	Jerusalem Talmud, *Sotah*
Shab.	*Shabbat*	v., vv.	verse, verses

Note: The abbreviation "Q," unless specified as "Quelle" ("Source") for the posited New Testament document of non-Markan common material in Matthew and Luke, refers to Qumran, and manuscripts from Qumran are identified by the cave number, which precedes the Q, and the official manuscript number, which follows it; thus, 1Q34 = Manuscript 34 from Cave 1 at Qumran; 4Q174 = Manuscript 174 from Cave 4; etc.

THE EDITORS' PREFACE

For nearly five decades *The Oxford Annotated Bible* and its successor *The New Oxford Annotated Bible* have served generations of readers and students as a study Bible. That extraordinary longevity alone is eloquent testimony to its success. This new edition retains the format and features that have proven so attractive. At the same time, the field of biblical studies has not been static, and this edition is a thoroughgoing revision of the previous ones. In particular, the editors have recruited contributors from a wide diversity of backgrounds and of scholarly approaches to the biblical traditions. In order to present this diversity more fully, the introductions to the biblical books, the maps and charts, the annotations, and the study materials at the end of the book have been significantly enhanced and lengthened since the third edition.

We recognize that no single interpretation or approach is sufficient for informed reading of these ancient texts, and have aimed at inclusivity of interpretive strategies. On a great number of issues there is a consensus among scholars, and the contributors have been encouraged to present such consensus when it exists. Where it has broken down, and has not yet re-formed, alternatives are mentioned. Moreover, in order to respect the canonical status of various parts of the Bible for different communities, and to avoid privileging any book or part of the Bible, we have kept both introductions and annotations roughly proportionate to the length of the books, while recognizing that some parts require more elaboration than others.

The editorial process was collaborative. Each contribution was read in its entirety by at least three of the editors, and revised with a view toward consistency of tone, coherence of approach, and completeness of coverage. We have also wanted to allow the contributors' own voices to be heard, and we have avoided imposing a superficial uniformity of style and approach. Throughout, we have kept the needs of the general audience firmly in mind during the editorial stages, and our aim has been a congruity of experience as a reader turns from book to book and from section to section of the finished volume.

CONTENTS OF THE ANNOTATED BIBLE

The biblical text stands apart from any editorial contributions, in both placement and format. This will enable anyone who wishes to do so to read the text unprejudiced by editorial judgments.

The footnotes that are part of the New Revised Standard Version (indicated by an italic superscript letter after the word or phrase in question) are printed at the bottom of the right-hand column of the biblical text on each page where they occur. In these notes, divergent textual readings and alternate translations are printed in italics. The phrase "Other ancient authorities read" means that the reading (i.e., the wording) of the passage is different in various manuscripts and early versions, and the word "Or" signifies that the Hebrew, Aramaic, Greek, or Latin text permits an alternate rendering besides the one given in the text.

Each book is preceded by its own introduction, which sketches the book's structure, main themes, literary history, and historical context, as well as broad lines of interpretation; they therefore present a clear overview and guide to reading. For this edition we have not only made the introductions longer than in previous editions but have also organized them so that they cover the same topics in the same order.

At the bottom of each page of the biblical text, in a different font from it and in a single column, are the annotations. The annotations are just that, notes rather than paraphrase or commentary, although these genres admittedly overlap. They are intended to enhance the reader's understanding of the text, providing essential information, background, and interpretation, rather than only summarizing what it says. The boldface headings delineate the larger units of the book and provide a detailed consecutive outline of its contents. The word or phrase being glossed is given in italics. Quotation marks are used for words quoted from elsewhere in the Bible as well as for transliterations of ancient languages. Since we desire each book to stand on its own, as much as possible the annotations are self-contained. We have thus tried to avoid both cross-references to fuller discussions elsewhere, and the misconception that a book or larger part of the Bible is merely a perfunctory reworking of other material, or that a particular passage can only be understood fully in the light of later biblical traditions. At the same time, we recognize that the Bible is often a progressive text, and that later parts of the Bible often contain the oldest interpretations of earlier traditions. The best starting point for interpreting a particular passage is often another passage, and we have encouraged contributors to point out interconnections in the biblical material by means of cross-references. (The cross-references that end with "n." refer to the annotation as well as to the biblical text.)

A listing of abbreviations for the books of the Apocrypha used in this edition is found on p. viii. The chapter and verse divisions in a reference are separated by a period; thus, Tob 3.8 refers to the book of Tobit, chapter 3, verse 8. Inclusive references are used for both chapters and verses; thus, Sir 1–15 refers to the first fifteen chapters of the book of Sirach; 1 Macc 11.33–36 to verses 33 through 36 of chapter 11 of the letter to the First Maccabees; and so forth. When a book of the Apocrypha is referred to within an annotation on that book, the name of the book is not repeated unless there is ambiguity.

In keeping with our general desire to take account of the diversity of the users of this study Bible, we have cited all dates in the notes as BCE or CE ("Before the Common Era" and "Common Era") instead of BC or AD ("Before Christ" and "Anno Domini" ["in the year of the Lord"]), which imply a Christian view of the status of Jesus of Nazareth. Use of the title "Old Testament" for those books here designated as "the Hebrew Bible" is confined to instances expressing the historical view of various Christian interpreters. These conventions are followed in the study materials that we have produced; the translation has its own conventions, which we are not at liberty to alter.

ACKNOWLEDGMENTS

It remains to express our gratitude, first and above all to the contributors, whose learning has made this a work of which we are immensely proud, and whose uncommon patience with the editorial process made our task light. Donald Kraus, Executive Editor in the Bible department at Oxford University Press, U.S.A., has guided this edition from its inception with wisdom and tact. Elisabeth Nelson carried out with efficiency and accuracy a wide variety of editorial tasks that are needed in a project of this complexity. Mary Sutherland prepared the text for composition, and 2Krogh AS, Denmark, designed and typeset the entire text. We thank them all.

MICHAEL D. COOGAN, MARC Z. BRETTLER,
CAROL A. NEWSOM, PHEME PERKINS
August, 2009

TO THE READER

When the King James or Authorized Version of the Bible was published in 1611, it contained, between the Old and the New Testaments, the books of the Apocrypha. These are books and portions of books that appear in the Latin Vulgate, either as part of the Old Testament or as an appendix, but are not in the Hebrew Bible. With the exception of 2 Esdras, these books appear also in the Greek version of the Old Testament that is known as the Septuagint.

In the course of time printers began to issue editions of the King James Bible without the books of the Apocrypha, and when the American Standard Version of the Bible was published in 1901, it did not include the Apocrypha. After the Revised Standard Version of the Bible was published in 1952, a request came from the General Convention of the Protestant Episcopal Church that the Standard Bible Committee undertake also the revision of the English translation of the Apocrypha. This work was accomplished in 1957. It was on the basis of this version that the text of a "Common Bible" (approved by both Roman Catholics and Protestants, was issued in 1973. Subsequently, in order to include all the texts accepted as Deuterocanonical by Eastern Orthodox Churches, the Standard Bible Committee prepared a version of 3 and 4 Maccabees and Psalm 151. These were issued in 1977, and the expanded edition of the Apocryphal/Deuterocanonical Books was endorsed by representatives of Orthodox communions. Since the contents of the collection known as Deuterocanonical Books vary among the churches that recognize them as authoritative, in the interest of clear identification they have been arranged in the New Revised Standard Version in four sections (see the Table of Contents).

For the translation of the Apocryphal/Deuterocanonical Books the Committee made use of a number of texts. In the case of most of the books the basic text was the standard edition of the Greek Septuagint prepared by Alfred Rahlfs and published by the Wurttemberg Bible Society (Stuttgart, 1935). For several of the books the more recently published individual volumes of Göttingen Septuagint project were utilized. For the book of Tobit it was decided to follow the form of the Greek text found in codex Sinaiticus (supported as it is by evidence from Qumran); where this text is defective, it was supplemented and corrected by other Greek manuscripts. For the three Additions to Daniel (namely, Susanna, the Prayer of Azariah and the Song of the Three Jews, and Bel and the Dragon) the Committee continued to use the Greek version attributed to Theodotion (the so-called "Theodotion-Daniel"). In translating Ecclesiasticus (Sirach), while constant reference was made to the Hebrew fragments of a large portion of this book (those discovered at Qumran and Masada as well as those recovered from the Cairo Geniza), the Committee generally followed the Greek text (including verse numbers) published by Joseph Ziegler in the Göttingen Septuagint (1965). But in many places the Committee has translated the Hebrew text when this provides a reading that is clearly superior to the Greek; the Syriac and Latin versions were also consulted throughout and occasionally adopted. The basic text adopted in rendering 2 Esdras is the Latin version given in the Biblia Sacra, edited by Robert Weber (Stuttgart, 1971). This was supplemented by consulting the Latin text as edited by R.L. Bensly (1895) and by Bruno Violet (1910), as well as the several Oriental versions of 2 Esdras, namely, the Syriac, Ethiopic, Arabic (two forms, referred to as Arabic 1 and Arabic 2), Armenian, and Georgian versions. Finally, since the Additions to the Book of Esther are disjointed and unintelligible as they stand in most editions of the Apocrypha, we have provided them with their original context by translating the whole of the Greek version of Esther from Robert Hanhart's Göttingen edition (1983).

For the Committee,
BRUCE M. METZGER

THE GEOGRAPHY OF THE BIBLE

The geographical territory encompassed by the Bible (if one includes all identifiable places that are mentioned in it) includes most countries that border the Mediterranean Sea as well as those to its east. The majority of the narratives of the Hebrew Bible and the Apocrypha, as well as the Gospels in the New Testament, are set in that subregion of the Middle East known as the Levant and now governed by Lebanon, Syria, Jordan, Israel, and the Palestinian Authority. Egypt to the southwest, Asia Minor (modern Turkey) to the north, and Mesopotamia (largely modern Iraq) and Persia (Iran) to the northeast are also part of the biblical landscape.

In Mesopotamia—the Greek term for the region between the Euphrates and Tigris Rivers (see color Maps 6 and 14 at the end of this volume)—as in Egypt, urban civilization developed by the fourth millennium BCE in the river valleys that provided the essential water for a region where rainfall was at best seasonal and at worst, especially in the case of Egypt, insufficient for agriculture. But the regular summer flooding of the Nile Valley enabled the early and continuous existence of a remarkably long-lasting culture in Egypt, which because of its proximity to the Middle East was an important player in that region's history and the locale for several episodes in biblical narrative, most notably the Exodus. In Mesopotamia the inhabitants had harnessed the two rivers to provide, by means of an elaborate irrigation system, sufficient water for agriculture as well as for consumption. The successive imperial powers that originated in Mesopotamia were able to use this productive region as a base for expansion, especially to the west, over which they exercised control throughout most of the first millennium BCE, until the Hellenistic period.

Although surrounded by vast deserts, there is a narrow stretch of land where agriculture can flourish, which extends from the Nile Valley around to the Persian Gulf. The western part of this "fertile crescent," the Levant, has the same environment as much of the rest of the region adjacent to the Mediterranean, which today as for the last several millennia is characterized by almost ideal growing conditions for grapes and olives and for raising sheep and goats; grains and legumes and other fruits can also be grown in much of the region. Its climate is moderate, without excessively high or low temperatures for the most part, and with abundant rainfall that occurs mainly during the winter months. Jerusalem, for example, receives on average about 22 in (550 mm) of rain annually, most of it falling between November and February, with January being the rainiest month. Higher elevations to

the north receive still more rainfall, and the southern and easternmost regions considerably less.

Within the Levant itself, the primary focus of biblical narratives, there is a wide variety of environments, the result of the geological substructure of the region, which presents dramatic changes in a relatively small area. Moving from west to east, the Mediterranean coast is occupied by a coastal plain that is about 15 mi (25 km) wide in the south but narrows as one moves north. It is interrupted by Mount Carmel, which juts into it, and virtually disappears in northern Israel and Lebanon. The coast itself has several excellent harbors in the north, from which the Canaanites and their successors the Phoenicians conducted a flourishing maritime trade. Farther south the coast is relatively even, and there are few natural harbors. Phoenician influence eventually extended to such port cities as Acco, Dor, Joppa, and Ashkelon, and in the late first century Herod the Great constructed an impressive artificial harbor at Caesarea. Along the coastal plain was a major route used by traders and by armies of conquest between Egypt and Damascus. This route ran to the point where the coast narrows below Mount Carmel, from which passes led from the coastal plain to the Jezreel (Esdraelon) Valley; from there, several routes could be taken to the northeast.

Adjacent to the coastal plain in the south is an uplift of smaller, gentler hills called "the Shephelah" ("lowland"). As the natural western boundary of the kingdom of Judah in the Iron Age, and of other entities in the same region before and after, it was protected by such important cities as Lachish and Gezer. The Shephelah forms the foothills of the mountainous region immediately to its east. This is the "hill country" of the biblical writers, with higher elevations to the north. For example, Jerusalem, about 35 mi (55 km) east of the Mediterranean, is 2,500 ft (760 m) above sea level, and many mountains in northern Galilee have elevations of over 3,300 ft (1,000 m). The highest peak in the region is Mount Hermon, which at 9,200 ft (2,800 m) is snow-covered year-round. The hill country is the setting for many of the key locales in biblical narrative, including the relatively inaccessible sites of Jerusalem, the capital of the kingdom of Judah (later Judea), and Samaria, the capital of the Northern Kingdom of Israel and later of the province with the same name. This central mountainous ridge is bisected by the broad, fertile Jezreel Valley, the major route to the interior and hence the location of important ancient cities, including Jokneam, Megiddo, Taanach, Ibleam, and Jezreel. Mount Tabor rises from the floor of the Jezreel Valley in splendid isolation to an elevation of 1,929 ft (588 m) above sea level. The village of Nazareth, home of Jesus, is in the hills on the northern side of the valley.

To the north of the Jezreel Valley lies Galilee. Because of its abundant springs, Galilee was dotted by settlements from prehistoric times, but it plays little role in biblical narratives until the end of the first millennium BCE, when it is the setting both for some of the campaigns of the Maccabees and, in the early first century CE, of the ministry of Jesus in the Gospels.

Just east of this central mountainous region is the Rift Valley. This major depression in the earth's crust extends from southern Turkey into East Africa; in Israel and Jordan it is almost entirely below sea level. Included in it are the Huleh Basin in northern Galilee, 230 ft (70 m) above sea level, where the site of Hazor was a major fortified city from early in the second millennium BCE until its destruction by the Assyrians in 732 BCE. Some 12 mi (20 km) south of Lake Huleh is the Sea of Chinnereth, or the Sea of Galilee (also called the Sea of Tiberias), a large freshwater lake about 12 mi (20 km) long that fills the valley. It lies 210 m (700 ft) below sea level, and is fed by the Jordan River, which flows into it from the north. It is habitat to nearly two dozen species of fish, and the fishing industry has been an important part of the local economy since prehistoric times. Many of the events narrated in the Gospels are set in the many towns and cities near the lake; the region was a center of resistance against the Romans during the First Jewish Revolt of 66–73 CE.

The Jordan River continues its flow south from the Sea of Galilee 65 mi (105 km) to the Dead Sea. The valley itself is about 12 mi (20 km) wide and is entirely below sea level, with a semitropical climate that produces lush vegetation, even though because of its low elevation it receives relatively little rain. Important cities in the valley include Beth-shan (later Scythopolis) in the north and Jericho in the south. The valley was another important north-south route, especially during the Roman period, when Jews often avoided the district controlled by the Samaritans between Galilee and Judea.

The Dead Sea, lying 1,300 ft (400 m) below sea level, is the lowest point on the land mass of the earth. Because of evaporation due to high temperatures (a record 124°F [51°C] was measured here), the composition of the water is about 25 percent salt and other minerals, making organic life impossible and giving this lake its ancient name, "the salt sea" (Num 34.3,12; NRSV "Dead Sea"). The

desolate region that surrounds it is the narrative setting for the legendary cities of Sodom and Gomorrah. On its western shore are Qumran, where the Dead Sea Scrolls were found, and Masada, a palace constructed by Herod that was the last Jewish outpost to be captured in the First Jewish Revolt.

East of the Rift Valley there is a rapid rise to the relatively level Transjordanian plateau to the east, with the elevation of modern Amman (ancient Rabbah, later Philadelphia) at ca. 2,700 ft (820 m) about average. This region also receives sufficient rainfall to sustain agriculture and, moreover, is watered by two tributaries of the Jordan, the Yarmuk and the Jabbok, and by the Arnon, which flows into the Dead Sea. The northern part of the plateau, biblical Bashan, was famous for its cattle and for its oak forests, and in the Hellenistic and Roman periods was the location of several of the cities of the Decapolis. Traversing the Transjordanian plateau from south to north is another major route, called in the Bible the "King's Highway" (Num 20.17), used throughout antiquity as a conduit for the incense and spice trade from Arabia to Damascus. East of the plateau is a vast desert region, a continuation of the Arabian desert that extends northward to the Euphrates Valley, and thus limits the Fertile Crescent on both east and west. Apart from a few oases, especially Tadmor (later Palmyra) northeast of Damascus, this desert was mostly uninhabited in historic times.

South of the hill country of Judah lies the Negeb, a region of limited rainfall and hence marginal agriculture. The city of Beer-sheba is located in the extreme northern Negeb, just south of the Judean hill country. The Negeb merges into the Sinai peninsula, which is formed by the two northern arms of the Red Sea, separating the Sinai from the North African desert to its west and the Arabian desert to its east.

The small size of this region is out of proportion to its importance in ancient times and to the importance of the biblical texts which are set in it. West of the Jordan, the traditional limits of ancient Israel were Dan in the north and Beer-sheba in the south, separated by a distance of about 150 mi (240 km). Between these two cities, and between the Mediterranean and the Rift Valley, is a region with an area approximately the same as that of the state of Vermont. From another perspective, Jerusalem is about 35 mi (55 km) east of the Mediterranean and 16 mi (25 km) west of the Dead Sea. In the right conditions, both bodies of water are visible from Jerusalem's hills.

CULTURAL CONTEXTS
THE PERSIAN AND HELLENISTIC PERIODS

THE PERSIAN PERIOD (539–333 BCE)

The Babylonian exile and the period of Persian domination that followed was a time of great transformation for Judean institutions, religious practices, and culture, but it was equally a time in which the fundamental continuity with preexilic traditions was reaffirmed and secured. When Nebuchadrezzar put down the rebellion of Judah in 586 BCE, he exiled to Babylonia a portion of the population, including the ruling class and the skilled artisans. Some, however, remained in Judah, where a subsistence economy was soon reestablished. Although the system of regular sacrifices at the Temple was disrupted, the ruined Temple remained a focus for religious observances. The book of Lamentations may preserve liturgical poems used on days commemorating the destruction of Jerusalem and its Temple. Little is known about the circumstances of those who went into exile, although it appears that the exiles were settled in many local communities in Babylonia, where they were able to oversee their own internal and cultural affairs under the leadership of Jewish elders and prophets (see Ezek; Isa 40–55).

The conquest of Babylon by the Persian king Cyrus the Great in 539 BCE brought significant changes. In keeping with his policy of respecting the various deities worshiped throughout the empire, a decree by Cyrus in 538 (see Ezra 1.1–4; 6.1–5) authorized the rebuilding of the Temple in Jerusalem and the return of the Temple vessels captured by Nebuchadrezzar. In addition, Cyrus allowed any of the exiles who wished to return to Judah to do so. Within the exilic community in Babylon the anonymous prophet known as "Second Isaiah" (Isa 40–55) strongly supported Cyrus and urged the exiles to return to Judah. Although the historical sources are few and not always easy to interpret, it appears that only a small minority of the exiles and their descendants returned to Judah, most choosing to remain in Babylonia. This latter group became the nucleus of a large and highly significant Jewish Diaspora community (Jews of "the dispersion," that is, living outside the promised land), which strongly influenced the development of Judaism and Jewish culture during the following centuries.

Despite the decree of Cyrus, the Temple in Jerusalem was not rebuilt until 520–515 BCE. The reasons for the delay were various. Persian control over the western territories may actually have been tentative until after the Persians conquered Egypt in 525. The economy of Yehud (the name by which the Persian province of Judah was known) was weak, and there appears to have been friction between the population that had remained in the land and the small but powerful group who returned from exile with the authorization and financial backing of the Persian king. Conflicts with the neighboring territories of Samaria and Geshur and Ammon in Transjordan also complicated the situation. Within the Bible the prophetic books of Haggai and Zechariah and portions of Ezra 1–6 refer to this period, but these sources have to be read and interpreted critically, for they are neither consistent with one another nor easy to understand on their own terms. At least during the early part of Persian rule the governors of Judah appear to have been prominent Jews from the Diaspora community, one of whom, Zerubbabel, was actually a member of the Davidic royal family. The province of Yehud itself was very small, consisting of Jerusalem and the territory surrounding it within a radius of about 15–20 mi (24–32 km).

Once the Temple was rebuilt, it became the nucleus of the restored community, and consequently a focus of conflict (Isa 56–66; Mal). The high priestly family, which had also returned from the Diaspora, became very powerful, and at least on occasion was in conflict with the governor appointed by the Persian king. Although the details are often not clear, there appears to have been continuing conflict during the fifth century between those Jews whose ancestors had been in exile and those whose ancestors had remained in the land. Those who returned from the Diaspora styled themselves the "children of the exile" and referred rather contemptuously to the rest as "people of the land," as though their very status as Jews was in question. In fact, the question of the limits of the community was one of the most contentious issues of the period, reflected both in the controversy over mixed marriages between Jewish men and ethnically foreign women (Ezra 10; Neh 13) and also in conflicts within the Jewish community over who had the right to claim the traditional identity as descendants of "Abraham" and "Israel" (see Isa 63.16 and more generally "Third Isaiah," Isa 56–66). Although the conflicts between various contending groups in early Persian period Yehud are largely cast in religious terms, there is no question that they were also in part socioeconomic (see Neh 5). All of these conflicts and efforts toward redefinition of the community, however, took place within the reality of Persian imperial control. Thus it is not by accident that the two most prominent figures involved in various reforms of mid-fifth century Yehud, Ezra and Nehemiah, were Diaspora Jews of high standing, carrying out tasks that had been specifically authorized by the Persian kings.

Because this was a period of self-conscious reconstruction, it was also a time of immense literary activity, as traditional materials were collected, revised, and edited, and new works composed. Although much of the Pentateuch may have existed in various forms during the time of the monarchy, it was probably reworked during the Persian period into something close to its final form. Indeed, some scholars have suggested that this revision may have been undertaken under the sponsorship of the Persian government, reflecting Persia's interest in achieving stability throughout its empire by means of religious and legal reforms in the provinces. Although a history of Israel and Judah known as the Deuteronomistic History (Deut through 2 Kings) had been composed during the latter years of the monarchy and updated during the exile, a new version of that history, 1–2 Chronicles, was prepared during the Persian period (ca. 350 BCE). It clearly reflects the concerns of the postexilic community, focusing almost exclusively on the history of Judah and giving particular emphasis to the institution of the Temple. The books of Ezra and Nehemiah interpret events from the decree of Cyrus in 538 until the late fifth century.

In addition to the prophetic books composed at this time (Isa 56–66, Hag, Zech, Mal, and perhaps Joel), there is evidence that the texts of older prophets were also edited and reinterpreted. Psalmody had been an important element of worship at the First Temple but appears to have taken on an even more significant role in the Second Temple. Although the expansion and revision of the book of Psalms may have continued until well into the Hellenistic or even Roman period, an important shaping of the psalter, perhaps including its division into five "books," was part of Persian period activity. Wisdom writing, too, flourished during this time. The book of Job, parts of the book of Proverbs, and perhaps Ecclesiastes were likely composed then.

THE HELLENISTIC PERIOD (333–363 BCE)

The westward expansion of the Persian Empire into the area of Asia Minor had brought it into conflict with Greece, since many of the cities of Asia Minor that came under Persian control had been founded and populated by Greeks. Twice the Persians had even invaded the Greek

mainland but were defeated on both occasions. Eventually, Philip of Macedon developed a plan to free the Greek cities of Asia Minor from Persian domination. Although he died before he could undertake the campaign, it was taken up by his son Alexander the Great in 334 BCE. Alexander, however, did not stop with the accomplishment of that initial goal. In 333 he continued down the Phoenician coast, subduing any city that resisted, conquered Egypt, then turned to the Persian heartland, defeating Darius III, the last Persian emperor, in 331. Alexander continued his conquest into the eastern reaches of the Persian Empire before returning in 324 to Babylon, which he apparently intended to establish as the capital of the empire he now controlled. He died in 323 before he could successfully organize his enormous territory. After Alexander's death, his generals fought for control of portions of the empire. By 301 an agreement gave Egypt to Ptolemy and Mesopotamia and Syria-Palestine to Seleucus. Ptolemy, however, occupied Palestine and southern Syria. Through a series of five wars extending over more than a hundred years, the Ptolemaic kings managed to hold onto their Palestinian territory, finally losing it to the Seleucids in 198 BCE.

Jerusalem had surrendered to Alexander in 333 and was relatively undisturbed by the events of his conquest. Samaria, too, surrendered but rebelled in 332 and was severely punished, its inhabitants killed or sold into slavery, and the city refounded as a Macedonian military colony. Documents belonging to a group of Samaritans who fled and were later tracked down and killed by Alexander's troops have been excavated from the Wadi Daliyeh in the Jordan Valley. In contrast to the relatively settled conditions following Alexander's conquest, however, the dispute between the Ptolemies and the Seleucids over control of Palestine had serious consequences for Jerusalem and Judea. Not only did the wars sometimes affect Judean territory, but the nation's leaders had to make difficult choices concerning which power to support. The conflict between pro-Ptolemaic and pro-Seleucid factions within the Judean community was a significant factor in internal politics during the third century BCE.

Although the high priest was the primary representative of the Judeans, the Ptolemaic system of government and taxation had significant effects on the power structure of the country. The Ptolemies considered their territories primarily as a source of revenue. Rather than collecting funds directly, they employed "tax farmers," often local persons who bought the right to collect taxes for a specified area. Their profit was the difference between the amount they raised and the amount they had pledged to the government. Some of these positions were quite lucrative. Moreover, the Ptolemies also engaged prominent landowners to keep the peace as the heads of locally organized military villages. The Jewish historian Josephus preserves a long account of the Tobiad family, which served the Ptolemaic government in both capacities. From his lively narrative one has a sense not only of the power and wealth such positions could afford but also of the dangers and conflict they often entailed.

Culturally, the most significant effect of Ptolemaic rule was the establishment of a large Jewish Diaspora community in Egypt, centered in the new city of Alexandria, founded by Alexander the Great. Jews had often migrated to Egypt during times of economic or political trouble (see Jer 42–44). In the fifth century a Jewish military colony in the service of the Persian army was established at Elephantine (near modern Aswan). They had their own temple, though they remained in correspondence with Jerusalem concerning various religious matters, including the proper celebration of Passover and assistance in securing Persian permission for the rebuilding of the Elephantine temple after it was destroyed by local Egyptians. The various Aramaic documents found there (letters, contracts, marriage documents, records of legal disputes, etc.) provide an important glimpse into the daily life of this Jewish community in Egypt. Among the papyri was a copy of the book of Ahikar, a legendary story about an official in the Assyrian court at the time of Sennacherib and Esarhaddon (late eighth to early seventh century). Although the story was not Jewish in origin, it became popular among the Jews. The book of Tobit in the Apocrypha makes reference to Ahikar, even calling him Tobit's nephew (Tob 1.21–22).

The Hellenistic-era Egyptian Diaspora, however, was much larger and more influential than the previous small communities of Jews living in Egypt. Its origins are not clear, but during the initial Ptolemaic conquest of Palestine, Ptolemy I apparently captured Jerusalem and took many prisoners back to Egypt, where they settled. Later many other Jews migrated there, presumably for economic reasons. The community continued to grow, both in numbers and in prosperity, until in the Roman period the Jewish population numbered in the hundreds of thousands, including many wealthy and prominent families.

By the middle of the third century BCE the largely Greek-speaking Jewish community in Egypt had translated the books of the Torah (Genesis–Deuteronomy) into Greek, and over the next century or so, the other books of the Hebrew Bible were also translated. A legendary account of this project is contained in the Letter of Aristeas. According to that narrative, the impetus for the project came from the king himself, Ptolemy II Philadelphus (285–246 BCE), who wished to have a copy for the library of Alexandria. Seventy-two Jewish translators were brought to Egypt from Jerusalem for the task; hence the translation came to be known as the Septuagint, from the Greek word for "seventy." Scholars largely reject this account as unhistorical and maintain that the translation was undertaken for the religious needs of a Jewish community that no longer understood Hebrew. (See the essays "The Canons of the Bible" and "Hebrew Bible: Texts and Versions" for more information about the Septuagint.)

In addition to the translation of the scriptures, the Jewish Diaspora in Egypt produced a rich and varied literature in Greek. One should not assume, however, that every Jewish writing in Greek originated in Alexandria, for during the Hellenistic period Greek became the most important international language. Educated Jews in Palestine and in the eastern Diaspora were nearly as likely to speak Greek as their counterparts in Egypt. Nevertheless, Alexandria remained unparalleled in the richness of its intellectual culture.

Throughout the Hellenistic world the increasing contact between different ethnic groups led to a new self-consciousness within communities about their own historical traditions and how these traditions related to those of other peoples. Thus historiographical writing, from the scholarly to the popular, became an important type of literary activity. In the late third century BCE an Alexandrian Jew named Demetrius investigated the chronologies of the biblical tradition, attempting to explain apparent contradictions and logical inconsistencies. A more entertaining work is Eupolemus's *Concerning the Kings in Judea*. A friend of Judas Maccabeus (see below), Eupolemus retold the biblical narrative with many embellishments and legendary details in an attempt to glorify Israel's traditions and accomplishments. In Eupolemus's history Moses appears as a culture-bringer, the inventor of the alphabet, which the Phoenicians and the Greeks later borrowed. Eupolemus particularly emphasizes the power and influence of the Israelite kingdom under David and Solomon, as well as the splendor of the Solomonic Temple. Not only was the Temple decorated with gifts from the kings of Tyre and Egypt, but Solomon reciprocated, sending a golden pillar to the temple of Zeus in Tyre.

The tendency to make connections between one's own traditions and those of other ethnic groups and to claim priority in the arts of civilization is reflected in the highly legendary history written in the second century BCE by an anonymous Samaritan. He identifies Enoch with Greek Atlas and claims that Abraham was the inventor of astrology, which he taught to the Egyptians when he sojourned there. A similar tendency is evident in the work of Artapanus. In his history Moses becomes the inventor of the technologies basic to civilization.

Moreover, this Moses serves as a general in the Egyptian army, organizes Egyptian religion, and comes to be treated virtually as a god by the Egyptians, who identify him with Hermes (the Greek equivalent of the Egyptian god Thoth). The interest of Egyptian Jews in the biblical figure of Joseph is reflected in the romance, *Joseph and Asenath*, which tells the story of Joseph's marriage to the Egyptian noblewoman Asenath. She is depicted as a model convert to Judaism, and the story depicts some of the complications that attended Jewish-Gentile relations in Hellenistic Egypt.

Jewish poetic works composed in Greek also reflect a blending of cultural traditions. The Hellenistic genre of poetry praising cities and countries is represented in the work of Theodotus and Philo the Epic Poet, who wrote poems about Shechem and Jerusalem, respectively. Even more ambitious was the work of Ezekiel the Tragedian, whose play *The Exodus* retold the account of Ex 1–15 in a style influenced by the Greek dramatists Aeschylus and Euripides.

Greek philosophy, too, left its imprint on Hellenistic Jewish culture. Already in the second century BCE an Alexandrian Jew named Aristobulus produced a philosophical commentary on the Torah in which he claimed that the law of Moses anticipated many of the fundamental tenets of Greek philosophy and that the Greek philosophers Pythagoras, Socrates, and Plato derived their ideas from the Jewish law. Written toward the end of the Hellenistic period, the Wisdom of Solomon continues the biblical tradition of wisdom books like Proverbs but incorporates many elements of Greek rhetoric, philosophy, and literary style.

Less is known about the Jews of the eastern Diaspora who remained under Seleucid control than about the Jews of Egypt and Palestine, but it appears that peoples of various ethnic groups had access to economic and political advancement within the Seleucid Empire. Several writings from this time—Tobit, Dan 1–6, and Esther—suggest something of the outlook of Jews in the eastern Diaspora. Written originally in Hebrew or Aramaic and later enlarged when they were translated into Greek, these books are works of fiction, edifying entertainments that tell the stories of Jews who achieved high status in foreign courts, were threatened by jealous rivals, and yet succeeded in securing personal power and the good will of the king. Though the stories are all set in the pre-Hellenistic period (Tobit in the Assyrian Empire, Daniel in the Babylonian exile, and Esther in the Persian court), they were probably written during the Seleucid period. While they acknowledge that faithful Jews may be vulnerable because of their religion, on the whole these are optimistic stories with a positive view of the Gentile kings.

The eastern Diaspora was also the conduit for important religious developments that arose from the contact between Judaism and the religions of Babylon and Persia. This influence is most clearly seen in the development of apocalyptic literature. Parts of the book of *1 Enoch* composed in the third century BCE reflect astronomical lore and traditions about antediluvian sages that derive from Babylonian sources. Although it is more difficult to trace the path of influence in its earliest stages, the dualistic religious beliefs of Persian Zoroastrianism almost certainly contributed to the development of Jewish apocalyptic thought and to some of the ideas of the sectarians at Qumran.

The eventual triumph of the Seleucid kingdom over the Ptolemies in the fifth Syrian war (198 BCE) obviously had a greater significance for the Jews of Judea than for those of Egypt. The Seleucid ruler Antiochus III treated the Judeans generously in appreciation for the support he received from the pro-Seleucid faction, granting an allowance for the Temple and various tax concessions, as well as confirming the Judeans' right to live "according to the laws of their country." Although relations began well, the way the Seleucid Empire governed its territories set the stage for a terrible conflict. Unlike the Ptolemaic system of centralized government administered with the cooperation of local leaders, the Seleucid regime was more decentralized. It derived some unity, however, from a network of Greek cities established throughout the empire. These were not necessarily ethnically Greek but were cities that had received a charter to organize as a *polis*, the Greek form of city government. Cultural prestige and economic advantages often led the leadership of Near Eastern cities to request such a charter.

The events leading up to the conflict between Judea and the Seleucid king Antiochus IV Epiphanes (175–164 BCE) are complex and not fully understood. In part they involved a struggle for succession to the high priesthood and the attempts of various contenders to secure the support of the king by paying him large sums of money. The first of the contenders, Jason, also paid to have Jerusalem established as a Greek *polis*, Antioch at Jerusalem. Neither of these acts in itself seems to have aroused much opposition in Jerusalem. The conflict was not a cultural conflict between Judaism and Hellenism, for Palestinian Jews had already incorporated significant elements of Hellenistic culture, which they considered quite compatible with their religious identity.

The crisis was sparked by the attempt by another contender, Menelaus, to buy the office of high priest. When he promised the king more than he could pay, he attempted to raise the money by taking golden vessels from the Temple. At this, a riot broke out in Jerusalem. Subsequent fighting between the forces of Jason and Menelaus convinced Antiochus that Judea was in revolt, and he retook the city and plundered the Temple, either in 169 or 168. Sometime later there were further disturbances, and Antiochus sent Syrian troops, which remained garrisoned in Jerusalem. Whether the status of Jerusalem at this point was a *polis* or a military colony is uncertain, but in either case in 167 the Temple was reorganized to accommodate the religious needs of the Syrian troops. The Temple was dedicated to Zeus Olympius, the Greek name for the Syrian god Baal Shamem, and an altar established for sacrifice to him. Though Menelaus continued to preside as high priest, most Jews considered these actions to have profaned the Temple. In addition, the traditional practice of Judaism was suppressed by Antiochus, perhaps with the cooperation of Menelaus. Since religious persecution was virtually unknown in antiquity, it is difficult to know how Antiochus understood this repression and what he hoped to accomplish by it. Its actual result was to ignite the resistance known as the Maccabean revolt.

The Hasmoneans, Mattathias and his sons Judas Maccabeus, Jonathan, Simon, John, and Eleazar, were the leaders of the revolt. Although Judas managed to retake control of the Temple in 164 (its rededication being the occasion for the institution of the festival of Hanukkah), it was not until 142 that the last of the Seleucid army was expelled and actual independence was secured by Simon. From then until the Roman conquest of Judea in 63 BCE the small kingdom was ruled by the Hasmonean family, which in addition to being kings also assumed the office of high priest.

Religious and cultural life in Judea during the Seleucid and Hasmonean periods was rich and varied, with a remarkable quantity of literature produced in Hebrew, Aramaic, and to some extent in Greek. Sirach (Ecclesiasticus), Jesus Ben Sira's book of wisdom teachings, was probably composed in Hebrew about 180 BCE. Though largely traditional, it embodies several innovations: Ben Sira's identification of wisdom with the law of Moses, his praise of the contemporary high priest Simon II, and his own explicit claim to authorship. Ben Sira disapproved of apocalyptic speculation, but the crisis under Antiochus IV produced an upsurge in apocalyptic writings, not only Dan 7–12, but also 1 Enoch 83–90 and *The Testament of Moses*. After the establishment of the Hasmonean monarchy, a supporter of the dynasty composed an account of the war in Hebrew (1 Maccabees), modeling it after the earlier books of Kings and Chronicles. An Egyptian Jewish writer, Jason of Cyrene, also wrote a history of the war in Greek (2 Maccabees), which was strongly influenced by forms of Hellenistic history writing.

Our knowledge of the literature of this time has been greatly increased by the discovery of the Dead Sea Scrolls at Qumran. Although this library was the property of a sectarian religious group related to the Essenes, it contained many Hebrew and Aramaic texts that were not sectarian compositions. Several of these scrolls contain noncanonical psalms, blessings, and other liturgical material. There are also many examples of what is called "the rewritten Bible," fairly free retellings of parts of the biblical story, embellished with new narrative episodes, prayers, and other elements (e.g., *Jubilees, The Genesis Apocryphon, The Apocryphon of Joshua*). Some texts elaborate on the apocalyptic elements of the books of Ezekiel and Daniel or place apocalyptic pronouncements in the mouths of other biblical figures, such as Levi, Qahat, and Amram. Several texts, often having to do with matters of religious law, purport to be discourses of Moses. Perhaps the most remarkable document is the Temple Scroll, which apparently takes the form of an address by God to Moses. Although it incorporates material from the books of Exodus through Deuteronomy, it also contains much new material, including detailed instructions for building the Temple.

These documents and others pertaining to the Qumran sect itself help to clarify issues of religious controversy that shaped the period of Hasmonean rule. The Temple and the Torah were central institutions for Judaism, which made them focal points for conflict. The Qumran scrolls show that conflict over the proper calendar (i.e., a solar or lunar calendar) for the conduct of Temple sacrifices was a major issue dividing the Qumran Essenes from their rivals, the Pharisees. Though the Hasmoneans were not always on good terms with the Pharisees, they adopted the lunar calendar favored by them. Many other writings from Qumran also elaborate their understanding of disputed issues such as purity, marriage, and sabbath observance, concerning which they were at odds with the Pharisees. Although the Qumran community did not compose apocalypses (i.e., reports of revelatory visions), they were strongly influenced by apocalyptic ideas and considered themselves to be living in the last times, just before God would intervene to restore proper order to the world. They supported their ideas in part by writing commentaries (*pesharim*) on biblical texts, which they read as referring to themselves and their opponents.

In general, the Hellenistic period presents a picture of Judaism that is much more diverse than is often imagined. Not only did Jews live in a vast range of lands from Egypt to Parthia, they also creatively adapted many elements from the varied Hellenistic cultures of these lands. Nevertheless, important symbols and institutions, including the Temple in Jerusalem, the scriptures, and common religious practices based in the Torah, provided a sense of unity and common identity.

CALENDAR

The year was composed of twelve lunar months (beginning on the day of the new moon), with an intercalary month added periodically (see perhaps 1 Kings 12.33). In some traditions, and perhaps originally, the year began in the fall, at the autumnal equinox (see Ex 23.16; 34.22). In others, following Babylonian practice, the new year was celebrated in the spring. The fall new year became standard in postbiblical Judaism.

Months in the Bible are usually identified by ordinal numbers, beginning with the spring new year. Some months (in boldface in the following list) are also designated with names derived either from a Canaanite calendar or, in postexilic texts, from a Babylonian one; the names of months not found in the Bible are known from other ancient sources.

	CANAANITE NAME	BABYLONIAN NAME	MODERN EQUIVALENT
First	**Abib**	**Nisan**	March–April
Second	**Ziv**	Iyyar	April–May
Third		**Sivan**	May–June
Fourth		Tammuz	June–July
Fifth		Ab	July–August
Sixth		**Elul**	August–September
Seventh	**Ethanim**	Tishri	September–October
Eighth	**Bul**	Marheshvan	October–November
Ninth		Chislev	November–December
Tenth		**Tebeth**	December–January
Eleventh		**Shebat**	January–February
Twelfth		**Adar**	February–March

CHRONOLOGICAL TABLE OF RULERS

DATE	EGYPT	SYRIA
	HELLENISTIC PERIOD	**Alexander** (the Great) (336–323)
300 BCE	Ptolemy I Soter (305–282)	**Seleucus I Nicator** (305–281)
	Ptolemy II Philadelphus (285–246)	Antiochus I Soter (281–261)
		Antiochus II Theos (261–246)
	Ptolemy III Euergetes (246–221)	Seleucus II Callinicus (246–225)
	Ptolemy IV Philopator (221–204)	Seleucus III Soter Ceraunos (225–223)
	Ptolemy V Epiphanes (204–180);	**Antiochus III** (the Great) (223–187)
	Cleopatra I (180–176)	**Seleucus IV Philopator** (187–175)
		Antiochus IV Epiphanes (175–164)
	Ptolemy VI Philometor (180–145);	**Antiochus V Eupator** (164–162)
	Cleopatra II (175–116)	**Demetrius I Soter** (162–150)
	Ptolemy VII Neos Philopator (145)	**Alexander Epiphanes** (Balas) (150–145)
	Ptolemy VIII Euergetes II Physcon (170–116)	**Demetrius II Nicator** (145–141 and 129–125)
		Antiochus VI Epiphanes (145–142)
		Trypho (142–138)
		Antiochus VII Sidetes (138–129)
		Cleopatra Thea (126–121)
		Antiochus VIII Grypus (125–121 and 121–96)
	Cleopatra III (116–101)	Seleucus V (125)
	Ptolemy IX Soter II (116–107 and 88–80)	Antiochus IX Cyzicenus (115–95)
100 BCE	Ptolemy X Alexander I (107–88)	Seleucus VI (95)
		Antiochus X Eusebes (95–83)
		Antiochus XI Philadelphus (95)
	Cleopatra Berenice (101–88)	Demetrius III Eukairos (95–88)
		Philip I Epiphanes Philadelphus (95–84)
	Ptolemy XI Alexander II (80)	Antiochus XII Dionysus Epiphanes (87–84)
		Philip II (67–66)
	Ptolemy XII Auletes (80–59 and 55–51)	Antiochus XIII Asiaticus (69–68 and 65–64)
50 BCE	Cleopatra VII (51–30)	
	Ptolemy XIII (51–47)	
	Ptolemy XIV (47–44)	

Note: Names in boldface occur in the Bible. Overlapping dates indicate coregencies. Date ranges are reigns, not life spans.

PALESTINE

HASMONEAN RULERS
[Mattathias d. 166]

Judas Maccabeus, son of Mattathias (165–160)

Jonathan, son of Mattathias (160–142)

Simon, son of Mattathias (142–135)

John Hyrcanus I, son of Simon (135–104)

Judah Aristobulus I , son of John Hyrcanus (104–103)

Alexander Janneus, son of John Hyrcanus (103–76)

Salome Alexandra, wife of Alexander Jannaeus (76–67)

Aristobulus II, son of Alexander Jannaeus and Salome Alexandra (67–63)

Hyrcanus II, son of Alexander Jannaeus and Salome Alexandra (63–40)

Mattathias Antigonus, son of Aristobulus II (40–37)

THE NEW OXFORD ANNOTATED APOCRYPHA

Fully Revised
Fourth Edition

New Revised Standard Version

THE APOCRYPHA

The Apocryphal/
Deuterocanonical books
of The Old Testament

New Revised Standard Version

INTRODUCTION TO THE APOCRYPHAL/ DEUTEROCANONICAL BOOKS

DEFINITIONS

The apocryphal/Deuterocanonical books are those works that were included in the Septuagint (the ancient Greek translation of the Hebrew Bible, referred to as LXX) or in the Old Latin and Vulgate translations, but are not included in the Hebrew text that forms both the canon for Judaism and the Protestant Old Testament. All of these works, whether they are individual books or additions to the Hebrew texts of Esther and Daniel, have been regarded as canonical by one or more Christian communities, but not by all. (The exception is 4 Macc, which appears only in an appendix to the Greek Bible.)

"Apocrypha" means "hidden things," but it is not clear why the term was chosen to describe these books. In antiquity "hidden books" sometimes referred to books that were restricted because they contained mysterious or esoteric teaching, too profound to be communicated to any except the initiated (see 2 Esd 14.45–46). Some early Christian writers used the term to describe works they considered to be spurious or heretical. But neither usage aptly describes the set of books that now goes by this name. The use of the term to refer to this group of books can be traced to the Christian scholar Jerome at the turn of the fifth century CE. It serves to distinguish them from books of the Christian Old Testament that are also found in the Jewish canon.

"Deuterocanonical," along with its coordinate term "protocanonical," is used in Roman Catholic tradition to describe the status of the two groups of books of the Old Testament. The "protocanon" consists of the books of the Hebrew Bible, concerning which there was no debate as to their canonical status. The "Deuterocanon" refers to those additional books whose canonical status was reaffirmed at a later date. This distinction, introduced by Sixtus of Sienna in 1566, acknowledges the differences between the two categories while making clear that Roman Catholics accept as fully canonical those books and parts of books that Protestants call the Apocrypha (except the Prayer of Manasseh, Psalm 151, 3 and 4 Maccabees, and 1 and 2 Esdras, which both groups regard as apocryphal). Thus, although the terms "Deuterocanonical" and "Apocryphal" can describe the same collections of writings, they clearly indicate the difference in status of the writings among different groups. In the NRSV translation, subheadings in the table of contents for these books, and in the text itself, explain the differing canonical status of various writings.

THE ROMAN CATHOLIC, ORTHODOX, AND PROTESTANT CANONS OF THE OLD TESTAMENT

Toward the end of the fourth century CE, Pope Damasus commissioned Jerome, the most learned Christian biblical scholar of his day, to prepare a standard Latin version of the scriptures (the translation that was to become known as the Latin Vulgate). In the Old Testament Jerome followed the Hebrew canon; though he also translated the apocryphal books, he called attention to their distinct status in prefaces. Subsequent copyists of the Latin Bible, however, did not always include Jerome's prefaces, and during the medieval period the Western Church generally regarded these books as scripture, without differentiation. After the Protestant reformers had denied the canonical status of these books, in 1546 the Council of Trent decreed that the canon of the Old Testament includes them (with the exceptions listed earlier). Subsequent editions of the Latin Vulgate text, officially approved by the Roman Catholic Church, placed these books within the Christian sequence of the Old Testament books. Thus Tobit and Judith come after Nehemiah; the Wisdom of Solomon and Ecclesiasticus (Sirach) come after the Song of Solomon; Baruch (with the Letter of Jeremiah as ch 6) comes after Lamentations; and 1 and 2 Maccabees conclude the books of the Old Testament. Esther is given in its longer (Greek) form rather than in the version based solely on the Hebrew text; the Prayer of Azariah and Song of the Three Jews appear as vv. 24–90 of ch 3 of Daniel, and the stories of Susanna and Bel and the Dragon as chs 13 and 14 of Daniel. An appendix after the New Testament contains the Prayer of Manasseh and 1 and 2 Esdras, without implying canonical status.

The Eastern Orthodox Churches recognize several other books as authoritative. Editions of the Old Testament approved by the Holy Synod of the Greek Orthodox Church contain, besides the Roman Catholic Deuterocanonical books, 1 Esdras, Psalm 151, the Prayer of Manasseh, and 3 Maccabees, while 4 Maccabees appears in an appendix. Slavonic Bibles approved by the Russian Orthodox Church contain, besides the Deuterocanonical books, 1 and 2 Esdras (called 2 and 3 Esdras), Psalm 151, and 3 Maccabees.

Protestant Bibles have followed the Hebrew canon, though in a different order. The disputed books, if they are included at all, have generally been placed in a separate section, usually bound between the Old and New Testaments, but occasionally placed after the close of the New Testament.

Here is a list of the Apocryphal/Deuterocanonical books in the order in which they are found in this Bible, showing which religious communities accept them as scripture:

	ROMAN CATHOLIC	GREEK ORTHODOX	SLAVONIC (RUSSIAN ORTHODOX)	LATIN VULGATE APPENDIX	GREEK APPENDIX	PROTESTANT/ ANGLICAN APOCRYPHA
Tobit	•	•	•			•
Judith	•	•	•			•
Additions to Esther	•	•	•			•
Wisdom of Solomon	•	•	•			•
Ecclesiasticus[1]	•	•	•			•
Baruch	•	•	•			•
Letter of Jeremiah (Baruch ch.6)	•	•	•			•
Additions to Daniel	•	•	•			•
1 Maccabees	•	•	•			•
2 Maccabees	•	•	•			•
1 Esdras[2]		•	•	•		•
Prayer of Manasseh		•	•	•		•
Psalm 151		•	•			
3 Maccabees		•	•			
2 Esdras[3]			•	•		•
4 Maccabees					•	

[1] Also called The Wisdom of Jesus, Son of Sirach, or simply Sirach.
[2] 2 Esdras in Slavonic; 3 Esdras in Appendix to Vulgate; In the Vulgate, Ezra-Nehemiah are 1 and 2 Esdras.
[3] 3 Esdras in Slavonic; 4 Esdras in Vulgate Appendix.

THE STATUS OF THE APOCRYPHAL/DEUTEROCANONICAL BOOKS IN CHRISTIANITY

During the first centuries of the Common Era, early Christian theologians (most of whom knew no Hebrew) quoted, in Greek, passages both from books in the Hebrew canon and from these additional works without making any distinction between them. Such citations were usually preceded by a word or phrase making it clear that the writer regarded the text being cited as canonical. During this time, only a few thinkers investigated the Jewish canon or distinguished between, for instance, the Hebrew text of Daniel and the addition of the story of Susanna in the Greek version.

By the fourth century, theologians in the Eastern (Greek) churches had begun to recognize a distinction between the books in the Hebrew canon and the rest, though they continued to cite all of them as scripture. During the following centuries the matter was debated and, consequently, practice varied in the East, but at the Synod of Jerusalem in 1672 (which expressed the Orthodox churches' reaction to the Protestant Reformation), Tobit, Judith, Ecclesiasticus (Sirach), Wisdom, Additions to Daniel, and 1 and 2 Maccabees were expressly designated as canonical.

In the Western (Latin) church, on the other hand, though there was some variety of opinion, in general theologians regarded these books as canonical. More than one local synodical council (e.g., Hippo, 393, and Carthage, 397 and 419) justified and authorized their use as scripture. The so-called *Decretum Gelasianum*, a Latin document probably dating to the sixth century, contains lists of the books to be read as scripture and of books to be avoided as apocryphal. The former list, which is not present in all the manuscripts, includes among the biblical books Tobit, Judith, Wisdom, Ecclesiasticus (Sirach), and 1 and 2 Maccabees.

Occasionally, however, theologians questioned the status of these books. Jerome, near the end of the fourth century, thought that books not in the Hebrew canon should be designated as apocryphal, and other thinkers, though always a minority, followed his view, at least theoretically. Toward the close of the fourteenth century John Wycliffe and his disciples produced the first English version of the Bible. This translation of the Latin Vulgate included all of the disputed books, with the exception of 2 Esdras. In the Prologue to the Old Testament, however, it makes a distinction between the books of the Hebrew canon, listed there, and the others which, the writer says, "shall be set among apocrypha, that is, without authority of belief." In the books of Esther and Daniel, the translators included a rendering of Jerome's notes calling the reader's attention to the additions.

At the time of the Reformation, Protestant thinkers came to the conclusion fairly early that they would need to determine which books were authoritative for the establishment of doctrine and which were not. For instance, disputes over the doctrine of purgatory and of the usefulness of prayers and masses for the dead involved the authority of 2 Maccabees, which contains what was held to be scriptural warrant for them (12.43–45). The first extensive Protestant discussion of the canon was Andreas Bodenstein's treatise *De Canonicis Scripturis Libellus* (1520). Bodenstein (or Carlstadt, after his place of birth) distinguished the books of the Hebrew Bible from the books of the Apocrypha, classifying the Apocrypha into two divisions. Concerning Wisdom, Ecclesiasticus (Sirach), Judith, Tobit, and 1 and 2 Maccabees, he says, "These are Apocrypha, that is, are outside the Hebrew canon; yet they are holy writings" (sect. 114). He continues:

> What they contain is not to be despised at once; still it is not right that Christians should relieve, much less slake, their thirst with them. . . . Before all things the best books must be read, that is, those that are canonical beyond all controversy; afterwards, if one has the time, it is allowed to peruse the controverted books, provided that you have the set purpose of comparing and collating the non-canonical books with those which are truly canonical (sect. 118).

The second group, 1 and 2 Esdras, Baruch, Prayer of Manasseh, and the Additions to Daniel, he declared without worth.

The first Bible in a modern vernacular language to segregate the apocryphal books from the others was the Dutch Bible published by Jacob van Liesveldt in 1526 at Antwerp. After Malachi there follows a section embodying the Apocrypha titled "The books which are not in the canon, that is to say, which one does not find among the Jews in the Hebrew."

The first edition of the Swiss-German Bible was published in six volumes (Zurich, 1527–29), the fifth of which contains the Apocrypha. The title page of this volume states, "These are the books which are not reckoned as biblical by the ancients, nor are found among the Hebrews." A one-volume edition of the Zurich Bible, which appeared in 1530, contains the apocryphal books grouped together after the New Testament. One Swiss reformer, Oecolampadius, declared in 1530: "We do not despise Judith, Tobit, Ecclesiasticus, Baruch, the last two books of Esdras, the three books of Maccabees, the Additions to Daniel; but we do not allow them divine authority with the others."

In reaction to Protestant criticism of the disputed books, in 1546 the Council of Trent gave what is regarded by Roman Catholics as the definitive declaration on the canon of the scriptures. After enumerating the books, which in the Old Testament include Tobit, Judith, Wisdom, Ecclesiasticus (Sirach), Baruch, and the two books of Maccabees, the decree pronounces an anathema upon anyone who "does not accept as sacred and canonical the aforesaid books in their entirety and with all their parts, as they have been accustomed to be read in the Catholic Church and as they are contained in the old Latin Vulgate Edition" (trans. H. J. Schroeder). The reference to "books in their entirety and with all their parts" is intended to cover the Letter of Jeremiah as ch 6 of Baruch, the Additions to Esther, and the chapters in Daniel including the Prayer of Azariah, the Song of the Three Jews, Susanna, and Bel and the Dragon. It is noteworthy, however, that the Prayer of Manasseh and 1 and 2 Esdras, although included in some manuscripts of the Latin Vulgate, were denied canonical status by the Council of Trent. In the official edition of the Vulgate, published in 1592, these three are printed as an appendix after the New Testament, "lest they should perish altogether."

In England, even though Protestants were unanimous in declaring that the apocryphal books were not to be used to establish any doctrine, differences arose as to the proper use and place of noncanonical books. A milder view prevailed in the Church of England, and the lectionary attached to the Book of Common Prayer, from 1549 on, has always contained prescribed lessons from the Apocrypha. In addition, portions of the Song of the Three Jews are used as a canticle, or song of praise, alongside selected Psalms in the service of Morning Prayer. In reply to those who urged the discontinuance of reading lessons from apocryphal books, as being inconsistent with the sufficiency of scripture, the bishops at the Savoy Conference, held in 1661, replied that the same objection could be raised against the preaching of sermons, and that it was much to be desired that all sermons should give as useful instruction as did the chapters selected from the Apocrypha.

The Puritans took a stricter view, and some Geneva Bibles, printed in 1599 mainly in the Low Countries, excluded the Apocrypha. The omission of the Apocrypha was presumably due to those responsible for binding the copies, since the titles of the apocryphal books occur in the table of contents. During subsequent centuries Bibles that lacked the books of the Apocrypha came to outnumber those that included them, and soon it became difficult to obtain ordinary editions of the King James Version containing the Apocrypha.

(For a more complete account of the formation of the various canons of scripture, see "The Canons of the Bible" on p 2185.)

THE HISTORICAL BACKGROUND TO THE APOCRYPHAL/DEUTEROCANONICAL BOOKS

With the destruction of Jerusalem and the Temple by the Babylonians under Nebuchadnezzar in 586 BCE, and the subsequent exile of many Judeans to Babylon, the history of Israel underwent a decisive break. Henceforth there would always be Jewish communities outside the land of Israel (the Diaspora), and even after the Persian king Cyrus allowed the exiles to return in 538 BCE, large communities flourished in Babylon and elsewhere.

For two centuries the Persians controlled the Near East. The rebuilt Temple became the institutional focus of the province of Judah. Although details are uncertain, this era probably saw important work on the editing of the Pentateuch and the prophetic writings, as well as the composition of other literature. The Persian period came to an end when Alexander the Great completed a series of conquests that put him in control of the former Persian empire, including Egypt. When Alexander died in 323, his empire was divided among his warring generals, and two of them—Seleucus, king of Syria, and Ptolemy, king of Egypt—and their successors fought over the territory of Judah, which fell first under Ptolemaic and then Seleucid dynastic control. Despite the political changes, however, the overall cultural influence remained: This was the era of the triumph of Hellenistic culture, including the use of the Greek language as the standard for the whole empire.

There had already been, in the Hebrew Bible, contention about such issues as intermarriage (Ezra 9.1–10.44; Neh 13.23–31). Now, with large numbers of Jews living outside the land as minorities within much larger and more dominant cultures, this issue and those of other religious observances came to be much more important. Stories of faithfully observant Jews among non-Jewish populations (Tobit, 3 Macc) were joined by expanded versions of books that strengthened this point (Greek Esther, the Prayer of Azariah, and Song of the Three Jews in ch 3 of Daniel).

Jews both in the Diaspora and in Judah appropriated many elements of Hellenistic culture, usually without incident. During the second century BCE, however, an attempt to establish Hellenistic educational and civic institutions in Jerusalem created a crisis when the persons involved bribed King Antiochus IV Epiphanes (175–164) to appoint Hellenizing high priests (Jason and Menelaus) and funds were taken from the Temple itself to pay the king. In response to the ensuing violence, Antiochus invaded Jerusalem in 169; in 167 he effectively outlawed the Jewish religion, making the teaching of the Torah a crime and establishing polytheistic worship in the Temple. This final provocation led to the ultimately successful Jewish revolt under the Hasmonean family, led by Mattathias and his five sons, one of whom, Judas, was known as Maccabeus, "the hammer." The revolt and the subsequent establishment of a Jewish government (which took more than twenty years to accomplish) are therefore referred to as Maccabean. This rule lasted for eighty years, until (because of constant power struggles among the various factions of Jews) the Romans were able to intervene and take direct control of the territory in 63 BCE.

The Apocryphal/Deuterocanonical books contain several different literary genres, including histories, historical fiction, wisdom, devotional writings, letters, and an apocalypse. Though several of the books combine more than one of these genres, most of the books can be classified as predominantly one type or another. Thus 1 Esdras, 1 Maccabees, and in a certain sense, 2 Maccabees are histories. First Esdras summarizes 2 Chr 35.1–36.23 and reproduces all of Ezra and Neh 7.38–8.12. Only 1 Esd 3.1–5.6 is a significant addition. First Maccabees recounts the history of the Seleucid persecutions and the rebellion and rise of the Maccabees. Second Maccabees, with its bombastic rhetoric and abundant use of invectives against the Seleucid tyrants and Hellenizing Jews, is an example of a popular Hellenistic genre, the "pathetic history," which uses highly charged language, exhortation, exaggeration, and other methods to stimulate the imaginations and emotions ("pathos") of readers. Third Maccabees is misleadingly named: It actually has nothing to do with the Maccabean period or the Seleucid dynasty, but deals with a period a half-century earlier and concerns the sufferings of the Jewish community in Egypt under the Ptolemaic rulers. It is a religious novel, written in Greek by an Alexandrian Jew sometime after 30 BCE. Using legendary elements, it tells three stories of conflict between Ptolemy IV (221–204) and the Jewish community in Egypt. The most dramatic section (5.1–6.21) describes Ptolemy's scheme to martyr the Jews: They were to be herded into an arena near Alexandria to be trampled under the feet of five hundred intoxicated elephants. The king's plan was finally foiled when angelic intervention terrorized those supervising the persecutions and also frightened the elephants into turning upon the Egyptian soldiers.

Fourth Maccabees is not a historical narrative but rather a Greek philosophical treatise addressed to Jews on the supremacy of reason over the passions of body and soul. In the form of a Stoic diatribe, or popular address, it uses narratives of exemplary behavior, and the conversations and arguments of characters in the narratives, to explore philosophical issues. The author begins with a theoretical exposition of his theme, which he then illustrates at length with examples of the martyrs drawn from 2 Maccabees, who preferred death to committing apostasy. The book was probably written by a Hellenistic Jew before 70 CE. In early Christianity the Maccabean martyrs were venerated as saints and eventually accorded a yearly festival in the ecclesiastical calendar (August 1).

Judith, Tobit, Susanna, and Bel and the Dragon are short historical fictions written to convey a moral point, as well as to entertain. Except for Judith, which is set in Judah, the rest are sometimes referred to as "Diaspora novels" since they are all set in the Jewish Diaspora of Mesopotamia. Yet they differ from one another in other respects. Like the canonical stories of Daniel 1–6, Bel and the Dragon is a court tale, in which the hero's relationship with the king and other members of the court provides the conflict of the plot. The motif of the lion's den, which occurs in Daniel 6, also occurs in the story of the dragon. In contrast to the earlier Daniel tales, however, Bel and the Dragon is preoccupied with the theme of the exposure of idols as false gods and their priests as fraudulent (see also the Letter of Jeremiah). Bel and the Dragon and Susanna are sometimes referred to as ancient examples of the detective story. Whereas Daniel functioned as an interpreter of dreams and visions in Daniel 1–6, in these stories Daniel uses cleverness and logical deduction to uncover deception.

Although Tobit, like Daniel, is presented as a court official of a Mesopotamian king, the story is concerned with personal and family affairs, not a rivalry at court. Thematically, Tobit may be compared with the prose story of Job, since it concerns the suffering of the righteous (both Tobit and his daughter-in-law Sarah). The book of Tobit is distinguished by the use of various folktale motifs (e.g., the motifs of the grateful dead, the angel in disguise, the dangerous bride, and the demon lover), and by its references to Ahikar, the hero of a non-Jewish folktale from Mesopotamia.

Judith might seem to bear comparison with 1 and 2 Maccabees, since it concerns a threat to the people from a foreign army. But whereas 1 and 2 Maccabees are histories, the fictional nature of Judith is evident from the story's flagrant historical inaccuracies, such as describing Nebuchadnezzar as king of Assyria and the invasion as taking place after the people's return from exile. A better comparison might be between Judith and Esther. Though set in Judah rather than the Diaspora, Judith, like Esther, tells how a courageous Jewish woman saves her people from enemies bent on destroying them.

Didactic literature is represented in the Apocrypha by the two treatises on wisdom: the Wisdom of Solomon, and the Wisdom of Jesus son of Sirach (also known as Ecclesiasticus). Sirach, which was originally composed in Hebrew ca. 180 BCE, shows particularly close connections with the style and content of the book of Proverbs in the Hebrew Bible, from which it is a natural development. The Wisdom of Solomon, by contrast, contains no proverbial material, such as characterizes the Hebrew wisdom tradition. It does, however, share with Proverbs and Sirach an interest in the figure of wisdom personified as a woman. What makes the Wisdom of Solomon distinctive is the strong influence of Greek literary styles and philosophical ideas. Thus, it comes from the Greek-speaking Diaspora, most probably from Alexandria in Egypt.

The Prayer of Manasseh is a hymnic lament of great feeling and literary skill. The Prayer of Azariah and the Song of the Three Jews are both modeled on psalms that are liturgical in form. In addition to the 150 psalms comprising the book of Psalms in the Hebrew Bible, during the Hellenistic and Roman periods such hymns were composed in Hebrew and in other languages; there are a number of such compositions in the Dead Sea Scrolls. Another, which celebrates the prowess of young David in slaying Goliath, is appended (as Ps 151) to the book of Psalms in Greek manuscripts.

The Hebrew Bible contains no books that are in the form of a letter, although letters or excerpts from letters occur at various places. There are decrees (Ezra 1.1–6), diplomatic correspondence (1 Kings 5.2–6), royal commands (2 Sam 11.14–15), even forgeries (1 Kings 21.8–10), but all are used to advance the narratives in which they occur, or explain incidents that follow, so it is unclear how representative they are. Twenty-one of the twenty-seven books of the New Testament are in the form of letters, but some (for instance, Hebrews) are more like sermons than letters. The Letter of Jeremiah, which dates from the Hellenistic period, may have provided later, Christian writers with an example of how this literary form could be used for religious purposes, combining theological content with a direct personal approach.

Finally, 2 Esdras, a book that purports to reveal the future, belongs to the genre of apocalypse, a word that literally means "an unveiling." Like the last six chapters of Daniel in the Hebrew Bible and the book of Revelation in the New Testament, which also are apocalypses, 2 Esdras uses metaphoric language, symbolic numbers, and angelic messengers who reveal hidden information.

Despite this diversity of genres, most of which parallel or are developed from similar ones in the Hebrew Bible, there is no correlative to classical prophecy. Even within the prophetic books of the Hebrew Bible, apocalyptic elements had already begun to supplant strict prophecy (for instance, Isa chs 24–27; Ezek chs 38–39; Joel ch 2; Zech chs 9–14). This absence perhaps supports the view of the late first-century CE historian Josephus (*Ag. Ap.* 1.8), that "the exact succession of the prophets" had been broken after the Persian period; a similar idea is found in later rabbinic literature. Sometimes there is a direct statement that "prophets ceased to appear" (1 Macc 9.27); at other times the writers express the hope that prophecy might one day return (1 Macc 4.46; 14.41). When a writer imitates prophetic style, as in the book of Baruch, he repeats with slight modifications the language of the older prophets. But the introductory phrase, "Thus says the Lord," which occurs so frequently in the prophetic literature of the Hebrew Bible, is absent from the Apocryphal/Deuterocanonical Books.

THE APOCRYPHAL/DEUTEROCANONICAL BOOKS WITHIN JUDAISM

All of the writings in the Apocryphal/Deuterocanonical books are Jewish in origin, but it is not clear that they were collected by any particular community of Jews. Some of them (for instance, Sirach) were quoted by rabbis, but for others no evidence exists that they were regarded as central to the Jewish community at any point. Some (Tobit, parts of Sirach, the Letter of Jeremiah, and Psalm 151) are among the Dead Sea Scrolls, and were therefore presumably of importance to the Essene community there, but whether or not they were considered canonical is not clear.

Nevertheless, influences from some of these works are apparent within Judaism. As mentioned above, rabbinic literature quotes and appropriates sayings from Sirach. The martyrdom of the woman and her seven sons (2 Macc 7.1–42; 4 Macc 8.3–18.24) is recounted in several places (*Lam. Rab.* 1.50; b. Git. 57b; *Seder Eliyahu R.* 29).

First and Second Maccabees (1 Macc 4.36–59; 2 Macc 10.1–8) provide the original accounts of the purification of the Temple in 164 BCE, which is commemorated in the festival of Hanukkah. The Talmudic legend (*b. Shabb.* 21b) that oil in the Temple, though only enough for one day nevertheless burned for eight—the supposed reason for the eight-day length of the observance—is not found in the books of Maccabees. Judith was, during the Middle Ages, associated with Hanukkah as well, on the grounds that both had to do with rallying an oppressed Jewish population to overthrow a threatening or occupying power.

Both Tobit and 2 Esdras influenced later Jewish literature and were popular during the Middle Ages. Baruch may have been read in synagogues at one time (see Bar 1.14), and Baruch himself, and therefore his writing, were regarded in some rabbinic writings as sharing Jeremiah's prophetic status (*Sifre Num.* 78; *Seder Olam R.* 20; b. B. Bat. 14b; Jer. Sot. 9.12). Susanna's story is recounted in the Babylonian Talmud (*b. San.* 93a).

The sense of a canon of scripture emerged only gradually in Judaism. During the time in which the Apocryphal/Deuterocanonical books were composed, the Torah (Pentateuch), the Prophets, and possibly the book of Psalms were considered authoritative. Many other writings, both those now in the Jewish canon and additional ones, were widely popular but did not have the status of scripture. A sense of a closed set of authoritative books emerged only in the first century CE, and even then there was some uncertainty about its extent. Josephus, however, says that "there are not with us myriads of books, discordant and discrepant, but only twenty-two, comprising the history of all time, which are justly accredited" (*Ag. Ap.*1.43).

Even if these additional writings were not considered scripture, they were often read and cited. Josephus himself makes use of 1 Esdras, 1 Maccabees, and the additions to Esther. Early rabbinic literature, however, makes no mention of any of these books except for Sirach, which is frequently quoted. The rabbis were, however, aware of the festival of Hanukkah, which is described in 1 and 2 Maccabees. During the Middle Ages, Jews became reacquainted with some of the Apocryphal/Deuterocanonical works from Christian sources and retranslated Tobit and Judith into Hebrew. The entire Apocrypha/Deuterocanon was translated into Hebrew in the early sixteenth century.

NEW TESTAMENT USES OF THE APOCRYPHAL/DEUTEROCANONICAL BOOKS

None of the books of the New Testament quotes directly from any Apocryphal book, in contrast to the frequent quotation of the thirty-nine books in the Hebrew Bible. Several New Testament writers, however, do allude to one or more apocryphal books. For example, what seem to be literary echoes from the Wisdom of Solomon are present in Paul's Letter to the Romans (compare Rom 1.20–29 with Wis 13.5,8; 14.24,27; and Rom 9.20–23 with Wis 12.12,20; 15.7) and in his correspondence with the Corinthians (compare 2 Cor 5.1,4 with Wis 9.15). The short Letter of James, a typical bit of "wisdom literature" in the New Testament, contains allusions not only to the book of Proverbs in the Hebrew Bible but to gnomic sayings in Sirach as well (compare Jas 1.19 with Sir 5.11; and Jas 1.13 with Sir 15.11–12).

THE FURTHER INFLUENCE OF THE APOCRYPHAL/DEUTEROCANONICAL BOOKS

The influence of the Apocrypha has been widespread, inspiring homilies, meditations, and liturgical forms, and providing subjects for poets, dramatists, composers, and artists. Some common expressions and proverbs have come from the Apocrypha. The sayings, "A good name endures forever" and "You can't touch pitch without being defiled," are derived from Sir 41.13 and 13.1. The affirmation in 1 Esd 4.41, "Great is Truth, and mighty above all things" (King James Version), or its Latin form, *Magna est veritas et praevalet,* has been used as a motto or maxim in a wide variety of contexts.

The importance of these books extends to the information they supply concerning the development of Jewish life and thought just prior to the beginning of the Common Era. The stirring political fortunes of the Jews in the time of the Maccabees; the rise of what has been called normative Judaism, and the emergence of the sects of the Pharisees and the Sadducees; the lush growth of popular belief in the activities of angels and demons, and the use of magic to drive away malevolent influences; the first reflections on "original sin" and its relation to the "evil inclination" present in every person; the blossoming of apocalyptic hopes relating to the messiah, the resurrection of the body, and the vindication of the righteous—all these and many other topics are to be found in the Apocryphal/Deuterocanonical books.

TOBIT

NAME AND CANONICAL STATUS

The book is named for its principal character, Tobit. The name is the Greek form of Hebrew *Tobi*, meaning "my good," possibly an abbreviation for *Tobiah*, "Yahweh is my good," or *Tobiel*, "God is my good." The book is not included in the Protestant or Jewish canons, but it is canonical in the Roman Catholic and Orthodox Churches. The Anglican Church and some other communions also recognize Tobit as Scripture for the purpose of edification but not for doctrine.

AUTHORSHIP, TEXT, AND DATE OF COMPOSITION

The author of the book is unknown. Although the original language was likely Aramaic, only fragments of that text have survived. The translation below is based on the Greek text of Codex Sinaiticus; other versions include two additional Greek recensions, the Old Latin, Jerome's Vulgate, a medieval Aramaic rendering, Coptic, Syriac, Ethiopic, and Armenian. Fragments in both Hebrew and Aramaic were found among the Dead Sea Scrolls. The book likely dates to sometime in the third or possibly early second century BCE; its place of composition remains unknown, with plausible suggestions including the eastern Diaspora, Egypt, and Israel.

CONTENTS AND STRUCTURE

After the Assyrian conquest of the Northern Kingdom of Israel in 722 BCE, Tobit, his wife Anna, and his son Tobias were exiled from their home in Galilee to Assyria. There Tobit, like Joseph (in Gen 39–50), Mordecai (in the book of Esther), and Daniel (in the book of Daniel), found himself in the service of a foreign ruler, as an officer in the court of the Assyrian king Shalmaneser. This pious Israelite too was tested: Shalmaneser's successor removed Tobit from his official position and then persecuted him for his insistence on burying the unattended corpses of his fellow Jews. One evening, following yet another burial, Tobit was blinded by a bird with unfortunate aim. Dependent on others, including his wife, for economic support, and following an argument with her in which she questioned the value of his piety, Tobit prayed for death. At the same time his relative Sarah was also praying for death. The demon Asmodeus, who was in love with her, had killed each of her seven successive grooms on their wedding nights. To resolve these improbable situations, the angel Raphael, in disguise as Tobias's traveling companion, escorts the young man first to Media to exorcise the demon and marry Sarah and then back to Nineveh to cure Tobit.

The complex plot is tied together by the parallel situations of Tobit and Sarah, prayers of praise and references to almsgiving, and frequent supernatural events. Its humorous aspects—from the angel in disguise to the attack of a magical fish—make the stories of Tobit and Sarah almost farcical and so prevent the book from becoming tragic or maudlin. Readers familiar with biblical literature will recognize familiar motifs and themes in the narrative: wisdom sayings; the antipathy between the matriarch Sarah and her slave Hagar (Gen 16; 21); the search for a bride for Isaac (Gen 24); the successes and trials of the Jew in the royal court; the problems of life in the Diaspora; Job's trials; the role of angels; the centrality of Jerusalem; the fulfillment of prophecy; and, especially, the importance of charity. The numerous personal prayers, similar to those found in the stories of Judith, Daniel (including the Additions), the Greek Additions to Esther, and elsewhere in postexilic Jewish literature, emphasize the universal authority and righteousness of God.

INTERPRETATION AND GUIDE TO READING

Combining ethical exhortation and prayers with broad humor, a rollicking plot, and vivid characters, the book of Tobit is both entertaining and edifying. It offers to a Diaspora community guidelines on how to preserve their identity, to historians indirect information about the postexilic period, and to theologians a view of a God who tests the faithful, responds to prayers, and redeems the covenant community.

The book of Tobit is also replete with information concerning family life, travel, burial and eating customs, gender roles, and medicine. These matters testify to the author's interest in providing guidance for life in Diaspora: Where Temple sacrifice is unavailable and the people are scattered, the story insists that Jews maintain their identity not only through piety and practice but also through strong bonds between parents and children, between husbands and wives, and with family members and fellow Jews. To preserve the community, Tobit insists that his son imitate Abraham, Isaac, and Jacob, who "took wives from among their kindred" (4.12–13).

The book also has connections to well-known folktale motifs, including the dangerous bride, the monster in the nuptial chamber, the supernatural being in disguise, the miraculous animal, and the grateful dead. Specifically mentioned are the characters of an Assyrian official Ahikar and his nephew, from a story well known in antiquity; there may also be hints of Homer's *Odyssey* and Sophocles's *Antigone*.

Amy-Jill Levine

1 This book tells the story of Tobit son of Tobiel son of Hananiel son of Aduel son of Gabael son of Raphael son of Raguel of the descendants[a] of Asiel, of the tribe of Naphtali, [2] who in the days of King Shalmaneser[b] of the Assyrians was taken into captivity from Thisbe, which is to the south of Kedesh Naphtali in Upper Galilee, above Asher toward the west, and north of Phogor.

[3] I, Tobit, walked in the ways of truth and righteousness all the days of my life. I performed many acts of charity for my kindred and my people who had gone with me in exile to Nineveh in the land of the Assyrians. [4] When I was in my own country, in the land of Israel, while I was still a young man, the whole tribe of my ancestor Naphtali deserted the house of David and Jerusalem. This city had been chosen from among all the tribes of Israel, where all the tribes of Israel should offer sacrifice and where the temple, the dwelling of God, had been consecrated and established for all generations forever.

[5] All my kindred and our ancestral house of Naphtali sacrificed to the calf[c] that King Jeroboam of Israel had erected in Dan and on all the mountains of Galilee. [6] But I alone went often to Jerusalem for the festivals, as it is prescribed for all Israel by an everlasting decree. I would hurry off to Jerusalem with the first fruits of the crops and the firstlings of the flock, the tithes of the cattle, and the first shearings of the sheep. [7] I would give these to the priests, the sons of Aaron, at the altar; likewise the tenth of the grain, wine, olive oil, pomegranates, figs, and the rest of the fruits to the sons of Levi who ministered

---

[a] Other ancient authorities lack *of Raphael son of Raguel of the descendants*

[b] Gk *Enemessaros*

[c] Other ancient authorities read *heifer*

1.1–2: Exilic context. The superscription establishes Tobit's location and genealogy. **1:** *Tobiel*, "God is my good"; *Hananiel*, "God has shown mercy"; the names of his family members have the suffix *el*, meaning "God." Genealogy becomes increasingly important in Second Temple Judaism (see Ezra 2; 8.1–20; Neh 7.5–73; 11.1–12.26; Jdt 8; Mt 1; Lk 3). **2:** *Shalmaneser* V, ruled 727–722 BCE. Shalmaneser's predecessor, Tiglath-pileser III (ruled 745–727) deported the Naphtalites to Assyria (2 Kings 15.29); in 722 Sargon of Assyria, Shalmaneser's brother and successor, conquered Samaria, Israel's capital and resettled substantial portions of the population (2 Kings 17.1–6). *Kedesh*, in northern Galilee, defeated by Joshua (Josh 12.22; 19.37), was the home of Deborah's general Barak (Judg 4.6) and site of a Maccabean victory (1 Macc 11.63,73). *Asher* may be a Greek spelling of Hazor, ca. 6 mi (10 km) south-southeast of Kedesh. *Thisbe* and *Phogor* have not been identified.

1.3–9: Tobit's background. 3–4: Tobit, who speaks in the first person in 1.3–3.1, consistently emphasizes his own righteousness despite Israel's apostasy. Walking *in the ways of truth and righteousness* is a prominent motif of the Israelite wisdom tradition (see Prov 2.7–9; 4.11). **3:** *Nineveh*, the capital of Assyria. **4:** Tobit's life span, ranging from before 928 to after 722 BCE (but see 14.2), indicates the tale's fictional nature (the book of Judith similarly displays chronological fiction). *Naphtali* was one of the ten northern tribes that rebelled in 928 BCE against the dynasty founded by David (1 Kings 12.19–20); Tobit nevertheless consistently expresses concern for Jerusalem, the capital of the Southern Kingdom of Judah. **5:** *Calf*, 1 Kings 12.28–29; *Dan* is northeast of Kedesh (see 1.2n.). **6:** Participation in the pilgrimage *festivals* (Deut 12.11) of Booths (Sukkot), Passover (Pesach), and Weeks (Shavuot/Pentecost) entailed the giving of *first fruits* (Deut 26.1–11), *firstlings* (Ex 13.12), *tithes of the cattle* (Lev 27.32), and *first shearings of the sheep* (Deut 18.4). The extent of Tobit's pilgrimages and sacrificial activity emphasizes his faithfulness to the Torah, in contrast to his kin. **7–8:** For tithing of produce, see Lev 27.30; Deut

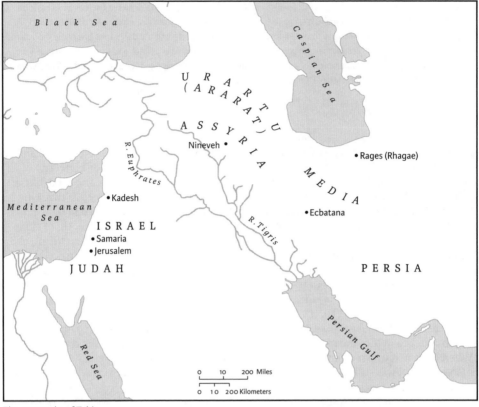

The geography of Tobit.

at Jerusalem. Also for six years I would save up a second tenth in money and go and distribute it in Jerusalem. ⁸ A third tenthᵃ I would give to the orphans and widows and to the converts who had attached themselves to Israel. I would bring it and give it to them in the third year, and we would eat it according to the ordinance decreed concerning it in the law of Moses and according to the instructions of Deborah, the mother of my father Tobiel,ᵇ for my father had died and left me an orphan. ⁹ When I became a man I married a woman,ᶜ a member of our own family, and by her I became the father of a son whom I named Tobias.

¹⁰ After I was carried away captive to Assyria and came as a captive to Nineveh, everyone of my kindred and my people ate the food of the Gentiles, ¹¹ but I kept myself from eating the food of the Gentiles. ¹² Because I was mindful of God with all my heart, ¹³ the Most High gave me favor and good

a   *A third tenth* added from other ancient authorities
b   Lat: Gk *Hananiel*
c   Other ancient authorities add *Anna*

14.22. For the distribution of tithes to *Levites, orphans, and widows,* see Deut 14.27–29. **8:** *Deborah* indicates women's roles in religious education (see Prov 1.8; Sir 3.2); the name may have some connection to Kedesh and Naphtali (Judg 4–5; Tob 1.2n.). **9:** Endogamy, i.e., marriage within the kinship group, is a major theme (3.17; 4.12–13; 6.11–12; 7.10–11; cf. Gen 11.29; 24.3–4; 27.46–28.2; Deut 7.3–4; Ezra 9–10; Neh 10.28–30; but contrast the marriages of Ruth and Esther). Intermarriage became a particularly acute issue in the Diaspora.

   1.10–22: Early captivity. The setting and Tobit's initial political success resemble that of Dan 1–6. Like Daniel and his companions (Dan 1.8–20), Esther (Add Esth 14.17), and Judith (Jdt 12.1–3), Tobit follows Jewish dietary laws (e.g., Lev 11.1–47; Deut 14.3–21). **13:** Tobit regards his political office as steward as a reward for righteous-

standing with Shalmaneser,[a] and I used to buy everything he needed. [14] Until his death I used to go into Media, and buy for him there. While in the country of Media I left bags of silver worth ten talents in trust with Gabael, the brother of Gabri. [15] But when Shalmaneser[a] died, and his son Sennacherib reigned in his place, the highways into Media became unsafe and I could no longer go there.

[16] In the days of Shalmaneser[a] I performed many acts of charity to my kindred, those of my tribe. [17] I would give my food to the hungry and my clothing to the naked; and if I saw the dead body of any of my people thrown out behind the wall of Nineveh, I would bury it. [18] I also buried any whom King Sennacherib put to death when he came fleeing from Judea in those days of judgment that the king of heaven executed upon him because of his blasphemies. For in his anger he put to death many Israelites; but I would secretly remove the bodies and bury them. So when Sennacherib looked for them he could not find them. [19] Then one of the Ninevites went and informed the king about me, that I was burying them; so I hid myself. But when I realized that the king knew about me and that I was being searched for to be put to death, I was afraid and ran away. [20] Then all my property was confiscated; nothing was left to me that was not taken into the royal treasury except my wife Anna and my son Tobias.

[21] But not forty[b] days passed before two of Sennacherib's[c] sons killed him, and they fled to the mountains of Ararat, and his son Esar-haddon[d] reigned after him. He appointed Ahikar, the son of my brother Hanael[e] over all the accounts of his kingdom, and he had authority over the entire administration. [22] Ahikar interceded for me, and I returned to Nineveh. Now Ahikar was chief cupbearer, keeper of the signet, and in charge of administration of the accounts under King Sennacherib of Assyria; so Esar-haddon[d] reappointed him. He was my nephew and so a close relative.

2 Then during the reign of Esar-haddon[d] I returned home, and my wife Anna and my son Tobias were restored to me. At our festival of Pentecost, which is the sacred festival of weeks, a good dinner was prepared for me and I reclined to eat. [2] When the table was set for me and an abundance of food placed before me, I said to my son Tobias, "Go, my child, and bring whatever poor person you may find of our people among the exiles in Nineveh, who is wholeheartedly mindful of God,[f] and he shall eat together with me. I will wait for you, until you come back." [3] So Tobias went to look for some poor person of our people. When he had returned he said, "Father!" And I replied, "Here I am, my child."

[a] Gk *Enemessaros*
[b] Other ancient authorities read either *forty-five* or *fifty*
[c] Gk *his*
[d] Gk *Sacherdonos*
[e] Other authorities read *Hananael*
[f] Lat: Gk *wholeheartedly mindful*

ness; later events temporarily question such justice. *Shalmaneser,* see 1.2n. **14:** *Media* (northern Iran) is east of Assyria; on Israelites exiled there, see 2 Kings 17.6. *Ten talents* is approximately 750 lb (350 kg). **15:** Sargon II (ruled 721–705 BCE), not Shalmaneser, was *Sennacherib's* father (see 1.2n.,18–20n.). Similar historical inaccuracies mark the opening of the book of Judith. **16–17:** Tobit continues his earlier charitable works (1.3). Burying corpses is his principal sign of righteousness (1.18–20; 2.3–8; 4.3–4; 6.15; 14.10–133); their unburied presence indicates Assyria's brutality (Deut 28.26; 1 Kings 14.11; 21.24; Jer 7.33; Ezek 29.5), for even executed criminals deserved proper burial (Deut 21.22–23). *Nineveh,* see 1.3n. **18:** Sennacherib (ruled 705–681) succeeded his father Sargon II in 705 BCE. *Fleeing . . . in those days of judgment,* a reference to the defeat of Sennacherib by divine intervention; see 2 Kings 19.35–36. **19:** Like Sophocles's Antigone, Tobit is threatened with death for burying the executed; cf. 2 Sam 21.8–14. **20:** Like Daniel and his companions (Dan 3; 6), Tobit is persecuted for practicing Jewish piety. **21:** *Killed him,* see 2 Kings 19.37. *Esar-haddon* reigned 681–669 BCE. **21–22:** *Ahikar* is a well-known figure in Semitic stories; a copy of the Aramaic book of Ahikar, dating to the early fifth century BCE, was found among a cache of papyri from a Jewish colony in Elephantine in southern Egypt. Ahikar's relationship to Tobit, noted only in this book, enhances Tobit's status. Ahikar's own story is summarized in 14.10; cf. 2.10; 11.18.

2.1–10: Tobit's blindness. Tobit's charity toward others results in his being blinded. **1:** *Pentecost,* the spring harvest of Weeks, also known as Shavuot (Lev 23.15–21; Deut 16.9–12; 2 Chr 8.13). **2:** Tobit consistently demon-

Then he went on to say, "Look, father, one of our own people has been murdered and thrown into the market place, and now he lies there strangled." [4] Then I sprang up, left the dinner before even tasting it, and removed the body[a] from the square[b] and laid it[a] in one of the rooms until sunset when I might bury it.[a] [5] When I returned, I washed myself and ate my food in sorrow. [6] Then I remembered the prophecy of Amos, how he said against Bethel,[c]

> "Your festivals shall be turned into mourning,
> and all your songs into lamentation."

And I wept.

[7] When the sun had set, I went and dug a grave and buried him. [8] And my neighbors laughed and said, "Is he still not afraid? He has already been hunted down to be put to death for doing this, and he ran away; yet here he is again burying the dead!" [9] That same night I washed myself and went into my courtyard and slept by the wall of the courtyard; and my face was uncovered because of the heat. [10] I did not know that there were sparrows on the wall; their fresh droppings fell into my eyes and produced white films. I went to physicians to be healed, but the more they treated me with ointments the more my vision was obscured by the white films, until I became completely blind. For four years I remained unable to see. All my kindred were sorry for me, and Ahikar took care of me for two years before he went to Elymais.

[11] At that time, also, my wife Anna earned money at women's work. [12] She used to send what she made to the owners and they would pay wages to her. One day, the seventh of Dystrus, when she cut off a piece she had woven and sent it to the owners, they paid her full wages and also gave her a young goat for a meal. [13] When she returned to me, the goat began to bleat. So I called her and said, "Where did you get this goat? It is surely not stolen, is it? Return it to the owners; for we have no right to eat anything stolen." [14] But she said to me, "It was given to me as a gift in addition to my wages." But I did not believe her, and told her to return it to the owners. I became flushed with anger against her over this. Then she replied to me, "Where are your acts of charity? Where are your righteous deeds? These things are known about you!"[d]

3 Then with much grief and anguish of heart I wept, and with groaning began to pray:

> [2] "You are righteous, O Lord,
> and all your deeds are just;
> all your ways are mercy and truth;
> you judge the world.[e]

---

a   Gk *him*
b   Other ancient authorities lack *from the square*
c   Other ancient authorities read *against Bethlehem*
d   Or *to you;* Gk *with you*
e   Other ancient authorities read *you render true and righteous judgment forever*

---

strates charity toward his people in exile (4.7–11,16). **5**: *Washed,* Num 19.11–13 commands washing as purification after contact with a corpse. **6**: *Amos* 8.10, one of the few scriptural citations in the book and another sign of composition in the Second Temple period. **9**: It is unclear why Tobit sleeps outside, especially since after moving the corpse he did return home to eat dinner (v. 5). If the concern is for ritual purity following contact with a corpse, see Num 19.11–22. A similar connection of dinner and gravedigging, but with humorous overtones, appears in 8.9–11. **10**: *Droppings,* Tobit is blinded in an ignominious and perhaps farcical manner. *Ahikar,* see 1.21–22n. *Elymais,* earlier Elam, a region in northwestern Persia.

2.11–14: **The argument.** Now dependent on others, Tobit becomes increasingly despondent. **11**: *Women's work* is weaving (cf. Prov 31.13,24); Tobit's earlier source of income, aside from investments, is unmentioned. **12**: At this verse and at 2.15–16, the Vulgate adds a comparison of Tobit to Job and thus an implied comparison of Anna to Job's wife. *Dystrus,* the fifth month in the Macedonian calendar (February/March), corresponding to the Jewish month of Shebat. The use of the Macedonian name is an indication of the Hellenistic date of Tobit. **13**: The outburst nuances Tobit's claims of righteousness and may also reflect his feeling of dishonor in being supported by a woman (Sir 25.22). **14**: Like Job's wife (Job 2.9), Anna questions the relationship between *righteous deeds* and a good life.

3.1–6: **Tobit's prayer.** The fight, coupled with Anna's observations about justice, not Tobit's blindness, causes him to seek death. Personal prayer is a major motif of this book (3.11–15; 8.4–8,15–17; 13.1–17) as well as

³ And now, O Lord, remember me
and look favorably upon me.
Do not punish me for my sins
and for my unwitting offenses
and those that my ancestors committed
before you.
They sinned against you,
⁴ and disobeyed your commandments.
So you gave us over to plunder, exile, and
death,
to become the talk, the byword, and an
object of reproach
among all the nations among whom
you have dispersed us.
⁵ And now your many judgments are true
in exacting penalty from me for my sins.
For we have not kept your commandments
and have not walked in accordance with
truth before you.
⁶ So now deal with me as you will;
command my spirit to be taken from
me,
so that I may be released from the face
of the earth and become dust.
For it is better for me to die than to live,
because I have had to listen to
undeserved insults,
and great is the sorrow within me.
Command, O Lord, that I be released from
this distress;
release me to go to the eternal home,
and do not, O Lord, turn your face away
from me.

For it is better for me to die
than to see so much distress in my life
and to listen to insults."

⁷ On the same day, at Ecbatana in Media,
it also happened that Sarah, the daughter of
Raguel, was reproached by one of her father's
maids. ⁸ For she had been married to seven
husbands, and the wicked demon Asmodeus
had killed each of them before they had
been with her as is customary for wives. So
the maid said to her, "You are the one who
kills[a] your husbands! See, you have already
been married to seven husbands and have
not borne the name of[b] a single one of them.
⁹ Why do you beat us? Because your husbands are dead? Go with them! May we never
see a son or daughter of yours!"
¹⁰ On that day she was grieved in spirit and
wept. When she had gone up to her father's
upper room, she intended to hang herself. But
she thought it over and said, "Never shall they
reproach my father, saying to him, 'You had
only one beloved daughter but she hanged
herself because of her distress.' And I shall
bring my father in his old age down in sorrow to Hades. It is better for me not to hang
myself, but to pray the Lord that I may die
and not listen to these reproaches anymore."

a Other ancient authorities read *strangles*
b Other ancient authorities read *have had no benefit
from*

in Hellenistic Jewish literature in general (see Jdt 9; Esth 14.1–9; Song of Thr; Sus; 1 Macc 7.37–38). **3–4:** Tobit admits his own sin and the sin of his *ancestors* (see Ex 20.5–6). The theology, which posits that plunder, exile, and death are occasioned by sin, is complicated by the plot, in which the righteous Tobit and Sarah suffer. Attribution of the exile to the people's sin is a common biblical idea. **6:** *Command my spirit to be taken from me*, Moses (Num 11.15), Elijah (1 Kings 19.4), and Jonah (Jon 4.8) similarly pray for release from suffering. *Undeserved insults* were directed at Tobit by his neighbors (2.8); Tobit does not reflect upon his undeserved insult to Anna. To *become dust* evokes Gen 3.19. The request for death is reminiscent of Job 3; cf. Jer 20.14–18. *The eternal home* likely refers not to immortality of the soul or eternal life, but either to the grave (see Job 34.15; Ps 104.29) or to Sheol, the realm of the dead (see Job 7.9–10; 14.10–13).

3.7–15: Sarah's plight and prayer. The scene shifts to Ecbatana in Media (modern Hamadan, in Iran), ca. 325 mi (525 km) east-southeast of Nineveh, and the narration shifts from first to third person as, *on the same day*, Sarah's plight parallels that of Tobit. **7:** *Reproached*, like Sarah of Gen 16.4–6, this Sarah also has no children and abuses her tormentor. **8:** The earliest literary mention of *Asmodeus*; his name derives from either the Persian expression "aeshma Daeva" meaning "demon of wrath," or Heb "shamad," meaning "to destroy." **10:** Sarah *intended to hang herself*, but concern for her father prevents suicide. The Bible does not condemn those who commit suicide (e.g. Saul [1 Sam 31.4–5], Ahithophel [2 Sam 17.23], Zimri [1 Kings 16.18], Razis [2 Macc 14.41–46]), but suicide is implicitly forbidden in Gen 9.4–6 and Ex 20.13. *Hades*, for this text the Greek equivalent of Sheol, the abode of the dead. Like Tobit, Sarah seeks to escape a woman's reproaches. **11:** *Hands outstretched* is a com-

¹¹ At that same time, with hands outstretched toward the window, she prayed and said,
"Blessed are you, merciful God!
  Blessed is your name forever;
  let all your works praise you forever.
¹² And now, Lord,ᵃ I turn my face to you,
  and raise my eyes toward you.
¹³ Command that I be released from the earth
  and not listen to such reproaches any
      more.
¹⁴ You know, O Master, that I am innocent
  of any defilement with a man,
¹⁵ and that I have not disgraced my name
  or the name of my father in the land of
      my exile.
I am my father's only child;
  he has no other child to be his heir;
and he has no close relative or other
      kindred
  for whom I should keep myself as wife.
Already seven husbands of mine have died.
  Why should I still live?
But if it is not pleasing to you, O Lord, to
      take my life,
  hear me in my disgrace."

¹⁶ At that very moment, the prayers of both of them were heard in the glorious presence of God. ¹⁷ So Raphael was sent to heal both of them: Tobit, by removing the white films from his eyes, so that he might see God's light with his eyes; and Sarah, daughter of Raguel, by giving her in marriage to Tobias son of Tobit, and by setting her free from the wicked demon Asmodeus. For Tobias was entitled to have her before all others who had desired to marry her. At the same time that Tobit returned from the courtyard into his house, Sarah daughter of Raguel came down from her upper room.

4 That same day Tobit remembered the money that he had left in trust with Gabael at Rages in Media, ² and he said to himself, "Now I have asked for death. Why do I not call my son Tobias and explain to him about the money before I die?" ³ Then he called his son Tobias, and when he came to him he said, "My son, when I die,ᵇ give me a proper burial. Honor your mother and do not abandon her all the days of her life. Do whatever pleases her, and do not grieve her in anything. ⁴ Remember her, my son, because she faced many dangers for you while you were in her womb. And when she dies, bury her beside me in the same grave.

⁵ "Revere the Lord all your days, my son, and refuse to sin or to transgress his commandments. Live uprightly all the days of your life, and do not walk in the ways of wrongdoing; ⁶ for those who act in accordance with truth will prosper in all their activities. To all those who practice righteousnessᶜ ⁷ give alms from your possessions,

---

ᵃ Other ancient authorities lack *Lord*
ᵇ Lat
ᶜ The text of codex Sinaiticus goes directly from verse 6 to verse 19, reading *To those who practice righteousness ¹⁹the Lord will give good counsel.* In order to fill the lacuna verses 7 to 18 are derived from other ancient authorities

---

mon posture for prayer (Ezra 9.5; Dan 6.10). *Blessed are you* is the traditional opening of Jewish prayers (8.5,15; Jdt 13.17). **13–15:** Sarah more quickly than Tobit pleads for death, though, unlike Tobit, she adds only if death is *pleasing* to God; in contrast to Tobit, she does not confess sins but instead protests her innocence. **14–15:** Women's chastity and honor are also prominent themes in the books of Judith and Susanna. *A close relative* suggests levirate law (Deut 25.5–10); Sarah is not aware that another relative and thus a potential husband, Tobias, exists.

3.16–17: Divine response. The fates of the supplicants are intertwined by Raphael's dual mission. **16:** Seven angels stand *in the glorious presence of God* to express human prayers and fulfill God's replies (see 12.15n.). **17:** *Raphael's* name means "God has healed." *Entitled,* by being a near relation (6.12; see 3.14–15n.). The style shifts to third-person narration.

4.1–13: Tobit's advice on the family. Tobit offers a "testament" or "farewell discourse," a common literary genre in biblical texts (Gen 48–49 [Jacob]; the book of Deuteronomy [Moses]; Josh 22–24 [Joshua]; 1 Chr 28–29 [David]) as well as in Hellenistic writings (*1 Enoch* 81; *Testaments of the Twelve Patriarchs*), in which a father offers his children ethical advice and prophetic insight. Chapter 14 provides a second example. **1:** *Money,* see 1.14. *Rages* is just east of modern Teheran. **3:** *Burial,* Tobit asks for what he provided others (on this familial responsibility, see also Lk 9.59). *Honoring one's mother* is commanded in the Decalogue (Ex 20.12; Deut 5.16; see also Prov 23.22; Sir 3.12–15; 7.27–28). **6–7:** Tobit's circumstances (temporarily) conflict with the comments typical

and do not let your eye begrudge the gift when you make it. Do not turn your face away from anyone who is poor, and the face of God will not be turned away from you. ⁸ If you have many possessions, make your gift from them in proportion; if few, do not be afraid to give according to the little you have. ⁹ So you will be laying up a good treasure for yourself against the day of necessity. ¹⁰ For almsgiving delivers from death and keeps you from going into the Darkness. ¹¹ Indeed, almsgiving, for all who practice it, is an excellent offering in the presence of the Most High.

¹² "Beware, my son, of every kind of fornication. First of all, marry a woman from among the descendants of your ancestors; do not marry a foreign woman, who is not of your father's tribe; for we are the descendants of the prophets. Remember, my son, that Noah, Abraham, Isaac, and Jacob, our ancestors of old, all took wives from among their kindred. They were blessed in their children, and their posterity will inherit the land. ¹³ So now, my son, love your kindred, and in your heart do not disdain your kindred, the sons and daughters of your people, by refusing to take a wife for yourself from among them. For in pride there is ruin and great confusion. And in idleness there is loss and dire poverty, because idleness is the mother of famine.

¹⁴ "Do not keep over until the next day the wages of those who work for you, but pay them at once. If you serve God you will receive payment. Watch yourself, my son, in everything you do, and discipline yourself in all your conduct. ¹⁵ And what you hate, do not do to anyone. Do not drink wine to excess or let drunkenness go with you on your way. ¹⁶ Give some of your food to the hungry, and some of your clothing to the naked. Give all your surplus as alms, and do not let your eye begrudge your giving of alms. ¹⁷ Place your bread on the grave of the righteous, but give none to sinners. ¹⁸ Seek advice from every wise person and do not despise any useful counsel. ¹⁹ At all times bless the Lord God, and ask him that your ways may be made straight and that all your paths and plans may prosper. For none of the nations has understanding, but the Lord himself will give them good counsel; but if he chooses otherwise, he casts down to deepest Hades. So now, my child, remember these commandments, and do not let them be erased from your heart.

²⁰ "And now, my son, let me explain to you that I left ten talents of silver in trust with Gabael son of Gabrias, at Rages in Media. ²¹ Do not be afraid, my son, because we have become poor. You have great wealth if you fear God and flee from every sin and do what is good in the sight of the Lord your God."

---

of wisdom literature (e.g., Prov 10.27–30). **8:** Giving what one can is a prominent motif in Jewish-Hellenistic (*Testament of Issachar*), early Christian (Lk 21.1–4; 2 Cor 8.12), and rabbinic (*b. Git.* 7a) writing. **10:** *Delivers from death* probably suggests a long life, not an eternal one. *Darkness*, that is, the grave. **11:** *Almsgiving* is consistently emphasized (12.8–9; 14.10–11; see also Lev 23.22; Ps 112.9; Prov 14.21,31; Isa 58.6–8; Sir 3.30–31; 34.18–35.4). **12–13:** Consistent with the instructions of wisdom literature (Prov 5.20; 6.24), Tobit warns about the evils of sexual sin and foreign women. *Fornication* refers to any intercourse outside of marriage. On endogamy, see 1.9n. Genesis does not record the ancestry of Noah's wife, though *Jubilees* (4.33), an early Second Temple text, does. The reference to *pride* suggests Prov 16.18.

4.14–19: Popular wisdom. Following instructions on marriage, Tobit returns to the conventional advice begun in 4.5–10. **14:** *Do not keep over*, see Lev 19.13; Deut 24.15. **15:** The "golden rule" appears throughout ancient writing (*Ahikar*; Mt 7.12; Lk 6.31; *b. Shabb.* 31a). On *drunkenness*, see Prov 23.29–35; Sir 31.25–30; Tobit's point is not abstinence but avoiding excess. **16:** *Alms*, see v. 11n. **17:** *The grave of the righteous* may refer to food given to mourners (see Ps 106.28) or to meals offered to the dead. The *Tale of Ahikar* (see 1.21–22n.) mentions this latter forbidden (Deut 26:14) and decried (Sir 30.18) practice. **19:** *Ways . . . made straight*, see Prov 3.6; 11.5; Ps 5.8; Isa 45.13. The view that *none of the nations has understanding* (see Deut 32.28) comports with the condition of exile. *Hades*, see 3.10n.

4.20–5.3: Obtaining funds left in trust. Tobias is to obtain wealth from righteousness and, more directly, from his father's banked funds. The *fear* of God is a common theme in wisdom literature (see Prov 1.7; 10.27; 15.16; 22.4). **4.20:** *Ten talents*, see 1.14n. **5.1–2:** Tobias's positive response echoes Ex 19.8; Ruth 3.5. However, like Moses (Ex 3), he also questions his commission.

5 Then Tobias answered his father Tobit, "I will do everything that you have commanded me, father; [2] but how can I obtain the money[a] from him, since he does not know me and I do not know him? What evidence[b] am I to give him so that he will recognize and trust me, and give me the money? Also, I do not know the roads to Media, or how to get there." [3] Then Tobit answered his son Tobias, "He gave me his bond and I gave him my bond. I[c] divided his in two; we each took one part, and I put one with the money. And now twenty years have passed since I left this money in trust. So now, my son, find yourself a trustworthy man to go with you, and we will pay him wages until you return. But get back the money from Gabael."[d]

[4] So Tobias went out to look for a man to go with him to Media, someone who was acquainted with the way. He went out and found the angel Raphael standing in front of him; but he did not perceive that he was an angel of God. [5] Tobias[e] said to him, "Where do you come from, young man?" "From your kindred, the Israelites," he replied, "and I have come here to work." Then Tobias[f] said to him, "Do you know the way to go to Media?" [6] "Yes," he replied, "I have been there many times; I am acquainted with it and know all the roads. I have often traveled to Media, and would stay with our kinsman Gabael who lives in Rages of Media. It is a journey of two days from Ecbatana to Rages; for it lies in a mountainous area, while Ecbatana is in the middle of the plain." [7] Then Tobias said to him, "Wait for me, young man, until I go in and tell my father; for I do need you to travel with me, and I will pay you your wages." [8] He replied, "All right, I will wait; but do not take too long."

[9] So Tobias[f] went in to tell his father Tobit and said to him, "I have just found a man who is one of our own Israelite kindred!" He replied, "Call the man in, my son, so that I may learn about his family and to what tribe he belongs, and whether he is trustworthy enough to go with you."

[10] Then Tobias went out and called him, and said, "Young man, my father is calling for you." So he went in to him, and Tobit greeted him first. He replied, "Joyous greetings to you!" But Tobit retorted, "What joy is left for me any more? I am a man without eyesight; I cannot see the light of heaven, but I lie in darkness like the dead who no longer see the light. Although still alive, I am among the dead. I hear people but I cannot see them." But the young man[f] said, "Take courage; the time is near for God to heal you; take courage." Then Tobit said to him, "My son Tobias wishes to go to Media. Can you accompany him and guide him? I will pay your wages, brother." He answered, "I can go with him and I know all the roads, for I have often gone to Media and have crossed all its plains, and I am familiar with its mountains and all of its roads."

[11] Then Tobit[f] said to him, "Brother, of what family are you and from what tribe? Tell me, brother." [12] He replied, "Why do you need to know my tribe?" But Tobit[f] said, "I want to be sure, brother, whose son you are and what your name is." [13] He replied, "I am Azariah, the son of the great Hananiah, one of your

a   Gk *it*
b   Gk *sign*
c   Other authorities read *He*
d   Gk *from him*
e   Gk *He*
f   Gk *he*

5.4–17: **Raphael's disguise**. Disguised heavenly beings are a stock motif in folklore (as in *The Odyssey*, in which Athena accompanies Telemachus), and angelic appearances are frequent in biblical stories (e.g., Gen 18.1–15; Judg 13). That readers know more than Tobit and his family adds to the entertainment of the tale. **4:** *Standing in front of him*, the immediacy of the angel's appearance suggests the miraculous. *Raphael*, see 3.17n. **5:** *Young man*: Tobias better fits this description; the humor of mistaken identities continues. **6:** *Two days*: *Rages* is 185 mi (300 km) from *Ecbatana*; this journey would take far longer for anyone other than an angel. Ecbatana is not in *the middle of a plain*, but in the mountains; the story is as loose with geographical as with chronological and historical details (see 1.4n.; 1.15n.). **10:** Having prayed for death (3.6), Tobit perceives himself as among the dead. The reference to divine healing recalls Raphael's name (see 3.17n.). **11–12:** The angel appears to be reluctant to reveal his *family* and *tribe*. **13:** The pseudonyms point to Raphael's roles: *Azariah* is Hebrew for "God

relatives." [14] Then Tobit said to him, "Welcome! God save you, brother. Do not feel bitter toward me, brother, because I wanted to be sure about your ancestry. It turns out that you are a kinsman, and of good and noble lineage. For I knew Hananiah and Nathan,[a] the two sons of Shemeliah,[b] and they used to go with me to Jerusalem and worshiped with me there, and were not led astray. Your kindred are good people; you come of good stock. Hearty welcome!"

[15] Then he added, "I will pay you a drachma a day as wages, as well as expenses for yourself and my son. So go with my son, [16] and[c] I will add something to your wages." Raphael[d] answered, "I will go with him; so do not fear. We shall leave in good health and return to you in good health, because the way is safe." [17] So Tobit[e] said to him, "Blessings be upon you, brother."

Then he called his son and said to him, "Son, prepare supplies for the journey and set out with your brother. May God in heaven bring you safely there and return you in good health to me; and may his angel, my son, accompany you both for your safety."

Before he went out to start his journey, he kissed his father and mother. Tobit then said to him, "Have a safe journey."

[18] But his mother[f] began to weep, and said to Tobit, "Why is it that you have sent my child away? Is he not the staff of our hand as he goes in and out before us? [19] Do not heap money upon money, but let it be a ransom for our child. [20] For the life that is given to us by the Lord is enough for us."

[21] Tobit[d] said to her, "Do not worry; our child will leave in good health and return to us in good health. Your eyes will see him on the day when he returns to you in good health. Say no more! Do not fear for them, my sister. [22] For a good angel will accompany him; his journey will be successful, and he will come back in good health." [1] So she stopped weeping.

6

The young man went out and the angel went with him; [2] and the dog came out with him and went along with them. So they both journeyed along, and when the first night overtook them they camped by the Tigris river. [3] Then the young man went down to wash his feet in the Tigris river. Suddenly a large fish leaped up from the water and tried to swallow the young man's foot, and he cried out. [4] But the angel said to the young man, "Catch hold of the fish and hang on to it!" So the young man grasped the fish and drew it up on the land. [5] Then the angel said to him, "Cut open the fish and take out its gall, heart, and liver. Keep them with you, but throw away the intestines. For its gall, heart, and liver are useful as medicine." [6] So after cutting open

---

a Other ancient authorities read *Jathan* or *Nathaniah*
b Other ancient authorities read *Shemaiah*
c Other ancient authorities add *when you return safely*
d Gk *He*
e Gk *he*
f Other ancient authorities add *Anna*

---

has helped"; *Hananiah* means "God is merciful." **14:** Reference to the righteous sons of *Shemeliah* belies Tobit's claim (1.5–6) that he alone was faithful. **15:** Tobit's financial arrangements are generous. **17:** Tobit's prayer for angelic accompaniment (also 5.22) is already answered, adding an ironic note to the scene. Tobias's journey will resemble earlier quests for brides, although he does not yet know this (cf. Gen 24.40).

5.18–6.1a: Anna's lament. The couple alternate between practical observations and theological reflection (cf. 10.1–7). **18:** *My child,* Anna's maternal worry is palpable. *The staff of our hand,* a reliable person upon whom they can lean (see 2 Kings 18.21). **19:** *Ransom* suggests that Gabael should keep the funds as though they were ransom for Tobias. **21:** *My sister,* a term of affection for a lover or spouse (see Song 4.9,10). **22:** *A good angel* does accompany Tobias, although Tobit does not know this.

6.1b–9: Dangerous journey. Still disguised, Raphael will protect Tobias from dangerous fish and provide instruction for protection against lecherous demons. **2:** The *dog* (see also 11.4) adds an intimate touch and may suggest Odysseus's faithful pet (*Odyssey* 17.289–327). The *Tigris* is west of Nineveh; the geography remains fanciful. **3:** The unexpected *large fish* may be a parody of the Jonah story (Jon 1.7), in which a large fish swallows someone heading eventually toward Nineveh. **5:** Raphael's instructions are consistent with ancient medical texts that provide instructions for the use of fish organs. *Gall,* i.e., bile, is a bitter digestive juice recognized as

the fish the young man gathered together the gall, heart, and liver; then he roasted and ate some of the fish, and kept some to be salted.

The two continued on their way together until they were near Media.[a] 7 Then the young man questioned the angel and said to him, "Brother Azariah, what medicinal value is there in the fish's heart and liver, and in the gall?" 8 He replied, "As for the fish's heart and liver, you must burn them to make a smoke in the presence of a man or woman afflicted by a demon or evil spirit, and every affliction will flee away and never remain with that person any longer. 9 And as for the gall, anoint a person's eyes where white films have appeared on them; blow upon them, upon the white films, and the eyes[b] will be healed."

10 When he entered Media and already was approaching Ecbatana,[c] 11 Raphael said to the young man, "Brother Tobias." "Here I am," he answered. Then Raphael[d] said to him, "We must stay this night in the home of Raguel. He is your relative, and he has a daughter named Sarah. 12 He has no male heir and no daughter except Sarah only, and you, as next of kin to her, have before all other men a hereditary claim on her. Also it is right for you to inherit her father's possessions. Moreover, the girl is sensible, brave, and very beautiful, and her father is a good man." 13 He continued, "You have every right to take her in marriage. So listen to me, brother; tonight I will speak to her father about the girl, so that we may take her to be your bride. When we return from Rages we will celebrate her marriage. For I know that Raguel can by no means keep her from you or promise her to another man without incurring the penalty

of death according to the decree of the book of Moses. Indeed he knows that you, rather than any other man, are entitled to marry his daughter. So now listen to me, brother, and tonight we shall speak concerning the girl and arrange her engagement to you. And when we return from Rages we will take her and bring her back with us to your house."

14 Then Tobias said in answer to Raphael, "Brother Azariah, I have heard that she already has been married to seven husbands and that they died in the bridal chamber. On the night when they went in to her, they would die. I have heard people saying that it was a demon that killed them. 15 It does not harm her, but it kills anyone who desires to approach her. So now, since I am the only son my father has, I am afraid that I may die and bring my father's and mother's life down to their grave, grieving for me—and they have no other son to bury them."

16 But Raphael[d] said to him, "Do you not remember your father's orders when he commanded you to take a wife from your father's house? Now listen to me, brother, and say no more about this demon. Take her. I know that this very night she will be given to you in marriage. 17 When you enter the bridal chamber, take some of the fish's liver and heart, and put them on the embers of the incense. An odor will be given off; 18 the demon will smell it and flee, and will never be seen near her any more. Now when you are

a   Other ancient authorities read *Ecbatana*
b   Gk *they*
c   Other ancient authorities read *Rages*
d   Gk *he*

having medicinal properties. **6:** No reference is made to the angel's eating (see Judg. 13.16). **8:** *To make a smoke,* or to fumigate, was a standard means for healing and exorcising demons. Explicit reference to a *woman* foreshadows Sarah's role.

6.10–18: Prenuptial instructions. Raphael now reveals the additional purpose of their journey; knowing Sarah's past luck with marriages, Tobias is understandably reluctant but quickly warms to the prospect of marrying her. **12:** *No male heir,* although Israelite inheritance laws were patrilineal, brotherless daughters could inherit if they married within the tribe (Num 27.1–11; 36.1–13). *Next of kin* refers to levirate law (3.14–15n.); by marrying Sarah, Tobias will obtain Raguel's estate. **13:** *Penalty of death*: no such law exists. **14–15:** Tobias's hesitancy—he mentions the death of Sarah's husbands four times in vv. 14–15—increases the tension; his fear is not primarily for his own life, but for the grief his death will cause his parents (see 3.10). **16:** Raphael eases Tobias's fear by repeating his concern for his parents, but changing his focus. **17:** On fumigating as an exorcism technique, see 6.8n. **18:** Raphael's advice, coupled with the announcement that the match was made in heaven and that Sarah is Tobias's relative, both calms the young man's fears and prompts his love.

about to go to bed with her, both of you must first stand up and pray, imploring the Lord of heaven that mercy and safety may be granted to you. Do not be afraid, for she was set apart for you before the world was made. You will save her, and she will go with you. I presume that you will have children by her, and they will be as brothers to you. Now say no more!" When Tobias heard the words of Raphael and learned that she was his kinswoman,[a] related through his father's lineage, he loved her very much, and his heart was drawn to her.

7 Now when they[b] entered Ecbatana, Tobias[c] said to him, "Brother Azariah, take me straight to our brother Raguel." So he took him to Raguel's house, where they found him sitting beside the courtyard door. They greeted him first, and he replied, "Joyous greetings, brothers; welcome and good health!" Then he brought them into his house. [2] He said to his wife Edna, "How much the young man resembles my kinsman Tobit!" [3] Then Edna questioned them, saying, "Where are you from, brothers?" They answered, "We belong to the descendants of Naphtali who are exiles in Nineveh." [4] She said to them, "Do you know our kinsman Tobit?" And they replied, "Yes, we know him." Then she asked them, "Is he[d] in good health?" [5] They replied, "He is alive and in good health." And Tobias added, "He is my father!" [6] At that Raguel jumped up and kissed him and wept. [7] He also spoke to him as follows, "Blessings on you, my child, son of a good and noble father![e] O most miserable of calamities that such an upright and beneficent man has become blind!" He then embraced his kinsman Tobias and wept. [8] His wife Edna also wept for him, and

their daughter Sarah likewise wept. [9] Then Raguel[c] slaughtered a ram from the flock and received them very warmly.

When they had bathed and washed themselves and had reclined to dine, Tobias said to Raphael, "Brother Azariah, ask Raguel to give me my kinswoman[a] Sarah." [10] But Raguel overheard it and said to the lad, "Eat and drink, and be merry tonight. For no one except you, brother, has the right to marry my daughter Sarah. Likewise I am not at liberty to give her to any other man than yourself, because you are my nearest relative. But let me explain to you the true situation more fully, my child. [11] I have given her to seven men of our kinsmen, and all died on the night when they went in to her. But now, my child, eat and drink, and the Lord will act on behalf of you both." But Tobias said, "I will neither eat nor drink anything until you settle the things that pertain to me." So Raguel said, "I will do so. She is given to you in accordance with the decree in the book of Moses, and it has been decreed from heaven that she be given to you. Take your kinswoman;[a] from now on you are her brother and she is your sister. She is given to you from today and forever. May the Lord of heaven, my child, guide and prosper you both this night and grant you mercy and peace." [12] Then Raguel summoned his daughter Sarah. When she came to him he took her by the hand and

---

[a] Gk *sister*

[b] Other ancient authorities read *he*

[c] Gk *he*

[d] Other ancient authorities add *alive and*

[e] Other ancient authorities add *When he heard that Tobit had lost his sight, he was stricken with grief and wept. Then he said,*

7.1–16: Tobit and Sarah marry. *Raguel* and Edna's welcome repeats the themes of family connections. **1:** *Raguel's* name is connected to Reuel, Moses' father-in-law (Ex 2.18; Num 10.29); the name is also shared with an archangel in *I Enoch* 20.4. *Ecbatana*, see 5.6n. **3:** *Edna* asks the more pertinent questions; the scene echoes Gen 28.1–5. **5:** Tobias does not mention his father's illness. **7:** The source of Raguel's knowledge of Tobit's blindness is not cited. **9:** *Bathed and washed* and *reclined to dine* indicate common customs of hospitality, cf. Gen 18.1–8; Lk 7.44–46. **10–11:** The juxtaposition of death threats and joyous feasting is humorous; not every groom would appreciate Sarah's *true situation*. Raguel must follow the *decree in the book of Moses* regarding the rightful spouse for Sarah (see 3.14–15n.), but he is also concerned about the fate of her husbands. *I will neither eat nor drink*, Tobias begins to take charge of his fate. *Sister*, see 5.21n. **12–15:** *The decree* is Num 36.8; Raguel repeats the idea (6.18) that Sarah is Tobias's divinely appointed wife. **12:** *Raguel summoned his daughter* because neither she nor

gave her to Tobias,[a] saying, "Take her to be your wife in accordance with the law and decree written in the book of Moses. Take her and bring her safely to your father. And may the God of heaven prosper your journey with his peace." [13] Then he called her mother and told her to bring writing material; and he wrote out a copy of a marriage contract, to the effect that he gave her to him as wife according to the decree of the law of Moses. [14] Then they began to eat and drink.

[15] Raguel called his wife Edna and said to her, "Sister, get the other room ready, and take her there." [16] So she went and made the bed in the room as he had told her, and brought Sarah[b] there. She wept for her daughter.[b] Then, wiping away the tears,[c] she said to her, "Take courage, my daughter; the Lord of heaven grant you joy[d] in place of your sorrow. Take courage, my daughter." Then she went out.

8 When they had finished eating and drinking they wanted to retire; so they took the young man and brought him into the bedroom. [2] Then Tobias remembered the words of Raphael, and he took the fish's liver and heart out of the bag where he had them and put them on the embers of the incense. [3] The odor of the fish so repelled the demon that he fled to the remotest parts[e] of Egypt. But Raphael followed him, and at once bound him there hand and foot. [4] When the parents[f] had gone out and shut the door of the room, Tobias got out of bed and said to Sarah,[b] "Sister, get up,

and let us pray and implore our Lord that he grant us mercy and safety." [5] So she got up, and they began to pray and implore that they might be kept safe. Tobias[g] began by saying,

"Blessed are you, O God of our ancestors,
and blessed is your name in all
generations forever.
Let the heavens and the whole creation
bless you forever.
[6] You made Adam, and for him you made
his wife Eve
as a helper and support.
From the two of them the human race
has sprung.
You said, 'It is not good that the man
should be alone;
let us make a helper for him like
himself.'
[7] I now am taking this kinswoman of mine,
not because of lust,
but with sincerity.
Grant that she and I may find mercy
and that we may grow old together."
[8] And they both said, "Amen, Amen." [9] Then they went to sleep for the night.

a Gk *him*
b Gk *her*
c Other ancient authorities read *the tears of her daughter*
d Other ancient authorities read *favor*
e Or *fled through the air to the parts*
f Gk *they*
g Gk *He*

her mother participated in the original conversation about her fate; the match is arranged by the men. **13:** The Jewish marriage *contract* (Heb "ketubah") protects the wife's financial interests; this is the first recorded literary reference to this well-known practice; the earliest preserved example of a ketubah, dating to ca. 440 BCE, comes from the Jewish colony at Elephantine in Egypt. **16:** Edna's emotions encompass both fear and hope; she exhorts her daughter to courage, as Raphael had exhorted Tobias (6.18).

8.1–9a: Asmodeus is exorcised. Raphael's advice proves sound as the demon is exorcised, and the couple offers a prayer of thanksgiving. **2:** *The words of Raphael*, 6.8. **3:** *Repelled the demon*, see 6.8n. *Bound*, since binding restrains demons (see *1 Enoch* 10.4). **4–5:** The couple's praying contrasts with both Raguel's grave-digging (8.9–11) and the descriptions of ardent love-making found in non-Jewish Hellenistic romances. *Sister*, see 5.21n. **5–7:** Prayers are frequently attributed to characters in Second Temple Jewish literature (Jdt 9; Add Est 13; 14; Sus; Song of Three). **5:** *Blessed are you*, see 3.11n. *God of our ancestors*, see Ex 3.13; Deut 4.1. **6:** *Adam* and *Eve*, one of the earliest biblical references to these figures outside of Genesis. *You said*, introducing a quotation of Gen 2.18. **7:** *Not because of lust*, chastity is a popular theme in Jewish-Hellenistic literature; see also 3.14–15n. **8:** The text, discreetly, does not note when the marriage was consummated. *Amen, Amen* are Sarah's only words aside from her prayer (3.11–15).

8.9b–18: Raguel's fears are assuaged. 9–10: Raguel's morbid planning contrasts with Tobias's piety; unlike

But Raguel arose and called his servants to him, and they went and dug a grave, [10] for he said, "It is possible that he will die and we will become an object of ridicule and derision." [11] When they had finished digging the grave, Raguel went into his house and called his wife, [12] saying, "Send one of the maids and have her go in to see if he is alive. But if he is dead, let us bury him without anyone knowing it." [13] So they sent the maid, lit a lamp, and opened the door; and she went in and found them sound asleep together. [14] Then the maid came out and informed them that he was alive and that nothing was wrong. [15] So they blessed the God of heaven, and Raguel[a] said,

"Blessed are you, O God, with every pure
blessing;
let all your chosen ones bless you.[b]
Let them bless you forever.
[16] Blessed are you because you have made
me glad.
It has not turned out as I expected,
but you have dealt with us according to
your great mercy.
[17] Blessed are you because you had
compassion
on two only children.
Be merciful to them, O Master, and keep
them safe;
bring their lives to fulfillment
in happiness and mercy."

[18] Then he ordered his servants to fill in the grave before daybreak.

[19] After this he asked his wife to bake many loaves of bread; and he went out to the herd and brought two steers and four rams and ordered them to be slaughtered. So they began to make preparations. [20] Then he called for Tobias and swore on oath to him in these words:[c] "You shall not leave here for fourteen days, but shall stay here eating and drinking with me; and you shall cheer up my daughter, who has been depressed. [21] Take at once half of what I own and return in safety to your father; the other half will be yours when my wife and I die. Take courage, my child. I am your father and Edna is your mother, and we belong to you as well as to your wife[d] now and forever. Take courage, my child."

9 Then Tobias called Raphael and said to him, [2] "Brother Azariah, take four servants and two camels with you and travel to Rages. Go to the home of Gabael, give him the bond, get the money, and then bring him with you to the wedding celebration. [4] For you know that my father must be counting the days, and if I delay even one day I will upset him very much. [3] You are witness to the oath Raguel has sworn, and I cannot violate his oath."[e] [5] So Raphael with the four servants and two camels went to Rages in Media and stayed with Gabael. Raphael[f] gave him the bond and informed him that Tobit's son Tobias had married and was inviting him to the wedding celebration. So Gabael[g] got up and counted out to him the money bags, with their seals intact; then they loaded

---

a   Gk *they*
b   Other ancient authorities lack this line
c   Other ancient authorities read *Tobias and said to him*
d   Gk *sister*
e   In other ancient authorities verse 3 precedes verse 4
f   Gk *He*
g   Gk *he*

Tobit, Raguel prepares a grave *before* finding a corpse. **10:** *Ridicule and derision*, Raguel fears for his reputation, not his daughter's happiness or his son-in-law's life; Sarah had already become an object of derision (3.7–9). **12:** *Without anyone knowing* ignores Azariah/Raphael, the servants, and the concerns of Tobit and Anna. **15–17:** The prayer continues Raguel's wry perspective: he praises God for his own good fortune before mentioning the mercy extended to the couple.

   8.19–9.6: The wedding celebrated and tasks fulfilled. 8.20: *Fourteen days*, often seen as twice as long as a usual wedding celebration. *Depressed* either because of past deaths or the prospect of leaving her home. **21:** *Take courage* is what Edna advised Sarah (7.16), but under much different circumstances. The language of *father* and *mother* together with promises of inheritance suggests an adoption formula (see 10.12). **9.1:** Tobias now commands Raphael to obtain Tobit's money from Gabael; no longer the youth, he has become an adult. **4:** *I will upset him*, as demonstrated in 10.1–3. **5:** *Rages*, see 4.1n. **6:** Gabael's blessing indicates that the two families are regarded as one.

them on the camels.[a] [6] In the morning they both got up early and went to the wedding celebration. When they came into Raguel's house they found Tobias reclining at table. He sprang up and greeted Gabael,[b] who wept and blessed him with the words, "Good and noble son of a father good and noble, upright and generous! May the Lord grant the blessing of heaven to you and your wife, and to your wife's father and mother. Blessed be God, for I see in Tobias the very image of my cousin Tobit."

10 Now, day by day, Tobit kept counting how many days Tobias[c] would need for going and for returning. And when the days had passed and his son did not appear, [2] he said, "Is it possible that he has been detained? Or that Gabael has died, and there is no one to give him the money?" [3] And he began to worry. [4] His wife Anna said, "My child has perished and is no longer among the living." And she began to weep and mourn for her son, saying, [5] "Woe to me, my child, the light of my eyes, that I let you make the journey." [6] But Tobit kept saying to her, "Be quiet and stop worrying, my dear;[d] he is all right. Probably something unexpected has happened there. The man who went with him is trustworthy and is one of our own kin. Do not grieve for him, my dear;[d] he will soon be here." [7] She answered him, "Be quiet yourself! Stop trying to deceive me! My child has perished." She would rush out every day and watch the road her son had taken, and would heed no one.[e] When the sun had set she would go in and mourn and weep all night long, getting no sleep at all.

Now when the fourteen days of the wedding celebration had ended that Raguel had sworn to observe for his daughter, Tobias came to him and said, "Send me back, for I know that my father and mother do not believe that they will see me again. So I beg of you, father, to let me go so that I may return to my own father. I have already explained to you how I left him." [8] But Raguel said to Tobias, "Stay, my child, stay with me; I will send messengers to your father Tobit and they will inform him about you." [9] But he said, "No! I beg you to send me back to my father." [10] So Raguel promptly gave Tobias his wife Sarah, as well as half of all his property: male and female slaves, oxen and sheep, donkeys and camels, clothing, money, and household goods. [11] Then he saw them safely off; he embraced Tobias[b] and said, "Farewell, my child; have a safe journey. The Lord of heaven prosper you and your wife Sarah, and may I see children of yours before I die." [12] Then he kissed his daughter Sarah and said to her, "My daughter, honor your father-in-law and your mother-in-law,[f] since from now on they are as much your parents as those who gave you birth. Go in peace, daughter, and may I hear a good report about you as long as I live." Then he bade them farewell and let

a   Other ancient authorities lack *on the camels*
b   Gk *him*
c   Gk *he*
d   Gk *sister*
e   Other ancient authorities read *and she would eat nothing*
f   Other ancient authorities lack parts of *Then ... mother-in-law*

10.1–7a: **Anxiety at home**. Tobit and Anna's concerns contrast with the celebration in Media. **1:** *And when the days had passed,* the two-week wedding celebrations, unknown to Tobit and Anna, extended the time of Tobias's absence long past what was required for the journey. **5:** *Light of my eyes,* perhaps a veiled reference to Tobit's blindness, recalls his words to Anna in 5.21. *I let you make the journey,* rather than again blaming Tobit (see 5.18), Anna suggests she had the power to prevent Tobias from leaving. **6:** In comforting Anna (cf. 5.21), Tobit masks his own fears. **7:** Unlike 5.21, here Anna does not heed Tobit's command to silence. Despite insisting that her *child has perished,* she continues to watch for him.

10.7b–13: **Return to Nineveh**. The couple's leave-taking is much less fraught with worry—and advice—than the parallel scene of 5.17–22. Tobias is mindful that his parents are likely worried (10.1–7a). **8:** Raguel desires his new son remain with him, but filial duty prompts Tobias to leave. **10:** Sarah's substantial dowry is part of the inheritance Tobias will receive (6.12). **12:** *Honor your father-in-law and your mother-in-law* extends the Decalogue's commandment (see 4.3n.). *Child and dear brother* intensifies the familial connection; more than just a marriage, the couple's relationship is the merging of two families. To *see children,* this prayer will be granted, as Raphael had remarked to Tobias (6.18). *Do nothing to grieve her,* the mother is vigilant for her daughter's happiness; the

them go. Then Edna said to Tobias, "My child and dear brother, the Lord of heaven bring you back safely, and may I live long enough to see children of you and of my daughter Sarah before I die. In the sight of the Lord I entrust my daughter to you; do nothing to grieve her all the days of your life. Go in peace, my child. From now on I am your mother and Sarah is your beloved wife.[a] May we all prosper together all the days of our lives." Then she kissed them both and saw them safely off. [13] Tobias parted from Raguel with happiness and joy, praising the Lord of heaven and earth, King over all, because he had made his journey a success. Finally, he blessed Raguel and his wife Edna, and said, "I have been commanded by the Lord to honor you all the days of my life."[b]

11

When they came near to Kaserin, which is opposite Nineveh, Raphael said, [2] "You are aware of how we left your father. [3] Let us run ahead of your wife and prepare the house while they are still on the way." [4] As they went on together Raphael[c] said to him, "Have the gall ready." And the dog[d] went along behind them.

[5] Meanwhile Anna sat looking intently down the road by which her son would come. [6] When she caught sight of him coming, she said to his father, "Look, your son is coming, and the man who went with him!"

[7] Raphael said to Tobias, before he had approached his father, "I know that his eyes will be opened. [8] Smear the gall of the fish on his eyes; the medicine will make the white films shrink and peel off from his eyes, and your father will regain his sight and see the light." [9] Then Anna ran up to her son and threw her arms around him, saying, "Now that I have seen you, my child, I am ready to die." And she wept. [10] Then Tobit got up and came

stumbling out through the courtyard door. Tobias went up to him, [11] with the gall of the fish in his hand, and holding him firmly, he blew into his eyes, saying, "Take courage, father." With this he applied the medicine on his eyes, [12] and it made them smart.[b] [13] Next, with both his hands he peeled off the white films from the corners of his eyes. Then Tobit[c] saw his son and[e] threw his arms around him, [14] and he wept and said to him, "I see you, my son, the light of my eyes!" Then he said,

"Blessed be God,
and blessed be his great name,
and blessed be all his holy angels.
May his holy name be blessed[f]
throughout all the ages.
[15] Though he afflicted me,
he has had mercy upon me.[g]
Now I see my son Tobias!"

So Tobit went in rejoicing and praising God at the top of his voice. Tobias reported to his father that his journey had been successful, that he had brought the money, that he had married Raguel's daughter Sarah, and that she was, indeed, on her way there, very near to the gate of Nineveh.

[16] Then Tobit, rejoicing and praising God, went out to meet his daughter-in-law at the gate of Nineveh. When the people of Nineveh saw him coming, walking along in full vigor and with no one leading him, they were

a   Gk *sister*
b   Lat: Meaning of Gk uncertain
c   Gk *he*
d   Codex Sinaiticus reads *And the Lord*
e   Other ancient authorities lack *saw his son and*
f   Codex Sinaiticus reads *May his great name be upon us and blessed be all the angels*
g   Lat: Gk lacks this line

reader may recall the grief Tobit's insults brought Anna (2.11–14). **13:** Tobias confirms his bond with his in-laws; Sarah remains silent.

11.1–6: Tobias returns. 3: *Let us run ahead* may indicate Raphael's concern to avoid Sarah's company; unlike Asmodeus, he will not be tempted. **4:** *Gall*, see 6.5n. *The dog*, see 6.2n. **6:** Anna, ever watchful (see 10.7), brings the good news to Tobit.

11.7–18: Tobit is healed. 8: *Gall*, see 6.9. **11–13:** See Acts 9.18. **14:** *Light of my eyes*, fulfilling v. 8, has both metaphoric and literal implications (cf. 10.5). **14–15:** Tobit's doxology resembles those of Tobias (8.5–7) and Raguel (8.15–17); see also 8.5–7n. *Holy angels* is ironic, since Raphael has not revealed his identity. *Afflicted* (lit. "scourged") and *had mercy*, conventional terms for divine punishment and reconciliation upon the community's repentance, are applied to Israel in 13.2,5 (see 2 Macc 6.12–16). **16:** *Amazement* is the standard reaction

amazed. [17] Before them all, Tobit acknowledged that God had been merciful to him and had restored his sight. When Tobit met Sarah the wife of his son Tobias, he blessed her saying, "Come in, my daughter, and welcome. Blessed be your God who has brought you to us, my daughter. Blessed be your father and your mother, blessed be my son Tobias, and blessed be you, my daughter. Come in now to your home, and welcome, with blessing and joy. Come in, my daughter." So on that day there was rejoicing among all the Jews who were in Nineveh. [18] Ahikar and his nephew Nadab were also present to share Tobit's joy. With merriment they celebrated Tobias's wedding feast for seven days, and many gifts were given to him.[a]

12 When the wedding celebration was ended, Tobit called his son Tobias and said to him, "My child, see to paying the wages of the man who went with you, and give him a bonus as well." [2] He replied, "Father, how much shall I pay him? It would do no harm to give him half of the possessions brought back with me. [3] For he has led me back to you safely, he cured my wife, he brought the money back with me, and he healed you. How much extra shall I give him as a bonus?" [4] Tobit said, "He deserves, my child, to receive half of all that he brought back." [5] So Tobias[b] called him and said, "Take for your wages half of all that you brought back, and farewell."

[6] Then Raphael[b] called the two of them privately and said to them, "Bless God and acknowledge him in the presence of all the living for the good things he has done for you. Bless and sing praise to his name. With fitting honor declare to all people the deeds[c] of God. Do not be slow to acknowledge him. [7] It is good to conceal the secret of a king, but to acknowledge and reveal the works of God, and with fitting honor to acknowledge him. Do good and evil will not overtake you. [8] Prayer with fasting[d] is good, but better than both is almsgiving with righteousness. A little with righteousness is better than wealth with wrongdoing.[e] It is better to give alms than to lay up gold. [9] For almsgiving saves from death and purges away every sin. Those who give alms will enjoy a full life, [10] but those who commit sin and do wrong are their own worst enemies.

[11] "I will now declare the whole truth to you and will conceal nothing from you. Already I have declared it to you when I said, 'It is good to conceal the secret of a king, but to reveal with due honor the works of God.' [12] So now when you and Sarah prayed, it was I who brought and read[f] the record of your prayer before the glory of the Lord, and likewise whenever you would bury the dead. [13] And that time when you did not hesitate to get up and leave your dinner to go and bury the dead, [14] I was sent to you to test you. And at the same time God sent me to heal you and

---

[a]   Other ancient authorities lack parts of this sentence

[b]   Gk *he*

[c]   Gk *words*; other ancient authorities read *words of the deeds*

[d]   Codex Sinaiticus *with sincerity*

[e]   Lat

[f]   Lat: Gk lacks *and read*

---

to a miraculous healing. **17**: *My daughter*, a repeated phrase, echoes the familial language of Raguel and Edna; Tobit greets the daughter-in-law for whom he had prayed (4.12–13). **18**: *Ahikar*, see 1.21–22n. *Nadab*, see 14.10n.

12.1–22: Raphael's revelations. Bringing the major plot lines to a conclusion, Raphael explains his role in testing Tobit and exhorts Tobit and his son to good deeds and piety. **2**: *How much shall I pay him?* The fee had been determined, but not the amount of the bonus (5.15–16). *Half of the possessions* is one-quarter of Raguel's estate plus half the loan. The generosity is consistent with Tobit's insistence on almsgiving. **6**: *Declare to all people* expresses a universalistic impulse (13.3–4,11; 14.6–7). **7**: *Secret of a king* anticipates Raphael's revelation in v. 11 and recalls Tobit's position at court (1.13–14); indeed, Tobit reveals no court secrets. *To acknowledge*, as Tobit had done in 11.17. **7b–10**: Proverbial sayings continue the emphasis on charitable deeds (4.6–11); for *fasting*, which becomes increasingly important in the postexilic period, see also 1 Macc 3.44–48; Esth 4.1–3,15; Mt 6.16–18; *almsgiving*, see 4.11n. **12–13**: The angelic task of conveying prayers and good deeds is mentioned in other Second Temple Jewish literature, such as *1 Enoch*. **14**: *To test* indicates that Tobit's blindness and his subsequent trials resulted from God's active effort (Gen 22.1–22; Job 1–2); unmentioned is whether Sarah's trials were

Sarah your daughter-in-law. [15] I am Raphael, one of the seven angels who stand ready and enter before the glory of the Lord."

[16] The two of them were shaken; they fell face down, for they were afraid. [17] But he said to them, "Do not be afraid; peace be with you. Bless God forevermore. [18] As for me, when I was with you, I was not acting on my own will, but by the will of God. Bless him each and every day; sing his praises. [19] Although you were watching me, I really did not eat or drink anything—but what you saw was a vision. [20] So now get up from the ground,[a] and acknowledge God. See, I am ascending to him who sent me. Write down all these things that have happened to you." And he ascended. [21] Then they stood up, and could see him no more. [22] They kept blessing God and singing his praises, and they acknowledged God for these marvelous deeds of his, when an angel of God had appeared to them.

13

Then Tobit[b] said:
"Blessed be God who lives forever,
  because his kingdom[c] lasts throughout
    all ages.
[2] For he afflicts, and he shows mercy;
  he leads down to Hades in the lowest
    regions of the earth,
  and he brings up from the great abyss,[d]
  and there is nothing that can escape his
    hand.
[3] Acknowledge him before the nations,
    O children of Israel;
  for he has scattered you among them.
[4] He has shown you his greatness even
    there.

Exalt him in the presence of every living
    being,
  because he is our Lord and he is our
    God;
  he is our Father and he is God forever.
[5] He will afflict[e] you for your iniquities,
  but he will again show mercy on all of
    you.
He will gather you from all the nations
  among whom you have been scattered.
[6] If you turn to him with all your heart and
    with all your soul,
  to do what is true before him,
then he will turn to you
  and will no longer hide his face from
    you.
So now see what he has done for you;
  acknowledge him at the top of your voice.
Bless the Lord of righteousness,
  and exalt the King of the ages.[f]
In the land of my exile I acknowledge him,
  and show his power and majesty to a
    nation of sinners:
'Turn back, you sinners, and do what is
    right before him;
  perhaps he may look with favor upon
    you and show you mercy.'

a   Other ancient authorities read *now bless the Lord on earth*
b   Gk *he*
c   Other ancient authorities read *forever, and his kingdom*
d   Gk *from destruction*
e   Other ancient authorities read *He afflicted*
f   The lacuna in codex Sinaiticus, verses 6b to 10a, is filled in from other ancient authorities

also tests. **15:** *Seven angels* (cf. Rev. 8.2) do not appear in earlier biblical material; Daniel mentions Gabriel (Dan 8.16; 9.21; cf. Lk 1.19,26) and Michael (Dan 10.13,21; 12.1; cf. Jude 9; Rev 12.7). *The glory of the Lord*, see 3.16. **16–17:** Fear and prostration are standard reactions to epiphanies (Dan 10.1–12), as is the response, *Do not be afraid*. **19:** *I really did not eat* reflects the traditional view that angels do not require food (Judg 13.16; see 6.6n.). **20:** Jesus' ascension in Acts 1.9 (cf. Jn 16.5) shares several motifs with this scene.

13.1–14.1: Tobit's hymn. The hymn expands upon 11.14–15; the vocabulary evokes Psalms 92–118, and the form may indicate liturgical models in use in the early Second Temple period. **2:** *Afflicts . . . and . . . shows mercy* (also v. 5), see 11.14–15n.; Tobit's (and Sarah's) trials encapsulate the difficulties of exile. Tobit repeats the Deuteronomic view that sin leads to punishment, and repentance to redemption (Deut 28–33; cf. Wis 12.22). Some interpreters see in *brings up from the great abyss* belief in resurrection; others associate the references with sickness and recovery, redemption from Sheol, or exile and return; see Deut 32.39; 1 Sam 2.6; Wis 16.13–15; 2 Macc 7.35. *Hades*, see 3.10n. **4:** *Our Father*, an address to God that becomes increasingly common in the post-exilic period (e.g., Isa 63.16; 64.8; Sir 23.1,4; Wis 14.3; Mt 6.9). **5:** The in-gathering of the exiles, a popular theme in Second Temple Jewish literature, becomes in Jewish tradition a sign of the messianic age (14.7; Sir 36.13; Bar

⁷ As for me, I exalt my God,
    and my soul rejoices in the King of
        heaven.
⁸ Let all people speak of his majesty,
    and acknowledge him in Jerusalem.
⁹ O Jerusalem, the holy city,
    he afflicted^a you for the deeds of your
        hands,^{b}
    but will again have mercy on the
        children of the righteous.
¹⁰ Acknowledge the Lord, for he is good,^{c}
    and bless the King of the ages,
    so that his tent^d may be rebuilt in you
        in joy.
May he cheer all those within you who are
    captives,
    and love all those within you who are
        distressed,
    to all generations forever.
¹¹ A bright light will shine to all the ends of
    the earth;
    many nations will come to you from far
        away,
the inhabitants of the remotest parts of
    the earth to your holy name,
    bearing gifts in their hands for the King
        of heaven.
Generation after generation will give
    joyful praise in you;
    the name of the chosen city will endure
        forever.
¹² Cursed are all who speak a harsh word
    against you;
    cursed are all who conquer you
    and pull down your walls,
all who overthrow your towers
    and set your homes on fire.
    But blessed forever will be all who
        revere you.^{e}
¹³ Go, then, and rejoice over the children of
    the righteous,
    for they will be gathered together
    and will praise the Lord of the ages.

¹⁴ Happy are those who love you,
    and happy are those who rejoice in your
        prosperity.
Happy also are all people who grieve with
    you
    because of your afflictions;
for they will rejoice with you
    and witness all your glory forever.
¹⁵ My soul blesses^f the Lord, the great King!
¹⁶ For Jerusalem will be built^g as his
    house for all ages.
How happy I will be if a remnant of my
    descendants should survive
    to see your glory and acknowledge the
        King of heaven.
The gates of Jerusalem will be built with
    sapphire and emerald,
    and all your walls with precious stones.
The towers of Jerusalem will be built with
    gold,
    and their battlements with pure gold.
The streets of Jerusalem will be paved
    with ruby and with stones of Ophir.
¹⁷ The gates of Jerusalem will sing hymns
    of joy,
    and all her houses will cry, 'Hallelujah!
Blessed be the God of Israel!'
    and the blessed will bless the holy name
        forever and ever."

14 So ended Tobit's words of praise.
² Tobit^h died in peace when he was one
hundred twelve years old, and was buried with
great honor in Nineveh. He was sixty-two^i

a   Other ancient authorities read *will afflict*
b   Other ancient authorities read *your children*
c   Other ancient authorities read *Lord worthily*
d   Or *tabernacle*
e   Other ancient authorities read *who build you up*
f   Or *O my soul, bless*
g   Other ancient authorities add *for a city*
h   Gk *He*
i   Other ancient authorities read *fifty-eight*

4.21–5.9). *Afflict* and *show mercy*, see 11.14–15n. **6**: *Heart* and *soul* are to be inclined toward God (Deut 6.5). **8–17**: A celebration of *Jerusalem*, a focus with which the book began (1.4–10); now Tobit speaks of Jerusalem's glory rather than its destruction. **11**: *Many nations will come* is another sign of the messianic age (Isa 60.1–5; Zech 14.16). **12**: *Who conquer you* is anachronistic for Tobit's ostensible date; the reference shows knowledge of Nebuchadnezzar's attack on Jerusalem in 586 BCE. **14**: *Happy are . . . you* is a macarism or beatitude, cf. Mt 5.3–11; Lk 6.20–22. **16–17**: For similar views of Jerusalem's restoration, see Isa 54.11–14; Rev 21.9–27.

    14.2–11a: Tobit's testament. Tobit's second testament (see 4.1–13n.) confirms his earlier insistence that piety will ultimately be rewarded. **2**: *Giving alms* and *blessing God* are the two major exhortations made throughout

years old when he lost his eyesight, and after regaining it he lived in prosperity, giving alms and continually blessing God and acknowledging God's majesty.

³ When he was about to die, he called his son Tobias and the seven sons of Tobias[a] and gave this command: "My son, take your children ⁴ and hurry off to Media, for I believe the word of God that Nahum spoke about Nineveh, that all these things will take place and overtake Assyria and Nineveh. Indeed, everything that was spoken by the prophets of Israel, whom God sent, will occur. None of all their words will fail, but all will come true at their appointed times. So it will be safer in Media than in Assyria and Babylon. For I know and believe that whatever God has said will be fulfilled and will come true; not a single word of the prophecies will fail. All of our kindred, inhabitants of the land of Israel, will be scattered and taken as captives from the good land; and the whole land of Israel will be desolate, even Samaria and Jerusalem will be desolate. And the temple of God in it will be burned to the ground, and it will be desolate for a while.[b]

⁵ "But God will again have mercy on them, and God will bring them back into the land of Israel; and they will rebuild the temple of God, but not like the first one until the period when the times of fulfillment shall come. After this they all will return from their exile and will rebuild Jerusalem in splendor; and in it the temple of God will be rebuilt, just as the prophets of Israel have said concerning it. ⁶ Then the nations in the whole world will all be converted and worship God in truth. They will all abandon their idols, which deceitfully

have led them into their error; ⁷ and in righteousness they will praise the eternal God. All the Israelites who are saved in those days and are truly mindful of God will be gathered together; they will go to Jerusalem and live in safety forever in the land of Abraham, and it will be given over to them. Those who sincerely love God will rejoice, but those who commit sin and injustice will vanish from all the earth. ⁸,⁹ So now, my children, I command you, serve God faithfully and do what is pleasing in his sight. Your children are also to be commanded to do what is right and to give alms, and to be mindful of God and to bless his name at all times with sincerity and with all their strength. So now, my son, leave Nineveh; do not remain here. ¹⁰ On whatever day you bury your mother beside me, do not stay overnight within the confines of the city. For I see that there is much wickedness within it, and that much deceit is practiced within it, while the people are without shame. See, my son, what Nadab did to Ahikar who had reared him. Was he not, while still alive, brought down into the earth? For God repaid him to his face for this shameful treatment. Ahikar came out into the light, but Nadab went into the eternal darkness, because he tried to kill Ahikar. Because he gave alms, Ahikar[c] escaped the fatal trap that Nadab had set for him, but Nadab fell into it himself, and was destroyed. ¹¹ So now, my children, see what almsgiving accomplishes, and what

---

a Lat: Gk lacks *and the seven sons of Tobias*
b Lat: Other ancient authorities read *of God will be in distress and will be burned for a while*
c Gk *he*; other ancient authorities read *Manasses*

---

the volume (see 3.1–6n.; 4.11n.). **3:** *Seven sons:* Edna's wish for grandchildren is granted (10.12; for the motif of seven sons, see Ruth 4.15; 2 Macc 7; 4 Macc 14.12). **4:** Unlike the first testament (ch 4), this one opens with predictions of the future; Tobit's comments are among the earliest claims that events are predetermined (see also Dan 10–12; Mk 13.7; Acts 1.7; Rev 1.1). The prophet *Nahum* predicted the destruction of *Assyria and Nineveh*; Babylon conquered Nineveh in 612 BCE (see v. 15; 13.12n.). **5–7:** With the restoration that began with the edict of Cyrus of Persia in 538 BCE, the hymn shifts to a vision of the splendid future of a renewed Jerusalem, glorified temple, return of the exiles (13.5n.), conversion of the Gentiles to the worship of the God of Israel, and elimination of sin. **10:** Recognizing that Anna will outlive him, Tobit insists his son provide for her in life and in death; reference to burial, now after a long life, contrasts positively with Tobit's interring of unburied corpses. *Nadab did to Ahikar:* see 1.21–22n. Nadab framed his uncle Ahikar, making it appear that he had committed treason against the king.

14.11b–15: Tobit and Anna die. Tobias is obedient to his father's command (v. 10) and fulfills his filial duty also by burying his in-laws. Of all the main characters, only Sarah's fate is left undeveloped in the final chapter.

injustice does—it brings death! But now my breath fails me."

Then they laid him on his bed, and he died; and he received an honorable funeral. [12] When Tobias's mother died, he buried her beside his father. Then he and his wife and children[a] returned to Media and settled in Ecbatana with Raguel his father-in-law. [13] He treated his parents-in-law[b] with great respect in their old age, and buried them in Ecbatana of Media. He inherited both the property of Raguel and that of his father Tobit. [14] He died highly respected at the age of one hundred seventeen[c] years. [15] Before he died he heard[d] of the destruction of Nineveh, and he saw its prisoners being led into Media, those whom King Cyaxares[e] of Media had taken captive. Tobias[f] praised God for all he had done to the people of Nineveh and Assyria; before he died he rejoiced over Nineveh, and he blessed the Lord God forever and ever. Amen.[g]

a   Codex Sinaiticus lacks *and children*
b   Gk *them*
c   Other authorities read other numbers
d   Codex Sinaiticus reads *saw and heard*
e   Cn: Codex Sinaiticus *Ahikar*; other ancient authorities read *Nebuchadnezzar and Ahasuerus*
f   Gk *He*
g   Other ancient authorities lack *Amen*

13: *Ecbatana of Media*, see 3.7–15n. 15: Reference to the destruction of Nineveh (see v. 4n.) suggests that Tobit's other predictions (vv. 4–7) will also come to pass. *Cyaxares* was ruler of Media ca. 625–585 BCE. Appropriately, the book ends with praise to God.

JUDITH

NAME, DATE OF COMPOSITION, AND CANONICAL STATUS

The book of Judith, which is named for its spirited heroine, is an entertaining narrative that has engaged Jewish and Christian imaginations for centuries and in many different ways. In Jewish tradition Judith was a heroine who protected her people, while in Christian tradition Judith has represented various virtues, such as chastity slaying lust. It was probably composed in Hebrew near the end of the second century BCE in the aftermath of the Maccabean Revolt, which it appears to idealize. No Hebrew manuscript survives, probably because the book was not accorded canonical status in Judaism, but the book was preserved in the Christian tradition in Greek, Latin, and other translations. It is considered canonical in Roman Catholic and Eastern Orthodox churches, and as part of the Apocrypha by Protestants.

GENRE, STRUCTURE, AND INTERPRETATION

Although the book of Judith came to be considered historical, it was composed as a fictional novella, much like other Hebrew stories with a central female protagonist, such as Esther, Tobit, and Susanna, as well as the apocryphal story of *Joseph and Aseneth,* and many Greek novels. The book's fictional nature is evident from its blending of history and fiction, beginning in the very first verse, and is too prevalent thereafter to be considered as the result of mere historical mistakes. Thus, the great villain is "Nebuchadnezzar, who ruled over the Assyrians" (1.1), yet the historical Nebuchadnezzar was the famous king of the Babylonians. Other details are also patently unbelievable, such as fictional place names, the immense size of armies and fortifications, the dating of events, and the actions of the Assyrian general Holofernes. Like the books of Jonah and Job and the more contemporary novellas, Judith would not have been taken to be a factual account even at the time of its composition. With its blend of fiction and ancient history, it should also be read in light of historical events at the time it was written. The "Assyrian" Nebuchadnezzar may be a cipher or coded name for the Syrian Antiochus IV Epiphanes, who had also tried to enforce a foreign religion on Israel. The Maccabees, like Judith, showed strength of resolve and won their freedom. Judith later recounts that Israel had destroyed the cults of those on the land (8.18–20), and this also recalls contemporary history, because the successors of the Maccabees destroyed the Samaritan temple on Mount Gerizim.

The book of Judith entertains and instructs by combining irony and humor, bombast and fascinating detail, sexual suggestiveness and pious self-denial bordering on asceticism, outrageous reversals of the period's gender roles and conservative religious values, escapism, and celebration of military success. Moreover, the plot's careful structure and the commanding figure of Judith herself make this a compelling tale. The story has two parts or acts of approximately equal length. Chapters 1–7 describe the rise of the threat to Israel, led by the evil king Nebuchadnezzar of the Assyrians and his sycophantic general Holofernes. This first part concludes as Holofernes' world-wide campaign has converged at the mountain pass where Judith's village, Bethulia, is located. The second part, chs 8–16, introduces Judith and depicts her heroic actions to save her people. Each of the two parts has a clear chiastic pattern in which the order of events is reversed at a central moment in the narrative (*abcc'b'a'*).

Part I (1.1–7.23)
- A. Campaign against disobedient nations; the people surrender (1.1–2.13)
    - B. Israel is "greatly terrified" (2.14–3.10)
        - C. Joakim prepares for war (4.1–15)
            - D. Holofernes talks with Achior (5.1–6.9)
                - E. Achior is expelled by Assyrians (6.10–13)
                - E.' Achior is received in village of Bethulia (6.14–15)
            - D.' Achior talks with the people (6.16–21)
        - C.' Holofernes prepares for war (7.1–3)
    - B.' Israel is "greatly terrified" (7.4–5)
- A.' Campaign against Bethulia; the people want to surrender (7.6–32)

Part II (8.1–16.25)
    A. Introduction of Judith (8.1–8)
        B. Judith plans to save Israel (8.9–10.8)
            C. Judith and her maid leave Bethulia (10.9–10)
                D. Judith beheads Holofernes (10.11–13.10a)
            C.' Judith and her maid return to Bethulia (13.10b–11)
        B.' Judith plans the destruction of Israel's enemy (13.12–16.20)
    A.' Conclusion about Judith (16.21–25)

Part I, although at times tedious in its description of the military developments, develops important themes by alternating battles with reflections and rousing action with rest. In contrast, the second half is devoted mainly to Judith's strength of character and the beheading scene, which is told quickly. Perhaps such terseness implies that the original audience would have known the story, but the artistry lies in describing not *what* will happen but *how* it will happen. Furthermore, that the scene is told quickly does not imply insignificance. On the contrary, its importance is evident in its position at the center of the story's second act. Other paired figures and expressions also contribute to the story's structure: Nebuchadnezzar and God each have a "general," Holofernes and Judith respectively, and each of them has a servant, Bagoas and Judith's maid.

    The character of Judith is also larger than life, and she has won a place in Jewish and Christian lore, art, poetry, and drama. Her name, which means "Jewish woman," is the feminine form of *Yehudi* and suggests that she represents the heroic spirit of the Jewish people. Because of her unswerving religious devotion, she is able to step outside of her widow's role, dress and act in a sexually provocative manner, lie to the opposing general Holofernes, seduce him, and behead him, all without a moment of self-doubt. Yet the book does not undermine accepted social conventions, for in the end Judith returns to her life as an exemplary pious widow. Thus, like many comedies, the book of Judith allows for a release of social tensions, explores transgressions of everyday rules, and then reconstitutes society on acceptable lines.

    The book constantly echoes biblical narratives, most notably the assassination of Sisera by Jael in Judg 4–5 and the revenge of Simeon and Levi on Shechem after the rape of Dinah in Gen 34. Judith's deliverance of her people from danger makes her like the judges of Israel. She echoes Moses, too, as when she responds to murmuring over water and the testing of God (8.9–27), and when her hand is likened to the hand of Moses (8.33; 13.14; cf. Ex 14.21). The story also recalls folk traditions about male heroes, but adds humor and irony by making the hero a pious widow who transgresses the social restrictions of her gender in order to save her people and defend her God. Although some modern interpreters have questioned Judith's morality, in the ancient world Judith was always remembered positively as a heroine of the faith.

Lawrence M. Wills

1

It was the twelfth year of the reign of Nebuchadnezzar, who ruled over the Assyrians in the great city of Nineveh. In those days Arphaxad ruled over the Medes in Ecbatana. ² He built walls around Ecbatana with hewn stones three cubits thick and six cubits long; he made the walls seventy cubits high and fifty cubits wide. ³ At its gates he raised towers one hundred cubits high and sixty cubits wide at the foundations. ⁴ He made its gates seventy cubits high and forty cubits wide to allow his armies to march out in force and his infantry to form their ranks. ⁵ Then King Nebuchadnezzar made war against King Arphaxad in the great plain that is on the borders of Ragau. ⁶ There rallied to him all the people of the hill country and all those who lived along the Euphrates, the Tigris, and the Hydaspes, and, on the plain, Arioch, king of the Elymeans. Thus, many nations joined the forces of the Chaldeans.ᵃ

⁷ Then Nebuchadnezzar, king of the Assyrians, sent messengers to all who lived in Persia and to all who lived in the west, those who lived in Cilicia and Damascus, Lebanon and Antilebanon, and all who lived along the seacoast, ⁸ and those among the nations of Carmel and Gilead, and Upper Galilee and the great plain of Esdraelon, ⁹ and all who were in Samaria and its towns, and beyond the Jordan as far as Jerusalem and Bethany and Chelous and Kadesh and the river of Egypt, and Tahpanhes and Raamses and the whole land of Goshen, ¹⁰ even beyond Tanis and Memphis, and all who lived in Egypt as far as the borders of Ethiopia. ¹¹ But all who lived in the whole region disregarded the summons of Nebuchadnezzar, king of the Assyrians, and refused to join him in the war; for they were not afraid of him, but regarded him as only one man.ᵇ So they sent back his messengers empty-handed and in disgrace.

¹² Then Nebuchadnezzar became very angry with this whole region, and swore by his throne and kingdom that he would take revenge on the whole territory of Cilicia and Damascus and Syria, that he would kill with his sword also all the inhabitants of the land of Moab, and the people of Ammon, and all Judea, and every one in Egypt, as far as the coasts of the two seas.

¹³ In the seventeenth year he led his forces against King Arphaxad and defeated him

ᵃ Syr: Gk *Cheleoudites*
ᵇ Or *a man*

1.1–7.32: Part I: A great empire rises up to attack Israel and other nations.

1.1–6: Nebuchadnezzar is introduced and declares war on Arphaxad, king of Media. 1: The dating of events in the reign of the great king is typical of histories, but although *Nebuchadnezzar* of Babylon had defeated the southern half of Israel (Judah) in 586 BCE (see 2 Kings 25.1–21) and the *Assyrians* had defeated the northern half of Israel in 722 BCE (see 2 Kings 17.5–6), the combination *Nebuchadnezzar* of the *Assyrians* is fictitious—yet it combines both bitter associations. There is also no known king of the *Medes* named *Arphaxad*.2–4: The massive fortifications of Arphaxad's capital *Ecbatana*, in northwestern Iran, are unrealistic: *walls seventy cubits high and fifty cubits wide* would measure 105 ft (32 m) by 75 ft (23 m). By beginning with the might and grandeur of Arphaxad, the threat of Nebuchadnezzar is made even more dramatic. 5–6: Although many of the place names in the book of Judith are well known, others are fictitious or unknown; together they give the impression that the entire world is involved. What seems repetitive to the modern reader serves to evoke the extent of the campaign. 6: *Euphrates, Tigris,* the principal rivers of Mesopotamia. *Chaldeans* is another name for Babylonians, reflecting the author's fictitious merging of the Assyrians and Babylonians for the purposes of the story.

1.7–11: Many nations rebuff Nebuchadnezzar's call to ally with him. Nebuchadnezzar's messengers move from east to west, through modern Iran, Syria, southern Turkey, Lebanon, Jordan, Palestine, Israel, and into Egypt. But all the nations reject his summons; he is nothing more than *one man* (v. 11). This judgment will be tested. 8: *Esdraelon* (older *Jezreel*), the *great plain* from Mount *Carmel* to the Jordan Valley. 9: *Samaria* and *Jerusalem* are mentioned only in passing; at this point there is a world-wide focus, which will first narrow to the area of Syria-Palestine, then to Samaria and Judea, and finally to the tiny mountain village of Bethulia (4.6). (See map on p. 36.)

1.12–16: Nebuchadnezzar vows to destroy the western nations and easily defeats Arphaxad without their aid. 12: Nebuchadnezzar swears to destroy the nations that figure so prominently in the Bible: *Damascus, Syria, Moab, Ammon, Egypt;* Judith and a small band of Jews will deliver all of the biblical lands. The *two seas* are pos-

in battle, overthrowing the whole army of Arphaxad and all his cavalry and all his chariots. ¹⁴ Thus he took possession of his towns and came to Ecbatana, captured its towers, plundered its markets, and turned its glory into disgrace. ¹⁵ He captured Arphaxad in the mountains of Ragau and struck him down with his spears, thus destroying him once and for all. ¹⁶ Then he returned to Nineveh, he and all his combined forces, a vast body of troops; and there he and his forces rested and feasted for one hundred twenty days.

2 In the eighteenth year, on the twenty-second day of the first month, there was talk in the palace of Nebuchadnezzar, king of the Assyrians, about carrying out his revenge on the whole region, just as he had said. ² He summoned all his ministers and all his nobles and set before them his secret plan and recounted fully, with his own lips, all the wickedness of the region.ᵃ ³ They decided that every one who had not obeyed his command should be destroyed.

⁴ When he had completed his plan, Nebuchadnezzar, king of the Assyrians, called Holofernes, the chief general of his army, second only to himself, and said to him, ⁵ "Thus says the Great King, the lord of the whole earth: Leave my presence and take with you men confident in their strength, one hundred twenty thousand foot soldiers and twelve thousand cavalry. ⁶ March out against all the land to the west, because they disobeyed my orders. ⁷ Tell them to prepare earth and water, for I am coming against them in my anger, and will cover the whole face of the earth with the feet of my troops, to whom I will hand them over to be plundered. ⁸ Their wounded shall fill their ravines and gullies, and the swelling river shall be filled with their dead. ⁹ I will lead them away captive to the ends of the whole earth. ¹⁰ You shall go and seize all their territory for me in advance. They must yield themselves to you, and you shall hold them for me until the day of their punishment. ¹¹ But to those who resist show no mercy, but hand them over to slaughter and plunder throughout your whole region. ¹² For as I live, and by the power of my kingdom, what I have spoken I will accomplish by my own hand. ¹³ And you—take care not to transgress any of your lord's commands, but carry them out exactly as I have ordered you; do it without delay."

¹⁴ So Holofernes left the presence of his lord, and summoned all the commanders, generals, and officers of the Assyrian army. ¹⁵ He mustered the picked troops by divisions as his lord had ordered him to do, one hundred twenty thousand of them, together with twelve thousand archers on horseback, ¹⁶ and he organized them as a great army is marshaled for a campaign. ¹⁷ He took along a vast number of camels and donkeys and mules for transport, and innumerable sheep and oxen and goats for food; ¹⁸ also ample rations for everyone, and a huge amount of gold and silver from the royal palace.

¹⁹ Then he set out with his whole army, to go ahead of King Nebuchadnezzar and to cover the whole face of the earth to the west with their chariots and cavalry and picked foot soldiers. ²⁰ Along with them went a mixed crowd like a swarm of locusts, like the

---

ᵃ Meaning of Gk uncertain

sibly the Red Sea and the Mediterranean. **16:** The army *rested and feasted for one hundred twenty days*. This is the first of a series of well-placed pauses in the military history of the first half of the book (cf. 2.28; 3.10; 6.21; 7.32).

2.1–13: Nebuchadnezzar makes plans to destroy all the nations who opposed him. 1: *The eighteenth year,* 587 BCE, when the siege of Jerusalem began; see 2 Kings 25.1. **2:** Nebuchadnezzar summons *all his ministers* and threatens to destroy the whole region (cf. Dan 2.2–5; 3.2–9). **4:** *Holofernes* was the name of a general in the Persian army of Artaxerxes III Ochus, who invaded this same region in 350 and 343 BCE. His officer was named Bagoas, a name that will appear in 12:11. Real persons have likely been used as fictional opponents. **5:** *The lord of the whole earth,* Nebuchadnezzar and Holofernes will have delusions of grandeur and attribute terms to Nebuchadnezzar that should be reserved for God alone (cf. 3.8). **7:** It was Persian practice to demand *earth and water* from foreign states as a sign of submission (Herodotus, *Histories* 6.48).

2.14–3.10: Holofernes begins the campaign to destroy the disobedient nations.

2.15–20: The enormousness of the Assyrian army is emphasized, including animals, rations, gold and silver, even hangers-on—*a mixed crowd* (cf. Ex 12.38) *like a swarm of locusts* (cf. Judg 6.5; Joel 1.4–7), *like the dust of the*

dust[a] of the earth—a multitude that could not be counted.

[21] They marched for three days from Nineveh to the plain of Bectileth, and camped opposite Bectileth near the mountain that is to the north of Upper Cilicia. [22] From there Holofernes[b] took his whole army, the infantry, cavalry, and chariots, and went up into the hill country. [23] He ravaged Put and Lud, and plundered all the Rassisites and the Ishmaelites on the border of the desert, south of the country of the Chelleans. [24] Then he followed[c] the Euphrates and passed through Mesopotamia and destroyed all the fortified towns along the brook Abron, as far as the sea. [25] He also seized the territory of Cilicia, and killed everyone who resisted him. Then he came to the southern borders of Japheth, facing Arabia. [26] He surrounded all the Midianites, and burned their tents and plundered their sheepfolds. [27] Then he went down into the plain of Damascus during the wheat harvest, and burned all their fields and destroyed their flocks and herds and sacked their towns and ravaged their lands and put all their young men to the sword.

[28] So fear and dread of him fell upon all the people who lived along the seacoast, at Sidon and Tyre, and those who lived in Sur and Ocina and all who lived in Jamnia. Those who lived in Azotus and Ascalon feared him greatly.

3 They therefore sent messengers to him to sue for peace in these words: [2] "We, the servants of Nebuchadnezzar, the Great King, lie prostrate before you. Do with us whatever you will. [3] See, our buildings and all our land and all our wheat fields and our flocks and

herds and all our encampments[d] lie before you; do with them as you please. [4] Our towns and their inhabitants are also your slaves; come and deal with them as you see fit."

[5] The men came to Holofernes and told him all this. [6] Then he went down to the seacoast with his army and stationed garrisons in the fortified towns and took picked men from them as auxiliaries. [7] These people and all in the countryside welcomed him with garlands and dances and tambourines. [8] Yet he demolished all their shrines[e] and cut down their sacred groves; for he had been commissioned to destroy all the gods of the land, so that all nations should worship Nebuchadnezzar alone, and that all their dialects and tribes should call upon him as a god.

[9] Then he came toward Esdraelon, near Dothan, facing the great ridge of Judea; [10] he camped between Geba and Scythopolis, and remained for a whole month in order to collect all the supplies for his army.

4 When the Israelites living in Judea heard of everything that Holofernes, the general of Nebuchadnezzar, the king of the Assyrians, had done to the nations, and how he had plundered and destroyed all their temples, [2] they were therefore greatly terrified at his approach; they were alarmed both for Jerusalem and for the temple of the Lord their God. [3] For they had only recently returned from exile, and all the people of Judea had

a   Gk *sand*
b   Gk *he*
c   Or *crossed*
d   Gk *all the sheepfolds of our tents*
e   Syr: Gk *borders*

earth. Such images depict the entire world at war. **21–27**: The campaign builds in intensity to include plundering, slaughter, and destruction, but the geography is confused. **21**: *Upper Cilicia*, in southeastern Asia Minor, is 400 mi (650 km) from Nineveh, a distance far too great to travel on foot in *three days*. **23**: *Put*, usually Libya; *Lud*, Lydia, in central Asia Minor; *Ishmaelites*, Arabs (Gen 16.11–12). **26**: *Midianites*, a group of people who lived in southern Transjordan, sometimes depicted as nomads (Gen 37.28; Judg 6.1–6).

2.28–3.10: The surrounding nations, who had caused trouble for Israel in the past, showed initial courage before Nebuchadnezzar (1.11), but now they succumb. **2.28**: *Sidon* and *Tyre* were two Phoenician cities on the Mediterranean coast north of Israel. *Jamnia, Azotus* (earlier Ashdod), and *Ascalon* (earlier Ashkelon), were on the Mediterranean coast of Palestine. **3.8**: *All nations, dialects, and tribes* (cf. Dan 3–4). **9**: *Dothan* was south of the plain of *Esdraelon* (see 1.8n.); *Scythopolis* (formerly Beth-shan) was at the plain's eastern end.

4.1–7: Israel, now standing alone, prepares for attack. The perspective now shifts to *the Israelites living in Judea* (v. 1), allowing an opportunity for a reflection on their history; however, it is telescoped: the Assyrians actually ruled before the Judeans *returned from exile* (v. 3). **3**: The consecration of the *sacred vessels, altar,* and

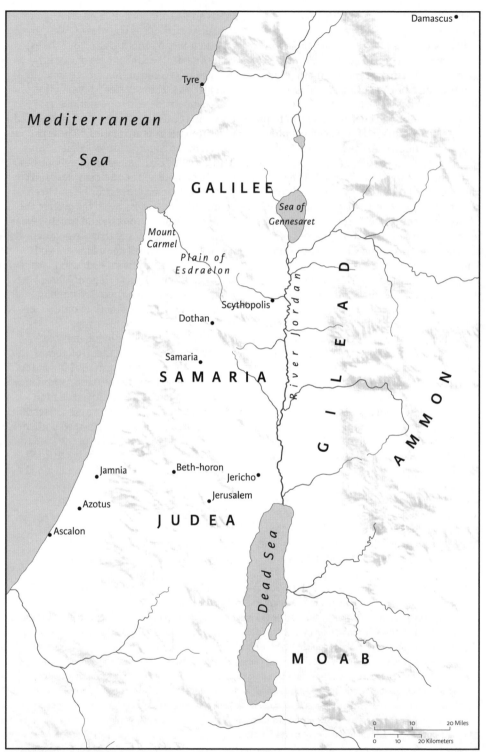

The geography of the book of Judith.

just now gathered together, and the sacred vessels and the altar and the temple had been consecrated after their profanation. ⁴ So they sent word to every district of Samaria, and to Kona, Beth-horon, Belmain, and Jericho, and to Choba and Aesora, and the valley of Salem. ⁵ They immediately seized all the high hilltops and fortified the villages on them and stored up food in preparation for war—since their fields had recently been harvested.

⁶ The high priest, Joakim, who was in Jerusalem at the time, wrote to the people of Bethulia and Betomesthaim, which faces Esdraelon opposite the plain near Dothan, ⁷ ordering them to seize the mountain passes, since by them Judea could be invaded; and it would be easy to stop any who tried to enter, for the approach was narrow, wide enough for only two at a time to pass.

⁸ So the Israelites did as they had been ordered by the high priest Joakim and the senate of the whole people of Israel, in session at Jerusalem. ⁹ And every man of Israel cried out to God with great fervor, and they humbled themselves with much fasting. ¹⁰ They and their wives and their children and their cattle and every resident alien and hired laborer and purchased slave—they all put sackcloth around their waists. ¹¹ And all the Israelite men, women, and children living at Jerusalem prostrated themselves before the temple and put ashes on their heads and spread out their sackcloth before the Lord.

¹² They even draped the altar with sackcloth and cried out in unison, praying fervently to the God of Israel not to allow their infants to be carried off and their wives to be taken as booty, and the towns they had inherited to be destroyed, and the sanctuary to be profaned and desecrated to the malicious joy of the Gentiles.

¹³ The Lord heard their prayers and had regard for their distress; for the people fasted many days throughout Judea and in Jerusalem before the sanctuary of the Lord Almighty. ¹⁴ The high priest Joakim and all the priests who stood before the Lord and ministered to the Lord, with sackcloth around their loins, offered the daily burnt offerings, the votive offerings, and freewill offerings of the people. ¹⁵ With ashes on their turbans, they cried out to the Lord with all their might to look with favor on the whole house of Israel.

5 It was reported to Holofernes, the general of the Assyrian army, that the people of Israel had prepared for war and had closed the mountain passes and fortified all the high hilltops and set up barricades in the plains. ² In great anger he called together all the princes of Moab and the commanders of Ammon and all the governors of the coastland, ³ and said to them, "Tell me, you Canaanites, what people is this that lives in the hill country? What towns do they inhabit? How large is their army, and in what does their power and strength consist? Who rules over them

temple ostensibly refers to the events in the late sixth century BCE after the exile (Ezra 6.13–22), but for the reader it would also evoke the more recent events after the victory of the Maccabees in 164 BCE (1 Macc 4:36–61; 2 Macc 10:1–8). Such telescoping distances the story from any specific historical event and so suggests that it concerns threats and responses in general. 4: *Beth-horon*, 11 miles (18 km) northwest of Jerusalem. 6: Judith's village, Bethulia ("virginity"), is named for the first time; if it is not a fictional place, its location is unknown. Although it is in Samaritan territory, Jerusalem and the Temple are always the focus.

4.8–15: Israel prays and fasts. The Israelites *humbled themselves with much fasting*, and *put sackcloth around their waists*—even the cattle! The humor is intentional (cf. Jon 3.8). The penitential theology found here became a staple of postexilic Judaism (cf. Ezra 9; Neh 9; Dan 9.4–19; Bar 1.1–3).13: *The Lord heard their prayers and had regard for their distress* (cf. Judg 3:9,15). Readers are assured that help is on the way, but in 7.23–31 this will be brought into question. Other novelistic texts of the period similarly predict happy endings despite building tension (Tob 3.16–17; Xenophon of Ephesus, *Ephesian Tale* 1.6). The question is not whether the protagonists will be saved, but how. 14: For the various types of *offerings*, see Ex 29.38–41 and Lev 22.18–30.

5.1–21: Holofernes learns from Achior about Israelite identity. 1–4: Holofernes' campaign pauses for him to inquire concerning these Israelites who dare to oppose him. His military questions call forth a reflection on Jewish identity within a larger world: *In what does their power and strength consist? Who rules over them as king?* For the reader, God is king, which profoundly qualifies reverence for any earthly king. This scene introduces a recurring irony: the opponents perceive a worldly frame of reference, but Judith—and the audience—under-

as king and leads their army? ⁴ And why have they alone, of all who live in the west, refused to come out and meet me?"

⁵ Then Achior, the leader of all the Ammonites, said to him, "May my lord please listen to a report from the mouth of your servant, and I will tell you the truth about this people that lives in the mountain district near you. No falsehood shall come from your servant's mouth. ⁶ These people are descended from the Chaldeans. ⁷ At one time they lived in Mesopotamia, because they did not wish to follow the gods of their ancestors who were in Chaldea. ⁸ Since they had abandoned the ways of their ancestors, and worshiped the God of heaven, the God they had come to know, their ancestorsᵃ drove them out from the presence of their gods. So they fled to Mesopotamia, and lived there for a long time. ⁹ Then their God commanded them to leave the place where they were living and go to the land of Canaan. There they settled, and grew very prosperous in gold and silver and very much livestock. ¹⁰ When a famine spread over the land of Canaan they went down to Egypt and lived there as long as they had food. There they became so great a multitude that their race could not be counted. ¹¹ So the king of Egypt became hostile to them; he exploited them and forced them to make bricks. ¹² They cried out to their God, and he afflicted the whole land of Egypt with incurable plagues. So the Egyptians drove them out of their sight. ¹³ Then God dried up the Red Sea before them, ¹⁴ and he led them by the way of Sinai and Kadesh-barnea. They drove out all the people of the desert, ¹⁵ and took up residence in the land of the Amorites, and by their might destroyed all the inhabitants of Heshbon; and crossing over the Jordan they took possession of all the hill country. ¹⁶ They drove out before them the Canaanites, the Perizzites, the Jebusites, the Shechemites, and all the Gergesites, and lived there a long time.

¹⁷ "As long as they did not sin against their God they prospered, for the God who hates iniquity is with them. ¹⁸ But when they departed from the way he had prescribed for them, they were utterly defeated in many battles and were led away captive to a foreign land. The temple of their God was razed to the ground, and their towns were occupied by their enemies. ¹⁹ But now they have returned to their God, and have come back from the places where they were scattered, and have occupied Jerusalem, where their sanctuary is, and have settled in the hill country, because it was uninhabited.

²⁰ "So now, my master and lord, if there is any oversight in this people and they sin

ᵃ Gk *they*

stand these discussions on a theological level. **5–21:** Achior's account of Israelite history is told from a Jewish, not an Ammonite, point of view and summarizes Israelite history from the time of Abraham until the return from exile. The character of the Ammonite Achior is probably inspired by the legendary Assyrian courtier Ahikar (cf. Tob 1.21–22; 14.10). He is similar to other righteous Gentiles (Josh 2–6; 2 Kings 5) and foreshadows Judith's role: he is heroic, in an almost prophetic way says many of the same things as she, and will attest to her achievements. **6–9:** The ancestral narratives from Gen 12–36. **6:** *Chaldeans,* Abraham came from Ur of the Chaldees (Gen 11.27–31), in southern Babylonia. It is characteristic of Greek and Roman ethnography to begin by noting the origins of a people. **7:** Early Jewish tradition explains that Abraham's family migrated from Chaldea because they wished to escape polytheism (*Jub.* 11.16–12.7; Josephus, *Ant.* 1.134–57). **10–13:** The descent into Egypt and the Exodus (Gen 37–Ex 18). **14:** *Sinai,* Ex 19–Num 10; *Kadesh-barnea,* Num 20.1. **15–16:** The conquests in Transjordan and Canaan (Num 20–Josh 11). **17–21:** Achior here states the Deuteronomic principle of God's conditional favor (Deut 28) that is prominent in the books of Joshua through Kings, later repeated by Judith (11. 9–15), and finally illustrated by the outcome of the story. **19:** The return from exile (Ezra 1–3).

5.22–6.21: Holofernes expels Achior, who is received in Bethulia. 6.2: *Ephraim,* the northern part of Israel. Holofernes understands Achior's words as an attempt at prophecy and uses prophetic idioms to report Nebuchadnezzar's will (v. 4). He thus defines the conflict as a question of who is God. **6.5:** *You shall not see my face again,* highly ironic, since Achior will see Holofernes' face again—separated from the rest of his body (14.6)! Achior will not die in battle but will become a Jew (14.10). At least some of Holofernes' words will indeed come true, but not as he assumes. **20:** His banquet upon being received will be balanced by Judith's smaller banquet when she is received by Holofernes (12.1).

against their God and we find out their offense, then we can go up and defeat them. ²¹ But if they are not a guilty nation, then let my lord pass them by; for their Lord and God will defend them, and we shall become the laughingstock of the whole world."

²² When Achior had finished saying these things, all the people standing around the tent began to complain; Holofernes' officers and all the inhabitants of the seacoast and Moab insisted that he should be cut to pieces. ²³ They said, "We are not afraid of the Israelites; they are a people with no strength or power for making war. ²⁴ Therefore let us go ahead, Lord Holofernes, and your vast army will swallow them up."

6 When the disturbance made by the people outside the council had died down, Holofernes, the commander of the Assyrian army, said to Achiorᵃ in the presence of all the foreign contingents:

² "Who are you, Achior and you mercenaries of Ephraim, to prophesy among us as you have done today and tell us not to make war against the people of Israel because their God will defend them? What god is there except Nebuchadnezzar? He will send his forces and destroy them from the face of the earth. Their God will not save them; ³ we the king'sᵇ servants will destroy them as one man. They cannot resist the might of our cavalry. ⁴ We will overwhelm them;ᶜ their mountains will be drunk with their blood, and their fields will be full of their dead. Not even their footprints will survive our attack; they will utterly perish. So says King Nebuchadnezzar, lord of the whole earth. For he has spoken; none of his words shall be in vain.

⁵ "As for you, Achior, you Ammonite mercenary, you have said these words in a moment of perversity; you shall not see my face again from this day until I take revenge on this race that came out of Egypt. ⁶ Then at my return the sword of my army and the spearᵈ of my servants shall pierce your sides, and you shall fall among their wounded. ⁷ Now my slaves are going to take you back into the hill country and put you in one of the towns beside the passes. ⁸ You will not die until you perish along with them. ⁹ If you really hope in your heart that they will not be taken, then do not look downcast! I have

spoken, and none of my words shall fail to come true."

¹⁰ Then Holofernes ordered his slaves, who waited on him in his tent, to seize Achior and take him away to Bethulia and hand him over to the Israelites. ¹¹ So the slaves took him and led him out of the camp into the plain, and from the plain they went up into the hill country and came to the springs below Bethulia. ¹² When the men of the town saw them,ᵉ they seized their weapons and ran out of the town to the top of the hill, and all the slingers kept them from coming up by throwing stones at them. ¹³ So having taken shelter below the hill, they bound Achior and left him lying at the foot of the hill, and returned to their master.

¹⁴ Then the Israelites came down from their town and found him; they untied him and brought him into Bethulia and placed him before the magistrates of their town, ¹⁵ who in those days were Uzziah son of Micah, of the tribe of Simeon, and Chabris son of Gothoniel, and Charmis son of Melchiel. ¹⁶ They called together all the elders of the town, and all their young men and women ran to the assembly. They set Achior in the midst of all their people, and Uzziah questioned him about what had happened. ¹⁷ He answered and told them what had taken place at the council of Holofernes, and all that he had said in the presence of the Assyrian leaders, and all that Holofernes had boasted he would do against the house of Israel. ¹⁸ Then the people fell down and worshiped God, and cried out:

¹⁹ "O Lord God of heaven, see their arrogance, and have pity on our people in their humiliation, and look kindly today on the faces of those who are consecrated to you."

²⁰ Then they reassured Achior, and praised him highly. ²¹ Uzziah took him from the assembly to his own house and gave a banquet for the elders; and all that night they called on the God of Israel for help.

ᵃ   Other ancient authorities add *and to all the Moabites*
ᵇ   Gk *his*
ᶜ   Other ancient authorities add *with it*
ᵈ   Lat Syr: Gk *people*
ᵉ   Other ancient authorities add *on the top of the hill*

7 The next day Holofernes ordered his whole army, and all the allies who had joined him, to break camp and move against Bethulia, and to seize the passes up into the hill country and make war on the Israelites. ² So all their warriors marched off that day; their fighting forces numbered one hundred seventy thousand infantry and twelve thousand cavalry, not counting the baggage and the foot soldiers handling it, a very great multitude. ³ They encamped in the valley near Bethulia, beside the spring, and they spread out in breadth over Dothan as far as Balbaim and in length from Bethulia to Cyamon, which faces Esdraelon.

⁴ When the Israelites saw their vast numbers, they were greatly terrified and said to one another, "They will now strip clean the whole land; neither the high mountains nor the valleys nor the hills will bear their weight." ⁵ Yet they all seized their weapons, and when they had kindled fires on their towers, they remained on guard all that night.

⁶ On the second day Holofernes led out all his cavalry in full view of the Israelites in Bethulia. ⁷ He reconnoitered the approaches to their town, and visited the springs that supplied their water; he seized them and set guards of soldiers over them, and then returned to his army.

⁸ Then all the chieftains of the Edomites and all the leaders of the Moabites and the commanders of the coastland came to him and said, ⁹ "Listen to what we have to say, my lord, and your army will suffer no losses. ¹⁰ This people, the Israelites, do not rely on their spears but on the height of the mountains where they live, for it is not easy to reach the tops of their mountains. ¹¹ Therefore, my lord, do not fight against them in regular formation, and not a man of your army will fall. ¹² Remain in your camp, and keep all the men in your forces with you; let your servants take possession of the spring of water that flows from the foot of the mountain, ¹³ for this is where all the people of Bethulia get their water. So thirst will destroy them, and they will surrender their town. Meanwhile, we and our people will go up to the tops of the nearby mountains and camp there to keep watch to see that no one gets out of the town. ¹⁴ They and their wives and children will waste away with famine, and before the sword reaches them they will be strewn about in the streets where they live. ¹⁵ Thus you will pay them back with evil, because they rebelled and did not receive you peaceably."

¹⁶ These words pleased Holofernes and all his attendants, and he gave orders to do as they had said. ¹⁷ So the army of the Ammonites moved forward, together with five thousand Assyrians, and they encamped in the valley and seized the water supply and the springs of the Israelites. ¹⁸ And the Edomites and Ammonites went up and encamped in the hill country opposite Dothan; and they sent some of their men toward the south and the east, toward Egrebeh, which is near Chusi beside the Wadi Mochmur. The rest of the Assyrian army encamped in the plain, and covered the whole face of the land. Their tents and supply trains spread out in great number, and they formed a vast multitude.

¹⁹ The Israelites then cried out to the Lord their God, for their courage failed, because all their enemies had surrounded them, and there was no way of escape from them. ²⁰ The whole Assyrian army, their infantry, chariots, and cavalry, surrounded them for thirty-four days, until all the water containers of every inhabitant of Bethulia were empty; ²¹ their cisterns were going dry, and on no day did they have enough water to drink, for their drinking water was rationed. ²² Their children were listless, and the women and young men fainted from thirst and were collapsing in the streets of the town and in the gateways; they no longer had any strength.

7.1–18: Holofernes advances on Bethulia and prepares for a siege. Again, the size of the army is emphasized, covering an entire valley (see 2.15–20n). They will *strip clean the whole land* like locusts. The action is drawn out and presented visually to give the full impression of the forces arrayed against Bethulia. **8:** The historical enemies of Israel, *Edomites* and *Moabites*, recommend a siege, so that Bethulia will fall for lack of water.

7.19–32: Israelites in Bethulia begin to despair. The predictions of Holofernes' advisers appear to be coming true. Just as lack of water led to murmuring in Ex 17.1–7, so also here; Moses' role is paralleled by both Uzziah

²³ Then all the people, the young men, the women, and the children, gathered around Uzziah and the rulers of the town and cried out with a loud voice, and said before all the elders, ²⁴ "Let God judge between you and us! You have done us a great injury in not making peace with the Assyrians. ²⁵ For now we have no one to help us; God has sold us into their hands, to be strewn before them in thirst and exhaustion. ²⁶ Now summon them and surrender the whole town as booty to the army of Holofernes and to all his forces. ²⁷ For it would be better for us to be captured by them.ᵃ We shall indeed become slaves, but our lives will be spared, and we shall not witness our little ones dying before our eyes, and our wives and children drawing their last breath. ²⁸ We call to witness against you heaven and earth and our God, the Lord of our ancestors, who punishes us for our sins and the sins of our ancestors; do today the things that we have described!"

²⁹ Then great and general lamentation arose throughout the assembly, and they cried out to the Lord God with a loud voice. ³⁰ But Uzziah said to them, "Courage, my brothers and sisters!ᵇ Let us hold out for five days more; by that time the Lord our God will turn his mercy to us again, for he will not forsake us utterly. ³¹ But if these days pass by, and no help comes for us, I will do as you say."

³² Then he dismissed the people to their various posts, and they went up on the walls and towers of their town. The women and children he sent home. In the town they were in great misery.

8 Now in those days Judith heard about these things: she was the daughter of Merari son of Ox son of Joseph son of Oziel son of Elkiah son of Ananias son of Gideon son of Raphain son of Ahitub son of Elijah son of Hilkiah son of Eliab son of Nathanael son of Salamiel son of Sarasadai son of Israel. ² Her husband Manasseh, who belonged to her tribe and family, had died during the barley harvest. ³ For as he stood overseeing those who were binding sheaves in the field, he was overcome by the burning heat, and took to his bed and died in his town Bethulia. So they buried him with his ancestors in the field between Dothan and Balamon. ⁴ Judith remained as a widow for three years and four months ⁵ at home where she set up a tent for herself on the roof of her house. She put sackcloth around her waist and dressed in widow's clothing. ⁶ She fasted all the days of her widowhood, except the day before the sabbath and the sabbath itself, the day before the new moon and the day of the new moon, and the festivals and days of rejoicing of the house of Israel. ⁷ She was beautiful in appearance, and was very lovely to behold. Her husband Manasseh had left her gold and silver, men and women slaves, livestock, and fields; and she

---

ᵃ Other ancient authorities add *than to die of thirst*
ᵇ Gk *Courage, brothers*

---

and Judith. **28**: *Our sins and the sins of our ancestors*, the Israelites blame themselves for their predicaments (cf. Judith's interpretation in 8.18,27). **30**: Uzziah urges that they *hold out for five days more*. A similar story is told of the Greek city of Lindos, in which the citizens, besieged by the Persians, pray to Athena to send rain within five days. The goddess comes to their aid by bringing rain to them and drought to the Persians. Judith, however, will later have none of this; she will condemn the Bethulians for setting a deadline on God's help (see 8.11–17). **7.32**: Calm descends on Bethulia, but it is the calm of despair. This makes an effective conclusion to the first half and a transition to the introduction of the person who will save Bethulia and thus Israel: Judith.

8.1–16.25: Part II: Judith rescues her people.

8.1–8: Judith is introduced. 1: Judith's name, in Greek "Ioudith," in Hebrew "Yehudit," is the feminine for Judean or Jew. Her name suggests that Bethulia and Jerusalem will be saved by the ideal Jewish woman, and it also echoes the name of one of the leaders of the Maccabean revolt, Judas Maccabeus. She is given the longest genealogy of any woman in the Bible, but it is likely fictitious. Many of the names are unknown, although it includes *Israel*, i.e., Jacob. **2–3**: The death of her husband from sunstroke provides an unheroic contrast to Judith's actions. Other male characters will also be passive in contrast to her. **4–6**: Judith's piety is exemplary, and her period of mourning is far greater than prescribed in Jewish law, suggesting a new mode of ascetic practice. In keeping with Jewish law, she does not fast on festive holidays. **7–8**: Judith's beauty and wealth give her a larger-than-life quality, but her devotion to God is the source of her strength.

maintained this estate. ⁸ No one spoke ill of her, for she feared God with great devotion.

⁹ When Judith heard the harsh words spoken by the people against the ruler, because they were faint for lack of water, and when she heard all that Uzziah said to them, and how he promised them under oath to surrender the town to the Assyrians after five days, ¹⁰ she sent her maid, who was in charge of all she possessed, to summon Uzziah andᵃ Chabris and Charmis, the elders of her town. ¹¹ They came to her, and she said to them:

"Listen to me, rulers of the people of Bethulia! What you have said to the people today is not right; you have even sworn and pronounced this oath between God and you, promising to surrender the town to our enemies unless the Lord turns and helps us within so many days. ¹² Who are you to put God to the test today, and to set yourselves up in the place ofᵇ God in human affairs? ¹³ You are putting the Lord Almighty to the test, but you will never learn anything! ¹⁴ You cannot plumb the depths of the human heart or understand the workings of the human mind; how do you expect to search out God, who made all these things, and find out his mind or comprehend his thought? No, my brothers, do not anger the Lord our God. ¹⁵ For if he does not choose to help us within these five days, he has power to protect us within any time he pleases, or even to destroy us in the presence of our enemies. ¹⁶ Do not try to bind the purposes of the Lord our God; for God is not like a human being, to be threatened, or like a mere mortal, to be won over by pleading. ¹⁷ Therefore, while we wait for his deliverance, let us call upon him to help us, and he will hear our voice, if it pleases him.

¹⁸ "For never in our generation, nor in these present days, has there been any tribe or family or people or town of ours that worships gods made with hands, as was done in days gone by. ¹⁹ That was why our ancestors were handed over to the sword and to pillage, and so they suffered a great catastrophe before our enemies. ²⁰ But we know no other god but him, and so we hope that he will not disdain us or any of our nation. ²¹ For if we are captured, all Judea will be captured and our sanctuary will be plundered; and he will make us pay for its desecration with our blood. ²² The slaughter of our kindred and the captivity of the land and the desolation of our inheritance—all this he will bring on our heads among the Gentiles, wherever we serve as slaves; and we shall be an offense and a disgrace in the eyes of those who acquire us. ²³ For our slavery will not bring us into favor, but the Lord our God will turn it to dishonor.

²⁴ "Therefore, my brothers, let us set an example for our kindred, for their lives depend upon us, and the sanctuary—both the temple and the altar—rests upon us. ²⁵ In spite of everything let us give thanks to the Lord our God, who is putting us to the test as he did our ancestors. ²⁶ Remember what he did with Abraham, and how he tested Isaac, and what happened to Jacob in Syrian Mesopotamia, while he was tending the sheep of Laban, his mother's brother. ²⁷ For he has not tried us with fire, as he did them, to search their hearts, nor has he taken vengeance on us; but the Lord scourges those who are close to him in order to admonish them."

²⁸ Then Uzziah said to her, "All that you have said was spoken out of a true heart, and there is no one who can deny your words. ²⁹ Today is not the first time your wisdom

ᵃ Other ancient authorities lack *Uzziah and* (see verses 28 and 35)

ᵇ Or *above*

8.9–27: Judith upbraids the town leaders. 10: Her unnamed *maid*, a slave, is responsible for her affairs. Slaves could wield the authority of their owners. **11:** That *they came to her* indicates Judith's important status in the community. **12:** Judith will insist that they pray to God (v.17), but they may not *put God to the test* by setting a date, a violation of Deut 6.16. **18–19:** A theme of this story is the Deuteronomic principle that if Jews sin, they will be defeated, but if they remain righteous, God will protect them (Deut 28). Judith's description of the present righteousness idealizes the period after the Maccabean Revolt when the Temple had been rededicated. **25–27:** Rather than testing God, it is God who tests Israel, as God tested *Abraham* (Gen 22), *Isaac*, and *Jacob* (Gen 29). Israelite history is echoed often in Judith.

8.28–36: Judith's powerful words win over Uzziah and the citizens. Just as Holofernes in the first half spends much of his time in war councils, Judith holds a war council with the Bethulians. **29:** The Bethulians have always

has been shown, but from the beginning of your life all the people have recognized your understanding, for your heart's disposition is right. ³⁰ But the people were so thirsty that they compelled us to do for them what we have promised, and made us take an oath that we cannot break. ³¹ Now since you are a God-fearing woman, pray for us, so that the Lord may send us rain to fill our cisterns. Then we will no longer feel faint from thirst."

³² Then Judith said to them, "Listen to me. I am about to do something that will go down through all generations of our descendants. ³³ Stand at the town gate tonight so that I may go out with my maid; and within the days after which you have promised to surrender the town to our enemies, the Lord will deliver Israel by my hand. ³⁴ Only, do not try to find out what I am doing; for I will not tell you until I have finished what I am about to do."

³⁵ Uzziah and the rulers said to her, "Go in peace, and may the Lord God go before you, to take vengeance on our enemies." ³⁶ So they returned from the tent and went to their posts.

9 Then Judith prostrated herself, put ashes on her head, and uncovered the sack-cloth she was wearing. At the very time when the evening incense was being offered in the house of God in Jerusalem, Judith cried out to the Lord with a loud voice, and said,

² "O Lord God of my ancestor Simeon, to whom you gave a sword to take revenge on those strangers who had torn off a virgin's clothing[a] to defile her, and exposed her thighs to put her to shame, and polluted her womb to disgrace her; for you said, 'It shall

not be done'—yet they did it; ³ so you gave up their rulers to be killed, and their bed, which was ashamed of the deceit they had practiced, was stained with blood, and you struck down slaves along with princes, and princes on their thrones. ⁴ You gave up their wives for booty and their daughters to captivity, and all their booty to be divided among your beloved children who burned with zeal for you and abhorred the pollution of their blood and called on you for help. O God, my God, hear me also, a widow.

⁵ "For you have done these things and those that went before and those that followed. You have designed the things that are now, and those that are to come. What you had in mind has happened; ⁶ the things you decided on presented themselves and said, 'Here we are!' For all your ways are prepared in advance, and your judgment is with foreknowledge.

⁷ "Here now are the Assyrians, a greatly increased force, priding themselves in their horses and riders, boasting in the strength of their foot soldiers, and trusting in shield and spear, in bow and sling. They do not know that you are the Lord who crushes wars; the Lord is your name. ⁸ Break their strength by your might, and bring down their power in your anger; for they intend to defile your sanctuary, and to pollute the tabernacle where your glorious name resides, and to break off the horns[b] of your altar with the sword. ⁹ Look at their pride, and send your

---

a   Cn: Gk *loosed her womb*
b   Syr: Gk *horn*

---

respected Judith's wisdom; her traits are similar to personified Wisdom (Prov 8.6) and the capable wife (Prov 31.10–31). However, her wisdom will exceed the usual standards for wise women. **30:** Thirst had rendered the people weak, and the passive leaders, unlike Judith, had acquiesced. **32–34:** Judith keeps her plan secret, in contrast to Nebuchadnezzar who reveals his secret plan to his advisors (2.2), and places her confidence in God that it will succeed. It will be remembered by *all generations* (cf. 16.21–25).

9.1–14: Judith prepares through prayer. 1: *Ashes* and *sackcloth* are signs of mourning and affliction. Judith's prayer coincides with the offering of evening incense (Ex 30.8). **2–8:** She invokes the sins of the invaders and the revenge of *my ancestor Simeon* on Shechem for raping Dinah (Gen 34). Although Simeon's revenge is characterized as excessive and foolhardy in Gen 34.30; 49.5–7, here it is considered justified, as in *Jub.* 30. **8:** The *horns* of the altar were projections with symbolic importance; see Ex 27.2; 1 Kings 1.50; 2.28; Am 3.14. **9–10:** Judith prays that God strike down Holofernes by the hand of a *widow* and a *woman,* a reversal found also at Judg 4; 5; 9.53–54. Like Simeon, Judith will use *deceit*—not a last-minute expedient but the basis of her plan and her prayer all along. By contrast, a weaker male, Achior, insisted rightly that he would speak only truth (5.5). Although rejected in wisdom texts (Prov 6.16–19; Wis 1.8; Jas 3.5–12), deceit is celebrated in this story, and

wrath upon their heads. Give to me, a widow, the strong hand to do what I plan. [10] By the deceit of my lips strike down the slave with the prince and the prince with his servant; crush their arrogance by the hand of a woman.

[11] "For your strength does not depend on numbers, nor your might on the powerful. But you are the God of the lowly, helper of the oppressed, upholder of the weak, protector of the forsaken, savior of those without hope. [12] Please, please, God of my father, God of the heritage of Israel, Lord of heaven and earth, Creator of the waters, King of all your creation, hear my prayer! [13] Make my deceitful words bring wound and bruise on those who have planned cruel things against your covenant, and against your sacred house, and against Mount Zion, and against the house your children possess. [14] Let your whole nation and every tribe know and understand that you are God, the God of all power and might, and that there is no other who protects the people of Israel but you alone!"

10

When Judith[a] had stopped crying out to the God of Israel, and had ended all these words, [2] she rose from where she lay prostrate. She called her maid and went down into the house where she lived on sabbaths and on her festal days. [3] She removed the sackcloth she had been wearing, took off her widow's garments, bathed her body with water, and anointed herself with precious ointment. She combed her hair, put on a tiara, and dressed herself in the festive attire that she used to wear while her husband Manasseh was living. [4] She put sandals on her feet, and put on her anklets, bracelets, rings,

earrings, and all her other jewelry. Thus she made herself very beautiful, to entice the eyes of all the men who might see her. [5] She gave her maid a skin of wine and a flask of oil, and filled a bag with roasted grain, dried fig cakes, and fine bread;[b] then she wrapped up all her dishes and gave them to her to carry.

[6] Then they went out to the town gate of Bethulia and found Uzziah standing there with the elders of the town, Chabris and Charmis. [7] When they saw her transformed in appearance and dressed differently, they were very greatly astounded at her beauty and said to her, [8] "May the God of our ancestors grant you favor and fulfill your plans, so that the people of Israel may glory and Jerusalem may be exalted." She bowed down to God.

[9] Then she said to them, "Order the gate of the town to be opened for me so that I may go out and accomplish the things you have just said to me." So they ordered the young men to open the gate for her, as she requested. [10] When they had done this, Judith went out, accompanied by her maid. The men of the town watched her until she had gone down the mountain and passed through the valley, where they lost sight of her.

[11] As the women[c] were going straight on through the valley, an Assyrian patrol met her [12] and took her into custody. They asked her, "To what people do you belong, and where are you coming from, and where are you going?" She replied, "I am a daughter of the Hebrews, but I am fleeing from them, for they are about

a Gk *she*
b Other ancient authorities add *and cheese*
c Gk *they*

---

elsewhere is often used by tricksters and those less powerful than their adversaries, such as Rebekah (Gen 27), Jacob (Gen 27), Rachel (Gen 31), Tamar (Gen 38), and Abraham (Gen 12; 20).

10.1–10: Judith puts her plan into motion. 1–4: Judith wore sackcloth while praying, but now dresses in beautiful clothes (cf. Add Esth 15). 3: Given the lack of water in Bethulia, Judith's decision to bathe *her body with water* indicates the significance of her mission. 5: Judith's provisions will allow her to keep the dietary laws while with the Assyrians (cf. Dan 1.8–16). Her maid will be a silent, efficient, loyal counterpart to Holofernes' talkative assistant, Bagoas. 6–10: The ritualized departure slows the rhythm of the story here, and the visual detail is striking. Once Judith passes through the gate of the city, almost every word out of her mouth will be deceitful and every action sexually provocative or murderous.

10.11–23: Judith meets the guards and is taken to Holofernes. 13–16: Ironically and humorously, readers already see that her *true report* will be a lie. Nearly every line of dialogue that follows can be read ironically as well: *You have saved your life by hurrying down to see our lord* (v. 15) can be heard by the audience as referring to God. The obtuseness of the Assyrians, even about the meanings of their own words, is likely intended as

to be handed over to you to be devoured. ¹³I am on my way to see Holofernes the commander of your army, to give him a true report; I will show him a way by which he can go and capture all the hill country without losing one of his men, captured or slain."

¹⁴When the men heard her words, and observed her face—she was in their eyes marvelously beautiful—they said to her, ¹⁵"You have saved your life by hurrying down to see our lord. Go at once to his tent; some of us will escort you and hand you over to him. ¹⁶When you stand before him, have no fear in your heart, but tell him what you have just said, and he will treat you well."

¹⁷They chose from their number a hundred men to accompany her and her maid, and they brought them to the tent of Holofernes. ¹⁸There was great excitement in the whole camp, for her arrival was reported from tent to tent. They came and gathered around her as she stood outside the tent of Holofernes, waiting until they told him about her. ¹⁹They marveled at her beauty and admired the Israelites, judging them by her. They said to one another, "Who can despise these people, who have women like this among them? It is not wise to leave one of their men alive, for if we let them go they will be able to beguile the whole world!"

²⁰Then the guards of Holofernes and all his servants came out and led her into the tent. ²¹Holofernes was resting on his bed under a canopy that was woven with purple and gold, emeralds and other precious stones. ²²When they told him of her, he came to the front of the tent, with silver lamps carried before him. ²³When Judith came into the presence of Holofernes^a and his servants, they all marveled at the beauty of her face. She prostrated herself and did obeisance to him, but his slaves raised her up.

11 Then Holofernes said to her, "Take courage, woman, and do not be afraid in your heart, for I have never hurt anyone

who chose to serve Nebuchadnezzar, king of all the earth. ²Even now, if your people who live in the hill country had not slighted me, I would never have lifted my spear against them. They have brought this on themselves. ³But now tell me why you have fled from them and have come over to us. In any event, you have come to safety. Take courage! You will live tonight and ever after. ⁴No one will hurt you. Rather, all will treat you well, as they do the servants of my lord King Nebuchadnezzar."

⁵Judith answered him, "Accept the words of your slave, and let your servant speak in your presence. I will say nothing false to my lord this night. ⁶If you follow out the words of your servant, God will accomplish something through you, and my lord will not fail to achieve his purposes. ⁷By the life of Nebuchadnezzar, king of the whole earth, and by the power of him who has sent you to direct every living being! Not only do human beings serve him because of you, but also the animals of the field and the cattle and the birds of the air will live, because of your power, under Nebuchadnezzar and all his house. ⁸For we have heard of your wisdom and skill, and it is reported throughout the whole world that you alone are the best in the whole kingdom, the most informed and the most astounding in military strategy.

⁹"Now as for Achior's speech in your council, we have heard his words, for the people of Bethulia spared him and he told them all he had said to you. ¹⁰Therefore, lord and master, do not disregard what he said, but keep it in your mind, for it is true. Indeed our nation cannot be punished, nor can the sword prevail against them, unless they sin against their God.

¹¹"But now, in order that my lord may not be defeated and his purpose frustrated, death

^a Gk *him*

---

humorous. **20–22:** Holofernes' tent is decorated with luxurious items like a harem chamber.

11.1–23: Judith's dialogue with Holofernes. 1: Holofernes also speaks a mixture of truth and lies (see 3.2–8). **6:** Judith's double meanings continue with the ambiguity in her statement: *My lord will not fail to achieve his purposes.* **7:** This grandiose view of Nebuchadnezzar is also played upon in Dan 2.37–38; 4.12 (cf. Jer 27.6; 28.14). Judith cleverly adapts the praise of Nebuchadnezzar to flatter Holofernes. **9–15:** That Holofernes would have believed any part of her story is preposterous, but this only makes the fictional world more enjoyable. **9:** *Achior's*

will fall upon them, for a sin has overtaken them by which they are about to provoke their God to anger when they do what is wrong. [12] Since their food supply is exhausted and their water has almost given out, they have planned to kill their livestock and have determined to use all that God by his laws has forbidden them to eat. [13] They have decided to consume the first fruits of the grain and the tithes of the wine and oil, which they had consecrated and set aside for the priests who minister in the presence of our God in Jerusalem—things it is not lawful for any of the people even to touch with their hands. [14] Since even the people in Jerusalem have been doing this, they have sent messengers there in order to bring back permission from the council of the elders. [15] When the response reaches them and they act upon it, on that very day they will be handed over to you to be destroyed.

[16] "So when I, your slave, learned all this, I fled from them. God has sent me to accomplish with you things that will astonish the whole world wherever people shall hear about them. [17] Your servant is indeed God-fearing and serves the God of heaven night and day. So, my lord, I will remain with you; but every night your servant will go out into the valley and pray to God. He will tell me when they have committed their sins. [18] Then I will come and tell you, so that you may go out with your whole army, and not one of them will be able to withstand you. [19] Then I will lead you through Judea, until you come to Jerusalem; there I will set your throne.[a] You will drive them like sheep that have no shepherd, and no dog will so much as growl at you. For this was told me to give me foreknowledge; it was announced to me, and I was sent to tell you."

[20] Her words pleased Holofernes and all his servants. They marveled at her wisdom and said, [21] "No other woman from one end of the earth to the other looks so beautiful or speaks so wisely!" [22] Then Holofernes said to her, "God has done well to send you ahead of the people, to strengthen our hands and bring destruction on those who have despised my lord. [23] You are not only beautiful in appearance, but wise in speech. If you do as you have said, your God shall be my God, and you shall live in the palace of King Nebuchadnezzar and be renowned throughout the whole world."

12 Then he commanded them to bring her in where his silver dinnerware was kept, and ordered them to set a table for her with some of his own delicacies, and with some of his own wine to drink. [2] But Judith said, "I cannot partake of them, or it will be an offense; but I will have enough with the things I brought with me." [3] Holofernes said to her, "If your supply runs out, where can we get you more of the same? For none of your people are here with us." [4] Judith replied, "As surely as you live, my lord, your servant will not use up the supplies I have with me before the Lord carries out by my hand what he has determined."

[5] Then the servants of Holofernes brought her into the tent, and she slept until midnight. Toward the morning watch she got up [6] and sent this message to Holofernes: "Let my lord now give orders to allow your servant to go out and pray." [7] So Holofernes commanded his guards not to hinder her. She remained in the camp three days. She went out each night to the valley of Bethulia, and bathed at the spring in the camp.[b] [8] After bathing, she prayed the Lord God of Israel to direct her way for the triumph of his[c] people. [9] Then she returned purified and stayed in the tent until she ate her food toward evening.

---

a Or *chariot*
b Other ancient authorities lack *in the camp*
c Other ancient authorities read *her*

---

speech, see 5.5–21. **13**: *First fruits*, Ex 23.19; *tithes*, Lev 27.30. **17**: Even Judith's piety is deceitful; she establishes a prayer discipline that will allow her to escape unnoticed (13.3,10), just as her pouch for kosher food will also serve a different and macabre purpose. **22–23**: Holofernes unknowingly speaks the truth in double meanings: *bring destruction on those who have despised my lord; your God shall be my God*—in judgment!

12.1–9: Judith's daily schedule within Holofernes' camp. Judith imposes her schedule on Holofernes, which allows her to keep the dietary laws and to pray (cf. Dan 1.8–19). **8:** Her daily *bathing* may be a ritual bath; similar rituals were practiced at Qumran.

[10] On the fourth day Holofernes held a banquet for his personal attendants only, and did not invite any of his officers. [11] He said to Bagoas, the eunuch who had charge of his personal affairs, "Go and persuade the Hebrew woman who is in your care to join us and to eat and drink with us. [12] For it would be a disgrace if we let such a woman go without having intercourse with her. If we do not seduce her, she will laugh at us."

[13] So Bagoas left the presence of Holofernes, and approached her and said, "Let this pretty girl not hesitate to come to my lord to be honored in his presence, and to enjoy drinking wine with us, and to become today like one of the Assyrian women who serve in the palace of Nebuchadnezzar." [14] Judith replied, "Who am I to refuse my lord? Whatever pleases him I will do at once, and it will be a joy to me until the day of my death." [15] So she proceeded to dress herself in all her woman's finery. Her maid went ahead and spread for her on the ground before Holofernes the lambskins she had received from Bagoas for her daily use in reclining.

[16] Then Judith came in and lay down. Holofernes' heart was ravished with her and his passion was aroused, for he had been waiting for an opportunity to seduce her from the day he first saw her. [17] So Holofernes said to her, "Have a drink and be merry with us!" [18] Judith said, "I will gladly drink, my lord, because today is the greatest day in my whole life." [19] Then she took what her maid had prepared and ate and drank before him. [20] Holofernes was greatly pleased with her, and drank a great quantity of wine, much more than he had ever drunk in any one day since he was born.

13 When evening came, his slaves quickly withdrew. Bagoas closed the tent from outside and shut out the attendants from his master's presence. They went to bed, for they all were weary because the banquet had lasted so long. [2] But Judith was left alone in the tent, with Holofernes stretched out on his bed, for he was dead drunk.

[3] Now Judith had told her maid to stand outside the bedchamber and to wait for her to come out, as she did on the other days; for she said she would be going out for her prayers. She had said the same thing to Bagoas. [4] So everyone went out, and no one, either small or great, was left in the bedchamber. Then Judith, standing beside his bed, said in her heart, "O Lord God of all might, look in this hour on the work of my hands for the exaltation of Jerusalem. [5] Now indeed is the time to help your heritage and to carry out my design to destroy the enemies who have risen up against us."

[6] She went up to the bedpost near Holofernes' head, and took down his sword that hung there. [7] She came close to his bed, took hold of the hair of his head, and said, "Give me strength today, O Lord God of Israel!" [8] Then she struck his neck twice with all her might, and cut off his head. [9] Next she rolled his body off the bed and pulled down the canopy from the posts. Soon afterward she went out and gave Holofernes' head to her maid, [10] who placed it in her food bag.

12.10–20: Holofernes invites Judith to a banquet. 11–13: *Bagoas,* see 2.4n. Both Holofernes and Bagoas reveal by their words that they are putty in Judith's hands, an ironic contrast with the power they think they have. In the Greek novels the beautiful heroine is often threatened with the prospect of being forced to marry a king or become a courtesan, but here Judith is fully in charge and can manipulate the suggestion. **15:** The lambskins may symbolically protect Judith from impurity (cf. Josephus, *Ant.* 3.270, *m. Sot.* 2:4). **16–20:** Holofernes thinks that he will seduce Judith, but it is *she* who seduces *him* into drinking *more than he had ever drunk* before. She seems as excited as Holofernes, but for an entirely different reason. Again, Judith speaks the truth that she intends to be misunderstood by Holofernes.

13.1–10a: Judith beheads Holofernes 1–3: Chs 1–12 have been building in tension for this moment. The story has been intentionally delayed before but proceeds quickly now, with the beheading scene told in seven verses. **6–10a:** Judith's actions and words also have biblical precedents, including David slaying Goliath (1 Sam 17.46) and Jael slaying Sisera (Judg 4–5). Holofernes' *canopy* and *head* are collected as trophies, which will be important later. The *food bag* is now seen to be part of her plan to kill Holofernes as well.

13.10b–20: Judith and her maid return to Bethulia. The daily prayers of Judith and her maid now make it

Then the two of them went out together, as they were accustomed to do for prayer. They passed through the camp, circled around the valley, and went up the mountain to Bethulia, and came to its gates. [11] From a distance Judith called out to the sentries at the gates, "Open, open the gate! God, our God, is with us, still showing his power in Israel and his strength against our enemies, as he has done today!"

[12] When the people of her town heard her voice, they hurried down to the town gate and summoned the elders of the town. [13] They all ran together, both small and great, for it seemed unbelievable that she had returned. They opened the gate and welcomed them. Then they lit a fire to give light, and gathered around them. [14] Then she said to them with a loud voice, "Praise God, O praise him! Praise God, who has not withdrawn his mercy from the house of Israel, but has destroyed our enemies by my hand this very night!"

[15] Then she pulled the head out of the bag and showed it to them, and said, "See here, the head of Holofernes, the commander of the Assyrian army, and here is the canopy beneath which he lay in his drunken stupor. The Lord has struck him down by the hand of a woman. [16] As the Lord lives, who has protected me in the way I went, I swear that it was my face that seduced him to his destruction, and that he committed no sin with me, to defile and shame me."

[17] All the people were greatly astonished. They bowed down and worshiped God, and said with one accord, "Blessed are you our God, who have this day humiliated the enemies of your people."

[18] Then Uzziah said to her, "O daughter, you are blessed by the Most High God above all other women on earth; and blessed be the Lord God, who created the heavens and the earth, who has guided you to cut off the head of the leader of our enemies. [19] Your praise[a] will never depart from the hearts of those who remember the power of God. [20] May God grant this to be a perpetual honor to you, and may he reward you with blessings, because you risked your own life when our nation was brought low, and you averted our ruin, walking in the straight path before our God." And all the people said, "Amen. Amen."

14 Then Judith said to them, "Listen to me, my friends. Take this head and hang it upon the parapet of your wall. [2] As soon as day breaks and the sun rises on the earth, each of you take up your weapons, and let every able-bodied man go out of the town; set a captain over them, as if you were going down to the plain against the Assyrian outpost; only do not go down. [3] Then they will seize their arms and go into the camp and rouse the officers of the Assyrian army. They will rush into the tent of Holofernes and will not find him. Then panic will come over them, and they will flee before you. [4] Then you and all who live within the borders of Israel will pursue them and cut them down in their tracks. [5] But before you do all this, bring Achior the Ammonite to me so that he may see and recognize the man who despised the house of Israel and sent him to us as if to his death."

[6] So they summoned Achior from the house of Uzziah. When he came and saw the head of Holofernes in the hand of one of the men in the assembly of the people, he fell down on his face in a faint. [7] When they raised him up he threw himself at Judith's feet, and did obeisance to her, and said, "Blessed are you in every tent of Judah! In every nation those who hear your name will be alarmed. [8] Now tell me what you have done during these days."

So Judith told him in the presence of the people all that she had done, from the day

---

[a] Other ancient authorities read *hope*

---

possible for them to arouse no suspicion as they escape (11.17; 12.7). **15**: *By the hand of a woman,* see 9.9–10n. **18–20**: Judith's deed is met with a blessing similar to Deborah's blessing of Jael for killing the Canaanite general Sisera (Judg 5.24).

14.1–10: **Judith plans for a military victory, and Achior converts.** Judith again orders the Bethulians into action and demonstrates her control over the Assyrians. On exhibiting the enemy's *head,* cf. 1 Sam 17.54; 31.9–10; 2 Kings 10.7–8; Matt 14.8; 1 Macc 7.47; 2 Macc 15.35. The last two are significant because Judith's name may be a play on that of Judas Maccabeus, whose exhibition of the head of Nicanor also resulted in an annual celebra-

she left until the moment she began speaking to them. ⁹ When she had finished, the people raised a great shout and made a joyful noise in their town. ¹⁰ When Achior saw all that the God of Israel had done, he believed firmly in God. So he was circumcised, and joined the house of Israel, remaining so to this day.

¹¹ As soon as it was dawn they hung the head of Holofernes on the wall. Then they all took their weapons, and they went out in companies to the mountain passes. ¹² When the Assyrians saw them they sent word to their commanders, who then went to the generals and the captains and to all their other officers. ¹³ They came to Holofernes' tent and said to the steward in charge of all his personal affairs, "Wake up our lord, for the slaves have been so bold as to come down against us to give battle, to their utter destruction."

¹⁴ So Bagoas went in and knocked at the entry of the tent, for he supposed that he was sleeping with Judith. ¹⁵ But when no one answered, he opened it and went into the bedchamber and found him sprawled on the floor dead, with his head missing. ¹⁶ He cried out with a loud voice and wept and groaned and shouted, and tore his clothes. ¹⁷ Then he went to the tent where Judith had stayed, and when he did not find her, he rushed out to the people and shouted, ¹⁸ "The slaves have tricked us! One Hebrew woman has brought disgrace on the house of King Nebuchadnezzar. Look, Holofernes is lying on the ground, and his head is missing!"

¹⁹ When the leaders of the Assyrian army heard this, they tore their tunics and were greatly dismayed, and their loud cries and shouts rose up throughout the camp.

15 When the men in the tents heard it, they were amazed at what had happened. ² Overcome with fear and trembling, they did not wait for one another, but with one impulse all rushed out and fled by every path across the plain and through the hill country. ³ Those who had camped in the hills around Bethulia also took to flight. Then the Israelites, everyone that was a soldier, rushed out upon them. ⁴ Uzziah sent men to Beto-masthaimª and Choba and Kola, and to all the frontiers of Israel, to tell what had taken place and to urge all to rush out upon the enemy to destroy them. ⁵ When the Israelites heard it, with one accord they fell upon the enemy,ᵇ and cut them down as far as Choba. Those in Jerusalem and all the hill country also came, for they were told what had happened in the camp of the enemy. The men in Gilead and in Galilee outflanked them with great slaughter, even beyond Damascus and its borders. ⁶ The rest of the people of Bethulia fell upon the Assyrian camp and plundered it, acquiring great riches. ⁷ And the Israelites, when they returned from the slaughter, took possession of what remained. Even the villages and towns in the hill country and in the plain got a great amount of booty, since there was a vast quantity of it.

⁸ Then the high priest Joakim and the elders of the Israelites who lived in Jerusalem came to witness the good things that the Lord

ª Other ancient authorities add *and Bebai*
ᵇ Gk *them*

tion. **6:** Cf. 6.5. It is ironic that Achior faints, since Judith was so resolute in taking the head. **10:** Like Judith, Achior recognizes that her heroism comes from God, and responds by converting. Although Deut 23.3 forbids the acceptance of Ammonites or Moabites to the tenth generation, in this romanticized narrative, he, like Ruth the Moabite, is permitted to join.

14.11–15.7: The Assyrians discover Holofernes' headless body and are put to flight. 14.11–14: Events occur just as Judith predicted (14.3), although the story is slowed somewhat so that the audience can relish the coming reversal. **18:** Honor and shame are now reversed; Judith has exhibited Holofernes' head, shaming him and his memory, and the status of weak and powerful is reversed: *Slaves* and *one Hebrew woman* prevail over and disgrace *the house of King Nebuchadnezzar.* **14.19–15.7:** Upon learning that Holofernes has lost his head, the Assyrians lose theirs as well: general chaos results, and they are easily vanquished by the outnumbered Israelites. Here the Assyrians experience the same *fear and trembling* that they caused other nations (cf. 2.3), including Israel (4.1–2). The depiction of victory and plundering is similar to 1 Macc 7.44–47 (cf. also Deut 20.10–18; Esth 9.1–19; Ps 48).

15.8–16.20: A series of celebrations. 15.8–10: The connection between Judith, Bethulia, and the Jerusalem

had done for Israel, and to see Judith and to wish her well. ⁹ When they met her, they all blessed her with one accord and said to her, "You are the glory of Jerusalem, you are the great boast of Israel, you are the great pride of our nation! ¹⁰ You have done all this with your own hand; you have done great good to Israel, and God is well pleased with it. May the Almighty Lord bless you forever!" And all the people said, "Amen."

¹¹ All the people plundered the camp for thirty days. They gave Judith the tent of Holofernes and all his silver dinnerware, his beds, his bowls, and all his furniture. She took them and loaded her mules and hitched up her carts and piled the things on them.

¹² All the women of Israel gathered to see her, and blessed her, and some of them performed a dance in her honor. She took ivy-wreathed wands in her hands and distributed them to the women who were with her; ¹³ and she and those who were with her crowned themselves with olive wreaths. She went before all the people in the dance, leading all the women, while all the men of Israel followed, bearing their arms and wearing garlands and singing hymns.

¹⁴ Judith began this thanksgiving before

16 all Israel, and all the people loudly sang this song of praise. ¹ And Judith said,

Begin a song to my God with tambourines,
    sing to my Lord with cymbals.
Raise to him a new psalm;ᵃ
    exalt him, and call upon his name.
² For the Lord is a God who crushes wars;
    he sets up his camp among his people;
he delivered me from the hands of my
    pursuers.

³ The Assyrian came down from the
    mountains of the north;
    he came with myriads of his warriors;
their numbers blocked up the wadis,
    and their cavalry covered the hills.
⁴ He boasted that he would burn up my
    territory,
    and kill my young men with the sword,
and dash my infants to the ground,
    and seize my children as booty,
    and take my virgins as spoil.

⁵ But the Lord Almighty has foiled them
    by the hand of a woman.ᵇ
⁶ For their mighty one did not fall by the
    hands of the young men,
    nor did the sons of the Titans strike him
        down,
    nor did tall giants set upon him;
but Judith daughter of Merari
    with the beauty of her countenance
        undid him.

⁷ For she put away her widow's clothing
    to exalt the oppressed in Israel.
She anointed her face with perfume;
    ⁸ she fastened her hair with a tiara
    and put on a linen gown to beguile
        him.
⁹ Her sandal ravished his eyes,
    her beauty captivated his mind,
    and the sword severed his neck!
¹⁰ The Persians trembled at her boldness,
    the Medes were daunted at her
        daring.

ᵃ Other ancient authorities read *a psalm and praise*
ᵇ Other ancient authorities add *he has confounded them*

Temple officials has often been emphasized in the story, and especially here in the co-celebration. **11:** A balanced and complete reversal of fortune can be seen here. Bethulia was under siege for thirty-four days (7.20) before Judith went to the Assyrian camp for four days, which the Israelites then plunder for thirty days. **12:** *The women . . . performed a dance in her honor,* women in Israel performed victory dances and songs (Ex 15.20–21; 1 Sam 18.6–7). *Ivy-wreathed wands* were Greek in origin, but 2 Macc 10.7 and 3 Macc 7.16 indicate that they had been adopted by Jews. **15.14–16.17:** Judith's victory song. This book, like Tobit, concludes with a long hymn of thanksgiving (cf. also Deut 32–33; Judg 5; 2 Sam 22; Jon 2; Prayer of Azariah, and the Song of the Three Jews). Especially close is Ex 15; Ex 15.3 (Greek) and Jdt 16.2 both read: *For the Lord is a God who crushes wars.* **16.1:** *Tambourines,* small hand-drums without the modern metal rattles, are known from ancient depictions (cf. Ps 150.4–5). *A new psalm* (cf. Ps 96.1; 98.1). **5:** *By the hand of a woman,* see 9.9–10n.; 13.15. **6:** *Titans* and *giants* are from Greek mythology, though here perhaps also referring to giants from Israelite tradition (Gen 6.4; Deut 3.11). **10:** The

¹¹ Then my oppressed people shouted;
  my weak people cried out,ᵃ and the
    enemyᵇ trembled;
  they lifted up their voices, and the
    enemyᵇ were turned back.
¹² Sons of slave-girls pierced them through
    and wounded them like the children of
      fugitives;
  they perished before the army of my Lord.

¹³ I will sing to my God a new song:
O Lord, you are great and glorious,
  wonderful in strength, invincible.
¹⁴ Let all your creatures serve you,
  for you spoke, and they were made.
You sent forth your spirit,ᶜ and it formed
    them;ᵈ
  there is none that can resist your voice.
¹⁵ For the mountains shall be shaken to
    their foundations with the waters;
  before your glance the rocks shall melt
    like wax.
But to those who fear you
  you show mercy.
¹⁶ For every sacrifice as a fragrant offering
    is a small thing,
  and the fat of all whole burnt offerings
    to you is a very little thing;
but whoever fears the Lord is great forever.

¹⁷ Woe to the nations that rise up against
    my people!
  The Lord Almighty will take vengeance
    on them in the day of judgment;
he will send fire and worms into their
    flesh;
  they shall weep in pain forever.

¹⁸ When they arrived at Jerusalem, they worshiped God. As soon as the people were purified, they offered their burnt offerings, their freewill offerings, and their gifts. ¹⁹ Judith also dedicated to God all the possessions of Holofernes, which the people had given her; and the canopy that she had taken for herself from his bedchamber she gave as a votive offering. ²⁰ For three months the people continued feasting in Jerusalem before the sanctuary, and Judith remained with them.

²¹ After this they all returned home to their own inheritances. Judith went to Bethulia, and remained on her estate. For the rest of her life she was honored throughout the whole country. ²² Many desired to marry her, but she gave herself to no man all the days of her life after her husband Manasseh died and was gathered to his people. ²³ She became more and more famous, and grew old in her husband's house, reaching the age of one hundred five. She set her maid free. She died in Bethulia, and they buried her in the cave of her husband Manasseh; ²⁴ and the house of Israel mourned her for seven days. Before she died she distributed her property to all those who were next of kin to her husband Manasseh, and to her own nearest kindred. ²⁵ No one ever again spread terror among the Israelites during the lifetime of Judith, or for a long time after her death.

ᵃ Other ancient authorities read *feared*
ᵇ Gk *they*
ᶜ Or *breath*
ᵈ Other ancient authorities read *they were created*

Persians and *Medes* are surprising here; they have not figured in the narrative before. **13:** *A new song* (cf. 16.1n.; Ps 33; 149.1; Isa 42.10). **14:** Cf. Ps 104.30. **15:** Cf. Ps. 97.5. **19:** Offerings of military booty were common; David offered the sword of Goliath (1 Sam 21.9). Ironically, Judith does not offer Holofernes' sword but the inner canopy of his tent, which she penetrated to kill him. Even in death Holofernes is unmanned and shamed.

16.21–25: Conclusion. The hero or heroine in stories of many cultures does not generally reintegrate into society after saving the people, although Judith's status is unclear. She does not marry, gives away her wealth (cf. Num 27.11), and frees her slave, but does she reenter her hut (8.5)? At any rate, like the judges she brings peace and safety to the land for a period (Judg 3.11,30; 5.31).

ESTHER
(THE GREEK VERSION CONTAINING
ADDITIONAL CHAPTERS)

NAME AND CANONICAL STATUS

The Greek version of Esther is a second- or first-century BCE translation for Greek-speaking Jews of the canonical Hebrew book of Esther (i.e., the one included in the "Hebrew Bible" portion of this edition). The earliest indication that the story was titled "Esther" after its Jewish heroine appears in connection with this Greek translation. The translator—very likely the Lysimachus of Jerusalem mentioned in 11.1—produced a systematic but relatively free translation of the Hebrew. Besides numerous small but often significant omissions and additions (see annotations that follow), the Greek version includes six extra sections with more than a hundred verses that have no counterparts in any Hebrew manuscript.

In the early centuries CE, as the rabbis worked out the official canon of Jewish scripture, they rejected the Greek translation of Esther, including its additional verses, along with all other non-Hebrew Jewish texts. By contrast the early Church adopted into its canon a number of Jewish writings in Greek, among them the "extra" verses in Greek Esther. Protestants follow the Jewish model and exclude the additional verses from their canon, while Roman Catholic and Orthodox Christians accept them. (Most editions of this Bible include these disputed Greek/Jewish texts in the Apocryphal/Deuterocanonical section.)

AUTHORSHIP, DATE, AND LITERARY HISTORY

The evidence from both Hebrew and Greek manuscripts suggests a complicated evolution of the Esther story that scholars have yet to disentangle fully. Originally, Additions A, C, D, and F were probably composed in either Hebrew or Aramaic, and if so may have already been part of the text from which the Greek translator worked. The florid rhetorical phraseology of B and E indicates that they must originally have been composed in Greek. It is impossible to say who authored either the Semitic or Greek Additions. Additions B and E may have been composed in a sophisticated Greek Jewish center, such as Alexandria, but a Palestinian provenance for the others is likely.

The additions were not composed at the same time. The latest possible date for B, C, D, and E is 93 CE when the historian Josephus paraphrased them in his *Jewish Antiquities*. The colophon's location (11.1) immediately after F suggests that A as well as F were part of the Semitic text at the time that Lysimachus made his Greek translation in the late second or first century BCE.

The additional sections are clearly intrusive and secondary, for they contradict the older Hebrew text at a number of points. What is clear, however, is that the Hellenistic author(s) of these extra portions of the story all followed the early Jewish tradition of biblical interpretation called *midrash* and felt called upon to resolve perceived narrative, theological, and moral ambiguities in Jewish scripture. Consequently, while the additions sometimes make the characters and events more vivid or dramatic, their main purpose is to transform the comparatively subtle and enigmatic Hebrew story of Esther into a more conventional tale of divine intervention and exemplary Jewish piety.

CONTENTS

The Greek Additions to the book of Esther comprise 105 verses. Their contents are as follows:

- Addition A: Mordecai's dream (11.2–12) and his discovery of a plot against the king (12.1–6)
- Addition B: The royal edict dictated by Haman, announcing a pogrom (a persecution to the death) against the Jews (13.1–7)
- Addition C: The prayers of Mordecai (13.8-18) and Esther (14.1–19)
- Addition D: Esther's appearance, unsummoned, before the king (15.4–19)
- Addition E: The royal edict dictated by Mordecai, counteracting the edict sent by Haman (16.1–24)
- Addition F: The interpretation of Mordecai's dream (10.4–13) and the colophon (an inscription at the end of a manuscript) to the Greek version (11.1)

Besides the Additions, the translators also made many minor changes as they interpreted the Hebrew text. These are mentioned in the annotations.

INTERPRETATION

Besides giving the story a more explicit religious character, the additions as they are arranged within the narrative create new emphases. A and F, which frame the story, graft onto it an apocalyptic perspective of cosmic struggle between good and evil. The juxtaposition of C's extensive praise of God with specific terms and phrases applied to Ahasuerus in D makes explicit the Greek version's intent throughout the story to contrast the capricious earthly king with God the faithful heavenly king. Similarly, the royal decrees in B and E highlight the theme of human commandments versus the divinely given Jewish law to which Esther also alludes when she prays in C.

There is no mention of God in the original Hebrew narrative, one important reason for the centuries of rabbinical debate over including Esther among the authoritative Jewish scriptures. By contrast, in the Greek Additions the terms "Lord" or "God" appear more than fifty times. Occasionally the Greek translation inserts references to God into verses that correspond to the original Hebrew text, as when Mordecai instructs Esther prior to her becoming queen that she should "fear God and keep his laws" (2.20) and then later urges her to "call upon the Lord" (4.8) before appearing unsummoned before the king. In 6.1 according to the Greek text, "That night the Lord took sleep from the king," whereas the Hebrew leaves the source of Ahasuerus's insomnia unspecified. Likewise in the Greek version, Haman's wife and his friends caution Haman that if Mordecai is Jewish, then "the living God is with him" (compare the Heb at 6.13).

The additions provide their authors with an opportunity to express their own particular theological views. Additions A and F introduce apocalyptic motifs to emphasize God's providential care for the people Israel in a universally hostile world. Addition C attests to the efficacy of prayer and expresses Queen Esther's abhorrence at being married to a Gentile, her loathing of all things worldly and courtly, and her strict observance of Jewish dietary laws—none of which are so much as hinted at in the Hebrew. Thanks largely to Addition D, the climax of the Greek version is reached when God miraculously changes to gentleness the king's "fierce anger" at Esther's unannounced entrance. This motif is lacking in the Hebrew. Taken together, the six additions deemphasize the establishment of Purim and express a deep distrust of Gentiles.

Mary Joan Winn Leith

11 [a] [2] In the second year of the reign of Artaxerxes the Great, on the first day of Nisan, Mordecai son of Jair son of Shimei[b] son of Kish, of the tribe of Benjamin, had a dream. [3] He was a Jew living in the city of Susa, a great man, serving in the court of the king. [4] He was one of the captives whom King Nebuchadnezzar of Babylon had brought from Jerusalem with King Jeconiah of Judea. And this was his dream: [5] Noises[c] and confusion, thunders and earthquake, tumult on the earth! [6] Then two great dragons came forward, both ready to fight, and they roared terribly. [7] At their roaring every nation prepared for war, to fight against the righteous nation. [8] It was a day of darkness and gloom, of tribulation and distress, affliction and great tumult on the earth! [9] And the whole righteous nation was troubled; they feared the evils that threatened them,[d] and were ready to perish. [10] Then they cried out to God; and at their outcry, as though from a tiny spring, there came a great river, with abundant water; [11] light came, and the sun rose, and the lowly were exalted and devoured those held in honor.

[12] Mordecai saw in this dream what God had determined to do, and after he awoke he had it on his mind, seeking all day to understand it in every detail.

12 Now Mordecai took his rest in the courtyard with Gabatha and Tharra, the two eunuchs of the king who kept watch in the courtyard. [2] He overheard their conversation and inquired into their purposes, and learned that they were preparing to lay hands on King Artaxerxes; and he informed the king concerning them. [3] Then the king examined the two eunuchs, and after they had confessed it, they were led away to execution. [4] The king made a permanent record of these

---

[a] Chapters 11.2—12.6 correspond to chapter A 1-17 in some translations.

[b] Gk *Semeios*

[c] Or *Voices*

[d] Gk *their own evils*

Addition A: 11.2–12: Mordecai's prophetic dream of impending danger to the Jews. 2: *Artaxerxes*, a mistranslation of the Heb "Ahasuerus," that is, Xerxes I (486–465 BCE); the *second year* would be 485. Month names in Esther are Babylonian; *Nisan*, March-April, is the first month of the new year. Thus, Mordecai's dream comes on New Year's Day. *Mordecai*'s name derives from the name of the Babylonian god Marduk, whose creation of the world was reenacted every new year in Babylon. Mordecai's genealogy connecting him with King Saul (1 Sam 9.1; 2 Sam 16.5–18) is repeated in 2.5. **3:** *Jew* (Heb "yehudi"), originally meaning someone from the kingdom of Judah (2 Kings 16.6), is used here in its later sense of an adherent to Judaism. *Susa*, westernmost of the three capital cities of the Persian empire in northwestern Iran. In contrast to Heb Esther, Mordecai is already an important royal official. **4:** Mordecai would be well over one hundred years old by 485 BCE if he, along with Judah's last king *Jeconiah* (Jehoiachin), had been exiled by *Nebuchadnezzar* in 597 (2 Kings 24.8–16). As in other historical novellas, the author takes liberties with actual chronology. **5:** *Noises . . . tumult on the earth*, the language of cosmic chaos is typical of apocalyptic texts (see Isa 24.17–20; Dan 12.1,4). **6:** *Two great dragons*, Mordecai and Haman (see Addition F 10.7). God defeated the chaos dragon (a sea monster) at the time of creation (Pss 74.13; 89.10; Isa 27.1; 51.9–10; Job 26.12–13); imagery from this primordial battle is frequently used in apocalyptic literature (Dan 7; Rev 12.3; 13.2; 20.2). Two dragons (see 2 Esd 6.49–52), one good, one evil, are unusual and may reflect Persian influence. **7:** *Righteous nation*, the Jews (see Dan 7.27). Unlike the Heb, Gk Esther perceives the entire Gentile (non-Jewish) world as a danger to the Jews. **10:** *Cried out*, Ex 3.7; Jdt 4.9,12,15. *Tiny spring* and *great river* refer to Esther (10.6). **11:** *Light* and morning, symbolizing joy, salvation, and new life (Pss 30.5; 46.5; 112.4; Isa 33.2). *Lowly were exalted*, 1 Sam 2.4–9. One *held in honor* is Haman (12.6). **12:** *What God had determined to do*, in contrast to the Heb, all events in Gk Esther are foreordained by God, although Mordecai does not yet fully understand the dream's symbolism (10.4–9).

12.1–6: Mordecai saves the king's life. It is unclear whether this conspiracy is the same as the one in Esth 2.19–23 of the Heb text or an earlier intrigue. **5:** The king *rewarded* Mordecai immediately (in contrast to 6.1–3). **6:** The Gk text suggests (in contrast to the Heb) that Haman took part in the eunuchs' foiled plot and thus provides a motivation for Mordecai's and Haman's subsequent actions. *Bougean* (see also 3.1) is apparently an attempt to translate the Heb word "Agagite," which connects Haman to the Amalekite king, Agag, Saul's vanquished enemy (see 1 Sam 15.8). Mordecai and Haman share an ancestral enmity (Ex 17.8–16; Num 24.7).

things, and Mordecai wrote an account of them. [5] And the king ordered Mordecai to serve in the court, and rewarded him for these things. [6] But Haman son of Hammedatha, a Bougean, who was in great honor with the king, determined to injure Mordecai and his people because of the two eunuchs of the king.

END OF ADDITION A

1 It was after this that the following things happened in the days of Artaxerxes, the same Artaxerxes who ruled over one hundred twenty-seven provinces from India to Ethiopia.[a] [2] In those days, when King Artaxerxes was enthroned in the city of Susa, [3] in the third year of his reign, he gave a banquet for his Friends and other persons of various nations, the Persians and Median nobles, and the governors of the provinces. [4] After this, when he had displayed to them the riches of his kingdom and the splendor of his bountiful celebration during the course of one hundred eighty days, [5] at the end of the festivity[b] the king gave a drinking party for the people of various nations who lived in the city. This was held for six days in the courtyard of the royal palace, [6] which was adorned with curtains of fine linen and cotton, held by cords of purple linen attached to gold and silver blocks on pillars of marble and other stones. Gold and silver couches were placed on a mosaic floor of emerald, mother-of-pearl, and marble. There were coverings of gauze, embroidered in various colors, with roses arranged around them. [7] The cups were of gold and silver, and

a miniature cup was displayed, made of ruby, worth thirty thousand talents. There was abundant sweet wine, such as the king himself drank. [8] The drinking was not according to a fixed rule; but the king wished to have it so, and he commanded his stewards to comply with his pleasure and with that of the guests.

[9] Meanwhile, Queen Vashti[c] gave a drinking party for the women in the palace where King Artaxerxes was.

[10] On the seventh day, when the king was in good humor, he told Haman, Bazan, Tharra, Boraze, Zatholtha, Abataza, and Tharaba, the seven eunuchs who served King Artaxerxes, [11] to escort the queen to him in order to proclaim her as queen and to place the diadem on her head, and to have her display her beauty to all the governors and the people of various nations, for she was indeed a beautiful woman. [12] But Queen Vashti[c] refused to obey him and would not come with the eunuchs. This offended the king and he became furious. [13] He said to his Friends, "This is how Vashti[c] has answered me.[d] Give therefore your ruling and judgment on this matter." [14] Arkesaeus, Sarsathaeus, and Malesear, then the governors of the Persians and Medes who were closest to the king—Arkesaeus, Sarsathaeus, and Malesear, who sat beside him in the chief seats—came to him [15] and told him what must be done

a   Other ancient authorities lack *to Ethiopia*
b   Gk *marriage feast*
c   Gk *Astin*
d   Gk *Astin has said thus and so*

1.1–9: **Artaxerxes' banquet. 1:** *Artaxerxes* see 11.2n. *Ethiopia* (Heb "Cush"), in the Bible this term refers to the territory of modern Sudan and Ethiopia. **3–4:** Greek writers mention fabulous feasts given by Persian kings; Ahasuerus's *banquet*, with its exaggerated length of *one hundred eighty days* (see Jdt 1.16), is the first of several that occur at key points in the story. *Friends*, a special class of courtiers. **5:** *Festivity*, or *marriage feast* (see textual note b), which would clarify the behavior of the king and Vashti (see 1.11). *Six days*, 1.10 (and Heb 1.5,10) says the party lasted seven days. **6–7:** The description, which emphasizes power and wealth, is more extravagant than in the Heb version. **8:** *According to a fixed rule*, ancient sources suggest that the king set the pace for drinking (Herodotus 1.33), and all guests drank when he drank. **9:** There are no ancient references to *Vashti*, whose name means "beloved"; Xerxes I's queen was Amestris (Herodotus 7.61). *Queen Vashti gave a drinking party for the women* emphasizes the separate gendered spheres of king and queen, a factor in Esther's later bravery.

1.10–22: **Queen Vashti's downfall. 10:** *Eunuchs* were castrated males who served in the Persian court. The list of their names lends the story an air of authenticity. **11:** *Proclaim her as queen*, in contrast to the Heb, Vashti is summoned for her official coronation as well as for display. **12:** The circumstances will be reversed when Esther approaches the king without having been summoned (4.11,16,15). **13–14:** Three *governors* rather than the seven

to Queen Vashti[a] for not obeying the order that the king had sent her by the eunuchs. [16] Then Muchaeus said to the king and the governors, "Queen Vashti[a] has insulted not only the king but also all the king's governors and officials" [17] (for he had reported to them what the queen had said and how she had defied the king). "And just as she defied King Artaxerxes, [18] so now the other ladies who are wives of the Persian and Median governors, on hearing what she has said to the king, will likewise dare to insult their husbands. [19] If therefore it pleases the king, let him issue a royal decree, inscribed in accordance with the laws of the Medes and Persians so that it may not be altered, that the queen may no longer come into his presence; but let the king give her royal rank to a woman better than she. [20] Let whatever law the king enacts be proclaimed in his kingdom, and thus all women will give honor to their husbands, rich and poor alike." [21] This speech pleased the king and the governors, and the king did as Muchaeus had recommended. [22] The king sent the decree into all his kingdom, to every province in its own language, so that in every house respect would be shown to every husband.

2 After these things, the king's anger abated, and he no longer was concerned about Vashti[a] or remembered what he had said and how he had condemned her. [2] Then the king's servants said, "Let beautiful and virtuous girls be sought out for the king. [3] The king shall appoint officers in all the provinces of his kingdom, and they shall select beautiful young virgins to be brought to the harem in Susa, the capital. Let them be entrusted to the king's eunuch who is in charge of the women, and let ointments and whatever else they need be given them. [4] And the woman who pleases the king shall be queen instead of Vashti."[a] This pleased the king, and he did so.

[5] Now there was a Jew in Susa the capital whose name was Mordecai son of Jair son of Shimei[b] son of Kish, of the tribe of Benjamin; [6] he had been taken captive from Jerusalem among those whom King Nebuchadnezzar of Babylon had captured. [7] And he had a foster child, the daughter of his father's brother, Aminadab, and her name was Esther. When her parents died, he brought her up to womanhood as his own. The girl was beautiful in appearance. [8] So, when the decree of the king was proclaimed, and many girls were gathered in Susa the capital in custody of Gai, Esther also was brought to Gai, who had custody of the women. [9] The girl pleased him

[a] Gk *Astin*
[b] Gk *Semeios*

officials named in the Heb. **16–18:** The fear of a feminine insurrection against patriarchal order lies just below the surface of many ancient myths and legends. Contrary to Muchaeus's dire imaginings, the real danger will come in the form of a conspiracy by palace bodyguards (2.21). **19:** There is no historical evidence that the *laws of the Medes and the Persians* (Esth 8.8; Dan 6.9,13) were unalterable. The phrase sets up a narrative tension between rigid legalism and the requirements of true justice. **20:** By issuing an absurdly unenforceable decree, the foolish king draws attention to his failure at ruling his own wife. **22:** The first of several decrees in the book (see 2.8; 3.12,13; 8.9–11; 9.20–22,29–32). Persian royal edicts were issued both in Aramaic, the official language of Persian diplomacy, and in the *languages* of subject peoples (see Ezra 6.3–5).

2.1–18: Esther becomes queen. 1–4: The king agrees to seek a new queen. 1: Here the search for a replacement occurs after the king forgets Vashti, while in the Heb the search begins because the king remembers Vashti's act. **2:** Consistent with its concern for moral rectitude, the Gk version adds that the winning *girl* (Heb "virgin") must be *virtuous* as well as *beautiful*. **3:** In patriarchal societies, a *virgin* bride ensures the paternity of children within the marriage (see Ex 22.16; Lev 21.13); here it may also be a convention of historical romance. Actual Persian law restricted kings to wives from certain noble Persian families.

2.5–7: Mordecai and Esther. 5–6: For a second time, the Gk introduces Mordecai (see 11.2–4n.). **7:** The name *Esther* derives from Ishtar, the Babylonian goddess of sexuality and war (the deities Marduk and Ishtar were cousins), or from the Persian word for "star," or both. The Gk fails to mention Esther's Heb name, Hadassah (see 2.7 in the Heb). *Aminadab*, in the Heb (2.15) Esther's father is Abihail. **8:** By beginning the book (11.2–12) with Mordecai's prophetic dream, the Gk version suggests that Esther arrives at court according to divine plan (see 10.4–6). Neither the Heb nor the Gk mentions Esther's feelings when she *was brought* to Susa. This is contra-

and won his favor, and he quickly provided her with ointments and her portion of food,[a] as well as seven maids chosen from the palace; he treated her and her maids with special favor in the harem. [10] Now Esther had not disclosed her people or country, for Mordecai had commanded her not to make it known. [11] And every day Mordecai walked in the courtyard of the harem, to see what would happen to Esther.

[12] Now the period after which a girl was to go to the king was twelve months. During this time the days of beautification are completed—six months while they are anointing themselves with oil of myrrh, and six months with spices and ointments for women. [13] Then she goes in to the king; she is handed to the person appointed, and goes with him from the harem to the king's palace. [14] In the evening she enters and in the morning she departs to the second harem, where Gai the king's eunuch is in charge of the women; and she does not go in to the king again unless she is summoned by name.

[15] When the time was fulfilled for Esther daughter of Aminadab, the brother of Mordecai's father, to go in to the king, she neglected none of the things that Gai, the eunuch in charge of the women, had commanded. Now Esther found favor in the eyes of all who saw her. [16] So Esther went in to King Artaxerxes in the twelfth month, which is Adar, in the seventh year of his reign. [17] And the king loved Esther and she found favor beyond all the other virgins, so he put on her the queen's diadem. [18] Then the king gave a banquet lasting seven days for all his Friends and the officers to celebrate his marriage to Esther; and he granted a remission of taxes to those who were under his rule.

[19] Meanwhile Mordecai was serving in the courtyard. [20] Esther had not disclosed her country—such were the instructions of Mordecai; but she was to fear God and keep his laws, just as she had done when she was with him. So Esther did not change her mode of life. [21] Now the king's eunuchs, who were chief bodyguards, were angry because of Mordecai's advancement, and they plotted to kill King Artaxerxes. [22] The matter became known to Mordecai, and he warned Esther, who in turn revealed the plot to the king. [23] He investigated the two eunuchs and hanged them. Then the king ordered a memorandum to be deposited in the royal library in praise of the goodwill shown by Mordecai.

3 After these events King Artaxerxes promoted Haman son of Hammedatha, a Bougean, advancing him and granting him precedence over all the king's[b] Friends. [2] So all who were at court used to do obeisance to Haman,[c] for so the king had commanded to be done. Mordecai, however, did not do obeisance. [3] Then the king's courtiers said to Mordecai, "Mordecai, why do you disobey the king's command?" [4] Day after day they spoke

---

a   Gk lacks *of food*
b   Gk *all his*
c   Gk *him*

---

dicted later in one of the Gk additions (14.15–18). **9:** In winning the *favor* of *Gai* (foreshadowing 2.15,17; 5.8; 7.3), Esther resembles Joseph in the house of Potiphar (Gen 39.2–6) and Daniel at the Babylonian court (Dan 1.9). **10:** Esther's silence about her Jewish identity (reiterated in v. 20) demonstrates her submissive nature even as it heightens narrative suspense.

2.12–18: **Esther becomes queen. 14:** The impossibility of seeing the king again unless *summoned by name* foreshadows Esther's dilemma in 4.11–16 and 15.1–6. **16:** *Adar*, February-March. The Heb gives a different month, Tebeth (December-January). *In the seventh year of his reign*, Ahasuerus has been testing queen candidates now for about four years. **18:** Another in the series of banquets (see 1.3n.) that will climax with the feast of Purim. *Remission of taxes*, the Gk correctly interprets the Hebrew term "holiday" in economic terms.

2.19–23: **Mordecai and Esther save the king's life.** This may be a second version of the plot in 12.1–6 or a different episode altogether. **20:** *Mode of life*, in contrast to the Heb, where Esther seems Jewish by ethnicity rather than religious observance. **21:** Unlike the Heb, the conspirators in the Gk are motivated by jealousy of Mordecai (see Dan 6.3–5). **23:** *Hanged*, impaled, not strangled with a rope, a foreshadowing of 5.14; 7.9–10; 9.13–14. *The royal library*, an official archive of royal decrees (cf. 10.2; 1 Kings 14.19,29; 2 Chr 25.26; 32.32).

3.1–13: **Haman plots to annihilate the Jews. 1:** *Bougean*, see 12.6n. **2:** The reasons for Mordecai's refusal to *do obeisance* are unclear but possibly explained in the Gk by Mordecai's prayer (13.14) or by the fact that Jews and

to him, but he would not listen to them. Then they informed Haman that Mordecai was resisting the king's command. Mordecai had told them that he was a Jew. ⁵ So when Haman learned that Mordecai was not doing obeisance to him, he became furiously angry, ⁶ and plotted to destroy all the Jews under Artaxerxes' rule.

⁷ In the twelfth year of King Artaxerxes Haman^a came to a decision by casting lots, taking the days and the months one by one, to fix on one day to destroy the whole race of Mordecai. The lot fell on the fourteenth^b day of the month of Adar.

⁸ Then Haman^a said to King Artaxerxes, "There is a certain nation scattered among the other nations in all your kingdom; their laws are different from those of every other nation, and they do not keep the laws of the king. It is not expedient for the king to tolerate them. ⁹ If it pleases the king, let it be decreed that they are to be destroyed, and I will pay ten thousand talents of silver into the king's treasury." ¹⁰ So the king took off his signet ring and gave it to Haman to seal the decree^c that was to be written against the Jews. ¹¹ The king told Haman, "Keep the money, and do whatever you want with that nation."

¹² So on the thirteenth day of the first month the king's secretaries were summoned, and in accordance with Haman's instructions they wrote in the name of King Artaxerxes to the magistrates and the governors in every province from India to Ethiopia. There were one hundred twenty-seven provinces in all, and the governors were addressed each in his own language. ¹³ Instructions were sent by couriers throughout all the empire of Artaxerxes to destroy the Jewish people on a given day of the twelfth month, which is Adar, and to plunder their goods.

ADDITION B

13^d This is a copy of the letter: "The Great King, Artaxerxes, writes the following to the governors of the hundred twenty-seven provinces from India to Ethiopia and to the officials under them:

² "Having become ruler of many nations and master of the whole world (not elated with presumption of authority but always acting reasonably and with kindness), I have determined to settle the lives of my subjects in lasting tranquility and, in order to make my kingdom peaceable and open to travel throughout all its extent, to restore the peace desired by all people.

³ "When I asked my counselors how this might be accomplished, Haman—who excels among us in sound judgment, and is distinguished for his unchanging goodwill and steadfast fidelity, and has attained the second place in the kingdom— ⁴ pointed out to us that among all the nations in the world there is scattered a certain hostile people, who have laws contrary to those of every nation and continually disregard the ordinances of kings, so that the unifying of the kingdom

---

^a Gk *he*
^b Other ancient witnesses read *thirteenth*; see 8.12
^c Gk lacks *the decree*
^d Chapter 13.1-7 corresponds to chapter B 1-7 in some translations.

Agagites were traditionally enemies; see 12.6n. **4:** *Day after day*, wording reminiscent of Joseph's resistance to the blandishments of Potiphar's wife (Gen 39.10). **7:** *The twelfth year*, Esther has been queen for five years. The Heb word for *lot*, "pur" (pl. "purim"), is borrowed from Babylonian. Haman resorts to this common form of divination (Herodotus 3.128) known also to the Israelites (1 Sam 14.42). *Adar*, February-March. Instead of the *fourteenth day*, 8.12 of the Gk and Heb rightly cite the thirteenth. **8:** Haman's manipulation of the pliable king (see 1.16–20) begins with the truth: the Jews were indeed *scattered* (Zech 7.14), and like other subject peoples in the Persian empire, their *laws* were different (Deut 4.5–6). He slides into falsehood in asserting that Jews *do not keep the laws of the king.* **9:** *Ten thousand talents of silver*, equal in value to hundreds of millions of US dollars. **10:** The king's *signet ring* gave Haman unlimited power to sign documents in the king's name (8.2,8; cf. Gen 41.41–42; 1 Kings 21.8–9). **12:** *In his own language*, see 1.22n. **13:** *Couriers*, the Persian empire's communication system was renowned (Herodotus 8.98). *A given day*, the thirteenth (see 8.12, Gk and Heb). *Adar*, February-March.

Addition B: 13.1–7: The text of the king's letter authorizing the slaughter of the Jews. This addition to the Gk version of Esther was composed in Gk by the same author as 16.1–24 (Addition E). The brazen tone of the letter seems inconsistent with the king's general demeanor as depicted earlier in the story and reflects Haman's

that we honorably intend cannot be brought about. [5] We understand that this people, and it alone, stands constantly in opposition to every nation, perversely following a strange manner of life and laws, and is ill-disposed to our government, doing all the harm they can so that our kingdom may not attain stability.

[6] "Therefore we have decreed that those indicated to you in the letters written by Haman, who is in charge of affairs and is our second father, shall all—wives and children included—be utterly destroyed by the swords of their enemies, without pity or restraint, on the fourteenth day of the twelfth month, Adar, of this present year, [7] so that those who have long been hostile and remain so may in a single day go down in violence to Hades, and leave our government completely secure and untroubled hereafter."

END OF ADDITION B

3 [14] Copies of the document were posted in every province, and all the nations were ordered to be prepared for that day. [15] The matter was expedited also in Susa. And while the king and Haman caroused together, the city of Susa[a] was thrown into confusion.

4 When Mordecai learned of all that had been done, he tore his clothes, put on sackcloth, and sprinkled himself with ashes; then he rushed through the street of the city, shouting loudly: "An innocent nation is being destroyed!" [2] He got as far as the king's gate, and there he stopped, because no one was allowed to enter the courtyard clothed in sackcloth and ashes. [3] And in every province where the king's proclamation had been posted there was a loud cry of mourning and lamentation among the Jews, and they put on sackcloth and ashes. [4] When the queen's[b] maids and eunuchs came and told her, she was deeply troubled by what she heard had happened, and sent some

clothes to Mordecai to put on instead of sackcloth; but he would not consent. [5] Then Esther summoned Hachratheus, the eunuch who attended her, and ordered him to get accurate information for her from Mordecai.[c]

[7] So Mordecai told him what had happened and how Haman had promised to pay ten thousand talents into the royal treasury to bring about the destruction of the Jews. [8] He also gave him a copy of what had been posted in Susa for their destruction, to show to Esther; and he told him to charge her to go in to the king and plead for his favor in behalf of the people. "Remember," he said, "the days when you were an ordinary person, being brought up under my care—for Haman, who stands next to the king, has spoken against us and demands our death. Call upon the Lord; then speak to the king in our behalf, and save us from death."

[9] Hachratheus went in and told Esther all these things. [10] And she said to him, "Go to Mordecai and say, [11] 'All nations of the empire know that if any man or woman goes to the king inside the inner court without being called, there is no escape for that person. Only the one to whom the king stretches out the golden scepter is safe—and it is now thirty days since I was called to go to the king.'"

[12] When Hachratheus delivered her entire message to Mordecai, [13] Mordecai told him to go back and say to her, "Esther, do not say to yourself that you alone among all the Jews will escape alive. [14] For if you keep quiet at such a time as this, help and protection will come to the Jews from another quarter,

a   Gk *the city*
b   Gk *When her*
c   Other ancient witnesses add *[6]So Hachratheus went out to Mordecai in the street of the city opposite the city gate.*

voice. **6:** *Fourteenth* day, a correction of the Gk's "thirteenth" (see the Hebrew text 3.13; 8.12; 9.1; cf. Gk 16.20; 8.12). *Adar*, February–March. **7:** *Hades*, the underworld and abode of the dead (Heb "sheol").

3.14–15: Haman and the king celebrate the publication of the decree.

4.1–17: Mordecai persuades Esther to risk her life to save her people. **1:** *Sackcloth* and *ashes* and torn clothing were traditional signs of mourning and repentance (2 Sam 3.31; Job 42.6; Jon 3.5; Dan 9.3). **2:** No one rendered ritually unclean by mourning could *enter the courtyard.* **4:** Esther has obeyed Mordecai and kept her Jewish identity a secret; she is unaware of the edict. **11:** Like other biblical heroes called upon to save their people (Ex 3.11; 4.10; 10.28; Judg 6.15; Jer 1.6), Esther initially objects. *Since I was called to go to the king,* see 2.14. **14:** *From another quarter,* divine providence according to Gk 10.4–5; the phrase is ambiguous in Heb Esther. *Who*

but you and your father's family will perish. Yet, who knows whether it was not for such a time as this that you were made queen?" [15] Then Esther gave the messenger this answer to take back to Mordecai: [16] "Go and gather all the Jews who are in Susa and fast on my behalf; for three days and nights do not eat or drink, and my maids and I will also go without food. After that I will go to the king, contrary to the law, even if I must die." [17] So Mordecai went away and did what Esther had told him to do.

---

13 [8] [a]Then Mordecai[b] prayed to the Lord, calling to remembrance all the works of the Lord.

[9] He said, "O Lord, Lord, you rule as King over all things, for the universe is in your power and there is no one who can oppose you when it is your will to save Israel, [10] for you have made heaven and earth and every wonderful thing under heaven. [11] You are Lord of all, and there is no one who can resist you, the Lord. [12] You know all things; you know, O Lord, that it was not in insolence or pride or for any love of glory that I did this, and refused to bow down to this proud Haman; [13] for I would have been willing to kiss the soles of his feet to save Israel! [14] But I did this so that I might not set human glory above the glory of God, and I will not bow down to anyone but you, who are my Lord; and I will not do these things in pride. [15] And now, O Lord God and King, God of Abraham, spare your people; for the eyes of our foes are upon us[c] to annihilate us, and they desire to destroy the inheritance that has been yours

from the beginning. [16] Do not neglect your portion, which you redeemed for yourself out of the land of Egypt. [17] Hear my prayer, and have mercy upon your inheritance; turn our mourning into feasting that we may live and sing praise to your name, O Lord; do not destroy the lips[d] of those who praise you."

[18] And all Israel cried out mightily, for their death was before their eyes.

14 Then Queen Esther, seized with deadly anxiety, fled to the Lord. [2] She took off her splendid apparel and put on the garments of distress and mourning, and instead of costly perfumes she covered her head with ashes and dung, and she utterly humbled her body; every part that she loved to adorn she covered with her tangled hair. [3] She prayed to the Lord God of Israel, and said: "O my Lord, you only are our king; help me, who am alone and have no helper but you, [4] for my danger is in my hand. [5] Ever since I was born I have heard in the tribe of my family that you, O Lord, took Israel out of all the nations, and our ancestors from among all their forebears, for an everlasting inheritance, and that you did for them all that you promised. [6] And now we have sinned before you, and you have handed us over to our enemies [7] because we glorified their gods. You are righteous, O Lord! [8] And now they are not satisfied that we are in bitter slavery, but they have covenanted with their idols [9] to abolish what your mouth has ordained, and to destroy

a Chapters 13.8—15.16 correspond to chapters C 1–30 and D 1-16 in some translations.
b Gk *he*
c Gk *for they are eying us*
d Gk *mouth*

---

knows? Often precedes an expression of hope for divine mercy (2 Sam 12.22; Joel 2.14; Jon 3.9). **16–17:** Resolving to act *contrary to the law* (see 4.11) on behalf of her people, Esther takes charge (anticipating 9.29). Communal or individual fasting was a rite of repentance believed to influence the deity (Lev 16.29–31; Judg 20.26; 2 Sam 12.16; 1 Kings 21.27; Jon 3.5,8; Ezra 8.21–23; Joel 1.14; 2.12,15; 1 Macc 3.47).

Addition C: **13.8–14.19:** The prayers of Mordecai and Esther give the book an explicitly religious tone. Both contain themes common to national laments (Neh 9; Dan 9).

13.8–17: Mordecai's prayer and the people's response. **12–14:** Mordecai justifies his refusal to bow down to Haman (3.2) on religious grounds (see Dan 3.12,16–18). **16:** Mordecai is confident in the god who liberated the Israelites, God's *portion* (Deut 32.9), from enslavement in *Egypt* (Ex 1–14).

14.1–19: Esther humbly petitions God. Her prayer (see especially Jdt 9) resembles Mordecai's in its sincere, if conventional, piety and concern for religious self-justification. **2:** Humble *garments*, filth, and disarray are appropriate to penitential prayer (2 Kings 19.1; Neh 1.4; Dan 9.3–4; Jdt 9.1). **8:** *Bitter slavery* interprets the exile and Diaspora in terms evocative of bondage in *Egypt* (Ex 1–14). **9:** *Your altar* and *your house* refer to the ruined

your inheritance, to stop the mouths of those who praise you and to quench your altar and the glory of your house, ¹⁰ to open the mouths of the nations for the praise of vain idols, and to magnify forever a mortal king.

¹¹ "O Lord, do not surrender your scepter to what has no being; and do not let them laugh at our downfall; but turn their plan against them, and make an example of him who began this against us. ¹² Remember, O Lord; make yourself known in this time of our affliction, and give me courage, O King of the gods and Master of all dominion! ¹³ Put eloquent speech in my mouth before the lion, and turn his heart to hate the man who is fighting against us, so that there may be an end of him and those who agree with him. ¹⁴ But save us by your hand, and help me, who am alone and have no helper but you, O Lord. ¹⁵ You have knowledge of all things, and you know that I hate the splendor of the wicked and abhor the bed of the uncircumcised and of any alien. ¹⁶ You know my necessity—that I abhor the sign of my proud position, which is upon my head on days when I appear in public. I abhor it like a filthy rag, and I do not wear it on the days when I am at leisure. ¹⁷ And your servant has not eaten at Haman's table, and I have not honored the king's feast or drunk the wine of libations. ¹⁸ Your servant has had no joy since the day that I was brought here until now, except in you, O Lord God of Abraham. ¹⁹ O God, whose might is over all, hear the voice of the despairing, and save us from the hands of evildoers. And save me from my fear!"

END OF ADDITION C

15 On the third day, when she ended her prayer, she took off the garments in which she had worshiped, and arrayed herself in splendid attire. ² Then, majestically adorned, after invoking the aid of the all-seeing God and Savior, she took two maids with her; ³ on one she leaned gently for support, ⁴ while the other followed, carrying her train. ⁵ She was radiant with perfect beauty, and she looked happy, as if beloved, but her heart was frozen with fear. ⁶ When she had gone through all the doors, she stood before the king. He was seated on his royal throne, clothed in the full array of his majesty, all covered with gold and precious stones. He was most terrifying.

⁷ Lifting his face, flushed with splendor, he looked at her in fierce anger. The queen faltered, and turned pale and faint, and collapsed on the head of the maid who went in front of her. ⁸ Then God changed the spirit of the king to gentleness, and in alarm he sprang from his throne and took her in his arms until she came to herself. He comforted her with soothing words, and said to her, ⁹ "What is it, Esther? I am your husband.ᵃ Take courage; ¹⁰ You shall not die, for our law applies only to our subjects.ᵇ Come near."

¹¹ Then he raised the golden scepter and touched her neck with it; ¹² he embraced her, and said, "Speak to me." ¹³ She said to him, "I saw you, my lord, like an angel of God, and my heart was shaken with fear at your glory.

ᵃ   Gk *brother*
ᵇ   Meaning of Gk uncertain

Temple in Jerusalem (2 Macc 14.33; 3 Macc 5.43), a subject ignored in the Heb. **13:** Despite her plea for *eloquent speech*, in 15.5 it is her beauty on which Esther initially relies. *Lion*, Artaxerxes (see Prov 19.12; 20.2). **15:** *Abhor the bed of the uncircumcised*, reflecting the Jewish prohibition of mixed marriage (Deut 7.3; Ezra 10.2; Neh 13.23–27). *Wicked, uncircumcised, alien*, non-Jews. Unlike the Heb text, Gk Esther takes a negative view of Gentiles. **16:** The *sign* upon Esther's *head* is the crown which she abhors as a *filthy* rag (lit. a rag soaked in menstrual blood; see Lev 15.19–24; Isa 64.6; contrast Deut 6.9). **17:** Esther observes the Jewish dietary laws (Lev 11; see Jdt 12.1–2).

    Addition D: 15.1–16: Esther approaches the king. This chapter expands 5.1–2 in the Heb text, heightening the suspense with added details and, consistent with the Gk version's theological perspective, crediting Esther's success to God's intervention. **1:** Esther's preparations call to mind an epic hero arming for battle (see *Iliad* 19.338–39; 360–91; 1 Sam 17.5–7,38–39; see Jdt 10.3; 12.15). **7–8:** This episode, absent in the Heb, portrays an Esther undone by feminine weakness and dependant upon God to succeed in her mission. *God changed the spirit of the king*, see 1 Sam 10.9. **9:** *Husband*, Gk "brother," a metaphorical expression of endearment found in Egyptian and Israelite love poetry (Song 4.9–10; 5.1–2). **13:** *Like an angel of God*, see 2 Sam 14.20. The phrase (not found in the Heb) implies wisdom and absence of evil intent. **15:** *Fainted*, see 15.7n.

¹⁴ For you are wonderful, my lord, and your countenance is full of grace." ¹⁵ And while she was speaking, she fainted and fell. ¹⁶ Then the king was agitated, and all his servants tried to comfort her.

END OF ADDITION D

5 ᵃ ³ The king said to her, "What do you wish, Esther? What is your request? It shall be given you, even to half of my kingdom." ⁴ And Esther said, "Today is a special day for me. If it pleases the king, let him and Haman come to the dinner that I shall prepare today." ⁵ Then the king said, "Bring Haman quickly, so that we may do as Esther desires." So they both came to the dinner that Esther had spoken about. ⁶ While they were drinking wine, the king said to Esther, "What is it, Queen Esther? It shall be granted you." ⁷ She said, "My petition and request is: ⁸ if I have found favor in the sight of the king, let the king and Haman come to the dinner that I shall prepare them, and tomorrow I will do as I have done today."

⁹ So Haman went out from the king joyful and glad of heart. But when he saw Mordecai the Jew in the courtyard, he was filled with anger. ¹⁰ Nevertheless, he went home and summoned his friends and his wife Zosara. ¹¹ And he told them about his riches and the honor that the king had bestowed on him, and how he had advanced him to be the first in the kingdom. ¹² And Haman said, "The queen did not invite anyone to the dinner with the king except me; and I am invited again tomorrow. ¹³ But these things give me no pleasure as long as I see Mordecai the Jew in the courtyard." ¹⁴ His wife Zosara and his friends said to him, "Let a gallows be made, fifty cubits high, and

in the morning tell the king to have Mordecai hanged on it. Then, go merrily with the king to the dinner." This advice pleased Haman, and so the gallows was prepared.

6 That night the Lord took sleep from the king, so he gave orders to his secretary to bring the book of daily records, and to read to him. ² He found the words written about Mordecai, how he had told the king about the two royal eunuchs who were on guard and sought to lay hands on King Artaxerxes. ³ The king said, "What honor or dignity did we bestow on Mordecai?" The king's servants said, "You have not done anything for him." ⁴ While the king was inquiring about the goodwill shown by Mordecai, Haman was in the courtyard. The king asked, "Who is in the courtyard?" Now Haman had come to speak to the king about hanging Mordecai on the gallows that he had prepared. ⁵ The servants of the king answered, "Haman is standing in the courtyard." And the king said, "Summon him." ⁶ Then the king said to Haman, "What shall I do for the person whom I wish to honor?" And Haman said to himself, "Whom would the king wish to honor more than me?" ⁷ So he said to the king, "For a person whom the king wishes to honor, ⁸ let the king's servants bring out the fine linen robe that the king has worn, and the horse on which the king rides, ⁹ and let both be given to one of the king's honored Friends, and let him robe the person whom the king loves and mount him on the horse, and let it be proclaimed through the open square of the city, saying, 'Thus shall it be done to everyone

ᵃ In Greek, Chapter D replaces verses 1 and 2 in Hebrew.

5.3–8: Esther invites the king and Haman to dinner. 3: *Half of my kingdom* is customary folktale hyperbole. **4:** Esther frames her invitation in self-effacing terms. *Dinner*, see 1.3n. Food, reassuring and nurturing, is a frequent motif in stories of women confronting powerful men; Esther works indirectly to achieve her goal (Judg 5.25; Jdt 10.5; 12.1,17–20).

5.9–14: Haman's happiness is spoiled. 11–12: Haman's boasting sets him up as an arrogant fool ripe for a fall, a theme also found in wisdom literature (Prov 11.28; 13.3; 16.5,18; 27.1; 29.20). **14:** *Zosara* is an exemplary son-bearing wife (9.7–10) whose husband heeds her loyal counsel. *Gallows* (also 9.13–14), see 2.23n. *Fifty cubits*, ca. 72 ft (22m), an exaggerated height. Only *the king* can order an execution.

6.1–13: Mordecai's triumph. 1: *The Lord took sleep from the king*, unlike the Heb, the Gk ascribes the events of the Esther story to divine intention and intervention (11.1–12; 10.4–12; 4.14n.; 15.1–16). A sleepless king appears in numerous folktales (Dan 6.18; 1 Esd 3.3). **3:** Herodotus (8.85,90) notes that Persian kings kept records of courtiers' noble deeds. *You have not done anything for him*, in contrast to Mordecai's royal reward for reporting the earlier plot in Gk Addition A (see 12.5). **8:** A *robe* and a *horse* were gestures of favor (Gen 37.3; 41.42; 1 Sam

whom the king honors.'" [10] Then the king said to Haman, "You have made an excellent suggestion! Do just as you have said for Mordecai the Jew, who is on duty in the courtyard. And let nothing be omitted from what you have proposed." [11] So Haman got the robe and the horse; he put the robe on Mordecai and made him ride through the open square of the city, proclaiming, "Thus shall it be done to everyone whom the king wishes to honor." [12] Then Mordecai returned to the courtyard, and Haman hurried back to his house, mourning and with his head covered. [13] Haman told his wife Zosara and his friends what had befallen him. His friends and his wife said to him, "If Mordecai is of the Jewish people, and you have begun to be humiliated before him, you will surely fall. You will not be able to defend yourself, because the living God is with him."

[14] While they were still talking, the eunuchs arrived and hurriedly brought Haman to the banquet that Esther had prepared.

7 [1] So the king and Haman went in to drink with the queen. [2] And the second day, as they were drinking wine, the king said, "What is it, Queen Esther? What is your petition and what is your request? It shall be granted to you, even to half of my kingdom." [3] She answered and said, "If I have found favor with the king, let my life be granted me at my petition, and my people at my request. [4] For we have been sold, I and my people, to be destroyed, plundered, and made slaves—we and our children—male and female slaves. This has come to my knowledge. Our antagonist brings shame on[a] the king's court." [5] Then the king said, "Who is the person that would dare

to do this thing?" [6] Esther said, "Our enemy is this evil man Haman!" At this, Haman was terrified in the presence of the king and queen.

[7] The king rose from the banquet and went into the garden, and Haman began to beg for his life from the queen, for he saw that he was in serious trouble. [8] When the king returned from the garden, Haman had thrown himself on the couch, pleading with the queen. The king said, "Will he dare even assault my wife in my own house?" Haman, when he heard, turned away his face. [9] Then Bugathan, one of the eunuchs, said to the king, "Look, Haman has even prepared a gallows for Mordecai, who gave information of concern to the king; it is standing at Haman's house, a gallows fifty cubits high." So the king said, "Let Haman be hanged on that." [10] So Haman was hanged on the gallows he had prepared for Mordecai. With that the anger of the king abated.

8 On that very day King Artaxerxes granted to Esther all the property of the persecutor[b] Haman. Mordecai was summoned by the king, for Esther had told the king[c] that he was related to her. [2] The king took the ring that had been taken from Haman, and gave it to Mordecai; and Esther set Mordecai over everything that had been Haman's.

[3] Then she spoke once again to the king and, falling at his feet, she asked him to avert all the evil that Haman had planned against the Jews. [4] The king extended his golden scepter to Esther, and she rose and stood

a Gk *is not worthy of*
b Gk *slanderer*
c Gk *him*

18.4; 1 Kings 1.33). **12:** Haman *covered* his *head* as a sign of grief (2 Sam 15.30; 19.4; Jer 14.4), foreshadowing his own demise, as his wife and friends recognize (v.13). **13:** *Because the living God is with him* (lacking in the Heb text), an example of Gentile wisdom, Zosara and Haman's friends make explicit the story's theme of divine retribution and Jewish triumph (11.1–12; 15.1–16; 6.1; 10.4–12; 4.14n.; see Josh 2.6–14; Jdt 5.20–21; 3 Macc 3.8–10,31).

6.14–7.10: Esther's second banquet and Haman's fall. **7.2:** *Half of my kingdom*, see 5.3n. **4:** *Sold*, probably an allusion to Haman's bribe in 3.11; (see 4.7; but note the metaphorical use of the verb in Deut 32.30; Judg 2.14; 3.8; 4.2,9; 10.7). *Shame on the king's court*, the king would be shamed if his queen were dishonored. **6:** Like Esther before the king in 15.5, now Haman is *terrified in the presence of the king and queen.* **8:** *Assault my wife*, Artaxerxes misinterprets Haman's gesture as a sexual assault on the queen, an unpardonable affront to both male and royal honor and, as such, a capital offense. **9–10:** *Bugathan*, Heb "Harbona." *Gallows*, see 2.23n., an ironic reversal of the death Haman intended for Mordecai.

8.1–12: The king shows favor to Esther, Mordecai, and the Jews. **1:** In 3.9, Haman offered the king money; now the king gives Haman's wealth to Esther. **2:** Haman's position as grand vizier (3.10) becomes Mordecai's with the transfer of the king's signet *ring* (see v. 8; 3.10n.), another ironic inversion of the two figures. **5:** *That*

before the king. [5] Esther said, "If it pleases you, and if I have found favor, let an order be sent rescinding the letters that Haman wrote and sent to destroy the Jews in your kingdom. [6] How can I look on the ruin of my people? How can I be safe if my ancestral nation[a] is destroyed?" [7] The king said to Esther, "Now that I[b] have granted all of Haman's property to you and have hanged him on a tree because he acted against the Jews, what else do you request? [8] Write in my name what you think best and seal it with my ring; for whatever is written at the king's command and sealed with my ring cannot be contravened."

[9] The secretaries were summoned on the twenty-third day of the first month, that is, Nisan, in the same year; and all that he commanded with respect to the Jews was given in writing to the administrators and governors of the provinces from India to Ethiopia, one hundred twenty-seven provinces, to each province in its own language. [10] The edict was written[c] with the king's authority and sealed with his ring, and sent out by couriers. [11] He ordered the Jews in every city to observe their own laws, to defend themselves, and to act as they wished against their opponents and enemies [12] on a certain day, the thirteenth of the twelfth month, which is Adar, throughout all the kingdom of Artaxerxes.

ADDITION E

16[d] The following is a copy of this letter: "The Great King, Artaxerxes, to the governors of the provinces from India to Ethiopia, one hundred twenty-seven provinces, and to those who are loyal to our government, greetings.

[2] "Many people, the more they are honored with the most generous kindness of their benefactors, the more proud do they become, [3] and not only seek to injure our subjects, but in their inability to stand prosperity, they even undertake to scheme against their own benefactors. [4] They not only take away thankfulness from others, but, carried away by the boasts of those who know nothing of goodness, they even assume that they will escape the evil-hating justice of God, who always sees everything. [5] And often many of those who are set in places of authority have been made in part responsible for the shedding of innocent blood, and have been involved in irremediable calamities, by the persuasion of friends who have been entrusted with the administration of public affairs, [6] when these persons by the false trickery of their evil natures beguile the sincere goodwill of their sovereigns.

[7] "What has been wickedly accomplished through the pestilent behavior of those who exercise authority unworthily can be seen, not so much from the more ancient records that we hand on, as from investigation of matters close at hand.[e] [8] In the future we will take care to render our kingdom quiet and peaceable for all, [9] by changing our methods and always judging what comes before our eyes with more equitable consideration. [10] For Haman son of Hammedatha, a Macedonian

a   Gk *country*
b   Gk *If I*
c   Gk *It was written*
d   Chapter 16.1-24 corresponds to chapter E 1-24 in some translations.
e   Gk *matters beside* (your) *feet*

Haman wrote, Esther diplomatically dissociates the king from the edict that condemned the Jews. **8:** The king's earlier edict *cannot be contravened* (1.19n.), but a new edict can neutralize the former's intent. **9:** *First month . . . Nisan* (March-April), Heb "third month . . . Sivan" (May-June). *In its own language*, see 1.22n. **11:** This explicit permission for the *Jews . . . to observe their own laws* (see 3.8n.; 13.4–5), which is a distinctly religious concern, is lacking in the Heb. **12:** The date of the intended extermination (3.7,13) becomes a day of triumph and relates to the Purim festival (see 9.21). *Adar*, February-March.

Addition E: 16.1–24: The king's second letter: Denunciation of Haman, praise of Mordecai and Esther, and direction to his subjects to help the Jews. Addition E to the Gk version of Esther provides a counterpoint to Addition C (13.1–17). Both were composed in Gk probably by the same author. The Gentile king refers in the most positive terms to the Jews and their God (Ex 9.27; 18.10–11; Num 22–24; 2 Kings 5.15; Dan 2.47; 3.29; 4.1–3,34–37; 6.26–27; Jdt 5.5–21). **2:** *Benefactors*, a reference to the king. **10:** Haman is actually a *Macedonian* scheming to overthrow Persian rule (v. 14; cf. 12.6), a plot twist not found in the Heb. This may be an allusion to the conquest of Persia by the Macedonian Alexander the Great in 333 BCE, an event already in the past when Addition E was composed.

(really an alien to the Persian blood, and quite devoid of our kindliness), having become our guest, [11] enjoyed so fully the goodwill that we have for every nation that he was called our father and was continually bowed down to by all as the person second to the royal throne. [12] But, unable to restrain his arrogance, he undertook to deprive us of our kingdom and our life,[a] [13] and with intricate craft and deceit asked for the destruction of Mordecai, our savior and perpetual benefactor, and of Esther, the blameless partner of our kingdom, together with their whole nation. [14] He thought that by these methods he would catch us undefended and would transfer the kingdom of the Persians to the Macedonians. [15] "But we find that the Jews, who were consigned to annihilation by this thrice-accursed man, are not evildoers, but are governed by most righteous laws [16] and are children of the living God, most high, most mighty,[b] who has directed the kingdom both for us and for our ancestors in the most excellent order.

[17] "You will therefore do well not to put in execution the letters sent by Haman son of Hammedatha, [18] since he, the one who did these things, has been hanged at the gate of Susa with all his household—for God, who rules over all things, has speedily inflicted on him the punishment that he deserved.

[19] "Therefore post a copy of this letter publicly in every place, and permit the Jews to live under their own laws. [20] And give them reinforcements, so that on the thirteenth day of the twelfth month, Adar, on that very day, they may defend themselves against those who attack them at the time of oppression. [21] For God, who rules over all things, has made this day to be a joy for his chosen people instead of a day of destruction for them.

[22] "Therefore you shall observe this with all good cheer as a notable day among your commemorative festivals, [23] so that both now and hereafter it may represent deliverance for you[c] and the loyal Persians, but that it may be a reminder of destruction for those who plot against us.

[24] "Every city and country, without exception, that does not act accordingly shall be destroyed in wrath with spear and fire. It shall be made not only impassable for human beings, but also most hateful to wild animals and birds for all time.

END OF ADDITION E

8 [13] "Let copies of the decree be posted conspicuously in all the kingdom, and let all the Jews be ready on that day to fight against their enemies."

[14] So the messengers on horseback set out with all speed to perform what the king had commanded; and the decree was published also in Susa. [15] Mordecai went out dressed in the royal robe and wearing a gold crown and a turban of purple linen. The people in Susa rejoiced on seeing him. [16] And the Jews had light and gladness [17] in every city and province wherever the decree was published; wherever the proclamation was made, the Jews had joy and gladness, a banquet and a holiday. And many of the Gentiles were circumcised and became Jews out of fear of the Jews.

9 Now on the thirteenth day of the twelfth month, which is Adar, the decree written by the king arrived. [2] On that same day the enemies of the Jews perished; no one resisted, because they feared them. [3] The chief provincial governors, the princes, and the royal secretaries were paying honor to the Jews, because fear of Mordecai weighed upon them. [4] The king's decree required that Mordecai's name be held in honor throughout the

---

a   Gk *our spirit*
b   Gk *greatest*
c   Other ancient authorities read *for us*

11: *Our father*, 13.6. *Second to the royal throne*, 13.3 (2 Chr 28.7; 1 Esd 3.7). **17:** *Letters sent by Haman*, see 8.8n. **18:** The Gk's reference to the death of Haman's family contradicts 7.9 and 9.7–10,13–14. **19:** *Their own laws* (absent in the Heb), see vv. 15–16; 8.11n. **21:** *Chosen people*, Deut 7.6; 1 Kings 3.8; 1 Chr 16.13; Ps 105.6; Isa 43.20 (see Esth 13.15–17). **22–23:** These verses, addressed to all the king's subjects, may hint at a non-Jewish origin for the Purim festival.

8.13–17: Dispatch of the king's decree. 14: See 3.13n. **17:** *Gentiles were circumcised and became Jews*, the Gk here interprets literally the ambiguous wording of the Heb.

9.1–19: The Jews triumph over their enemies. 2: *No one resisted*, contradicts the Heb ("no one could withstand them"), and vv. 11,16. **10:** The death of *the ten sons of Haman* agrees with the Heb but contradicts 16.18 (see

kingdom.[a] [6] Now in the city of Susa the Jews killed five hundred people, [7] including Pharsannestain, Delphon, Phasga, [8] Pharadatha, Barea, Sarbacha, [9] Marmasima, Aruphaeus, Arsaeus, Zabutheus, [10] the ten sons of Haman son of Hammedatha, the Bougean, the enemy of the Jews—and they indulged[b] themselves in plunder.

[11] That very day the number of those killed in Susa was reported to the king. [12] The king said to Esther, "In Susa, the capital, the Jews have destroyed five hundred people. What do you suppose they have done in the surrounding countryside? Whatever more you ask will be done for you." [13] And Esther said to the king, "Let the Jews be allowed to do the same tomorrow. Also, hang up the bodies of Haman's ten sons." [14] So he permitted this to be done, and handed over to the Jews of the city the bodies of Haman's sons to hang up. [15] The Jews who were in Susa gathered on the fourteenth and killed three hundred people, but took no plunder.

[16] Now the other Jews in the kingdom gathered to defend themselves, and got relief from their enemies. They destroyed fifteen thousand of them, but did not engage in plunder. [17] On the fourteenth day they rested and made that same day a day of rest, celebrating it with joy and gladness. [18] The Jews who were in Susa, the capital, came together also on the fourteenth, but did not rest. They celebrated the fifteenth with joy and gladness. [19] On this account then the Jews who are scattered around the country outside Susa keep the fourteenth of Adar as a joyful holiday, and send presents of food to one another, while those who live in the large cities keep the fifteenth day of Adar as their joyful holiday, also sending presents to one another.

[20] Mordecai recorded these things in a book, and sent it to the Jews in the kingdom of Artaxerxes both near and far, [21] telling them that they should keep the fourteenth and fifteenth days of Adar, [22] for on these days the Jews got relief from their enemies. The whole month (namely, Adar), in which their condition had been changed from sorrow into gladness and from a time of distress to a holiday, was to be celebrated as a time for feasting[c] and gladness and for sending presents of food to their friends and to the poor.

[23] So the Jews accepted what Mordecai had written to them [24]—how Haman son of Hammedatha, the Macedonian,[d] fought against them, how he made a decree and cast lots[e] to destroy them, [25] and how he went in to the king, telling him to hang Mordecai; but the wicked plot he had devised against the Jews came back upon himself, and he and his sons were hanged. [26] Therefore these days were called "Purim," because of the lots (for in their language this is the word that means "lots"). And so, because of what was written in this letter, and because of what they had experienced in this affair and what had befallen them, Mordecai established this festival,[f] [27] and the Jews took upon themselves, upon their descendants, and upon all who would join them, to observe it without fail.[g] These days of Purim should be a memorial and kept from generation to generation, in every city, family, and country. [28] These days of Purim were to be observed for all time, and the

---

a   Meaning of Gk uncertain. Some ancient authorities add verse 5, *So the Jews struck down all their enemies with the sword, killing and destroying them, and they did as they pleased to those who hated them.*
b   Other ancient authorities read *did not indulge*
c   Gk *of weddings*
d   Other ancient witnesses read *the Bougean*
e   Gk *a lot*
f   Gk *he established* (it)
g   Meaning of Gk uncertain

note). *Indulged themselves in plunder* contradicted by both the Heb and Gk 9:15–16. **12–15:** Notice of the extra day for observing the king's edict is probably included to explain why the Jews of Susa celebrated Purim on the fifteenth of Adar and country Jews on the fourteenth (see 9.18–19). *Plunder*, see v.10n. **16:** *Destroyed fifteen thousand*, Heb "seventy-five thousand."

18–19: Differences in Purim dates are explained (see vv. 12–15n.). Jews today continue to observe Purim with feasting and *presents of food*.

9.20–32: The inauguration of the feast of Purim. The emphasis here upon the written word, a particular concern in postexilic Judaism, was probably intended to legitimize a festival not mentioned in the Torah (cf. the origin of Hanukkah: 1 Macc 4.56–59; 2 Macc 1.1–2.28; 10.1–8). **21:** See 9.12–15n. **22:** Purim commemorates not the day of the Jews' military triumph, but the day they obtained their *relief. Sorrow into gladness,* see Isa

commemoration of them was never to cease among their descendants.

²⁹ Then Queen Esther daughter of Aminadab along with Mordecai the Jew wrote down what they had done, and gave full authority to the letter about Purim.ᵃ ³¹ And Mordecai and Queen Esther established this decision on their own responsibility, pledging their own well-being to the plan.ᵇ ³² Esther established it by a decree forever, and it was written for a memorial.

10 The king levied a tax upon his kingdom both by land and sea. ² And as for his power and bravery, and the wealth and glory of his kingdom, they were recorded in the annals of the kings of the Persians and the Medes. ³ Mordecai acted with authority on behalf of King Artaxerxes and was great in the kingdom, as well as honored by the Jews. His way of life was such as to make him beloved to his whole nation.

ADDITION F

⁴ᵇ And Mordecai said, "These things have come from God; ⁵ for I remember the dream that I had concerning these matters, and none of them has failed to be fulfilled. ⁶ There was the little spring that became a river, and there was light and sun and abundant water—the river is Esther, whom the king married and made queen. ⁷ The two dragons are Haman and myself. ⁸ The nations are those that gathered to destroy the name of the Jews. ⁹ And my nation, this is Israel, who cried out to God and

was saved. The Lord has saved his people; the Lord has rescued us from all these evils; God has done great signs and wonders, wonders that have never happened among the nations. ¹⁰ For this purpose he made two lots, one for the people of God and one for all the nations, ¹¹ and these two lots came to the hour and moment and day of decision before God and among all the nations. ¹² And God remembered his people and vindicated his inheritance. ¹³ So they will observe these days in the month of Adar, on the fourteenth and fifteenthᶜ of that month, with an assembly and joy and gladness before God, from generation to generation

11 forever among his people Israel." ¹ In the fourth year of the reign of Ptolemy and Cleopatra, Dositheus, who said that he was a priest and a Levite,ᵈ and his son Ptolemy brought to Egyptᵉ the preceding Letter about Purim, which they said was authentic and had been translated by Lysimachus son of Ptolemy, one of the residents of Jerusalem.

END OF ADDITION F

ᵃ   Verse 30 in Heb is lacking in Gk: *Letters were sent to all the Jews, to the one hundred twenty-seven provinces of the kingdom of Ahasuerus, in words of peace and truth.*

ᵇ   Chapter 10.4-13 and 11.1 correspond to chapter F 1-11 in some translations.

ᶜ   Other ancient authorities lack *and fifteenth*

ᵈ   Or *priest, and Levitas*

ᵉ   Cn: Gk *brought in*

61.3; Jer 31.13. **24–26:** This plot summary, which does not mention Esther, differs slightly from the Heb version. The festival came to be called *"Purim"* for the lot, "pur" (pl. "purim"), which Haman cast (see 3.7n.). **32:** *Esther established it,* Queen Esther is the only woman in the Bible credited with establishing a religious observance.

10.1–3: The greatness of Artaxerxes and Mordecai. 1: This seemingly irrelevant comment may imply that the king prospered with Mordecai's assistance (see Gen 47.1–26). **2:** *Recorded in the annals,* a standard formula for historical reports in Kings and Chronicles (1 Kings 14.19,29; 2 Chr 25.26; 32.32).

Addition F: 10.4–13: Epilogue: Mordecai's dream explained. This addition rounds out the Gk version of Esther with an explanation of Mordecai's dream with which the book began (11.2–12n.). **4:** *These things have come from God,* the theme of Gk Esther (11.12; 4.14; 15.8; 6.1,13; 16.4; see Ps 118.23). **6:** *Light and sun,* 11.11n.; 8.16. **8:** *Name,* in ancient times, the essence of one's identity resided largely in one's name. **10:** *Two lots,* not mentioned in 11.2–12. This verse may represent an alternative derivation for Purim. It assumes a different context for the "lots" that give Purim its name (9.23; 3.7n.), understanding them as symbols of destiny (Dan 12.13; Isa 17.14; Jer 13.25). A similar concept appears in the Dead Sea Scrolls (1QS 2.2,5; 3.1–4.26). **13:** *So they will observe these days,* see 9.20–22.

11.1: The colophon to Gk Esther provides a probable date reference for the Gk translation. *Ptolemy and Cleopatra,* because three kings of Egypt named Ptolemy had wives named Cleopatra, the *fourth year* could be 114–113, 78–77, or 49–48 BCE. *Dositheus,* a common Hellenistic name (2 Macc 12.19,35; 3 Macc 1.3); presumably a copyist, he affirms the text's authenticity and his own religious authority. *Letter about Purim,* probably the entire book of Esther. *Lysimachus,* a Greek name (cf. 2 Macc 4.29), likely the translator of Heb Esther into Gk.

THE WISDOM OF SOLOMON

NAME AND CANONICAL STATUS

The title of the book in most manuscripts is "The Wisdom of Solomon." It is a Jewish writing, but it was preserved in Christian circles, like other Jewish writings in Greek. There is no evidence that the writing was accepted as canonical by any Jewish group, or even read by Jewish readers until many centuries after it had been written. The work seems to have been known to Clement of Rome and possibly Ignatius (late first-early second century CE). The Wisdom of Solomon was certainly used as Scripture by such early third-century writers as Tertullian, Clement of Alexandria, and Pseudo-Hippolytus. On the other hand, its canonicity was doubted by Origen, although he sometimes quotes it as if it were canonical. The book became a part of the Roman Catholic and Eastern Orthodox canons but is considered one of the Apocrypha by many Protestant groups.

AUTHORSHIP, DATE, AND HISTORICAL CONTEXT

Although the author claims to be King Solomon (with parts of ch 9 based on his prayer for wisdom in 1 Kings 3.6–9), this ascription has been recognized as a literary fiction since ancient times. Instead, the author is an anonymous Hellenistic Jew writing some time in the late first century BCE or early first century CE. The author most likely came from the Jewish community in Alexandria in Egypt or possibly from another major center in the Hellenistic world. In spite of seeming to appeal to Greek readers, the work is evidently aimed at an internal audience, probably the Jewish youth of Alexandria who might be tempted by the Hellenistic culture around them.

Some recent commentators view the book as originating in the historical context of the troubles experienced by the Alexandrian Jewish community in the period 38–41 CE, but the book gives no hint of a period of trauma or threat. Others have argued that the book is earlier, dating from the reign of the Roman emperor Augustus (27 BCE–14 CE). Nothing prevents the book from being this early. Typologically, The Wisdom of Solomon represents an earlier stage of development in the trajectory of biblical interpretation that reached its culmination in the Jewish philosopher Philo of Alexandria. A date about 20 BCE would fit the contents of the book.

GENRE, STRUCTURE, AND CONTENTS

The genre of the book has been analyzed in two distinct ways. One is as an "encomium," defined by Aristotle as a work praising someone or, in this case, something—the quality of wisdom. Much of the content of the book can be seen as part of an encomium if the structure is understood as follows:

Introduction	chs 1–6
Encomium proper	chs 6–9
Comparison	10.1–19.9
Epilogue and conclusion	19.10–22

Another suggestion is that The Wisdom of Solomon is an "exhortatory discourse." This is a much more specialized type of writing that was cultivated in philosophical schools and argued for and extolled a philosophical lifestyle. In addition to these two literary forms, The Wisdom of Solomon also has much in common with the "diatribe." The Hellenistic diatribe was a specific rhetorical form and should not be confused with the English term "diatribe"; it was essentially a type of moral discourse in the form of a speech or address, much favored by the philosophical street preachers among the Cynics and Stoics, though recent study has emphasized its home in an academic context. Its aim was to convince the hearers of a particular course of action, and it always had a moral theme.

Some scholars have argued that a concentric internal structure (or "chiastic" structure) with parallel elements can be found in various passages of The Wisdom of Solomon, indicating a deliberate arrangement of material. Some of these arrangements affect only individual passages of a few verses or so (for example, see chs 7–8). Others suggest an overall structure to the book. For example:

1–6	Book of Eschatology
7–10	Book of Wisdom
11–19	Book of History

Arguments about how to divide the book are often based on an inclusio, in which a section is delimited by having the same device (e.g., a word, a phrase, a sentence, a subject) at the beginning and the end. For example, the Book of Eschatology begins with an address to the rulers of the earth (ch 1) and ends with an address to the kings of the earth (ch 6), suggesting that chs 1–6 formed a complete unit in the mind of the author.

The Book of Eschatology (chs 1–6) contrasts the lives of the just and the wicked, dramatizing the eschatological destinies of the two groups. The next section, the Book of Wisdom (chs 7–10), celebrates the figure of divine Sophia (Wisdom). The author's persona as Solomon emerges most clearly here, as the king describes wisdom and his pursuit of her. The third section, the Book of History (chs 11–19), adopts the approach of historical comparison, presenting an elaborate system of contrasts based largely on Ex 7–14. A series of digressions in 11.17–15.19 explains why God's judgment manifested itself differently in dealing with the Egyptians and the Israelites. This adaptation of the Exodus story is meant to complement the arguments of the first two sections, providing biblical examples of the righteous and the unrighteous, and demonstrating how the power of divine wisdom operates in human history.

GUIDE TO READING

As a carefully crafted work, the book is best read in its entirety. For an understanding of its distinctive style and philosophical approach, comparing its summaries of biblical history in 10.1–11.14 with the corresponding passages in Genesis and Exodus will be fruitful.

Lester L. Grabbe

1 Love righteousness, you rulers of the
   earth,
think of the Lord in goodness
and seek him with sincerity of heart;
² because he is found by those who do not
   put him to the test,
and manifests himself to those who do not
   distrust him.
³ For perverse thoughts separate people
   from God,
and when his power is tested, it exposes
   the foolish;

⁴ because wisdom will not enter a deceitful
   soul,
or dwell in a body enslaved to sin.
⁵ For a holy and disciplined spirit will flee
   from deceit,
and will leave foolish thoughts behind,
and will be ashamed at the approach of
   unrighteousness.

⁶ For wisdom is a kindly spirit,
but will not free blasphemers from the
   guilt of their words;

1.1–6.21: The Book of Eschatology. Many scholars see this "book" as having a concentric structure, as follows:
A. Address to judges: exhortation to justice (1.1–15)
   B. Speech of the wicked (1.16–2.24)
      C. Four paired contrasts of the just and the wicked (3.1–4.20)
   B.' Speech of the wicked (5.1–23)
A.' Address to kings: exhortation to wisdom (6.1–21).
For those who analyze the book as an encomium (see Introduction), chs 1–6 function as the introduction ("exordium") whose theme is Wisdom's gift of immortality to the righteous. This section addresses "rulers of the earth" in what is mainly a discourse on righteousness and wickedness.

1.1–15: An exhortation to justice. The figure of Wisdom is introduced (v. 4) and seems to be equated with a *holy . . . spirit* (v. 5) or *the spirit of the Lord* (v. 7). Specific references to wisdom then disappear until ch 6. Much of the passage is framed negatively, focusing on those things that are the opposite of wisdom and God's spirit: *perverse thoughts* (v. 3), *sin* (v. 4), injustice (vv. 5,8), blasphemy (v. 6), *counsels of the ungodly* (v. 9), *lawless deeds* (v. 9), and so on. **1:** The verse is reminiscent of Ps 2.2; other passages seem to presuppose this Psalm (see 2.10–20; 4.8,19; 6.1,21). The book begins with the literary device of the apostrophe, a direct address to the hearers or readers, though the actual audience is the Hellenistic Jewish community, not their Gentile rulers. This is one of the features of the diatribe that has influenced the rhetoric of Wisdom of Solomon; see also 2.10–20n. **5:**

because God is witness of their inmost
feelings,
and a true observer of their hearts, and a
hearer of their tongues.
[7] Because the spirit of the Lord has filled
the world,
and that which holds all things together
knows what is said,
[8] therefore those who utter unrighteous
things will not escape notice,
and justice, when it punishes, will not pass
them by.
[9] For inquiry will be made into the
counsels of the ungodly,
and a report of their words will come to
the Lord,
to convict them of their lawless deeds;
[10] because a jealous ear hears all
things,
and the sound of grumbling does not go
unheard.
[11] Beware then of useless grumbling,
and keep your tongue from slander;
because no secret word is without
result,[a]
and a lying mouth destroys the soul.

[12] Do not invite death by the error of your
life,
or bring on destruction by the works of
your hands;
[13] because God did not make death,
and he does not delight in the death of the
living.
[14] For he created all things so that they
might exist;

the generative forces[b] of the world are
wholesome,
and there is no destructive poison in them,
and the dominion[c] of Hades is not on
earth.
[15] For righteousness is immortal.

[16] But the ungodly by their words and
deeds summoned death;[d]
considering him a friend, they pined away
and made a covenant with him,
because they are fit to belong to his
company.

2 For they reasoned unsoundly, saying to
themselves,
"Short and sorrowful is our life,
and there is no remedy when a life comes
to its end,
and no one has been known to return from
Hades.
[2] For we were born by mere chance,
and hereafter we shall be as though we
had never been,
for the breath in our nostrils is smoke,
and reason is a spark kindled by the
beating of our hearts;
[3] when it is extinguished, the body will
turn to ashes,
and the spirit will dissolve like empty air.
[4] Our name will be forgotten in time,
and no one will remember our works;

---

[a] Or *will go unpunished*
[b] Or *the creatures*
[c] Or *palace*
[d] Gk *him*

Wisdom is a product of the *spirit* of God; cf. Isa 2.11. **6**: *A kindly spirit*, literally "a philanthropic spirit," i.e., loving humanity (cf. 7.22–23; 12.19; 15.1). **7**: See 12.1n. **11**: *Tongue*, counsel on the vices of human speech is ubiquitous in wisdom literature (e.g., Prov 2.12; 4.24; 10.11,18–19,31–32; Sir 9.18; 20.24–26; 28.12–26). **12–15**: These verses anticipate the discussion on immortality that follows in chs 2–6. **13**: *Death* is eternal separation from God, the condition of the sinner. Here the author does not refer to the reality of physical death. **14**: *Hades*, the abode of the dead in Greek tradition; comparable to Heb "Sheol." **15**: Immortality is not an innate condition of the soul but God's gift to the righteous (see Philo, *On the Confusion of Tongues*, 149); see 2.23–24n.

1.16–2.24: The deluded reasoning of the ungodly. The passage's style resembles that of the Greco-Roman diatribe, which often included argumentative exchanges with a fictional adversary. Here the ungodly are made to explain their actions and motives *to themselves* (2.1–20). The writer then disproves the reasoning of the ungodly (vv. 21–24). The view expressed is Epicurean or a caricature of the Epicurean belief, which argued that everything was material, that life and the universe came about by accident, and that death was the end of the person. Epicureans were accused of being atheists and of promoting a sensual lifestyle. Some of this was broadly true, but in reality the Epicurean lifestyle was one of moderation, not excess. **1.16**: For the *covenant* with *death* cf. Isa 28.15. **2.1–5**: This view of death is reflected also in Job 7.9–10; 14.1–2; Eccl 2.14,16,24; 3.12,19; 6.12;

our life will pass away like the traces of a
cloud,
and be scattered like mist
that is chased by the rays of the sun
and overcome by its heat.
⁵ For our allotted time is the passing of a
shadow,
and there is no return from our death,
because it is sealed up and no one turns
back.

⁶ "Come, therefore, let us enjoy the good
things that exist,
and make use of the creation to the full as
in youth.
⁷ Let us take our fill of costly wine and
perfumes,
and let no flower of spring pass us by.
⁸ Let us crown ourselves with rosebuds
before they wither.
⁹ Let none of us fail to share in our revelry;
everywhere let us leave signs of
enjoyment,
because this is our portion, and this our lot.
¹⁰ Let us oppress the righteous poor man;
let us not spare the widow
or regard the gray hairs of the aged.
¹¹ But let our might be our law of right,
for what is weak proves itself to be useless.

¹² "Let us lie in wait for the righteous man,
because he is inconvenient to us and
opposes our actions;
he reproaches us for sins against the law,
and accuses us of sins against our training.
¹³ He professes to have knowledge of God,
and calls himself a childᵃ of the Lord.
¹⁴ He became to us a reproof of our
thoughts;

¹⁵ the very sight of him is a burden to us,
because his manner of life is unlike that of
others,
and his ways are strange.
¹⁶ We are considered by him as something
base,
and he avoids our ways as unclean;
he calls the last end of the righteous
happy,
and boasts that God is his father.
¹⁷ Let us see if his words are true,
and let us test what will happen at the end
of his life;
¹⁸ for if the righteous man is God's child, he
will help him,
and will deliver him from the hand of his
adversaries.
¹⁹ Let us test him with insult and torture,
so that we may find out how gentle he is,
and make trial of his forbearance.
²⁰ Let us condemn him to a shameful
death,
for, according to what he says, he will be
protected."

²¹ Thus they reasoned, but they were led
astray,
for their wickedness blinded them,
²² and they did not know the secret
purposes of God,
nor hoped for the wages of holiness,
nor discerned the prize for blameless
souls;
²³ for God created us for incorruption,
and made us in the image of his own
eternity,ᵇ

ᵃ Or *servant*
ᵇ Other ancient authorities read *nature*

9.2,7–9). 1: *Hades*, see 1.14n. 6–9: In the reasoning of the ungodly, the threat of death warrants sensuality (see Isa 22.13). In Eccl 9.7 enjoyment of pleasure is recommended as a proper response to life under the shadow of death. 10–20: The wicked are misled by an irrational antipathy for the righteous and the weak, persecuting those who call *God* their *father*. This passage draws on Isa 52.13–53.12: vv. 13 and 16 describe the righteous as *child*, Gk "pais," which can also be translated "servant" (as in LXX Isa 52.13); cf. also vv. 19–20 with Isa 53.7–9. Other parallels in following chapters include 3.2–3 and Isa 53.4; 3.6 and Isa 53.7–10; 4.19 and Isa 52.15; 5.2 and Isa 52.14; 5.3–4 and Isa 53.3,10; 5.6 and Isa 53.6. The passage also shows affinities with *1 Enoch* 62–63, probably indicating that both *1 Enoch* and Wis have drawn on Isa 52–53. 13: *Knowledge of God*, a gift of wisdom illuminating the path to immortality (6.22; 7.12,17; 8.4,9; 10.10; 15.2–3; 18.6). Conversely the wicked refuse to know God (2.22; 12.27; 13.1,9; 14.22; 15.11; 16.16). 22: For the idea of the afterlife as part of *the secret purposes of God*, see also 1 Cor 4.5; 15.51; *1 Enoch* 103.2; and the *Book of Mysteries* in the Dead Sea Scrolls, 1Q27 1.3–4. 23–24: These verses explain further what has already been asserted in 1.13–14: Humanity was created for immortality. *Through the*

[24] but through the devil's envy death entered the world,
and those who belong to his company experience it.

3 But the souls of the righteous are in the hand of God,
and no torment will ever touch them.
[2] In the eyes of the foolish they seemed to have died,
and their departure was thought to be a disaster,
[3] and their going from us to be their destruction;
but they are at peace.
[4] For though in the sight of others they were punished,
their hope is full of immortality.
[5] Having been disciplined a little, they will receive great good,
because God tested them and found them worthy of himself;
[6] like gold in the furnace he tried them,
and like a sacrificial burnt offering he accepted them.
[7] In the time of their visitation they will shine forth,
and will run like sparks through the stubble.
[8] They will govern nations and rule over peoples,
and the Lord will reign over them forever.
[9] Those who trust in him will understand truth,
and the faithful will abide with him in love,
because grace and mercy are upon his holy ones,
and he watches over his elect.[a]

[10] But the ungodly will be punished as their reasoning deserves,
those who disregarded the righteous[b]
and rebelled against the Lord;
[11] for those who despise wisdom and instruction are miserable.
Their hope is vain, their labors are unprofitable,
and their works are useless.
[12] Their wives are foolish, and their children evil;
[13] their offspring are accursed.
For blessed is the barren woman who is undefiled,
who has not entered into a sinful union;
she will have fruit when God examines souls.

[a] Text of this line uncertain; omitted by some ancient authorities. Compare 4.15
[b] Or *what is right*

devil's envy death entered refers to Gen 3.1–24 (see 6.23; 2 Enoch 31.3–6). Consequently, immortality (*incorruption*) is no longer a natural condition but a reward from God, contrasted with the view of this time in the Greek world that the soul was naturally immortal (see 1.16–2.24n., however, for the Epicurean view).

3.1–4.20: Four pairs contrasting the just and the wicked. 3.1–11: The souls of the righteous will be rewarded, and the wicked, punished; 3.12–19: the offspring of the righteous and the wicked; 4.1–6: better the childlessness of the righteous than the fertility of the wicked; 4.7–20: better a short life and righteousness than long life and wickedness.

3.1–11: First contrast, on suffering and death. The suffering and even death of the righteous is only apparent (vv. 1–9; cf. 1 Enoch 102.4–103.4; 103.9–104.6), in contrast to the wicked (vv. 10–11; cf. 1 Enoch 103.5–8; 104.7–10) who are rightly punished. **1**: *Souls*, the author repeatedly emphasizes the primacy of the soul in constituting human identity (1.4,11; 2.22; 3.13; 4.14; 7.27; 8.19; 9.15; 10.16; 15.8,11). **4**: The emphasis on *immortality* rather than bodily resurrection reflects Greek influence (1.15; 2.23; 4.1; 6.18–19; 8.13, 17; 12.1; 15.3; 2 Esd 2.45; 7.13,96; 8.54; 4 Macc 9.22). **5–6**: The value of divine discipline; cf. 11.8–10; 12.20–22; 16.3–6,11; 18.20; Deut 8.5; Job 5.17; Prov 3.11–12; Sir 2.1–5; 4.17; 18.13–14; 32.14; 2 Macc 6.12–16; 7.33. **7**: *Shine forth*, the star-like appearance of the glorified righteous is frequently mentioned in apocalyptic literature (cf. Dan 12.3; 2 Esd 7.97; 1 Enoch 104.2). **9**: *Watches over his elect*, see 4.15; Ps 1.6; 145.20; Sir 46.14; 2 Macc 7.6.

3.12–19: Second contrast, on offspring. Better is childlessness than children through adultery and unlawful union. Since children were considered a blessing in the ancient world (e.g., Ps 127.3–5; 128.3–4), the author shows how the apparent good fortune of the ungodly in having children is illusory. See also 3.16–19; 4.3–6; cf. Sir 16.1–4; 23.22–27. 41.5–9. In contrast, barrenness, which was often thought to indicate divine displeasure

¹⁴ Blessed also is the eunuch whose hands
have done no lawless deed,
and who has not devised wicked things
against the Lord;
for special favor will be shown him for his
faithfulness,
and a place of great delight in the temple
of the Lord.
¹⁵ For the fruit of good labors is
renowned,
and the root of understanding does not
fail.
¹⁶ But children of adulterers will not come
to maturity,
and the offspring of an unlawful union will
perish.
¹⁷ Even if they live long they will be held of
no account,
and finally their old age will be without
honor.
¹⁸ If they die young, they will have no
hope
and no consolation on the day of
judgment.
¹⁹ For the end of an unrighteous generation
is grievous.

4 Better than this is childlessness with
virtue,
for in the memory of virtue[a] is
immortality,
because it is known both by God and by
mortals.
² When it is present, people imitate[b] it,
and they long for it when it has gone;
throughout all time it marches, crowned in
triumph,
victor in the contest for prizes that are
undefiled.

³ But the prolific brood of the ungodly will
be of no use,
and none of their illegitimate seedlings
will strike a deep root
or take a firm hold.
⁴ For even if they put forth boughs for a
while,
standing insecurely they will be shaken by
the wind,
and by the violence of the winds they will
be uprooted.
⁵ The branches will be broken off before
they come to maturity,
and their fruit will be useless,
not ripe enough to eat, and good for
nothing.
⁶ For children born of unlawful unions
are witnesses of evil against their parents
when God examines them.[c]
⁷ But the righteous, though they die early,
will be at rest.
⁸ For old age is not honored for length of
time,
or measured by number of years;
⁹ but understanding is gray hair for
anyone,
and a blameless life is ripe old age.

¹⁰ There were some who pleased God and
were loved by him,
and while living among sinners were taken
up.
¹¹ They were caught up so that evil might
not change their understanding
or guile deceive their souls.

a Gk *it*
b Other ancient authorities read *honor*
c Gk *at their examination*

(Gen 30.23) if not sin (*1 Enoch* 98.5), may be the condition of the morally pure. **14:** Although Deut 23.1 excluded eunuchs from the cultic assembly, this author assures the virtuous eunuch a place in *the temple of the Lord*, referring perhaps to the heavenly temple; cf. Isa 56.4–5.

4.1–6: Third contrast, parallel to 3.13–19 on offspring. 1: *The memory of virtue*, God's remembrance of the virtuous is their guarantee of eternal life (cf. 8.13; Ps 112.6; Prov 10.7; Sir 44.8–15; 2 Esd 12.47). Conversely, the memory of the wicked will perish (4.19; see 2.4; Eccl 9.5). **3–5:** Cf. Sir 23.22–27. For the imagery, cf. Job 15.32–34; Ps 1.4–5; Ezek 17.9; 31.10–14; Dan 4.14. **6:** *Witnesses . . . against their parents,* see 4.20.

4.7–20: Fourth contrast, parallel to 3.1–9, returning to the theme of suffering and death. A similar idea, that the righteous were taken away in order that they be removed from evil, is found in Isa 57.1–2. **7–9:** In contrast to the traditional association of old age with wisdom (Job 15.7–10), *understanding*, not *length of time*, is the true measure of righteousness (see 4.15; Philo, *On Abraham* 271). **10–11:** An allusion to Enoch who was *taken up* by God (Gen 5.24; cf. Sir 44.16). *Gen Rab* 25.1 also claims that the purpose of Enoch's removal was to

¹² For the fascination of wickedness
　　obscures what is good,
and roving desire perverts the innocent
　　mind.
¹³ Being perfected in a short time, they
　　fulfilled long years;
¹⁴ for their souls were pleasing to the Lord,
therefore he took them quickly from the
　　midst of wickedness.
¹⁵ Yet the peoples saw and did not
　　understand,
or take such a thing to heart,
that God's grace and mercy are with his
　　elect,
and that he watches over his holy ones.

¹⁶ The righteous who have died will
　　condemn the ungodly who are living,
and youth that is quickly perfectedᵃ will
　　condemn the prolonged old age of
　　the unrighteous.
¹⁷ For they will see the end of the wise,
and will not understand what the Lord
　　purposed for them,
and for what he kept them safe.
¹⁸ The unrighteousᵇ will see, and will have
　　contempt for them,
but the Lord will laugh them to scorn.
After this they will become dishonored
　　corpses,
and an outrage among the dead forever;
¹⁹ because he will dash them speechless to
　　the ground,
and shake them from the foundations;
they will be left utterly dry and barren,
and they will suffer anguish,
and the memory of them will perish.

²⁰ They will come with dread when their
　　sins are reckoned up,

and their lawless deeds will convict them
　　to their face.

5 Then the righteous will stand with great
　　confidence
in the presence of those who have
　　oppressed them
and those who make light of their labors.
² When the unrighteousᶜ see them, they
　　will be shaken with dreadful fear,
and they will be amazed at the unexpected
　　salvation of the righteous.
³ They will speak to one another in
　　repentance,
and in anguish of spirit they will groan,
　　and say,
⁴ "These are persons whom we once held
　　in derision
and made a byword of reproach—fools
　　that we were!
We thought that their lives were
　　madness
and that their end was without honor.
⁵ Why have they been numbered among
　　the children of God?
And why is their lot among the saints?
⁶ So it was we who strayed from the way of
　　truth,
and the light of righteousness did not
　　shine on us,
and the sun did not rise upon us.
⁷ We took our fill of the paths of
　　lawlessness and destruction,
and we journeyed through trackless
　　deserts,
but the way of the Lord we have not
　　known.

ᵃ　Or *ended*
ᵇ　Gk *They*
ᶜ　Gk *they*

preserve his character. **12:** *Roving desire,* see 15.5–6; Eccl 6.9; 11.9; Sir 18.30–19.3. **14–15,17:** Premature death is interpreted not as a curse (cf. Ps 109.8–9) but as a sign of God's favor. These verses may be based on Isa 57.1–2. **17:** *They will see,* answering 2.17 (cf. 5.2). **18:** *The Lord will laugh,* cf. Ps 2.4; Prov 1.26. **18b–19:** These threats are familiar from prophetic announcements of judgment (Isa 13.6–16; 24.17–23; 66.24; Jer 15.7–9). **19:** *Memory,* see 4.1n.

　　5.1–23: Final judgment and the speech of the impious. In contrast to their arrogant speech of 2.1–20, *the unrighteous* now speak with remorse and self-condemnation (5.4–13). **1–8:** The reaction of *the unrighteous* to *the righteous* parallels the so-called servant song of Isa 52.13–53.12, which describes the astonishing restoration of Israel after terrible affliction. Cf. also *1 Enoch* 62–63. **4–13:** An imaginary monologue is placed in the mouths of the wicked, as in 2.1–20, a device common in diatribe. **5:** The righteous eventually become part of the heavenly host, a kind of astral immortality; cf. Dan. 12.2–3; *1 Enoch* 39.5; 104.2,6; 1QH 3.19–23; *2 Baruch* 51.5–13. **6–8:** Con-

⁸What has our arrogance profited us?
And what good has our boasted wealth
brought us?

⁹"All those things have vanished like a
shadow,
and like a rumor that passes by;
¹⁰like a ship that sails through the billowy
water,
and when it has passed no trace can be
found,
no track of its keel in the waves;
¹¹or as, when a bird flies through the air,
no evidence of its passage is found;
the light air, lashed by the beat of its
pinions
and pierced by the force of its rushing
flight,
is traversed by the movement of its wings,
and afterward no sign of its coming is
found there;
¹²or as, when an arrow is shot at a target,
the air, thus divided, comes together at
once,
so that no one knows its pathway.
¹³So we also, as soon as we were born,
ceased to be,
and we had no sign of virtue to show,
but were consumed in our wickedness."
¹⁴Because the hope of the ungodly is like
thistledown[a] carried by the wind,
and like a light frost[b] driven away by a
storm;
it is dispersed like smoke before the wind,
and it passes like the remembrance of a
guest who stays but a day.

¹⁵But the righteous live forever,
and their reward is with the Lord;
the Most High takes care of them.
¹⁶Therefore they will receive a glorious
crown

and a beautiful diadem from the hand of
the Lord,
because with his right hand he will cover
them,
and with his arm he will shield them.
¹⁷The Lord[c] will take his zeal as his whole
armor,
and will arm all creation to repel[d] his
enemies;
¹⁸he will put on righteousness as a
breastplate,
and wear impartial justice as a helmet;
¹⁹he will take holiness as an invincible
shield,
²⁰and sharpen stern wrath for a sword,
and creation will join with him to fight
against his frenzied foes.
²¹Shafts of lightning will fly with true aim,
and will leap from the clouds to the target,
as from a well-drawn bow,
²²and hailstones full of wrath will be
hurled as from a catapult;
the water of the sea will rage against
them,
and rivers will relentlessly overwhelm
them;
²³a mighty wind will rise against them,
and like a tempest it will winnow them
away.
Lawlessness will lay waste the whole
earth,
and evildoing will overturn the thrones of
rulers.

6 Listen therefore, O kings, and
understand;
learn, O judges of the ends of the earth.

ᵃ Other ancient authorities read *dust*
ᵇ Other ancient authorities read *spider's web*
ᶜ Gk *He*
ᵈ Or *punish*

---

fession of guilt by the wicked (cf. Isa 59.2–3,7–10). **6:** *The light . . . did not shine*, see 17.2–21. **9–14:** The ephemeral
existence of *the ungodly*, cf. Ps. 1.4–5; Hos 13.3; 2 Esd 7.61; Jas 4.14. **10–11:** *A ship . . . a bird*, cf. Prov 30.18–19. **17–22:**
The armor of virtues (see also 18.14–16; 19.13–17). The imagery of God putting on various attributes as divine armor derives from Isa 59.17; cf. Eph. 6.11–17. **16:** *Crown . . . diadem*, cf. Isa 62.3. **17:** *Will arm all creation*, see 5.20–23;
19.6; Sir 39.28–31. **21–22:** *Lightning . . . hailstones . . . water*, cf. 16.15–29.

6.1–21: An exhortation to wisdom. This section is parallel to 1.1–15, forming an inclusio that marks off 1.1–
6.21 as a unit: just as the section began with an address to "the rulers of the earth" (1.1–15), it ends with an address to "the kings of the earth" (6.1–21). Some of the passage's themes are familiar from philosophical treatises
on kingship (e.g., Plutarch, *To an Uneducated Ruler*), which generally stressed the need for rulers to be wise and

² Give ear, you that rule over multitudes,
and boast of many nations.
³ For your dominion was given you from
the Lord,
and your sovereignty from the Most High;
he will search out your works and inquire
into your plans.
⁴ Because as servants of his kingdom you
did not rule rightly,
or keep the law,
or walk according to the purpose of God,
⁵ he will come upon you terribly and
swiftly,
because severe judgment falls on those in
high places.
⁶ For the lowliest may be pardoned in
mercy,
but the mighty will be mightily tested.
⁷ For the Lord of all will not stand in awe of
anyone,
or show deference to greatness;
because he himself made both small and
great,
and he takes thought for all alike.
⁸ But a strict inquiry is in store for the
mighty.
⁹ To you then, O monarchs, my words are
directed,
so that you may learn wisdom and not
transgress.
¹⁰ For they will be made holy who observe
holy things in holiness,

and those who have been taught them will
find a defense.
¹¹ Therefore set your desire on my words;
long for them, and you will be instructed.

¹² Wisdom is radiant and unfading,
and she is easily discerned by those who
love her,
and is found by those who seek her.
¹³ She hastens to make herself known to
those who desire her.
¹⁴ One who rises early to seek her will have
no difficulty,
for she will be found sitting at the gate.
¹⁵ To fix one's thought on her is perfect
understanding,
and one who is vigilant on her account will
soon be free from care,
¹⁶ because she goes about seeking those
worthy of her,
and she graciously appears to them in
their paths,
and meets them in every thought.

¹⁷ The beginning of wisdom[a] is the most
sincere desire for instruction,
and concern for instruction is love of her,
¹⁸ and love of her is the keeping of her laws,
and giving heed to her laws is assurance of
immortality,

---

[a] Gk *Her beginning*

---

benevolent (cf. 12.15–18n.). Kingship is also an important theme in Proverbs (e.g., 16.10–19; 20.26–28; 25.1–7; 29.4,12–14; 30.21–31), another book attributed to Solomon. **1–11:** Rulers of other nations are often condemned in the Bible and Jewish literature (e.g., Isa 14.3–21), yet this passage seems to assume that the ruler who heeds and gains wisdom will rule the world and gain many benefits. Thus, even Gentile rulers can gain favor in the eyes of God by living according to the law and God's will (6.4). *Law* (v. 4) here probably refers to universal law rather the specific Jewish Torah, though some Jewish writers of the time equated the two (*Ep. Aris.* 161,168–69; Philo, *Abraham*, especially 16,60–61,133–37). **1–2:** An apostrophe (see 1.1n.). **3:** Political authority is granted by God (cf. Prov 8.15–16; Jer 27.5–7; Dan 2.37–38; 4.17; Sir 10.4–5). **4–6:** For God's judgment against *the mighty*, cf. 1 Sam 2.3–5; Job 12.17–25; 34.24–30; Ps 2; Isa 2.11–17; Jer 25.15–29; Ezek 21.25–27; Sir 10.8–18. **7:** *Small and great*, cf. Job 34.19. **12:** *Wisdom* has been mentioned in passing at several points (1.4–6; 3.11; 6.9), but with this verse a discourse on the figure of personified Wisdom begins, continuing to the end of ch 10. The figure of Wisdom or Lady Wisdom occurs frequently in late Israelite and Jewish literature, especially Prov 1.20–33; 8; 9.1–6; Job 28.12–28; Sir 1.1–27; 4.11–19; 6.18–37; 14.20–15.10; 24; Bar 3.9–4.4. Later, Wisdom came to be equated with the Torah or elements of the Torah, rather than just intellectual or practical wisdom (e.g., Sir 24.23–29; Bar 4.1). **14:** *The gate*, the place in a city where legal and commercial transactions were carried out (Deut 22.15,24; Prov 22.22; Isa 29.21; Am 5.10–12,15); cf. Prov 1.20–21. **17–20:** The literary form called a "sorites" in Greek, defined as a set of statements that proceed step by step to a conclusion, with each statement picking up the last key word or phrase of the preceding one. The author of Wis clearly knows of the form and makes effective use of it. **18–19:** *Immortality*, see 3.4n.

¹⁹ and immortality brings one near to God;
²⁰ so the desire for wisdom leads to a
kingdom.

²¹ Therefore if you delight in thrones and
scepters, O monarchs over the peoples,
honor wisdom, so that you may reign
forever.
²² I will tell you what wisdom is and how
she came to be,
and I will hide no secrets from you,
but I will trace her course from the
beginning of creation,
and make knowledge of her clear,
and I will not pass by the truth;
²³ nor will I travel in the company of sickly
envy,
for envy[a] does not associate with wisdom.
²⁴ The multitude of the wise is the
salvation of the world,
and a sensible king is the stability of any
people.
²⁵ Therefore be instructed by my words,
and you will profit.

7 I also am mortal, like everyone else,
a descendant of the first-formed child of
earth;
and in the womb of a mother I was molded
into flesh,
² within the period of ten months,
compacted with blood,

from the seed of a man and the pleasure of
marriage.
³ And when I was born, I began to breathe
the common air,
and fell upon the kindred earth;
my first sound was a cry, as is true of all.
⁴ I was nursed with care in swaddling
cloths.
⁵ For no king has had a different beginning
of existence;
⁶ there is for all one entrance into life, and
one way out.
⁷ Therefore I prayed, and understanding
was given me;
I called on God, and the spirit of wisdom
came to me.
⁸ I preferred her to scepters and thrones,
and I accounted wealth as nothing in
comparison with her.
⁹ Neither did I liken to her any priceless
gem,
because all gold is but a little sand in her
sight,
and silver will be accounted as clay before
her.
¹⁰ I loved her more than health and
beauty,
and I chose to have her rather than
light,
because her radiance never ceases.

[a] Gk *this*

6.22–10.21: The Book of Wisdom.

6.22–25: Introduction: the promise is made to reveal the mysteries of wisdom to the reader.

7.1–9.18: In this section the implied author speaks in the persona of Solomon, describing his life and quest for wisdom and the benefits wisdom is able to bestow. The pseudo-autobiographical narrative serves the dual function of gaining the empathy of the hearers and commending the quest for wisdom.

7.1–8.21: The first part of the autobiographical narrative consists of a speech by Solomon that has a concentric framework:

A. Birth of Solomon (7.1–6)
   B. Solomon asks for wisdom from God (7.7–12)
      C. Solomon given wealth and power (7.13–22a)
         D. Description of wisdom (7.22b–8.1)
      C.' Wisdom brings all good things (8.2–8)
   B.' Solomon becomes a great king through Wisdom (8.9–16)
A.' Wisdom available only through prayer (8.17–21).

7.1–6: By describing his birth *like everyone else*, "Solomon" shows his common humanity with the hearers. **2:** The conventional 40 weeks or 280 days of human gestation was usually interpreted as *ten months* in antiquity, because of the use of lunar rather than solar months. *Compacted with blood*, on conception as the coagulation of semen in the womb, cf. Job 10.10. **7–14:** Solomon prays for wisdom from God, as also in 1 Kings 3.4–14. God grants Solomon not only wisdom but also wealth and other benefits (cf. 1 Kings 3.10–14). **8–9:** Cf. Job 28.15–19;

¹¹ All good things came to me along with
her,
and in her hands uncounted wealth.
¹² I rejoiced in them all, because wisdom
leads them;
but I did not know that she was their
mother.
¹³ I learned without guile and I impart
without grudging;
I do not hide her wealth,
¹⁴ for it is an unfailing treasure for mortals;
those who get it obtain friendship with
God,
commended for the gifts that come from
instruction.

¹⁵ May God grant me to speak with
judgment,
and to have thoughts worthy of what I
have received;
for he is the guide even of wisdom
and the corrector of the wise.
¹⁶ For both we and our words are in his
hand,
as are all understanding and skill in crafts.
¹⁷ For it is he who gave me unerring
knowledge of what exists,
to know the structure of the world and the
activity of the elements;
¹⁸ the beginning and end and middle of
times,
the alternations of the solstices and the
changes of the seasons,
¹⁹ the cycles of the year and the
constellations of the stars,
²⁰ the natures of animals and the tempers
of wild animals,
the powers of spirits[a] and the thoughts of
human beings,

the varieties of plants and the virtues of
roots;
²¹ I learned both what is secret and what is
manifest,
²² for wisdom, the fashioner of all things,
taught me.

There is in her a spirit that is intelligent,
holy,
unique, manifold, subtle,
mobile, clear, unpolluted,
distinct, invulnerable, loving the good,
keen,
irresistible, ²³ beneficent, humane,
steadfast, sure, free from anxiety,
all-powerful, overseeing all,
and penetrating through all spirits
that are intelligent, pure, and altogether
subtle.
²⁴ For wisdom is more mobile than any
motion;
because of her pureness she pervades and
penetrates all things.
²⁵ For she is a breath of the power of God,
and a pure emanation of the glory of the
Almighty;
therefore nothing defiled gains entrance
into her.
²⁶ For she is a reflection of eternal light,
a spotless mirror of the working of God,
and an image of his goodness.
²⁷ Although she is but one, she can do all
things,
and while remaining in herself, she renews
all things;
in every generation she passes into holy
souls

a   Or *winds*

Prov 2.4; 3.14–16. **14:** Abraham in particular was known for his *friendship with* God (2 Chr 20.7; Isa 41.8; Jas 2.23);
see also 7.27; 8.18; Job 29.4; Ps 25.14; Jer 3.4. **15–22:** Divine wisdom is presented in scientific and philosophical
terms; this sort of encyclopedic knowledge was a common interest of ancient wisdom literature; cf. 1 Kings
4.33.
   7.22b–8.1: A description of wisdom, with two sets of lists. **7.22b–24:** The first list consists of 21 attributes
(a multiple of 7 and 3, numbers signifying completeness and perfection). Most of the epithets have parallels in
Greek philosophy (cf. Pseudo-Aristotle, *On the Cosmos* 400B–401B); a similar litany of attributes, glorifying the
deity, is used in the *Apocalypse of Abraham* 17.8–15. **7.25–8.1:** The second list is made up of metaphors, a five-
fold description of wisdom's relationship with God (breath, emanation, reflection, mirror, image). **25:** *Breath,*
see 11.20; Sir 24.3. The description of wisdom as a *pure emanation* or effluence of God reflects the influence of
philosophical concepts (e.g., Cicero, *The Nature of the Gods* 2.79; cf. Sir 1.9; 24.23–33). **26:** *Mirror,* cf. 2 Cor 3.18;
Philo, *Quest. in Gen.* 1.57.

and makes them friends of God, and
    prophets;
²⁸ for God loves nothing so much as the
    person who lives with wisdom.
²⁹ She is more beautiful than the sun,
and excels every constellation of the stars.
Compared with the light she is found to be
    superior,
³⁰ for it is succeeded by the night,
but against wisdom evil does not prevail.

8 She reaches mightily from one end of the
    earth to the other,
and she orders all things well.
² I loved her and sought her from my youth;
I desired to take her for my bride,
and became enamored of her beauty.
³ She glorifies her noble birth by living
    with God,
and the Lord of all loves her.
⁴ For she is an initiate in the knowledge of
    God,
and an associate in his works.
⁵ If riches are a desirable possession in life,
what is richer than wisdom, the active
    cause of all things?
⁶ And if understanding is effective,
who more than she is fashioner of what
    exists?
⁷ And if anyone loves righteousness,
her labors are virtues;
for she teaches self-control and prudence,
justice and courage;
nothing in life is more profitable for
    mortals than these.
⁸ And if anyone longs for wide experience,
she knows the things of old, and infers the
    things to come;
she understands turns of speech and the
    solutions of riddles;
she has foreknowledge of signs and
    wonders
and of the outcome of seasons and times.
⁹ Therefore I determined to take her to live
    with me,

knowing that she would give me good
    counsel
and encouragement in cares and grief.
¹⁰ Because of her I shall have glory among
    the multitudes
and honor in the presence of the elders,
    though I am young.
¹¹ I shall be found keen in judgment,
and in the sight of rulers I shall be
    admired.
¹² When I am silent they will wait for me,
and when I speak they will give heed;
if I speak at greater length,
they will put their hands on their
    mouths.
¹³ Because of her I shall have immortality,
and leave an everlasting remembrance to
    those who come after me.
¹⁴ I shall govern peoples,
and nations will be subject to me;
¹⁵ dread monarchs will be afraid of me
    when they hear of me;
among the people I shall show myself
    capable, and courageous in war.
¹⁶ When I enter my house, I shall find rest
    with her;
for companionship with her has no
    bitterness,
and life with her has no pain, but gladness
    and joy.
¹⁷ When I considered these things inwardly,
and pondered in my heart
that in kinship with wisdom there is
    immortality,
¹⁸ and in friendship with her, pure delight,
and in the labors of her hands, unfailing
    wealth,
and in the experience of her company,
    understanding,
and renown in sharing her words,
I went about seeking how to get her for
    myself.
¹⁹ As a child I was naturally gifted,
and a good soul fell to my lot;

8.2–16: The extended metaphor of Solomon making Wisdom his bride. Erotic imagery in connection with Wisdom is found elsewhere, as in Prov. 9.1–6, which makes Wisdom a seductress. Even more erotically explicit is the Hebrew version of Sir 51.13–30, which circulated separately at Qumran as part of a Psalms scroll (11QPsa 21). **4–6:** On wisdom's agency in creation, see Prov 8.22–31. **7:** The four cardinal virtues of Greek thought: *self-control, prudence, justice,* and *courage.* Cf. 4 Macc 1.2–4. **8:** *Turns of speech ... riddles,* cf. Prov. 1.5–6. **10–12:** Cf. Job 29.7–11,21–23; Sir 15.4–6. **13:** *Everlasting remembrance,* see 4.1n. **15–16:** *Rest,* see Sir 6.28.

    8.17–21: Wisdom is available only as a gift from God. 17: *Immortality,* see 3.4n. **18:** *Friendship,* see 7.8–9n.

20 or rather, being good, I entered an undefiled body. 21 But I perceived that I would not possess wisdom unless God gave her to me— and it was a mark of insight to know whose gift she was— so I appealed to the Lord and implored him, and with my whole heart I said:

9 "O God of my ancestors and Lord of mercy, who have made all things by your word, 2 and by your wisdom have formed humankind to have dominion over the creatures you have made, 3 and rule the world in holiness and righteousness, and pronounce judgment in uprightness of soul, 4 give me the wisdom that sits by your throne, and do not reject me from among your servants. 5 For I am your servant[a] the son of your serving girl, a man who is weak and short-lived, with little understanding of judgment and laws; 6 for even one who is perfect among human beings will be regarded as nothing without the wisdom that comes from you. 7 You have chosen me to be king of your people and to be judge over your sons and daughters. 8 You have given command to build a temple on your holy mountain, and an altar in the city of your habitation, a copy of the holy tent that you prepared from the beginning.

9 With you is wisdom, she who knows your works and was present when you made the world; she understands what is pleasing in your sight and what is right according to your commandments. 10 Send her forth from the holy heavens, and from the throne of your glory send her, that she may labor at my side, and that I may learn what is pleasing to you. 11 For she knows and understands all things, and she will guide me wisely in my actions and guard me with her glory. 12 Then my works will be acceptable, and I shall judge your people justly, and shall be worthy of the throne[b] of my father. 13 For who can learn the counsel of God? Or who can discern what the Lord wills? 14 For the reasoning of mortals is worthless, and our designs are likely to fail; 15 for a perishable body weighs down the soul, and this earthy tent burdens the thoughtful[c] mind. 16 We can hardly guess at what is on earth, and what is at hand we find with labor; but who has traced out what is in the heavens? 17 Who has learned your counsel, unless you have given wisdom and sent your holy spirit from on high?

a Gk *slave*
b Gk *thrones*
c Or *anxious*

19–20: The Platonic view of the soul as preexistent is reflected here, as in other Hellenistic Jewish writings (cf. Philo, *Giants* 6–14; *2 Enoch* 23.4–5). The author may be referring also to Hellenistic theories about the transmigration of souls, a belief attributed by Josephus to the Pharisees (*J.W.* 2.8.14).

9.1–18: Solomon's prayer (cf. 1 Kings 3.6–9; 2 Chr 1.8–10). Verses 1–5 parallel vv. 7–12: Address to God (vv. 1–3; 7–9); petition (vv. 4; 10a); motive (vv. 5; 10b–12). Verses 13–18 are a meditation on humanity's insignificance before God. **2:** *Dominion*, see 10.2; Gen 1.26,28; Ps 8.6; Sir 17.2–4. **4:** *Wisdom . . . sits by your throne*, see 9.10; 18.15; Prov 8.30; Sir 24.4; 1 Enoch 84.3. **5:** *Your servant*, see Pss 86.16; 116.16. **8:** That the earthly temple on Mount Zion was only a *copy* of a heavenly archetype may be an interpretation of Ex 25.9,40; 26.30 (cf. Heb 8.2–5; Rev 11.19; 1 Enoch 14.10–20). **9:** Cf. Prov. 8.22–31. **12:** *My father*, David. **13:** Cf. Isa 40.12–14; Sir 1.2–6; Bar 3.29–31.15: That

¹⁸ And thus the paths of those on earth
were set right,
and people were taught what pleases you,
and were saved by wisdom."

10

Wisdom[a] protected the first-formed
father of the world, when he alone
had been created;
she delivered him from his transgression,
² and gave him strength to rule all things.
³ But when an unrighteous man departed
from her in his anger,
he perished because in rage he killed his
brother.
⁴ When the earth was flooded because of
him, wisdom again saved it,
steering the righteous man by a paltry
piece of wood.

⁵ Wisdom[a] also, when the nations in
wicked agreement had been put to
confusion,
recognized the righteous man and
preserved him blameless before God,
and kept him strong in the face of his
compassion for his child.

⁶ Wisdom[a] rescued a righteous man when
the ungodly were perishing;
he escaped the fire that descended on the
Five Cities.[b]
⁷ Evidence of their wickedness still
remains:
a continually smoking wasteland,
plants bearing fruit that does not ripen,
and a pillar of salt standing as a
monument to an unbelieving soul.
⁸ For because they passed wisdom by,
they not only were hindered from
recognizing the good,

but also left for humankind a reminder of
their folly,
so that their failures could never go
unnoticed.

⁹ Wisdom rescued from troubles those
who served her.
¹⁰ When a righteous man fled from his
brother's wrath,
she guided him on straight paths;
she showed him the kingdom of God,
and gave him knowledge of holy
things;
she prospered him in his labors,
and increased the fruit of his toil.
¹¹ When his oppressors were covetous,
she stood by him and made him rich.
¹² She protected him from his
enemies,
and kept him safe from those who lay in
wait for him;
in his arduous contest she gave him the
victory,
so that he might learn that godliness is
more powerful than anything else.

¹³ When a righteous man was sold,
wisdom[c] did not desert him,
but delivered him from sin.
She descended with him into the
dungeon,
¹⁴ and when he was in prison she did not
leave him,
until she brought him the scepter of a
kingdom
and authority over his masters.

ᵃ   Gk *She*
ᵇ   Or *on Pentapolis*
ᶜ   Gk *she*

---

the body *weighs down the soul* was a common philosophical belief (see Plato, *Phaedr* 81C). **18:** *Saved by wisdom*, the attribution of a saving role to wisdom is one of the book's distinctive features; here as elsewhere activities usually reserved for God are assigned to wisdom.

10.1–21: Biblical history illustrates wisdom's saving and punishing power. The author presents seven righteous heroes as evidence of wisdom's providential ordering of Israelite history, each contrasted with some unrighteous villain. Personal names are avoided in favor of generic categories, but the descriptions make it clear who they are. This chapter provides a transition to the third part of the book. **1–2:** The interpretation of Adam is different in emphasis from the account in Gen 1.26–5.5. **2:** *Rule*, see 9.2n. **3:** Cain and Abel (Gen 4.1–16). **4:** *Because of him*, Cain's crime is interpreted by the author as the cause of the Flood. *The righteous man*, Noah (Gen 5.28–9.29). **5:** Abraham (Gen 11.26–25.10). *The nations*, referring to the Tower of Babel story (Gen 11.1–9). *Compassion for his child*, cf. Gen 22.1–19. **6–8:** Lot (Gen 19.1–29). **9–12:** Jacob (Gen 27–33). **10:** *The kingdom of God,*

Those who accused him she showed to be
false,
and she gave him everlasting honor.

¹⁵ A holy people and blameless race
wisdom delivered from a nation of
oppressors.
¹⁶ She entered the soul of a servant of the
Lord,
and withstood dread kings with wonders
and signs.
¹⁷ She gave to holy people the reward of
their labors;
she guided them along a marvelous
way,
and became a shelter to them by day,
and a starry flame through the night.
¹⁸ She brought them over the Red Sea,
and led them through deep waters;
¹⁹ but she drowned their enemies,
and cast them up from the depth of the
sea.
²⁰ Therefore the righteous plundered the
ungodly;
they sang hymns, O Lord, to your holy
name,
and praised with one accord your
defending hand;
²¹ for wisdom opened the mouths of those
who were mute,
and made the tongues of infants speak
clearly.

11 Wisdomᵃ prospered their works by the
hand of a holy prophet.
² They journeyed through an uninhabited
wilderness,
and pitched their tents in untrodden places.
³ They withstood their enemies and fought
off their foes.
⁴ When they were thirsty, they called upon
you,
and water was given them out of flinty rock,
and from hard stone a remedy for their
thirst.
⁵ For through the very things by which
their enemies were punished,
they themselves received benefit in their
need.
⁶ Instead of the fountain of an ever-flowing
river,
stirred up and defiled with blood
⁷ in rebuke for the decree to kill the infants,
you gave them abundant water
unexpectedly,
⁸ showing by their thirst at that time
how you punished their enemies.
⁹ For when they were tried, though they
were being disciplined in mercy,
they learned how the ungodly were
tormented when judged in wrath.
¹⁰ For you tested them as a parentᵇ does in
warning,

ᵃ Gk *She*
ᵇ Gk *a father*

see Gen 28.12,17,22. **12:** *Arduous contest* (Gen 32.22–32; Hos 12.3–4). **13–14:** Joseph (Gen 37–50). **15–21:** Moses
(Ex 1–17).

11.1–19.22: The Book of History, a historical meditation contrasting God's dealings with the Israelites and
the Egyptians. The presentation of Moses in the preceding passage leads without a break into an elaborate
comparison consisting of seven historical contrasts, supplemented by a digression in 11.17–15.19. Although
based on the events of Ex 7–14, the author's interpretation is apologetic in nature, underscoring the Egyptians' culpability while omitting reference to any of Israel's failures. Three principles seem have been used in
constructing these historical contrasts: Israel would benefit from those things that were a punishment of the
Egyptians (11.5); the Egyptians' sins would themselves act as a punishment of them (11.16); Israel would also
suffer a mild form of the punishments, but this would be a means of understanding God's mercies (cf. 16.4).

11.1–14: First contrast: plague of the Nile versus water from the rock. The sin of the Egyptians was killing
the Israelite infants in the Nile (11.7); the punishment is that the Nile becomes undrinkable. The Israelite counterpart is the water brought forth from the rock in the desert (Ex 17.1–7; Num 20.1–13). **1–3:** Without making
specific references, the author establishes the historical setting for what follows, the Israelites' struggle in
the *wilderness*. **4,6–8:** See Ex 7.14–25; 17.1–7; Num 20.2–13. **5:** The principle behind all the contrasts: God uses
the same means for aiding Israel and punishing her *enemies* (see 11.13; 16.24; 18.8). **8–10:** The righteous must
also experience God's punishment, though not as a matter of condemnation but of compassionate testing and
discipline (see 3.5).

but you examined the ungodly[a] as a stern king does in condemnation.

[11] Whether absent or present, they were equally distressed,

[12] for a twofold grief possessed them, and a groaning at the memory of what had occurred.

[13] For when they heard that through their own punishments the righteous[b] had received benefit, they perceived it was the Lord's doing.

[14] For though they had mockingly rejected him who long before had been cast out and exposed, at the end of the events they marveled at him, when they felt thirst in a different way from the righteous.

[15] In return for their foolish and wicked thoughts, which led them astray to worship irrational serpents and worthless animals, you sent upon them a multitude of irrational creatures to punish them,

[16] so that they might learn that one is punished by the very things by which one sins.

[17] For your all-powerful hand, which created the world out of formless matter, did not lack the means to send upon them a multitude of bears, or bold lions,

[18] or newly-created unknown beasts full of rage, or such as breathe out fiery breath, or belch forth a thick pall of smoke, or flash terrible sparks from their eyes;

[19] not only could the harm they did destroy people,[c] but the mere sight of them could kill by fright.

[20] Even apart from these, people[b] could fall at a single breath when pursued by justice and scattered by the breath of your power.

But you have arranged all things by measure and number and weight.

[21] For it is always in your power to show great strength, and who can withstand the might of your arm?

[22] Because the whole world before you is like a speck that tips the scales, and like a drop of morning dew that falls on the ground.

[23] But you are merciful to all, for you can do all things, and you overlook people's sins, so that they may repent.

[24] For you love all things that exist, and detest none of the things that you have made, for you would not have made anything if you had hated it.

[25] How would anything have endured if you had not willed it? Or how would anything not called forth by you have been preserved?

[26] You spare all things, for they are yours, O Lord, you who love the living.

[a] Gk those
[b] Gk they
[c] Gk them

11.15–16: **Second contrast: the plague of small animals** (see Ex 8.1–19; 9.1–7). Here the positive parallel with the Israelites is not developed; see further 16.1–4.

11.17–15.19: **Two digressions** that interrupt the interpretation of the Exodus, explaining how and why God judges the nations, contrasting the results of true worship (Jewish monotheism) and false worship (idolatry).

11.17–12.27: **First digression.** God's power and mercy, composed of two parallel sections and a conclusion: God punished the Egyptians by degrees so that they will have a chance to repent (11.17–12.2); God's punishment of the Canaanites was gradual, in spite of their heinous sins (12.3–18); God's punishment of Israel is very mild compared to that of their enemies (12.19–22).

11.17–12.2: **God exercises power and mercy in judgment** so as to free all creation from wickedness. **11.17:** *Formless matter,* a concept of Greek philosophy (see Plato, *Timaeus* 50D-E), here describing the chaos of Gen 1.2. **18–19:** Cf. Job 41.12–21. **21:** See 12.12n. **23:** *Merciful to all,* see 12.13,16,18; 15.1; Sir 16.11–14; 18.11–14; 2 Esd

12 For your immortal spirit is in all things.
² Therefore you correct little by little
those who trespass,
and you remind and warn them of the
things through which they sin,
so that they may be freed from wickedness
and put their trust in you, O Lord.

³ Those who lived long ago in your holy
land
⁴ you hated for their detestable practices,
their works of sorcery and unholy rites,
⁵ their merciless slaughter[a] of children,
and their sacrificial feasting on human
flesh and blood.
These initiates from the midst of a
heathen cult,[b]
⁶ these parents who murder helpless
lives,
you willed to destroy by the hands of our
ancestors,
⁷ so that the land most precious of all to
you
might receive a worthy colony of the
servants[c] of God.
⁸ But even these you spared, since they
were but mortals,
and sent wasps[d] as forerunners of your
army
to destroy them little by little,
⁹ though you were not unable to give
the ungodly into the hands of the
righteous in battle,
or to destroy them at one blow by dread
wild animals or your stern word.
¹⁰ But judging them little by little you gave
them an opportunity to repent,
though you were not unaware that their
origin[e] was evil
and their wickedness inborn,

and that their way of thinking would never
change.
¹¹ For they were an accursed race from the
beginning,
and it was not through fear of anyone that
you left them unpunished for their
sins.

¹² For who will say, "What have you done?"
or will resist your judgment?
Who will accuse you for the destruction of
nations that you made?
Or who will come before you to plead as an
advocate for the unrighteous?
¹³ For neither is there any god besides you,
whose care is for all people,[f]
to whom you should prove that you have
not judged unjustly;
¹⁴ nor can any king or monarch confront
you about those whom you have
punished.
¹⁵ You are righteous and you rule all things
righteously,
deeming it alien to your power
to condemn anyone who does not deserve
to be punished.
¹⁶ For your strength is the source of
righteousness,
and your sovereignty over all causes you to
spare all.
¹⁷ For you show your strength when people
doubt the completeness of your
power,

---

a Gk *slaughterers*
b Meaning of Gk uncertain
c Or *children*
d Or *hornets*
e Or *nature*
f Or *all things*

8.45. **12.1**: *Your . . . spirit is in all things*, see 1.7; 15.11; cf. Gen 6.3; Ps 104.30; Jdt 16.14. **2**: *You remind . . . them*, see 16.6,11n.

12.3–11: **Divine judgment of the ancient Canaanites**, a common theme of Jewish apologetic (see *Jub.*10.27–34; 22.20–22), gives an illustration for the preceding argument; although hating their *wickedness*, God showed forbearance in destroying them. **5**: Cf. Lev 20.2–5. **8**: *Wasps*, see Ex 23.28; Deut 7.20; Josh 24.12. **10**: *Little by little*, see 12.2,8; Ex 23.28–30. *Their origin was evil* (see textual note *e*), cf. Sir 33.10–15. **11**: *An accursed race*, see the curse placed on Canaan in Gen 9.25–27.

12.12–27: **Divine righteousness and forbearance**. God gives opportunity for *repentance* (v. 19; see also 11.23; 12.10) but condemns the obstinate. **12–14**: The affirmation of divine providence, making use of legal terminology. **12**: For similar rhetorical questions, see 9.13; 11.21; Job 9.12,19; Ps 76.7; Isa 40.13–14. **13**: *Any god besides you*, see Deut 32.39; cf. Ex 20.3. **15–18**: The portrayal of God's universal *power* and *forbearance* shares themes used

and you rebuke any insolence among
those who know it.[a]
[18] Although you are sovereign in strength,
you judge with mildness,
and with great forbearance you govern us;
for you have power to act whenever you
choose.

[19] Through such works you have taught
your people
that the righteous must be kind,
and you have filled your children with
good hope,
because you give repentance for sins.
[20] For if you punished with such great care
and indulgence[b]
the enemies of your servants[c] and those
deserving of death,
granting them time and opportunity to
give up their wickedness,
[21] with what strictness you have judged
your children,
to whose ancestors you gave oaths and
covenants full of good promises!
[22] So while chastening us you scourge our
enemies ten thousand times
more,
so that, when we judge, we may meditate
upon your goodness,
and when we are judged, we may expect
mercy.

[23] Therefore those who lived
unrighteously, in a life of folly,
you tormented through their own
abominations.
[24] For they went far astray on the paths of
error,

accepting as gods those animals that even
their enemies[d] despised;
they were deceived like foolish infants.
[25] Therefore, as though to children who
cannot reason,
you sent your judgment to mock them.
[26] But those who have not heeded the
warning of mild rebukes
will experience the deserved judgment of
God.
[27] For when in their suffering they became
incensed
at those creatures that they had thought
to be gods, being punished by means
of them,
they saw and recognized as the true God
the one whom they had before
refused to know.
Therefore the utmost condemnation came
upon them.

13 For all people who were ignorant of
God were foolish by nature;
and they were unable from the good
things that are seen to know the one
who exists,
nor did they recognize the artisan while
paying heed to his works;
[2] but they supposed that either fire or wind
or swift air,
or the circle of the stars, or turbulent
water,

---

a   Meaning of Gk uncertain
b   Other ancient authorities lack *and indulgence*;
     others read *and entreaty*
c   Or *children*
d   Gk *they*

---

to describe the ideal ruler in philosophical treatises on kingship (see 6.1–21n.). **17:** *You rebuke any insolence*,
see Ps 119.21; Isa 13.11; Jer 48.28–33; Sir 35.22–26; Bar 4.34; 3 Macc 2.3,21. **19–22:** Divine judgment is a model of
goodness and *mercy* for God's children. **20–21:** If repentance is available to the wicked, it is all the more available
to the heirs of God's *promises*. **23–27:** Condemnation of animal worshipers (see 11.15–16; 13.14; 15.18–19); divine
judgment forces them to recognize *the true God*. On their refusal *to know* God, see 2.13n. **25:** *To mock them*, cf.
Ex 10.2; Isa 66.4.

13.1–15.19: Second digression. False worship of nature, idols, and animals is castigated at length. The material is divided into two sections: a short section on worship of the natural world (13.1–9), and a much longer and
detailed section on idol worship (13.10–15.19).

13.1–9: Worship of the natural world. The natural philosophers are to be blamed, because they sought the
Creator but were unable to find him in spite of his works. **1:** *The one who exists* is used of the Supreme Being by
Platonists, whereas it is used by Jews (e.g., LXX Ex 3.14) to refer to the only God. Platonists considered the Su-
preme Being to be separate from the material creator. For Jews the Supreme Being is also the creator or *artisan*.

or the luminaries of heaven were the gods
  that rule the world.
³ If through delight in the beauty of these
  things people assumed them to be
  gods,
let them know how much better than
  these is their Lord,
for the author of beauty created them.
⁴ And if peopleᵃ were amazed at their
  power and working,
let them perceive from them
how much more powerful is the one who
  formed them.
⁵ For from the greatness and beauty of
  created things
comes a corresponding perception of their
  Creator.
⁶ Yet these people are little to be blamed,
for perhaps they go astray
while seeking God and desiring to find
  him.
⁷ For while they live among his works, they
  keep searching,
and they trust in what they see, because
  the things that are seen are beautiful.
⁸ Yet again, not even they are to be
  excused;
⁹ for if they had the power to know so
  much

that they could investigate the world,
how did they fail to find sooner the Lord of
  these things?

¹⁰ But miserable, with their hopes set on
  dead things, are those
who give the name "gods" to the works of
  human hands,
gold and silver fashioned with skill,
and likenesses of animals,
or a useless stone, the work of an ancient
  hand.
¹¹ A skilled woodcutter may saw down a
  tree easy to handle
and skillfully strip off all its bark,
and then with pleasing workmanship
make a useful vessel that serves life's needs,
¹² and burn the cast-off pieces of his work
to prepare his food, and eat his fill.
¹³ But a cast-off piece from among them,
  useful for nothing,
a stick crooked and full of knots,
he takes and carves with care in his leisure,
and shapes it with skill gained in idleness;ᵇ
he forms it in the likeness of a human
  being,

ᵃ Gk *they*
ᵇ Other ancient authorities read *with intelligent skill*

In Hellenistic literature, *ignorance* in this sort of context often implied impiety. **2:** The elements worshiped by those who do not know God. Associated with them are several philosophical terms; for example, the phrase *gods that rule the world* seems to refer to astral piety, the worship of the heavenly bodies (cf. 2 Kings 17.16; 23.4; Job 31.26–28; Cicero, *The Nature of the Gods* 2.15). **4:** Another technical philosophical expression, known from Aristotle (*Metaphysics*, 9.6.1–2 1048a), is *power and working*. **5:** The type of argumentation used here is Hellenistic, not biblical. It includes the common Hellenistic form of reasoning from analogy, and it argues that the beauty of the creation requires some overseer and source of beauty behind it. **6:** *Seeking God*, cf. Philo, *Abraham* 124–30; Acts 17.26–27. **9:** In Hellenistic speculation, the word translated *world* (Gk "aion") could mean both "world" and "age," but in Hellenistic speculation it was used of a mystical concept, the personification of a kind of world-soul, as in Plato's *Timaeus* 37D. The Stoics believed in an analogous cosmic "reason" or mind that governed all things.

13.10–15.19: Polemic against idolatry. The Jews came to regard idolatry as one of the most disgusting traits of paganism. Here it is stated that idolatry is "the beginning and cause and end of every evil" (14.27), leading to child murder, secret rites, pollution of marriages, adultery, bloodshed, murder, theft, deceit, sexual perversion, and debauchery. Jer 10.1–16 and Isa 44.9–20 engage in a similar polemic, describing at length the way in which a piece of wood could partly be burned for warmth and preparing food, and partly used to make a god for worship. This was a simplistic criticism, of course, since no pagans regarded themselves as worshiping a piece of wood, stone, or metal. The criticism is aimed at a Jewish audience, however, and the polemic may have been effective in this context. Yet similar comments about idols can be found in some Greco-Roman writers (Horace, *Satires* 1.8.1–7; Sophocles, according to a quotation in Clement of Alexandria, *Strom.* 5.14 113.1–2).

13.10–16: A sarcastic description of how idol "gods" are created from discarded wood (see 15.7–19). **13:** *In the*

¹⁴ or makes it like some worthless animal,
giving it a coat of red paint and coloring its
surface red
and covering every blemish in it with
paint;
¹⁵ then he makes a suitable niche for it,
and sets it in the wall, and fastens it there
with iron.
¹⁶ He takes thought for it, so that it may
not fall,
because he knows that it cannot help
itself,
for it is only an image and has need of
help.
¹⁷ When he prays about possessions and
his marriage and children,
he is not ashamed to address a lifeless
thing.
¹⁸ For health he appeals to a thing that is
weak;
for life he prays to a thing that is dead;
for aid he entreats a thing that is utterly
inexperienced;
for a prosperous journey, a thing that
cannot take a step;
¹⁹ for money-making and work and success
with his hands
he asks strength of a thing whose hands
have no strength.

14 Again, one preparing to sail and about
to voyage over raging waves
calls upon a piece of wood more fragile
than the ship that carries him.
² For it was desire for gain that planned
that vessel,
and wisdom was the artisan who built it;
³ but it is your providence, O Father, that
steers its course,
because you have given it a path in the sea,
and a safe way through the waves,
⁴ showing that you can save from every
danger,
so that even a person who lacks skill may
put to sea.
⁵ It is your will that works of your wisdom
should not be without effect;
therefore people trust their lives even to
the smallest piece of wood,
and passing through the billows on a raft
they come safely to land.
⁶ For even in the beginning, when arrogant
giants were perishing,
the hope of the world took refuge on a raft,
and guided by your hand left to the world
the seed of a new generation.
⁷ For blessed is the wood by which
righteousness comes.

⁸ But the idol made with hands is accursed,
and so is the one who made it—
he for having made it, and the perishable
thing because it was named a god.
⁹ For equally hateful to God are the
ungodly and their ungodliness;
¹⁰ for what was done will be punished
together with the one who did it.
¹¹ Therefore there will be a visitation also
upon the heathen idols,
because, though part of what God created,
they became an abomination,
snares for human souls
and a trap for the feet of the foolish.

¹² For the idea of making idols was the
beginning of fornication,
and the invention of them was the
corruption of life;

likeness of a human being, cf. 14.19; Deut 4.16.

13.17–14.2: The ironically ineffective prayer of the idolater contrasts with that of Solomon in 9.1–18.

14.3–11: Safety and salvation come from God, not idols. 3: *Providence*, see 17.2,4; 4 Macc 9.24. *O Father*, cf. Isa 63.16; Tob 13.4; Sir 23.1; 3 Macc 6.3. 6–7: *Arrogant giants*, see Gen 6.1–4; cf. Sir 16.7; Bar 3.26–28; 3 Macc 2.4. A *raft*, Noah's ark (Gen 6.5–9.29). 8–11: The author's premise is that one takes on the status of what one worships; in this case both idols and idolaters are *accursed* by God. 11: *Visitation*, the occasion of God's judgment; see 3.7; Sir 16.18. *Abomination*, a common term for idolatry (see 12.23; 2 Chr 34.33; Ezra 9.1,11,14; Jer 2.7–8; Ezek 8.6–17; 18.12–13; Mal 2.11; 1 Macc 1.43–49).

14.12–31: **Origins and repercussions of idolatry.** The idea that the gods were originally human beings who have been elevated to divine status goes back to the Greek writer Euhemerus (ca. 300 BCE). He told a story about islands with a utopian society, in which the local gods (with Greek names) were originally kings who were promoted to divine status and worshiped by the people after their death (Diodorus Siculus 6.1). Although

¹³ for they did not exist from the beginning,
nor will they last forever.
¹⁴ For through human vanity they entered
the world,
and therefore their speedy end has been
planned.

¹⁵ For a father, consumed with grief at an
untimely bereavement,
made an image of his child, who had been
suddenly taken from him;
he now honored as a god what was once a
dead human being,
and handed on to his dependents secret
rites and initiations.
¹⁶ Then the ungodly custom, grown strong
with time, was kept as a law,
and at the command of monarchs carved
images were worshiped.
¹⁷ When people could not honor
monarchs[a] in their presence, since
they lived at a distance,
they imagined their appearance far away,
and made a visible image of the king
whom they honored,
so that by their zeal they might flatter the
absent one as though present.

¹⁸ Then the ambition of the artisan
impelled
even those who did not know the king to
intensify their worship.
¹⁹ For he, perhaps wishing to please his ruler,
skillfully forced the likeness to take more
beautiful form,
²⁰ and the multitude, attracted by the
charm of his work,
now regarded as an object of worship the
one whom shortly before they had
honored as a human being.
²¹ And this became a hidden trap for
humankind,
because people, in bondage to misfortune
or to royal authority,

bestowed on objects of stone or wood the
name that ought not to be shared.

²² Then it was not enough for them to err
about the knowledge of God,
but though living in great strife due to
ignorance,
they call such great evils peace.
²³ For whether they kill children in their
initiations, or celebrate secret
mysteries,
or hold frenzied revels with strange
customs,
²⁴ they no longer keep either their lives or
their marriages pure,
but they either treacherously kill one
another, or grieve one another by
adultery,
²⁵ and all is a raging riot of blood and
murder, theft and deceit, corruption,
faithlessness, tumult, perjury,
²⁶ confusion over what is good,
forgetfulness of favors,
defiling of souls, sexual perversion,
disorder in marriages, adultery, and
debauchery.
²⁷ For the worship of idols not to be
named
is the beginning and cause and end of
every evil.
²⁸ For their worshipers[b] either rave in
exultation,
or prophesy lies, or live unrighteously, or
readily commit perjury;
²⁹ for because they trust in lifeless idols
they swear wicked oaths and expect to
suffer no harm.
³⁰ But just penalties will overtake them on
two counts:
because they thought wrongly about God
in devoting themselves to idols,

a Gk *them*
b Gk *they*

the idea was not widespread among Greeks, the Jews latched on to it as an explanation for pagan worship, and it appears in several Jewish writings (e.g., Aristeas 135; Artapanus [Eusebius, *Praep. Ev.* 9.18,23,27; Clement of Alexandria, *Strom.* 1.23.154]; *Sib. Or.* 3.110–58). **12:** *Fornication,* the prophets sometimes spoke of idolatry metaphorically as sexual immorality (Jer 3.1–3; Ezek 16.28–41; Hos 2.2–15). **22–31.** The repercussions of idolatry include *strife, murder, adultery,* and *perjury.* **23:** Cf. 11.7; 12.4–5. **25:** Similar crimes are enumerated in Jer 7.9; Hos 4.2. **27:** Cf. 14.12. **29:** *They swear wicked oaths,* for the seriousness with which false oaths were regarded, see Hos 10.4; Sir 23.11; 41.19; 1 Macc 7.18; 1 Esd 1.48.

and because in deceit they swore
    unrighteously through contempt for
    holiness.
[31] For it is not the power of the things by
    which people swear,[a]
but the just penalty for those who sin,
that always pursues the transgression of
    the unrighteous.

15 But you, our God, are kind and true,
    patient, and ruling all things[b] in mercy.
[2] For even if we sin we are yours, knowing
    your power;
but we will not sin, because we know that
    you acknowledge us as yours.
[3] For to know you is complete
    righteousness,
and to know your power is the root of
    immortality.
[4] For neither has the evil intent of human
    art misled us,
nor the fruitless toil of painters,
a figure stained with varied colors,
[5] whose appearance arouses yearning in
    fools,
so that they desire[c] the lifeless form of a
    dead image.
[6] Lovers of evil things and fit for such
    objects of hope[d]
are those who either make or desire or
    worship them.

[7] A potter kneads the soft earth
and laboriously molds each vessel for our
    service,
fashioning out of the same clay
both the vessels that serve clean uses
and those for contrary uses, making all
    alike;
but which shall be the use of each of them
the worker in clay decides.
[8] With misspent toil, these workers form a
    futile god from the same clay—

these mortals who were made of earth a
    short time before
and after a little while go to the earth from
    which all mortals are taken,
when the time comes to return the souls
    that were borrowed.
[9] But the workers are not concerned that
    mortals are destined to die
or that their life is brief,
but they compete with workers in gold and
    silver,
and imitate workers in copper;
and they count it a glorious thing to mold
    counterfeit gods.
[10] Their heart is ashes, their hope is
    cheaper than dirt,
and their lives are of less worth than
    clay,
[11] because they failed to know the one who
    formed them
and inspired them with active souls
and breathed a living spirit into them.
[12] But they considered our existence an idle
    game,
and life a festival held for profit,
for they say one must get money however
    one can, even by base means.
[13] For these persons, more than all others,
    know that they sin
when they make from earthy matter fragile
    vessels and carved images.

[14] But most foolish, and more miserable
    than an infant,
are all the enemies who oppressed your
    people.
[15] For they thought that all their heathen
    idols were gods,

a   Or *of the oaths people swear*
b   Or *ruling the universe*
c   Gk *and he desires*
d   Gk *such hopes*

15.1–6: **The benefits of true worship** include *righteousness* and *immortality.* 1–3: An apostrophe (direct address) to the deity. Allusion to Ex 34.6–9 makes it clear that the author associates authentic worship with the Sinai covenant. 5–6: *Desire,* cf. 4.12; 6.11,13,17,20; 8.2; 13.6; 15.19.

15.7–19: **The fabrication of idols** (cf. 13.10–19). The image of clay and the potter occurs frequently (Isa 41.25; 45.9; 64.8; Jer 18.1–10), but it is usually about God as the potter and humans as clay. The image is turned here into the choice of the potter to turn the clay into base objects (e.g., a sewage pipe) or divine images, thus making the same point as at 13.11–19. 8: That *souls* are *borrowed* was a philosophical conception (cf. 15.16). 12: The image of life as a *game* or *festival* was common in ancient literature, e.g. Isa 22.12–13; Mt 11.16–17; Epictetus,

though these have neither the use of their
    eyes to see with,
nor nostrils with which to draw breath,
nor ears with which to hear,
nor fingers to feel with,
and their feet are of no use for walking.
¹⁶ For a human being made them,
and one whose spirit is borrowed formed
    them;
for none can form gods that are like
    themselves.
¹⁷ People are mortal, and what they make
    with lawless hands is dead;
for they are better than the objects they
    worship,
sinceᵃ they have life, but the idolsᵇ never
    had.

¹⁸ Moreover, they worship even the most
    hateful animals,
which are worse than all others when
    judged by their lack of intelligence;
¹⁹ and even as animals they are not so
    beautiful in appearance that one
    would desire them,
but they have escaped both the praise of
    God and his blessing.

16 Therefore those peopleᶜ were deservedly
    punished through such creatures,
and were tormented by a multitude of
    animals.
² Instead of this punishment you showed
    kindness to your people,
and you prepared quails to eat,
a delicacy to satisfy the desire of
    appetite;
³ in order that those people, when they
    desired food,
might lose the least remnant of appetiteᵈ

because of the odious creatures sent to
    them,
while your people,ᶜ after suffering want a
    short time,
might partake of delicacies.
⁴ For it was necessary that upon those
    oppressors inescapable want should
    come,
while to these others it was merely shown
    how their enemies were being
    tormented.

⁵ For when the terrible rage of wild animals
    came upon your peopleᵉ
and they were being destroyed by the bites
    of writhing serpents,
your wrath did not continue to the end;
⁶ they were troubled for a little while as a
    warning,
and received a symbol of deliverance to
    remind them of your law's command.

⁷ For the one who turned toward it was
    saved, not by the thing that was
    beheld,
but by you, the Savior of all.
⁸ And by this also you convinced our
    enemies
that it is you who deliver from every
    evil.
⁹ For they were killed by the bites of
    locusts and flies,

ᵃ Other ancient authorities read *of which*
ᵇ Gk *but they*
ᶜ Gk *they*
ᵈ Gk *loathed the necessary appetite*
ᵉ Gk *them*

Discourses 2.14.23–29. **14:** *Most foolish* are the Egyptians who *oppressed* the Israelites. **18–19:** Egyptian animal worship was denounced by Romans as well as Jews, e.g., Juvenal, *Satire* 15.1–11; cf. Philo, *Decalogue* 76–80. **19:** *They have escaped . . . blessing*, referring perhaps to Gen 3.14–15 (cf. Wis 11.15; 1.5,10).

    16.1–14: The contrasts, resumed (see 11.1–16). Each of the "elements" of classical antiquity (water, earth, air, and fire) is associated with one of the plagues in this section of the book; see 16.1–4; 16.5–14; 16.15–29; 17.1–18.4.

    16.1–4: The second contrast, continued (see 11.15–16). The plague of frogs (cf. Ex 7.25–8.11) that came up from the Nile as punishment for the Egyptian attempt to kill the Israelite baby boys in the Nile is contrasted with the gift of God to the Israelites in the form of the quails from the sea to provide food in the wilderness (Ex 16.12–13; Num 11.31–34; Wis ignores the context in Num in which the demand for meat is actually criticized). This section also represents the element of water, with references to the river and the sea.

    16.5–14: The third contrast: the plague of insects and the bronze serpent (Ex 8.20–32; 10.1–20; Num 21.4–9). Whereas the Egyptians were plagued by locusts and flies, the Israelites were saved from a plague of poisonous

and no healing was found for them,
because they deserved to be punished by
such things.
¹⁰ But your children were not conquered
even by the fangs of venomous
serpents,
for your mercy came to their help and
healed them.
¹¹ To remind them of your oracles they
were bitten,
and then were quickly delivered,
so that they would not fall into deep
forgetfulness
and become unresponsiveᵃ to your
kindness.
¹² For neither herb nor poultice cured
them,
but it was your word, O Lord, that heals all
people.
¹³ For you have power over life and death;
you lead mortals down to the gates of
Hades and back again.
¹⁴ A person in wickedness kills another,
but cannot bring back the departed spirit,
or set free the imprisoned soul.

¹⁵ To escape from your hand is impossible;
¹⁶ for the ungodly, refusing to know you,
were flogged by the strength of your arm,
pursued by unusual rains and hail and
relentless storms,
and utterly consumed by fire.
¹⁷ For—most incredible of all—in water,
which quenches all things,
the fire had still greater effect,
for the universe defends the righteous.
¹⁸ At one time the flame was restrained,
so that it might not consume the creatures
sent against the ungodly,
but that seeing this they might know
that they were being pursued by the
judgment of God;

¹⁹ and at another time even in the midst of
water it burned more intensely than
fire,
to destroy the crops of the unrighteous land.
²⁰ Instead of these things you gave your
people food of angels,
and without their toil you supplied them
from heaven with bread ready to eat,
providing every pleasure and suited to
every taste.
²¹ For your sustenance manifested your
sweetness toward your children;
and the bread, ministeringᵇ to the desire of
the one who took it,
was changed to suit everyone's liking.
²² Snow and ice withstood fire without
melting,
so that they might know that the crops of
their enemies
were being destroyed by the fire that
blazed in the hail
and flashed in the showers of rain;
²³ whereas the fire,ᶜ in order that the
righteous might be fed,
even forgot its native power.

²⁴ For creation, serving you who made it,
exerts itself to punish the unrighteous,
and in kindness relaxes on behalf of those
who trust in you.
²⁵ Therefore at that time also, changed into
all forms,
it served your all-nourishing bounty,
according to the desire of those who had
need,ᵈ
²⁶ so that your children, whom you loved,
O Lord, might learn

ᵃ Meaning of Gk uncertain
ᵇ Gk *and it, ministering*
ᶜ Gk *this*
ᵈ Or *who made supplication*

serpents through God's "word." **9:** Ex 8.16–32 and 10.12–20 do not speak of deaths from the lice/gnats/flies and
locusts, but Josephus mentions them in connection with this plague (*Ant.* 2.14.3).
    16.15–29: The fourth contrast: the plague of storms (cf. Ex 9.13–35). Because the Egyptians sinned by refus-
ing to recognize God (16.16), their crops were destroyed by fire and hail. The Israelite counterpart of this plague
is the rain of manna from heaven (Ex 16.11–35; Num. 11.6–9). **17:** *Water . . . fire,* referring to the hail and lightning
of Ex 9.23–24. **18:** *So that it might not consume,* cf. 19.21. *The creatures,* the animals and insects of 16.1–14; apparently the author assumes that the plagues occurred at one time. **20:** *Food of angels,* cf. Ps 78.24–25. **21:** *Changed
to suit everyone's liking,* a tradition also reflected in *Tosefta to Yoma* 75a and *Mekilta* on Ex 16.23. **24:** Since it was
fashioned in accordance with wisdom, *creation* inherently assists providence, functioning as an instrument of

that it is not the production of crops that
feeds humankind
but that your word sustains those who
trust in you.
27 For what was not destroyed by fire
was melted when simply warmed by a
fleeting ray of the sun,
28 to make it known that one must rise
before the sun to give you thanks,
and must pray to you at the dawning of the
light;
29 for the hope of an ungrateful person will
melt like wintry frost,
and flow away like waste water.

17 Great are your judgments and hard to
describe;
therefore uninstructed souls have gone
astray.
2 For when lawless people supposed that
they held the holy nation in their
power,
they themselves lay as captives of
darkness and prisoners of long night,
shut in under their roofs, exiles from
eternal providence.
3 For thinking that in their secret sins they
were unobserved
behind a dark curtain of forgetfulness,
they were scattered, terribly[a] alarmed,
and appalled by specters.
4 For not even the inner chamber that held
them protected them from fear,
but terrifying sounds rang out around
them,
and dismal phantoms with gloomy faces
appeared.
5 And no power of fire was able to give light,
nor did the brilliant flames of the stars
avail to illumine that hateful night.

6 Nothing was shining through to them
except a dreadful, self-kindled fire,
and in terror they deemed the things that
they saw
to be worse than that unseen appearance.
7 The delusions of their magic art lay
humbled,
and their boasted wisdom was scornfully
rebuked.
8 For those who promised to drive off the
fears and disorders of a sick soul
were sick themselves with ridiculous
fear.
9 For even if nothing disturbing frightened
them,
yet, scared by the passing of wild animals
and the hissing of snakes
10 they perished in trembling fear,
refusing to look even at the air, though it
nowhere could be avoided.
11 For wickedness is a cowardly thing,
condemned by its own testimony;[b]
distressed by conscience, it has always
exaggerated[c] the difficulties.
12 For fear is nothing but a giving up of the
helps that come from reason;
13 and hope, defeated by this inward
weakness,
prefers ignorance of what causes the
torment.
14 But throughout the night, which was
really powerless
and which came upon them from the
recesses of powerless Hades,

a   Other ancient authorities read *unobserved,*
      they were darkened behind a dark curtain of
      forgetfulness, terribly
b   Meaning of Gk uncertain
c   Other ancient authorities read *anticipated*

both condemnation and blessing; see 8.4–6; 19.18–21 (cf. Josh 10.11–14; Judg 5.20–21). **28**: *Rise before the sun*, cf.
Ps 119.147; Sir 39.5. **29**: *Hope . . . will melt*, cf. 5.14; Job 14.19.

   17.1–18.4: The fifth contrast: the plague of darkness and the pillar of fire (Ex. 10.21–29; 13.21–22; 14.24–15).
Because the Egyptians sinned by taking the Israelites captive, they suffer by being taken captive by the darkness, which contrasts with the pillar of fire that goes with the Israelites day and night (18.3). This plague represents the element of air, since the darkness was caused by a strange atmosphere. **17.2–21**: The description of
the Egyptians' *terror* is reminiscent of the Greco-Roman genre of the "descent into Hades," of which Book 6 of
Virgil's *Aeneid* was a popular example. **3**: *A dark curtain of forgetfulness*, those who thought their sins were hidden are themselves concealed in darkness (cf. 16.11). **7**: See Ex 7.11,22; 8.7,18; 9.11. **11**: *Conscience*, a common topic
in moral literature (e.g., *T. Reuben* 4.3; Philo, *The Worse Attacks the Better* 22–26). **14**: *Powerless Hades*, see 1.14; cf.
Ps 88.10–12; Eccl 9.10; Isa 14.9–11. *Sleep*, the divine penalty includes nightmares (cf. 18.17–19; Job 7.14; Dan 4.5; Sir

they all slept the same sleep,
[15] and now were driven by monstrous specters,
and now were paralyzed by their souls' surrender;
for sudden and unexpected fear overwhelmed them.
[16] And whoever was there fell down,
and thus was kept shut up in a prison not made of iron;
[17] for whether they were farmers or shepherds
or workers who toiled in the wilderness,
they were seized, and endured the inescapable fate;
for with one chain of darkness they all were bound.
[18] Whether there came a whistling wind,
or a melodious sound of birds in wide-spreading branches,
or the rhythm of violently rushing water,
[19] or the harsh crash of rocks hurled down,
or the unseen running of leaping animals,
or the sound of the most savage roaring beasts,
or an echo thrown back from a hollow of the mountains,
it paralyzed them with terror.
[20] For the whole world was illumined with brilliant light,
and went about its work unhindered,
[21] while over those people alone heavy night was spread,
an image of the darkness that was destined to receive them;
but still heavier than darkness were they to themselves.

18

But for your holy ones there was very great light.
Their enemies[a] heard their voices but did not see their forms,
and counted them happy for not having suffered,

[2] and were thankful that your holy ones,[b]
though previously wronged, were doing them no injury;
and they begged their pardon for having been at variance with them.[b]
[3] Therefore you provided a flaming pillar of fire
as a guide for your people's[c] unknown journey,
and a harmless sun for their glorious wandering.
[4] For their enemies[d] deserved to be deprived of light and imprisoned in darkness,
those who had kept your children imprisoned,
through whom the imperishable light of the law was to be given to the world.

[5] When they had resolved to kill the infants of your holy ones,
and one child had been abandoned and rescued,
you in punishment took away a multitude of their children;
and you destroyed them all together by a mighty flood.
[6] That night was made known beforehand to our ancestors,
so that they might rejoice in sure knowledge of the oaths in which they trusted.
[7] The deliverance of the righteous and the destruction of their enemies
were expected by your people.
[8] For by the same means by which you punished our enemies
you called us to yourself and glorified us.
[9] For in secret the holy children of good people offered sacrifices,

a   Gk *They*
b   Meaning of Gk uncertain
c   Gk *their*
d   Gk *those persons*

40.5–7). **18–19:** They experience *terror* even at ordinary sounds (cf. 17.4; Lev 26.36–37; Job 15.20–21). **18.2:** This verse, the meaning of which is unclear, may be referring to Ex 12.31–33. **3:** See Ex 13.21–22; 14.24. **4:** *The law was to be given to the world*, cf. Isa 2.2–3; 42.6; 49.6; 2 Esd 7.20–24; 14.20–22.

18.5–25: The sixth contrast: the plague of the Egyptian firstborn and Israel's rescue (cf. Ex 11.1–12.32). The Egyptians sinned by killing the infants in the Nile. Their punishment is to have their firstborn die by the hand of the angel of death **5:** *One child*, Moses (Ex 1.15–2.10). **6–9:** A poetic description of the first Passover (Ex 12.1–28).

and with one accord agreed to the divine
    law,
so that the saints would share alike the
    same things,
both blessings and dangers;
and already they were singing the praises
    of the ancestors.[a]
[10] But the discordant cry of their enemies
    echoed back,
and their piteous lament for their children
    was spread abroad.
[11] The slave was punished with the same
    penalty as the master,
and the commoner suffered the same loss
    as the king;
[12] and they all together, by the one form[b]
    of death,
had corpses too many to count.
For the living were not sufficient even to
    bury them,
since in one instant their most valued
    children had been destroyed.
[13] For though they had disbelieved
    everything because of their magic arts,
yet, when their firstborn were destroyed,
    they acknowledged your people to be
    God's child.
[14] For while gentle silence enveloped all
    things,
and night in its swift course was now half
    gone,
[15] your all-powerful word leaped from
    heaven, from the royal throne,
into the midst of the land that was
    doomed,
a stern warrior
[16] carrying the sharp sword of your
    authentic command,
and stood and filled all things with death,
and touched heaven while standing on the
    earth.
[17] Then at once apparitions in dreadful
    dreams greatly troubled them,
and unexpected fears assailed them;
[18] and one here and another there, hurled
    down half dead,

made known why they were dying;
[19] for the dreams that disturbed them
    forewarned them of this,
so that they might not perish without
    knowing why they suffered.

[20] The experience of death touched also
    the righteous,
and a plague came upon the multitude in
    the desert,
but the wrath did not long continue.
[21] For a blameless man was quick to act as
    their champion;
he brought forward the shield of his
    ministry,
prayer and propitiation by incense;
he withstood the anger and put an end to
    the disaster,
showing that he was your servant.
[22] He conquered the wrath[c] not by strength
    of body,
not by force of arms,
but by his word he subdued the avenger,
appealing to the oaths and covenants
    given to our ancestors.
[23] For when the dead had already fallen on
    one another in heaps,
he intervened and held back the wrath,
and cut off its way to the living.
[24] For on his long robe the whole world
    was depicted,
and the glories of the ancestors were
    engraved on the four rows of
    stones,
and your majesty was on the diadem upon
    his head.
[25] To these the destroyer yielded, these he[d]
    feared;
for merely to test the wrath was enough.

---

a Other ancient authorities read *dangers, the*
    ancestors already leading the songs of praise
b Gk *name*
c Cn: Gk *multitude*
d Other ancient authorities read *they*

9: *Already they were singing*, cf. 2 Chr 30.21. **13**: *God's child*, cf. 5.5; Ex 4.22–23; Jer 31.9; Hos 11.1. **15**: *A stern warrior*,
cf. 5.17–20. **17–19**: Cf. 17.14n. **20–25**: *A blameless man*, Aaron makes atonement for the Israelites' rebellion against
God by burning *incense*, ending *a plague* that killed 14,700 people (Num 16.41–50). **22**: *The avenger*, cf. Ps 99.8;
1 Thess 4.6. **24**: See Ex 28.15–38. On the symbolism of the high priest's vestments, see Josephus, *Ant.* 3.7.7; Philo,
Moses 2.117–26 **25**: *The destroyer*, cf. 1 Cor 10:10.

19 But the ungodly were assailed to the
end by pitiless anger,
for God[a] knew in advance even their future
actions:
[2] how, though they themselves had
permitted[b] your people to depart
and hastily sent them out,
they would change their minds and pursue
them.
[3] For while they were still engaged in
mourning,
and were lamenting at the graves of their
dead,
they reached another foolish decision,
and pursued as fugitives those whom they
had begged and compelled to leave.
[4] For the fate they deserved drew them on
to this end,
and made them forget what had happened,
in order that they might fill up the
punishment that their torments still
lacked,
[5] and that your people might experience[c]
an incredible journey,
but they themselves might meet a strange
death.

[6] For the whole creation in its nature was
fashioned anew,
complying with your commands,
so that your children[d] might be kept
unharmed.
[7] The cloud was seen overshadowing the
camp,
and dry land emerging where water had
stood before,
an unhindered way out of the Red Sea,
and a grassy plain out of the raging
waves,
[8] where those protected by your hand
passed through as one nation,
after gazing on marvelous wonders.
[9] For they ranged like horses,
and leaped like lambs,
praising you, O Lord, who delivered them.
[10] For they still recalled the events of their
sojourn,

how instead of producing animals the
earth brought forth gnats,
and instead of fish the river spewed out
vast numbers of frogs.
[11] Afterward they saw also a new kind[e] of
birds,
when desire led them to ask for luxurious
food;
[12] for, to give them relief, quails came up
from the sea.

[13] The punishments did not come upon the
sinners
without prior signs in the violence of
thunder,
for they justly suffered because of their
wicked acts;
for they practiced a more bitter hatred of
strangers.
[14] Others had refused to receive strangers
when they came to them,
but these made slaves of guests who were
their benefactors.
[15] And not only so—but, while punishment
of some sort will come upon the
former
for having received strangers with
hostility,
[16] the latter, having first received them
with festal celebrations,
afterward afflicted with terrible sufferings
those who had already shared the same
rights.
[17] They were stricken also with loss of sight—
just as were those at the door of the
righteous man—
when, surrounded by yawning darkness,
all of them tried to find the way through
their own doors.

a   Gk *he*
b   Other ancient authorities read *had changed their
    minds to permit*
c   Other ancient authorities read *accomplish*
d   Or *servants*
e   Or *production*

19.1–21: The seventh contrast: death and salvation at the Red Sea (Ex 14.1–31). 1: *The ungodly,* the Egyptians.
4: *Made them forget,* cf. 4.1; 17.3. *Fill up the punishment,* cf. Dan 8.23; 2 Macc 6.14. 6: See 19.18–21. 7: *Cloud,* Ex
13.21–22. 10: Ex 8.1–19. 11–12: See 16.1–4; cf. Num 11.31–32. 14: *Others,* those of Sodom (Gen 19.1–11). *These,* the
Egyptians. *Guests,* see Gen 45.16–20. *Benefactors,* referring to Joseph's service to Egypt. 17: *Righteous man,* Lot;

18 For the elements changed[a] places with
  one another,
as on a harp the notes vary the nature of
  the rhythm,
while each note remains the same.[b]
This may be clearly inferred from the sight
  of what took place.
19 For land animals were transformed into
  water creatures,
and creatures that swim moved over to the
  land.
20 Fire even in water retained its normal
  power,
and water forgot its fire-quenching
  nature.

21 Flames, on the contrary, failed to
  consume
the flesh of perishable creatures that
  walked among them,
nor did they melt[c] the crystalline, quick-
  melting kind of heavenly food.

22 For in everything, O Lord, you have
  exalted and glorified your people,
and you have not neglected to help them
  at all times and in all places.

a   Gk *changing*
b   Meaning of Gk uncertain
c   Cn: Gk *nor could be melted*

cf. Gen 19.11; Ex 14.20. **18–21:** In the plagues and at the Red Sea nature *changed* its customary actions so as to bring about God's purpose (16.24; 19.6). That the material elements could be transformed in various ways was an assumption of ancient physics, e.g., Cicero, *The Nature of the Gods* 3.39.92.

  19.22: A final doxology or praise of God concludes the book.

ECCLESIASTICUS, OR THE WISDOM OF JESUS, SON OF SIRACH

NAME

In most Greek manuscripts the title given to this book is "The Wisdom of Jesus the Son of Sirach." Latin manuscripts refer to it as "The Book of Jesus the Son of Sirach." In the Latin tradition it is also known as "Ecclesiasticus," which means "church book" and was probably intended as a statement about the book's acceptance in the Christian canon of scripture. If the Hebrew original had a title, it was something like "The Wisdom of Yeshua the Son of Sira." Today some scholars refer to the book as "Sirach" and the original author as Ben Sira. Others use the title "Sirach" for the Greek version, "Ecclesiasticus" for the Latin text, and "Ben Sira" for the Hebrew original and/or its author.

CANONICAL STATUS

The book of Sirach was never part of the Hebrew canon of scripture, even though it was composed in Hebrew and was often quoted in Hebrew by later Jewish writers. It may have been considered too recent in its composition (early second century BCE) in comparison with the other canonical books. The Greek translation made by Ben Sira's grandson, however, was transmitted as part of the larger collection of Jewish writings in Greek known as the Septuagint (LXX). The Christian churches generally followed the wider Greek canon of scripture, and for fifteen centuries most Christians regarded Sirach as part of their Old Testament. When Martin Luther and other early Reformers sought to limit the Protestant Old Testament canon to the Jewish Hebrew canon, Sirach and other "deuterocanonical" books were relegated to the "Apocrypha" (see p. 5). Roman Catholics and Orthodox Christians regard Sirach as canonical and place it among the other Old Testament books. Some Protestant Bibles today have revived the practice of the early Reformers and place it as part of the separate section between the Old and the New Testaments that is known as the Apocrypha.

AUTHOR AND HISTORICAL CONTEXT

Near the end of the Greek version of the book, the original author identifies himself as "Jesus son of Eleazar son of Sirach" (50.27). His Hebrew name would have been "Yeshua ben Eleazar ben Sira." He conducted a school ("a house of instruction," 51.23) for prospective scribes and sages, perhaps in association with the Jerusalem Temple complex. His book is a summary or compendium of his teachings, written down in Hebrew ca. 180 BCE. His grandson produced the Greek version in Egypt ca. 117 BCE.

If Ben Sira wrote his book ca. 180 BCE, he would have lived through the transition in control of Judea from the Ptolemies in Egypt to the Seleucids in Syria, and the political turmoil associated with that transition, which took place around 200 BCE. He may have died before the conflicts about the Jewish high priesthood beginning ca. 175 BCE, when the Seleucid ruler Antiochus IV Epiphanes and his Jewish collaborators attempted to eradicate the distinctive features of Jewish life (the Jerusalem Temple and the Torah) and sparked the Maccabean revolt (see Daniel and 1 and 2 Maccabees). Ben Sira was a traditional and conservative person by nature, and a strong supporter of the Temple and the Jewish high priesthood. Nevertheless, it is difficult to find clear references in his book to contemporary historical events (but perhaps 35.21–26 and 36.1–22 constitute exceptions) and figures (except for Simon the high priest in 50.1–24). For Ben Sira's autobiographical notices scattered throughout the book, see 24.30–34; 33.16–19; 34.9–13; 39.12–13; 50.27; and 51.13–30.

Ben Sira was a man of his place and time, that is, Palestine in the early second century BCE. His opinions on many social issues, especially on women and slaves, may strike modern readers as benighted, even outrageous. Ben Sira and his contemporaries perceived themselves as embedded in various groups (family, clan, village, city, etc.). They judged their own importance by what others thought of them, in what anthropologists call an honor-shame society. His social world was hierarchical, with everyone having a relatively fixed place and little opportunity for upward social mobility. People then considered wives to be naturally subordinate to their husbands, and children and slaves under the ultimate control of the male head of the household.

LITERARY HISTORY

The book of Sirach is best known through the grandson's Greek translation, which provides the basis for the present English version. As the Greek version became canonical for Christians, the Hebrew form became increasingly marginal for Jews. Large parts of the Hebrew text, however, have been found among the Dead Sea Scrolls (at Qumran and Masada) and in the Genizah (storehouse) of a medieval Jewish synagogue in Cairo. Nearly two-thirds of the Hebrew version has been retrieved in one form or another. Even in antiquity the Hebrew and Greek textual traditions developed short and long editions or recensions. The additional sayings in the longer recension appear in small type at the foot of the pages in this translation; this explains the "missing numbers" for verses throughout the main text of the book. Moreover, it appears that all the Greek manuscripts contained a textual displacement by which Sir 30.25–33.13a and 33.13b–36.16a changed places; this explains discrepancies in references between older and more recent translations and scholarly studies.

Sirach remains a valuable resource for understanding Judaism in the Second Temple period and the world in which Jesus and the early Christians lived. It was translated into various ancient languages and received much attention from patristic and medieval writers. It was treasured for its practical advice on many different topics and its emphasis on love of learning and the desire for God.

STRUCTURE AND CONTENTS

As with other ancient wisdom books, Sirach is an anthology or collection of short units on various topics. In many parts it is difficult to discover a logical progression of thought or to discern the principles of arrangement. However, a series of poems on seeking and finding wisdom (1.1–10; 4.11–19; 6.18–37; 14.20–15.10; 24.1–33; 38.24–39.11) seem to divide the book into something like chapters. The book reaches its climax with the praise of God's glory manifest in creation (42.15–43.33) and in the heroes of faith in ancient Israel's history (44.1–50.24).

In conveying his wisdom teachings, Ben Sira used a wide array of literary forms: analogies or comparisons (*meshalim*), maxims or proverbs, beatitudes and woes, numerical sayings, questions and answers, refrains and repetitions, "there is" sayings, "better than" sayings, prohibitions or admonitions ("Do not . . ."), instructions, prayers of petition, hymns, aretalogy (self-praise), autobiographical accounts, and biblical paraphrases. Many of these literary devices lend themselves to easy memorization, thus supplying Ben Sira's students and readers with a treasury of wisdom sayings by which to interpret the world around them and to conduct themselves wisely and righteously.

INTERPRETATION

Sirach is the largest wisdom book that we have from antiquity. It provides a window into life in ancient Israel at a pivotal point in Jewish history, illustrating how and what Jewish wisdom teachers taught, and offering wise teachings that have inspired and challenged readers for more than two millennia. Ben Sira gives his opinions on topics such as creation, death, fear of the Lord, friendship, happiness, and honor and shame. While conservative by nature, Ben Sira was an innovator in joining the wisdom traditions of the ancient Near East and the distinctive traditions of ancient Israel (cf. 24.23). The students at his school were expected to become equally adept at practical wisdom and biblical learning (39.1–5).

Ben Sira's students were mainly well-to-do young men preparing for careers as teachers and counselors in the public arena (39.6–11). He insisted that they view true wisdom as a gift from God and that they pray regularly for wisdom. He was an enthusiastic supporter of the Jerusalem Temple and high priesthood. As a teacher of young men, he issued warnings about the troubles that the wrong kinds of women might bring upon them. At several points, however, his caution borders on misogyny. With regard to human suffering, Ben Sira accepts the traditional understanding of theodicy, or divine justice, according to which wise and righteous persons prosper, while foolish and wicked persons suffer. He generally ignores the problem of innocent suffering raised by the book of Job, and at some points he may have been responding to the skepticism displayed by the book of Ecclesiastes. He takes a tentative stab at the problem of evil with his doctrine of the "pairs" (33.7–15), without proposing a full-fledged dualism. His poems about God's action in creation and in Israel's history urge his readers to seek and find the glory of God in all things (42.15–50.24). He viewed immortality mainly in terms of the good name or reputation that one leaves behind (38.16–23; 41.1–13).

GUIDE TO READING

One can read Sirach straight through from beginning to end, just as the book has come down to us. However, many find it difficult to read an anthology that way. Moreover, the various units in the book demand meditation, personal appropriation, and application. The reflections on wisdom and fear of the Lord in chapters 1 and 2 provide the theological framework for all that follows. The poem about wisdom personified and Ben Sira's identification of her with the covenant and the Torah in chapter 24 is the key to his integration of secular wisdom and biblical revelation. The other wisdom poems (4.11–19; 6.18–37; 14.20–15.10; 38.34–39.11) are also important for catching the flavor of Ben Sira's project. The description of Israel's heroes of faith as manifestations of God's glory in chapters 44–50 opens up fresh perspectives on the Bible as a whole. For the rest of the book, tracking specific themes through the various parts can be quite fruitful. For example, one might pursue several or all of the following ten topics: creation (16.24–17.24; 18.1–14; 33.7–15; 39.12–35; 42.15–43.33), death (11.26–28; 22.11–12; 38.16–23; 41.1–13), friendship (6.5–17; 9.10–16; 19.13–17; 22.19–26; 27.16–21; 36.23–37.15), happiness (25.1–11; 30.14–25; 40.1–30), honor and shame (4.20–6.4; 10.19–11.6; 41.14–42.8), money matters (3.30–4.10; 11.7–28; 13.1–14.19; 29.1–28; 31.1–11), sin (7.1–17; 15.11–20; 16.1–17.32; 18.30–19.3; 21.1–10; 22.27–23.27; 26.28–28.7), social justice (4.1–10; 34.21–27; 35.14–26), speech (5.9–15; 18.15–29; 19.4–17; 20.1–31; 23.7–15; 27.4–7; 27.11–15; 28.8–26), and women (9.1–9; 23.22–27; 25.13–26.27; 36.26–31; 42.9–14).

Daniel J. Harrington

THE PROLOGUE

Many great teachings have been given to us through the Law and the Prophets and the others[a] that followed them, and for these we should praise Israel for instruction and wisdom. Now, those who read the scriptures must not only themselves understand them, but must also as lovers of learning be able through the spoken and written word to help the outsiders. So my grandfather Jesus, who had devoted himself especially to the reading of the Law and the Prophets and the other books of our ancestors, and had acquired considerable proficiency in them, was himself also led to write something pertaining to instruction and wisdom, so that by becoming familiar also with his book[b] those who love learning might make even greater progress in living according to the law.

You are invited therefore to read it with goodwill and attention, and to be indulgent in cases where, despite our diligent labor in translating, we may seem to have rendered some phrases imperfectly. For what was originally expressed in Hebrew does not have exactly the same sense when translated into another language. Not only this book, but even the Law itself, the Prophecies, and the rest of the books differ not a little when read in the original.

When I came to Egypt in the thirty-eighth year of the reign of Euergetes and stayed for some time, I found opportunity for no little instruction.[c] It seemed highly necessary that

[a] Or *other books*
[b] Gk *with these things*
[c] Other ancient authorities read *I found a copy affording no little instruction*

Prologue: Written in an elevated Greek style, the prologue to the Greek version of the book provides in three long sentences basic information about the original author and his purposes, the problems facing the translator, and the circumstances of the translation. It contains the earliest references to the threefold division of the Hebrew scriptures: *the Law and the Prophets and the other books* (cf. Lk 24.44). *Jesus* is the Greek form of the original author's Hebrew name, which was probably "Yeshua" or some other form of Joshua (50.27). In contrast to this translator, who admits that his book, as well as *the Law, the Prophecies, and the rest,* differ *not a little* from the *Hebrew* original, other early Jewish and Christian writers defended the accuracy of the Septuagint (LXX) in legends that have miraculous elements (Philo, *Life of Moses* 2.25–44). Ben Sira's grandson came to Egypt (most likely Alexandria) in *the thirty-eighth year* of the reign of Ptolemy VII Psychon *Euergetes* II, that is, in 132 BCE. He probably completed his work shortly after Ptolemy VII's death in 117 BCE. He intended his Greek translation especially for his fellow Jews *living abroad,* and in particular for the large Jewish community in Egypt. Thus he hoped that Diaspora Jews might profit from reading his grandfather's work in Greek just as Jews in Palestine had profited from the Hebrew original.

I should myself devote some diligence and labor to the translation of this book. During that time I have applied my skill day and night to complete and publish the book for those living abroad who wished to gain learning and are disposed to live according to the law.

1 All wisdom is from the Lord,
and with him it remains forever.
² The sand of the sea, the drops of rain,
and the days of eternity—who can
count them?
³ The height of heaven, the breadth of the
earth,
the abyss, and wisdom[a]—who can
search them out?
⁴ Wisdom was created before all other things,
and prudent understanding from
eternity.[b]
⁶ The root of wisdom—to whom has it
been revealed?
Her subtleties—who knows them?[c]
⁸ There is but one who is wise, greatly to be
feared,
seated upon his throne—the Lord.
⁹ It is he who created her;
he saw her and took her measure;
he poured her out upon all his works,
¹⁰ upon all the living according to his gift;
he lavished her upon those who love him.[d]

¹¹ The fear of the Lord is glory and exultation,
and gladness and a crown of rejoicing.
¹² The fear of the Lord delights the heart,
and gives gladness and joy and long life.[e]
¹³ Those who fear the Lord will have a
happy end;
on the day of their death they will be
blessed.

¹⁴ To fear the Lord is the beginning of wisdom;
she is created with the faithful in the
womb.
¹⁵ She made[f] among human beings an
eternal foundation,
and among their descendants she will
abide faithfully.
¹⁶ To fear the Lord is fullness of wisdom;
she inebriates mortals with her fruits;
¹⁷ she fills their[g] whole house with
desirable goods,
and their[g] storehouses with her produce.
¹⁸ The fear of the Lord is the crown of
wisdom,
making peace and perfect health to
flourish.[h]
¹⁹ She rained down knowledge and
discerning comprehension,
and she heightened the glory of those
who held her fast.

a   Other ancient authorities read *the depth of the abyss*
b   Other ancient authorities add as verse 5, *The source of wisdom is God's word in the highest heaven, and her ways are the eternal commandments.*
c   Other ancient authorities add as verse 7, *The knowledge of wisdom—to whom was it manifested? And her abundant experience—who has understood it?*
d   Other ancient authorities add *Love of the Lord is glorious wisdom; to those to whom he appears he apportions her, that they may see him.*
e   Other ancient authorities add *The fear of the Lord is a gift from the Lord; also for love he makes firm paths.*
f   Gk *made as a nest*
g   Other ancient authorities read *her*
h   Other ancient authorities add *Both are gifts of God for peace; glory opens out for those who love him. He saw her and took her measure.*

1.1-10: Wisdom's origin. Wisdom, described as a feminine figure, was created by God and is given to humans as a gift. **1:** *From the Lord,* created by and residing with God (Prov 8.22–23; Wis 7.25–26). **2-3:** The rhetorical questions (cf. 1.6) indicate that true wisdom is beyond mere human understanding (Job 38–39). **4:** *Created before all other things,* 24.3–7; Prov 8.22–26. **6-10:** God, the truly wise one, *created* wisdom and bestows *her* on those who *love him* (Job 28.23–27).

1.11-30: Wisdom and fear of the Lord. A programmatic statement of the proper response to God's gift of wisdom: *fear of the Lord*—the gratitude, respect, and conduct owed to God. **12:** *Long life,* v. 20; cf. Prov 3.16. In wisdom literature generally, the good are rewarded with a long, healthy, prosperous life. **13:** *Happy end,* immortality for Ben Sira consists primarily in the good name or reputation that one leaves behind (41.11–13). **14:** *The beginning of wisdom,* cf. Prov 1.7; 9.10; Ps 111.10. *In the womb,* a prophetic motif (49.7; Jer 1.5; Isa 44.2,24; 49.1,5; see also Ps 139.13). **15:** *Abide faithfully,* for wisdom's dwelling place, cf. 24.10–12; Prov 8.31; Wis 1.7. **20:** *Root,* wis-

²⁰ To fear the Lord is the root of wisdom,
and her branches are long life.ᵃ

²² Unjust anger cannot be justified,
for anger tips the scale to one's ruin.
²³ Those who are patient stay calm until
the right moment,
and then cheerfulness comes back to
them.
²⁴ They hold back their words until the
right moment;
then the lips of many tell of their good
sense.

²⁵ In the treasuries of wisdom are wise
sayings,
but godliness is an abomination to a
sinner.
²⁶ If you desire wisdom, keep the
commandments,
and the Lord will lavish her upon you.
²⁷ For the fear of the Lord is wisdom and
discipline,
fidelity and humility are his delight.

²⁸ Do not disobey the fear of the Lord;
do not approach him with a divided
mind.
²⁹ Do not be a hypocrite before others,
and keep watch over your lips.
³⁰ Do not exalt yourself, or you may fall
and bring dishonor upon yourself.
The Lord will reveal your secrets
and overthrow you before the whole
congregation,
because you did not come in the fear of
the Lord,
and your heart was full of deceit.

2 My child, when you come to serve the Lord,
prepare yourself for testing.ᵇ
² Set your heart right and be steadfast,
and do not be impetuous in time of
calamity.
³ Cling to him and do not depart,
so that your last days may be
prosperous.
⁴ Accept whatever befalls you,
and in times of humiliation be patient.
⁵ For gold is tested in the fire,
and those found acceptable, in the
furnace of humiliation.ᶜ
⁶ Trust in him, and he will help you;
make your ways straight, and hope in
him.

⁷ You who fear the Lord, wait for his mercy;
do not stray, or else you may fall.
⁸ You who fear the Lord, trust in him,
and your reward will not be lost.
⁹ You who fear the Lord, hope for good
things,
for lasting joy and mercy.ᵈ
¹⁰ Consider the generations of old and see:
has anyone trusted in the Lord and
been disappointed?
Or has anyone persevered in the fear of the
Lordᵉ and been forsaken?

ᵃ Other ancient authorities add as verse 21, *The fear
of the Lord drives away sins; and where it abides, it
will turn away all anger.*
ᵇ Or *trials*
ᶜ Other ancient authorities add *in sickness and
poverty put your trust in him*
ᵈ Other ancient authorities add *For his reward is an
everlasting gift with joy.*
ᵉ Gk *of him*

dom is the tree that gives life (24.13–17; Prov 3.18; Gen 3.22). **22–24:** For the dangers of yielding to *unjust anger,*
cf. 27.30–28.11; Prov 12.16; 29.22. **25–27:** *The treasuries of wisdom* include proverbs and other sayings, while the
commandments are laws in the Torah (cf. 24.23). Sirach is the first wisdom book to relate Torah and wisdom in
this way; cf. Bar 4.1. **28:** *Divided mind,* 2.12. **29:** *Hypocrite,* 32.15; 33.2. **30:** Honor and *dishonor* are major themes in
Sirach (3.2–11; 4.21; 7.7; 10.19–11.6; 41.17–42.8).
   2.1–18: Fear of the Lord. What it means to remain faithful to God and to the pursuit of wisdom. **1–6:** Those
who serve God must expect testing, remain patient, and accept suffering as a discipline. **1:** *My child,* literally
"my son," a common way for Ben Sira the teacher to address a pupil (3.17; 4.1; 6.8; 7.3; etc.; cf. Prov 1.8,10, etc.).
Testing reveals one's true character (4.17; 6.20–21; 44.20; Prov 3.11–12). **5.** *Tested in the fire,* cf. Prov 17.3; 27.21;
Wis 3.6. **7–9:** Those who *fear the Lord* must *wait, trust,* and *hope* during this life. Note another threefold repeti-
tion of *fear of the Lord* in 2.15–17. **10–11:** The three questions (cf. Pss 22.4–5; 37.25) expect negative responses,
though the case of Job renders dubious such easy answers. **11:** *The Lord is compassionate and merciful,* Ex 34.6–7;

Or has anyone called upon him and
  been neglected?
¹¹ For the Lord is compassionate and
  merciful;
  he forgives sins and saves in time of
    distress.

¹² Woe to timid hearts and to slack hands,
  and to the sinner who walks a double
    path!
¹³ Woe to the fainthearted who have no trust!
  Therefore they will have no shelter.
¹⁴ Woe to you who have lost your nerve!
  What will you do when the Lord's
    reckoning comes?

¹⁵ Those who fear the Lord do not disobey
  his words,
  and those who love him keep his ways.
¹⁶ Those who fear the Lord seek to please
  him,
  and those who love him are filled with
    his law.
¹⁷ Those who fear the Lord prepare their
  hearts,
  and humble themselves before him.
¹⁸ Let us fall into the hands of the Lord,
  but not into the hands of mortals;
for equal to his majesty is his mercy,
  and equal to his name are his works.ᵃ

3 Listen to me your father, O children;
  act accordingly, that you may be kept in
    safety.
² For the Lord honors a father above his
  children,
  and he confirms a mother's right over
    her children.

³ Those who honor their father atone for
  sins,
⁴ and those who respect their mother
  are like those who lay up treasure.
⁵ Those who honor their father will have
  joy in their own children,
  and when they pray they will be heard.
⁶ Those who respect their father will have
  long life,
  and those who honorᵇ their mother
  obey the Lord;
⁷ they will serve their parents as their
  masters.ᶜ
⁸ Honor your father by word and deed,
  that his blessing may come upon you.
⁹ For a father's blessing strengthens the
  houses of the children,
  but a mother's curse uproots their
    foundations.
¹⁰ Do not glorify yourself by dishonoring
  your father,
  for your father's dishonor is no glory
    to you.
¹¹ The glory of one's father is one's own
  glory,
  and it is a disgrace for children not to
    respect their mother.

¹² My child, help your father in his old age,
  and do not grieve him as long as he lives;
¹³ even if his mind fails, be patient with him;
  because you have all your faculties do
    not despise him.

ᵃ Syr: Gk lacks this line
ᵇ Heb: Other ancient authorities read *comfort*
ᶜ In other ancient authorities this line is preceded by
   Those who fear the Lord honor their father,

Pss 103.8–9; 145.8; Jon 4.2. For God as one who *forgives sins* and saves, cf. Pss 37.39–40; 103.3; 145.18–19. **12–14:** The three *woes* (41.8) are warnings or threats to the conflicted or *fainthearted*. The *Lord's reckoning* refers to the consequences during this life rather than to the last judgment. **15–17:** *Those who fear the Lord* observe God's commandments and approach God with proper reverence (cf. 2.7–9). **18:** *Fall into the hands of the Lord,* 2 Sam 24.14; 1 Chr 21.13. The *name* of the Lord here is "the merciful one"; see 2.11n.; 50.19.

3.1–16: Parents and children. Wisdom and fear of the Lord should extend to family relationships (Ex 20.12; Deut 5.16); those addressed (*O children*) are adults. **1–2:** The social order decreed by God places parents above their children. For the *father* as head of the family, see 7.23–26; 22.3–5; 26.1–27. Respect for the *mother* is also stressed here (cf. 3.16; Prov 1.8; 6.20; etc.). **3–7:** *Those who honor* their parents can expect spiritual and material benefits, including atonement for their sins (3.14) and a long life (Deut 5.16).

8–11: Honoring parents brings *honor* to the child, while *dishonoring* them brings shame (1.30; 4.21; 7.7; 10.19–11.6; 41.17–42.8). **12–16:** Caring for elderly parents will be rewarded by God and will provide atonement for sins (3.3), while dishonoring parents is the equivalent of blasphemy (3.1–2).

¹⁴ For kindness to a father will not be
forgotten,
and will be credited to you against your
sins;
¹⁵ in the day of your distress it will be
remembered in your favor;
like frost in fair weather, your sins will
melt away.
¹⁶ Whoever forsakes a father is like a
blasphemer,
and whoever angers a mother is cursed
by the Lord.

¹⁷ My child, perform your tasks with
humility;ᵃ
then you will be loved by those whom
God accepts.
¹⁸ The greater you are, the more you must
humble yourself;
so you will find favor in the sight of the
Lord.ᵇ
²⁰ For great is the might of the Lord;
but by the humble he is glorified.
²¹ Neither seek what is too difficult for you,
nor investigate what is beyond your
power.
²² Reflect upon what you have been
commanded,
for what is hidden is not your concern.
²³ Do not meddle in matters that are
beyond you,
for more than you can understand has
been shown you.
²⁴ For their conceit has led many astray,
and wrong opinion has impaired their
judgment.

²⁵ Without eyes there is no light;
without knowledge there is no
wisdom.ᶜ
²⁶ A stubborn mind will fare badly at the
end,
and whoever loves danger will perish in it.

²⁷ A stubborn mind will be burdened by
troubles,
and the sinner adds sin to sins.
²⁸ When calamity befalls the proud, there
is no healing,
for an evil plant has taken root in him.
²⁹ The mind of the intelligent appreciates
proverbs,
and an attentive ear is the desire of the
wise.

³⁰ As water extinguishes a blazing fire,
so almsgiving atones for sin.
³¹ Those who repay favors give thought to
the future;
when they fall they will find support.

4 My child, do not cheat the poor of their
living,
and do not keep needy eyes waiting.
² Do not grieve the hungry,
or anger one in need.
³ Do not add to the troubles of the desperate,
or delay giving to the needy.
⁴ Do not reject a suppliant in distress,
or turn your face away from the poor.
⁵ Do not avert your eye from the needy,
and give no one reason to curse you;
⁶ for if in bitterness of soul some should
curse you,
their Creator will hear their prayer.

⁷ Endear yourself to the congregation;
bow your head low to the great.
⁸ Give a hearing to the poor,
and return their greeting politely.
⁹ Rescue the oppressed from the oppressor;
and do not be hesitant in giving a verdict.

ᵃ Heb: Gk *meekness*
ᵇ Other ancient authorities add as verse 19, *Many are
lofty and renowned, but to the humble he reveals
his secrets.*
ᶜ Heb: Other ancient authorities lack verse 25

3.17–29: **Humility before God.** Humility brings favor from God, while intellectual pride is to be avoided.
17–20: Humility (or meekness) glorifies God and wins favor from those *loved* by God (7.16–17; 10.28). **21–29:**
What is too difficult may refer to Greek philosophical and Jewish apocalyptic speculations. True wisdom is found
in *what you have been commanded* (in the Torah) and in *proverbs* (the teachings of the sages)—the two major
sources of wisdom in Ben Sira's school and his book.
3.30–4.10: **Almsgiving.** The instructions assume that the sage will have sufficient wealth to act as a benefactor (cf. Job 29). **30:** *Atones for sin,* cf. 3.4,14. **4.1–5:** Ten things not to do when giving alms. The advice acknowledges and attempts to address the social and power differences that are present in acts of charity. **6:** *Curse,* cf.

¹⁰ Be a father to orphans,
and be like a husband to their mother;
you will then be like a son of the Most
High,
and he will love you more than does
your mother.

¹¹ Wisdom teachesᵃ her children
and gives help to those who seek her.
¹² Whoever loves her loves life,
and those who seek her from early
morning are filled with joy.
¹³ Whoever holds her fast inherits glory,
and the Lord blesses the place sheᵇ
enters.
¹⁴ Those who serve her minister to the
Holy One;
the Lord loves those who love her.
¹⁵ Those who obey her will judge the
nations,
and all who listen to her will live secure.
¹⁶ If they remain faithful, they will inherit
her;
their descendants will also obtain her.
¹⁷ For at first she will walk with them on
tortuous paths;
she will bring fear and dread upon
them,
and will torment them by her discipline
until she trusts them,ᶜ
and she will test them with her
ordinances.
¹⁸ Then she will come straight back to them
again and gladden them,
and will reveal her secrets to them.
¹⁹ If they go astray she will forsake them,
and hand them over to their ruin.

²⁰ Watch for the opportune time, and
beware of evil,
and do not be ashamed to be yourself.

²¹ For there is a shame that leads to sin,
and there is a shame that is glory and
favor.
²² Do not show partiality, to your own harm,
or deference, to your downfall.
²³ Do not refrain from speaking at the
proper moment,ᵈ
and do not hide your wisdom.ᵉ
²⁴ For wisdom becomes known through
speech,
and education through the words of the
tongue.
²⁵ Never speak against the truth,
but be ashamed of your ignorance.
²⁶ Do not be ashamed to confess your sins,
and do not try to stop the current of a
river.
²⁷ Do not subject yourself to a fool,
or show partiality to a ruler.
²⁸ Fight to the death for truth,
and the Lord God will fight for you.

²⁹ Do not be reckless in your speech,
or sluggish and remiss in your deeds.
³⁰ Do not be like a lion in your home,
or suspicious of your servants.
³¹ Do not let your hand be stretched out to
receive
and closed when it is time to give.

5 Do not rely on your wealth,
or say, "I have enough."
² Do not follow your inclination and strength
in pursuing the desires of your heart.

ᵃ Heb Syr: Gk *exalts*
ᵇ Or *he*
ᶜ Or *until they remain faithful in their heart*
ᵈ Heb: Gk *at a time of salvation*
ᵉ So some Gk Mss and Heb Syr Lat: Other Gk Mss
lack *and do not hide your wisdom*

Deut 15.9. **10:** *Orphans,* cf. Ex 22.21–23; for God as father of orphans, see Ps 68.5.
4.11–19. Wisdom's benefits. While the search for wisdom brings many benefits, it also involves testing and discipline. As often, wisdom is personified as a woman (cf. Prov 1.20–33; 8; Sir 24). **12:** Prov 8.35. **14:** Serving wisdom is the same as serving *the Holy One.* **15:** The expressions *judge the nations* and *live secure* probably refer to earthly existence rather than life after death. **17–19:** Wisdom as harsh disciplinarian but also giver of joy and security are key themes in Prov 1–9. **17:** *Discipline,* cf. 2.1. **18:** *Secrets,* 39.7; Dan 2.22.
4.20–31: The need for self-restraint and truthfulness. 20–21: For proper and improper *shame,* see 41.17–42.8. **20–31:** The admonitions (*Do not . . .*) deal mainly with speech, especially truthfulness in speech, a frequent topic in wisdom literature (e.g., Prov 13.3; 25.11). **26:** *Stop the current of a river,* that is, trying to conceal one's sins from God is impossible. **30:** *Lion,* a frequent symbol of overpowering force (13.19; 21.2; 25.16; 27.10,28; 28.23; 47.3).

³ Do not say, "Who can have power over
    me?"
  for the Lord will surely punish you.

⁴ Do not say, "I sinned, yet what has
    happened to me?"
  for the Lord is slow to anger.
⁵ Do not be so confident of forgivenessᵃ
    that you add sin to sin.
⁶ Do not say, "His mercy is great,
  he will forgiveᵇ the multitude of my
    sins,"
for both mercy and wrath are with him,
  and his anger will rest on sinners.
⁷ Do not delay to turn back to the Lord,
  and do not postpone it from day to day;
for suddenly the wrath of the Lord will
    come upon you,
  and at the time of punishment you will
    perish.
⁸ Do not depend on dishonest wealth,
  for it will not benefit you on the day of
    calamity.

⁹ Do not winnow in every wind,
  or follow every path.ᶜ
¹⁰ Stand firm for what you know,
  and let your speech be consistent.
¹¹ Be quick to hear,
  but deliberate in answering.
¹² If you know what to say, answer your
    neighbor;
  but if not, put your hand over your
    mouth.

¹³ Honor and dishonor come from
    speaking,
  and the tongue of mortals may be their
    downfall.

¹⁴ Do not be called double-tonguedᵈ
    and do not lay traps with your
      tongue;
  for shame comes to the thief,
    and severe condemnation to the
      double-tongued.
¹⁵ In great and small matters cause no
    harm,ᵉ

6 ¹ and do not become an enemy instead of
    a friend;
for a bad name incurs shame and
    reproach;
  so it is with the double-tongued
    sinner.

² Do not fall into the grip of passion,ᶠ
  or you may be torn apart as by
    a bull.ᵍ
³ Your leaves will be devoured and your
    fruit destroyed,
  and you will be left like a withered tree.
⁴ Evil passion destroys those who have it,
  and makes them the laughingstock of
    their enemies.

⁵ Pleasant speech multiplies friends,
  and a gracious tongue multiplies
    courtesies.

ᵃ Heb: Gk *atonement*
ᵇ Heb: Gk *he* (or *it*) *will atone for*
ᶜ Gk adds *so it is with the double-tongued sinner* (see
   6.1)
ᵈ Heb: Gk *a slanderer*
ᵉ Heb Syr: Gk *be ignorant*
ᶠ Heb: Meaning of Gk uncertain
ᵍ Meaning of Gk uncertain

5.1–8. Avoid presumption. Do not rely on wealth or presume on God's mercy as excuses for putting off repentance. **4:** *Slow to anger,* Ex 34.6. This ancient liturgical formula is frequently cited and adapted; cf. Num 14.18; Neh 9.17; Pss 86.15; 103.8; 145.8; Jon 4.2; etc. **6:** *Mercy and wrath,* although God is merciful, God's just demands cannot be ignored (16.11–12). **7:** *Wrath of the Lord,* Ex 32.10; Num 16.46; Deut 29.23; etc. The notion of sudden punishment, especially of the powerful, is a common motif in wisdom literature (10.10–11; Job 34.20–25; cf. Dan 5).

5.9–6.4: The need for truthfulness and self-restraint. Here speech is treated mainly in an honor-shame context (see 4.20–31).

10: For other treatments of *speech,* see 19.6–17; 20.16–20; 22.27–23.15; 28.12–26. **12:** *Hand over your mouth,* a gesture of humility and circumspection (Job 29.9; 40.4–5; Prov 30.32). **14:** *Double-tongued,* one who is duplicitous in speech or a slanderer (cf. 5.9 in Greek; 6.1). **6.2–4:** *Passion,* most likely sexual desire (18.30–19.3), though anger or envy is also possible. **6.3:** Cf. Ps 1.3.

⁶ Let those who are friendly with you be
   many,
   but let your advisers be one in a
      thousand.
⁷ When you gain friends, gain them
      through testing,
   and do not trust them hastily.
⁸ For there are friends who are such when
      it suits them,
   but they will not stand by you in time of
      trouble.
⁹ And there are friends who change into
      enemies,
   and tell of the quarrel to your disgrace.
¹⁰ And there are friends who sit at your table,
   but they will not stand by you in time of
      trouble.
¹¹ When you are prosperous, they become
      your second self,
   and lord it over your servants;
¹² but if you are brought low, they turn
      against you,
   and hide themselves from you.
¹³ Keep away from your enemies,
   and be on guard with your friends.

¹⁴ Faithful friends are a sturdy shelter:
   whoever finds one has found a treasure.
¹⁵ Faithful friends are beyond price;
   no amount can balance their worth.
¹⁶ Faithful friends are life-saving medicine;
   and those who fear the Lord will find
      them.
¹⁷ Those who fear the Lord direct their
      friendship aright,
   for as they are, so are their neighbors
      also.

¹⁸ My child, from your youth choose
      discipline,
   and when you have gray hair you will
      still find wisdom.
¹⁹ Come to her like one who plows and
      sows,
   and wait for her good harvest.
For when you cultivate her you will toil
      but little,
   and soon you will eat of her produce.
²⁰ She seems very harsh to the
      undisciplined;
   fools cannot remain with her.
²¹ She will be like a heavy stone to test
      them,
   and they will not delay in casting her
      aside.
²² For wisdom is like her name;
   she is not readily perceived by many.

²³ Listen, my child, and accept my
      judgment;
   do not reject my counsel.
²⁴ Put your feet into her fetters,
   and your neck into her collar.
²⁵ Bend your shoulders and carry her,
   and do not fret under her bonds.
²⁶ Come to her with all your soul,
   and keep her ways with all your might.
²⁷ Search out and seek, and she will
      become known to you;
   and when you get hold of her, do not let
      her go.
²⁸ For at last you will find the rest she gives,
   and she will be changed into joy for you.
²⁹ Then her fetters will become for you a
      strong defense,
   and her collar a glorious robe.

6.5–17: Friendship. While caution is necessary in making friends, a faithful friend is a treasure (cf. 9.10–16; 19.13–17; 22.19–26; 27.16–21; 37.1–6). Although the topic of friendship occasionally appears in earlier Israelite wisdom literature (Prov 17.17; 18.24; 27.6,10), it was particularly prominent theme in Hellenistic writings. 6–7: The difference between *those who are friendly* and true friends becomes clear only over time (*testing*). 8–13: False *friends* can easily turn into enemies. 14–17: *Faithful friends* are best sought and found among *those who fear the Lord*.

6.18–37: Discipline and the way to wisdom. Those who seek to become wise must accept the religious, intellectual, and moral formation (*discipline*) that produces wisdom and its rewards. 18–22: Those who accept wisdom's *discipline* are like farmers who work hard and so enjoy abundant harvests, whereas discipline is *like a heavy stone* to those who refuse it. 18: *My child*, each of the three segments begins with this address (vv.18,23,32); see 2.1n. 22: *Wisdom is like her name*, probably a play on the Hebrew words "musar" (*discipline*, v. 18) and "sar" ("turn aside," i.e., become distant). 23–31: The process of accepting wisdom's discipline is illustrated by images of the *yoke* and *rest* (51.26) and *glorious* royal apparel. 26: *All your soul, and . . . all your might*, Deut

30 Her yoke[a] is a golden ornament,
and her bonds a purple cord.
31 You will wear her like a glorious robe,
and put her on like a splendid crown.[b]

32 If you are willing, my child, you can be
disciplined,
and if you apply yourself you will
become clever.
33 If you love to listen you will gain
knowledge,
and if you pay attention you will
become wise.
34 Stand in the company of the elders.
Who is wise? Attach yourself to such a
one.
35 Be ready to listen to every godly
discourse,
and let no wise proverbs escape you.
36 If you see an intelligent person, rise
early to visit him;
let your foot wear out his doorstep.
37 Reflect on the statutes of the Lord,
and meditate at all times on his
commandments.
It is he who will give insight to[c] your
mind,
and your desire for wisdom will be
granted.

7 Do no evil, and evil will never overtake
you.
2 Stay away from wrong, and it will turn
away from you.
3 Do[d] not sow in the furrows of injustice,
and you will not reap a sevenfold
crop.

4 Do not seek from the Lord high office,
or the seat of honor from the king.
5 Do not assert your righteousness before
the Lord,
or display your wisdom before the king.

6 Do not seek to become a judge,
or you may be unable to root out
injustice;
you may be partial to the powerful,
and so mar your integrity.
7 Commit no offense against the public,
and do not disgrace yourself among the
people.

8 Do not commit a sin twice;
not even for one will you go
unpunished.
9 Do not say, "He will consider the great
number of my gifts,
and when I make an offering to the
Most High God, he will accept it."
10 Do not grow weary when you pray;
do not neglect to give alms.
11 Do not ridicule a person who is
embittered in spirit,
for there is One who humbles and
exalts.
12 Do not devise[e] a lie against your
brother,
or do the same to a friend.
13 Refuse to utter any lie,
for it is a habit that results in no
good.
14 Do not babble in the assembly of the
elders,
and do not repeat yourself when you
pray.

15 Do not hate hard labor
or farm work, which was created by the
Most High.

---

a Heb: Gk *Upon her*
b Heb: Gk *crown of gladness*
c Heb: Gk *will confirm*
d Gk *My child, do*
e Heb: Gk *plow*

6.5. **30:** *Purple cord*; see Num 15.38–40. Although wisdom is often likened to an ornament (e.g., Prov 1.9; 3.22; 4.8–9), here the language evokes ritual garments like those of the high priest (50.11). **32–37:** The prospective sage should spend time in listening to the *elders*, attending to *godly discourse* and *wise proverbs*, and reflecting on and carrying out God's *commandments* (in the Torah).

7.1–17: Evildoing and its consequences. Most of these instructions are presented as negative admonitions (*Do not* . . . ; cf. Prov 3.1–4; 22.22–29). **1–3:** Avoiding *evil, wrong,* and *injustice* will protect one from their damaging consequences. **4–7:** Ambition for high offices and public prestige can be dangerous (Prov 25.6–7). **8–9:** For an earlier warning about presuming on God's mercy and patience, see 5.6–7. **10–14:** The unit begins and ends with

¹⁶ Do not enroll in the ranks of sinners;
　remember that retribution does not
　　delay.
¹⁷ Humble yourself to the utmost,
　for the punishment of the ungodly is
　　fire and worms.ᵃ

¹⁸ Do not exchange a friend for money,
　or a real brother for the gold of Ophir.
¹⁹ Do not dismissᵇ a wise and good wife,
　for her charm is worth more than gold.
²⁰ Do not abuse slaves who work
　　faithfully,
　or hired laborers who devote
　　themselves to their task.
²¹ Let your soul love intelligent slaves;ᶜ
　do not withhold from them their
　　freedom.

²² Do you have cattle? Look after them;
　if they are profitable to you, keep them.
²³ Do you have children? Discipline them,
　and make them obedientᵈ from their
　　youth.
²⁴ Do you have daughters? Be concerned
　for their chastity,ᵉ
　and do not show yourself too indulgent
　　with them.
²⁵ Give a daughter in marriage, and you
　complete a great task;
　but give her to a sensible man.
²⁶ Do you have a wife who pleases you?ᶠ Do
　not divorce her;
　but do not trust yourself to one whom
　　you detest.

²⁷ With all your heart honor your father,
　and do not forget the birth pangs of
　　your mother.

²⁸ Remember that it was of your parentsᵍ
　you were born;
　how can you repay what they have
　　given to you?

²⁹ With all your soul fear the Lord,
　and revere his priests.
³⁰ With all your might love your Maker,
　and do not neglect his ministers.
³¹ Fear the Lord and honor the priest,
　and give him his portion, as you have
　　been commanded:
the first fruits, the guilt offering, the gift of
　the shoulders,
　the sacrifice of sanctification, and the
　　first fruits of the holy things.

³² Stretch out your hand to the poor,
　so that your blessing may be complete.
³³ Give graciously to all the living;
　do not withhold kindness even from
　　the dead.
³⁴ Do not avoid those who weep,
　but mourn with those who mourn.
³⁵ Do not hesitate to visit the sick,
　because for such deeds you will be
　　loved.
³⁶ In all you do, remember the end of your
　life,
　and then you will never sin.

ᵃ　Heb *for the expectation of mortals is worms*
ᵇ　Heb: Gk *deprive yourself of*
ᶜ　Heb *Love a wise slave as yourself*
ᵈ　Gk *bend their necks*
ᵉ　Gk *body*
ᶠ　Heb Syr lack *who pleases you*
ᵍ　Gk *them*

comments on prayer; the intervening material concerns faults connected with speech. **17:** *Fire and worms*, cf. Isa 66.24. The Hebrew has *worms* only.

7.18–36: Social relations. Directed to the male head of a household, these instructions pertain to his relationships with his *friend* or *brother*, *wife*, *slaves*, and *hired laborers*, *cattle*, *children*, *daughters*, *wife* again, *father* and *mother*, *priests*, the *poor*, the *dead*, and the *sick*. **18:** *Ophir* in southern Arabia or east Africa was famous for its *gold* (1 Kings 9.28; 10.11; Job 22.24; 28.16; Ps 45.9; Isa 13.12). **19:** *Dismiss a . . . wife*, Deut 24.1–4. **21:** *Freedom*, Ex 21.2; Lev 25.39–43; Deut 15.12–15. **24–25:** *Daughters*, cf. 22.3–6n.; 42.9–13. **27–28:** *Father . . . mother*, 3.1–16; cf. Ex 20.12; Deut 5.16.

31: *His portion*, Ex 29.27; Lev 7.31–34; Num 18.8–20; Deut 18.3. Earlier Israelite wisdom literature does not mention priests and seldom refers to ritual obligations; Prov 3.9 is a rare exception. **32:** *Poor*, Deut 14.28–29. **33:** *Dead*, cf. 38.16–18; Tob 1.17. **36:** *The end of your life* probably refers to one's good name at death (1.13; 28.6) rather than rewards in life after death.

8 Do not contend with the powerful,
 or you may fall into their hands.
2 Do not quarrel with the rich,
 in case their resources outweigh yours;
for gold has ruined many,
 and has perverted the minds of kings.
3 Do not argue with the loud of mouth,
 and do not heap wood on their fire.

4 Do not make fun of one who is ill-bred,
 or your ancestors may be insulted.
5 Do not reproach one who is turning away
 from sin;
 remember that we all deserve
 punishment.
6 Do not disdain one who is old,
 for some of us are also growing old.
7 Do not rejoice over anyone's death;
 remember that we must all die.

8 Do not slight the discourse of the sages,
 but busy yourself with their maxims;
because from them you will learn
 discipline
 and how to serve princes.
9 Do not ignore the discourse of the
 aged,
 for they themselves learned from their
 parents;[a]
from them you learn how to understand
 and to give an answer when the need
 arises.

10 Do not kindle the coals of sinners,
 or you may be burned in their flaming
 fire.
11 Do not let the insolent bring you to your
 feet,
 or they may lie in ambush against your
 words.

12 Do not lend to one who is stronger than
 you;
 but if you do lend anything, count it as
 a loss.
13 Do not give surety beyond your means;
 but if you give surety, be prepared to
 pay.

14 Do not go to law against a judge,
 for the decision will favor him because
 of his standing.
15 Do not go traveling with the reckless,
 or they will be burdensome to you;
for they will act as they please,
 and through their folly you will perish
 with them.
16 Do not pick a fight with the quick-
 tempered,
 and do not journey with them through
 lonely country,
because bloodshed means nothing to
 them,
 and where no help is at hand, they will
 strike you down.
17 Do not consult with fools,
 for they cannot keep a secret.
18 In the presence of strangers do nothing
 that is to be kept secret,
 for you do not know what they will
 divulge.[b]
19 Do not reveal your thoughts to
 anyone,
 or you may drive away your
 happiness.[c]

a Or *ancestors*
b Or *it will bring forth*
c Heb: Gk *and let him not return a favor to you*

8.1–19: Caution in social relations. These negative admonitions (*Do not . . .*) are accompanied by reasons why certain persons and social situations should be avoided. The goal is to help one avoid public disgrace and shame. 1–2: The *powerful* and *rich* as social categories are more prominent in Sirach than in earlier wisdom literature and may reflect the changing socio-economic realities of the Hellenistic world. 3: The dangers of arguing with those who cannot control their speech is already a topic in ancient Egyptian wisdom literature (see, e.g., *Ptahhotep*). 5–7: These motive clauses are more philosophical than the mainly pragmatic reasons given elsewhere in this instruction. 8–9: *The discourse of the sages* and *of the aged* contain the wise learning of tradition, highly valued by the wisdom tradition (cf. Prov 4.1–4; Job 8.8–10). 10: Flaming fire, 8.3; 28.8–12. 12–13: Although Ben Sira was not opposed in principle to making loans and standing *surety* (29.1–7; cf. Prov 6.1–5; 11.15), he urges great caution. 17–19: Avoiding self–revelation to *fools* and *strangers* is a prudent way to protect one's social standing. 18: The Hebrew makes a play on words between "zar" (*stranger*) and "raz" (*secret*).

9 Do not be jealous of the wife of your bosom,
  or you will teach her an evil lesson to
    your own hurt.
2 Do not give yourself to a woman
  and let her trample down your strength.
3 Do not go near a loose woman,
  or you will fall into her snares.
4 Do not dally with a singing girl,
  or you will be caught by her tricks.
5 Do not look intently at a virgin,
  or you may stumble and incur penalties
    for her.
6 Do not give yourself to prostitutes,
  or you may lose your inheritance.
7 Do not look around in the streets of a city,
  or wander about in its deserted sections.
8 Turn away your eyes from a shapely
    woman,
  and do not gaze at beauty belonging to
    another;
many have been seduced by a woman's
    beauty,
  and by it passion is kindled like a fire.
9 Never dine with another man's wife,
  or revel with her at wine;
or your heart may turn aside to her,
  and in blood[a] you may be plunged into
    destruction.

10 Do not abandon old friends,
  for new ones cannot equal them.
A new friend is like new wine;
  when it has aged, you can drink it with
    pleasure.

11 Do not envy the success of sinners,
  for you do not know what their end will
    be like.

12 Do not delight in what pleases the
    ungodly;
  remember that they will not be held
    guiltless all their lives.

13 Keep far from those who have power to
    kill,
  and you will not be haunted by the fear
    of death.
But if you approach them, make no
    misstep,
  or they may rob you of your life.
Know that you are stepping among snares,
  and that you are walking on the city
    battlements.

14 As much as you can, aim to know your
    neighbors,
  and consult with the wise.
15 Let your conversation be with intelligent
    people,
  and let all your discussion be about the
    law of the Most High.
16 Let the righteous be your dinner
    companions,
  and let your glory be in the fear of the
    Lord.

17 A work is praised for the skill of the
    artisan;
  so a people's leader is proved wise by
    his words.
18 The loud of mouth are feared in their
    city,
  and the one who is reckless in speech
    is hated.

a   Heb: Gk *by your spirit*

9.1–9: Caution in relations with women. These admonitions concern the various types of women who can bring public disgrace and shame upon a sage. They continue the cautious tone of the preceding passage. **3–4:** *Loose*, literally "strange" woman (Heb. "zarah"); see Prov 2.16; 5.3,20; 7.5. The *singing girl* is apparently a prostitute (cf. Isa 23.15–16). **5:** The penalty for seducing a *virgin* involved financial payments to her father and marriage (Ex 22.16–17). **7:** *In the streets of a city*, cf. Prov 7.7–10. **9:** The penalty for adultery with *another man's wife* was death (Lev 20.10; Deut 22.22).

9.10–16: Caution in choosing and making friends. The best friends share the same spiritual values—*the law of the Most High* and *fear of the Lord*. See 6.5–17; 19.13–17; 22.19–26; 27.16–21; 37.1–6. **10:** As with *wine, old friends* are better than *new* ones.

11–13: *Sinners* and the *ungodly* pose a threat because they may entangle one in their own bad *end* (cf. Prov 1.10–19), but kings and rulers are dangerous because they themselves *have power to kill* (cf. Prov 16.14). **13:** *Battlements*, high on the city walls where one is exposed and easy to kill.

9.17–10.5: Wise rulers. The wise ruler is the good ruler (see Prov 25.4–5; 28.2–3,16; 29.4,12,14). **17–18:** Wise

10

A wise magistrate educates his people,
and the rule of an intelligent person is
well ordered.

² As the people's judge is, so are his
officials;
as the ruler of the city is, so are all its
inhabitants.

³ An undisciplined king ruins his people,
but a city becomes fit to live in through
the understanding of its rulers.

⁴ The government of the earth is in the
hand of the Lord,
and over it he will raise up the right
leader for the time.

⁵ Human success is in the hand of the Lord,
and it is he who confers honor upon the
lawgiver.ᵃ

⁶ Do not get angry with your neighbor for
every injury,
and do not resort to acts of insolence.

⁷ Arrogance is hateful to the Lord and to
mortals,
and injustice is outrageous to both.

⁸ Sovereignty passes from nation to nation
on account of injustice and insolence
and wealth.ᵇ

⁹ How can dust and ashes be proud?
Even in life the human body decays.ᶜ

¹⁰ A long illness baffles the physician;ᵈ
the king of today will die tomorrow.

¹¹ For when one is dead
he inherits maggots and verminᵉ and
worms.

¹² The beginning of human pride is to
forsake the Lord;
the heart has withdrawn from its
Maker.

¹³ For the beginning of pride is sin,
and the one who clings to it pours out
abominations.

Therefore the Lord brings upon them
unheard-of calamities,
and destroys them completely.

¹⁴ The Lord overthrows the thrones of
rulers,
and enthrones the lowly in their place.

¹⁵ The Lord plucks up the roots of the
nations,ᶠ
and plants the humble in their place.

¹⁶ The Lord lays waste the lands of the
nations,
and destroys them to the foundations of
the earth.

¹⁷ He removes some of them and destroys
them,
and erases the memory of them from
the earth.

¹⁸ Pride was not created for human beings,
or violent anger for those born of
women.

¹⁹ Whose offspring are worthy of honor?
Human offspring.
Whose offspring are worthy of honor?
Those who fear the Lord.
Whose offspring are unworthy of honor?
Human offspring.
Whose offspring are unworthy of honor?
Those who break the commandments.

²⁰ Among family members their leader is
worthy of honor,

ᵃ Heb: Gk *scribe*
ᵇ Other ancient authorities add here or after verse
9a, *Nothing is more wicked than one who loves
money, for such a person puts his own soul up for
sale.*
ᶜ Heb: Meaning of Gk uncertain
ᵈ Heb Lat: Meaning of Gk uncertain
ᵉ Heb: Gk *wild animals*
ᶠ Other ancient authorities read *proud nations*

---

words are the tools of the good ruler. **10.1–3:** Rulers can have positive or negative effects on their city's *inhabitants* (Prov 28.3,16; 29.4,12). **4–5:** *The hand of the Lord*, Prov 8.15–16; Wis 6.1–3.

10.6–18: Avoid arrogance and pride. Such behavior is hateful to not only to God but also to other people and has disastrous effects. Although arrogance is a traditional topic in wisdom literature, Sirach applies it specifically to rulers and nations, perhaps as a critique of the Ptolemaic and Seleucid kings of his day. **9–11:** Death is the great equalizer among humans (22.11–22; 38.16–23; 41.1–13), and the best remedy for pride. **9:** *Dust and ashes*, Gen 18.27; Job 30.19; 42.6. **12:** *To forsake the Lord* is the root of foolish *pride*, and pride is not what God intended for humankind (10.18). **14–17:** *Overthrows the thrones of rulers*, cf. 1 Sam 2.1–10; Lk 1.47–55.

10.19–11.6: Honor and shame. True honor belongs not to the wealthy and powerful but rather to those who *fear the Lord* and keep God's *commandments* (cf. 4.20–6.4; 41.14–42.8; Prov 1.7; 9.10). **19:** *Human offspring*, giving

but those who fear the Lord are worthy
of honor in his eyes.[a]

²² The rich, and the eminent, and the
poor—
their glory is the fear of the Lord.

²³ It is not right to despise one who is
intelligent but poor,
and it is not proper to honor one who
is sinful.

²⁴ The prince and the judge and the ruler
are honored,
but none of them is greater than the
one who fears the Lord.

²⁵ Free citizens will serve a wise servant,
and an intelligent person will not
complain.

²⁶ Do not make a display of your wisdom
when you do your work,
and do not boast when you are in need.

²⁷ Better is the worker who has goods in
plenty
than the boaster who lacks bread.

²⁸ My child, honor yourself with humility,
and give yourself the esteem you
deserve.

²⁹ Who will acquit those who condemn[b]
themselves?
And who will honor those who
dishonor themselves?[c]

³⁰ The poor are honored for their
knowledge,
while the rich are honored for their
wealth.

³¹ One who is honored in poverty, how
much more in wealth!
And one dishonored in wealth, how
much more in poverty!

11 The wisdom of the humble lifts their
heads high,
and seats them among the great.

² Do not praise individuals for their good
looks,

or loathe anyone because of appearance
alone.

³ The bee is small among flying creatures,
but what it produces is the best of sweet
things.

⁴ Do not boast about wearing fine clothes,
and do not exalt yourself when you are
honored;
for the works of the Lord are wonderful,
and his works are concealed from
humankind.

⁵ Many kings have had to sit on the ground,
but one who was never thought of has
worn a crown.

⁶ Many rulers have been utterly disgraced,
and the honored have been handed
over to others.

⁷ Do not find fault before you investigate;
examine first, and then criticize.

⁸ Do not answer before you listen,
and do not interrupt when another is
speaking.

⁹ Do not argue about a matter that does not
concern you,
and do not sit with sinners when they
judge a case.

¹⁰ My child, do not busy yourself with
many matters;
if you multiply activities, you will not
be held blameless.
If you pursue, you will not overtake,
and by fleeing you will not escape.

¹¹ There are those who work and struggle
and hurry,
but are so much the more in want.

¹² There are others who are slow and need
help,

---

a   Other ancient authorities add as verse 21, *The fear
    of the Lord is the beginning of acceptance; obduracy
    and pride are the beginning of rejection.*
b   Heb: Gk *sin against*
c   Heb Lat: Gk *their own life*

---

the same answer to opposite questions is a form of riddle, designed to provoke reflection. **26–27**: Boasting by
those in need brings only shame. **28**: *Humility* is appropriate to the wise (cf. 11.1). **11.3**: *The bee,* for other comparisons between animal and human behaviors, see Prov 6.6–8; 30.15–19,24–31.

11.7–9: Avoid hasty judgments. See 5.11–12.

11.10–28: True wealth. Since God is the real source of wealth, it is foolish to rely on earthly riches for security (cf. Prov 13.11; 20.21; 23.4–5; Eccl 5.10–12). **10–13**: Divine favor (*the eyes of the Lord*), and not human activity

who lack strength and abound in poverty;
but the eyes of the Lord look kindly upon
   them;
   he lifts them out of their lowly condition
¹³ and raises up their heads
   to the amazement of the many.

¹⁴ Good things and bad, life and death,
   poverty and wealth, come from the Lord.ᵃ
¹⁷ The Lord's gift remains with the devout,
   and his favor brings lasting success.
¹⁸ One becomes rich through diligence and
   self-denial,
   and the reward allotted to him is this:
¹⁹ when he says, "I have found rest,
   and now I shall feast on my goods!"
he does not know how long it will be
   until he leaves them to others and dies.

²⁰ Stand by your agreement and attend to it,
   and grow old in your work.
²¹ Do not wonder at the works of a sinner,
   but trust in the Lord and keep at your
   job;
for it is easy in the sight of the Lord
   to make the poor rich suddenly, in an
   instant.
²² The blessing of the Lord isᵇ the reward of
   the pious,
   and quickly God causes his blessing to
   flourish.
²³ Do not say, "What do I need,
   and what further benefit can be mine?"
²⁴ Do not say, "I have enough,
   and what harm can come to me now?"
²⁵ In the day of prosperity, adversity is
   forgotten,
   and in the day of adversity, prosperity is
   not remembered.
²⁶ For it is easy for the Lord on the day of
   death
   to reward individuals according to their
   conduct.

²⁷ An hour's misery makes one forget past
   delights,
   and at the close of one's life one's deeds
   are revealed.
²⁸ Call no one happy before his death;
   by how he ends, a person becomes
   known.ᶜ

²⁹ Do not invite everyone into your home,
   for many are the tricks of the crafty.
³⁰ Like a decoy partridge in a cage, so is the
   mind of the proud,
   and like spies they observe your
   weakness;ᵈ
³¹ for they lie in wait, turning good into
   evil,
   and to worthy actions they attach blame.
³² From a spark many coals are kindled,
   and a sinner lies in wait to shed blood.
³³ Beware of scoundrels, for they devise evil,
   and they may ruin your reputation
   forever.
³⁴ Receive strangers into your home and
   they will stir up trouble for you,
   and will make you a stranger to your
   own family.

12 If you do good, know to whom you do it,
   and you will be thanked for your good
   deeds.
² Do good to the devout, and you will be
   repaid—

ᵃ Other ancient authorities add as verses 15 and 16,
   ¹⁵ *Wisdom, understanding, and knowledge of the*
   law come from the Lord; affection and the ways of
   good works come from him. ¹⁶ *Error and darkness*
   were created with sinners; evil grows old with those
   who take pride in malice.
ᵇ Heb: Gk *is in*
ᶜ Heb: Gk *and through his children a person becomes*
   known
ᵈ Heb: Gk *downfall*

alone, often brings success to some unlikely persons. **19:** A rich fool can be quickly deprived of material security
by death (cf. 11.26–28; Eccl 2.21; 4.8; 5.12–14). **26–28:** The *reward* most likely refers to the sage's good name
rather than to the last judgment and eternal rewards (22.11–22; 38.16–23; 41.1–13).

   11.29–12.18: Caution in social relations. Even for those who approach them innocently and with good will,
social relations can be full of danger. **29–34:** *Scoundrels* and *strangers* can ruin one's reputation and turn a whole
household against its master. The Hebrew text makes a pun between "zar" (*stranger*) and "zahir" (*make you a*
stranger). **12.1–7:** Reserve almsgiving for the *devout, humble,* and *good* (cf. 18.15–18; 29.8–13). **8–18:** A warning
against potential enemies.

if not by them, certainly by the Most
High.
³ No good comes to one who persists in evil
or to one who does not give alms.
⁴ Give to the devout, but do not help the
sinner.
⁵ Do good to the humble, but do not give
to the ungodly;
hold back their bread, and do not give it to
them,
for by means of it they might subdue you;
then you will receive twice as much evil
for all the good you have done to them.
⁶ For the Most High also hates sinners
and will inflict punishment on the
ungodly.^a
⁷ Give to the one who is good, but do not
help the sinner.
⁸ A friend is not known^b in prosperity,
nor is an enemy hidden in adversity.
⁹ One's enemies are friendly^c when one
prospers,
but in adversity even one's friend
disappears.
¹⁰ Never trust your enemy,
for like corrosion in copper, so is his
wickedness.
¹¹ Even if he humbles himself and walks
bowed down,
take care to be on your guard against
him.
Be to him like one who polishes a mirror,
to be sure it does not become
completely tarnished.
¹² Do not put him next to you,
or he may overthrow you and take your
place.
Do not let him sit at your right hand,
or else he may try to take your own seat,
and at last you will realize the truth of my
words,
and be stung by what I have said.

¹³ Who pities a snake charmer when he is
bitten,
or all those who go near wild animals?
¹⁴ So no one pities a person who associates
with a sinner

and becomes involved in the other's sins.
¹⁵ He stands by you for a while,
but if you falter, he will not be there.
¹⁶ An enemy speaks sweetly with his lips,
but in his heart he plans to throw you
into a pit;
an enemy may have tears in his eyes,
but if he finds an opportunity he will
never have enough of your blood.
¹⁷ If evil comes upon you, you will find him
there ahead of you;
pretending to help, he will trip you up.
¹⁸ Then he will shake his head, and clap his
hands,
and whisper much, and show his true
face.

13 Whoever touches pitch gets dirty,
and whoever associates with a proud
person becomes like him.
² Do not lift a weight too heavy for you,
or associate with one mightier and
richer than you.
How can the clay pot associate with the
iron kettle?
The pot will strike against it and be
smashed.
³ A rich person does wrong, and even adds
insults;
a poor person suffers wrong, and must
add apologies.
⁴ A rich person^d will exploit you if you can
be of use to him,
but if you are in need he will abandon
you.
⁵ If you own something, he will live with
you;
he will drain your resources without a
qualm.
⁶ When he needs you he will deceive you,
and will smile at you and encourage
you;

---

^a Other ancient authorities add *and he is keeping
them for the day of their punishment*
^b Other ancient authorities read *punished*
^c Heb: Gk *grieved*
^d Gk *He*

13.1–23: Rich and poor. Associating with rich persons poses dangers to those dedicated to wisdom and
fear of the Lord. **1–7:** The rich abuse and exploit the poor; they defile (like *pitch*) and destroy (like an *iron kettle*
striking a *clay pot*) poor persons. Although a prominent citizen, Sirach speaks from the perspective of the poor

he will speak to you kindly and say,
  "What do you need?"
[7] He will embarrass you with his delicacies,
  until he has drained you two or three
    times,
  and finally he will laugh at you.
Should he see you afterwards, he will pass
    you by
  and shake his head at you.

[8] Take care not to be led astray
  and humiliated when you are enjoying
    yourself.[a]
[9] When an influential person invites you,
  be reserved,
  and he will invite you more insistently.
[10] Do not be forward, or you may be rebuffed;
  do not stand aloof, or you will be
    forgotten.
[11] Do not try to treat him as an equal,
  or trust his lengthy conversations;
for he will test you by prolonged talk,
  and while he smiles he will be
    examining you.
[12] Cruel are those who do not keep your
    secrets;
  they will not spare you harm or
    imprisonment.
[13] Be on your guard and very careful,
  for you are walking about with your
    own downfall.[b]

[15] Every creature loves its like,
  and every person the neighbor.
[16] All living beings associate with their own
    kind,
  and people stick close to those like
    themselves.
[17] What does a wolf have in common with
    a lamb?
  No more has a sinner with the devout.
[18] What peace is there between a hyena and
    a dog?

And what peace between the rich and
    the poor?
[19] Wild asses in the wilderness are the prey
    of lions;
  likewise the poor are feeding grounds
    for the rich.
[20] Humility is an abomination to the proud;
  likewise the poor are an abomination to
    the rich.

[21] When the rich person totters, he is
    supported by friends,
  but when the humble[c] falls, he is
    pushed away even by friends.
[22] If the rich person slips, many come to
    the rescue;
  he speaks unseemly words, but they
    justify him.
If the humble person slips, they even
    criticize him;
  he talks sense, but is not given a hearing.
[23] The rich person speaks and all are silent;
  they extol to the clouds what he says.
The poor person speaks and they say,
  "Who is this fellow?"
  And should he stumble, they even push
    him down.
[24] Riches are good if they are free from sin;
  poverty is evil only in the opinion of the
    ungodly.

[25] The heart changes the countenance,
  either for good or for evil.[d]
[26] The sign of a happy heart is a cheerful face,

---

a Other ancient authorities read *in your folly*
b Other ancient authorities add as verse 14, *When
   you hear these things in your sleep, wake up!
   During all your life love the Lord, and call on him
   for your salvation.*
c Other ancient authorities read *poor*
d Other ancient authorities add *and a glad heart
   makes a cheerful countenance*

rather than from the perspective of the rich. **8–13:** In dealing with the rich and powerful, one must always be on guard, since they can easily bring about one's *downfall*; see also 31.12–18. Similar cautious advice is found in Egyptian wisdom literature (*Amenemope*, ch. 23), in Prov 23.1–3, and in later Jewish wisdom literature (*m. Abot* 2.3). **15–20:** The incompatibility between rich and poor is illustrated by comparisons taken from the animal kingdom, which serve to naturalize the social antagonism. **17:** Cf. Isa 11.6. **21–23:** The *rich* customarily receive better treatment than the *poor*.

13.24–14.2: Wealth and happiness. Happiness of *heart* (in biblical understanding where thinking and feeling take place) is reflected in a *cheerful face* and in a clear conscience.

but to devise proverbs requires painful
thinking.

14 Happy are those who do not blunder
with their lips,
and need not suffer remorse for sin.
2 Happy are those whose hearts do not
condemn them,
and who have not given up their hope.

3 Riches are inappropriate for a small-
minded person;
and of what use is wealth to a miser?
4 What he denies himself he collects for
others;
and others will live in luxury on his
goods.
5 If one is mean to himself, to whom will
he be generous?
He will not enjoy his own riches.
6 No one is worse than one who is grudging
to himself;
this is the punishment for his
meanness.
7 If ever he does good, it is by mistake;
and in the end he reveals his meanness.
8 The miser is an evil person;
he turns away and disregards people.
9 The eye of the greedy person is not
satisfied with his share;
greedy injustice withers the soul.
10 A miser begrudges bread,
and it is lacking at his table.

11 My child, treat yourself well, according to
your means,
and present worthy offerings to the
Lord.
12 Remember that death does not tarry,
and the decree[a] of Hades has not been
shown to you.
13 Do good to friends before you die,
and reach out and give to them as much
as you can.

14 Do not deprive yourself of a day's
enjoyment;
do not let your share of desired good
pass by you.
15 Will you not leave the fruit of your labors
to another,
and what you acquired by toil to be
divided by lot?
16 Give, and take, and indulge yourself,
because in Hades one cannot look for
luxury.
17 All living beings become old like a
garment,
for the decree[b] from of old is, "You must
die!"
18 Like abundant leaves on a spreading
tree
that sheds some and puts forth others,
so are the generations of flesh and
blood:
one dies and another is born.
19 Every work decays and ceases to exist,
and the one who made it will pass away
with it.

20 Happy is the person who meditates on[c]
wisdom
and reasons intelligently,
21 who[d] reflects in his heart on her ways
and ponders her secrets,
22 pursuing her like a hunter,
and lying in wait on her paths;
23 who peers through her windows
and listens at her doors;
24 who camps near her house
and fastens his tent peg to her
walls;

a Heb Syr: Gk *covenant*
b Heb: Gk *covenant*
c Other ancient authorities read *dies in*
d The structure adopted in verses 21-27 follows
the Heb

14.3–10: **The miser.** While devoted to making money, the *miser* never really enjoys life and so leads a miserable existence, doing harm to himself and little good for others (cf. Prov 11.24–26).
14.11–19: **Money and death.** Now is the time to use money to serve God, help others, and enjoy oneself. **12:**
Hades, the abode of the dead; Sheol in Hebrew. **14:** Cf. Eccl 8.15; 9.7. **17:** *Like a garment,* cf. Ps 102.26; Isa 50.9. *The
decree from of old,* see Gen 2.17; 3.3,19. **18–19:** Cf. Eccl 1.2–4; *Iliad* 6.146–49.
14.20–27: **The search for wisdom.** One who seeks and finds wisdom may be declared *happy* (cf. Prov 3.13).
20: *Happy is* takes the form of a beatitude or makarism (cf. Ps 1.1; Prov 3.13; 8.34; etc.; Mt 5.3–11; Lk 6.20–23).
22–27: The search for wisdom is compared to going on a hunt, camping out by *her house,* and finding her as a

25 who pitches his tent near her,
    and so occupies an excellent lodging
        place;
26 who places his children under her
        shelter,
    and lodges under her boughs;
27 who is sheltered by her from the heat,
    and dwells in the midst of her glory.

15 Whoever fears the Lord will do this,
    and whoever holds to the law will
        obtain wisdom.[a]
2 She will come to meet him like a mother,
    and like a young bride she will welcome
        him.
3 She will feed him with the bread of
        learning,
    and give him the water of wisdom to
        drink.
4 He will lean on her and not fall,
    and he will rely on her and not be put
        to shame.
5 She will exalt him above his neighbors,
    and will open his mouth in the midst of
        the assembly.
6 He will find gladness and a crown of
        rejoicing,
    and will inherit an everlasting name.
7 The foolish will not obtain her,
    and sinners will not see her.
8 She is far from arrogance,
    and liars will never think of her.
9 Praise is unseemly on the lips of a sinner,
    for it has not been sent from the Lord.

10 For in wisdom must praise be uttered,
    and the Lord will make it prosper.
11 Do not say, "It was the Lord's doing that I
        fell away";
    for he does not do[b] what he hates.
12 Do not say, "It was he who led me astray";
    for he has no need of the sinful.
13 The Lord hates all abominations;
    such things are not loved by those who
        fear him.
14 It was he who created humankind in the
        beginning,
    and he left them in the power of their
        own free choice.
15 If you choose, you can keep the
        commandments,
    and to act faithfully is a matter of your
        own choice.
16 He has placed before you fire and water;
    stretch out your hand for whichever
        you choose.
17 Before each person are life and death,
    and whichever one chooses will be given.
18 For great is the wisdom of the Lord;
    he is mighty in power and sees
        everything;
19 his eyes are on those who fear him,
    and he knows every human action.
20 He has not commanded anyone to be
        wicked,

a Gk *her*
b Heb: Gk *you ought not to do*

shady tree. **23:** *Peers through her windows,* cf. Song 2.9. **24:** *Her house,* cf. the description of Ben Sira's school as the "house of instruction" in 51.23; see also Prov 8.32–35. **26:** *Her boughs,* for wisdom as a tree, see 1.20; 24.13–17; Prov 3.18.

15.1–10: The benefits of wisdom. Wisdom is eager to be found and wants to lavish gifts on those who seek her out. **1:** The three major theological themes of Sirach—*fear of Lord, the law,* and *wisdom*—come together in this verse (cf. 1.1–30; 6.32–37; 24.23). **2–6:** Portrayed as a *mother* and as a *bride,* wisdom brings to those who seek her love, sustenance, security, success, and *an everlasting name* (immortality by remembrance). Cf. Prov 7.4; Wis 7.12; 8.2. **3:** *Bread* and *water,* cf. 1.16; 24.19–21; Prov 9.1–5; Isa 55.1–2. **7–10:** Wisdom has nothing to do with fools and sinners; only the wise can praise God properly.

15.11–20: Human choice and sin. Since God has given humans free will, they must take responsibility for their sins. **11–13:** For texts that could suggest that God makes people sin, see Ex 11.10 and 2 Sam 24.1. **14–17:** No attention is given here to Adam's sin (Gen 3.1–24) or the sins of "the sons of God" (Gen 6.1–4; but see Sir 16.7). Rather, the human person is regarded as free to choose between life and death (Deut 30.15–20) and so must be ready to accept the consequences. **14:** *Free choice* (Heb "yetser") is a technical term, sometimes used in a good sense (Isa 26.3; 1 Chr 29.18), but usually to refer to an evil tendency or inclination toward sin (Gen 6.5; 8.21; cf. 2 Esd 4.30–31). In postbiblical times the doctrine arose of a good and an evil "yetser" that every person possesses (cf. 37.3). **18–20:** God has no part in sin (cf. 15.11–13).

and he has not given anyone
permission to sin.

16

Do not desire a multitude of
worthless[a] children,
and do not rejoice in ungodly offspring.
[2] If they multiply, do not rejoice in them,
unless the fear of the Lord is in them.
[3] Do not trust in their survival,
or rely on their numbers;[b]
for one can be better than a thousand,
and to die childless is better than to
have ungodly children.
[4] For through one intelligent person a city
can be filled with people,
but through a clan of outlaws it
becomes desolate.

[5] Many such things my eye has seen,
and my ear has heard things more
striking than these.
[6] In an assembly of sinners a fire is kindled,
and in a disobedient nation wrath
blazes up.
[7] He did not forgive the ancient giants
who revolted in their might.
[8] He did not spare the neighbors of Lot,
whom he loathed on account of their
arrogance.
[9] He showed no pity on the doomed nation,
on those dispossessed because of their
sins;[c]
[10] or on the six hundred thousand foot
soldiers
who assembled in their stubbornness.[d]
[11] Even if there were only one stiff-necked
person,
it would be a wonder if he remained
unpunished.
For mercy and wrath are with the Lord;[e]
he is mighty to forgive—but he also
pours out wrath.

[12] Great as is his mercy, so also is his
chastisement;
he judges a person according to his or
her deeds.
[13] The sinner will not escape with plunder,
and the patience of the godly will not be
frustrated.
[14] He makes room for every act of mercy;
everyone receives in accordance with
his or her deeds.[f]

[17] Do not say, "I am hidden from the Lord,
and who from on high has me in
mind?
Among so many people I am unknown,
for what am I in a boundless creation?
[18] Lo, heaven and the highest heaven,
the abyss and the earth, tremble at his
visitation![g]
[19] The very mountains and the foundations
of the earth
quiver and quake when he looks upon
them.

a   Heb: Gk *unprofitable*
b   Other ancient authorities add *For you will groan in
untimely mourning, and will know of their sudden
end.*
c   Other ancient authorities add *All these things
he did to the hard-hearted nations, and by the
multitude of his holy ones he was not appeased.*
d   Other ancient authorities add *Chastising, showing
mercy, striking, healing, the Lord persisted in mercy
and discipline.*
e   Gk *him*
f   Other ancient authorities add *[15]The Lord hardened
Pharaoh so that he did not recognize him, in order
that his works might be known under heaven. [16]His
mercy is manifest to the whole of creation, and he
divided his light and darkness with a plumb line.*
g   Other ancient authorities add *The whole world past
and present is in his will.*

16.1–23: Responsibility for sin. God holds both individuals and groups responsible for their sins. **1–4:** In
a society in which having many children was regarded as a sign of divine blessing (Prov 17.6; Ps 127.3–5), the
author counters that one good child *can be better than a thousand* bad ones. Cf. 40.15–16; 41.5–9. **5–10:** God
has punished groups of sinners such as *the ancient giants* (Gen 6.1–4), *the neighbors of Lot* (Gen 18.16–19.29),
the doomed nation of Canaanites (Lev 18.3,24–25), and *the six hundred thousand foot soldiers* in the desert (Ex
12.37; Num 14.38). **11–14:** God judges individuals according to their deeds (Ps 62.12; Ezek 18). **15–23:** The speaker
quoted here claims that God is distant and has no concern for individuals and their moral responsibility (cf. Wis
2.1–20). The target may be Qoheleth/Ecclesiastes. The monologue is prefaced by an admonition (*Do not say*)
and is concluded with a judgment (16.23) that whoever says such things is a fool.

20 But no human mind can grasp this,
  and who can comprehend his ways?
21 Like a tempest that no one can see,
  so most of his works are concealed.ᵃ
22 Who is to announce his acts of justice?
  Or who can await them? For his decreeᵇ
    is far off."ᶜ
23 Such are the thoughts of one devoid of
    understanding;
  a senseless and misguided person
    thinks foolishly.

24 Listen to me, my child, and acquire
    knowledge,
  and pay close attention to my words.
25 I will impart discipline preciselyᵈ
  and declare knowledge accurately.

26 When the Lord createdᵉ his works from
    the beginning,
  and, in making them, determined their
    boundaries,
27 he arranged his works in an eternal order,
  and their dominionᶠ for all generations.
They neither hunger nor grow weary,
  and they do not abandon their tasks.
28 They do not crowd one another,
  and they never disobey his word.
29 Then the Lord looked upon the earth,
  and filled it with his good things.
30 With all kinds of living beings he
    covered its surface,
  and into it they must return.

17 The Lord created human beings out of
    earth,
  and makes them return to it again.
2 He gave them a fixed number of days,
  but granted them authority over
    everything on the earth.ᵍ
3 He endowed them with strength like his
    own,ʰ

and made them in his own image.
4 He put the fear of themⁱ in all living
    beings,
  and gave them dominion over beasts
    and birds.ʲ
6 Discretion and tongue and eyes,
  ears and a mind for thinking he gave
    them.
7 He filled them with knowledge and
    understanding,
  and showed them good and evil.
8 He put the fear of him intoᵏ their hearts
  to show them the majesty of his works.ˡ
10 And they will praise his holy name,
  9 to proclaim the grandeur of his works.
11 He bestowed knowledge upon them,
  and allotted to them the law of life.ᵐ
12 He established with them an eternal
    covenant,
  and revealed to them his decrees.

a   Meaning of Gk uncertain: Heb Syr *If I sin, no eye
    can see me, and if I am disloyal in secret, who is
    to know?*
b   Heb *the decree*: Gk *the covenant*
c   Other ancient authorities add *and a scrutiny for all
    comes at the end*
d   Gk *by weight*
e   Heb: Gk *judged*
f   Or *elements*
g   Lat: Gk *it*
h   Lat: Gk *proper to them*
i   Syr: Gk *him*
j   Other ancient authorities add as verse 5, *They
    obtained the use of the five faculties of the Lord; as
    sixth he distributed to them the gift of mind, and as
    seventh, reason, the interpreter of one's faculties.*
k   Other ancient authorities read *He set his eye upon*
l   Other ancient authorities add *and he gave them to
    boast of his marvels forever*
m   Other ancient authorities add *so that they may
    know that they who are alive now are mortal*

16.24–17.24: Creation and responsibility. God has put order into the world that can be discerned by reason and the law of Moses (the Torah), and God knows and judges the actions of every person. **16.26–17.4:** A paraphrase of Gen 1–3 and related texts, with an emphasis on the orderliness of creation. **26:** *Beginning*, Gen 1.1; Prov 8.22–23. *Their boundaries*, Job 38.10; Pss 104.9; 148.6. **27b–28:** Apparently referring to the heavenly bodies; see Ps 104.19; but cf. *1 En* 21. **29:** *Good things*, Gen 1.4,10,12, etc. **30:** *Must return*, 17.1; Gen 3.19. **17.1:** *Out of earth*, Gen 2.7 **2:** *Authority*, Gen 1.28. **3:** *His own image*, Gen 1.26. **4:** *Dominion*, Gen 1.28; 9.2. **6–10:** God has endowed humans with reason, and their proper response to God is *fear* and *praise* of the Lord. Thus there is no excuse for sin. **11–14:** The *law* (the Torah) is a further gift from God, and it enables humans to discern good from evil. **11:** *The law of life*, 45.5; Deut 30.15–20. **12–13:** When God made a *covenant* with the Israelites on Mount Sinai, they saw his *glorious majesty* (Ex 19).

¹³ Their eyes saw his glorious majesty,
   and their ears heard the glory of his voice.
¹⁴ He said to them, "Beware of all evil."
   And he gave commandment to each of
      them concerning the neighbor.
¹⁵ Their ways are always known to him;
   they will not be hid from his eyes.ᵃ
¹⁷ He appointed a ruler for every nation,
   but Israel is the Lord's own portion.ᵇ
¹⁹ All their works are as clear as the sun
      before him,
   and his eyes are ever upon their ways.
²⁰ Their iniquities are not hidden from him,
   and all their sins are before the Lord.ᶜ
²² One's almsgiving is like a signet ring
      with the Lord,ᵈ
   and he will keep a person's kindness
      like the apple of his eye.ᵉ
²³ Afterward he will rise up and repay them,
   and he will bring their recompense on
      their heads.
²⁴ Yet to those who repent he grants a return,
   and he encourages those who are losing
      hope.

²⁵ Turn back to the Lord and forsake your
      sins;
   pray in his presence and lessen your
      offense.
²⁶ Return to the Most High and turn away
      from iniquity,ᶠ
   and hate intensely what he abhors.
²⁷ Who will sing praises to the Most High
      in Hades
   in place of the living who give thanks?
²⁸ From the dead, as from one who does
      not exist, thanksgiving has ceased;
   those who are alive and well sing the
      Lord's praises.
²⁹ How great is the mercy of the Lord,
   and his forgiveness for those who
      return to him!
³⁰ For not everything is within human
      capability,

since human beings are not immortal.
³¹ What is brighter than the sun? Yet it can
      be eclipsed.
   So flesh and blood devise evil.
³² He marshals the host of the height of
      heaven;
   but all human beings are dust and ashes.

18 He who lives forever created the whole
   universe;
   ² the Lord alone is just.ᵍ
⁴ To none has he given power to proclaim
      his works;
   and who can search out his mighty deeds?
⁵ Who can measure his majestic power?
   And who can fully recount his mercies?
⁶ It is not possible to diminish or increase
      them,
   nor is it possible to fathom the wonders
      of the Lord.

ᵃ Other ancient authorities add ¹⁶*Their ways from
   youth tend toward evil, and they are unable to
   make for themselves hearts of flesh in place of their
   stony hearts. ¹⁷For in the division of the nations of
   the whole earth, he appointed*
ᵇ Other ancient authorities add as verse 18, *whom,
   being his firstborn, he brings up with discipline,
   and allotting to him the light of his love, he does not
   neglect him.*
ᶜ Other ancient authorities add as verse 21, *But the
   Lord, who is gracious and knows how they are
   formed, has neither left them nor abandoned them,
   but has spared them.*
ᵈ Gk *him*
ᵉ Other ancient authorities add *apportioning
   repentance to his sons and daughters*
ᶠ Other ancient authorities add *for he will lead you
   out of darkness to the light of health.*
ᵍ Other ancient authorities add *and there is no other
   beside him; ³he steers the world with the span of his
   hand, and all things obey his will; for he is king of
   all things by his power, separating among them the
   holy things from the profane.*

14: *Neighbor,* Ex 20.13–17; Lev 19.18; Deut 5.17–21. **15–23:** Although God will judge each person with justice, almsgiving and repentance can delay or even temper God's judgment. **17:** *The Lord's own portion,* Deut 32.8–9. **22:** *Signet ring*
(Jer 22.24; Hag 2.23) and *apple of his eye* (Deut 32.10; Ps 17.8; Prov 7.2) suggest a close personal relationship with God.
   17.25–32: A call to repent. God's mercy makes repentance possible. **27:** *Hades,* Heb "Sheol," the abode of
the dead, where there is no praising God (Pss 6.5; 30.9; 88.10–12; 115.17–18; Isa 38.18; Bar 2.17). **31:** *Eclipsed,* if the
sun can fail by way of an eclipse, so mortal humans can also be expected to fail. **32:** *Dust and ashes,* see 10.9n.
   18.1–14: God's majesty and mercy. The all-powerful and just God shows mercy to weak and mortal humans.

⁷ When human beings have finished, they
  are just beginning,
  and when they stop, they are still
  perplexed.
⁸ What are human beings, and of what use
  are they?
  What is good in them, and what is evil?
⁹ The number of days in their life is great if
  they reach one hundred years.ᵃ
¹⁰ Like a drop of water from the sea and a
  grain of sand,
  so are a few years among the days of
  eternity.
¹¹ That is why the Lord is patient with them
  and pours out his mercy upon them.
¹² He sees and recognizes that their end is
  miserable;
  therefore he grants them forgiveness all
  the more.
¹³ The compassion of human beings is for
  their neighbors,
  but the compassion of the Lord is for
  every living thing.
  He rebukes and trains and teaches them,
  and turns them back, as a shepherd his
  flock.
¹⁴ He has compassion on those who accept
  his discipline
  and who are eager for his precepts.

¹⁵ My child, do not mix reproach with your
  good deeds,
  or spoil your gift by harsh words.
¹⁶ Does not the dew give relief from the
  scorching heat?
  So a word is better than a gift.
¹⁷ Indeed, does not a word surpass a good gift?
  Both are to be found in a gracious person.
¹⁸ A fool is ungracious and abusive,
  and the gift of a grudging giver makes
  the eyes dim.

¹⁹ Before you speak, learn;
  and before you fall ill, take care of your
  health.
²⁰ Before judgment comes, examine yourself;
  and at the time of scrutiny you will find
  forgiveness.
²¹ Before falling ill, humble yourself;
  and when you have sinned, repent.
²² Let nothing hinder you from paying a
  vow promptly,
  and do not wait until death to be
  released from it.
²³ Before making a vow, prepare yourself;
  do not be like one who puts the Lord to
  the test.
²⁴ Think of his wrath on the day of death,
  and of the moment of vengeance when
  he turns away his face.
²⁵ In the time of plenty think of the time of
  hunger;
  in days of wealth think of poverty and
  need.
²⁶ From morning to evening conditions
  change;
  all things move swiftly before the Lord.

²⁷ One who is wise is cautious in
  everything;
  when sin is all around, one guards
  against wrongdoing.
²⁸ Every intelligent person knows wisdom,
  and praises the one who finds her.
²⁹ Those who are skilled in words become
  wise themselves,
  and pour forth apt proverbs.ᵇ

ᵃ Other ancient authorities add *but the death of each
  one is beyond the calculation of all*
ᵇ Other ancient authorities add *Better is confidence
  in the one Lord than clinging with a dead heart to a
  dead one.*

8: *What are human beings*, Ps 8.4. 9: *The number of days*, Ps. 90.10. 13: *As a shepherd his flock*, cf. Pss 23.1–4; 80.1;
Isa 40.11; Ezek 34.11–16.

18.15–18: Words and gifts. Good gifts can be spoiled by bad words, whereas good words are better than material gifts and are the mark of a gracious person. For more texts on speech, see 18.19–29; 19.4–17; 20.1–8,18–31.

18.19–29: Reflection and action. Before, during, and after action there is need for planning and assessment.
22–23: For similar advice see Prov 20.25; Eccl 5.4–5. *Test*, cf. Ex 17.2; Deut 6.16. 29: *Apt proverbs* are intended as
both interpretations of life experiences and guides to living wisely and correctly.

18.30–19.3: Self-control. Matters that need control are *base desires* such as greed and lust. Their negative
effects include shame, poverty, debauchery (Prov 20.1; 31.3–5), and death.

SELF-CONTROL[a]

30 Do not follow your base desires,
   but restrain your appetites.
31 If you allow your soul to take pleasure in
      base desire,
   it will make you the laughingstock of
      your enemies.
32 Do not revel in great luxury,
   or you may become impoverished by its
      expense.
33 Do not become a beggar by feasting with
      borrowed money,
   when you have nothing in your purse.[b]

19 The one who does this[c] will not
      become rich;
   one who despises small things will fail
      little by little.
2 Wine and women lead intelligent men
      astray,
   and the man who consorts with
      prostitutes is reckless.
3 Decay and worms will take possession of
      him,
   and the reckless person will be
      snatched away.

4 One who trusts others too quickly has a
      shallow mind,
   and one who sins does wrong to himself.
5 One who rejoices in wickedness[d] will be
      condemned,[e]
6 but one who hates gossip has less evil.
7 Never repeat a conversation,
   and you will lose nothing at all.
8 With friend or foe do not report it,
   and unless it would be a sin for you, do
      not reveal it;
9 for someone may have heard you and
      watched you,
   and in time will hate you.
10 Have you heard something? Let it die
      with you.
   Be brave, it will not make you burst!

11 Having heard something, the fool suffers
      birth pangs
   like a woman in labor with a child.
12 Like an arrow stuck in a person's thigh,
   so is gossip inside a fool.

13 Question a friend; perhaps he did not do it;
   or if he did, so that he may not do it again.
14 Question a neighbor; perhaps he did not
      say it;
   or if he said it, so that he may not repeat it.
15 Question a friend, for often it is slander;
   so do not believe everything you hear.
16 A person may make a slip without
      intending it.
   Who has not sinned with his tongue?
17 Question your neighbor before you
      threaten him;
   and let the law of the Most High take its
      course.[f]

20 The whole of wisdom is fear of the Lord,
   and in all wisdom there is the
      fulfillment of the law.[g]

a   This heading is included in the Gk text.
b   Other ancient authorities add *for you will be
    plotting against your own life*
c   Heb: Gk *A worker who is a drunkard*
d   Other ancient authorities read *heart*
e   Other ancient authorities add *but one who
    withstands pleasures crowns his life. 6One who
    controls the tongue will live without strife,*
f   Other ancient authorities add *and do not be
    angry. 18The fear of the Lord is the beginning of
    acceptance, and wisdom obtains his love. 19The
    knowledge of the Lord's commandments is life-
    giving discipline; and those who do what is pleasing
    to him enjoy the fruit of the tree of immortality.*
g   Other ancient authorities add *and the knowledge of
    his omnipotence. 21When a slave says to his master,
    "I will not act as you wish," even if later he does it,
    he angers the one who supports him.*

19.4–17: **The evils of gossip.** Loose talk is destructive not only to its subject but also to its purveyors. **4–12:** A wise person should not accept slander or gossip too quickly and repeat it *unless it would be a sin* (19.8) to with-hold it (cf. Lev 5.1). **13–17:** When a *friend* or *neighbor* is the subject of gossip, it is best to question that person directly. **17:** *The law of the Most High,* cf. Lev 19.17–18.
   18–19: The verses included in the translators' note to 19.17 are generally regarded as a later addition to the text, since they refer explicitly to *immortality,* which is inconsistent with Sirach's statements elsewhere about the finality of death.
   19.20–30: Wisdom and cleverness. Without *fear of the Lord* and fulfilling God's *law,* what may seem like

22 The knowledge of wickedness is not
  wisdom,
  nor is there prudence in the counsel of
  sinners.
23 There is a cleverness that is detestable,
  and there is a fool who merely lacks
  wisdom.
24 Better are the God-fearing who lack
  understanding
  than the highly intelligent who
  transgress the law.
25 There is a cleverness that is exact but
  unjust,
  and there are people who abuse favors
  to gain a verdict.
26 There is the villain bowed down in
  mourning,
  but inwardly he is full of deceit.
27 He hides his face and pretends not to
  hear,
  but when no one notices, he will take
  advantage of you.
28 Even if lack of strength keeps him from
  sinning,
  he will nevertheless do evil when he
  finds the opportunity.
29 A person is known by his appearance,
  and a sensible person is known when
  first met, face to face.
30 A person's attire and hearty laughter,
  and the way he walks, show what he is.

20 There is a rebuke that is untimely,
  and there is the person who is wise
  enough to keep silent.
2 How much better it is to rebuke than to
  fume!
3 And the one who admits his fault will be
  kept from failure.
4 Like a eunuch lusting to violate a girl
  is the person who does right under
  compulsion.
5 Some people keep silent and are thought
  to be wise,

while others are detested for being
  talkative.
6 Some people keep silent because they
  have nothing to say,
  while others keep silent because they
  know when to speak.
7 The wise remain silent until the right
  moment,
  but a boasting fool misses the right
  moment.
8 Whoever talks too much is detested,
  and whoever pretends to authority is
  hated.[a]

9 There may be good fortune for a person
  in adversity,
  and a windfall may result in a loss.
10 There is the gift that profits you nothing,
  and the gift to be paid back double.
11 There are losses for the sake of glory,
  and there are some who have raised
  their heads from humble
  circumstances.
12 Some buy much for little,
  but pay for it seven times over.
13 The wise make themselves beloved by
  only few words,[b]
  but the courtesies of fools are wasted.
14 A fool's gift will profit you nothing,[c]
  for he looks for recompense sevenfold.[d]
15 He gives little and upbraids much;
  he opens his mouth like a town crier.
  Today he lends and tomorrow he asks it
  back;
  such a one is hateful to God and humans.[e]

a Other ancient authorities add *How good it is to
   show repentance when you are reproved, for so you
   will escape deliberate sin!*
b Heb: Gk *by words*
c Other ancient authorities add *so it is with the
   envious who give under compulsion*
d Syr: Gk *he has many eyes instead of one*
e Other ancient authorities lack *to God and humans*

wisdom may be only *detestable cleverness.* **20**: *Fear of the Lord,* cf. Prov 1.7; 9.10. **29**: A person's *appearance* may
be either deceiving or revealing.

20.1–31: Speech and related topics. These sayings concerning rebukes, silence, gifts and money, the fool,
inappropriate speech, shame, lies, and other matters are connected more by catchwords and topics than by logical progression or argument. The appeal throughout is to human experience and natural reasoning, not to fear
of the Lord or the commandments. **4**: *Like a eunuch,* a sinner cannot be forced to do *right* any more than a eunuch
can engage in sexual intercourse. **5–6**: *Keep silent,* Prov 17.27–28. **9–12**: Although wisdom literature attempted to

¹⁶ The fool says, "I have no friends,
and I get no thanks for my good deeds.
Those who eat my bread are evil-
tongued."
¹⁷ How many will ridicule him, and how
often!^a

¹⁸ A slip on the pavement is better than a
slip of the tongue;
the downfall of the wicked will occur
just as speedily.
¹⁹ A coarse person is like an inappropriate
story,
continually on the lips of the ignorant.
²⁰ A proverb from a fool's lips will be rejected,
for he does not tell it at the proper time.

²¹ One may be prevented from sinning by
poverty;
so when he rests he feels no remorse.
²² One may lose his life through shame,
or lose it because of human respect.^b
²³ Another out of shame makes promises
to a friend,
and so makes an enemy for nothing.

²⁴ A lie is an ugly blot on a person;
it is continually on the lips of the
ignorant.
²⁵ A thief is preferable to a habitual liar,
but the lot of both is ruin.
²⁶ A liar's way leads to disgrace,
and his shame is ever with him.

PROVERBIAL SAYINGS^c

²⁷ The wise person advances himself by his
words,
and one who is sensible pleases the great.
²⁸ Those who cultivate the soil heap up
their harvest,
and those who please the great atone
for injustice.
²⁹ Favors and gifts blind the eyes of the wise;
like a muzzle on the mouth they stop
reproofs.

³⁰ Hidden wisdom and unseen treasure,
of what value is either?
³¹ Better are those who hide their folly
than those who hide their wisdom.^d

21 Have you sinned, my child? Do so no
more,
but ask forgiveness for your past sins.
² Flee from sin as from a snake;
for if you approach sin, it will bite you.
Its teeth are lion's teeth,
and can destroy human lives.
³ All lawlessness is like a two-edged sword;
there is no healing for the wound it inflicts.

⁴ Panic and insolence will waste away riches;
thus the house of the proud will be laid
waste.^e
⁵ The prayer of the poor goes from their
lips to the ears of God,^f
and his judgment comes speedily.
⁶ Those who hate reproof walk in the
sinner's steps,
but those who fear the Lord repent in
their heart.
⁷ The mighty in speech are widely known;
when they slip, the sensible person
knows it.

⁸ Whoever builds his house with other
people's money
is like one who gathers stones for his
burial mound.^g

[a] Other ancient authorities add *for he has not honestly received what he has, and what he does not have is unimportant to him*
[b] Other ancient authorities read *his foolish look*
[c] This heading is included in the Gk text.
[d] Other ancient authorities add ³²*Unwearied endurance in seeking the Lord is better than a masterless charioteer of one's own life.*
[e] Other ancient authorities read *uprooted*
[f] Gk *his ears*
[g] Other ancient authorities read *for the winter*

discern clear cause-and-effect relationships, it also acknowledged the possibility of paradox and uncertainty; cf. Prov 14.12; 16.25; Eccl 9.11–12. **24–26:** For the evil effects of a *lie*, see 7.13; 25.2; Prov 6.17; 12.22; Ps 5.6.

21.1–10: The destructive effects of sin. Sin can destroy a person and lead to shame and death. **2–3:** Sin is subtle and tempting like a *snake* (Gen 3.1–5), strong and destructive like a *lion's teeth* (27.10), and deadly like a *two-edged sword* (Prov 5.4). **5:** The prayer of the poor, cf. 35.17–21. **9:** *Bundle of tow,* that is, combustible fibers. *Fire* here refers to the sinner's destruction in this life rather than punishment after death. **10:** *Hades,* the abode

9 An assembly of the wicked is like a
bundle of tow,
and their end is a blazing fire.
10 The way of sinners is paved with smooth
stones,
but at its end is the pit of Hades.

11 Whoever keeps the law controls his
thoughts,
and the fulfillment of the fear of the
Lord is wisdom.
12 The one who is not clever cannot be
taught,
but there is a cleverness that increases
bitterness.
13 The knowledge of the wise will increase
like a flood,
and their counsel like a life-giving spring.
14 The mind[a] of a fool is like a broken jar;
it can hold no knowledge.

15 When an intelligent person hears a wise
saying,
he praises it and adds to it;
when a fool[b] hears it, he laughs at[c] it
and throws it behind his back.
16 A fool's chatter is like a burden on a
journey,
but delight is found in the speech of the
intelligent.
17 The utterance of a sensible person is
sought in the assembly,
and they ponder his words in their
minds.

18 Like a house in ruins is wisdom to a fool,
and to the ignorant, knowledge is talk
that has no meaning.
19 To a senseless person education is fetters
on his feet,
and like manacles on his right hand.
20 A fool raises his voice when he laughs,
but the wise[d] smile quietly.

21 To the sensible person education is like a
golden ornament,
and like a bracelet on the right arm.

22 The foot of a fool rushes into a house,
but an experienced person waits
respectfully outside.
23 A boor peers into the house from the
door,
but a cultivated person remains outside.
24 It is ill-mannered for a person to listen
at a door;
the discreet would be grieved by the
disgrace.

25 The lips of babblers speak of what is not
their concern,[e]
but the words of the prudent are
weighed in the balance.
26 The mind of fools is in their mouth,
but the mouth of the wise is in[f] their
mind.
27 When an ungodly person curses an
adversary,[g]
he curses himself.
28 A whisperer degrades himself
and is hated in his neighborhood.

22 The idler is like a filthy stone,
and every one hisses at his disgrace.
2 The idler is like the filth of dunghills;
anyone that picks it up will shake it off
his hand.

a Syr Lat: Gk *entrails*
b Syr: Gk *reveler*
c Syr: Gk *dislikes*
d Syr Lat: Gk *clever*
e Other ancient authorities read *of strangers speak of
these things*
f Other ancient authorities omit *in*
g Or *curses Satan*

of the dead (Heb "Sheol").
  21.11–28: The sage and the fool. The opening saying gives the series of comparisons a specifically Jewish religious context by linking them to the *law, fear of the Lord,* and *wisdom*—the major themes of the book. Otherwise,
the appeal is to common human experience and reason. The contrasts between the sage and the fool are especially evident with regard to speech (21.16–17,25–28), attitudes toward education (21.15,19,21), and behavior (21.22–24).
  22.1–18: Dealing with fools. While the *idler* and the *fool* can be avoided, dealing with one's own foolish children
is especially difficult. **1:** *Filthy stone,* a rock used for wiping oneself after a bowel movement. **3–6:** *Daughter,* sons
were prized in Ben Sira's patriarchal society, whereas daughters were often regarded as a source of trouble for their

³ It is a disgrace to be the father of an
    undisciplined son,
  and the birth of a daughter is a loss.
⁴ A sensible daughter obtains a husband of
    her own,
  but one who acts shamefully is a grief
    to her father.
⁵ An impudent daughter disgraces father
    and husband,
  and is despised by both.
⁶ Like music in time of mourning is ill-
    timed conversation,
  but a thrashing and discipline are at all
    times wisdom.ᵃ

⁹ Whoever teaches a fool is like one who
    glues potsherds together,
  or who rouses a sleeper from deep
    slumber.
¹⁰ Whoever tells a story to a fool tells it to a
    drowsy man;
  and at the end he will say, "What is it?"
¹¹ Weep for the dead, for he has left the
    light behind;
  and weep for the fool, for he has left
    intelligence behind.
  Weep less bitterly for the dead, for he is at
    rest;
  but the life of the fool is worse than death.
¹² Mourning for the dead lasts seven days,
  but for the foolish or the ungodly it
    lasts all the days of their lives.

¹³ Do not talk much with a senseless person
    or visit an unintelligent person.ᵇ
  Stay clear of him, or you may have trouble,
    and be spattered when he shakes
    himself off.
  Avoid him and you will find rest,
    and you will never be wearied by his
    lack of sense.

¹⁴ What is heavier than lead?
  And what is its name except "Fool"?
¹⁵ Sand, salt, and a piece of iron
  are easier to bear than a stupid person.

¹⁶ A wooden beam firmly bonded into a
    building
  is not loosened by an earthquake;
  so the mind firmly resolved after due
    reflection
  will not be afraid in a crisis.
¹⁷ A mind settled on an intelligent thought
  is like stucco decoration that makes a
    wall smooth.
¹⁸ Fencesᶜ set on a high place
  will not stand firm against the wind;
  so a timid mind with a fool's resolve
  will not stand firm against any fear.

¹⁹ One who pricks the eye brings tears,
  and one who pricks the heart makes
    clear its feelings.
²⁰ One who throws a stone at birds scares
    them away,
  and one who reviles a friend destroys a
    friendship.
²¹ Even if you draw your sword against a
    friend,
  do not despair, for there is a way back.
²² If you open your mouth against your
    friend,
  do not worry, for reconciliation is
    possible.

ᵃ Other ancient authorities add ⁷Children who are
    brought up in a good life, conceal the lowly birth of
    their parents. ⁸Children who are disdainfully and
    boorishly haughty stain the nobility of their kindred.
ᵇ Other ancient authorities add For being without
    sense he will despise everything about you
ᶜ Other ancient authorities read Pebbles

fathers (cf. 7.24–25; 42.9–13). **6:** *Thrashing,* corporal punishment was acceptable in this society (30.1–13; Prov 13.24; 23.13–14). **7–8:** Translated in the marginal notes, these verses are probably not part of the original composition. **9:** *Glues potsherds together,* reassembling a broken clay pot is futile and nearly impossible. **11–12:** *The fool* is more deserving of pity and mourning than a dead person (cf. 38.16–23). **13:** *Avoid him,* the best strategy for dealing with a fool. **14–15:** The comparisons illustrate how burdensome a fool can be (cf. 21.16). Verse 14 has the structure of a riddle. **16–18:** *A fool's resolve,* the comparisons contrast the strong resolve of the sage and the weak resolve of the fool.

22.19–26: Preserving friendships. Friendships are best preserved by keeping confidences and avoiding harsh words. A true friend remains faithful both in prosperity and in hard times (cf. 6.5–17; 9.10–16; 19.13–17; 27.16–21; 37.1–6). **19:** *Eye,* just as the eye is sensitive to being hurt, so the heart (the place of thinking and feeling) suffers and expresses its own hurt *feelings.*

But as for reviling, arrogance, disclosure of
  secrets, or a treacherous blow—
in these cases any friend will take to
  flight.

²³ Gain the trust of your neighbor in his
  poverty,
  so that you may rejoice with him in his
    prosperity.
Stand by him in time of distress,
  so that you may share with him in his
    inheritance.ᵃ
²⁴ The vapor and smoke of the furnace
  precede the fire;
  so insults precede bloodshed.
²⁵ I am not ashamed to shelter a friend,
  and I will not hide from him.
²⁶ But if harm should come to me because
    of him,
  whoever hears of it will beware of him.

²⁷ Who will set a guard over my mouth,
  and an effective seal upon my lips,
so that I may not fall because of them,
  and my tongue may not destroy me?

23 O Lord, Father and Master of my life,
  do not abandon me to their designs,
  and do not let me fall because of them!
² Who will set whips over my thoughts,
  and the discipline of wisdom over my
    mind,
so as not to spare me in my errors,
  and not overlook myᵇ sins?
³ Otherwise my mistakes may be multiplied,
  and my sins may abound,
and I may fall before my adversaries,
  and my enemy may rejoice over me.ᶜ
⁴ O Lord, Father and God of my life,
  do not give me haughty eyes,
  ⁵ and remove evil desire from me.
⁶ Let neither gluttony nor lust overcome me,
  and do not give me over to shameless
    passion.

DISCIPLINE OF THE TONGUEᵈ

⁷ Listen, my children, to instruction
  concerning the mouth;

the one who observes it will never be
  caught.
⁸ Sinners are overtaken through their
  lips;
  by them the reviler and the arrogant are
    tripped up.
⁹ Do not accustom your mouth to oaths,
  nor habitually utter the name of the
    Holy One;
¹⁰ for as a servant who is constantly under
    scrutiny
  will not lack bruises,
so also the person who always swears and
    utters the Name
  will never be cleansedᵉ from sin.
¹¹ The one who swears many oaths is full of
    iniquity,
  and the scourge will not leave his
    house.
If he swears in error, his sin remains on
    him,
  and if he disregards it, he sins doubly;
if he swears a false oath, he will not be
    justified,
  for his house will be filled with
    calamities.

¹² There is a manner of speaking
  comparable to death;ᶠ
  may it never be found in the inheritance
    of Jacob!
Such conduct will be far from the godly,
  and they will not wallow in sins.
¹³ Do not accustom your mouth to coarse,
    foul language,
  for it involves sinful speech.

ᵃ Other ancient authorities add *For one should not
  always despise restricted circumstances, or admire
  a rich person who is stupid.*
ᵇ Gk *their*
ᶜ Other ancient authorities add *From them the hope
  of your mercy is remote*
ᵈ This heading is included in the Gk text.
ᵉ Syr *be free*
ᶠ Other ancient authorities read *clothed about with
  death*

22.27–23.6: Prayers for self-control. Two short units consisting of a question and a prayer ask for God's help
in the areas of speech and sexuality. **23.1,4:** *O Lord, Father,* cf. 51.10.
  23.7–15: Sins of speech. Recognition of the need for self-control in matters of speech flows from the question and prayer in 22.27–23.1. **9:** *Oaths,* for avoiding rash or false oaths sworn in God's *name,* see Ex 20.7; Lev

¹⁴ Remember your father and mother
    when you sit among the great,
or you may forget yourself in their
        presence,
    and behave like a fool through bad habit;
then you will wish that you had never
        been born,
    and you will curse the day of your birth.
¹⁵ Those who are accustomed to using
        abusive language
    will never become disciplined as long as
        they live.

¹⁶ Two kinds of individuals multiply sins,
    and a third incurs wrath.
Hot passion that blazes like a fire
    will not be quenched until it burns
        itself out;
one who commits fornication with his
        near of kin
    will never cease until the fire burns
        him up.
¹⁷ To a fornicator all bread is sweet;
    he will never weary until he dies.
¹⁸ The one who sins against his marriage
        bed
    says to himself, "Who can see me?
Darkness surrounds me, the walls hide me,
    and no one sees me. Why should I
        worry?
The Most High will not remember sins."
¹⁹ His fear is confined to human eyes
    and he does not realize that the eyes of
        the Lord
    are ten thousand times brighter than
        the sun;
they look upon every aspect of human
        behavior
    and see into hidden corners.
²⁰ Before the universe was created, it was
        known to him,
    and so it is since its completion.

²¹ This man will be punished in the streets
        of the city,
    and where he least suspects it, he will
        be seized.

²² So it is with a woman who leaves her
        husband
    and presents him with an heir by
        another man.
²³ For first of all, she has disobeyed the law
        of the Most High;
    second, she has committed an offense
        against her husband;
and third, through her fornication she has
        committed adultery
    and brought forth children by another
        man.
²⁴ She herself will be brought before the
        assembly,
    and her punishment will extend to her
        children.
²⁵ Her children will not take root,
    and her branches will not bear fruit.
²⁶ She will leave behind an accursed
        memory
    and her disgrace will never be blotted
        out.
²⁷ Those who survive her will recognize
    that nothing is better than the fear of
        the Lord,
and nothing sweeter than to heed the
    commandments of the Lord.ᵃ

THE PRAISE OF WISDOMᵇ

24 Wisdom praises herself,
    and tells of her glory in the midst of
        her people.

ᵃ Other ancient authorities add as verse 28, *It is a
    great honor to follow God, and to be received by him
    is long life.*

ᵇ This heading is included in the Gk text.

5.4; Deut 5.11. **12:** *Death,* the biblical penalty for blasphemy (Lev 24.16). *The inheritance of Jacob,* the Israelites. **14:** *Curse the day of your birth,* see Job 3.3–5; Jer 20.14–18.

23.16–27: Sexual sins. This unit flows from the question and prayer in 23.2–6. **16–17:** *Two kinds . . . a third,* the numerical proverb (cf. 25.1–2,7–11; 26.5–6,28; 50.25–26) condemns three kinds of sexual sins: *hot passion,* incest, and *fornication.* **18–21:** How adulterers delude themselves. **21:** *Punished,* cf. Lev 20.10; Deut 22.22–27. **22–27:** An adulteress who bears a child by another man offends both God and her husband (Ex 20.14; Deut. 5.18). **24:** *Before the assembly,* cf. Deut 22.22–24. **27:** The punishments visited upon those who commit adultery highlight the importance of the *fear of the Lord* and God's *commandments.*

24.1–22: Wisdom praises herself. Wisdom is personified as a female figure (cf. Prov 8.22–36; Job 28; Bar

2 In the assembly of the Most High she
   opens her mouth,
   and in the presence of his hosts she
   tells of her glory:
3 "I came forth from the mouth of the Most
   High,
   and covered the earth like a mist.
4 I dwelt in the highest heavens,
   and my throne was in a pillar of cloud.
5 Alone I compassed the vault of heaven
   and traversed the depths of the abyss.
6 Over waves of the sea, over all the earth,
   and over every people and nation I have
   held sway.ᵃ
7 Among all these I sought a resting place;
   in whose territory should I abide?

8 "Then the Creator of all things gave me a
   command,
   and my Creator chose the place for my
   tent.
He said, 'Make your dwelling in Jacob,
   and in Israel receive your inheritance.'
9 Before the ages, in the beginning, he
   created me,
   and for all the ages I shall not cease to be.
10 In the holy tent I ministered before him,
   and so I was established in Zion.
11 Thus in the beloved city he gave me a
   resting place,
   and in Jerusalem was my domain.
12 I took root in an honored people,
   in the portion of the Lord, his heritage.

13 "I grew tall like a cedar in Lebanon,
   and like a cypress on the heights of
   Hermon.
14 I grew tall like a palm tree in En-gedi,ᵇ
   and like rosebushes in Jericho;

like a fair olive tree in the field,
   and like a plane tree beside waterᶜ I
   grew tall.
15 Like cassia and camel's thorn I gave forth
   perfume,
   and like choice myrrh I spread my
   fragrance,
like galbanum, onycha, and stacte,
   and like the odor of incense in the tent.
16 Like a terebinth I spread out my branches,
   and my branches are glorious and
   graceful.
17 Like the vine I bud forth delights,
   and my blossoms become glorious and
   abundant fruit.ᵈ

19 "Come to me, you who desire me,
   and eat your fill of my fruits.
20 For the memory of me is sweeter than
   honey,
   and the possession of me sweeter than
   the honeycomb.
21 Those who eat of me will hunger for more,
   and those who drink of me will thirst
   for more.
22 Whoever obeys me will not be put to
   shame,
   and those who work with me will not
   sin."

ᵃ Other ancient authorities read *I have acquired a
   possession*
ᵇ Other ancient authorities read *on the beaches*
ᶜ Other ancient authorities omit *beside water*
ᵈ Other ancient authorities add as verse 18, *I am the
   mother of beautiful love, of fear, of knowledge, and
   of holy hope; being eternal, I am given to all my
   children, to those who are named by him.*

3.9–4.4) who dwells in the Jerusalem Temple. **1–2:** *Her glory,* both the Hebrew (*hokhma*) and Greek (*sophia*)
terms for *wisdom* are feminine in gender. The use of first-person singular language in praise of oneself (aretalogy) is characteristic of ancient texts associated with the Egyptian goddess Isis. *Her people,* i.e., Israel, and
the assembly of the Most High, i.e., the divine council, cf. Ps 82.1,6–7. **3–7:** Wisdom was created by God and has
cosmic significance (Prov 8.22–31; Wis 1.7; 7.22–30). **4:** *Pillar of cloud,* see Ex 13.21–22; 33.9–10. **7:** *Resting place,* cf.
Job 28.12–28; Wis 7.22–30; 1 Enoch 42. **8–12:** *Zion,* wisdom's dwelling place in Jacob (cf. Bar 3.36–37) is the Jerusalem Temple. **9:** Cf. Prov 8.22–23. **10:** *Holy tent,* i.e., the tabernacle; see Ex 25.8–9. **13–17:** The comparisons stress
wisdom's attractiveness and her life-giving power. **13:** *Lebanon,* a high mountain range in modern Lebanon and
Syria, famous in antiquity for its forests. *Hermon,* a high mountain on the border between modern Israel and
Syria. **14:** *En-gedi* and *Jericho* are oases in the Judean desert region, near the Dead Sea. **15:** These items were in-
gredients for the *perfume* and *incense* used in the Jerusalem Temple; see Ex 30.22–38. **19–22:** Wisdom's banquet
provides delights and keeps one from sin (cf. 51.23–30; Prov 9.1–6).

²³ All this is the book of the covenant of
the Most High God,
the law that Moses commanded us
as an inheritance for the congregations
of Jacob.ᵃ
²⁵ It overflows, like the Pishon, with wisdom,
and like the Tigris at the time of the
first fruits.
²⁶ It runs over, like the Euphrates, with
understanding,
and like the Jordan at harvest time.
²⁷ It pours forth instruction like the Nile,ᵇ
like the Gihon at the time of vintage.
²⁸ The first man did not know wisdomᶜ
fully,
nor will the last one fathom her.
²⁹ For her thoughts are more abundant
than the sea,
and her counsel deeper than the great
abyss.

³⁰ As for me, I was like a canal from a river,
like a water channel into a garden.
³¹ I said, "I will water my garden
and drench my flower-beds."
And lo, my canal became a river,
and my river a sea.
³² I will again make instruction shine forth
like the dawn,
and I will make it clear from far away.
³³ I will again pour out teaching like
prophecy,
and leave it to all future generations.
³⁴ Observe that I have not labored for
myself alone,
but for all who seek wisdom.ᶜ

25 I take pleasure in three things,
and they are beautiful in the sight of
God and of mortals:ᵈ

agreement among brothers and sisters,
friendship among neighbors,
and a wife and a husband who live in
harmony.
² I hate three kinds of people,
and I loathe their manner of life:
a pauper who boasts, a rich person who lies,
and an old fool who commits adultery.

³ If you gathered nothing in your youth,
how can you find anything in your old
age?
⁴ How attractive is sound judgment in the
gray-haired,
and for the aged to possess good
counsel!
⁵ How attractive is wisdom in the aged,
and understanding and counsel in the
venerable!
⁶ Rich experience is the crown of the aged,
and their boast is the fear of the Lord.

⁷ I can think of nine whom I would call
blessed,
and a tenth my tongue proclaims:
a man who can rejoice in his children;
a man who lives to see the downfall of
his foes.
⁸ Happy the man who lives with a sensible
wife,

ᵃ Other ancient authorities add as verse 24, *"Do not
cease to be strong in the Lord, cling to him so that
he may strengthen you; the Lord Almighty alone is
God, and besides him there is no savior."*
ᵇ Syr: Gk *It makes instruction shine forth like light*
ᶜ Gk *her*
ᵈ Syr Lat: Gk *In three things I was beautiful and I
stood in beauty before the Lord and mortals.*

24.23–34: Ben Sira's commentary on the preceding poem about Wisdom. The identification of wisdom with
the *covenant* and the *law* (24.23; Ex 24.7; Deut 33.4) combines the two great traditions taught at Ben Sira's
school. **25–27:** Four of the rivers—Pishon, Tigris, Euphrates, and Gihon—appear in Gen 2.10–14. **28–29:** *The
first man,* Adam did not know the Torah, the true wisdom, which was given first to Moses. **30–34:** As a wisdom
teacher, Ben Sira regarded himself as a *canal* and a *water channel* for the wisdom conveyed in the Torah and the
ancient Near Eastern wisdom tradition. See 33.16–19 and 51.13–30 for further autobiographical reflections on
his role as a wisdom teacher.

25.1–11: Happiness. Two sets of numerical sayings (25.1–2,7–11) bracket an ideal picture of old age (25.3–6).
1–2: The scenes of harmony stand in contrast with pictures of persons who act inappropriately. **3–6:** At their
best the elderly manifest the value of *wisdom* and *fear of the Lord.* **7–11:** Ten beatitudes declare certain persons
happy in the present. **8:** Plowing with an *ox and ass together* is forbidden by Deut 22.10. The reference here may

and the one who does not plow with ox
and ass together.[a]
Happy is the one who does not sin with
the tongue,
and the one who has not served an
inferior.
⁹ Happy is the one who finds a friend,[b]
and the one who speaks to attentive
listeners.
¹⁰ How great is the one who finds wisdom!
But none is superior to the one who
fears the Lord.
¹¹ Fear of the Lord surpasses everything;
to whom can we compare the one who
has it?[c]

¹³ Any wound, but not a wound of the
heart!
Any wickedness, but not the
wickedness of a woman!
¹⁴ Any suffering, but not suffering from
those who hate!
And any vengeance, but not the
vengeance of enemies!
¹⁵ There is no venom[d] worse than a snake's
venom,[d]
and no anger worse than a woman's[e]
wrath.

¹⁶ I would rather live with a lion and a
dragon
than live with an evil woman.
¹⁷ A woman's wickedness changes her
appearance,
and darkens her face like that of a bear.
¹⁸ Her husband sits[f] among the neighbors,
and he cannot help sighing[g] bitterly.
¹⁹ Any iniquity is small compared to a
woman's iniquity;
may a sinner's lot befall her!
²⁰ A sandy ascent for the feet of the aged—
such is a garrulous wife to a quiet
husband.

²¹ Do not be ensnared by a woman's beauty,
and do not desire a woman for her
possessions.[h]
²² There is wrath and impudence and great
disgrace
when a wife supports her husband.
²³ Dejected mind, gloomy face,
and wounded heart come from an evil
wife.
Drooping hands and weak knees
come from the wife who does not make
her husband happy.
²⁴ From a woman sin had its beginning,
and because of her we all die.
²⁵ Allow no outlet to water,
and no boldness of speech to an evil wife.
²⁶ If she does not go as you direct,
separate her from yourself.

26 Happy is the husband of a good wife;
the number of his days will be doubled.
² A loyal wife brings joy to her husband,
and he will complete his years in peace.
³ A good wife is a great blessing;
she will be granted among the blessings
of the man who fears the Lord.
⁴ Whether rich or poor, his heart is
content,
and at all times his face is cheerful.

a Heb Syr: Gk lacks *and the one who does not plow with ox and ass together*
b Lat Syr: Gk *good sense*
c Other ancient authorities add as verse 12, *The fear of the Lord is the beginning of love for him, and faith is the beginning of clinging to him.*
d Syr: Gk *head*
e Other ancient authorities read *an enemy's*
f Heb Syr: Gk *loses heart*
g Other ancient authorities read *and listening he sighs*
h Heb Syr: Other Gk authorities read *for her beauty*

be to polygamy with incompatible wives (cf. 26.6; 37.11).
25.13–26.18: Bad and good wives. Alternating sections describe a bad wife (25.13–26; 26.5–12) and a good wife (26.1–4; 26.13–18). **25.13–26:** Advice for young male students about the bad effects of living with an evil and angry woman. Sirach's very negative remarks about women are striking even in the context of a patriarchal culture. **16:** Prov 21.19; 25.24; 27.15. **22:** *Disgrace,* for a husband to be dependent financially on his wife was regarded as a cause for shame. **24:** *From a woman sin had its beginning,* see Gen 3.6. Sirach's interpretation exceeds Gen 3 in placing blame upon the woman (cf. 2 Cor 11.3; 1 Tim 2.14). **26:** *Separate,* only the husband could initiate divorce proceedings (Deut 24.1–4). **26.1–4:** A *good wife* is a *great blessing* to her husband, and brings him a long

⁵ Of three things my heart is frightened,
  and of a fourth I am in great fear:ᵃ
Slander in the city, the gathering of
    a mob,
  and false accusation—all these are
    worse than death.
⁶ But it is heartache and sorrow when a
    wife is jealous of a rival,
  and a tongue-lashing makes it known
    to all.
⁷ A bad wife is a chafing yoke;
  taking hold of her is like grasping a
    scorpion.
⁸ A drunken wife arouses great anger;
  she cannot hide her shame.
⁹ The haughty stare betrays an unchaste
    wife;
  her eyelids give her away.

¹⁰ Keep strict watch over a headstrong
    daughter,
  or else, when she finds liberty, she will
    make use of it.
¹¹ Be on guard against her impudent eye,
  and do not be surprised if she sins
    against you.
¹² As a thirsty traveler opens his mouth
    and drinks from any water near him,
so she will sit in front of every tent peg
  and open her quiver to the arrow.

¹³ A wife's charm delights her husband,
  and her skill puts flesh on his bones.
¹⁴ A silent wife is a gift from the Lord,
  and nothing is so precious as her self-
    discipline.
¹⁵ A modest wife adds charm to charm,
  and no scales can weigh the value of her
    chastity.
¹⁶ Like the sun rising in the heights of the
    Lord,

so is the beauty of a good wife in her
    well-ordered home.
¹⁷ Like the shining lamp on the holy
    lampstand,
  so is a beautiful face on a stately figure.
¹⁸ Like golden pillars on silver bases,
  so are shapely legs and steadfast feet.

Other ancient authorities add verses 19-27:

¹⁹ *My child, keep sound the bloom of your*
    youth,
  and do not give your strength to
    strangers.
²⁰ *Seek a fertile field within the whole plain,*
  and sow it with your own seed, trusting
    in your fine stock.
²¹ *So your offspring will prosper,*
  and, having confidence in their good
    descent, will grow great.
²² *A prostitute is regarded as spittle,*
  and a married woman as a tower of
    death to her lovers.
²³ *A godless wife is given as a portion to a*
    lawless man,
  but a pious wife is given to the man who
    fears the Lord.
²⁴ *A shameless woman constantly acts*
    disgracefully,
  but a modest daughter will even be
    embarrassed before her husband.
²⁵ *A headstrong wife is regarded as a dog,*
  but one who has a sense of shame will
    fear the Lord.
²⁶ *A wife honoring her husband will seem*
    wise to all,
  but if she dishonors him in her pride she
    will be known to all as ungodly.
  Happy is the husband of a good wife;

ᵃ Syr: Meaning of Gk uncertain

life, joy, and peace (cf. Prov. 31.10–31). **26.5–12:** Warnings about a *jealous, bad, drunken,* and *unchaste wife* lead into advice about keeping strict control over a *headstrong daughter.* **5–6:** In numerical proverbs (see 23.16–17n) the last element is the climax. **6:** *Jealous of a rival,* probably referring to hostility among wives in a polygamous household. **12:** *Tent peg . . . quiver,* the language here about illicit sexual relations is very graphic. **26.13–18:** A good wife is praised for her virtues and physical beauty. **13:** *Her skill,* cf. Prov 31.10–31. **17–18:** Cf. Song 4.1–7.

27.19–27: More about women. While not in the Hebrew text, these verses appear in Greek and Syriac manuscripts and seem to have been part of Ben Sira's original work. **19–21:** The ideal for the young Jewish man is to marry a Jewish woman and raise up many children from her (Prov 5.7–23). **20:** An agricultural metaphor for reproduction. **22–27:** These further contrasts between bad and good wives (cf. 25.13–26.18) allow the positive ideal of the good Jewish wife to emerge more clearly.

for the number of his years will be doubled.
²⁷ *A loud-voiced and garrulous wife is like a trumpet sounding the charge,*
and every person like this lives in the anarchy of war.

---

²⁸ At two things my heart is grieved,
and because of a third anger comes over me:
a warrior in want through poverty,
intelligent men who are treated contemptuously,
and a man who turns back from righteousness to sin—
the Lord will prepare him for the sword!

²⁹ A merchant can hardly keep from wrongdoing,
nor is a tradesman innocent of sin.

27 Many have committed sin for gain,[a]
and those who seek to get rich will avert their eyes.
² As a stake is driven firmly into a fissure between stones,
so sin is wedged in between selling and buying.
³ If a person is not steadfast in the fear of the Lord,
his house will be quickly overthrown.

⁴ When a sieve is shaken, the refuse appears;
so do a person's faults when he speaks.
⁵ The kiln tests the potter's vessels;
so the test of a person is in his conversation.
⁶ Its fruit discloses the cultivation of a tree;
so a person's speech discloses the cultivation of his mind.
⁷ Do not praise anyone before he speaks,
for this is the way people are tested.

⁸ If you pursue justice, you will attain it
and wear it like a glorious robe.

⁹ Birds roost with their own kind,
so honesty comes home to those who practice it.
¹⁰ A lion lies in wait for prey;
so does sin for evildoers.

¹¹ The conversation of the godly is always wise,
but the fool changes like the moon.
¹² Among stupid people limit your time,
but among thoughtful people linger on.
¹³ The talk of fools is offensive,
and their laughter is wantonly sinful.
¹⁴ Their cursing and swearing make one's hair stand on end,
and their quarrels make others stop their ears.
¹⁵ The strife of the proud leads to bloodshed,
and their abuse is grievous to hear.

¹⁶ Whoever betrays secrets destroys confidence,
and will never find a congenial friend.
¹⁷ Love your friend and keep faith with him;
but if you betray his secrets, do not follow after him.
¹⁸ For as a person destroys his enemy,
so you have destroyed the friendship of your neighbor.
¹⁹ And as you allow a bird to escape from your hand,
so you have let your neighbor go, and will not catch him again.
²⁰ Do not go after him, for he is too far off,
and has escaped like a gazelle from a snare.
²¹ For a wound may be bandaged,
and there is reconciliation after abuse,
but whoever has betrayed secrets is without hope.

---

a   Other ancient authorities read *a trifle*

26.28–27.29: Sin and speech. 26.28–27.7: How speech often reveals a person's character. 28: Another numerical proverb (see 23.16–17; 26.5–6). *Warrior,* the Greek translator may have mistaken *warrior* for the Hebrew word for "wealthy man." 27.2: *Sin is wedged,* business dealings often involve corruption (cf. Prov 11.1; 20.10,14). 4–7: Good speech is a paramount virtue in the wisdom tradition. A series of three comparisons from daily life disclose its diagnostic quality. 8–10: The contrasting effects of honesty and sin. 11–15: The contrast in the speech of the godly person and the fool. 16–21: Betraying confidences or *secrets* often brings friendships to an

²² Whoever winks the eye plots mischief,
    and those who know him will keep their
        distance.
²³ In your presence his mouth is all
        sweetness,
    and he admires your words;
but later he will twist his speech
    and with your own words he will trip
        you up.
²⁴ I have hated many things, but him above
        all;
    even the Lord hates him.
²⁵ Whoever throws a stone straight up
        throws it on his own head,
    and a treacherous blow opens up many
        wounds.
²⁶ Whoever digs a pit will fall into it,
    and whoever sets a snare will be caught
        in it.
²⁷ If a person does evil, it will roll back
        upon him,
    and he will not know where it came
        from.
²⁸ Mockery and abuse issue from the
        proud,
    but vengeance lies in wait for them like
        a lion.
²⁹ Those who rejoice in the fall of the godly
        will be caught in a snare,
    and pain will consume them before
        their death.

³⁰ Anger and wrath, these also are
        abominations,
    yet a sinner holds on to them.

28 The vengeful will face the Lord's
        vengeance,
    for he keeps a strict account of[a] their sins.
² Forgive your neighbor the wrong he has
        done,
    and then your sins will be pardoned
        when you pray.

³ Does anyone harbor anger against
        another,
    and expect healing from the Lord?
⁴ If one has no mercy toward another like
        himself,
    can he then seek pardon for his own sins?
⁵ If a mere mortal harbors wrath,
    who will make an atoning sacrifice for
        his sins?
⁶ Remember the end of your life, and set
        enmity aside;
    remember corruption and death, and be
        true to the commandments.
⁷ Remember the commandments, and do
        not be angry with your neighbor;
    remember the covenant of the Most
        High, and overlook faults.

⁸ Refrain from strife, and your sins will be
        fewer;
    for the hot-tempered kindle strife,
⁹ and the sinner disrupts friendships
    and sows discord among those who are
        at peace.
¹⁰ In proportion to the fuel, so will the fire
        burn,
    and in proportion to the obstinacy, so
        will strife increase;[b]
in proportion to a person's strength will be
        his anger,
    and in proportion to his wealth he will
        increase his wrath.
¹¹ A hasty quarrel kindles a fire,
    and a hasty dispute sheds blood.
¹² If you blow on a spark, it will glow;
    if you spit on it, it will be put out;
    yet both come out of your mouth.

a   Other ancient authorities read *for he firmly
    establishes*
b   Other ancient authorities read *burn*

end (Prov 20.19; 25.9). **21:** *Without hope,* of reconciliation (cf. 22.22). **22–24:** The hatefulness of the hypocrite.
25–29: How people destroy themselves with their own evil devices; cf. Prov 26.27; Eccl 10.8.

27.30–28.7: Forgiveness of sins. Two very important attributes of God are justice and mercy. **27.30–28.1:**
Those who demand strict justice from others will have to face God's own strict justice (cf. Deut 32.35–36). **2–5:**
Those who seek God's mercy must be willing to show mercy to others (cf. Lev 19.18). **6–7:** Remembering *death,*
the commandments, and God's *covenant* can provide encouragement to forgive others. Death is frequently mentioned as a motivation for proper conduct in Sirach; see 7.36; 8.7; 14.12; 18.24; 38.20.

28.8–26: Destructive speech. The mouth can be the instrument for all kinds of bad speech, and so it must
be carefully controlled. **8–12:** The mouth can either ignite or extinguish anger and *strife* (cf. Prov 26.20–21).

¹³ Curse the gossips and the double-
tongued,
    for they destroy the peace of many.
¹⁴ Slander[a] has shaken many,
    and scattered them from nation to
        nation;
it has destroyed strong cities,
    and overturned the houses of the
        great.
¹⁵ Slander[a] has driven virtuous women
    from their homes,
    and deprived them of the fruit of their
        toil.
¹⁶ Those who pay heed to slander[b] will not
    find rest,
    nor will they settle down in peace.
¹⁷ The blow of a whip raises a welt,
    but a blow of the tongue crushes the
        bones.
¹⁸ Many have fallen by the edge of the
    sword,
    but not as many as have fallen because
        of the tongue.
¹⁹ Happy is the one who is protected from
    it,
    who has not been exposed to its
        anger,
who has not borne its yoke,
    and has not been bound with its
        fetters.
²⁰ For its yoke is a yoke of iron,
    and its fetters are fetters of bronze;
²¹ its death is an evil death,
    and Hades is preferable to it.
²² It has no power over the godly;
    they will not be burned in its flame.
²³ Those who forsake the Lord will fall into
    its power;
    it will burn among them and will not be
        put out.
It will be sent out against them like a lion;
    like a leopard it will mangle them.
²⁴ᵃ As you fence in your property with
    thorns,

²⁵ᵇ so make a door and a bolt for your
    mouth.
²⁴ᵇ As you lock up your silver and gold,
    ²⁵ᵃ so make balances and scales for your
        words.
²⁶ Take care not to err with your tongue,[c]
    and fall victim to one lying in wait.

29 The merciful lend to their neighbors;
    by holding out a helping hand they
        keep the commandments.
² Lend to your neighbor in his time of
    need;
    repay your neighbor when a loan falls
        due.
³ Keep your promise and be honest with
    him,
    and on every occasion you will find
        what you need.
⁴ Many regard a loan as a windfall,
    and cause trouble to those who help
        them.
⁵ One kisses another's hands until he gets
    a loan,
    and is deferential in speaking of his
        neighbor's money;
but at the time for repayment he delays,
    and pays back with empty promises,
    and finds fault with the time.
⁶ If he can pay, his creditor[d] will hardly get
    back half,
    and will regard that as a windfall.
If he cannot pay, the borrower[d] has robbed
    the other of his money,
    and he has needlessly made him an
        enemy;

a Gk *A third tongue*
b Gk *it*
c Gk *with it*
d Gk *he*

13–16: *Slander* can and does ruin lives (51.2–6). 17–23: A series of comparisons illustrates the destructive effects of speech. 17: *Bones*, cf. Prov 25.15. 21: *Hades* (Heb "Sheol") is the abode of the dead. 24–26: Various images highlight the need to guard against destructive speech. One's *words* should be guarded as carefully as one's prized possessions.

29.1–20: Money matters. 1–7: *Lend*ing. While loans could be given to fellow Jews without charging interest (Ex 22.25; Lev 25.35–37; Deut 15.7–11; 23.19–20; 24.10–13; Neh 5.10–11), charging interest was allowed when one loaned to non-Jews (Deut 23.20–21). Ben Sira encourages a willingness to make loans, but warns that there is

he will repay him with curses and
reproaches,
and instead of glory will repay him with
dishonor.
⁷ Many refuse to lend, not because of
meanness,
but from fearᵃ of being defrauded
needlessly.

⁸ Nevertheless, be patient with someone in
humble circumstances,
and do not keep him waiting for your
alms.
⁹ Help the poor for the commandment's sake,
and in their need do not send them
away empty-handed.
¹⁰ Lose your silver for the sake of a brother
or a friend,
and do not let it rust under a stone and
be lost.
¹¹ Lay up your treasure according to the
commandments of the Most High,
and it will profit you more than gold.
¹² Store up almsgiving in your treasury,
and it will rescue you from every disaster;
¹³ better than a stout shield and a sturdy
spear,
it will fight for you against the enemy.

¹⁴ A good person will be surety for his
neighbor,
but the one who has lost all sense of
shame will fail him.
¹⁵ Do not forget the kindness of your
guarantor,
for he has given his life for you.
¹⁶ A sinner wastes the property of his
guarantor,
¹⁷ and the ungrateful person abandons
his rescuer.
¹⁸ Being surety has ruined many who were
prosperous,
and has tossed them about like waves of
the sea;

it has driven the influential into exile,
and they have wandered among foreign
nations.
¹⁹ The sinner comes to grief through surety;
his pursuit of gain involves him in
lawsuits.
²⁰ Assist your neighbor to the best of your
ability,
but be careful not to fall yourself.

²¹ The necessities of life are water, bread,
and clothing,
and also a house to assure privacy.
²² Better is the life of the poor under their
own crude roof
than sumptuous food in the house of
others.
²³ Be content with little or much,
and you will hear no reproach for being
a guest.ᵇ
²⁴ It is a miserable life to go from house to
house;
as a guest you should not open your
mouth;
²⁵ you will play the host and provide drink
without being thanked,
and besides this you will hear rude
words like these:
²⁶ "Come here, stranger, prepare the table;
let me eat what you have there."
²⁷ "Be off, stranger, for an honored guest
is here;
my brother has come for a visit, and I
need the guest-room."
²⁸ It is hard for a sensible person to bear
scolding about lodgingᶜ and the insults
of the moneylender.

ᵃ Other ancient authorities read *many refuse to lend, therefore, because of such meanness; they are afraid*
ᵇ Lat: Gk *reproach from your family*; other ancient authorities lack this line
ᶜ Or *scolding from the household*

no guarantee that one will be repaid and so one must always be cautious (cf. 8.12–13). **8–13**: Alms. Giving *alms* is in accord with the Torah (Deut 15.7) and will contribute to one's spiritual treasury (cf. 3.30–4.10). **14–20**: *Surety*. Ben Sira's encouragement to provide *surety* or collateral for another person contrasts with the advice given repeatedly in Prov 6.1–5; 11.15; 17.18; 20.16; 22.2; 27.13.

29.21–28: Not depending on others. While the Torah directs caring for indigent relatives (Lev 25.35), receiving such care can become demeaning and even shameful. **21**: *Necessities*, cf. the longer list in 39.26. **25**: *You will play the host*, that is, you will be pressed into service in the household.

CONCERNING CHILDREN[a]

30 He who loves his son will whip him often,
so that he may rejoice at the way he turns out.

[2] He who disciplines his son will profit by him,
and will boast of him among acquaintances.

[3] He who teaches his son will make his enemies envious,
and will glory in him among his friends.

[4] When the father dies he will not seem to be dead,
for he has left behind him one like himself,

[5] whom in his life he looked upon with joy
and at death, without grief.

[6] He has left behind him an avenger against his enemies,
and one to repay the kindness of his friends.

[7] Whoever spoils his son will bind up his wounds,
and will suffer heartache at every cry.

[8] An unbroken horse turns out stubborn,
and an unchecked son turns out headstrong.

[9] Pamper a child, and he will terrorize you;
play with him, and he will grieve you.

[10] Do not laugh with him, or you will have sorrow with him,
and in the end you will gnash your teeth.

[11] Give him no freedom in his youth,
and do not ignore his errors.

[12] Bow down his neck in his youth,[b]
and beat his sides while he is young,
or else he will become stubborn and disobey you,
and you will have sorrow of soul from him.[c]

[13] Discipline your son and make his yoke heavy,[d]

so that you may not be offended by his shamelessness.

[14] Better off poor, healthy, and fit
than rich and afflicted in body.

[15] Health and fitness are better than any gold,
and a robust body than countless riches.

[16] There is no wealth better than health of body,
and no gladness above joy of heart.

[17] Death is better than a life of misery,
and eternal sleep[e] than chronic sickness.

CONCERNING FOODS[f]

[18] Good things poured out upon a mouth that is closed
are like offerings of food placed upon a grave.

[19] Of what use to an idol is a sacrifice?
For it can neither eat nor smell.
So is the one punished by the Lord;

[20] he sees with his eyes and groans
as a eunuch groans when embracing a girl.[g]

[21] Do not give yourself over to sorrow,
and do not distress yourself deliberately.

a   This heading is included in the Gk text.
b   Other ancient authorities lack this line and the preceding line
c   Other ancient authorities lack this line
d   Heb: Gk *take pains with him*
e   Other ancient authorities lack *eternal sleep*
f   This heading is included in the Gk text; other ancient authorities place the heading before verse 16
g   Other ancient authorities add *So is the person who does right under compulsion*

30.1–13: Fathers and sons. A father's discipline of his son will benefit the son and add to the father's good reputation before others. **1–6:** Ben Sira's harsh views on raising children (cf. 22.6) were not unique (cf. Prov 13.24; 19.18; 22.15; 23.13–14; 29.15,17). **4:** The child is the image of the father (cf. Gen 5.3; Tob 9.6). **6:** *Avenger*, one who can vindicate his father's honor (cf. Ps 127.5). **7–13:** Lack of *discipline* will lead to shame and sorrow for both parent and child (Deut 21.18–21).

30.14–25: Happiness. Three elements that lead to happiness are good health, good food, and a good disposition. **17:** *Death is better,* cf. Job 3.11,13,17; Eccl 4.2–3; 6.3,10,13; Tob 3.6,10,13. **18–20:** *Food placed on a grave* (Tob

22 A joyful heart is life itself,
    and rejoicing lengthens one's life span.
23 Indulge yourself[a] and take comfort,
    and remove sorrow far from you,
for sorrow has destroyed many,
    and no advantage ever comes from it.
24 Jealousy and anger shorten life,
    and anxiety brings on premature old
        age.
25 Those who are cheerful and merry at
        table
    will benefit from their food.

31 Wakefulness over wealth wastes away
    one's flesh,
    and anxiety about it drives away
        sleep.
2 Wakeful anxiety prevents slumber,
    and a severe illness carries off sleep.[b]
3 The rich person toils to amass a fortune,
    and when he rests he fills himself with
        his dainties.
4 The poor person toils to make a meager
        living,
    and if ever he rests he becomes needy.

5 One who loves gold will not be justified;
    one who pursues money will be led
        astray[c] by it.
6 Many have come to ruin because of gold,
    and their destruction has met them face
        to face.
7 It is a stumbling block to those who are
        avid for it,
    and every fool will be taken captive by
        it.
8 Blessed is the rich person who is found
        blameless,
    and who does not go after gold.
9 Who is he, that we may praise him?
    For he has done wonders among his
        people.

10 Who has been tested by it and been
        found perfect?
    Let it be for him a ground for
        boasting.
Who has had the power to transgress and
        did not transgress,
    and to do evil and did not do it?
11 His prosperity will be established,[d]
    and the assembly will proclaim his acts
        of charity.

12 Are you seated at the table of the great?[e]
    Do not be greedy at it,
    and do not say, "How much food there
        is here!"
13 Remember that a greedy eye is a bad
        thing.
    What has been created more greedy
        than the eye?
    Therefore it sheds tears for any reason.
14 Do not reach out your hand for
        everything you see,
    and do not crowd your neighbor[f] at the
        dish.
15 Judge your neighbor's feelings by your
        own,
    and in every matter be thoughtful.
16 Eat what is set before you like a well
        brought-up person,[g]
    and do not chew greedily, or you will
        give offense.
17 Be the first to stop, as befits good
        manners,

a   Other ancient authorities read *Beguile yourself*
b   Other ancient authorities read *sleep carries off a
    severe illness*
c   Heb Syr: Gk *pursues destruction will be filled*
d   Other ancient authorities add *because of this*
e   Heb Syr: Gk *at a great table*
f   Gk *him*
g   Heb: Gk *like a human being*

4.17) is useless. An *idol* (Deut 4.28; Isa 44.9–20) and a *eunuch* (20.4) are unable to enjoy the pleasures of life. **23:**
Indulge yourself, cf. Eccl 2.10; 11.9–10.

   31.1–11: Riches and righteousness. Wealth does not guarantee happiness or righteousness (cf. Prov 30.8–9;
Eccl 5.10). **8–11:** The beatitude acknowledges that it is possible (by exception) for a rich person to be righteous
(cf. 13.24; Prov 28.20). **8:** *Gold,* the Hebrew text has *mammon* (cf. Mt 6.24; Lk 16.9,13).

   31.12–32.13: Table manners and moderation. In the upper-class milieu supposed here, cautious public behavior could help in establishing and maintaining one's good reputation. The topic of proper behavior at banquets was a frequent theme in ancient Egyptian wisdom literature, including *Ptahhotep* and *Amenemope*. **12–18:**
The goal behind observing good table manners (cf. Prov 23.1–3) is to avoid drawing undue and unwelcome

and do not be insatiable, or you will give offense.

¹⁸ If you are seated among many persons, do not help yourself[a] before they do.

¹⁹ How ample a little is for a well-disciplined person!
He does not breathe heavily when in bed.

²⁰ Healthy sleep depends on moderate eating;
he rises early, and feels fit.
The distress of sleeplessness and of nausea
and colic are with the glutton.

²¹ If you are overstuffed with food, get up to vomit, and you will have relief.

²² Listen to me, my child, and do not disregard me,
and in the end you will appreciate my words.
In everything you do be moderate,[b]
and no sickness will overtake you.

²³ People bless the one who is liberal with food,
and their testimony to his generosity is trustworthy.

²⁴ The city complains of the one who is stingy with food,
and their testimony to his stinginess is accurate.

²⁵ Do not try to prove your strength by wine-drinking,
for wine has destroyed many.

²⁶ As the furnace tests the work of the smith,[c]
so wine tests hearts when the insolent quarrel.

²⁷ Wine is very life to human beings if taken in moderation.
What is life to one who is without wine?
It has been created to make people happy.

²⁸ Wine drunk at the proper time and in moderation
is rejoicing of heart and gladness of soul.

²⁹ Wine drunk to excess leads to bitterness of spirit,
to quarrels and stumbling.

³⁰ Drunkenness increases the anger of a fool to his own hurt,
reducing his strength and adding wounds.

³¹ Do not reprove your neighbor at a banquet of wine,
and do not despise him in his merrymaking;
speak no word of reproach to him,
and do not distress him by making demands of him.

32 If they make you master of the feast, do not exalt yourself;
be among them as one of their number.
Take care of them first and then sit down;
² when you have fulfilled all your duties, take your place,
so that you may be merry along with them
and receive a wreath for your excellent leadership.

³ Speak, you who are older, for it is your right,
but with accurate knowledge, and do not interrupt the music.

⁴ Where there is entertainment, do not pour out talk;
do not display your cleverness at the wrong time.

⁵ A ruby seal in a setting of gold is a concert of music at a banquet of wine.

⁶ A seal of emerald in a rich setting of gold is the melody of music with good wine.

⁷ Speak, you who are young, if you are obliged to,
but no more than twice, and only if asked.

a Gk *reach out your hand*
b Heb Syr: Gk *industrious*
c Heb: Gk *tests the hardening of steel by dipping*

attention to oneself. **19–31:** The bad effects of drinking too much *wine* (cf. Prov 20.1; 23.29–35; 31.4–5) are contrasted with the good effects of the moderate use of wine (cf. Ps 104.15). **32.1–13:** Advice to various participants at a banquet. **1:** *Master of the feast,* the one who cares for the needs of those who are eating (2 Macc 2.27). **3–10:**

⁸ Be brief; say much in few words;
  be as one who knows and can still hold
    his tongue.
⁹ Among the great do not act as their equal;
  and when another is speaking, do not
    babble.

¹⁰ Lightning travels ahead of the thunder,
  and approval goes before one who is
    modest.
¹¹ Leave in good time and do not be the last;
  go home quickly and do not linger.
¹² Amuse yourself there to your heart's
    content,
  but do not sin through proud speech.
¹³ But above all bless your Maker,
  who fills you with his good gifts.

¹⁴ The one who seeks God[a] will accept his
    discipline,
  and those who rise early to seek him[b]
    will find favor.
¹⁵ The one who seeks the law will be filled
    with it,
  but the hypocrite will stumble at it.
¹⁶ Those who fear the Lord will form true
    judgments,
  and they will kindle righteous deeds
    like a light.
¹⁷ The sinner will shun reproof,
  and will find a decision according to his
    liking.

¹⁸ A sensible person will not overlook a
    thoughtful suggestion;
  an insolent[c] and proud person will not
    be deterred by fear.[d]
¹⁹ Do nothing without deliberation,
  but when you have acted, do not regret
    it.
²⁰ Do not go on a path full of hazards,
  and do not stumble at an obstacle
    twice.[e]

²¹ Do not be overconfident on a smooth[f]
    road,
  ²² and give good heed to your paths.[g]
²³ Guard[h] yourself in every act,
  for this is the keeping of the
    commandments.

²⁴ The one who keeps the law preserves
    himself,[i]
  and the one who trusts the Lord will
    not suffer loss.

33 No evil will befall the one who fears
    the Lord,
  but in trials such a one will be rescued
    again and again.
² The wise will not hate the law,
  but the one who is hypocritical about it
    is like a boat in a storm.
³ The sensible person will trust in the law;
  for such a one the law is as dependable
    as a divine oracle.

⁴ Prepare what to say, and then you will be
    listened to;
  draw upon your training, and give your
    answer.
⁵ The heart of a fool is like a cart wheel,
  and his thoughts like a turning axle.
⁶ A mocking friend is like a stallion
  that neighs no matter who the rider is.

---

a   Heb: Gk *who fears the Lord*
b   Other ancient authorities lack *to seek him*
c   Heb: Gk *alien*
d   Meaning of Gk uncertain. Other ancient authorities
    add *and after acting, with him, without deliberation*
e   Heb: Gk *stumble on stony ground*
f   Or *an unexplored*
g   Heb Syr: Gk *and beware of your children*
h   Heb Syr: Gk *Trust*
i   Heb: Gk *who believes the law heeds the
    commandments*

Directions to *older* persons and the *young.* **11–13:** Advice meant for all. **13:** *Bless your Maker,* by saying a prayer of
thanksgiving after the meal.
  32.14–33.6: The law, fear of the Lord, and wisdom. Ben Sira's ideal sage combines these three elements
(which are the book's central themes), and so differs sharply from fools and sinners. **14:** *Discipline,* a frequent
topic in the book; see 1.27; 4.17; 6.18,22; 21.19,21; 26.14; 42.5,8; 50.27). *Rise early,* for prayer (cf. 39.5). **15:** *The law,*
here and elsewhere in the passage the reference is to the law of Moses (the Torah). **17:** *Decision,* an interpretation of the Torah. **33.1:** Cf. Wis 10.1–21. **2:** Hebrew, "He who hates the law is not wise, and is tossed about like a
boat in a storm." **3:** *Divine oracle,* the Urim and Thummim (45.10; Ex 28.30; Num 27.21; 1 Sam 14.41–42).

⁷ Why is one day more important than
another,
when all the daylight in the year is from
the sun?
⁸ By the Lord's wisdom they were
distinguished,
and he appointed the different seasons
and festivals.
⁹ Some days he exalted and hallowed,
and some he made ordinary days.
¹⁰ All human beings come from the ground,
and humankind[a] was created out of the
dust.
¹¹ In the fullness of his knowledge the Lord
distinguished them
and appointed their different ways.
¹² Some he blessed and exalted,
and some he made holy and brought
near to himself;
but some he cursed and brought low,
and turned them out of their place.
¹³ Like clay in the hand of the potter,
to be molded as he pleases,
so all are in the hand of their Maker,
to be given whatever he decides.

¹⁴ Good is the opposite of evil,
and life the opposite of death;
so the sinner is the opposite of the
godly.
¹⁵ Look at all the works of the Most High;
they come in pairs, one the opposite of
the other.

¹⁶ Now I was the last to keep vigil;
I was like a gleaner following the grape-
pickers;

¹⁷ by the blessing of the Lord I arrived first,
and like a grape-picker I filled my wine
press.
¹⁸ Consider that I have not labored for
myself alone,
but for all who seek instruction.
¹⁹ Hear me, you who are great among the
people,
and you leaders of the congregation,
pay heed!

²⁰ To son or wife, to brother or friend,
do not give power over yourself, as long
as you live;
and do not give your property to another,
in case you change your mind and must
ask for it.
²¹ While you are still alive and have breath
in you,
do not let anyone take your place.
²² For it is better that your children should
ask from you
than that you should look to the hand
of your children.
²³ Excel in all that you do;
bring no stain upon your honor.
²⁴ At the time when you end the days of
your life,
in the hour of death, distribute your
inheritance.

²⁵ Fodder and a stick and burdens for a
donkey;
bread and discipline and work for a
slave.

---

a   Heb: Gk *Adam*

33.7–15: The pairs. God's plan for creation is based on opposites. Nevertheless, since the absolute sovereignty of God is assumed, this is not a full-scale dualism. Ben Sira may be influenced by Stoic philosophy. **7–9:** Some days are holy days and others are *ordinary* (Gen 1.14; 2.3; Deut 16.1–15). **10–13:** A similar dualism occurs among humans. Although all are made from *dust* (Gen 3.19), some are *blessed* and some are *cursed*; perhaps referring to the different status of Israel (Gen 12.2–3; Ex 19.5) and the Canaanites (Gen 9.25–27; 12.6–7). **13:** *Clay,* cf. Isa 29.16; 45.9; 64.8; Jer 18.1–12. **14–15:** The dualism of the pairs is modified, since the *Most High* remains sovereign over all (Isa 45.7).

33.16–19: Ben Sira's vocation. For other autobiographical notices, see 24.30–34; 34.9–13; 39.12–13; 50.27; 51.13–30. **16–17:** A *gleaner* collects the leftovers during the harvest. By study and hard work Ben Sira became a *grape-picker,* that is, a wisdom teacher. **18–19:** *For all,* cf. 24.34.

33.20–33: Master of the household. The advice given here is intended for an adult male with a family, financial resources, and slaves. **20–24:** Preserve your financial independence and do not distribute your property until the hour of death. **25–33:** Human slavery was a socially and religiously sanctioned institution, and integral to the economy, in Ben Sira's world (cf. 7.20–21). His harsh advice is tempered by recognizing the self-interest

26 Set your slave to work, and you will find
    rest;
    leave his hands idle, and he will seek
        liberty.
27 Yoke and thong will bow the neck,
    and for a wicked slave there are racks
        and tortures.
28 Put him to work, in order that he may
    not be idle,
29 for idleness teaches much evil.
30 Set him to work, as is fitting for him,
    and if he does not obey, make his fetters
        heavy.
Do not be overbearing toward anyone,
    and do nothing unjust.

31 If you have but one slave, treat him like
    yourself,
    because you have bought him with
        blood.
If you have but one slave, treat him like a
    brother,
    for you will need him as you need your
        life.
32 If you ill-treat him, and he leaves you
    and runs away,
33 which way will you go to seek him?

34 The senseless have vain and false
    hopes,
    and dreams give wings to fools.
2 As one who catches at a shadow and
    pursues the wind,
    so is anyone who believes in[a] dreams.
3 What is seen in dreams is but a
    reflection,
    the likeness of a face looking at itself.
4 From an unclean thing what can be
    clean?
    And from something false what can be
        true?

5 Divinations and omens and dreams are
    unreal,
    and like a woman in labor, the mind has
        fantasies.
6 Unless they are sent by intervention from
    the Most High,
    pay no attention to them.
7 For dreams have deceived many,
    and those who put their hope in them
        have perished.
8 Without such deceptions the law will be
    fulfilled,
    and wisdom is complete in the mouth
        of the faithful.

9 An educated[b] person knows many
    things,
    and one with much experience knows
        what he is talking about.
10 An inexperienced person knows few
    things,
11 but he that has traveled acquires much
        cleverness.
12 I have seen many things in my travels,
    and I understand more than I can
        express.
13 I have often been in danger of death,
    but have escaped because of these
        experiences.

14 The spirit of those who fear the Lord will
    live,
15 for their hope is in him who saves
        them.
16 Those who fear the Lord will not be
    timid,
    or play the coward, for he is their
        hope.

a   Syr: Gk *pays heed to*
b   Other ancient authorities read *A traveled*

of someone who owns only *one slave* (33.31–33). **30:** *Do nothing unjust,* that is, act according to the biblical laws
pertaining to slaves (Ex 21.2–6,20–21,26–27; Lev 25.46; Deut 15.12–18). **32:** *Runs away,* Deut 23.15–16.

34.1–8: A critique of dreams. It is better to fulfill the law and to practice perfect wisdom than to rely on
dreams for wisdom and direction. Ben Sira may be criticizing the Jewish apocalyptic movement, which relied
extensively on dreams and visions for divine guidance (see the book of Daniel). **1:** *Dreams give wings to fools,* cf.
Deut 13.2–5; 18.9–14; Eccl 5.7; Jer 29.8. **2:** *Pursues the wind,* cf. Eccl 1.14; Hos 12.1. **3:** *Reflection,* dreams are often
merely mirrors of one's own concerns. **4:** *Unclean . . . clean,* cf. Job 14.4. **6:** *From the Most High,* an exception is
made for dreams that definitely come from God (as in Gen 37.5–10; Judg 7.13–15; Dan 2).

34.9–13: The value of experience through travel. See 39.4; 51.13.

34.14–20: Fear of the Lord. Blessings accompany *those who fear the Lord,* which is the proper human re-

¹⁷ Happy is the soul that fears the Lord!
　¹⁸ To whom does he look? And who is
　　his support?
¹⁹ The eyes of the Lord are on those who
　　love him,
　a mighty shield and strong support,
a shelter from scorching wind and a shade
　　from noonday sun,
　a guard against stumbling and a help
　　against falling.
²⁰ He lifts up the soul and makes the eyes
　　sparkle;
　he gives health and life and blessing.

²¹ If one sacrifices ill-gotten goods, the
　　offering is blemished;ᵃ
　²² the giftsᵇ of the lawless are not
　　acceptable.
²³ The Most High is not pleased with the
　　offerings of the ungodly,
　nor for a multitude of sacrifices does he
　　forgive sins.
²⁴ Like one who kills a son before his
　　father's eyes
　is the person who offers a sacrifice from
　　the property of the poor.
²⁵ The bread of the needy is the life of the
　　poor;
　whoever deprives them of it is a
　　murderer.
²⁶ To take away a neighbor's living is to
　　commit murder;
　²⁷ to deprive an employee of wages is to
　　shed blood.

²⁸ When one builds and another tears
　　down,
　what do they gain but hard work?

²⁹ When one prays and another curses,
　to whose voice will the Lord listen?
³⁰ If one washes after touching a corpse,
　　and touches it again,
　what has been gained by washing?
³¹ So if one fasts for his sins,
　and goes again and does the same
　　things,
who will listen to his prayer?
　And what has he gained by humbling
　　himself?

35 The one who keeps the law makes
　　many offerings;
　² one who heeds the commandments
　　makes an offering of well-being.
³ The one who returns a kindness offers
　　choice flour,
　⁴ and one who gives alms sacrifices a
　　thank offering.
⁵ To keep from wickedness is pleasing to
　　the Lord,
　and to forsake unrighteousness is an
　　atonement.
⁶ Do not appear before the Lord empty-
　　handed,
　⁷ for all that you offer is in fulfillment of
　　the commandment.
⁸ The offering of the righteous enriches the
　　altar,
　and its pleasing odor rises before the
　　Most High.
⁹ The sacrifice of the righteous is
　　acceptable,
　and it will never be forgotten.

ᵃ　Other ancient authorities read *is made in mockery*
ᵇ　Other ancient authorities read *mockeries*

sponse to true wisdom (cf. 1.11–30; 2.1–18). **19:** *The eyes of the Lord,* cf. Ps 34.15. *Shelter,* cf. Pss 61.2–4; 91.1–4; 121.5–6; Isa 25.4.

　34.21–31: True religion and social justice. Religious practices must be animated by and accomplished with a concern for social justice (cf. 1 Sam 15.22; Ps 51.16–19; Prov 15.8; 21.3: Hos 6.6; Amos 5.21–24). **21:** *Blemished,* cf. Lev 22.18–25. **26–27:** *Deprive an employee,* cf. Lev 19.13. **28:** *One builds and another tears down,* both the poor and the rich lose. **29:** *To whose voice,* cf. 4.5–6; 35.17–21. **30:** *Touching a corpse* makes a person ritually impure (Num 19.11). **31:** *Fasts for his sins,* most likely a reference to the Day of Atonement (Lev 23.27–32).

　35.1–13: Good deeds and sacrifices. While Ben Sira was an enthusiastic supporter of the Jerusalem Temple and its priesthood (cf. 50.1–24), he also insisted that sacrifices be offered in the proper spirit and be accompanied by ethical obedience to the Torah (cf. Isa 1.11–18; Mic 6.6–8; Tob 1.6–8). **1–5:** Observing the *commandments,* performing kind actions, and avoiding sin are equivalent to offering sacrifices to God (cf. Ps 51.17; 1QS 8.1–4). **6–13:** But such observances are neither in opposition to the offering of material sacrifices nor substitutes for them. Here Ben Sira offers his endorsement of the sacrificial system carried out at the Jerusalem Temple.

¹⁰ Be generous when you worship the Lord,
and do not stint the first fruits of your
hands.
¹¹ With every gift show a cheerful face,
and dedicate your tithe with gladness.
¹² Give to the Most High as he has given to
you,
and as generously as you can afford.
¹³ For the Lord is the one who repays,
and he will repay you sevenfold.
¹⁴ Do not offer him a bribe, for he will not
accept it;
¹⁵ and do not rely on a dishonest
sacrifice;
for the Lord is the judge,
and with him there is no partiality.
¹⁶ He will not show partiality to the poor;
but he will listen to the prayer of one
who is wronged.
¹⁷ He will not ignore the supplication of the
orphan,
or the widow when she pours out her
complaint.
¹⁸ Do not the tears of the widow run down
her cheek
¹⁹ as she cries out against the one who
causes them to fall?
²⁰ The one whose service is pleasing to the
Lord will be accepted,
and his prayer will reach to the clouds.
²¹ The prayer of the humble pierces the
clouds,
and it will not rest until it reaches its
goal;
it will not desist until the Most High
responds
²² and does justice for the righteous, and
executes judgment.
Indeed, the Lord will not delay,
and like a warrior[a] will not be
patient

until he crushes the loins of the
unmerciful
²³ and repays vengeance on the nations;
until he destroys the multitude of the
insolent,
and breaks the scepters of the
unrighteous;
²⁴ until he repays mortals according to
their deeds,
and the works of all according to their
thoughts;
²⁵ until he judges the case of his people
and makes them rejoice in his mercy.
²⁶ His mercy is as welcome in time of
distress
as clouds of rain in time of drought.

36 Have mercy upon us, O God[b] of all,
² and put all the nations in fear of you.
³ Lift up your hand against foreign nations
and let them see your might.
⁴ As you have used us to show your
holiness to them,
so use them to show your glory to us.
⁵ Then they will know,[c] as we have known,
that there is no God but you, O Lord.
⁶ Give new signs, and work other
wonders;
⁷ make your hand and right arm
glorious.
⁸ Rouse your anger and pour out your
wrath;
⁹ destroy the adversary and wipe out the
enemy.
¹⁰ Hasten the day, and remember the
appointed time,[d]

a   Heb: Gk *and with them*
b   Heb: Gk *O Master, the God*
c   Heb: Gk *And let them know you*
d   Other ancient authorities read *remember your oath*

35.14–26: God's justice. As a just judge God will not be bribed by *dishonest sacrifice*. God will answer the prayers of those most in need. **15:** *No partiality,* cf. Deut 10.17; Job 34.19; Wis 6.7. **17:** *Orphan . . . widow,* God will defend the most vulnerable in society (cf. 4.9–10; Ps 68.5; Prov 23.10–11). **22–26:** This passage prepares for the prayer in 36.1–22. It may allude to political turmoil in Ben Sira's own time. **25:** *His people,* this suggests that the oppressors threatened here were foreign enemies of Israel, perhaps the Seleucids who had recently replaced the Ptolemies as rulers over the land of Israel.

36.1–22: Prayers for God's people. 1–12: A plea for deliverance from Israel's enemies, perhaps from the Seleucid rulers after 198 BCE (cf. Ps 44.1–8; 2 Macc 1.24–29). **1:** *God of all,* cf. 36.5,12; 50.22. **4:** As God manifested *holiness* in rescuing Israel from exile (Ezek 20.41; 28.25), so may God display *glory* by subduing its enemies now. **6–7:** *Signs . . . wonders . . . hand . . . right arm,* allusions to the Exodus from Egypt (Ex 11.9–10; 15.6; Deut 4.34; 7.19;

and let people recount your mighty
deeds.
[11] Let survivors be consumed in the fiery
wrath,
and may those who harm your people
meet destruction.
[12] Crush the heads of hostile rulers
who say, "There is no one but
ourselves."
[13] Gather all the tribes of Jacob,[a]
[16] and give them their inheritance, as at
the beginning.
[17] Have mercy, O Lord, on the people called
by your name,
on Israel, whom you have named[b] your
firstborn,
[18] Have pity on the city of your sanctuary,[c]
Jerusalem, the place of your dwelling.[d]
[19] Fill Zion with your majesty,[e]
and your temple[f] with your glory.
[20] Bear witness to those whom you created
in the beginning,
and fulfill the prophecies spoken in
your name.
[21] Reward those who wait for you
and let your prophets be found
trustworthy.
[22] Hear, O Lord, the prayer of your
servants, according to your goodwill
toward[g] your people,
and all who are on the earth will know
that you are the Lord, the God of the ages.

[23] The stomach will take any food,
yet one food is better than another.
[24] As the palate tastes the kinds of game,
so an intelligent mind detects false
words.
[25] A perverse mind will cause grief,
but a person with experience will pay
him back.
[26] A woman will accept any man as a
husband,

but one girl is preferable to another.
[27] A woman's beauty lights up a man's
face,
and there is nothing he desires more.
[28] If kindness and humility mark her
speech,
her husband is more fortunate than
other men.
[29] He who acquires a wife gets his best
possession,[h]
a helper fit for him and a pillar of
support.[i]
[30] Where there is no fence, the property
will be plundered;
and where there is no wife, a man
will become a fugitive and a
wanderer.[j]
[31] For who will trust a nimble robber
that skips from city to city?
So who will trust a man that has no nest,
but lodges wherever night overtakes
him?

37 Every friend says, "I too am a friend";
but some friends are friends only in
name.
[2] Is it not a sorrow like that for death itself
when a dear friend turns into an
enemy?

[a] Owing to a dislocation in the Greek Mss of Sirach,
the verse numbers 14 and 15 are not used in
chapter 36, though no text is missing.
[b] Other ancient authorities read *you have likened to*
[c] Or *on your holy city*
[d] Heb: Gk *your rest*
[e] Heb Syr: Gk *the celebration of your wondrous deeds*
[f] Heb Syr: Gk Lat *people*
[g] Heb and two Gk witnesses: Lat and most Gk
witnesses read *according to the blessing of Aaron for*
[h] Heb: Gk *enters upon a possession*
[i] Heb: Gk *rest*
[j] Heb: Gk *wander about and sigh*

Neh 9.10). **10:** *The appointed time,* when Israel will be freed from its foreign oppressors. **13–22:** A prayer for the
ingathering of Israel and God's blessing on the Jerusalem Temple. **17:** *Called by your name,* see Deut 28.10; Jer
14.9. *Firstborn,* see Ex 4.22. **18:** *Your dwelling,* cf. Pss 26.8; 63.2; 102.16; 132.13–14.

36.23–31: On choosing a wife. 23–25: On discernment in general.

26–31: On choosing a wife in particular (cf. 26.13–18). **26:** *Accept,* marriages were often arranged by the fathers (cf. 7.25). **29:** In a patriarchal family, the wife was regarded as the husband's *possession. A helper fit for him,*
see Gen 2.18. **30:** *A fugitive and a wanderer,* like Cain (Gen 4.12,14).

37.1–15: On choosing a friend and a counselor. 1–7: More warnings against false and fair-weather friends (cf.

³ O inclination to evil, why were you
formed
to cover the land with deceit?
⁴ Some companions rejoice in the
happiness of a friend,
but in time of trouble they are against
him.
⁵ Some companions help a friend for their
stomachs' sake,
yet in battle they will carry his shield.
⁶ Do not forget a friend during the battle,ᵃ
and do not be unmindful of him when
you distribute your spoils.ᵇ

⁷ All counselors praise the counsel they give,
but some give counsel in their own
interest.
⁸ Be wary of a counselor,
and learn first what is his interest,
for he will take thought for himself.
He may cast the lot against you
⁹ and tell you, "Your way is good,"
and then stand aside to see what
happens to you.
¹⁰ Do not consult the one who regards you
with suspicion;
hide your intentions from those who
are jealous of you.
¹¹ Do not consult with a woman about her
rival
or with a coward about war,
with a merchant about business
or with a buyer about selling,
with a miser about generosityᶜ
or with the merciless about kindness,
with an idler about any work
or with a seasonal laborer about
completing his work,
with a lazy servant about a big task—
pay no attention to any advice they give.
¹² But associate with a godly person
whom you know to be a keeper of the
commandments,
who is like-minded with yourself,
and who will grieve with you if you fail.

¹³ And heedᵈ the counsel of your own
heart,
for no one is more faithful to you than
it is.
¹⁴ For our own mind sometimes keeps us
better informed
than seven sentinels sitting high on a
watchtower.
¹⁵ But above all pray to the Most High
that he may direct your way in truth.

¹⁶ Discussion is the beginning of every
work,
and counsel precedes every
undertaking.
¹⁷ The mind is the root of all conduct;
¹⁸ it sprouts four branches,ᵉ
good and evil, life and death;
and it is the tongue that continually
rules them.
¹⁹ Some people may be clever enough to
teach many,
and yet be useless to themselves.
²⁰ A skillful speaker may be hated;
he will be destitute of all food,
²¹ for the Lord has withheld the gift of
charm,
since he is lacking in all wisdom.
²² If a person is wise to his own
advantage,
the fruits of his good sense will be
praiseworthy.ᶠ
²³ A wise person instructs his own people,
and the fruits of his good sense will
endure.
²⁴ A wise person will have praise heaped
upon him,

ᵃ Heb: Gk *in your heart*
ᵇ Heb: Gk *him in your wealth*
ᶜ Heb: Gk *gratitude*
ᵈ Heb: Gk *establish*
ᵉ Heb: Gk *As a clue to changes of heart four kinds of
destiny appear*
ᶠ Other ancient witnesses read *trustworthy*

6.5–17; 9.10–16; 19.13–17; 22.19–26; 27.16–21). **3:** *O inclination to evil,* the evil impulse (Heb *yetser*) is the origin of
sins and offenses against friendships (cf. 15.14n). **5:** *Carry his shield,* defend from attack (cf. Ps 35.2). **8–11:** By finding out a prospective counselor's own agenda, one can avoid relying on inappropriate counselors. **11:** *Her rival,*
perhaps another wife (26.6). **12–15:** The best sources of good counsel are *those who keep the commandments,*
one's own heart, and *the Most High.*

    37.16–26: Wisdom and action. 16–18: Wise action demands consultation, thought, and articulation. **19–26:**

and all who see him will call him happy.
²⁵ The days of a person's life are numbered,
but the days of Israel are without
number.
²⁶ One who is wise among his people will
inherit honor,^a
and his name will live forever.

²⁷ My child, test yourself while you live;
see what is bad for you and do not give
in to it.
²⁸ For not everything is good for
everyone,
and no one enjoys everything.
²⁹ Do not be greedy for every delicacy,
and do not eat without restraint;
³⁰ for overeating brings sickness,
and gluttony leads to nausea.
³¹ Many have died of gluttony,
but the one who guards against it
prolongs his life.

38 Honor physicians for their services,
for the Lord created them;
² for their gift of healing comes from the
Most High,
and they are rewarded by the king.
³ The skill of physicians makes them
distinguished,
and in the presence of the great they are
admired.
⁴ The Lord created medicines out of the
earth,
and the sensible will not despise them.
⁵ Was not water made sweet with a tree
in order that its^b power might be
known?
⁶ And he gave skill to human beings
that he^c might be glorified in his
marvelous works.
⁷ By them the physician^d heals and takes
away pain;
⁸ the pharmacist makes a mixture from
them.

God's^e works will never be finished;
and from him health^f spreads over all
the earth.

⁹ My child, when you are ill, do not delay,
but pray to the Lord, and he will heal
you.
¹⁰ Give up your faults and direct your
hands rightly,
and cleanse your heart from all sin.
¹¹ Offer a sweet-smelling sacrifice, and a
memorial portion of choice flour,
and pour oil on your offering, as much
as you can afford.^g
¹² Then give the physician his place, for the
Lord created him;
do not let him leave you, for you need
him.
¹³ There may come a time when recovery
lies in the hands of physicians,^h
¹⁴ for they too pray to the Lord
that he grant them success in
diagnosisⁱ
and in healing, for the sake of
preserving life.
¹⁵ He who sins against his Maker,
will be defiant toward the physician.^j

¹⁶ My child, let your tears fall for the
dead,
and as one in great pain begin the
lament.

^a Other ancient authorities read *confidence*
^b Or *his*
^c Or *they*
^d Heb: Gk *he*
^e Gk *His*
^f Or *peace*
^g Heb: Lat lacks *as much as you can afford*; Meaning
of Gk uncertain
^h Gk *in their hands*
ⁱ Heb: Gk *rest*
^j Heb: Gk *may he fall into the hands of the physician*

There are *clever* persons who lack wisdom, while truly wise persons benefit themselves and their *people*. **25:** *The days of Israel are without number*, 2 Macc 14.15.

37.27–31: Moderation. Cf. 31.12–31. **28:** *Not everything is good for everyone*, Num 11.18–20.

38.1–15: Sickness and physicians. The wise person is respectful toward and cooperative with doctors, and regards medicines as gifts from God. **5:** *Water made sweet*, see Ex 15.23–25. **9–15:** The assumption is that illness is the effect of sin (Deut 28.21–22,27–28; Prov 3.7–8; Job 5.17–18), and so the sick must engage in prayer, repentance, and *sacrifice*.

Lay out the body with due ceremony,
and do not neglect the burial.
¹⁷ Let your weeping be bitter and your
wailing fervent;
make your mourning worthy of the
departed,
for one day, or two, to avoid criticism;
then be comforted for your grief.
¹⁸ For grief may result in death,
and a sorrowful heart saps one's
strength.
¹⁹ When a person is taken away, sorrow is
over;
but the life of the poor weighs down the
heart.
²⁰ Do not give your heart to grief;
drive it away, and remember your own
end.
²¹ Do not forget, there is no coming back;
you do the dead[a] no good, and you
injure yourself.
²² Remember his[b] fate, for yours is like it;
yesterday it was his,[c] and today it is
yours.
²³ When the dead is at rest, let his
remembrance rest too,
and be comforted for him when his
spirit has departed.

²⁴ The wisdom of the scribe depends on
the opportunity of leisure;
only the one who has little business can
become wise.
²⁵ How can one become wise who handles
the plow,
and who glories in the shaft of a goad,
who drives oxen and is occupied with their
work,
and whose talk is about bulls?
²⁶ He sets his heart on plowing
furrows,
and he is careful about fodder for the
heifers.

²⁷ So it is with every artisan and master
artisan
who labors by night as well as by day;
those who cut the signets of seals,
each is diligent in making a great
variety;
they set their heart on painting a lifelike
image,
and they are careful to finish their
work.
²⁸ So it is with the smith, sitting by the
anvil,
intent on his iron-work;
the breath of the fire melts his flesh,
and he struggles with the heat of the
furnace;
the sound of the hammer deafens his
ears,[d]
and his eyes are on the pattern of the
object.
He sets his heart on finishing his
handiwork,
and he is careful to complete its
decoration.
²⁹ So it is with the potter sitting at his
work
and turning the wheel with his feet;
he is always deeply concerned over his
products,
and he produces them in quantity.
³⁰ He molds the clay with his arm
and makes it pliable with his feet;
he sets his heart to finish the glazing,
and he takes care in firing[e] the kiln.

³¹ All these rely on their hands,
and all are skillful in their own work.

a Gk *him*
b Heb: Gk *my*
c Heb: Gk *mine*
d Cn: Gk *renews his ear*
e Cn: Gk *cleaning*

38.16–23: Mourning. Grief over the death of a loved one (cf. 22.11–12; Tob 1.17–18; 4.3–4; 6.15; 12.12; 14.12–13) should be intense but circumscribed, lest the mourner suffer harm. **23:** *The dead is at rest,* while there is no explicit denial of life after death, there is no affirmation of it either.

38.24–34: Tradesmen and the scribe. Scribes trained at Ben Sira's school (51.23–28) learned not only to copy and produce legal documents but were also expected to become intellectuals, public figures, and leaders (cf. 39.1–11). **24:** *Leisure,* the scribe has time and circumstances to study, whereas farmers, artisans, smiths, and potters (38.25–30) are too occupied with working on their trades to do so. The contrast between the scribe and other occupations is also a topic in several Egyptian wisdom compositions, including the *Satire on the Trades*

³² Without them no city can be inhabited,
and wherever they live, they will not go
hungry.ᵃ
Yet they are not sought out for the council
of the people,ᵇ
³³ nor do they attain eminence in the
public assembly.
They do not sit in the judge's seat,
nor do they understand the decisions of
the courts;
they cannot expound discipline or
judgment,
and they are not found among the
rulers.ᶜ
³⁴ But they maintain the fabric of the world,
and their concern is forᵈ the exercise of
their trade.

How different the one who devotes
himself
to the study of the law of the Most
High!

39 He seeks out the wisdom of all the
ancients,
and is concerned with prophecies;
² he preserves the sayings of the famous
and penetrates the subtleties of
parables;
³ he seeks out the hidden meanings of
proverbs
and is at home with the obscurities of
parables.
⁴ He serves among the great
and appears before rulers;
he travels in foreign lands
and learns what is good and evil in the
human lot.
⁵ He sets his heart to rise early
to seek the Lord who made him,
and to petition the Most High;
he opens his mouth in prayer
and asks pardon for his sins.

⁶ If the great Lord is willing,
he will be filled with the spirit of
understanding;
he will pour forth words of wisdom of his
own
and give thanks to the Lord in prayer.
⁷ The Lordᵉ will direct his counsel and
knowledge,
as he meditates on his mysteries.
⁸ He will show the wisdom of what he has
learned,
and will glory in the law of the Lord's
covenant.
⁹ Many will praise his understanding;
it will never be blotted out.
His memory will not disappear,
and his name will live through all
generations.
¹⁰ Nations will speak of his wisdom,
and the congregation will proclaim his
praise.
¹¹ If he lives long, he will leave a name
greater than a thousand,
and if he goes to rest, it is enoughᶠ for
him.

¹² I have more on my mind to express;
I am full like the full moon.
¹³ Listen to me, my faithful children, and
blossom
like a rose growing by a stream of water.
¹⁴ Send out fragrance like incense,
and put forth blossoms like a lily.
Scatter the fragrance, and sing a hymn of
praise;
bless the Lord for all his works.

ᵃ Syr: Gk *and people can neither live nor walk there*
ᵇ Most ancient authorities lack this line
ᶜ Cn: Gk *among parables*
ᵈ Syr: Gk *prayer is in*
ᵉ Gk *He himself*
ᶠ Cn: Meaning of Gk uncertain

and the *Instruction of Kheti.* **32–33:** *Without them no city can be inhabited,* Ben Sira acknowledges the positive contributions of tradesmen to society. But they are not present in the *public assembly,* the *courts,* or *among the rulers.* **34:** *Law,* the Torah was an essential component in Ben Sira's curriculum (cf. Ezra 7.6,10).

39.1–11: Scribal education. The scribes dealt with the law, *wisdom,* and *prophecies* (see the Prologue for the threefold division of the Hebrew scriptures). **2–3:** Cf. Prov 1.5–6; 25.1. **4:** *Travels,* cf. 34.11; 51.13. **5:** *Prayer,* since God is the source of true wisdom (1.1–10), prayer must be part of the scribe's formation. **9:** *His memory* and *name will live,* cf. 37.26; 44.10–15. **11:** *Greater than a thousand,* cf. Job 9.3; 33.23; Eccl 7.28.

39.12–35: God's creation and evil. God can use everything, both *good* and *bad,* to carry out the divine pur-

¹⁵ Ascribe majesty to his name
  and give thanks to him with praise,
with songs on your lips, and with harps;
  this is what you shall say in
    thanksgiving:

¹⁶ "All the works of the Lord are very good,
  and whatever he commands will be
    done at the appointed time.
¹⁷ No one can say, 'What is this?' or 'Why is
    that?'—
  for at the appointed time all such
    questions will be answered.
At his word the waters stood in a heap,
  and the reservoirs of water at the word
    of his mouth.
¹⁸ When he commands, his every purpose
    is fulfilled,
  and none can limit his saving power.
¹⁹ The works of all are before him,
  and nothing can be hidden from his
    eyes.
²⁰ From the beginning to the end of time
    he can see everything,
  and nothing is too marvelous for him.
²¹ No one can say, 'What is this?' or 'Why is
    that?'—
  for everything has been created for its
    own purpose.

²² "His blessing covers the dry land like a
    river,
  and drenches it like a flood.
²³ But his wrath drives out the nations,
  as when he turned a watered land into
    salt.
²⁴ To the faithful his ways are straight,
  but full of pitfalls for the wicked.
²⁵ From the beginning good things were
    created for the good,
  but for sinners good things and bad.ᵃ
²⁶ The basic necessities of human life
  are water and fire and iron and salt
and wheat flour and milk and honey,
  the blood of the grape and oil and
    clothing.

²⁷ All these are good for the godly,
  but for sinners they turn into evils.

²⁸ "There are winds created for
    vengeance,
  and in their anger they can dislodge
    mountains;ᵇ
on the day of reckoning they will pour out
    their strength
  and calm the anger of their Maker.
²⁹ Fire and hail and famine and
    pestilence,
  all these have been created for
    vengeance;
³⁰ the fangs of wild animals and scorpions
    and vipers,
  and the sword that punishes the
    ungodly with destruction.
³¹ They take delight in doing his bidding,
  always ready for his service on earth;
  and when their time comes they never
    disobey his command."

³² So from the beginning I have been
    convinced of all this
  and have thought it out and left it in
    writing:
³³ All the works of the Lord are good,
  and he will supply every need in its
    time.
³⁴ No one can say, "This is not as good as
    that,"
  for everything proves good in its
    appointed time.
³⁵ So now sing praise with all your heart
    and voice,
  and bless the name of the Lord.

40 Hard work was created for everyone,
  and a heavy yoke is laid on the
    children of Adam,
from the day they come forth from their
    mother's womb

ᵃ Heb Lat: Gk *sinners bad things*
ᵇ Heb Syr: Gk *can scourge mightily*

pose. **16–31**: A hymn of praise (v. 14). **16**: *Very good,* cf. Gen 1.4,10,12,18,21,25,31. **17**: *The waters stood in a heap,* see Ex 15.8; Josh 3.16. *Water at the word of his mouth,* see Gen 1.9–10. **21**: *Created for its own purpose* may reflect the influence of Stoic philosophy. **23**: *Watered land into salt,* see Gen 19.24–26. **26**: *The basic necessities,* cf. 29.21. **28–30**: Things with bad effects punish the wicked. **33–34**: *Good,* cf. 39.16; 33.7–15.
  40.1–30: Miseries and joys. **1–11**: Fears and anxieties stem from the *heavy yoke* laid on *Adam's* descendants

until the day they return to[a] the mother
of all the living.[b]

[2] Perplexities and fear of heart are theirs,
and anxious thought of the day of their
death.

[3] From the one who sits on a splendid
throne
to the one who grovels in dust and
ashes,

[4] from the one who wears purple and a
crown
to the one who is clothed in burlap,

[5] there is anger and envy and trouble and
unrest,
and fear of death, and fury and strife.
And when one rests upon his bed,
his sleep at night confuses his mind.

[6] He gets little or no rest;
he struggles in his sleep as he did by
day.[c]
He is troubled by the visions of his mind
like one who has escaped from the
battlefield.

[7] At the moment he reaches safety he
wakes up,
astonished that his fears were
groundless.

[8] To all creatures, human and animal,
but to sinners seven times more,

[9] come death and bloodshed and strife and
sword,
calamities and famine and ruin and
plague.

[10] All these were created for the wicked,
and on their account the flood came.

[11] All that is of earth returns to earth,
and what is from above returns above.[d]

[12] All bribery and injustice will be blotted
out,
but good faith will last forever.

[13] The wealth of the unjust will dry up like
a river,
and crash like a loud clap of thunder in
a storm.

[14] As a generous person has cause to
rejoice,
so lawbreakers will utterly fail.

[15] The children of the ungodly put out few
branches;
they are unhealthy roots on sheer
rock.

[16] The reeds by any water or river bank
are plucked up before any grass;

[17] but kindness is like a garden of
blessings,
and almsgiving endures forever.

[18] Wealth and wages make life sweet,[e]
but better than either is finding a
treasure.

[19] Children and the building of a city
establish one's name,
but better than either is the one who
finds wisdom.
Cattle and orchards make one
prosperous;[f]
but a blameless wife is accounted better
than either.

[20] Wine and music gladden the heart,
but the love of friends[g] is better than
either.

[21] The flute and the harp make sweet
melody,
but a pleasant voice is better than
either.

[22] The eye desires grace and beauty,
but the green shoots of grain more than
either.

[23] A friend or companion is always
welcome,
but a sensible wife[h] is better than
either.

[24] Kindred and helpers are for a time of
trouble,
but almsgiving rescues better than
either.

[a] Other Gk and Lat authorities read *are buried in*
[b] Heb: Gk *of all*
[c] Arm: Meaning of Gk uncertain
[d] Heb Syr: Gk Lat *from the waters returns to the sea*
[e] Heb: Gk *Life is sweet for the self-reliant worker*
[f] Heb Syr: Gk lacks *but better ... prosperous*
[g] Heb: Gk *wisdom*
[h] Heb Compare Syr: Gk *wife with her husband*

(Gen 3.17–19). **1:** *Mother's womb . . . mother,* cf. Job 1.21. **5–7:** For restless *sleep* and bad dreams, see 34.1–8; Job
7.4; Eccl 2.23. **10:** *Flood,* see Gen 6–8. **11:** *Returns to earth,* cf. Gen 3.19. *What is from above,* cf. Eccl 12.7. **12–17:** In
the end righteousness will prevail. **15:** Cf. Job 18.16. **18–27:** The numerical sayings name two good things and

²⁵ Gold and silver make one stand firm,
　　but good counsel is esteemed more
　　　than either.
²⁶ Riches and strength build up
　　confidence,
　　but the fear of the Lord is better than
　　　either.
There is no want in the fear of the Lord,
　　and with it there is no need to seek for
　　　help.
²⁷ The fear of the Lord is like a garden of
　　blessing,
　　and covers a person better than any
　　　glory.

²⁸ My child, do not lead the life of a beggar;
　　it is better to die than to beg.
²⁹ When one looks to the table of another,
　　one's way of life cannot be considered
　　　a life.
One loses self-respect with another
　　person's food,
　　but one who is intelligent and well
　　　instructed guards against that.
³⁰ In the mouth of the shameless begging
　　is sweet,
　　but it kindles a fire inside him.

41 O death, how bitter is the thought of
　　you
　　to the one at peace among possessions,
who has nothing to worry about and is
　　prosperous in everything,
　　and still is vigorous enough to enjoy
　　　food!
² O death, how welcome is your sentence
　　to one who is needy and failing in
　　　strength,
worn down by age and anxious about
　　everything;
　　to one who is contrary, and has lost all
　　　patience!
³ Do not fear death's decree for you;
　　remember those who went before you
　　　and those who will come after.

⁴ This is the Lord's decree for all flesh;
　　why then should you reject the will of
　　　the Most High?
Whether life lasts for ten years or a
　　hundred or a thousand,
　　there are no questions asked in Hades.

⁵ The children of sinners are abominable
　　children,
　　and they frequent the haunts of the
　　　ungodly.
⁶ The inheritance of the children of sinners
　　will perish,
　　and on their offspring will be a
　　　perpetual disgrace.
⁷ Children will blame an ungodly father,
　　for they suffer disgrace because of him.
⁸ Woe to you, the ungodly,
　　who have forsaken the law of the Most
　　　High God!
⁹ If you have children, calamity will be
　　theirs;
　　you will beget them only for groaning.
When you stumble, there is lasting joy;ᵃ
　　and when you die, a curse is your lot.
¹⁰ Whatever comes from earth returns to
　　earth;
　　so the ungodly go from curse to
　　　destruction.

¹¹ The human body is a fleeting thing,
　　but a virtuous name will never be
　　　blotted out.ᵇ
¹² Have regard for your name, since it will
　　outlive you
　　longer than a thousand hoards of gold.
¹³ The days of a good life are numbered,
　　but a good name lasts forever.

¹⁴ My children, be true to your training and
　　be at peace;

ᵃ　Heb: Meaning of Gk uncertain
ᵇ　Heb: Gk *People grieve over the death of the body,*
　　but the bad name of sinners will be blotted out

---

assert that a third is even *better.* **26–27:** *Fear of the Lord* is best of all (cf. 1.11–30). **28–30:** The worst misery is to be reduced to begging (29.24–28; 30.17).

　　41.1–13: Death and reputation. The most important mode of immortality for Ben Sira is through one's *name,* the reputation that one leaves behind (cf. 14.11–19; 17.25–28; 38.16–23). **4:** *Decree for all,* cf. Gen 3.19. *Hades,* Heb "Sheol," the abode of the dead (cf. Ps 88.10–12). **5:** *Abominable children,* merely having offspring does not guarantee immortality (Wis 3.12–13,16–18; 4.3–6). **11:** *Virtuous name,* cf. Prov 22.1; Eccl 7.1.

hidden wisdom and unseen treasure—
of what value is either?
15 Better are those who hide their folly
than those who hide their wisdom.
16 Therefore show respect for my words;
for it is not good to feel shame in every
circumstance,
nor is every kind of abashment to be
approved.[a]

17 Be ashamed of sexual immorality, before
your father or mother;
and of a lie, before a prince or a ruler;
18 of a crime, before a judge or magistrate;
and of a breach of the law, before the
congregation and the people;
of unjust dealing, before your partner or
your friend;
19 and of theft, in the place where you
live.
Be ashamed of breaking an oath or
agreement,[b]
and of leaning on your elbow at meals;
of surliness in receiving or giving,
20 and of silence, before those who greet
you;
of looking at a prostitute,
21 and of rejecting the appeal of a
relative;
of taking away someone's portion or gift,
and of gazing at another man's wife;
22 of meddling with his servant-girl—
and do not approach her bed;
of abusive words, before friends—
and do not be insulting after making a
gift.

42 Be ashamed of repeating what you
hear,
and of betraying secrets.
Then you will show proper shame,
and will find favor with everyone.

Of the following things do not be
ashamed,
and do not sin to save face:

2 Do not be ashamed of the law of the Most
High and his covenant,
and of rendering judgment to acquit the
ungodly;
3 of keeping accounts with a partner or
with traveling companions,
and of dividing the inheritance of
friends;
4 of accuracy with scales and weights,
and of acquiring much or little;
5 of profit from dealing with merchants,
and of frequent disciplining of
children,
and of drawing blood from the back of a
wicked slave.
6 Where there is an untrustworthy wife, a
seal is a good thing;
and where there are many hands, lock
things up.
7 When you make a deposit, be sure it is
counted and weighed,
and when you give or receive, put it all
in writing.
8 Do not be ashamed to correct the stupid
or foolish
or the aged who are guilty of sexual
immorality.
Then you will show your sound training,
and will be approved by all.

9 A daughter is a secret anxiety to her
father,
and worry over her robs him of sleep;
when she is young, for fear she may not
marry,
or if married, for fear she may be
disliked;
10 while a virgin, for fear she may be
seduced
and become pregnant in her father's
house;

a   Heb: Gk *and not everything is confidently esteemed
by everyone*
b   Heb: Gk *before the truth of God and the covenant*

41.14–42.8: True and false shame. Cf. 4.20–6.4; 10.19–11.6. After an introduction (41.14–16), Ben Sira describes behaviors that properly bring shame (sexual misconduct, dishonesty, rudeness, 41.17–42.1a) and notes things of which one should not be ashamed (fidelity to the law, honesty, controlling one's household, giving reproof where needed, 42.1b–8). **42.2:** *The law of the Most High* leads the list of things not to be ashamed of.
42.9–14: A father's anxiety over his daughters. Cf. 7.24–25; 22.3–6. The major concern here is the father's good reputation (cf. 30.1–13). **9–10:** *Worry over her,* the father was responsible for arranging his daughter's

or having a husband, for fear she may go
astray,
or, though married, for fear she may be
barren.
¹¹ Keep strict watch over a headstrong
daughter,
or she may make you a laughingstock to
your enemies,
a byword in the city and the assembly ofᵃ
the people,
and put you to shame in public
gatherings.ᵇ
See that there is no lattice in her room,
no spot that overlooks the approaches
to the house.ᶜ
¹² Do not let her parade her beauty before
any man,
or spend her time among married
women;ᵃ
¹³ for from garments comes the moth,
and from a woman comes woman's
wickedness.
¹⁴ Better is the wickedness of a man than a
woman who does good;
it is woman who brings shame and
disgrace.

¹⁵ I will now call to mind the works of the
Lord,
and will declare what I have seen.
By the word of the Lord his works are
made;
and all his creatures do his will.ᵈ
¹⁶ The sun looks down on everything with
its light,
and the work of the Lord is full of his
glory.
¹⁷ The Lord has not empowered even his
holy ones
to recount all his marvelous works,
which the Lord the Almighty has
established

so that the universe may stand firm in
his glory.
¹⁸ He searches out the abyss and the
human heart;
he understands their innermost secrets.
For the Most High knows all that may be
known;
he sees from of old the things that are
to come.ᵉ
¹⁹ He discloses what has been and what is
to be,
and he reveals the traces of hidden things.
²⁰ No thought escapes him,
and nothing is hidden from him.
²¹ He has set in order the splendors of his
wisdom;
he is from all eternity one and the same.
Nothing can be added or taken away,
and he needs no one to be his
counselor.
²² How desirable are all his works,
and how sparkling they are to see!ᶠ
²³ All these things live and remain forever;
each creature is preserved to meet a
particular need.ᵍ
²⁴ All things come in pairs, one opposite
the other,
and he has made nothing incomplete.
²⁵ Each supplements the virtues of the
other.
Who could ever tire of seeing his glory?

ᵃ Heb: Meaning of Gk uncertain
ᵇ Heb: Gk *to shame before the great multitude*
ᶜ Heb: Gk lacks *See . . . house*
ᵈ Syr Compare Heb: most Gk witnesses lack *and
all . . . will*
ᵉ Heb: Gk *he sees the sign(s) of the age*
ᶠ Meaning of Gk uncertain
ᵍ Heb: Gk *forever for every need, and all are obedient*

---

marriage, and a high premium was placed on her virginity and fertility (cf. Deut 22.13–29). **11–12:** *Headstrong daughter,* a father who was unable to control the women of his household was subject to shame. Thus the life of unmarried daughters was closely supervised. **13:** *From a woman comes woman's wickedness,* the woman is Eve (cf. Gen 3.6; 1 Tim 3.14). **14:** *Better is the wickedness of a man,* the lowest point in Ben Sira's misogyny (cf. 25.13–26.27; 36.26–31).

42.15–43.33: God's glory made manifest in all creation. 15–25: The order and splendor of the whole cosmos reflect God's omniscience and purpose. **15:** *By the word,* cf. Gen 1.1–31; Ps 33.6; Jdt 16.14; Wis 9.1. **17:** *Holy ones,* that is, angels or members of the heavenly court. **19:** *What has been and what is to be,* cf. Isa 41.22–23; 44.7. *Reveals . . . hidden things,* cf. Dan 2.22. **21:** *Counselor,* cf. Isa 40.13. **24:** *All things come in pairs,* cf. 33.7–15; 39.12–35;

43

The pride of the higher realms is the clear vault of the sky,
as glorious to behold as the sight of the heavens.

2 The sun, when it appears, proclaims as it rises
what a marvelous instrument it is, the work of the Most High.

3 At noon it parches the land,
and who can withstand its burning heat?

4 A man tending[a] a furnace works in burning heat,
but three times as hot is the sun scorching the mountains;
it breathes out fiery vapors,
and its bright rays blind the eyes.

5 Great is the Lord who made it;
at his orders it hurries on its course.

6 It is the moon that marks the changing seasons,[b]
governing the times, their everlasting sign.

7 From the moon comes the sign for festal days,
a light that wanes when it completes its course.

8 The new moon, as its name suggests, renews itself;[c]
how marvelous it is in this change,
a beacon to the hosts on high,
shining in the vault of the heavens!

9 The glory of the stars is the beauty of heaven,
a glittering array in the heights of the Lord.

10 On the orders of the Holy One they stand in their appointed places;
they never relax in their watches.

11 Look at the rainbow, and praise him who made it;
it is exceedingly beautiful in its brightness.

12 It encircles the sky with its glorious arc;
the hands of the Most High have stretched it out.

13 By his command he sends the driving snow
and speeds the lightnings of his judgment.

14 Therefore the storehouses are opened,
and the clouds fly out like birds.

15 In his majesty he gives the clouds their strength,
and the hailstones are broken in pieces.

17a The voice of his thunder rebukes the earth;

16 when he appears, the mountains shake.

At his will the south wind blows;

17b so do the storm from the north and the whirlwind.

He scatters the snow like birds flying down,
and its descent is like locusts alighting.

18 The eye is dazzled by the beauty of its whiteness,
and the mind is amazed as it falls.

19 He pours frost over the earth like salt,
and icicles form like pointed thorns.

20 The cold north wind blows,
and ice freezes on the water;
it settles on every pool of water,
and the water puts it on like a breastplate.

21 He consumes the mountains and burns up the wilderness,
and withers the tender grass like fire.

22 A mist quickly heals all things;
the falling dew gives refreshment from the heat.

23 By his plan he stilled the deep
and planted islands in it.

24 Those who sail the sea tell of its dangers,
and we marvel at what we hear.

25 In it are strange and marvelous creatures,
all kinds of living things, and huge sea-monsters.

---

a Other ancient authorities read *blowing upon*
b Heb: Meaning of Gk uncertain
c Heb: Gk *The month is named after the moon*

40.8–10. 43.1–12: God's glory in the heavenly bodies (cf. Job 38.1–38; Ps 104). 7: *The sign for festal days*, this may suggest preference for a lunar rather than a solar calendar. 11: *Rainbow*, see Gen 9.12–17. 43.13–26: God's glory in storms (cf. Ps 29; Job 38–39). 16–17: The imagery is evocative of divine theophanies, cf. Ps 18.7–15. 23–25: Cf.

26 Because of him each of his messengers
      succeeds,
   and by his word all things hold
      together.

27 We could say more but could never say
      enough;
   let the final word be: "He is the all."
28 Where can we find the strength to praise
      him?
   For he is greater than all his works.
29 Awesome is the Lord and very great,
   and marvelous is his power.
30 Glorify the Lord and exalt him as much
      as you can,
   for he surpasses even that.
   When you exalt him, summon all your
      strength,
   and do not grow weary, for you cannot
      praise him enough.
31 Who has seen him and can describe
      him?
   Or who can extol him as he is?
32 Many things greater than these lie
      hidden,
   for I[a] have seen but few of his works.
33 For the Lord has made all things,
   and to the godly he has given wisdom.

HYMN IN HONOR OF OUR ANCESTORS[b]

44 Let us now sing the praises of famous
      men,
   our ancestors in their generations.
2 The Lord apportioned to them[c] great
      glory,
   his majesty from the beginning.
3 There were those who ruled in their
      kingdoms,
   and made a name for themselves by
      their valor;
   those who gave counsel because they were
      intelligent;
   those who spoke in prophetic oracles;

4 those who led the people by their
      counsels
   and by their knowledge of the people's
      lore;
   they were wise in their words of
      instruction;
5 those who composed musical tunes,
   or put verses in writing;
6 rich men endowed with resources,
   living peacefully in their homes—
7 all these were honored in their
      generations,
   and were the pride of their times.
8 Some of them have left behind a
      name,
   so that others declare their praise.
9 But of others there is no memory;
   they have perished as though they had
      never existed;
   they have become as though they had
      never been born,
   they and their children after them.
10 But these also were godly men,
   whose righteous deeds have not been
      forgotten;
11 their wealth will remain with their
      descendants,
   and their inheritance with their
      children's children.[d]
12 Their descendants stand by the
      covenants;
   their children also, for their sake.
13 Their offspring will continue forever,
   and their glory will never be blotted
      out.
14 Their bodies are buried in peace,
   but their name lives on generation after
      generation.

a   Heb: Gk *we*
b   This title is included in the Gk text.
c   Heb: Gk *created*
d   Heb Compare Lat Syr: Meaning of Gk uncertain

Pss 104.24–26; 107.23–24. **27–33:** God is *the all* in the sense that all creation reveals the presence of God as its creator and lord. The proper response from humans is praise and humility.

44.1–50.24: In praise of Israel's ancestors. Ben Sira celebrates the covenant with the patriarchs and Israel by recounting the great figures of Israel's history (44.1–49.16), culminating in the high priest Simon II (50.1–24).

44.1–15: God's glory made manifest in Israel. The great heroes in Israel's history are best understood as manifestations of God's glory (cf. 1 Macc 2.51–64). **1.** *Famous men,* the Hebrew and Syriac read *men of piety.* **3–8:** Twelve types of heroes are listed. **9–10:** Some good people have left no memorial, but they will not be *forgotten.* **14:** *Their name,* cf. 41.11–13.

¹⁵ The assembly declares[a] their wisdom,
  and the congregation proclaims their
    praise.

¹⁶ Enoch pleased the Lord and was taken
    up,
  an example of repentance to all
    generations.

¹⁷ Noah was found perfect and righteous;
  in the time of wrath he kept the race
    alive;[b]
therefore a remnant was left on the earth
  when the flood came.
¹⁸ Everlasting covenants were made with
    him
  that all flesh should never again be
    blotted out by a flood.

¹⁹ Abraham was the great father of a
    multitude of nations,
  and no one has been found like him in
    glory.
²⁰ He kept the law of the Most High,
  and entered into a covenant with him;
he certified the covenant in his flesh,
  and when he was tested he proved
    faithful.
²¹ Therefore the Lord[c] assured him with an
    oath
  that the nations would be blessed
    through his offspring;
that he would make him as numerous as
    the dust of the earth,
  and exalt his offspring like the stars,
and give them an inheritance from sea to
    sea
  and from the Euphrates[d] to the ends of
    the earth.
²² To Isaac also he gave the same assurance
  for the sake of his father Abraham.

The blessing of all people and the
    covenant
  ²³ he made to rest on the head of Jacob;
he acknowledged him with his blessings,
  and gave him his inheritance;
he divided his portions,
  and distributed them among twelve
    tribes.

From his descendants the Lord[c] brought
    forth a godly man,
  who found favor in the sight of all

45 ¹ and was beloved by God and people,
  Moses, whose memory is blessed.
² He made him equal in glory to the holy
    ones,
  and made him great, to the terror of his
    enemies.
³ By his words he performed swift
    miracles;[e]
  the Lord[c] glorified him in the presence
    of kings.
He gave him commandments for his
    people,
  and revealed to him his glory.
⁴ For his faithfulness and meekness he
    consecrated him,
  choosing him out of all humankind.
⁵ He allowed him to hear his voice,
  and led him into the dark cloud,
and gave him the commandments face to
    face,
  the law of life and knowledge,

---

a Heb: Gk *Peoples declare*
b Heb: Gk *was taken in exchange*
c Gk *he*
d Syr: Heb Gk *River*
e Heb: Gk *caused signs to cease*

44.16–23: The patriarchs. 16: *Enoch* also ends the list (49.14). For his being *taken up,* see Gen 5.24. Why he is called an *example of repentance* is not clear. **17–18:** *Noah* was *perfect* (Gen 6.9) and *righteous* (Gen 7.1), and the vehicle for *everlasting covenants* (Gen 9.8–17). **19–21:** *Abraham,* the *great father* (Gen 17.4–5), *kept the law* before it was given to Moses on Sinai, entered into the *covenant* by circumcision (Gen 17), and *was tested* in the binding of Isaac (Gen 22.1–14). **21:** See Gen 12.3; 13.16; 15.5,18; 22.17–18. **22:** *Isaac,* Gen 17.19; 26.3–5. **23:** *Jacob,* Gen 27.27–29; 28.13–15; *his inheritance* is the promised land (Gen 28.4). The *twelve tribes* of Israel, descended from Jacob's sons; see Gen 49.

45.1–5: Moses as a miracle worker and teacher. 2: *Glory,* Ex 33.18–23. **3:** *Miracles,* specifically the signs and plagues in Egypt; Ex 7.1–11.10; 12.29–32. *Commandments,* the Decalogue (Ex 20.1–17; Deut 5.1–33); *glory* (Ex 33.18–23). **4:** *Meekness,* Num 12.3. **5:** *Dark cloud,* Ex 20.21; 24.18. *Face to face,* Num 12.8. *Teach,* Deut 4.1.

so that he might teach Jacob the covenant,
and Israel his decrees.

⁶ He exalted Aaron, a holy man like
Mosesª
who was his brother, of the tribe of
Levi.
⁷ He made an everlasting covenant with
him,
and gave him the priesthood of the
people.
He blessed him with stateliness,
and put a glorious robe on him.
⁸ He clothed him in perfect splendor,
and strengthened him with the symbols
of authority,
the linen undergarments, the long robe,
and the ephod.
⁹ And he encircled him with
pomegranates,
with many golden bells all around,
to send forth a sound as he walked,
to make their ringing heard in the
temple
as a reminder to his people;
¹⁰ with the sacred vestment, of gold and
violet
and purple, the work of an
embroiderer;
with the oracle of judgment, Urim and
Thummim;
¹¹ with twisted crimson, the work of an
artisan;
with precious stones engraved like seals,
in a setting of gold, the work of a
jeweler,
to commemorate in engraved letters
each of the tribes of Israel;
¹² with a gold crown upon his turban,
inscribed like a seal with "Holiness,"
a distinction to be prized, the work of an
expert,
a delight to the eyes, richly adorned.
¹³ Before him such beautiful things did not
exist.
No outsider ever put them on,

but only his sons
and his descendants in perpetuity.
¹⁴ His sacrifices shall be wholly burned
twice every day continually.
¹⁵ Moses ordained him,
and anointed him with holy oil;
it was an everlasting covenant for him
and for his descendants as long as the
heavens endure,
to minister to the Lordª and serve as
priest
and bless his people in his name.
¹⁶ He chose him out of all the living
to offer sacrifice to the Lord,
incense and a pleasing odor as a memorial
portion,
to make atonement for theᵇ people.
¹⁷ In his commandments he gave him
authority and statutes andᶜ
judgments,
to teach Jacob the testimonies,
and to enlighten Israel with his law.
¹⁸ Outsiders conspired against him,
and envied him in the wilderness,
Dathan and Abiram and their followers
and the company of Korah, in wrath
and anger.
¹⁹ The Lord saw it and was not pleased,
and in the heat of his anger they were
destroyed;
he performed wonders against them
to consume them in flaming fire.
²⁰ He added glory to Aaron
and gave him a heritage;
he allotted to him the best of the first
fruits,
and prepared bread of first fruits in
abundance;
²¹ for they eat the sacrifices of the Lord,
which he gave to him and his
descendants.

ª Gk *him*
ᵇ Other ancient authorities read *his* or *your*
ᶜ Heb: Gk *authority in covenants of*

45.6–26: Aaron and Phinehas. Attention to the priesthood prepares for the climactic description of Simon the high priest in 50.1–24. **6:** *His brother, of the tribe of Levi,* Ex 4.14. **7:** *Everlasting covenant* of *priesthood,* Ex 29.9; 40.15. **8–13:** *Perfect splendor,* see Ex 28–29 for the various priestly vestments. **10:** *Urim and Thummim,* see Ex 28.30; Num 27.21; 1 Sam 14.41–42. **14:** *Sacrifices,* Lev 6.8–15; Num 28.3–4. **15:** *Moses ordained . . . anointed,* Ex 28.41; Lev 8.1–30. *Bless his people,* see Num 6.22–27. **17:** *Teach,* Lev 10.11; Deut 33.10; Mal 2.7. **18–19:** *Dathan and Abiram*

22 But in the land of the people he has no
inheritance,
and he has no portion among the
people;
for the Lord[a] himself is his[b] portion and
inheritance.

23 Phinehas son of Eleazar ranks third in
glory
for being zealous in the fear of the
Lord,
and standing firm, when the people turned
away,
in the noble courage of his soul;
and he made atonement for Israel.
24 Therefore a covenant of friendship was
established with him,
that he should be leader of the
sanctuary and of his people,
that he and his descendants should
have
the dignity of the priesthood forever.
25 Just as a covenant was established with
David
son of Jesse of the tribe of Judah,
that the king's heritage passes only from
son to son,
so the heritage of Aaron is for his
descendants alone.

26 And now bless the Lord
who has crowned you with glory.[c]
May the Lord[a] grant you wisdom of
mind
to judge his people with justice,
so that their prosperity may not vanish,
and that their glory may endure
through all their generations.

46 Joshua son of Nun was mighty in war,
and was the successor of Moses in the
prophetic office.
He became, as his name implies,
a great savior of God's[d] elect,
to take vengeance on the enemies that
rose against them,

so that he might give Israel its
inheritance.
2 How glorious he was when he lifted his
hands
and brandished his sword against the
cities!
3 Who before him ever stood so firm?
For he waged the wars of the Lord.
4 Was it not through him that the sun
stood still
and one day became as long as two?
5 He called upon the Most High, the
Mighty One,
when enemies pressed him on every
side,
and the great Lord answered him
with hailstones of mighty power.
6 He overwhelmed that nation in
battle,
and on the slope he destroyed his
opponents,
so that the nations might know his
armament,
that he was fighting in the sight of the
Lord;
for he was a devoted follower of the
Mighty One.
7 And in the days of Moses he proved his
loyalty,
he and Caleb son of Jephunneh:
they opposed the congregation,[e]
restrained the people from sin,
and stilled their wicked grumbling.
8 And these two alone were spared
out of six hundred thousand
infantry,
to lead the people[f] into their inheritance,
the land flowing with milk and honey.

a   Gk *he*
b   Other ancient authorities read *your*
c   Heb: Gk lacks *And ... glory*
d   Gk *his*
e   Other ancient authorities read *the enemy*
f   Gk *them*

... *Korah*, Num 16.1–35. **21:** *Eat the sacrifices*, Num 18.8–19. **22:** *No inheritance*, Num 18.20; Deut 12.12. **23–25:**
Phinehas, Num 25.10–13; Ps 106.30; 1 Macc 2.54. **26:** *You*, perhaps directed to Simon (50.1–24) and his successors.
    46.1–20: Joshua and Caleb, the judges, and Samuel. 1–10: For Joshua's military exploits, see Josh 6–11. **1:**
Successor of Moses, Deut 34.9; Josh 1.1,5; 3.7. Joshua's *name* means "the Lord is salvation." **4:** *Sun stood still*, Josh
10.12–14. **5:** *Hailstones*, Josh 10.11. **7:** *Proved his loyalty*, Num 14.6–10. **8:** *Two alone*, Num 14.38; 26.65. *Six hundred*

⁹ The Lord gave Caleb strength,
    which remained with him in his old
        age,
so that he went up to the hill country,
    and his children obtained it for an
        inheritance,
¹⁰ so that all the Israelites might see
    how good it is to follow the Lord.

¹¹ The judges also, with their respective
        names,
    whose hearts did not fall into idolatry
and who did not turn away from the
        Lord—
    may their memory be blessed!
¹² May their bones send forth new life from
        where they lie,
    and may the names of those who have
        been honored
    live again in their children!

¹³ Samuel was beloved by his Lord;
    a prophet of the Lord, he established
        the kingdom
    and anointed rulers over his people.
¹⁴ By the law of the Lord he judged the
        congregation,
    and the Lord watched over Jacob.
¹⁵ By his faithfulness he was proved to be a
        prophet,
    and by his words he became known as a
        trustworthy seer.
¹⁶ He called upon the Lord, the Mighty
        One,
    when his enemies pressed him on every
        side,
    and he offered in sacrifice a suckling
        lamb.
¹⁷ Then the Lord thundered from
        heaven,
    and made his voice heard with a mighty
        sound;
¹⁸ he subdued the leaders of the enemyᵃ
    and all the rulers of the Philistines.

¹⁹ Before the time of his eternal sleep,
    Samuelᵇ bore witness before the Lord
        and his anointed:
"No property, not so much as a pair of
        shoes,
    have I taken from anyone!"
    And no one accused him.
²⁰ Even after he had fallen asleep, he
        prophesied
    and made known to the king his death,
and lifted up his voice from the ground
    in prophecy, to blot out the wickedness
        of the people.

47 After him Nathan rose up
    to prophesy in the days of David.
² As the fat is set apart from the offering of
        well-being,
    so David was set apart from the
        Israelites.
³ He played with lions as though they were
        young goats,
    and with bears as though they were
        lambs of the flock.
⁴ In his youth did he not kill a giant,
    and take away the people's disgrace,
when he whirled the stone in the sling
    and struck down the boasting
        Goliath?
⁵ For he called on the Lord, the Most
        High,
    and he gave strength to his right arm
to strike down a mighty warrior,
    and to exalt the powerᶜ of his people.
⁶ So they glorified him for the tens of
        thousands he conquered,
    and praised him for the blessings
        bestowed by the Lord,
    when the glorious diadem was given to
        him.

ᵃ Heb: Gk *leaders of the people of Tyre*
ᵇ Gk *he*
ᶜ Gk *horn*

thousand, Ex 12.37; Num 11.21. **9:** Caleb's *inheritance*, Josh 14.6–14. **11–12:** Only those *judges* who did not fall into idolatry (as Gideon did; Judg 8.22–35) are blessed. **12:** *Bones send forth new life*, 2 Kings 13.21. **13–20:** Samuel *anointed rulers* (1 Sam 10.1; 16.13) and served as a *judge* (1 Sam 7.3–17), *prophet* (1 Sam 3.19–20), and *priest* (1 Sam 7.9). **16–18:** 1 Sam 7.9–11. **19:** See 1 Sam 12.3. **20:** *Lifted up his voice from the ground*, 1 Sam 28.8–19.
    47.1–25: Early kings. 1: *Nathan*, 2 Sam 7.2–3; 12.1; 1 Chr 17.1. **2–11:** *David* was chosen by God (1 Sam 16.1–12), was a great warrior, and initiated public worship in Jerusalem (1 Chr 16.4; 23.1–6,24–32). **2:** *The fat*, Lev 3.3–5. **3:** *Played with lions . . . and with bears*, 1 Sam 17.34–36. **4:** *Kill a giant*, Goliath (1 Sam 17.49–51). **6:** *Tens of thousands*,

⁷ For he wiped out his enemies on every
    side,
    and annihilated his adversaries the
        Philistines;
    he crushed their power^a to our own
        day.
⁸ In all that he did he gave thanks
    to the Holy One, the Most High,
        proclaiming his glory;
he sang praise with all his heart,
    and he loved his Maker.
⁹ He placed singers before the altar,
    to make sweet melody with their
        voices.^b
¹⁰ He gave beauty to the festivals,
    and arranged their times throughout
        the year,^c
while they praised God's^d holy name,
    and the sanctuary resounded from
        early morning.
¹¹ The Lord took away his sins,
    and exalted his power^a forever;
he gave him a covenant of kingship
    and a glorious throne in Israel.

¹² After him a wise son rose up
    who because of him lived in security:^e
¹³ Solomon reigned in an age of peace,
    because God made all his borders
        tranquil,
so that he might build a house in his
    name
    and provide a sanctuary to stand
        forever.
¹⁴ How wise you were when you were
    young!
    You overflowed like the Nile^f with
        understanding.
¹⁵ Your influence spread throughout the
    earth,
    and you filled it with proverbs having
        deep meaning.
¹⁶ Your fame reached to far-off islands,
    and you were loved for your peaceful
        reign.
¹⁷ Your songs, proverbs, and parables,
    and the answers you gave astounded
        the nations.

¹⁸ In the name of the Lord God,
    who is called the God of Israel,
you gathered gold like tin
    and amassed silver like lead.
¹⁹ But you brought in women to lie at your
    side,
    and through your body you were
        brought into subjection.
²⁰ You stained your honor,
    and defiled your family line,
so that you brought wrath upon your
    children,
    and they were grieved^g at your folly,
²¹ because the sovereignty was divided
    and a rebel kingdom arose out of
        Ephraim.
²² But the Lord will never give up his
    mercy,
    or cause any of his works to perish;
he will never blot out the descendants of
    his chosen one,
    or destroy the family line of him who
        loved him.
So he gave a remnant to Jacob,
    and to David a root from his own
        family.

²³ Solomon rested with his ancestors,
    and left behind him one of his sons,
broad in^h folly and lacking in sense,
    Rehoboam, whose policy drove the
        people to revolt.
Then Jeroboam son of Nebat led Israel into
    sin
    and started Ephraim on its sinful
        ways.

^a Gk *horn*
^b Other ancient authorities add *and daily they sing
    his praises*
^c Gk *to completion*
^d Gk *his*
^e Heb: Gk *in a broad place*
^f Heb: Gk *a river*
^g Other ancient authorities read *I was grieved*
^h Heb (with a play on the name Rehoboam) Syr: Gk
    the people's

1 Sam 18.7. **11:** *His sins*, 2 Sam 11–12. *Covenant of kingship*, 2 Sam 7.12–16; Ps 89.19–37. **12–22:** *Solomon* built the
Jerusalem Temple (1 Kings 5–8), became *wise* and wealthy (1 Kings 3.12–13; 4.21–34; 10.14–29) but succumbed
to lust and idolatry (1 Kings 11.1–11). **21:** When Solomon died, what had been one kingdom was *divided* into

²⁴ Their sins increased more and more,
    until they were exiled from their land.
²⁵ For they sought out every kind of
    wickedness,
    until vengeance came upon them.

48 Then Elijah arose, a prophet like fire,
    and his word burned like a torch.
² He brought a famine upon them,
    and by his zeal he made them few in
    number.
³ By the word of the Lord he shut up the
    heavens,
    and also three times brought down
    fire.
⁴ How glorious you were, Elijah, in your
    wondrous deeds!
    Whose glory is equal to yours?
⁵ You raised a corpse from death
    and from Hades, by the word of the
    Most High.
⁶ You sent kings down to destruction,
    and famous men, from their sickbeds.
⁷ You heard rebuke at Sinai
    and judgments of vengeance at Horeb.
⁸ You anointed kings to inflict
    retribution,
    and prophets to succeed you.ᵃ
⁹ You were taken up by a whirlwind of fire,
    in a chariot with horses of fire.
¹⁰ At the appointed time, it is written, you
    are destinedᵇ
    to calm the wrath of God before it
    breaks out in fury,
    to turn the hearts of parents to their
    children,
    and to restore the tribes of Jacob.
¹¹ Happy are those who saw you
    and were adornedᶜ with your love!
    For we also shall surely live.ᵈ

¹² When Elijah was enveloped in the
    whirlwind,
    Elisha was filled with his spirit.
He performed twice as many signs,
    and marvels with every utterance of his
    mouth.ᵉ
Never in his lifetime did he tremble before
    any ruler,
    nor could anyone intimidate him at all.
¹³ Nothing was too hard for him,
    and when he was dead, his body
    prophesied.
¹⁴ In his life he did wonders,
    and in death his deeds were marvelous.

¹⁵ Despite all this the people did not
    repent,
    nor did they forsake their sins,
until they were carried off as plunder from
    their land,
    and were scattered over all the earth.
The people were left very few in number,
    but with a ruler from the house of
    David.
¹⁶ Some of them did what was right,
    but others sinned more and more.

¹⁷ Hezekiah fortified his city,
    and brought water into its midst;
he tunneled the rock with iron tools,
    and built cisterns for the water.
¹⁸ In his days Sennacherib invaded the
    country;
    he sent his commanderᶠ and departed;

ᵃ Heb: Gk *him*
ᵇ Heb: Gk *are for reproofs*
ᶜ Other ancient authorities read *and have died*
ᵈ Text and meaning of Gk uncertain
ᵉ Heb: Gk lacks *He performed … mouth*
ᶠ Other ancient authorities add *from Lachish*

two; 1 Kings 11.11–13,31–39; 12.15–20. **22:** *Root,* see Isa 11.10. **23–25:** *Rehoboam* and *Jeroboam,* 1 Kings 11.43–12.20; 12.28–30. **24:** *Exiled,* 2 Kings 17.6–8,18.

    48.1–16: Elijah and Elisha. 1–11: How *Elijah* the *prophet* manifested God's glory. **3:** *Shut up the heavens,* 1 Kings 17.1. *Brought down fire,* 1 Kings 18.38; 2 Kings 1.10–12. **5:** *Raised a corpse,* 1 Kings 17.21–22. *Hades,* Heb "Sheol," the abode of the dead. **6:** *Sent kings,* 2 Kings 1.16. **7:** *Heard rebuke at Sinai,* 1 Kings 19.8. **8:** *Anointed kings,* 1 Kings 19.15–16. **9:** *Taken up,* 2 Kings 2.11. **10:** *It is written,* Mal 4.5–6. **12–14:** How the prophet *Elisha* manifested God's glory. **12:** *Filled with his spirit,* 2 Kings 2.9,13. **13:** *His body prophesied,* 2 Kings 13.20–21. **15–16:** The prophets could not overcome the people's sinfulness, which led to the defeat and exile of the northern kingdom of Israel in the eighth century BCE. **15:** *Were carried off,* 2 Kings 18.11–12.

    48.17–49.16: Kings, prophets, and leaders of Judah. 17–22: The reign of King *Hezekiah.* **17:** *Water,* 2 Kings

he shook his fist against Zion,
and made great boasts in his
arrogance.
¹⁹ Then their hearts were shaken and their
hands trembled,
and they were in anguish, like women
in labor.
²⁰ But they called upon the Lord who is
merciful,
spreading out their hands toward him.
The Holy One quickly heard them from
heaven,
and delivered them through Isaiah.
²¹ The Lordᵃ struck down the camp of the
Assyrians,
and his angel wiped them out.
²² For Hezekiah did what was pleasing to
the Lord,
and he kept firmly to the ways of his
ancestor David,
as he was commanded by the prophet
Isaiah,
who was great and trustworthy in his
visions.
²³ In Isaiah'sᵇ days the sun went
backward,
and he prolonged the life of the king.
²⁴ By his dauntless spirit he saw the
future,
and comforted the mourners in Zion.
²⁵ He revealed what was to occur to the
end of time,
and the hidden things before they
happened.

49
The nameᶜ of Josiah is like blended
incense
prepared by the skill of the perfumer;
his memoryᵈ is as sweet as honey to every
mouth,
and like music at a banquet of wine.
² He did what was right by reforming the
people,
and removing the wicked
abominations.

³ He kept his heart fixed on the Lord;
in lawless times he made godliness
prevail.

⁴ Except for David and Hezekiah and
Josiah,
all of them were great sinners,
for they abandoned the law of the Most
High;
the kings of Judah came to an end.
⁵ Theyᵉ gave their power to others,
and their glory to a foreign nation,
⁶ who set fire to the chosen city of the
sanctuary,
and made its streets desolate,
as Jeremiah had foretold.ᶠ
⁷ For they had mistreated him,
who even in the womb had been
consecrated a prophet,
to pluck up and ruin and destroy,
and likewise to build and to plant.

⁸ It was Ezekiel who saw the vision of
glory,
which Godᵃ showed him above the
chariot of the cherubim.
⁹ For Godᵍ also mentioned Job
who held fast to all the ways of
justice.ʰ
¹⁰ May the bones of the Twelve Prophets
send forth new life from where they lie,
for they comforted the people of Jacob
and delivered them with confident
hope.

ᵃ Gk *He*
ᵇ Gk *his*
ᶜ Heb: Gk *memory*
ᵈ Heb: Gk *it*
ᵉ Heb *He*
ᶠ Gk *by the hand of Jeremiah*
ᵍ Gk *he*
ʰ Heb Compare Syr: Meaning of Gk uncertain

20.20. **18:** *Sennacherib,* the Assyrian king (705–681 BCE); 2 Kings 18.13,17; Isa 36.1. **20:** *Called upon the Lord,*
2 Kings 19.15–20. **21:** *The Lord struck down,* 2 Kings 19.35; Isa 37.36. **23–25:** The deeds of the prophet *Isaiah.* **23:**
Sun went backward, 2 Kings 20.8–11; Isa 38.7–8. **24–25:** *He saw the future,* Isa 40.1–2; 42.9. **49.1–3:** The reign
of King *Josiah.* **1:** *His memory,* 2 Kings 22.1–23.30. **6–7:** The prophet *Jeremiah,* 2 Chr 36.17–19; Jer 1.5–10; 38.2. **8:**
The prophet *Ezekiel,* Ezek 1.3–15; 10.1–3; **9:** *Job,* Job 1–2; 42. **10:** *Twelve Prophets,* Hosea—Malachi, the so-called
Minor Prophets, probably considered a single book by Ben Sira. **11–13:** Leaders after the exile: *Zerubbabel* (Ezra

¹¹ How shall we magnify Zerubbabel?
  He was like a signet ring on the right
    hand,
¹² and so was Jeshua son of Jozadak;
in their days they built the house
  and raised a temple[a] holy to the Lord,
    destined for everlasting glory.
¹³ The memory of Nehemiah also is lasting;
  he raised our fallen walls,
and set up gates and bars,
  and rebuilt our ruined houses.

¹⁴ Few have[b] ever been created on earth
    like Enoch,
  for he was taken up from the earth.
¹⁵ Nor was anyone ever born like Joseph;[c]
  even his bones were cared for.
¹⁶ Shem and Seth and Enosh were
    honored,[d]
  but above every other created living
    being was Adam.

50 The leader of his brothers and the
  pride of his people[e]
  was the high priest, Simon son of Onias,
who in his life repaired the house,
  and in his time fortified the temple.
² He laid the foundations for the high
    double walls,
  the high retaining walls for the temple
    enclosure.
³ In his days a water cistern was dug,[f]
  a reservoir like the sea in
    circumference.
⁴ He considered how to save his people
    from ruin,
  and fortified the city against siege.
⁵ How glorious he was, surrounded by the
    people,
  as he came out of the house of the
    curtain.
⁶ Like the morning star among the clouds,
  like the full moon at the festal season;[f]
⁷ like the sun shining on the temple of the
    Most High,

like the rainbow gleaming in splendid
    clouds;
⁸ like roses in the days of first fruits,
  like lilies by a spring of water,
  like a green shoot on Lebanon on a
    summer day;
⁹ like fire and incense in the censer,
  like a vessel of hammered gold
    studded with all kinds of precious
      stones;
¹⁰ like an olive tree laden with fruit,
  and like a cypress towering in the
    clouds.
¹¹ When he put on his glorious robe
  and clothed himself in perfect
    splendor,
when he went up to the holy altar,
  he made the court of the sanctuary
    glorious.

¹² When he received the portions from the
    hands of the priests,
  as he stood by the hearth of the altar
with a garland of brothers around him,
  he was like a young cedar on
    Lebanon
  surrounded by the trunks of palm
    trees.
¹³ All the sons of Aaron in their splendor
  held the Lord's offering in their hands
  before the whole congregation of
    Israel.
¹⁴ Finishing the service at the altars,[g]
  and arranging the offering to the Most
    High, the Almighty,

a Other ancient authorities read *people*
b Heb Syr: Gk *No one has*
c Heb Syr: Gk adds *the leader of his brothers, the
   support of the people*
d Heb: Gk *Shem and Seth were honored by people*
e Heb Syr: Gk lacks this line. Compare 49.15
f Heb: Meaning of Gk uncertain
g Other ancient authorities read *altar*

3.2; Hag 2.23), *Jeshua* (Ezra 3.2; Hag 1.12; 2.2; Zech 3.1); *Nehemiah* (Neh 7.1). **14–16:** Mentions of *Enoch* (44.16; Gen 5.18–24) and *Joseph* (Gen 39–50) as well as *Shem* (Gen 9.18), *Seth* (Gen 5.3) and *Enosh* (Gen 5.6–11) lead back to *Adam* (Gen 1.26–31).

  50.1–24: Simon the high priest. Simon II, son of Onias, was the high priest from 219 to 196 BCE (Josephus, *Ant.* 12.4.10). **1–4:** A summary of Simon's public works projects. **5–13:** For an earlier description of the high priest's vestments, cf. 45.6–13; cf. Ex 28.2–43; 39.1–31. **14–21:** A vivid description of the Temple ritual and sac-

¹⁵ he held out his hand for the cup
　and poured a drink offering of the blood
　　of the grape;
he poured it out at the foot of the altar,
　a pleasing odor to the Most High, the
　　king of all.
¹⁶ Then the sons of Aaron shouted;
　they blew their trumpets of hammered
　　metal;
they sounded a mighty fanfare
　as a reminder before the Most High.
¹⁷ Then all the people together quickly
　fell to the ground on their faces
to worship their Lord,
　the Almighty, God Most High.

¹⁸ Then the singers praised him with their
　　voices
　in sweet and full-toned melody.ᵃ
¹⁹ And the people of the Lord Most High
　　offered
　their prayers before the Merciful One,
until the order of worship of the Lord was
　　ended,
　and they completed his ritual.
²⁰ Then Simonᵇ came down and raised his
　　hands
　over the whole congregation of
　　Israelites,
to pronounce the blessing of the Lord with
　　his lips,
　and to glory in his name;
²¹ and they bowed down in worship a
　　second time,
　to receive the blessing from the Most
　　High.

²² And now bless the God of all,
　who everywhere works great wonders,
who fosters our growth from birth,
　and deals with us according to his
　　mercy.
²³ May he give usᶜ gladness of heart,

and may there be peace in ourᵈ days
　in Israel, as in the days of old.
²⁴ May he entrust to us his mercy,
　and may he deliver us in ourᵉ days!

²⁵ Two nations my soul detests,
　and the third is not even a people:
²⁶ Those who live in Seir,ᶠ and the
　　Philistines,
　and the foolish people that live in
　　Shechem.

²⁷ Instruction in understanding and
　　knowledge
　I have written in this book,
Jesus son of Eleazar son of Sirachᵍ of
　　Jerusalem,
　whose mind poured forth wisdom.
²⁸ Happy are those who concern
　　themselves with these things,
　and those who lay them to heart will
　　become wise.
²⁹ For if they put them into practice, they
　　will be equal to anything,
　for the fearʰ of the Lord is their path.

PRAYER OF JESUS SON OF SIRACHⁱ

51

I give you thanks, O Lord and King,
　and praise you, O God my Savior.
I give thanks to your name,
　²for you have been my protector and
　　helper

ᵃ　Other ancient authorities read *in sweet melody*
　　throughout the house
ᵇ　Gk *he*
ᶜ　Other ancient authorities read *you*
ᵈ　Other ancient authorities read *your*
ᵉ　Other ancient authorities read *his*
ᶠ　Heb Compare Lat: Gk *on the mountain of Samaria*
ᵍ　Heb: Meaning of Gk uncertain
ʰ　Heb: Other ancient authorities read *light*
ⁱ　This title is included in the Gk text.

rifices, most likely for the Day of Atonement (Lev 16). **16:** *Trumpets*, Num 10.2; 31.6. **18:** *Singers*, 2 Chr 29.26–30. **20:** *The blessing*, Num 6.24–27. *His name*, only the high priest (and only once a year, on the Day of Atonement) could utter the ineffable name, YHWH. **22–24:** A concluding benediction.

　50.25–26: A final numerical proverb. **26:** *Seir* (Edom) and the *Philistines* were historic enemies of the Israelites; here they refer to those who threatened them in Ben Sira's time, the Idumeans and the Greeks, along with the Samaritans, in *Shechem*.

　50.27–29: Postscript. **27:** *Jesus*, the author's Hebrew name was probably Yeshua ben Eleazar ben Sira. **29:** *Fear of the Lord*, one of the book's major themes (1.11–30).

and have delivered me from destruction
 and from the trap laid by a slanderous
  tongue,
 from lips that fabricate lies.
In the face of my adversaries
 you have been my helper ³ and delivered
  me,
 in the greatness of your mercy and of
  your name,
from grinding teeth about to devour me,
 from the hand of those seeking my life,
 from the many troubles I endured,
⁴ from choking fire on every side,
 and from the midst of fire that I had not
  kindled,
⁵ from the deep belly of Hades,
 from an unclean tongue and lying
  words—
  ⁶ the slander of an unrighteous tongue
   to the king.
My soul drew near to death,
 and my life was on the brink of Hades
  below.
⁷ They surrounded me on every side,
 and there was no one to help me;
I looked for human assistance,
 and there was none.
⁸ Then I remembered your mercy,
  O Lord,
 and your kindnessª from of old,
for you rescue those who wait for you
 and save them from the hand of their
  enemies.
⁹ And I sent up my prayer from the
  earth,
 and begged for rescue from death.
¹⁰ I cried out, "Lord, you are my Father;ᵇ
 do not forsake me in the days of
  trouble,
 when there is no help against the
  proud.
¹¹ I will praise your name continually,
 and will sing hymns of thanksgiving."
My prayer was heard,
 ¹² for you saved me from destruction
 and rescued me in time of trouble.
For this reason I thank you and praise you,
 and I bless the name of the Lord.

Heb adds:

Give thanks to the LORD, for he is good,
 for his steadfast love endures forever;

Give thanks to the God of praises,
 for his steadfast love endures forever;

Give thanks to the guardian of Israel,
 for his steadfast love endures forever;

Give thanks to him who formed all things,
 for his steadfast love endures forever;

Give thanks to the redeemer of Israel,
 for his steadfast love endures forever;

Give thanks to him who gathers the
  dispersed of Israel,
 for his steadfast love endures forever;

Give thanks to him who rebuilt his city and
  his sanctuary,
 for his steadfast love endures forever;

Give thanks to him who makes a horn to
  sprout for the house of David,
 for his steadfast love endures forever;

Give thanks to him who has chosen the
  sons of Zadok to be priests,
 for his steadfast love endures forever;

Give thanks to the shield of Abraham,
 for his steadfast love endures forever;

Give thanks to the rock of Isaac,
 for his steadfast love endures forever;

Give thanks to the mighty one of Jacob,
 for his steadfast love endures forever;

Give thanks to him who has chosen Zion,
 for his steadfast love endures forever;

Give thanks to the King of the kings of kings,

ª Other ancient authorities read *work*
ᵇ Heb: Gk *the Father of my lord*

51.1–30: Three appendixes. 1–12: A hymn in thanksgiving for deliverance. 5,6: *Hades*, Heb "Sheol," the abode of the dead. 10: *Father*, cf. 23.1,4. 12: Following v. 12, the medieval Hebrew text includes a thanksgiving

*for his steadfast love endures
 forever;*

*He has raised up a horn for his people,
 praise for all his loyal ones.*

*For the children of Israel, the people close
 to him.
 Praise the* Lord!

————————————

¹³ While I was still young, before I went on
 my travels,
 I sought wisdom openly in my prayer.
¹⁴ Before the temple I asked for her,
 and I will search for her until the end.

¹⁵ From the first blossom to the ripening
 grape
 my heart delighted in her;
my foot walked on the straight path;
 from my youth I followed her steps.

¹⁶ I inclined my ear a little and received her,
 and I found for myself much
 instruction.
¹⁷ I made progress in her;
 to him who gives wisdom I will give
 glory.

¹⁸ For I resolved to live according to
 wisdom,ᵃ
 and I was zealous for the good,
 and I shall never be disappointed.
¹⁹ My soul grappled with wisdom,ᵃ
 and in my conduct I was strict;ᵇ

I spread out my hands to the heavens,
 and lamented my ignorance of her.
²⁰ I directed my soul to her,
 and in purity I found her.

With her I gained understanding from the
 first;
 therefore I will never be forsaken.

²¹ My heart was stirred to seek her;
 therefore I have gained a prize
 possession.
²² The Lord gave me my tongue as a reward,
 and I will praise him with it.

²³ Draw near to me, you who are
 uneducated,
 and lodge in the house of instruction.
²⁴ Why do you say you are lacking in these
 things,ᶜ
 and why do you endure such great thirst?
²⁵ I opened my mouth and said,
 Acquire wisdomᵈ for yourselves without
 money.

²⁶ Put your neck under herᵉ yoke,
 and let your souls receive instruction;
 it is to be found close by.

²⁷ See with your own eyes that I have
 labored but little
 and found for myself much serenity.
²⁸ Hear but a little of my instruction,
 and through me you will acquire silver
 and gold.ᶠ

²⁹ May your soul rejoice in God'sᵍ mercy,
 and may you never be ashamed to
 praise him.
³⁰ Do your work in good time,
 and in his own time Godʰ will give you
 your reward.

ᵃ Gk *her*
ᵇ Meaning of Gk uncertain
ᶜ Cn Compare Heb Syr: Meaning of Gk uncertain
ᵈ Heb: Gk lacks *wisdom*
ᵉ Heb: other ancient authorities read *the*
ᶠ Syr Compare Heb: Gk *Get instruction with a large
   sum of silver, and you will gain by it much gold.*
ᵍ Gk *his*
ʰ Gk *he*

hymn based on Ps 136. **13–30:** An autobiographical, acrostic poem on the search for wisdom. Another (somewhat more erotic) version of this text appears in a Psalms scroll from Qumran (11QPsa). **13:** *Travels,* cf. 34.11; 39.4. **23:** *Draw near to me,* cf. 14.20–27; Prov 9.1–6. *House of instruction,* a wisdom school, presumably Ben Sira's own in Jerusalem. **26:** *Yoke,* cf. 6.23–31.

BARUCH

NAME AND AUTHORSHIP

The title of the book comes from its opening verse, which attributes the book to Baruch son of Neriah, the scribe of Jeremiah (cf. Jer 32.12; 36.4). This verse places Baruch in the Babylonian exile of the early sixth century BCE, but according to Jer 43.1–7, he and Jeremiah went to Egypt (not Babylon) in 582 BCE. This, along with historical errors in the introduction (1.1–14), suggests that the work was not actually written by Baruch. Following 1.1, later rabbinic tradition places Baruch in Babylon (*Mid. Rab. Song* 5.5; *b. Meg.* 16b; *Seder Olam R.* 26). The book is often referred to as 1 Baruch to distinguish it from several other books also attributed to Baruch, dating from the second century CE.

CANONICAL STATUS AND LOCATION IN CANON

In the Protestant tradition the book of Baruch is included in the Apocrypha; in the Roman Catholic and Eastern Orthodox churches it is one of the deuterocanonical books of the Old Testament. In Catholic Bibles the book is located between Lamentations and Ezekiel, with the Letter of Jeremiah (see p. 179) appended as the final chapter of Baruch. In the Orthodox churches the book is between Lamentations and the Letter of Jeremiah. Baruch is not included in the Jewish canon of scripture.

DATE OF COMPOSITION AND HISTORICAL CONTEXT

Scholars often date the book of Baruch to the second or first centuries BCE. The book's themes of communal repentance, the gift of the Torah to Israel, and the glorification of Jerusalem through the return of the exiles may indicate a date during the national revival led by the Maccabees that began during the revolt against the Seleucid king Antiochus IV Epiphanes (175–164 BCE).

LITERARY HISTORY, STRUCTURE, AND CONTENTS

The existing text of Baruch is in Greek. On the basis of its literary style scholars think that the book was originally written in Hebrew and then translated into Greek; however, no Hebrew manuscript of Baruch is known. Ancient versions of Baruch in other languages, such as Latin and Syriac, are translations from the Greek.

The book has four major sections:

A. Historical Introduction (1.1–14)
B. Confession of Sin (1.15–3.8)
C. Wisdom Poem (3.9–4.4)
D. Poem of Consolation (4.5–5.9)

While themes such as confession of sin and exile are found throughout the work, these four sections differ significantly from one another in form and content (see, for example, 3.10n. and 4.10n.). Also, different names for God are used in the confession ("Lord"), in the Wisdom poem ("God"), and in the poem of consolation ("the Everlasting"). Thus the different sections may have been written separately and combined later. Much of the book is a pastiche of quotations and paraphrases of biblical texts (see the annotations). This type of composition, popular in the late Second Temple period, provided a means of interpreting canonical literature and creating new works.

INTERPRETATION

The Babylonian exile was not a living reality for the author of Baruch but a context for reflection on maintaining the vitality of the relationship between God and Israel. The book attributes the Babylonian exile to national sin (1.21–2.1). The curses of the covenant have now come upon the people (1.20; 2.2; compare 2.3 and Deut 28.53). The book offers a way to alleviate this difficult situation: confess your sins and turn to God. The people need to renew their dedication to God and the covenant. This is the core message of the prayer in 1.15–3.8. The poem in 3.9–4.4 encourages Israel to learn "where there is wisdom" (3.14)—God has found Wisdom, and he has given it to Israel in the form of the Torah (3.36–4.1a). Wisdom, as elsewhere in wisdom literature, is associated with life

(3.9; 4.1b; Prov 3.16). God, the book promises, will reward repentance by returning the exiles to Judah (4.36–5.9). The exile represents death and sin (2.17; 3.4,10–11); return to Zion symbolizes life and devotion to God.

Although the book of Baruch originated in the Jewish community, like other such works written in the Hellenistic and Roman eras, it fell out of use in rabbinic Judaism. Early Christian writers, however, frequently quoted the book as scripture. Baruch 3.36–37, which refers to Wisdom appearing on earth and living with humankind, was often cited because of its Christological interpretation (cf. Jn 1.14).

GUIDE TO READING

The opening verses of Baruch describe the book as having been read to the Jews exiled in Babylon; reading aloud was a common practice in antiquity. Modern readers can also appreciate the book's rhetorical appeal by listening to it rather than reading it silently. Even though the book consists of stylistically different sections, readers can experience its unity by noticing verses that reflect its main themes: sin and exile, repentance and the restoration of Zion. In antiquity Jewish education often involved memorizing large sections of scripture. Thus early readers would have recognized the many phrases adapted from biblical books, in particular Deuteronomy, Jeremiah, and Isaiah. The annotations will aid modern readers to identify and recognize these echoes of scripture.

Matthew Goff

1 These are the words of the book that Baruch son of Neriah son of Mahseiah son of Zedekiah son of Hasadiah son of Hilkiah wrote in Babylon, ² in the fifth year, on the seventh day of the month, at the time when the Chaldeans took Jerusalem and burned it with fire.

³ Baruch read the words of this book to Jeconiah son of Jehoiakim, king of Judah, and to all the people who came to hear the book, ⁴ and to the nobles and the princes, and to the elders, and to all the people, small and great, all who lived in Babylon by the river Sud.

⁵ Then they wept, and fasted, and prayed before the Lord; ⁶ they collected as much money as each could give, ⁷ and sent it to Jerusalem to the high priestᵃ Jehoiakim son of Hilkiah son of Shallum, and to the priests, and to all the people who were present with him in Jerusalem. ⁸ At the same time, on the tenth day of Sivan, Baruchᵇ took the vessels of the house of the Lord, which had been carried away from the temple, to return them to the land of Judah—the silver vessels that Zedekiah son of Josiah, king of Judah, had made, ⁹ after King Nebuchadnezzar of Babylon had carried away from Jerusalem Jeconiah and the princes and the prisoners and the nobles and the people of the land, and brought them to Babylon.

¹⁰ They said: Here we send you money; so buy with the money burnt offerings and sin offerings and incense, and prepare a grain offering, and offer them on the altar of the Lord our God; ¹¹ and pray for the life of King

---

ᵃ Gk *the priest*
ᵇ Gk *he*

1.1–14: Historical introduction. 1–2: Authorship and date. **1:** *Baruch*, Jeremiah's scribe (Jer 36.4,15; 45.1). The genealogy here is more extensive than in Jer 32.12. **2:** *Fifth year*, after the destruction of Jerusalem in 586 BCE (2 Kings 25.8–12) by the Babylonians (*the Chaldeans*). **3–4:** Baruch reads his book to the other exiles (cf. Jer 36.10). **3:** *Jeconiah*, also called Jehoiachin. He was regarded by the exiles as king (2 Kings 24.15; 25.27–30; Jer 24.1; Ezek 1.2). **4:** *Sud*, the name is otherwise unknown. Perhaps a reference to the river Ahava (Ezra 8.15,21,31). **5–7:** The exiles react to Baruch's reading. **5:** In the book of Baruch the word *Lord* occurs only in 1.1–3.8. **6:** *They collected*, see Ezra 1.4,6. **7:** *The high priest Jehoiakim*, otherwise unknown. The Greek reads "the priest." The genealogy is derived from 1 Chr 6.13–15. **8:** *Sivan*, the third month of the Jewish calendar (May–June). This verse does not agree with Ezra 1.7–11, which states that Sheshbazzar returned the gold and *silver vessels* to Jerusalem after the edict of the Persian king Cyrus (538 BCE). *Zedekiah*, the king of Judah when Jerusalem fell (2 Kings 24.18–25.7). 2 Kings never claims that Zedekiah fashioned temple vessels. **9:** Jer 24.1; 2 Kings 24.10–16. **10–14:** Instruction that accompanies the scroll sent by exiles to the Jews who remained in Jerusalem. **10:** Jer 41.5 indicates that

Nebuchadnezzar of Babylon, and for the life of his son Belshazzar, so that their days on earth may be like the days of heaven. ¹² The Lord will give us strength, and light to our eyes; we shall live under the protectionᵃ of King Nebuchadnezzar of Babylon, and under the protection of his son Belshazzar, and we shall serve them many days and find favor in their sight. ¹³ Pray also for us to the Lord our God, for we have sinned against the Lord our God, and to this day the anger of the Lord and his wrath have not turned away from us. ¹⁴ And you shall read aloud this scroll that we are sending you, to make your confession in the house of the Lord on the days of the festivals and at appointed seasons.

¹⁵ And you shall say: The Lord our God is in the right, but there is open shame on us today, on the people of Judah, on the inhabitants of Jerusalem, ¹⁶ and on our kings, our rulers, our priests, our prophets, and our ancestors, ¹⁷ because we have sinned before the Lord. ¹⁸ We have disobeyed him, and have not heeded the voice of the Lord our God, to walk in the statutes of the Lord that he set before us. ¹⁹ From the time when the Lord brought our ancestors out of the land of Egypt until today, we have been disobedient to the Lord our God, and we have been negligent, in not heeding his voice. ²⁰ So to this day there have clung to us the calamities and the curse that the Lord declared through his servant Moses at the time when he brought our ancestors out of the land of Egypt to give to us a land flowing with milk and honey. ²¹ We did not listen to the voice of the Lord our God in all the words of the prophets whom he sent to us, ²² but all of us followed the intent of our own wicked hearts by serving other gods and doing what is evil in the sight of the Lord our God.

2 So the Lord carried out the threat he spoke against us: against our judges who ruled Israel, and against our kings and our rulers and the people of Israel and Judah. ² Under the whole heaven there has not been done the like of what he has done in Jerusalem, in accordance with the threats that wereᵇ written in the law of Moses. ³ Some of us ate the flesh of their sons and others the flesh of their daughters. ⁴ He made them subject to all the kingdoms around us, to be an object of scorn and a desolation among all the surrounding peoples, where the Lord has scattered them. ⁵ They were brought down and not raised up, because our nationᶜ sinned against the Lord our God, in not heeding his voice.

⁶ The Lord our God is in the right, but there is open shame on us and our ancestors this very day. ⁷ All those calamities with which the Lord threatened us have come upon us. ⁸ Yet we have not entreated the favor of the Lord by turning away, each of us, from the thoughts of our wicked hearts. ⁹ And the Lord has kept the calamities ready, and the Lord has brought them upon us, for the Lord is just in all the works that he has commanded us to do. ¹⁰ Yet we have not obeyed his voice, to walk in the statutes of the Lord that he set before us.

¹¹ And now, O Lord God of Israel, who brought your people out of the land of Egypt with a mighty hand and with signs and wonders and with great power and outstretched arm, and made yourself a name that continues to this day, ¹² we have sinned, we have

ᵃ Gk *in the shadow*
ᵇ Gk *in accordance with what is*
ᶜ Gk *because we*

incense and *grain* offerings continued at the ruined temple; cf. Jer 17.26. **11:** Jer 29.7. Belshazzar was the son of Nabonidus. Dan 5 makes the same error.

1.15–3.8: Confession of sin. This prayer draws on numerous biblical texts, including Lev 26, Deut 28, and parts of Jeremiah. It also has many links with Dan 9.4–19. Bar 1.15–2.5 appears to be intended for the Jewish community in Palestine and 2.6–3.8 for Jews in exile; compare 1.15–16 and 2.13–14. **1.15–18:** The Jews in Judah confess their disobedience to God and his commandments (Dan 9.7–10). This refrain is similar to 2.6–10, which helps mark the division between the two sections of 1.15–3.8. **15:** *Open shame*, repeated in 2.6. See Dan 9.7–8; Ezra 9.7. **18:** 2.10; Dan 9.10. **1.19–2.5:** Israel's disobedience is given a historical context, from the Exodus to the Babylonian exile. **19:** 2 Kings 21.15; Jer 7.25. **20:** *Curse*, Lev 26; Deut 28; Jer 11.3–5. **21:** Jer 7.25–26; 26.4–5; Dan 9.5–6,10. **22:** 2.8. **2.1–2:** Dan 9.12–13. **3:** Lev 26.29; Deut 28.53; Jer 19.9; Lam 4.10. **4:** Cf. Jer 42.18. **5:** Deut 28.13. **6–10:** Confession of guilt. See 1.15–18; Dan 9.12–14. **11–26:** Supplication and confession. **11–14:** Dan 9.15–17. **11:**

been ungodly, we have done wrong, O Lord our God, against all your ordinances. [13] Let your anger turn away from us, for we are left, few in number, among the nations where you have scattered us. [14] Hear, O Lord, our prayer and our supplication, and for your own sake deliver us, and grant us favor in the sight of those who have carried us into exile; [15] so that all the earth may know that you are the Lord our God, for Israel and his descendants are called by your name.

[16] O Lord, look down from your holy dwelling, and consider us. Incline your ear, O Lord, and hear; [17] open your eyes, O Lord, and see, for the dead who are in Hades, whose spirit has been taken from their bodies, will not ascribe glory or justice to the Lord; [18] but the person who is deeply grieved, who walks bowed and feeble, with failing eyes and famished soul, will declare your glory and righteousness, O Lord.

[19] For it is not because of any righteous deeds of our ancestors or our kings that we bring before you our prayer for mercy, O Lord our God. [20] For you have sent your anger and your wrath upon us, as you declared by your servants the prophets, saying: [21] Thus says the Lord: Bend your shoulders and serve the king of Babylon, and you will remain in the land that I gave to your ancestors. [22] But if you will not obey the voice of the Lord and will not serve the king of Babylon, [23] I will make to cease from the towns of Judah and from the region around Jerusalem the voice of mirth and the voice of gladness, the voice of the bridegroom and the voice of the bride, and the whole land will be a desolation without inhabitants.

[24] But we did not obey your voice, to serve the king of Babylon; and you have carried out your threats, which you spoke by your servants the prophets, that the bones of our kings and the bones of our ancestors would be brought out of their resting place; [25] and indeed they have been thrown out to the heat of day and the frost of night. They perished in great misery, by famine and sword and pestilence. [26] And the house that is called by your name you have made as it is today, because of the wickedness of the house of Israel and the house of Judah.

[27] Yet you have dealt with us, O Lord our God, in all your kindness and in all your great compassion, [28] as you spoke by your servant Moses on the day when you commanded him to write your law in the presence of the people of Israel, saying, [29] "If you will not obey my voice, this very great multitude will surely turn into a small number among the nations, where I will scatter them. [30] For I know that they will not obey me, for they are a stiff-necked people. But in the land of their exile they will come to themselves [31] and know that I am the Lord their God. I will give them a heart that obeys and ears that hear; [32] they will praise me in the land of their exile, and will remember my name [33] and turn from their stubbornness and their wicked deeds; for they will remember the ways of their ancestors, who sinned before the Lord. [34] I will bring them again into the land that I swore to give to their ancestors, to Abraham, Isaac, and Jacob, and they will rule over it; and I will increase them, and they will not be diminished. [35] I will make an everlasting covenant with them to be their God and they shall be my people; and I will never again remove my people Israel from the land that I have given them."

3 O Lord Almighty, God of Israel, the soul in anguish and the wearied spirit cry out to you. [2] Hear, O Lord, and have mercy, for we have sinned before you. [3] For you are enthroned forever, and we are perishing

Ex 15.11–16; Jer 32.20–21. **12:** Cf. 1 Kings 8.47 and Ps 106.6. **13:** Deut 4.27; Jer 42.2. **15:** Cf. Deut 28.10; Jer 14.9. **16:** Deut 26.15; 1 Kings 8.39; Isa 63.15; Dan 9.18. **17:** Pss 6.5; 30.9; Isa 38.18; Sir 17.27–28. *Hades*, in Hebrew "Sheol," the underworld abode of the dead. **18:** Deut 28.65–66. **20:** Jer 36.7. **21:** Jer 27.11–12. **23:** Jer 7.34; 16.9; 33.10–11. **24:** Jer 8.1–2. **25:** Jer 36.30. **26:** Jer 7.14. **27–35:** Repentance and restoration illustrate God's compassion for Israel. The words attributed to Moses in vv. 29–34 have no verbatim match in the Hebrew Bible but resemble phrases from Deuteronomy and Jeremiah. **29:** Deut 28.58,62. **30:** 1 Kings 8.47. **31:** Jer 24.7. **34:** Lev 26.42–45; Deut 6.10; 30.1–5; Jer 32.37. **35:** Jer 24.6; 32.38–40. **3.1–8:** Appeal to God to hear the prayer of the exiles. **4:** The Greek word *dead* (see textual note *a*) may represent the confusion of two similar Hebrew terms, one which means "dead" and the other "men." Note, however, that elsewhere in the book exile is symbolically depicted as a form of death (2.17;

forever. [4] O Lord Almighty, God of Israel,
hear now the prayer of the people[a] of Israel,
the children of those who sinned before
you, who did not heed the voice of the Lord
their God, so that calamities have clung to
us. [5] Do not remember the iniquities of our
ancestors, but in this crisis remember your
power and your name. [6] For you are the Lord
our God, and it is you, O Lord, whom we will
praise. [7] For you have put the fear of you in
our hearts so that we would call upon your
name; and we will praise you in our exile,
for we have put away from our hearts all the
iniquity of our ancestors who sinned against
you. [8] See, we are today in our exile where
you have scattered us, to be reproached and
cursed and punished for all the iniquities
of our ancestors, who forsook the Lord our
God.

[9] Hear the commandments of life, O Israel;
  give ear, and learn wisdom!
[10] Why is it, O Israel, why is it that you are
    in the land of your enemies,
  that you are growing old in a foreign
    country,
that you are defiled with the dead,
  [11] that you are counted among those in
    Hades?
[12] You have forsaken the fountain of
    wisdom.
[13] If you had walked in the way of God,
  you would be living in peace forever.
[14] Learn where there is wisdom,
  where there is strength,
  where there is understanding,

so that you may at the same time discern
  where there is length of days, and life,
  where there is light for the eyes, and
    peace.

[15] Who has found her place?
  And who has entered her storehouses?
[16] Where are the rulers of the nations,
  and those who lorded it over the
    animals on earth;
[17] those who made sport of the birds of the
    air,
  and who hoarded up silver and gold
in which people trust,
  and there is no end to their getting;
[18] those who schemed to get silver, and
    were anxious,
  but there is no trace of their works?
[19] They have vanished and gone down to
    Hades,
  and others have arisen in their place.

[20] Later generations have seen the light of
    day,
  and have lived upon the earth;
but they have not learned the way to
    knowledge,
  nor understood her paths,
  nor laid hold of her.
[21] Their descendants have strayed far from
    her[b] way.
[22] She has not been heard of in Canaan,
  or seen in Teman;

---

a   Gk *dead*
b   Other ancient authorities read *their*

3.10–11). **7**: 1 Kings 8.47–48; Jer 32.40b. **8**: 2.4. The exile is punishment for sins committed by earlier generations (2.33; 3.4–5; Ex 20.5; 34.7; Lam 5.7; cf. Jer 31.29–30; Ezek 18).

3.9–4.4: Wisdom poem. Wisdom, personified as a woman, is elusive but known to God, who gave her to Israel as the Torah. This section has many affinities with Sir 24 and Job 28. **3.9–14**: Introduction to the poem, exhorting Israel to learn wisdom. **9**: *The commandments of life,* Deut 30.15–20; Sir 45.5. **10**: This verse connects the Wisdom poem of 3.9–4.4 to the confession of sin in 1.15–3.8. *Growing old,* the exile has continued for a long time (contrast 1.2). **11**: Pss 28.1; 88.4. *Hades,* see 2.17n. **12**: Prov 18.4; Jer 2.13; 2 Esd 14.47. **14**: Prov 3.2,13–18; Job 12.13. **15–23**: Gentile kings and nations do not possess wisdom. **15**: Job 28.12,20. **16b–17a**: Jer 27.6; Dan 2.37–38; Jdt 11.7. **17b–19**: Those who searched for riches were unable to avoid death. The Torah, by contrast, is associated with life (4.1; cf. Prov 8.10–11,19). **22**: *Canaan,* here probably a reference to the Phoenicians (cf. Gen 10.15), whose coastal cities Tyre and Sidon were associated with wisdom and mercantile skill (Isa 23.8; Ezek 28.3–5; Zech 9.2). *Teman,* in Edom, a region known for its wisdom (Jer 49.7; Ob 8–9; cf. Gen 36.9–11). **23**: *The descendants of Hagar,* the Ishmaelites, who were Arabian tribal groups with a reputation for trade and commerce (Gen 25.12–15; 37.25). *Merran,* the word occurs nowhere else in the Bible. It may be a corruption of "Midian," an area well-known for its traders in the northern Hejaz region of Arabia, east of the Gulf of Aqaba

²³ the descendants of Hagar, who seek for
    understanding on the earth,
  the merchants of Merran and Teman,
  the story-tellers and the seekers for
    understanding,
have not learned the way to wisdom,
  or given thought to her paths.

²⁴ O Israel, how great is the house of God,
  how vast the territory that he possesses!
²⁵ It is great and has no bounds;
  it is high and immeasurable.
²⁶ The giants were born there, who were
    famous of old,
  great in stature, expert in war.
²⁷ God did not choose them,
  or give them the way to knowledge;
²⁸ so they perished because they had no
    wisdom,
  they perished through their folly.

²⁹ Who has gone up into heaven, and taken
    her,
  and brought her down from the clouds?
³⁰ Who has gone over the sea, and found
    her,
  and will buy her for pure gold?
³¹ No one knows the way to her,
  or is concerned about the path to her.
³² But the one who knows all things knows
    her,
  he found her by his understanding.
The one who prepared the earth for all time
  filled it with four-footed creatures;
³³ the one who sends forth the light, and
    it goes;
  he called it, and it obeyed him,
    trembling;

³⁴ the stars shone in their watches, and
    were glad;
  he called them, and they said, "Here we
    are!"
  They shone with gladness for him who
    made them.
³⁵ This is our God;
  no other can be compared to him.
³⁶ He found the whole way to knowledge,
  and gave her to his servant Jacob
  and to Israel, whom he loved.
³⁷ Afterward she appeared on earth
  and lived with humankind.

4 She is the book of the commandments
    of God,
  the law that endures forever.
All who hold her fast will live,
  and those who forsake her will die.
² Turn, O Jacob, and take her;
  walk toward the shining of her light.
³ Do not give your glory to another,
  or your advantages to an alien people.
⁴ Happy are we, O Israel,
  for we know what is pleasing to God.

⁵ Take courage, my people,
  who perpetuate Israel's name!
⁶ It was not for destruction
  that you were sold to the nations,
but you were handed over to your enemies
  because you angered God.
⁷ For you provoked the one who made you
  by sacrificing to demons and not to God.
⁸ You forgot the everlasting God, who
    brought you up,
  and you grieved Jerusalem, who reared
    you.

(Gen 25.2; 37.28; Isa 60.6). **24–28:** This section praises the magnitude of God's creation. **24:** *The house of God*, the context suggests that this refers to the created world rather than the Jerusalem temple. **26:** *The giants*, the legendary offspring of angels and women recounted in Gen 6.1–4; cf. *1 En.* 6–8; *Jub.* 5. **28:** Sir 16.7; Wis 14.6; 3 Macc 2.4. **29–37:** Only God has Wisdom, and he gives it to Israel. **29:** Deut 30.12–14; cf. Prov 30.4; Sir 24.4. **30:** Job 28.14–15. **32:** Job 28.23. God finds Wisdom (see v. 36), whereas in Ben Sira he creates Wisdom (Sir 24.3,9; cf. Prov 8:22). **33:** The trembling of *the light* denotes its fear and obedience before God (cf. Gen 1.3; Job 38.35). **34:** Job 38.7; Ps 148.3; Sir 43.10. **36:** Sir 24.8. **37:** Divine Wisdom appears on earth in Prov 8 and Sir 24.6–12 (cf. Wis 1.7; 9.10). Contrast *1 En.* 42. **4.1–4:** Identification of Wisdom as the Torah, which Israel should embrace. The personification of Wisdom as a woman is more prominent in Prov 8 and Sir 24 (cf. Wis 6–9). **1:** Prov 3.18; Sir 24.23 (cf. 6.37; 15.1). **4:** Deut 33.29.

    4.5–5.9: Poem of consolation. 4.5–8: Introductory exhortation, stressing that God wished to punish, not destroy, Israel because of its sins. **5:** *Take courage*, a refrain of the poem (vv. 21,27,30; cf. Isa 40.1). **6:** Isa 50.1b; 52.3. **7:** Deut 32.16–17; Ps 106.37. **8:** Gen 21.33; Isa 40.28. **9b–16:** Jerusalem personified addresses neighboring

⁹ For she saw the wrath that came upon
   you from God,
and she said:
Listen, you neighbors of Zion,
   God has brought great sorrow upon me;
¹⁰ for I have seen the exile of my sons and
   daughters,
   which the Everlasting brought upon
      them.
¹¹ With joy I nurtured them,
   but I sent them away with weeping and
      sorrow.
¹² Let no one rejoice over me, a widow
   and bereaved of many;
I was left desolate because of the sins of
   my children,
   because they turned away from the law
      of God.
¹³ They had no regard for his statutes;
   they did not walk in the ways of God's
      commandments,
   or tread the paths his righteousness
      showed them.
¹⁴ Let the neighbors of Zion come;
   remember the capture of my sons and
      daughters,
   which the Everlasting brought upon
      them.
¹⁵ For he brought a distant nation against
      them,
   a nation ruthless and of a strange
      language,
which had no respect for the aged
   and no pity for a child.
¹⁶ They led away the widow's beloved sons,
   and bereaved the lonely woman of her
      daughters.

¹⁷ But I, how can I help you?
¹⁸ For he who brought these calamities
      upon you
   will deliver you from the hand of your
      enemies.
¹⁹ Go, my children, go;
   for I have been left desolate.

²⁰ I have taken off the robe of peace
   and put on sackcloth for my
      supplication;
   I will cry to the Everlasting all my days.

²¹ Take courage, my children, cry to God,
   and he will deliver you from the power
      and hand of the enemy.
²² For I have put my hope in the Everlasting
      to save you,
   and joy has come to me from the Holy
      One,
because of the mercy that will soon come
      to you
   from your everlasting savior.[a]
²³ For I sent you out with sorrow and
      weeping,
   but God will give you back to me with
      joy and gladness forever.
²⁴ For as the neighbors of Zion have now
      seen your capture,
   so they soon will see your salvation by
      God,
which will come to you with great glory
   and with the splendor of the
      Everlasting.
²⁵ My children, endure with patience the
      wrath that has come upon you from
      God.
Your enemy has overtaken you,
   but you will soon see their destruction
      and will tread upon their necks.
²⁶ My pampered children have traveled
      rough roads;
   they were taken away like a flock
      carried off by the enemy.

²⁷ Take courage, my children, and cry to God,
   for you will be remembered by the one
      who brought this upon you.
²⁸ For just as you were disposed to go
      astray from God,
   return with tenfold zeal to seek him.

---

a   Or *from the Everlasting, your savior*

cities. **9:** Lam 1.12. **10:** *Everlasting*, a term for God characteristic of this poem that is not found in other sections
of the book of Baruch (vv. 14,20,22,24,35; 5.2). **12:** Isa 49.21; 54.4; Lam 1.1. **15:** Deut 28.49–50; Isa 33.19. **17–29:**
Jerusalem personified speaks to the exiles. **20:** Contrast Isa 52.1. *Robe of peace*, worn during a time of prosperity.
Sackcloth, worn in times of mourning and penitence (e.g., Isa 3.24; Jer 6.26; Lam 2.10). **22:** *The Holy One*, a name
for God that is prominent in Isaiah (e.g., 5.19; 12.6; 43.3; 47.4; 60.9) found also in 4.37; 5.5 but not elsewhere in
the book of Baruch. **23:** Ps 126.6; Isa 35.10; 51.11; Jer 31.12–13. **24:** Isa 60.1–3. **25:** Deut 33.29; Isa 51.23. *The wrath*

²⁹ For the one who brought these
    calamities upon you
  will bring you everlasting joy with your
    salvation.

³⁰ Take courage, O Jerusalem,
  for the one who named you will
    comfort you.
³¹ Wretched will be those who mistreated
    you
  and who rejoiced at your fall.
³² Wretched will be the cities that your
    children served as slaves;
  wretched will be the city that received
    your offspring.
³³ For just as she rejoiced at your fall
  and was glad for your ruin,
  so she will be grieved at her own
    desolation.
³⁴ I will take away her pride in her great
    population,
  and her insolence will be turned to
    grief.
³⁵ For fire will come upon her from the
    Everlasting for many days,
  and for a long time she will be inhabited
    by demons.

³⁶ Look toward the east, O Jerusalem,
  and see the joy that is coming to you
    from God.
³⁷ Look, your children are coming, whom
    you sent away;
  they are coming, gathered from east
    and west,
at the word of the Holy One,
  rejoicing in the glory of God.

5 Take off the garment of your sorrow and
    affliction, O Jerusalem,
  and put on forever the beauty of the
    glory from God.
² Put on the robe of the righteousness that
    comes from God;
  put on your head the diadem of the
    glory of the Everlasting;
³ for God will show your splendor
    everywhere under heaven.
⁴ For God will give you evermore the name,
  "Righteous Peace, Godly Glory."

⁵ Arise, O Jerusalem, stand upon the
    height;
  look toward the east,
and see your children gathered from west
    and east
  at the word of the Holy One,
  rejoicing that God has remembered
    them.
⁶ For they went out from you on foot,
  led away by their enemies;
but God will bring them back to you,
  carried in glory, as on a royal throne.
⁷ For God has ordered that every high
    mountain and the everlasting hills be
    made low
  and the valleys filled up, to make level
    ground,
  so that Israel may walk safely in the
    glory of God.
⁸ The woods and every fragrant tree
  have shaded Israel at God's command.
⁹ For God will lead Israel with joy,
  in the light of his glory,
  with the mercy and righteousness that
    come from him.

---

has a short duration (cf. Isa 54.7–8). **4.30–5.9:** The narrator consoles Jerusalem with the prospect of the exiles' return. **30–35:** Jerusalem is encouraged by the fall of her enemies, referring to Babylon and perhaps Edom (Ps 137.7–8; Isa 63.1–6; cf. Isa 13–14; 47; Jer 50–51). Contrast the attitude toward Babylon in 1.11–12. **30:** *The one who named you,* see 5.4n. Cf. Isa 51.3. **35:** *Fire,* Jer 51.58; *demons,* Isa 13.21; 34.14. **4.36–5.4:** Jerusalem is exhorted to watch the exiles return from the east. **36–37:** See 5.5n. **5.1–2:** 4.20; Isa 52.1; 61.3,10; *Pss. Sol.* 11.7. **4:** The renaming of Jerusalem, which marks a change in status, is a theme in the prophetic books (Isa 1.26; 60.14; 62.2–4; Jer 33.16; Ezek 48.35). *Righteous Peace,* Isa 32.17; 60.17. **5.5–9:** A second call for Jerusalem to watch God bring the exiles to her. **5:** 4.36; Isa 40.9–11; 43.5; 49.18; 51.17; 60.4; *Pss. Sol.* 11.2–3. **6:** Isa 49.22; 66.20. **7:** Isa 40.4–5; 42.16; *Pss. Sol.* 11.4. **8:** *Pss. Sol.* 11.5–6. Cf. Isa 41.19.

THE LETTER OF JEREMIAH

NAME AND AUTHORSHIP

The work claims to be a copy of a letter written by the prophet Jeremiah for Judeans about to be exiled to Babylonia in 597 BCE. The Letter, however, never gives the impression that the siege of Jerusalem and the Babylonian exile are recent calamities. Moreover, it draws on the canonical book of Jeremiah and other biblical texts (see next sections). Thus the Letter was probably written much later and attributed to Jeremiah, inspired by the account in Jer 29 of Jeremiah's writing to the exilic community.

CANONICAL STATUS AND LOCATION IN CANON

The Letter is not part of the Jewish or Protestant canons. In the Roman Catholic and Orthodox traditions it is deuterocanonical. Major Greek Septuagint manuscripts, such as Vaticanus (fourth century CE) and Alexandrinus (fifth century CE), treat the Letter as a distinct work placed between Lamentations and Ezekiel. The Latin Vulgate, which is prominent in the Roman Catholic tradition, considers the text the sixth chapter of Baruch. The Letter appears in the NRSV as an independent book because it differs markedly from Baruch in terms of style and content; there is no strong evidence that it was originally part of Baruch (but see also note *a*).

DATE OF COMPOSITION AND HISTORICAL CONTEXT

Although the Letter purports to be sent to the Judeans about to be exiled to Babylonia in the early sixth century BCE, many scholars date the Letter to the Hellenistic period. The reference in v. 3 to an exile lasting seven generations (280 years) could, if taken literally, indicate that the text was written in 317 BCE. The "seven generations," however, should probably be read symbolically. 2 Macc 2.1–3 refers to the Letter, and a fragment of a Greek papyrus from Cave 7 of Qumran (7Q2) contains a portion of Let Jer 43–44; these factors indicate that the work was written before 100 BCE.

LITERARY HISTORY, STRUCTURE, AND CONTENTS

Although the oldest surviving manuscripts of the Letter are in Greek, there are indications that it was originally written in Hebrew or Aramaic and then translated into Greek (see 12n. and 72n.).

After a historical introduction (vv. 1–7), the body of the composition consists of ten warnings about idolatry. Each unit ends with a refrain that idols are not gods and that they should not be feared (vv. 16,23,29,40,44,52,56,65,69,72).

INTERPRETATION

The Letter of Jeremiah warns Jews to avoid pagan religion and asserts that idols are false gods that have no power. Since the veneration of idols was widespread, the text would have had relevance not only to Jewish exiles living in Babylon but to Jews living anywhere in the ancient world. The work is influenced by biblical condemnations of idolatry such as Deut 4.27–28; Isa 44.9–20; 46.5–7; Pss 115.3–8; 135.15–18; cf. Wis 13–15. The Letter also relies upon and expands Jer 10. Despite the identification of the composition as a letter, inspired by the prophet's epistle to the exiles in Jer 29, the work does not belong to the genre of ancient letters and is better classified as a homily or sermon.

GUIDE TO READING

The homiletical style of the Letter, with its vivid imagery, repeated refrains, reliance on formulaic biblical denunciations of idolatry, and sarcastic humor is intended to reinforce beliefs and values already held by its Jewish audience. The author shows no sympathy for actual pagan customs, and the Letter cannot be read as an accurate description of the way in which pagans understood their own religious practices.

Matthew Goff

6 [a] A copy of a letter that Jeremiah sent to those who were to be taken to Babylon as exiles by the king of the Babylonians, to give them the message that God had commanded him.

[2] Because of the sins that you have committed before God, you will be taken to Babylon as exiles by Nebuchadnezzar, king of the Babylonians. [3] Therefore when you have come to Babylon you will remain there for many years, for a long time, up to seven generations; after that I will bring you away from there in peace. [4] Now in Babylon you will see gods made of silver and gold and wood, which people carry on their shoulders, and which cause the heathen to fear. [5] So beware of becoming at all like the foreigners or of letting fear for these gods[b] possess you [6] when you see the multitude before and behind them worshiping them. But say in your heart, "It is you, O Lord, whom we must worship." [7] For my angel is with you, and he is watching over your lives.

[8] Their tongues are smoothed by the carpenter, and they themselves are overlaid with gold and silver; but they are false and cannot speak. [9] People[c] take gold and make crowns for the heads of their gods, as they might for a girl who loves ornaments. [10] Sometimes the priests secretly take gold and silver from their gods and spend it on themselves, [11] or even give some of it to the prostitutes on the terrace. They deck their gods[d] out with garments like human beings—these gods of silver and gold and wood [12] that cannot save themselves from rust and corrosion. When they have been dressed in purple robes, [13] their faces are wiped because of the dust from the temple, which is thick upon them. [14] One of them holds a scepter, like a district judge, but is unable to destroy anyone who offends it. [15] Another has a dagger in its right hand, and an ax, but cannot defend itself from war and robbers. [16] From this it is evident that they are not gods; so do not fear them.

[17] For just as someone's dish is useless when it is broken, [18] so are their gods when they have been set up in the temples. Their eyes are full of the dust raised by the feet of those who enter. And just as the gates are shut on every side against anyone who has offended a king, as though under sentence of death, so the priests make their temples secure with doors and locks and bars, in order that they may not be plundered by robbers. [19] They light more lamps for them than they light for themselves, though their gods[e] can see none of them. [20] They are[f] just like a beam of the temple, but their hearts, it is said, are eaten away when crawling creatures from the earth devour them and their robes. They do not notice [21] when their faces have been blackened by the smoke

[a] The King James Version (like the Latin Vulgate) prints The Letter of Jeremiah as Chapter 6 of the Book of Baruch, and the chapter and verse numbers are here retained. In the Greek Septuagint, the Letter is separated from Baruch by the Book of Lamentations.
[b] Gk *for them*
[c] Gk *They*
[d] Gk *them*
[e] Gk *they*
[f] Gk *It is*

6.1–7: Historical introduction. 1: The exile of 597 BCE (2 Kings 24.10–17). *Who were to be taken*, the work is composed for people about to be exiled. The letter in Jer 29 is written by the prophet to Jews already in exile. **3:** *Seven generations*, taken literally, the duration of the exile in Babylon. Contrast the different figures given in Jer 25.12; 29.10 (seventy years), Ezek 4.6 (forty years) and Dan 9.24 (seventy weeks of years). **4:** *Silver and gold*, overlaid on wood (v. 55; Jer 10.3–4; cf. Isa 40.19). *Which people carry on their shoulders*, this may refer to the procession that was part of the *Akitu*, the Babylonian New Year festival (see v. 26). **5:** Jer 10.2.

6.8–73: Warnings against idolatry. 8–16: First warning: the helplessness of idols. 8: *Carpenter*, Isa 40.20; 44.13; Jer. 10.3–4. *Cannot speak*, Pss 115.4–5; 135.15–16. **11:** *Prostitutes* may refer to women who earned money for vows through prostitution (cf. v. 43). **12:** *Purple robes*, a symbol of authority (cf. Jer 10.9). *Corrosion*, several Greek manuscripts give this word as either "food" or "meat." It is most likely a mistranslation of a Hebrew word for "moth." **15:** Vv. 48–49,57.

6.17–23: Second warning: the uselessness of idols. 17: V. 59; Jer 22.28; Hos 8.8. **18:** *Robbers*, see vv. 57–58n. **19:** Despite many lamps, the idols cannot see (Deut 4.28; Pss 115.5; 135.16; Isa 44.18). **20:** Being wooden, the idols are subject to decay and infestation. **22:** The earliest reference in Jewish literature to *cats*, first domesticated in Egypt.

of the temple. [22] Bats, swallows, and birds alight on their bodies and heads; and so do cats. [23] From this you will know that they are not gods; so do not fear them.

[24] As for the gold that they wear for beauty—it[a] will not shine unless someone wipes off the tarnish; for even when they were being cast, they did not feel it. [25] They are bought without regard to cost, but there is no breath in them. [26] Having no feet, they are carried on the shoulders of others, revealing to humankind their worthlessness. And those who serve them are put to shame [27] because, if any of these gods falls[b] to the ground, they themselves must pick it up. If anyone sets it upright, it cannot move itself; and if it is tipped over, it cannot straighten itself. Gifts are placed before them just as before the dead. [28] The priests sell the sacrifices that are offered to these gods[c] and use the money themselves. Likewise their wives preserve some of the meat[d] with salt, but give none to the poor or helpless. [29] Sacrifices to them may even be touched by women in their periods or at childbirth. Since you know by these things that they are not gods, do not fear them.

[30] For how can they be called gods? Women serve meals for gods of silver and gold and wood; [31] and in their temples the priests sit with their clothes torn, their heads and beards shaved, and their heads uncovered. [32] They howl and shout before their gods as some do at a funeral banquet. [33] The priests take some of the clothing of their gods[e] to clothe their wives and children. [34] Whether one does evil to them or good,

they will not be able to repay it. They cannot set up a king or depose one. [35] Likewise they are not able to give either wealth or money; if one makes a vow to them and does not keep it, they will not require it. [36] They cannot save anyone from death or rescue the weak from the strong. [37] They cannot restore sight to the blind; they cannot rescue one who is in distress. [38] They cannot take pity on a widow or do good to an orphan. [39] These things that are made of wood and overlaid with gold and silver are like stones from the mountain, and those who serve them will be put to shame. [40] Why then must anyone think that they are gods, or call them gods?

Besides, even the Chaldeans themselves dishonor them; for when they see someone who cannot speak, they bring Bel and pray that the mute may speak, as though Bel[f] were able to understand! [41] Yet they themselves cannot perceive this and abandon them, for they have no sense. [42] And the women, with cords around them, sit along the passageways, burning bran for incense. [43] When one of them is led off by one of the passers-by and is taken to bed by him, she derides the woman next to her, because she was not as attractive as herself and her cord was not broken. [44] Whatever is done for these idols[g] is

---

a   Lat Syr: Gk *they*
b   Gk *if they fall*
c   Gk *to them*
d   Gk *of them*
e   Gk *some of their clothing*
f   Gk *he*
g   Gk *them*

6.24–29: Third warning: the lifelessness of idols. 25: *No breath*, Ps 135.17; Jer 10.14; 51.17; Hab 2.19. **26:** V. 4; Isa 46.1, 7a; Jer 10.5. **27:** Isa 46.7b; Jer 10.4 (cf. 1 Sam 5.3). *Gifts* for *the dead*, Ps 106.28; Tob 4.17; Sir 30.18–19. **29:** Biblical purity regulations state that women during and shortly after menstruation and childbirth are not allowed to participate in worship (Lev 12.2–5; 15.19–24).

6.30–40a: Fourth warning: the powerlessness of idols. 30: Only men were priests in the Temple in Jerusalem; but see Ex 38.8; 1 Sam 2.22. **31–32:** Ritual mourning, presumably for gods such as the Mesopotamian deity Tammuz, whose descent into the netherworld was annually observed with similar practices (Ezek 8.14; cf. Lev 21.5). *Funeral banquets*, Jer 16.5–9. **34b:** V. 53; cf. Job 12.18; Dan 2.21. **35b:** Deut 23.21. **36:** Deut 32.39; 1 Sam 2.6. **37:** Ps 146.8. **38:** Deut 10.18; Ps 146.9. **39:** Isa 44.11; Hab 2.19.

6.40b–44: Fifth warning: the folly of revering idols. 40b: *Chaldeans*, often a synonym for "Babylonians." The term can also refer to astrologers or diviners (e.g., Dan 2.2,4). *Bel* ("Lord"), a title for Marduk, the patron god of the city of Babylon (Isa 46.1; Jer 50.2; 51.44; Bel 1.3). **43:** The Greek historian Herodotus (1.199) describes a similar practice among the Babylonians (cf. v. 11).

6.45–52: Sixth warning: idols are not divine but the work of human hands. 45: Isa 40.15; Jer 10.9; Pss 115.4;

false. Why then must anyone think that they are gods, or call them gods?

⁴⁵ They are made by carpenters and goldsmiths; they can be nothing but what the artisans wish them to be. ⁴⁶ Those who make them will certainly not live very long themselves; ⁴⁷ how then can the things that are made by them be gods? They have left only lies and reproach for those who come after. ⁴⁸ For when war or calamity comes upon them, the priests consult together as to where they can hide themselves and their gods.ᵃ ⁴⁹ How then can one fail to see that these are not gods, for they cannot save themselves from war or calamity? ⁵⁰ Since they are made of wood and overlaid with gold and silver, it will afterward be known that they are false. ⁵¹ It will be manifest to all the nations and kings that they are not gods but the work of human hands, and that there is no work of God in them. ⁵² Who then can fail to know that they are not gods?ᵇ

⁵³ For they cannot set up a king over a country or give rain to people. ⁵⁴ They cannot judge their own cause or deliver one who is wronged, for they have no power; ⁵⁵ they are like crows between heaven and earth. When fire breaks out in a temple of wooden gods overlaid with gold or silver, their priests will flee and escape, but the godsᶜ will be burned up like timbers. ⁵⁶ Besides, they can offer no resistance to king or enemy. Why then must anyone admit or think that they are gods?

⁵⁷ Gods made of wood and overlaid with silver and gold are unable to save themselves from thieves or robbers. ⁵⁸ Anyone who can will strip them of their gold and silver and of the robes they wear, and go off with this booty, and they will not be able to help themselves. ⁵⁹ So it is better to be a king who shows his courage, or a household utensil that serves its owner's need, than to be these false gods; better even the door of a house that protects its contents, than these false gods; better also a wooden pillar in a palace, than these false gods.

⁶⁰ For sun and moon and stars are bright, and when sent to do a service, they are obedient. ⁶¹ So also the lightning, when it flashes, is widely seen; and the wind likewise blows in every land. ⁶² When God commands the clouds to go over the whole world, they carry out his command. ⁶³ And the fire sent from above to consume mountains and woods does what it is ordered. But these idolsᵈ are not to be compared with them in appearance or power. ⁶⁴ Therefore one must not think that they are gods, nor call them gods, for they are not able either to decide a case or to do good to anyone. ⁶⁵ Since you know then that they are not gods, do not fear them.

⁶⁶ They can neither curse nor bless kings; ⁶⁷ they cannot show signs in the heavens for the nations, or shine like the sun or give light like the moon. ⁶⁸ The wild animals are better than they are, for they can flee to shelter and help themselves. ⁶⁹ So we have no evidence whatever that they are gods; therefore do not fear them.

⁷⁰ Like a scarecrow in a cucumber bed, which guards nothing, so are their gods of wood, overlaid with gold and silver. ⁷¹ In the

ᵃ Gk *them*
ᵇ Meaning of Gk uncertain
ᶜ Gk *they*
ᵈ Gk *these things*

135.15. **47:** *Those who come after*, future generations. **50:** *Afterward*, when the idols' overlay is stripped off (cf. vv. 10,58).

6.53–56: Seventh warning: the impotence of idols. 53: See v. 34b and note. *Give rain*, Deut 11.14; 28.12; Ps 147.8; Jer 14.22. **54:** Vv. 36–37. **55:** *Crows*, the sense is unclear; perhaps a mistranslation into Greek of the Hebrew word for "clouds."

6.57–65: Eighth warning: the helplessness and uselessness of idols. 57–58: The author mentions the plundering of idols several times (vv. 15,18,33; cf. 10). **59:** V. 17. **60–63:** God controls the natural world; the idols do not (cf. Sir 16.26–30; 1 *En*. 2–5). **61:** Pss 97.4; 135.7. **64:** V. 54; Ex 18.19; Isa 41.21.

6.66–69: Ninth warning: idols cannot do what God can. Wild animals can do more than they can. 66: V. 34; Jer 10.5; for the idiom see Gen 12.3; Num 22.6. **67:** *Signs*, portents (cf. Jer 10.2; Joel 2.30).

6.70–73: Tenth warning: idols are compared to a scarecrow, a thornbush, and a corpse. 70: *Like a scarecrow in a cucumber bed*, the same comparison occurs in the Hebrew text of Jer 10.5 but not in its translation in the Greek Septuagint, suggesting that the Letter was originally written in Hebrew. **71:** *Thornbush*, a common, use-

same way, their gods of wood, overlaid with gold and silver, are like a thornbush in a garden on which every bird perches; or like a corpse thrown out in the darkness. [72] From the purple and linen[a] that rot upon them you will know that they are not gods; and they will finally be consumed themselves, and be a reproach in the land. [73] Better, therefore, is someone upright who has no idols; such a person will be far above reproach.

[a] Cn: Gk *marble*, Syr *silk*

less shrub (cf. Judg 9.14–15). *A corpse thrown out*, the body is crudely discarded and not buried (cf. Isa 34.3; Jer 14.16; 22.19). **72:** The Greek word "marble" (see textual note *a*) is a mistranslation based on the confusion of two Hebrew homonyms (*shesh*), one of which means "alabaster" (or "marble") and the other "linen."

THE ADDITIONS TO DANIEL

CANONICAL STATUS AND LOCATION

The original book of Daniel is comprised of twelve chapters, six in Aramaic and six in Hebrew. The Greek translations of the book of Daniel, however, both in the Septuagint (LXX) version and in a version attributed to the second-century CE Jewish scholar Theodotion, include three Additions to the twelve original chapters: "The Prayer of Azariah and the Song of the Three Jews," "Susanna," and "Bel and the Dragon." The names given to these poetic compositions are descriptive titles provided by later editors and do not appear in the texts of the ancient manuscripts themselves.

The Additions to Daniel are considered canonical in Roman Catholic and Orthodox Christian traditions, whereas Protestants place them with the Apocrypha. They are not considered scriptural in Judaism.

The Prayer of Azariah and the Song of the Three Jews are found in all Greek versions between Dan 3.23 and 3.24. The Septuagint locates the other two Additions at the end of the book of Daniel, after 12.13; Theodotion's version places Susanna at the opening of the book of Daniel, and Bel and the Dragon at the conclusion of ch 6. The NRSV follows Theodotion's text but places the Additions with the other Apocryphal/Deuterocanonical texts rather than integrating them into the book of Daniel.

DATE AND HISTORICAL CONTEXT

Behind the Greek Additions may lie Hebrew or Aramaic originals, although no versions of the three stories have been found, even among the Dead Sea Scrolls. Like the folktales in Dan 1–6, the Additions may well have been written prior to the Maccabean revolt of the mid-second century BCE; the Prayer of Azariah (vs. 9) may reflect the crisis that led to the revolt. Scholars debate the place of composition: A Semitic (Hebrew or Aramaic) original would strengthen the argument for an origin in Israel or the eastern Diaspora; a Greek original would suggest Alexandria in Egypt, where there was a major Jewish community. The Additions likely circulated independently and only later, perhaps ca. 100 BCE when the book of Daniel was translated into Greek, were they added to it. The first independent citations of the Additions date from the church fathers of the second century CE.

Amy-Jill Levine

THE PRAYER OF AZARIAH AND THE SONG OF THE THREE JEWS

LOCATION

The Prayer of Azariah (vv. 1–22) and the Song of the Three Jews (vv. 28–68), along with a brief prose paragraph (vv. 23–27) concerning the fate of the three in Nebuchadnezzar's furnace, appear in ancient manuscripts between Dan 3.23 and 3.24. The Prayer and Song (with the exception of the end of the Song) may have had no original connection to the book of Daniel. They appear as numbers seven and eight of the fifteen "Odes" added to the book of Psalms in a few manuscripts of the Septuagint, a placement that complements the resemblance of these Additions to Ps 148 in terms of theme and to Ps 136 in terms of structure. The narrative context of Dan 3 gives their general emphasis on hope for deliverance, national repentance, and divine faithfulness a poignant focus as the three Jews face death in Babylonian exile.

DATE AND HISTORICAL CONTEXT

Whether the Prayer and Song were initially written in Hebrew or Aramaic or Greek remains debated, as does their place of composition. The Prayer contains references that correspond to the reign of the Seleucid king Antiochus IV (175–164 BCE), and so a second- (or perhaps first-) century BCE date of composition is possible.

CONTENTS AND INTERPRETATION

Prayers and hymns are a hallmark of Second Temple Jewish texts, and they are found in such works as Judith, Tobit, and Baruch, as well as in Dan 9 and among the scrolls discovered at Qumran (the Dead Sea Scrolls). The Additions to Daniel are especially comparable to the Additions to Esther—in both, prose narrative is supplemented with prayer and song that emphasize the piety of the main characters. The Prayer of Azariah resembles other postexilic works in its condemnation of the covenant community for its lack of fidelity to God, its emphasis on divine righteousness and mercy, and its appeal for deliverance (Ps 106; Ezra 9.6–15; Neh 1.5–11; Bar 1.15–3.8; and some Qumran texts). The Song of the Three Jews has allusions to numerous psalmic and prophetic passages in its exhortations to the heavens (vv. 36–41), nature (vv. 42–51), earth and its creatures (vv. 52–59), and humanity (vv. 60–68). Unlike the book of Daniel and the Prayer of Azariah, however, it does not suggest a period of persecution or a time when the Temple was either destroyed or profaned.

Amy-Jill Levine

(ADDITIONS TO DANIEL, INSERTED BETWEEN 3.23 AND 3.24)

[1] They[a] walked around in the midst of the flames, singing hymns to God and blessing the Lord. [2] Then Azariah stood still in the fire and prayed aloud:

[3] "Blessed are you, O Lord, God of our
     ancestors, and worthy of praise;
     and glorious is your name forever!
[4] For you are just in all you have done;
     all your works are true and your ways
          right,
     and all your judgments are true.
[5] You have executed true judgments in all
          you have brought upon us
     and upon Jerusalem, the holy city of our
          ancestors;
     by a true judgment you have brought all
          this upon us because of our
          sins.
[6] For we have sinned and broken your law
          in turning away from you;
     in all matters we have sinned
          grievously.
[7] We have not obeyed your
          commandments,
     we have not kept them or done what
          you have commanded us for our
          own good.
[8] So all that you have brought upon us,
     and all that you have done to us,
     you have done by a true judgment.

[9] You have handed us over to our enemies,
          lawless and hateful rebels,
     and to an unjust king, the most wicked
          in all the world.
[10] And now we cannot open our mouths;
     we, your servants who worship you,
          have become a shame and a
          reproach.
[11] For your name's sake do not give us up
          forever,
     and do not annul your covenant.
[12] Do not withdraw your mercy from us,
     for the sake of Abraham your beloved
          and for the sake of your servant Isaac
          and Israel your holy one,
[13] to whom you promised
          to multiply their descendants like the
          stars of heaven
          and like the sand on the shore of the
          sea.
[14] For we, O Lord, have become fewer than
          any other nation,
     and are brought low this day in all the
          world because of our sins.
[15] In our day we have no ruler, or prophet,
          or leader,
     no burnt offering, or sacrifice, or
          oblation, or incense,

a   That is, Hananiah, Mishael, and Azariah (Dan 2.17), the original names of Shadrach, Meshach, and Abednego (Dan 1.6-7)

1–22: The prayer of Azariah. 1: *They* refers to Daniel's three friends, Hananiah (named Shadrach), Mishael (Meshach), and Azariah (Abednego) in v. 66; Dan 1.6–7; 3.22–23. The Babylonian names given here in parentheses do not appear in these Additions; the use of the Hebrew names reinforces the friends' Jewish identity. **3:** *Our ancestors*, see vv. 5,12,29; 1 Kings 8.53; Ezra 7.27; Dan 2.23; Tob 8.5. *Your name*, the praise of the divine name becomes increasingly common in Second Temple Jewish literature; cf. v. 30. **5:** *True judgments*, v. 8; Neh 9.33; Lam 1.18; Tobit; and other texts attribute the Babylonian exile to the community's sin. **6–8:** The confession of sin resembles Dan 9.5,15; Ezra 9.6; Neh 9.26. **9:** The *unjust king* in the context of the book of Daniel is Nebuchadnezzar (Dan 3.19), but the vague reference makes the statement applicable to other tyrants, such as Antiochus IV Epiphanes (see 1 Macc 1 and notes to Dan 10–12); *rebels* may refer to Jews who supported Antiochus and the Hellenization of Jerusalem (1 Macc 1.11–15,41–60). **10:** *Shame and a reproach*, see Dan 9.12. **11:** *Covenant*, see Gen 15.18; 17.7–8. **12:** *Abraham* is identified as beloved of God in Isa 41.8; 2 Chr 20.7; Jas 2.23, as well as the Qur'an (4.125). *Isaac* is called *servant* in Gen 24.14. *Israel*, i.e., Jacob (see Gen 32.28; 35.10). *Holy one* is more typically used for heavenly beings (Dan 4.10,20; 8.13). **13:** On the *promise*, with references to the *stars* or the *sand*, see, e.g., Gen 15.5; 22.17; Ex 32.13; Jer 33.22. **15:** *No ruler*, when read in the context of Dan 3, may refer to Nebuchadnezzar's blinding and exiling the Judean king (2 Kings 24.15); the lament is more generally expressed in Lam 2.9; Hos 3.4. No *prophet* is exaggerated for the Babylonian context, but it fits the early postexilic period (see Zech 13.3–6) and the time of Antiochus IV. *No burnt offering*, cessation of proper sacrifices occurred both when Nebuchadnezzar destroyed the Temple and when Antiochus IV profaned it. **16:** Contrition and humility substitute for sacrifice (1 Sam 15.22; Pss 51.16–17; 141.2; Hos 6.6); the context of the prayer, the impending martyrdom of the

no place to make an offering before you
and to find mercy.
¹⁶ Yet with a contrite heart and a humble
spirit may we be accepted,
¹⁷ as though it were with burnt offerings
of rams and bulls,
or with tens of thousands of fat lambs;
such may our sacrifice be in your sight
today,
and may we unreservedly follow you,ᵃ
for no shame will come to those who
trust in you.
¹⁸ And now with all our heart we follow you;
we fear you and seek your presence.
¹⁹ Do not put us to shame,
but deal with us in your patience
and in your abundant mercy.
²⁰ Deliver us in accordance with your
marvelous works,
and bring glory to your name, O Lord.
²¹ Let all who do harm to your servants be
put to shame;
let them be disgraced and deprived of
all power,
and let their strength be broken.
²² Let them know that you alone are the
Lord God,
glorious over the whole world."

²³ Now the king's servants who threw them
in kept stoking the furnace with naphtha,
pitch, tow, and brushwood. ²⁴ And the flames
poured out above the furnace forty-nine
cubits, ²⁵ and spread out and burned those
Chaldeans who were caught near the furnace.
²⁶ But the angel of the Lord came down

into the furnace to be with Azariah and his
companions, and drove the fiery flame out of
the furnace, ²⁷ and made the inside of the furnace as though a moist wind were whistling
through it. The fire did not touch them at all
and caused them no pain or distress.
²⁸ Then the three with one voice praised
and glorified and blessed God in the furnace:
²⁹ "Blessed are you, O Lord, God of our
ancestors,
and to be praised and highly exalted
forever;
³⁰ And blessed is your glorious, holy name,
and to be highly praised and highly
exalted forever.
³¹ Blessed are you in the temple of your
holy glory,
and to be extolled and highly glorified
forever.
³² Blessed are you who look into the depths
from your throne on the cherubim,
and to be praised and highly exalted
forever.
³³ Blessed are you on the throne of your
kingdom,
and to be extolled and highly exalted
forever.
³⁴ Blessed are you in the firmament of
heaven,
and to be sung and glorified forever.

³⁵ "Bless the Lord, all you works of the Lord;
sing praise to him and highly exalt him
forever.

ᵃ Meaning of Gk uncertain

three, makes the point acute. **21:** *Put to shame*, in the context of the book of Daniel, anticipates Nebuchadnezzar's madness in Dan 4. See also Sir 36.9 on the hope for the enemy's demise.

23–27: Protection in the furnace. The plot follows Dan 3.22. **23:** *Naphthah* is a type of petroleum (see
2 Macc 1.20–22,30–36). **24:** *Forty-nine cubits* is 71 ft (22 m); the multiple of seven suggests Dan 3.19, in which
Nebuchadnezzar orders the furnace heated to seven times its usual temperature **25:** *Burned those Chaldeans* is
noted in Dan 3:22; the king's agents die from the flames. **26:** The protecting *angel* is an increasingly common
figure in Second Temple literature (Tobit; Sus 44–45 in the Old Greek version; *1 Enoch*); this verse makes the
angelic presence, implicit in the reference to a "fourth man" who appeared like a "son of the gods" in Dan 3.25,
explicit. **27:** The verse is evoked in 3 Macc 6.6. *Moist* wind is dew; cf. Isa 26.19; Hos 14.5; Mic 5.7; etc., where dew
indicates God's salvation.

28–34: Song of thanksgiving. 29: The song begins with direct address to God. Verses 29–30 resemble Tob
8.5. **31:** *Temple* may refer to the heavenly, not the Jerusalem, sanctuary, as in Ps 11.4; Hab 2.20. **32:** *Cherubim* are
winged creatures who serve as the divine throne (Ex 25.18–20; 2 Sam 6.2; 22:11; Ps 18:10).

30–68: The litany of praise. 30: *Glorious, holy name*, Pss 29.2; 66.2; 79.9; etc. **31:** *Temple of your . . . glory* may
indicate a heavenly temple, or the earthly one in a restored, purified state. **35:** The song shifts to exhortations

36 Bless the Lord, you heavens;
    sing praise to him and highly exalt him
        forever.
37 Bless the Lord, you angels of the Lord;
    sing praise to him and highly exalt him
        forever.
38 Bless the Lord, all you waters above the
        heavens;
    sing praise to him and highly exalt him
        forever.
39 Bless the Lord, all you powers of the Lord;
    sing praise to him and highly exalt him
        forever.
40 Bless the Lord, sun and moon;
    sing praise to him and highly exalt him
        forever.
41 Bless the Lord, stars of heaven;
    sing praise to him and highly exalt him
        forever.

42 "Bless the Lord, all rain and dew;
    sing praise to him and highly exalt him
        forever.
43 Bless the Lord, all you winds;
    sing praise to him and highly exalt him
        forever.
44 Bless the Lord, fire and heat;
    sing praise to him and highly exalt him
        forever.
45 Bless the Lord, winter cold and summer
        heat;
    sing praise to him and highly exalt him
        forever.
46 Bless the Lord, dews and falling snow;
    sing praise to him and highly exalt him
        forever.
47 Bless the Lord, nights and days;
    sing praise to him and highly exalt him
        forever.
48 Bless the Lord, light and darkness;
    sing praise to him and highly exalt him
        forever.
49 Bless the Lord, ice and cold;
    sing praise to him and highly exalt him
        forever.
50 Bless the Lord, frosts and snows;
    sing praise to him and highly exalt him
        forever.

51 Bless the Lord, lightnings and clouds;
    sing praise to him and highly exalt him
        forever.

52 "Let the earth bless the Lord;
    let it sing praise to him and highly exalt
        him forever.
53 Bless the Lord, mountains and hills;
    sing praise to him and highly exalt him
        forever.
54 Bless the Lord, all that grows in the
        ground;
    sing praise to him and highly exalt him
        forever.
55 Bless the Lord, seas and rivers;
    sing praise to him and highly exalt him
        forever.
56 Bless the Lord, you springs;
    sing praise to him and highly exalt him
        forever.
57 Bless the Lord, you whales and all that
        swim in the waters;
    sing praise to him and highly exalt him
        forever.
58 Bless the Lord, all birds of the air;
    sing praise to him and highly exalt him
        forever.
59 Bless the Lord, all wild animals and
        cattle;
    sing praise to him and highly exalt him
        forever.

60 "Bless the Lord, all people on earth;
    sing praise to him and highly exalt him
        forever.
61 Bless the Lord, O Israel;
    sing praise to him and highly exalt him
        forever.
62 Bless the Lord, you priests of the Lord;
    sing praise to him and highly exalt him
        forever.
63 Bless the Lord, you servants of the Lord;
    sing praise to him and highly exalt him
        forever.
64 Bless the Lord, spirits and souls of the
        righteous;
    sing praise to him and highly exalt him
        forever.

to creation and thereby recalls the refrains of Pss 136 and 148. **38**: *Waters above*, see Gen 1.7; Ps 148.4. **39**: *Powers* suggests the heavenly host (see Ps 148.2–3). **57**: *Whales*, or sea monsters, suggest Leviathan (Isa 27.1; Ps 104.26; Job 41). **62**: *Priests* implies a Temple setting, but the song does not restrict its recitation to the Temple.

⁶⁵ Bless the Lord, you who are holy and
    humble in heart;
sing praise to him and highly exalt him
    forever.

⁶⁶ "Bless the Lord, Hananiah, Azariah, and
    Mishael;
sing praise to him and highly exalt him
    forever.
For he has rescued us from Hades and
    saved us from the power[a] of death,
and delivered us from the midst of the
    burning fiery furnace;

from the midst of the fire he has
    delivered us.
⁶⁷ Give thanks to the Lord, for he is good,
    for his mercy endures forever.
⁶⁸ All who worship the Lord, bless the God
    of gods,
sing praise to him and give thanks to
    him,
    for his mercy endures forever."

a   Gk *hand*

63: *Servants* could also refer to priests or other Temple functionaries, but the term is not limited to them. 66: The friends are identified by their Hebrew names, as in Dan 1.6; 1 Macc 2.59. *Hananiah* means "the Lᴏʀᴅ is gracious"; *Azariah* is "the Lᴏʀᴅ has helped" (in the book of Tobit, the disguised angel Raphael assumes this name); and *Mishael* is "who is like God?" *Hades*, the abode of the dead. Their song strikes the same chord as numerous biblical comments on rescue from Sheol, e.g., 1 Sam 2.6; Pss 16.10; 30.3; 49.15; 86.13; Prov 23.14; Jon 2.2. 67: *Give thanks . . . for his mercy endures forever*, see Ps 136; Sir 51; 1 Macc 4.24.

SUSANNA

NAME AND LOCATION

This addition to the book of Daniel is named for its heroine. Often called the first detective story, it appears in two different forms and locations in the early textual traditions. The Septuagint (and the Vulgate) locate it after Daniel 13; Theodotion, the version followed in this as well as most modern translations, locates the story at the beginning of the book of Daniel, since Sus 45 describes Daniel as a "young man." Perhaps composed as early as the Persian period (539–333 BCE), Susanna's tale was added to the cycle of tales about Daniel, probably ca. 100 BCE. The story may originally not have been about Daniel; the identification of the rescuing lad as Daniel would then be a secondary attribute of the story, added when the tale was attached to the other materials concerning Daniel, just as the Prayer of Azariah and the Song of the Three Jews may not have had an original connection to Dan 3. Susanna's setting in peaceful Babylon, in which the enemies are not wicked pagan kings but corrupt Jewish judges, contrasts with the threats emphasized in Dan 1–6.

CONTENT AND CANONICAL STATUS

Like Greek Esther, Judith, and Sarah of the book of Tobit, Susanna is beautiful and chaste, and, as in those books, prayer and piety are major motifs. Indeed, with the exception of the villainous elders, all the characters—including the narrator—mention God. First cited as having canonical status by the church father Irenaeus of Lyons in the late second century CE, Roman Catholic and Orthodox churches consider it canonical, while Protestants include it in the Apocrypha. Although the addition is not considered scriptural in Judaism, Susanna's story was also adapted by Samaritan and medieval Jewish writers.

Amy-Jill Levine

¹There was a man living in Babylon whose name was Joakim. ²He married the daughter of Hilkiah, named Susanna, a very beautiful woman and one who feared the Lord. ³Her parents were righteous, and had trained their daughter according to the law of Moses. ⁴Joakim was very rich, and had a fine garden adjoining his house; the Jews used to come to him because he was the most honored of them all.
⁵That year two elders from the people were appointed as judges. Concerning them the Lord had said: "Wickedness came forth from Babylon, from elders who were judges, who were supposed to govern the people." ⁶These men were frequently at Joakim's house, and all who had a case to be tried came to them there.
⁷When the people left at noon, Susanna would go into her husband's garden to walk. ⁸Every day the two elders used to see her, going in and walking about, and they began to lust for her. ⁹They suppressed their

1–4: Introduction. 1: Set in *Babylon*, the story is typically dated during the Babylonian exile (587–538 BCE) because of its connection to Daniel; however, an exact date is never specified. *Joakim* does not appear to be connected with others of the same name (2 Kings 24.15; Neh 12.10,12,26; Jdt 4.6; 15.8). 2: *Susanna*, the name, which means "lily," appears in Lk 8.3, but not elsewhere in the Jewish or Christian canons. It is attested in late Babylonian sources. *Hilkiah* was a common name in priestly circles (2 Kings 22.4; Neh 12.7; Jer 1.1) and so perhaps suggests that Susanna's father was a priest. Beauty and piety are typically associated with heroines in the Deuterocanonical literature (Jdt 8.7–8; Tob 6.12; Est 2.7,20 [LXX]). 4: The prosperity of some Jews in Babylon is attested by archaeological findings (see also Jer 29.5–7; 2 Esd 3.1b–2). *Joakim's* honor appears based on wealth. *Garden* (Gk "Paradeisos") recalls Eden (Gen 2–3).
5–14: The elders' plot. 5: The *year* is not identified. *Elders*, community leaders (Ruth 4.2–12; Ezek 8.1; 14.1; 20.1; Jer 29.1). The phrase *wickedness* (Gk "anomia," lit. "lawlessness") *came forth* is unattested in existing prophetic books, but see Jer 23.14–15; the church fathers Origin and Jerome associate the reference with Jer 29.20–23. The occasional suggestion that the Jewish community denied this story canonical status because it

consciences and turned away their eyes from looking to Heaven or remembering their duty to administer justice. [10] Both were overwhelmed with passion for her, but they did not tell each other of their distress, [11] for they were ashamed to disclose their lustful desire to seduce her. [12] Day after day they watched eagerly to see her.

[13] One day they said to each other, "Let us go home, for it is time for lunch." So they both left and parted from each other. [14] But turning back, they met again; and when each pressed the other for the reason, they confessed their lust. Then together they arranged for a time when they could find her alone.

[15] Once, while they were watching for an opportune day, she went in as before with only two maids, and wished to bathe in the garden, for it was a hot day. [16] No one was there except the two elders, who had hidden themselves and were watching her. [17] She said to her maids, "Bring me olive oil and ointments, and shut the garden doors so that I can bathe." [18] They did as she told them: they shut the doors of the garden and went out by the side doors to bring what they had been commanded; they did not see the elders, because they were hiding.

[19] When the maids had gone out, the two elders got up and ran to her. [20] They said, "Look, the garden doors are shut, and no one can see us. We are burning with desire for you; so give your consent, and lie with us. [21] If you refuse, we will testify against you that a young man was with you, and this was why you sent your maids away."

[22] Susanna groaned and said, "I am completely trapped. For if I do this, it will mean death for me; if I do not, I cannot escape your hands. [23] I choose not to do it; I will fall into your hands, rather than sin in the sight of the Lord."

[24] Then Susanna cried out with a loud voice, and the two elders shouted against her. [25] And one of them ran and opened the garden doors. [26] When the people in the house heard the shouting in the garden, they rushed in at the side door to see what had happened to her. [27] And when the elders told their story, the servants felt very much ashamed, for nothing like this had ever been said about Susanna.

[28] The next day, when the people gathered at the house of her husband Joakim, the two elders came, full of their wicked plot to have Susanna put to death. In the presence of the people they said, [29] "Send for Susanna daughter of Hilkiah, the wife of Joakim." [30] So they sent for her. And she came with her parents, her children, and all her relatives.

[31] Now Susanna was a woman of great refinement and beautiful in appearance. [32] As

criticized the elders is belied by the remarkable amount of self-critique the biblical text generates. **8:** *Lust*, in violation of Ex 20.17. **9:** *Turned away their eyes*, although they had no hesitance in looking at Susanna. *Heaven* is a circumlocution for God. **14:** *Pressed the other*, as if in cross-examination: their true testimony here will contrast with their false testimony regarding Susanna.

15–21: The attempted rape. 15: Contrary to most artistic depictions, Susanna never actually bathes. *In the garden*, the scene recollects depictions both of luxuriant beauty and physical love in the Song of Solomon, and of the garden of Eden (Gen 2–3) as a site of temptation. *Bathe* suggests both Bathsheba (2 Sam 11.2) and observations in Jewish-Hellenistic literature (*Jubilees* 22; *Testament of Reuben* 3) that Reuben sinned with his father's wife Bilhah after seeing her bathe; cf. Gen 35.22; 49.4. *Maids* frequently accompany heroines in the Deuterocanonical texts (Jdt, Tob, Add Esth). **17:** *Oil and ointments*, compare 2 Sam 12.20; Ruth 3.3; Jdt 10.3. *Shut the garden doors* attests to Susanna's modesty. **20:** *Give your consent*, Susanna's choice is adultery or death.

22–27: Susanna's response. 22: *Death*, because adultery was a capital crime (Lev 20.10; Deut 22.21–24; see also Jn 8.4–5). Susanna knows the "law of Moses" (v. 3). **23:** *Sin in the sight of the Lord* is the same concern voiced by Joseph in similar circumstances (Gen 39.9). **24:** Deut 22.24 legislates that a woman, facing rape, is to *cry out with a loud voice*; Susanna shows knowledge of and fidelity to the law. On crying out at times of oppression, see also Gen 21.16; Ex 2.23; 14.10; Deut 26.7; 1 Sam 4.13; 3 Macc 5.51; and elsewhere. **27:** That servants would be ashamed indicates the dishonor to the household. Although the elders (v. 11) and servants feel shame, Susanna is never described in this manner, despite being placed in a situation of public humiliation (vv. 31–32). *Nothing like this*, although she had an unblemished reputation, Susanna is presumed guilty.

28–41: Accusation. 30: Susanna is accompanied by all her family except Joakim. The Septuagint (LXX) notes

she was veiled, the scoundrels ordered her to be unveiled, so that they might feast their eyes on her beauty. ³³ Those who were with her and all who saw her were weeping.

³⁴ Then the two elders stood up before the people and laid their hands on her head. ³⁵ Through her tears she looked up toward Heaven, for her heart trusted in the Lord. ³⁶ The elders said, "While we were walking in the garden alone, this woman came in with two maids, shut the garden doors, and dismissed the maids. ³⁷ Then a young man, who was hiding there, came to her and lay with her. ³⁸ We were in a corner of the garden, and when we saw this wickedness we ran to them. ³⁹ Although we saw them embracing, we could not hold the man, because he was stronger than we, and he opened the doors and got away. ⁴⁰ We did, however, seize this woman and asked who the young man was, ⁴¹ but she would not tell us. These things we testify."

Because they were elders of the people and judges, the assembly believed them and condemned her to death.

⁴² Then Susanna cried out with a loud voice, and said, "O eternal God, you know what is secret and are aware of all things before they come to be; ⁴³ you know that

these men have given false evidence against me. And now I am to die, though I have done none of the wicked things that they have charged against me!"

⁴⁴ The Lord heard her cry. ⁴⁵ Just as she was being led off to execution, God stirred up the holy spirit of a young lad named Daniel, ⁴⁶ and he shouted with a loud voice, "I want no part in shedding this woman's blood!"

⁴⁷ All the people turned to him and asked, "What is this you are saying?" ⁴⁸ Taking his stand among them he said, "Are you such fools, O Israelites, as to condemn a daughter of Israel without examination and without learning the facts? ⁴⁹ Return to court, for these men have given false evidence against her."

⁵⁰ So all the people hurried back. And the rest of theᵃ elders said to him, "Come, sit among us and inform us, for God has given you the standing of an elder." ⁵¹ Daniel said to them, "Separate them far from each other, and I will examine them."

⁵² When they were separated from each other, he summoned one of them and said to him, "You old relic of wicked days, your sins have now come home, which you have

ᵃ Gk lacks *rest of the*

that Susanna had four children. **31:** *Refinement* and beauty are attributes of (Gk) Esther. **32:** *Veiled* emphasizes her modesty; although the trial occurs in her home, the proceedings are public. The LXX describes Susanna as being uncovered (see Hos 2.3–10; Ezek 16.37–39). **34:** *Laid their hands* indicates that the elders serve as witnesses (Lev 24.14; see Lev 8.14,18,22; Ex 29.10,15,19 for sacrificial imagery, and Lev 16.21–22 for the scapegoat ritual). The elders planned to lay their hands upon Susanna in order to rape her; now their gesture seeks to condemn her. Two witnesses are required (Num 35.30; Deut 17.6; 19.15). **41:** *Condemned her* without cross-examination (Deut 19.15–21) or Susanna's own testimony; the "trial" is illegal according to both biblical and later rabbinic regulations.

42–43: Susanna's prayer. Like (Gk) Esther (14.3–19), Judith (9.2–14), and Sarah (Tob 2.10–15), as well as Azariah of the Additions to Daniel, Susanna offers personal prayer in a time of distress. **42:** *Loud voice*, see v. 24. *Know what is secret* is a divine attribute stressed in Dan 2.22. **43:** *Given false evidence*, Susanna's prayer locates God as the (true) judge and jury even as it again shows her knowledge of the law (Deut 19.15–21). *Now I am to die* leaves Susanna's request for justice implicit.

44–47: Daniel responds. 44: God responds to Susanna's prayer, not to the events that prompted it. **45:** *Young lad* contrasts Daniel with the "elders"; the term indicates a youth of marriageable age (Tob 5.17) and subtly recalls the "young man" the elders claimed was with Susanna (37–39). *Holy spirit* is associated with both prophetic abilities and the possession of wisdom. The miraculous element in Susanna is not the work of an angel or a revelation of an undescribed dream, but the miracle of the inspired intellect. **46:** *I want no part*, since the community is responsible for justice (Deut 22.20–21; Mt 27.24; Acts 24.26).

48–63: Susanna's acquittal. 48: *Examination*, or cross-examination, is required by Deut 19.15–20. *Daughter of Israel*, see also v. 57, which describes Susanna as a *daughter of Judah*. **50:** Daniel's status appears miraculously granted. His youth contrasts with his *standing as an elder*. **50:** *Rest of the elders* indicates that not all the leaders

committed in the past, [53] pronouncing unjust judgments, condemning the innocent and acquitting the guilty, though the Lord said, 'You shall not put an innocent and righteous person to death.' [54] Now then, if you really saw this woman, tell me this: Under what tree did you see them being intimate with each other?" He answered, "Under a mastic tree."[a] [55] And Daniel said, "Very well! This lie has cost you your head, for the angel of God has received the sentence from God and will immediately cut[a] you in two."

[56] Then, putting him to one side, he ordered them to bring the other. And he said to him, "You offspring of Canaan and not of Judah, beauty has beguiled you and lust has perverted your heart. [57] This is how you have been treating the daughters of Israel, and they were intimate with you through fear; but a daughter of Judah would not tolerate your wickedness. [58] Now then, tell me: Under what tree did you catch them being intimate with each other?" He answered, "Under an evergreen oak."[b] [59] Daniel said to him, "Very

well! This lie has cost you also your head, for the angel of God is waiting with his sword to split[b] you in two, so as to destroy you both."

[60] Then the whole assembly raised a great shout and blessed God, who saves those who hope in him. [61] And they took action against the two elders, because out of their own mouths Daniel had convicted them of bearing false witness; they did to them as they had wickedly planned to do to their neighbor. [62] Acting in accordance with the law of Moses, they put them to death. Thus innocent blood was spared that day.

[63] Hilkiah and his wife praised God for their daughter Susanna, and so did her husband Joakim and all her relatives, because she was found innocent of a shameful deed. [64] And from that day onward Daniel had a great reputation among the people.

a   The Greek words for *mastic tree* and *cut* are similar, thus forming an ironic wordplay

b   The Greek words for *evergreen oak* and *split* are similar, thus forming an ironic wordplay

are wicked. **53:** *Pronouncing unjust judgments,* Daniel accuses the first elder of a pattern of injustice. The citation evokes Ex 23:7. **54–55:** *Mastic* (Gk "schinon") . . . *cut* (Gk "schisei"): "clove . . . cleave" provides an English approximation of the Greek pun. **55:** *Angels* become increasingly common in Jewish Hellenistic literature (including Daniel; also Isa 37.36; Ezek 9). Here they serve as agents of punishment rather than of revelation. **56–57:** The comment compares three nations. *Offspring of Canaan* suggests the sexual crimes attributed to the earlier inhabitants of the promised land (Lev 18.24–28); *daughters of Israel* refers to the Northern Kingdom, destroyed by Assyria in 722 BCE (2 Kings 17); *daughter of Judah,* Susanna is from the Southern Kingdom, whose exile in 586 BCE created the Babylonian Jewish community. **58–59:** *Evergreen oak* (Gk "prinon") . . . *split* (Gk "kataprisei"): "yew" and "hew" provides an English approximation of the Greek pun. **59:** *Sword* recalls Gen 3.24, as Susanna's garden suggests Eden (Gen 2–3). **62:** *Law of Moses* is Deut 19.15–21.

64: Epilogue. If Susanna is placed at the opening of the book of Daniel, Daniel's *great reputation* is seen to increase in the subsequent stories.

BEL AND THE DRAGON

LOCATION AND NAME

These stories appear as ch 14 of the Greek version of the book of Daniel. In the Septuagint, as opposed to Theo-dotion's version, which is printed here, Daniel is identified as a priest and thus as a positive foil to the deceptive priests of the false gods. The title of the stories in the Septuagint is "From the prophecy of Habakkuk, the son of Joshua [Gk Jesus], of the tribe of Levi."

DATE, CONTENTS, AND INTERPRETATION

Perhaps composed as early as the Persian period (539–333 BCE), these two idol parodies (compare Isa 44) display the foolishness of pagan worship, divine protection of faithful Jews, and the cleverness of the court favorite, Daniel. In the first story, concerning Bel, Daniel demonstrates that the idol is not a god by proving that it does not eat the food set out for it each night; the second story reverses this scenario as Daniel proves that the drag-on is not divine by feeding it a noxious concoction that kills it. This second story recapitulates the account of Daniel in the lion's den (Dan 6.16–24) and adds to it Daniel's own miraculous feeding by the prophet Habakkuk. Food references culminate at the end, when Daniel's enemies are eaten by the lions into whose den Daniel had been thrown. Perhaps this second story is based on Jer 51.34,44, which is also set in Babylon, the filling of a belly with delicacies, and the punishment of Bel by having him "disgorge what he has swallowed."

Amy-Jill Levine

¹ When King Astyages was laid to rest with his ancestors, Cyrus the Persian succeeded to his kingdom. ² Daniel was a companion of the king, and was the most honored of all his Friends.

³ Now the Babylonians had an idol called Bel, and every day they provided for it twelve bushels of choice flour and forty sheep and six measures^a of wine. ⁴ The king revered it and went every day to worship it. But Daniel worshiped his own God.

So the king said to him, "Why do you not worship Bel?" ⁵ He answered, "Because I do not revere idols made with hands, but the liv-ing God, who created heaven and earth and has dominion over all living creatures."

⁶ The king said to him, "Do you not think that Bel is a living god? Do you not see how much he eats and drinks every day?" ⁷ And Daniel laughed, and said, "Do not be deceived, O king, for this thing is only clay inside and bronze outside, and it never ate or drank anything."

⁸ Then the king was angry and called the priests of Bel^b and said to them, "If you do not tell me who is eating these provisions, you shall die. ⁹ But if you prove that Bel is eating them, Daniel shall die, because he has spoken blasphemy against Bel." Daniel said to the king, "Let it be done as you have said."

a   A little more than fifty gallons
b   Gk *his priests*

1–2: Daniel in the Persian court. 1: *Astyages*, last king of Media (585–550 BCE), was defeated by his grandson, *Cyrus the Persian* (Dan 6.28). **2:** *Companion of the king*, perhaps an official position (1 Macc 2.18), suggests a confidant. *Most honored*, see Dan 2.48.

3–7: The worship of Bel. 3: *Bel*, an epithet of Marduk, the god who headed the Babylonian pantheon (Jer 50.2). Ancient Babylonian sources confirm Bel's extensive diet. **4:** *The king revered it*, although ancient sources indicate that in actual practice, the "leftovers" were sent to the king, and their consumption was considered to provide blessings. The king's support for the priests who were consuming the food is therefore ironic. **4:** The question indicates the story's original independence from the book of Daniel, although in Dan 1–6 kings continually require reeducation about Daniel's faith and practices. **5:** Daniel boldly confesses his own faith and criticizes that of the king. **7:** *Laughed* (also in v. 19) indicates Daniel's familiarity with the king as well as his dis-dain for the worship of the idol; Bel is also ridiculed in Isa 46.1–2.

[10] Now there were seventy priests of Bel, besides their wives and children. So the king went with Daniel into the temple of Bel. [11] The priests of Bel said, "See, we are now going outside; you yourself, O king, set out the food and prepare the wine, and shut the door and seal it with your signet. [12] When you return in the morning, if you do not find that Bel has eaten it all, we will die; otherwise Daniel will, who is telling lies about us." [13] They were unconcerned, for beneath the table they had made a hidden entrance, through which they used to go in regularly and consume the provisions. [14] After they had gone out, the king set out the food for Bel. Then Daniel ordered his servants to bring ashes, and they scattered them throughout the whole temple in the presence of the king alone. Then they went out, shut the door and sealed it with the king's signet, and departed. [15] During the night the priests came as usual, with their wives and children, and they ate and drank everything.

[16] Early in the morning the king rose and came, and Daniel with him. [17] The king said, "Are the seals unbroken, Daniel?" He answered, "They are unbroken, O king." [18] As soon as the doors were opened, the king looked at the table, and shouted in a loud voice, "You are great, O Bel, and in you there is no deceit at all!"

[19] But Daniel laughed and restrained the king from going in. "Look at the floor," he said, "and notice whose footprints these are." [20] The king said, "I see the footprints of men and women and children."

[21] Then the king was enraged, and he arrested the priests and their wives and children. They showed him the secret doors through which they used to enter to consume what was on the table. [22] Therefore the king put them to death, and gave Bel over to Daniel, who destroyed it and its temple.

[23] Now in that place[a] there was a great dragon, which the Babylonians revered. [24] The king said to Daniel, "You cannot deny that this is a living god; so worship him." [25] Daniel said, "I worship the Lord my God, for he is the living God. [26] But give me permission, O king, and I will kill the dragon without sword or club." The king said, "I give you permission." [27] Then Daniel took pitch, fat, and hair, and boiled them together and made cakes, which he fed to the dragon. The dragon ate them, and burst open. Then Daniel said, "See what you have been worshiping!"

[28] When the Babylonians heard about it, they were very indignant and conspired against the king, saying, "The king has become a Jew; he has destroyed Bel, and killed the dragon, and slaughtered the priests." [29] Going to the king, they said, "Hand Daniel

---

8–22: Bel's trial. 8: The abruptness of *You shall die* (Dan 2.5; 3.6; 6.7) is conventional in folktales. 10: *Wives and children* contrasts Daniel's single status. 11: *Prepare the wine* by mixing it with water (2 Macc 15.39) or spices (Isa 5.22; Song 8.2). 14: *Ordered his servants*, unlike Dan chs 1–6, where Daniel relies on divine revelation and aid, here as well as in Susanna, he succeeds by his wits. The scene establishes what becomes a detective story convention, the "mystery of the locked room." 22: *Put them to death* echoes the punishment of the wicked elders (Sus 62; see Dan 2.12; 6.24); the corruption of the priests condemns also their wives and children. Bel's idol and *temple* were, according to the Greek historian Herodotus and other ancient sources, destroyed by the Persian king Xerxes in 479 BCE; Xerxes melted the temple's 20 ft (6 m) high statue of Bel into 800 lb (363 kg) of gold bullion. Daniel's action responds to Babylon's destruction of the Jerusalem Temple.

23–27: The destruction of the dragon. 23: *Great dragon*, dragons or snakes could symbolize the divine in ancient Near Eastern and Mediterranean cultures (see Num 2.8–9; 2 Kings 18.4), but there is no independent evidence of Babylonian snake worship. 24: *Living god* contrasts with the idol Bel, for the snake is clearly alive. 25: Daniel resists apostasy, a special concern for Jews in the Diaspora and during the persecution of Antiochus IV Epiphanes. 27: *Pitch, fat, and hair* would not necessarily be a noxious concoction; later versions of the story add details to increase the toxicity of the mixture. The snake eats and dies, unlike Bel who is proven false because he cannot eat; within the cycle of stories about Daniel, this detail offers subtle comparisons. Daniel and his friends prosper by restricting their diet (Dan 1); Belshazzar falls because of his blasphemous feasting (Dan 5).

28–42: Daniel in the lion pit. 28: *Become a Jew* anticipates v. 41, where the king affirms Daniel's God; he does not, however, convert. 29: The death threat repeats the punishment of Bel's priests and their families, but here

over to us, or else we will kill you and your household." ³⁰ The king saw that they were pressing him hard, and under compulsion he handed Daniel over to them.

³¹ They threw Daniel into the lions' den, and he was there for six days. ³² There were seven lions in the den, and every day they had been given two human bodies and two sheep; but now they were given nothing, so that they would devour Daniel.

³³ Now the prophet Habakkuk was in Judea; he had made a stew and had broken bread into a bowl, and was going into the field to take it to the reapers. ³⁴ But the angel of the Lord said to Habakkuk, "Take the food that you have to Babylon, to Daniel, in the lions' den." ³⁵ Habakkuk said, "Sir, I have never seen Babylon, and I know nothing about the den." ³⁶ Then the angel of the Lord took him by the crown of his head and carried him by his hair; with the speed of the wind[a] he set him down in Babylon, right over the den.

³⁷ Then Habakkuk shouted, "Daniel, Daniel! Take the food that God has sent you." ³⁸ Daniel said, "You have remembered me, O God, and have not forsaken those who love you." ³⁹ So Daniel got up and ate. And the angel of God immediately returned Habakkuk to his own place.

⁴⁰ On the seventh day the king came to mourn for Daniel. When he came to the den he looked in, and there sat Daniel! ⁴¹ The king shouted with a loud voice, "You are great, O Lord, the God of Daniel, and there is no other besides you!" ⁴² Then he pulled Daniel[b] out, and threw into the den those who had attempted his destruction, and they were instantly eaten before his eyes.

---

[a] Or *by the power of his spirit*

[b] Gk *him*

---

the king is threatened by his own people. **30**: The king's reluctance resembles that of Darius (Dan 6). **31**: *Lions' den*, see Dan 6.16–24, where Daniel spends one night, not six. Daniel destroyed Babylon's animal god; now the Babylonians anticipate that animals will destroy him. **32**: The description continues the author's interest in dietary matters, but it is only in this case that concerns for eating will be connected to the miraculous. **33**: *Habakkuk* prophesied ca. 612–597 BCE, well before the events recounted here. **34**: Angels appear in the book of Daniel as protectors (Dan 6.22) as well as apocalyptic revealers and interpreters (Dan 7–12). Along with the unlikely summoning of Habakkuk and his reluctance concerning this unexpected assignment, *the food* is part of the tale's humor: the lions, not Daniel, have the greater problem with hunger. **36**: *By his hair*, see Ezek 8.3. **41**: *You are great* replaces the king's praise of Bel in 18. **42**: References to food reach their conclusion as Daniel's accusers are consumed.

1 MACCABEES

NAME

The name "1 Maccabees" derives from the church fathers Hippolytus (ca. 170–236 CE), Origen (ca. 185–254 CE), and Jerome (ca. 342–420 CE), who notes that he found the first book of the Maccabees in Hebrew. The name "Maccabee," a nickname ("Hammer") given to Judas (1 Macc 3.4), was extended in Christian (but not Jewish) tradition to include his family. Origen said the book was titled *sarbethsabanaiel*, a Greek transliteration possibly suggesting an original Hebrew "The Book of the House of the Princes of Israel."

CANONICAL STATUS AND LOCATION

Jerome distinguished between Hebrew and Greek Jewish books, describing the latter as *apocrypha*, "hidden things." Perhaps because Jerome knew of a Hebrew version of 1 Maccabees, it was included in the Vulgate, the Latin Bible of the Western church. It is also one of the canonical scriptures of the Eastern Orthodox churches. The sixteenth-century Protestant reformers, unsympathetic toward non-Hebrew Jewish writings, placed it firmly among the Apocrypha, to be read for instruction in godly manners but not in Christian doctrine. The Roman Catholic church reaffirmed the canonical status of 1 Maccabees at the Council of Trent (1545–63). The book is not canonical in Jewish tradition, although it is an important religious text describing the origin of the festival of Hanukkah, the rededication of the Temple in 164 BCE. In Roman Catholic and Eastern Orthodox Bibles, 1 Maccabees is placed among the historical books, after the books of Tobit, Judith, and Esther. In Protestant Bibles it is included among the Apocrypha, usually after the Additions to Daniel.

AUTHORSHIP AND DATE

The author's identity is unknown. He was apparently an educated Jew, well versed in the Hebrew scriptures and the Temple liturgy, and with sufficient leisure and resources for authorship. He wrote in Hebrew but was able to use, translate, and incorporate Greek and Latin documents from Seleucid, Roman, and Spartan archives. His interests were political and historical rather than priestly; he firmly supported the Maccabean cause but was sufficiently scholarly and objective to avoid demonizing the Seleucid opposition (contrast 2 Maccabees).

The book covers Jewish history from the time of Alexander the Great to the high priesthood of John Hyrcanus (134–104 CE) and is thus usually dated to the later years of Hyrcanus's rule or soon after; the statements of 1 Macc 16.23–24, that his achievements were recorded in the chronicles of his high priesthood, and of 1 Macc 13.30, that the Maccabean family tomb built by Simon "remains to this day," suggest some passing of time. The book's positive attitude toward Rome makes it likely that it was written before the Roman general Pompey captured Jerusalem in 63 BCE.

LITERARY HISTORY

Sometime about the turn of the era, 1 Maccabees appeared in Greek translation; the late first-century BCE Jewish historian Josephus used this as a major source for his *Antiquities* (*Ant.* 12.242–13.212). Josephus perhaps found a copy in Jerusalem before the destruction of Jerusalem in 70 CE, or later in a Roman library. The fourth- and fifth-century manuscripts of Codex Sinaiticus and Codex Alexandrinus, and the eighth-century Codex Venetus preserve the Greek text; the presumed Hebrew original has been lost. The Old Latin translation, from the second or early third century CE, was later incorporated into the Vulgate tradition.

HISTORICAL CONTEXT

Judea had known a long period of relative peace and prosperity, first under Alexander the Great (332–323 BCE), then under the Ptolemies, the successors to Alexander's rule in Egypt. As a result of Alexander's rule, Hellenism (a mixture of Greek and Semitic cultures) had dominated all the countries of the eastern Mediterranean basin. By the second century BCE, however, when Judea came under the control of the Seleucids, the successors to Alexander's rule in Mesopotamia and Syria, Jews were divided over how to relate to Gentile culture. The upper classes in Jerusalem, the Hellenizers, had long adopted Greek ways, while the poorer people of the rural areas tended to cling to the customs of their ancestors. The book of 1 Maccabees consistently presents the Hellenizers as "renegades" or apostates (1 Macc 1.11–15), and their introduction of the Greek gymnasium and all that went with it (see 2 Macc 4.11–17) as the root of the following struggle.

In this situation of complex religious, economic, and political tensions, the actions of the Seleucid ruler Antiochus IV were a match in a tinderbox. In 169 BCE Antiochus IV invaded Egypt to reclaim Judea from Ptolemy IV Philometor. On Antiochus's return he pillaged the Jerusalem Temple (1 Macc 1.20–28) for purely financial reasons (he had at that point no political or religious quarrel with Judea). The following year, believing Judea to be in revolt (2 Macc 5.11), Antiochus attacked Jerusalem more viciously (1 Macc 1.29–40; cf. 2 Macc 5.11–14, Dan 11.29–31), and the subsequent attempt to suppress the Judeans by attacking the religious law (1 Macc 1.41–61), which apparently sustained the Jewish resistance, led to the war of independence and its horrors described in the following chapters of 1 Maccabees.

Into this crisis the author introduces the priestly family of Mattathias and his sons Judas, Jonathan, and Simon as the deliverers of Judea. Fearing that the policies of the Hellenizers would destroy Judaism, Judas Maccabeus and his men mounted a campaign of armed resistance against both enemies. Using a combination of guerrilla warfare and diplomacy, they succeeded in recovering and purifying the Temple after Antiochus had defiled it, fortifying Jerusalem and securing a measure of independence for Judea. By the end of the book three generations of Mattathias's family had fought for Judea's independence from the Seleucids and had established a ruling dynasty (called Hasmonean according to Josephus and other sources) that would remain in power until the Roman occupation in 63 BCE.

STRUCTURE AND CONTENTS

The book is clearly structured. Chapters 1 and 2 are introductory, giving the historical context and Mattathias's exhortation to his sons, and emphasizing the complementary roles of Simon and Judas (2.65–66). Chapters 3.1–9.22 describe the achievements of Judas, marked by an opening poetic eulogy of Judas (3.3–9) and a closure modeled on the regnal summaries in 1 and 2 Kings (9.22). Chapters 9.23–16.23 describe the activities of Jonathan, Simon, and Simon's son John, marked by the eulogy of Simon (14.4–15) and another regnal closure (16.23). Within this framework the author marshals his complex narrative. He presents the Maccabean relationships with the hostile Seleucids of Syria, the Ptolemies of Egypt, the cities of the Palestinian coast, and the tribes of Transjordan, and with two friendly Mediterranean powers, the Romans and the Spartans. The book condemns the "renegades" within Israel who would conform to the Greek way of life (1.11–15); Judas and Simon are presented as preserving the Jewish law and Temple against the enemies of their nation (14.29). The book ends with the firm establishment and solid achievements of the high priesthood of John Hyrcanus (16.23). For this author, it is through the Maccabean family alone that "deliverance was given to Israel" (5.62).

INTERPRETATION AND GUIDE TO READING

Historians value 1 Maccabees for its information on the second-century BCE Jewish-Hellenistic world. Jews and Christians alike have seen the Maccabees as champions against tyrants hostile to their faith aided by traitors within the fold. Some students of history, less sympathetic to the Jewish cause, have seen Antiochus as a cultivated Hellenistic monarch trying to unify his empire and control a disloyal subject on his borders. Others in modern times, less sympathetic to imperial causes, have interpreted the Maccabees as a rebel army struggling righteously on behalf of political minorities. Different circumstances make for different readings, as ever.

The reader will make sense of 1 Maccabees only by taking it as a coherent narrative from start to finish. Occasional dipping will yield only confusion. The author shapes his history clearly, quoting archival sources for information and adding short poems as theological commentary. Sympathetic reading will reveal, rewardingly, that the author was a man of scholarly ability, deep commitment to Israel, and trust in Israel's God.

John R. Bartlett

1 After Alexander son of Philip, the Macedonian, who came from the land of Kittim, had defeated[a] King Darius of the Persians and the Medes, he succeeded him as king. (He had previously become king of Greece.) ² He fought many battles, conquered strongholds, and put to death the kings of the earth. ³ He advanced to the ends of the earth, and plundered many nations. When the earth became quiet before him, he was exalted, and his heart was lifted up. ⁴ He gathered a very strong army and ruled over countries, nations, and princes, and they became tributary to him.

⁵ After this he fell sick and perceived that he was dying. ⁶ So he summoned his most honored officers, who had been brought up with him from youth, and divided his kingdom among them while he was still alive. ⁷ And after Alexander had reigned twelve years, he died.

⁸ Then his officers began to rule, each in his own place. ⁹ They all put on crowns after his death, and so did their descendants after them for many years; and they caused many evils on the earth.

¹⁰ From them came forth a sinful root, Antiochus Epiphanes, son of King Antiochus;

he had been a hostage in Rome. He began to reign in the one hundred thirty-seventh year of the kingdom of the Greeks.[b]

¹¹ In those days certain renegades came out from Israel and misled many, saying, "Let us go and make a covenant with the Gentiles around us, for since we separated from them many disasters have come upon us." ¹² This proposal pleased them, ¹³ and some of the people eagerly went to the king, who authorized them to observe the ordinances of the Gentiles. ¹⁴ So they built a gymnasium in Jerusalem, according to Gentile custom, ¹⁵ and removed the marks of circumcision, and abandoned the holy covenant. They joined with the Gentiles and sold themselves to do evil.

¹⁶ When Antiochus saw that his kingdom was established, he determined to become king of the land of Egypt, in order that he might reign over both kingdoms. ¹⁷ So he invaded Egypt with a strong force, with chariots and elephants and cavalry and with a large fleet. ¹⁸ He engaged King Ptolemy of

---

a Gk adds *and he defeated*

b 175 B.C.

1.1–10: Introduction. The author sketches the history of the Hellenistic world from Alexander the Great to Antiochus IV; cf. Dan 11.2–28. **1:** *Philip* II of Macedon (ruled 359–336 BCE) conquered the Greeks in 338 BCE; his son Alexander (336–323 BCE) marched from Greece (*the land of Kittim*) and defeated *Darius* III of Persia at Issus (333 BCE) and Gaugamela (331 BCE). Media (the land of *the Medes*) was south of the Caspian Sea. **2:** *Strongholds*, e.g., Tyre and Gaza. **3:** *To the ends of the earth*, i.e., present-day Afghanistan and India. *Exalted . . . his heart was lifted up* suggests deification as well as the biblical sin of pride (Isa 2.5–22; 2 Chr 26.16). **7:** Alexander *died* at Babylon, June 323 BCE. **8–9:** *Officers . . . descendants*, especially Seleucus I Nicator (305–281 BCE), who seized Babylonia and Syria, and Ptolemy I Soter (305–282 BCE), who took over Egypt and Palestine, and their successors in these regions. *Crowns* were white cloth rather than precious metal. **10:** *Antiochus* IV (175–164 BCE), son of *Antiochus* III "the Great" (223–187 BCE), used the title "Theos Epiphanes" ("god manifest") on some of his later coins, but probably took such implied divinity less seriously than his Jewish subjects. *Hostage in Rome*, after the Roman defeat of Antiochus III at Magnesia (190 BCE); he escaped, succeeding his brother Seleucus IV in 175 BCE. *One hundred thirty-seventh year of* the Seleucid era, which began in either 312 BCE or 311 BCE.

1.11–15: Conflicts over Hellenization. 11: The author sees the *renegades* as Jewish apostates; 2 Macc 4.7–17 identifies the usurping high priest Jason as their leader. They hoped for the economic and political advantages of belonging to the wider Hellenistic world, rejecting the separation from the Gentiles required by the Law (cf. Deut 7.1–6) and demanded by Nehemiah (Neh 13.1–3,23–27). **14:** *Gymnasium*, the essential place of education and recreation for citizens of a Hellenistic city. This development did not break the Law, but according to Greek custom, athletes competed in the nude (2 Macc 4.14). *Removing the marks of circumcision* by surgery (epispasm) to make participants resemble Greek athletes was elsewhere seen as showing "irreverence to the divine laws" (2 Macc 4.17).

1.16–19: Antiochus IV and Egypt. See Dan 11.25–27. In 170 BCE Egypt, under Ptolemy VI Philometor (180–145 BCE), claimed Palestine under the terms of an earlier marriage settlement; Antiochus *invaded Egypt*, defeated Ptolemy (v. 18) at Mons Casius, and captured the fortress of Pelusium.

Egypt in battle, and Ptolemy turned and fled before him, and many were wounded and fell. ¹⁹ They captured the fortified cities in the land of Egypt, and he plundered the land of Egypt.

²⁰ After subduing Egypt, Antiochus returned in the one hundred forty-third year.[a] He went up against Israel and came to Jerusalem with a strong force. ²¹ He arrogantly entered the sanctuary and took the golden altar, the lampstand for the light, and all its utensils. ²² He took also the table for the bread of the Presence, the cups for drink offerings, the bowls, the golden censers, the curtain, the crowns, and the gold decoration on the front of the temple; he stripped it all off. ²³ He took the silver and the gold, and the costly vessels; he took also the hidden treasures that he found. ²⁴ Taking them all, he went into his own land.

He shed much blood,
   and spoke with great arrogance.
²⁵ Israel mourned deeply in every
      community,
   ²⁶ rulers and elders groaned,
young women and young men became
      faint,
   the beauty of the women faded.

²⁷ Every bridegroom took up the lament;
   she who sat in the bridal chamber was
      mourning.
²⁸ Even the land trembled for its
      inhabitants,
   and all the house of Jacob was clothed
      with shame.

²⁹ Two years later the king sent to the cities of Judah a chief collector of tribute, and he came to Jerusalem with a large force. ³⁰ Deceitfully he spoke peaceable words to them, and they believed him; but he suddenly fell upon the city, dealt it a severe blow, and destroyed many people of Israel. ³¹ He plundered the city, burned it with fire, and tore down its houses and its surrounding walls. ³² They took captive the women and children, and seized the livestock. ³³ Then they fortified the city of David with a great strong wall and strong towers, and it became their citadel. ³⁴ They stationed there a sinful people, men who were renegades. These strengthened their position; ³⁵ they stored up arms and food, and collecting the spoils of Jerusalem they stored them there, and became a great menace,

---

a   169 B.C.

1.20–28: Antiochus's first attack on Jerusalem. In autumn 169 BCE Antiochus, en route home from Egypt, pillaged the Jerusalem Temple (cf. the earlier attempt of Seleucus IV, 2 Macc 3). His motive was financial (see Dan 11.28); he had no political or religious quarrel with Judah. A Hellenistic king would not hesitate to enter a city temple; the Jewish author saw the entry of anyone but the high priest into the sanctuary as arrogance (v. 21; cf. Dan 7.8,25), requiring divine punishment. **21–23:** *Golden altar* (of incense), Ex 30.1–10; *lampstand*, Ex 25.31–40; *table*, Ex 25.23–30; cf. 1 Kings 7.48–50. *The bread of the Presence*, see Lev 24.5–9; this symbolized the covenant between God and Israel, which 1 Macc sees as threatened by the current events. *Crowns*, diplomatic gifts stored in the Temple; see 13.37. *Gold decoration*, see 1 Kings 6.20–22. *Hidden treasures*, money deposited for safety by individuals; see 2 Macc 4.10–12. Later Judas restores these losses (4.49). **24b–28:** Poetic comment (cf. the book of Lamentations) on the events described, as also in 1.36–40; 2.7–13. *Blood*, vv. 20–24 record no bloodshed, but see 2 Macc 5.11–14.

1.29–40: Capture and fortification of Jerusalem. 29: *Two years later,* probably 168 BCE, after Antiochus's second invasion of Egypt (2 Macc 5.1). Ejected from Egypt by Roman legions, learning that in Jerusalem his appointee the high priest Menelaus was under attack from his deposed predecessor Jason (2 Macc 5.5–10), and believing Judea was in revolt, Antiochus attacked Jerusalem viciously (2 Macc 5.11–14), later sending Apollonius with troops to enslave the citizens (2 Macc 5.24). Apollonius is probably the *chief collector of tribute*, this title perhaps mistranslates "captain of the Mysians" (mercenary troops from Asia; see 2 Macc 5.24). **30:** *The city . . . many people*, the concern is political, to subjugate Jerusalem. **33:** *The city of David* indicates historical identity rather than topography; the precise location of the *citadel* (Gk "akra") is debated; it overlooked and controlled the Temple (Josephus, *Ant.* 12.252,362), from the northwest or southeast corner, and was finally captured by Simon (13.49–50). **34:** *Renegades:* see v. 11n. **36–40:** Poetic lament, emphasizing the citadel's effect on the *sanctuary*. But Antiochus has not yet threatened Jewish religion.

36 for the citadelᵃ became an ambush
    against the sanctuary,
  an evil adversary of Israel at all times.
37 On every side of the sanctuary they shed
    innocent blood;
  they even defiled the sanctuary.
38 Because of them the residents of
    Jerusalem fled;
  she became a dwelling of strangers;
she became strange to her offspring,
  and her children forsook her.
39 Her sanctuary became desolate like a
    desert;
  her feasts were turned into mourning,
her sabbaths into a reproach,
  her honor into contempt.
40 Her dishonor now grew as great as her
    glory;
  her exaltation was turned into
    mourning.

41 Then the king wrote to his whole kingdom that all should be one people, 42 and that all should give up their particular customs. 43 All the Gentiles accepted the command of the king. Many even from Israel gladly adopted his religion; they sacrificed to idols and profaned the sabbath. 44 And the king sent letters by messengers to Jerusalem and the towns of Judah; he directed them to follow customs strange to the land, 45 to forbid burnt offerings and sacrifices and drink offerings in the sanctuary, to profane sabbaths and festivals, 46 to defile the sanctuary and the priests, 47 to build altars and sacred precincts and shrines for idols, to sacrifice swine and other unclean animals, 48 and to leave their sons uncircumcised. They were to make themselves abominable by everything unclean and profane, 49 so that they would forget the law and change all the ordinances. 50 He added,ᵇ "And whoever does not obey the command of the king shall die."

51 In such words he wrote to his whole kingdom. He appointed inspectors over all the people and commanded the towns of Judah to offer sacrifice, town by town. 52 Many of the people, everyone who forsook the law, joined them, and they did evil in the land; 53 they drove Israel into hiding in every place of refuge they had.

54 Now on the fifteenth day of Chislev, in the one hundred forty-fifth year,ᶜ they erected a desolating sacrilege on the altar of burnt offering. They also built altars in the surrounding towns of Judah, 55 and offered incense at the doors of the houses and in the streets. 56 The books of the law that they found they tore to pieces and burned with fire. 57 Anyone found possessing the book of the covenant, or anyone who adhered to the law, was condemned to death by decree of the king. 58 They kept using violence against Israel, against those who were found month after month in the towns. 59 On the twenty-fifth day of the month they offered sacrifice on the altar that was on top of the altar of burnt offering. 60 According to the decree, they put to death the women who had their children circumcised, 61 and their families and those who circumcised them; and they hung the infants from their mothers' necks.

62 But many in Israel stood firm and were resolved in their hearts not to eat unclean food. 63 They chose to die rather than to be defiled by food or to profane the holy cov-

ᵃ Gk it
ᵇ Gk lacks He added
ᶜ 167 B.C.

1.41–64: The decree of Antiochus and its consequences. 41–43: Antiochus did not attempt religious coercion throughout his *whole kingdom*. His *letters* applied only to Jews in Jerusalem and Judea. 45–48: His prohibitions forced Jews to break the Law's fundamental commandments of *burnt offerings and sacrifices, sabbaths and festivals*, rejection of idolatry, practice of circumcision, and the offering of proper sacrifice at Jerusalem only (Ex 20.4–6; Deut 12.2–28). 51: Thus *inspectors* required sacrifice outside Jerusalem in *the towns of Judah* (cf. v. 55). 2 Macc 6.7 adds that Jews had to offer pagan sacrifices monthly to celebrate the king's birthday, and to honor the god Dionysus. 54: The date is December 168 or 167 BCE. *Desolating sacrilege* ("abomination of desolation"; cf. Dan 11.31; Mk 13.14) may pun on the Syrian "Ba'al Samen" ("Lord of Heaven"), identified as "Olympian Zeus" in 2 Macc 6.2, or more likely indicate a pagan altar erected above the Jewish altar of burnt offering outside the Temple (see v. 59). 56–57,60–61: The books of the Law, people owning copies, or keeping the Law, and those practicing circumcision (cf. 2 Macc 6.10) were targeted. *Decree*, the instructions contained in the king's letters (vv. 45–48 above). Antiochus's motives are debated; probably he wished to suppress rebellion by abolishing the

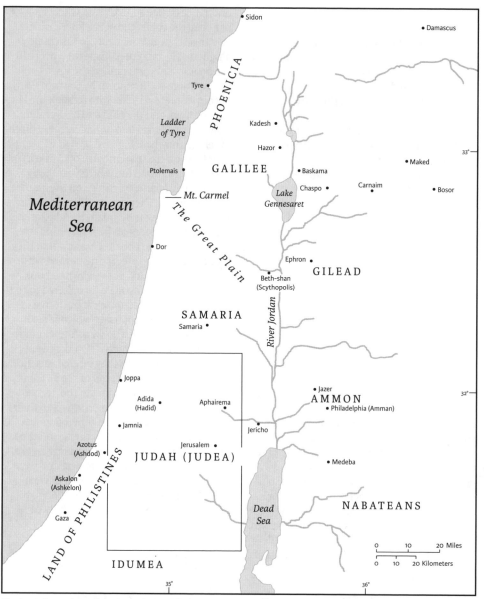

Chs 2–16: Campaigns of the Maccabees and Hasmoneans. See map on p. 205 for sites in the Jerusalem vicinity.

enant; and they did die. ⁶⁴ Very great wrath came upon Israel.

2 In those days Mattathias son of John son of Simeon, a priest of the family of Joarib, moved from Jerusalem and settled in Modein. ² He had five sons, John surnamed Gaddi, ³ Simon called Thassi, ⁴ Judas called Maccabeus, ⁵ Eleazar called Avaran, and Jonathan called Apphus. ⁶ He saw the blasphemies being committed in Judah and Jerusalem, ⁷ and said,

"Alas! Why was I born to see this,
    the ruin of my people, the ruin of the
        holy city,
and to live there when it was given over to
        the enemy,
    the sanctuary given over to aliens?
⁸ Her temple has become like a person
        without honor;ᵃ
    ⁹ her glorious vessels have been carried
        into exile.
Her infants have been killed in her streets,
    her youths by the sword of the foe.
¹⁰ What nation has not inherited her
        palacesᵇ
    and has not seized her spoils?
¹¹ All her adornment has been taken away;
    no longer free, she has become a slave.
¹² And see, our holy place, our beauty,
    and our glory have been laid waste;
the Gentiles have profaned them.
    ¹³ Why should we live any longer?"

¹⁴ Then Mattathias and his sons tore their clothes, put on sackcloth, and mourned greatly.

¹⁵ The king's officers who were enforcing the apostasy came to the town of Modein to make them offer sacrifice. ¹⁶ Many from Israel came to them; and Mattathias and his sons were assembled. ¹⁷ Then the king's officers spoke to Mattathias as follows: "You are a leader, honored and great in this town, and supported by sons and brothers. ¹⁸ Now be the first to come and do what the king commands, as all the Gentiles and the people of Judah and those that are left in Jerusalem have done. Then you and your sons will be numbered among the Friends of the king, and you and your sons will be honored with silver and gold and many gifts."

¹⁹ But Mattathias answered and said in a loud voice: "Even if all the nations that live under the rule of the king obey him, and have chosen to obey his commandments, every one of them abandoning the religion of their ancestors, ²⁰ I and my sons and my brothers will continue to live by the covenant of our ancestors. ²¹ Far be it from us to desert the law and the ordinances. ²² We will not obey the king's words by turning aside from our religion to the right hand or to the left."

²³ When he had finished speaking these words, a Jew came forward in the sight of all to offer sacrifice on the altar in Modein, according to the king's command. ²⁴ When Mattathias saw it, he burned with zeal and his heart was stirred. He gave vent to righteous anger; he ran and killed him on the altar. ²⁵ At the same time he killed the king's officer who was forcing them to sacrifice, and he tore down the altar. ²⁶ Thus he burned with zeal for the law, just as Phinehas did against Zimri son of Salu.

ᵃ Meaning of Gk uncertain
ᵇ Other ancient authorities read *has not had a part in her kingdom*

code that apparently sustained it. **64:** *Great wrath,* 1 Macc presents these events as God's punishment upon the sins of the renegades and their supporters.

2.1–14: Mattathias and his sons. 1: *Family of Joarib,* a senior priestly (not high priestly) family; 1 Chr 9.10; 24.7. *Modein* (cf. 13.25–30), a village near Lod, ca. 20 mi (32 km) northwest of Jerusalem. **2–5:** *Simon,* see chs 13–16; *Judas,* see 3.1–9.22. The nickname *Maccabeus* may mean "hammer" (see Introduction, 2 Macc). *Eleazar,* see 6.43. *Jonathan,* see 9.28–13.30. Jonathan and Simon became high priests. **7–13:** A poetic lament over Jerusalem personified as a captive woman, a comment on the events of 1.41–64; see Lam 1.

2.15–28: Confrontation at Modein. 15: *King's officers,* cf. "inspectors" (1.51). **18:** *What the king commands,* i.e., make local sacrifice away from Jerusalem, against the Jewish Law. *Friends of the king,* advisers at court appointed by the king. Jonathan was later enrolled among the king's "chief Friends" (10.65; cf. 10.20; 11.27) or "King's Kinsmen" (10.89). **22:** *Turning aside,* Mattathias rejects the invitation, quoting Deut 5.32. **23:** The Jew thus makes a direct challenge to Mattathias's leadership. **26:** Mattathias is directly compared with *Phinehas,* grandson of the high priest Aaron, who had killed an Israelite. The Israelite had compromised Israelite exclusivism by having

27 Then Mattathias cried out in the town with a loud voice, saying: "Let every one who is zealous for the law and supports the covenant come out with me!" 28 Then he and his sons fled to the hills and left all that they had in the town.

29 At that time many who were seeking righteousness and justice went down to the wilderness to live there, 30 they, their sons, their wives, and their livestock, because troubles pressed heavily upon them. 31 And it was reported to the king's officers, and to the troops in Jerusalem the city of David, that those who had rejected the king's command had gone down to the hiding places in the wilderness. 32 Many pursued them, and overtook them; they encamped opposite them and prepared for battle against them on the sabbath day. 33 They said to them, "Enough of this! Come out and do what the king commands, and you will live." 34 But they said, "We will not come out, nor will we do what the king commands and so profane the sabbath day." 35 Then the enemy[a] quickly attacked them. 36 But they did not answer them or hurl a stone at them or block up their hiding places, 37 for they said, "Let us all die in our innocence; heaven and earth testify for us that you are killing us unjustly." 38 So they attacked them on the sabbath, and they died, with their wives and children and livestock, to the number of a thousand persons.

39 When Mattathias and his friends learned of it, they mourned for them deeply. 40 And all said to their neighbors: "If we all do as our kindred have done and refuse to fight with the Gentiles for our lives and for our ordinances, they will quickly destroy us from the earth." 41 So they made this decision that day: "Let us fight against anyone who comes to attack us on the sabbath day; let us not all die as our kindred died in their hiding places."

42 Then there united with them a company of Hasideans, mighty warriors of Israel, all who offered themselves willingly for the law. 43 And all who became fugitives to escape their troubles joined them and reinforced them. 44 They organized an army, and struck down sinners in their anger and renegades in their wrath; the survivors fled to the Gentiles for safety. 45 And Mattathias and his friends went around and tore down the altars; 46 they forcibly circumcised all the uncircumcised boys that they found within the borders of Israel. 47 They hunted down the arrogant, and the work prospered in their hands. 48 They rescued the law out of the hands of the Gentiles and kings, and they never let the sinner gain the upper hand.

49 Now the days drew near for Mattathias to die, and he said to his sons: "Arrogance and scorn have now become strong; it is a time of ruin and furious anger. 50 Now, my children, show zeal for the law, and give your lives for the covenant of our ancestors.

51 "Remember the deeds of the ancestors, which they did in their generations; and you will receive great honor and an everlasting name. 52 Was not Abraham found faithful when tested, and it was reckoned to him as righteousness? 53 Joseph in the time of his distress kept the commandment, and became lord of Egypt. 54 Phinehas our ancestor, because he was deeply zealous, received the covenant of everlasting priesthood. 55 Joshua, because he fulfilled the command, became a judge in Israel. 56 Caleb, because he testified in the assembly, received an inheritance in

a   Gk they

intercourse with a Midianite woman who worshiped Baal of Peor (Num 25.1–16). **28:** *Fled to the hills*, 2 Macc 5.27–6.2 dates this before Antiochus's religious persecution.

2.29–41: Passive resistance. 29: Mattathias's violence for Law and covenant (2.27) is contrasted favorably with the passive reaction of another group *seeking righteousness and justice.* **41:** Mattathias's followers decide that the necessity of self-preservation overrides even the command to keep the sabbath.

2:42–48: The Hasideans and Mattathias. The *Hasideans* (Heb "ḥasidim," "the pious," cf. Pss 79.2; 149.1) are another militaristic group, which *united* with Mattathias's *friends*; in 2 Macc 14.6 they are under Judas's leadership. 1 Macc 7.12 reports them as naively and fatally supporting a peace mission.

2:49–70: Mattathias's death-bed speech. Jacob (Gen 49), Moses (Deut 33), and Samuel (1 Sam 12) utter similar speeches; compare also the praises of famous men in Sir 44–50. **52:** *Abraham . . . faithful when tested*, Gen 22.1–18; *reckoned . . . as righteousness*, Gen 15.6. **53:** *Joseph*, Gen 39–50. **54:** *Phinehas*, see v. 26n. **55–56:** *Joshua*

the land. [57] David, because he was merciful, inherited the throne of the kingdom forever. [58] Elijah, because of great zeal for the law, was taken up into heaven. [59] Hananiah, Azariah, and Mishael believed and were saved from the flame. [60] Daniel, because of his innocence, was delivered from the mouth of the lions.

[61] "And so observe, from generation to generation, that none of those who put their trust in him will lack strength. [62] Do not fear the words of sinners, for their splendor will turn into dung and worms. [63] Today they will be exalted, but tomorrow they will not be found, because they will have returned to the dust, and their plans will have perished. [64] My children, be courageous and grow strong in the law, for by it you will gain honor.

[65] "Here is your brother Simeon who, I know, is wise in counsel; always listen to him; he shall be your father. [66] Judas Maccabeus has been a mighty warrior from his youth; he shall command the army for you and fight the battle against the peoples.[a] [67] You shall rally around you all who observe the law, and avenge the wrong done to your people. [68] Pay back the Gentiles in full, and obey the commands of the law."

[69] Then he blessed them, and was gathered to his ancestors. [70] He died in the one hundred forty-sixth year[b] and was buried in the tomb of his ancestors at Modein. And all Israel mourned for him with great lamentation.

3 Then his son Judas, who was called Maccabeus, took command in his place. [2] All his brothers and all who had joined his father helped him; they gladly fought for Israel.

[3] He extended the glory of his people.
Like a giant he put on his breastplate;
he bound on his armor of war and waged battles,
protecting the camp by his sword.

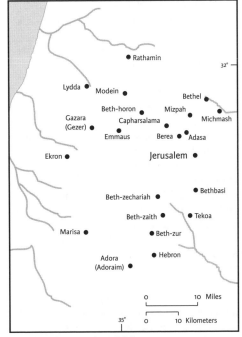

Chs 2–16: The Jerusalem vicinity.

[4] He was like a lion in his deeds,
like a lion's cub roaring for prey.
[5] He searched out and pursued those who broke the law;
he burned those who troubled his people.
[6] Lawbreakers shrank back for fear of him;
all the evildoers were confounded;
and deliverance prospered by his hand.
[7] He embittered many kings,
but he made Jacob glad by his deeds,
and his memory is blessed forever.

a   Or *of the people*
b   166 B.C.

and *Caleb* appear together in Num 14.5–10 and Sir 46.1–10. **57:** *David . . . merciful*, perhaps "pious" or "loyal" is meant. *Throne . . . forever*, see 2 Sam 7.13,16. **58:** *Elijah . . . zeal for the law*, cf. 1 Kings 21.17–29; *into heaven*, 2 Kings 2.9–12. **59:** *Hananiah, Azariah, and Mishael*, see Dan 1.6–20. **60:** *Daniel . . . lions*, Dan 6.16–24. Mattathias commends these heroes especially for their loyalty to the Law and readiness to testify under trial. **65–66:** *Simeon* (Simon), *wise in counsel*, and *Judas, a mighty warrior*, thus 1 Macc presents them, but in reverse order. **70:** *Tomb*, described in 13.27–30.

3.1–9: Introducing Judas. The poem pictures Judas in terms of earlier heroes. **4:** *Like a lion*, cf. Judah (Gen 49.9). **5–8:** Judas attacks two groups, the *lawbreakers* (vv. 5,6) who accept Antiochus's decree, and foreign *kings* (v. 7), i.e., Antiochus IV and Demetrius. *Turned away wrath from Israel*, cf. Phinehas (Num 25.11); thus Judas cancels God's wrath (1.64).

⁸ He went through the cities of Judah;
  he destroyed the ungodly out of the
    land;ᵃ
  thus he turned away wrath from Israel.
⁹ He was renowned to the ends of the
    earth;
  he gathered in those who were
    perishing.

¹⁰ Apollonius now gathered together Gentiles and a large force from Samaria to fight against Israel. ¹¹ When Judas learned of it, he went out to meet him, and he defeated and killed him. Many were wounded and fell, and the rest fled. ¹² Then they seized their spoils; and Judas took the sword of Apollonius, and used it in battle the rest of his life.

¹³ When Seron, the commander of the Syrian army, heard that Judas had gathered a large company, including a body of faithful soldiers who stayed with him and went out to battle, ¹⁴ he said, "I will make a name for myself and win honor in the kingdom. I will make war on Judas and his companions, who scorn the king's command." ¹⁵ Once again a strong army of godless men went up with him to help him, to take vengeance on the Israelites.

¹⁶ When he approached the ascent of Beth-horon, Judas went out to meet him with a small company. ¹⁷ But when they saw the army coming to meet them, they said to Judas, "How can we, few as we are, fight against so great and so strong a multitude? And we are faint, for we have eaten nothing today." ¹⁸ Judas replied, "It is easy for many to be hemmed in by few, for in the sight of Heaven there is no difference between saving by many or by few. ¹⁹ It is not on the size of the army that victory in battle depends, but strength comes from Heaven. ²⁰ They come against us in great insolence and lawlessness to destroy us and our wives and our children, and to despoil us; ²¹ but we fight for our lives and our laws. ²² He himself will crush them before us; as for you, do not be afraid of them."

²³ When he finished speaking, he rushed suddenly against Seron and his army, and they were crushed before him. ²⁴ They pursued themᵇ down the descent of Beth-horon to the plain; eight hundred of them fell, and the rest fled into the land of the Philistines. ²⁵ Then Judas and his brothers began to be feared, and terror fell on the Gentiles all around them. ²⁶ His fame reached the king, and the Gentiles talked of the battles of Judas.

²⁷ When King Antiochus heard these reports, he was greatly angered; and he sent and gathered all the forces of his kingdom, a very strong army. ²⁸ He opened his coffers and gave a year's pay to his forces, and ordered them to be ready for any need. ²⁹ Then he saw that the money in the treasury was exhausted, and that the revenues from the country were small because of the dissension and disaster that he had caused in the land by abolishing the laws that had existed from the earliest days. ³⁰ He feared that he might not have such funds as he had before for his expenses and for the gifts that he used to give more lavishly than preceding kings. ³¹ He was greatly perplexed in mind; then he determined to go to Persia and collect the revenues from those regions and raise a large fund.

ᵃ Gk *it*
ᵇ Other ancient authorities read *him*

3.10–26: Judas's campaigns against Apollonius and Seron. 10: *Apollonius,* possibly the Apollonius of 2 Macc 5.24, probably governor of Samaria (Josephus, *Ant.* 2.287). 1 Macc knows no details of this campaign. 12: *Sword of Apollonius,* cf. David's use of Goliath's sword (2 Sam 17.51). 13: *Seron . . . Syrian army,* in spite of the title, not a high-ranking officer, nor the main Syrian army, which in 166 BCE was on parade near Antioch. 16: *Ascent of Beth-horon,* a major pass ca. 12 mi (20 km) northwest of Jerusalem on the route from the coastal plain. The Seleucid general Bacchides later fortified it (9.50). Judas ambushed Seron here, as the Jews ambushed the Roman general Cestius in 65 CE (Josephus, *J.W.* 2.547). 18: *Heaven,* throughout 1 Macc, a pious substitution for the name of God; note "he himself" (v. 22). *Saving by many or by few,* an echo of 1 Sam 14.6. 24: *Philistines,* an anachronism illustrating the presentation of Judas as a latter-day David.

3.27–37: Antiochus's policy. 27: *Gathered all the forces* for a military review at Daphne near Antioch, 166 BCE. 29–30: Antiochus's shortage of cash was not caused, as the author likes to imagine, by *abolishing the* [Jewish] *laws* but by spending *lavishly* elsewhere. 31: Antiochus hoped to restore his finances by an expedition to *Persia.*

32 He left Lysias, a distinguished man of royal lineage, in charge of the king's affairs from the river Euphrates to the borders of Egypt. 33 Lysias was also to take care of his son Antiochus until he returned. 34 And he turned over to Lysias[a] half of his forces and the elephants, and gave him orders about all that he wanted done. As for the residents of Judea and Jerusalem, 35 Lysias was to send a force against them to wipe out and destroy the strength of Israel and the remnant of Jerusalem; he was to banish the memory of them from the place, 36 settle aliens in all their territory, and distribute their land by lot. 37 Then the king took the remaining half of his forces and left Antioch his capital in the one hundred and forty-seventh year.[b] He crossed the Euphrates river and went through the upper provinces.

38 Lysias chose Ptolemy son of Dorymenes, and Nicanor and Gorgias, able men among the Friends of the king, 39 and sent with them forty thousand infantry and seven thousand cavalry to go into the land of Judah and destroy it, as the king had commanded. 40 So they set out with their entire force, and when they arrived they encamped near Emmaus in the plain. 41 When the traders of the region heard what was said to them, they took silver and gold in immense amounts, and fetters,[c] and went to the camp to get the Israelites for slaves. And forces from Syria and the land of the Philistines joined with them.

42 Now Judas and his brothers saw that misfortunes had increased and that the forces were encamped in their territory. They also learned what the king had commanded to do to the people to cause their final destruction. 43 But they said to one another, "Let us restore the ruins of our people, and fight for our people and the sanctuary." 44 So the congregation assembled to be ready for battle, and to pray and ask for mercy and compassion.

45 Jerusalem was uninhabited like a
    wilderness;
    not one of her children went in or out.
The sanctuary was trampled down,
    and aliens held the citadel;
    it was a lodging place for the Gentiles.
Joy was taken from Jacob;
    the flute and the harp ceased to play.

46 Then they gathered together and went to Mizpah, opposite Jerusalem, because Israel formerly had a place of prayer in Mizpah. 47 They fasted that day, put on sackcloth and sprinkled ashes on their heads, and tore their clothes. 48 And they opened the book of the law to inquire into those matters about which the Gentiles consulted the likenesses of their gods. 49 They also brought the vestments of the priesthood and the first fruits and the tithes, and they stirred up the nazirites[d] who had completed their days; 50 and they cried aloud to Heaven, saying,

"What shall we do with these?
    Where shall we take them?
51 Your sanctuary is trampled down and
    profaned,
    and your priests mourn in humiliation.

---

a Gk *him*
b 165 B.C.
c Syr: Gk Mss, Vg *slaves*
d That is *those separated* or *those consecrated*

32: *Lysias . . . of royal lineage* was probably one of the King's "Kinsmen" (an honorary title; cf. 10.89) rather than a blood relative. 33: *His son Antiochus*, Antiochus V Eupator (ca. 164–162 BCE). 37: *Antioch*, modern Antakya in southern Turkey near the mouth of the Orontes River, founded by Seleucus I in 300 BCE. *Upper provinces*, Antiochus campaigned in Armenia, along the Persian Gulf, and in Elymais, probably in spring 165 BCE.

3.38–4.35: Judas's victory over Gorgias. 38: *Ptolemy son of Dorymenes*, probably the governor of Coelesyria and Phoenicia (2 Macc 8.8), and *Nicanor*, "son of Patroclus and one of the king's chief Friends" (2 Macc 8.9), play no further part in this campaign in 1 Macc; the enemy is led by *Gorgias*, another of the king's Friends (see 2.18) and governor of Idumea (2 Macc 12.32), but according to 2 Macc 8.10–29 by Nicanor (whose activities, however, seem to belong to Demetrius's reign; see 7.26–50). 40: *Emmaus* (not that of Lk 24.13), ca. 18 mi (28 km) west-northwest of Jerusalem, 8 mi (13 km) south of Modein. 41: *Slaves*, the sale of captured soldiers was usual in ancient warfare (see also 2 Macc 8.10–11). Some scholars think that *Syria* is an error for "Idumea" (cf. 4.29). *Philistines*, see v. 24n. 45–46: A poetic comment (cf. vv. 50–53). 46: *Mizpah*, 8 mi (13 km) north of Jerusalem, where Samuel gathered the Israelites against the Philistines (1 Sam 7.5–11). 48: A deliberate contrast: Jews consult *the book of the law*, Gentiles *their gods*. 49: *Nazirites* (cf. Num 6.1–21), perhaps a reminder of men like Samson (Judg

⁵²Here the Gentiles are assembled against
us to destroy us;
you know what they plot against us.
⁵³How will we be able to withstand them,
if you do not help us?"
⁵⁴Then they sounded the trumpets and
gave a loud shout. ⁵⁵After this Judas appointed leaders of the people, in charge of
thousands and hundreds and fifties and tens.
⁵⁶Those who were building houses, or were
about to be married, or were planting a vineyard, or were fainthearted, he told to go home
again, according to the law. ⁵⁷Then the army
marched out and encamped to the south of
Emmaus.

⁵⁸And Judas said, "Arm yourselves and be
courageous. Be ready early in the morning to
fight with these Gentiles who have assembled
against us to destroy us and our sanctuary.
⁵⁹It is better for us to die in battle than to
see the misfortunes of our nation and of the
sanctuary. ⁶⁰But as his will in heaven may be,
so shall he do."

4 Now Gorgias took five thousand infantry
and one thousand picked cavalry, and
this division moved out by night ²to fall upon
the camp of the Jews and attack them suddenly. Men from the citadel were his guides.
³But Judas heard of it, and he and his warriors moved out to attack the king's force in
Emmaus ⁴while the division was still absent
from the camp. ⁵When Gorgias entered the
camp of Judas by night, he found no one
there, so he looked for them in the hills, because he said, "These men are running away
from us."

⁶At daybreak Judas appeared in the plain
with three thousand men, but they did not
have armor and swords such as they desired.
⁷And they saw the camp of the Gentiles,
strong and fortified, with cavalry all around
it; and these men were trained in war. ⁸But

Judas said to those who were with him, "Do
not fear their numbers or be afraid when they
charge. ⁹Remember how our ancestors were
saved at the Red Sea, when Pharaoh with his
forces pursued them. ¹⁰And now, let us cry to
Heaven, to see whether he will favor us and
remember his covenant with our ancestors
and crush this army before us today. ¹¹Then
all the Gentiles will know that there is one
who redeems and saves Israel."

¹²When the foreigners looked up and saw
them coming against them, ¹³they went out
from their camp to battle. Then the men with
Judas blew their trumpets ¹⁴and engaged in
battle. The Gentiles were crushed, and fled
into the plain, ¹⁵and all those in the rear fell
by the sword. They pursued them to Gazara,
and to the plains of Idumea, and to Azotus
and Jamnia; and three thousand of them fell.
¹⁶Then Judas and his force turned back from
pursuing them, ¹⁷and he said to the people,
"Do not be greedy for plunder, for there is a
battle before us; ¹⁸Gorgias and his force are
near us in the hills. But stand now against our
enemies and fight them, and afterward seize
the plunder boldly."

¹⁹Just as Judas was finishing this speech,
a detachment appeared, coming out of the
hills. ²⁰They saw that their army[a] had been
put to flight, and that the Jews[a] were burning the camp, for the smoke that was seen
showed what had happened. ²¹When they
perceived this, they were greatly frightened,
and when they also saw the army of Judas
drawn up in the plain for battle, ²²they all
fled into the land of the Philistines. ²³Then
Judas returned to plunder the camp, and they
seized a great amount of gold and silver, and
cloth dyed blue and sea purple, and great
riches. ²⁴On their return they sang hymns

a   Gk they

13.7), Israel's champion against the Philistines. **55–56:** Judas *appointed leaders* (cf. Moses, Deut 1.15), sending
home some groups (cf. Deut 20.5–8) and giving a pre-battle sermon (like Jehoshaphat; 2 Chr 20.15–17). **4.2:** *The
citadel,* see 1.33n. **8:** *Do not fear their numbers,* the imbalance of Judas's 3,000 men opposing 35,000 infantry
and 6,000 cavalry (see 3.39 and 4.1) is emphasized. 2 Macc 8.9,24 give different numbers. **9–11:** Judas appeals to
Israel's victory at the Red Sea (Ex 14.21–31) and God's covenant with their *ancestors* Abraham, Isaac, and Jacob
(Gen 17.1–8; 26.2–5; 35.9–15). **15:** *Gazara,* Gezer (1 Kings 9.15–17), and *Jamnia,* Jabneh (2 Chr 26.6), were both west
of Emmaus, the site of the battle, and *Azotus,* Ashdod (1 Sam 5.5–6), was to the southwest. All were once Philistine cities. *Idumea* was south of Judah toward the Negeb. **23:** *Cloth dyed blue and sea purple,* luxury products of
the Phoenician coast; see Ezek 27.7. **24:** Pss 118.1; 136.1.

and praises to Heaven—"For he is good, for his mercy endures forever." [25] Thus Israel had a great deliverance that day.

[26] Those of the foreigners who escaped went and reported to Lysias all that had happened. [27] When he heard it, he was perplexed and discouraged, for things had not happened to Israel as he had intended, nor had they turned out as the king had ordered. [28] But the next year he mustered sixty thousand picked infantry and five thousand cavalry to subdue them. [29] They came into Idumea and encamped at Beth-zur, and Judas met them with ten thousand men.

[30] When he saw that their army was strong, he prayed, saying, "Blessed are you, O Savior of Israel, who crushed the attack of the mighty warrior by the hand of your servant David, and gave the camp of the Philistines into the hands of Jonathan son of Saul, and of the man who carried his armor. [31] Hem in this army by the hand of your people Israel, and let them be ashamed of their troops and their cavalry. [32] Fill them with cowardice; melt the boldness of their strength; let them tremble in their destruction. [33] Strike them down with the sword of those who love you, and let all who know your name praise you with hymns."

[34] Then both sides attacked, and there fell of the army of Lysias five thousand men; they fell in action.[a] [35] When Lysias saw the rout of his troops and observed the boldness that inspired those of Judas, and how ready they were either to live or to die nobly, he withdrew to Antioch and enlisted mercenaries in order to invade Judea again with an even larger army.

[36] Then Judas and his brothers said, "See, our enemies are crushed; let us go up to cleanse the sanctuary and dedicate it." [37] So all the army assembled and went up to Mount Zion. [38] There they saw the sanctuary desolate, the altar profaned, and the gates burned. In the courts they saw bushes sprung up as in a thicket, or as on one of the mountains. They saw also the chambers of the priests in ruins. [39] Then they tore their clothes and mourned with great lamentation; they sprinkled themselves with ashes [40] and fell face down on the ground. And when the signal was given with the trumpets, they cried out to Heaven.

[41] Then Judas detailed men to fight against those in the citadel until he had cleansed the sanctuary. [42] He chose blameless priests devoted to the law, [43] and they cleansed the sanctuary and removed the defiled stones to an unclean place. [44] They deliberated what to do about the altar of burnt offering, which had been profaned. [45] And they thought it best to tear it down, so that it would not be a lasting shame to them that the Gentiles had defiled it. So they tore down the altar, [46] and stored the stones in a convenient place on the temple hill until a prophet should come to tell what to do with them. [47] Then they took unhewn[b] stones, as the law directs, and built a new altar like the former one. [48] They also rebuilt the sanctuary and the interior of the temple, and consecrated the courts. [49] They made new holy vessels, and brought the lampstand, the altar of incense, and the table into the temple. [50] Then they offered incense on the altar and lit the lamps on the lampstand, and these gave light in the tem-

a Or *and some fell on the opposite side*
b Gk *whole*

4.26–35: Judas defeats Lysias. 26: *Lysias*, see 3.32n. 28: *The next year*, i.e., year 148 (cf. 3.37), probably beginning in autumn 165 BCE. 1 Macc emphasizes the size of Lysias's army. 29: *Beth-zur*, 16 mi (25 km) south-southeast of Jerusalem; cf. 2 Macc 11.25. 30–33: Judas's prayer (cf. 4.8–11) recalls David's killing of Goliath (*the mighty warrior*; cf. 1 Sam 17.4–54) and Jonathan's success against the Philistines (1 Sam 14.1–15); 1 Macc again presents the struggle in biblical terms. 35: *To invade Judea again*, cf. 6.28–63. Some scholars suspect that these two campaigns are really one.

4.36–61: The cleansing of the Temple and dedication of the altar. 37: *Mount Zion*, an old name for the city of David (2 Sam 5.7) and the Temple site (Ps 2.6; Joel 2.1). 38: *Sanctuary desolate . . . altar profaned*, cf. 1.54,59. *Gates burned*, by Jason's men in 168 BCE, cf. 2 Macc 1.8; 5.5–6; 8.33. 41: Judas attacks the *citadel*, which controlled access to the Temple (see 1.33n.). 43: *Defiled stones*, i.e., those forming the "desolating sacrilege," 1.54n. 44: See 1.54,59. 46: *Stored the stones*, though defiled, they were still part of the original altar. *Prophet should come*, the author believed that prophecy had ceased (9.27) but awaited a future prophet to advise the people (14.41;

ple. ⁵¹ They placed the bread on the table and hung up the curtains. Thus they finished all the work they had undertaken.

⁵² Early in the morning on the twenty-fifth day of the ninth month, which is the month of Chislev, in the one hundred forty-eighth year,^a ⁵³ they rose and offered sacrifice, as the law directs, on the new altar of burnt offering that they had built. ⁵⁴ At the very season and on the very day that the Gentiles had profaned it, it was dedicated with songs and harps and lutes and cymbals. ⁵⁵ All the people fell on their faces and worshiped and blessed Heaven, who had prospered them. ⁵⁶ So they celebrated the dedication of the altar for eight days, and joyfully offered burnt offerings; they offered a sacrifice of well-being and a thanksgiving offering. ⁵⁷ They decorated the front of the temple with golden crowns and small shields; they restored the gates and the chambers for the priests, and fitted them with doors. ⁵⁸ There was very great joy among the people, and the disgrace brought by the Gentiles was removed.

⁵⁹ Then Judas and his brothers and all the assembly of Israel determined that every year at that season the days of dedication of the altar should be observed with joy and gladness for eight days, beginning with the twenty-fifth day of the month of Chislev.

⁶⁰ At that time they fortified Mount Zion with high walls and strong towers all around, to keep the Gentiles from coming and trampling them down as they had done before. ⁶¹ Judas^b stationed a garrison there to guard it; he also fortified Beth-zur to guard it, so that the people might have a stronghold that faced Idumea.

5 When the Gentiles all around heard that the altar had been rebuilt and the sanctuary dedicated as it was before, they became very angry, ² and they determined to destroy the descendants of Jacob who lived among them. So they began to kill and destroy among the people. ³ But Judas made war on the descendants of Esau in Idumea, at Akrabattene, because they kept lying in wait for Israel. He dealt them a heavy blow and humbled them and despoiled them. ⁴ He also remembered the wickedness of the sons of Baean, who were a trap and a snare to the people and ambushed them on the highways. ⁵ They were shut up by him in their^c towers; and he encamped against them, vowed their complete destruction, and burned with fire their towers and all who were in them. ⁶ Then he crossed over to attack the Ammonites, where he found a strong band and many people, with Timothy as their leader. ⁷ He engaged in many battles with them, and they

^a 164 B.C.
^b Gk *He*
^c Gk *her*

cf. Deut 18.15; Mal 4.5; Jn 1.21). **47**: *As the law directs*, Ex 20.25; Deut 27.5–6. **49**: Cf. 1.21–23n. **51**: *Curtains*, see Ex 26.1–10,31–35. *Finished*, echoing the completion of Moses' work (Ex 40.33). **52**: *Chislev . . . the one hundred forty-eighth year*, i.e., December 165 BCE, exactly three years after the desecration (1.59); this dating places the Temple dedication, with 1 Macc, before Antiochus IV's death in 164 BCE. Some scholars, following 2 Macc 10.1–8, date the dedication soon after Antiochus's death in December 164 BCE. **56**: *Eight days*, as in Solomon's Temple dedication (1 Kings 8.66) and Hezekiah's purification (2 Chr 29.17). **57**: *Crowns*, cf. 1.22. **59**: *Assembly*, cf. 5.16; 14.19. Exactly who has authority to make this decision in 165 BCE is unclear. *Every year*, the letters of 2 Macc 1.1–9 and 1.10–2.18 instruct Egyptian Jews to keep this feast, associating it with lighting lamps (2 Macc 1.8) and holy fire (2 Macc 1.19–2.12). It is also called "the feast of Lights" (Josephus, *Ant.* 12.236) and "the festival of the Dedication" (Jn 10.22). **60–61**: *Mount Zion*, defending the Temple area against the citadel; *Beth-zur*, defending Jerusalem from the south (see 4.29n.).

5.1–68: Judas rescues Jews from neighboring peoples. The author inserts these undated events between chs 4 and 6 (2 Macc dates some of them later), constructing ch 5 carefully. Verses 1–8 show Judas attacking the sons of Esau and the Ammonites, balanced by 5.65–68 in which he attacks the sons of Esau again. In between, 5.9–64 show Simon rescuing Jews from Galilee (vv. 17,21–23), Judas rescuing Jews from Gilead (vv. 17,24–54), and Joseph and Azariah, left to guard Judea, being defeated (vv. 18–19,55–62). **3**: *Esau*, brother of Jacob, ancestor of Judah's enemy, Edom (see Gen 36). Judas defeats the Edomites as David did (2 Sam 8.13–14). *Idumea* (see 4.15n.). *Akrabattene*, located by Josephus (*J.W.* 2.235) in Samaria, by some scholars south of Judah (cf. Num 34.4). **4**: *Sons of Baean*, otherwise unknown. **6**: *Ammonites*, east of the Jordan; cf. Saul's victory (2 Sam 11). *Timothy*, cf.

were crushed before him; he struck them down. [8] He also took Jazer and its villages; then he returned to Judea.

[9] Now the Gentiles in Gilead gathered together against the Israelites who lived in their territory, and planned to destroy them. But they fled to the stronghold of Dathema, [10] and sent to Judas and his brothers a letter that said, "The Gentiles around us have gathered together to destroy us. [11] They are preparing to come and capture the stronghold to which we have fled, and Timothy is leading their forces. [12] Now then, come and rescue us from their hands, for many of us have fallen, [13] and all our kindred who were in the land of Tob have been killed; the enemy[a] have captured their wives and children and goods, and have destroyed about a thousand persons there."

[14] While the letter was still being read, other messengers, with their garments torn, came from Galilee and made a similar report; [15] they said that the people of Ptolemais and Tyre and Sidon, and all Galilee of the Gentiles,[b] had gathered together against them "to annihilate us." [16] When Judas and the people heard these messages, a great assembly was called to determine what they should do for their kindred who were in distress and were being attacked by enemies.[c] [17] Then Judas said to his brother Simon, "Choose your men and go and rescue your kindred in Galilee; Jonathan my brother and I will go to Gilead." [18] But he left Joseph, son of Zechariah, and Azariah, a leader of the people, with the rest of the forces, in Judea to guard it; [19] and he gave them this command, "Take charge of this people, but do not engage in battle with the Gentiles until we return." [20] Then three thousand men were assigned to Simon to go to Galilee, and eight thousand to Judas for Gilead.

[21] So Simon went to Galilee and fought many battles against the Gentiles, and the Gentiles were crushed before him. [22] He pursued them to the gate of Ptolemais; as many as three thousand of the Gentiles fell, and he despoiled them. [23] Then he took the Jews[d] of Galilee and Arbatta, with their wives and children, and all they possessed, and led them to Judea with great rejoicing.

[24] Judas Maccabeus and his brother Jonathan crossed the Jordan and made three days' journey into the wilderness. [25] They encountered the Nabateans, who met them peaceably and told them all that had happened to their kindred in Gilead: [26] "Many of them have been shut up in Bozrah and Bosor, in Alema and Chaspho, Maked and Carnaim"—all these towns were strong and large— [27] "and some have been shut up in the other towns of Gilead; the enemy[a] are getting ready to attack the strongholds tomorrow and capture and destroy all these people in a single day."

[28] Then Judas and his army quickly turned back by the wilderness road to Bozrah; and he took the town, and killed every male by the edge of the sword; then he seized all its spoils and burned it with fire. [29] He left the place at night, and they went all the way to the stronghold of Dathema.[e] [30] At dawn they looked out and saw a large company, which could not be counted, carrying ladders and engines of war to capture the stronghold, and attacking the Jews within.[f] [31] So Judas saw that the battle had begun and that the cry of the town went up to Heaven, with trumpets and loud shouts, [32] and he said to the men of his forces, "Fight today for your kindred!" [33] Then he came up behind them in three

a Gk *they*
b Gk *aliens*
c Gk *them*
d Gk *those*
e Gk lacks *of Dathema*. See verse 9
f Gk *and they were attacking them*

vv. 9,34,37,40 and 2 Macc 8.30–33. **8:** *Jazer*, ca. 12 mi (20 km) northwest of Philadelphia (modern Amman); see Num 32.3. **9:** *Gilead*, region north of Amman. *Dathema*, precise location uncertain. **13:** *Land of Tob*, in southern Syria; see Judg 11.3. **15:** *Ptolemais*, earlier Acco (Judg 1.31; modern Akko), renamed by Ptolemy II Philadelphus in 261 BCE, a Hellenistic port hostile to the Jews (see 2 Macc 6.8). **23:** *Arbatta*, precise location uncertain. **25:** *Nabateans*, people of northwest Arabia whose kings (e.g., Aretas, 2 Macc 5.8) ruled from Petra in southern Transjordan. **26:** *Bosrah*, modern Bostra in southern Syria. The identifications of *Bosor, Alema, Chaspho* (perhaps the Caspin of 2 Macc 12.13–16), and *Maked* are debated. *Carnaim* (cf. 2 Macc 12.21) is Sheik Sad in southern Syria.

companies, who sounded their trumpets and cried aloud in prayer. [34] And when the army of Timothy realized that it was Maccabeus, they fled before him, and he dealt them a heavy blow. As many as eight thousand of them fell that day.

[35] Next he turned aside to Maapha,[a] and fought against it and took it; and he killed every male in it, plundered it, and burned it with fire. [36] From there he marched on and took Chaspho, Maked, and Bosor, and the other towns of Gilead.

[37] After these things Timothy gathered another army and encamped opposite Raphon, on the other side of the stream. [38] Judas sent men to spy out the camp, and they reported to him, "All the Gentiles around us have gathered to him; it is a very large force. [39] They also have hired Arabs to help them, and they are encamped across the stream, ready to come and fight against you." And Judas went to meet them.

[40] Now as Judas and his army drew near to the stream of water, Timothy said to the officers of his forces, "If he crosses over to us first, we will not be able to resist him, for he will surely defeat us. [41] But if he shows fear and camps on the other side of the river, we will cross over to him and defeat him." [42] When Judas approached the stream of water, he stationed the officers[b] of the army at the stream and gave them this command, "Permit no one to encamp, but make them all enter the battle." [43] Then he crossed over against them first, and the whole army followed him. All the Gentiles were defeated before him, and they threw away their arms and fled into the sacred precincts at Carnaim. [44] But he took the town and burned the sacred precincts with fire, together with all who were in them. Thus Carnaim was conquered; they could stand before Judas no longer.

[45] Then Judas gathered together all the Israelites in Gilead, the small and the great, with their wives and children and goods, a very large company, to go to the land of Judah. [46] So they came to Ephron. This was a large and very strong town on the road, and they could not go around it to the right or to the left; they had to go through it. [47] But the people of the town shut them out and blocked up the gates with stones.

[48] Judas sent them this friendly message, "Let us pass through your land to get to our land. No one will do you harm; we will simply pass by on foot." But they refused to open to him. [49] Then Judas ordered proclamation to be made to the army that all should encamp where they were. [50] So the men of the forces encamped, and he fought against the town all that day and all the night, and the town was delivered into his hands. [51] He destroyed every male by the edge of the sword, and razed and plundered the town. Then he passed through the town over the bodies of the dead.

[52] Then they crossed the Jordan into the large plain before Beth-shan. [53] Judas kept rallying the laggards and encouraging the people all the way until he came to the land of Judah. [54] So they went up to Mount Zion with joy and gladness, and offered burnt offerings, because they had returned in safety; not one of them had fallen.

[55] Now while Judas and Jonathan were in Gilead and their[c] brother Simon was in Galilee before Ptolemais, [56] Joseph son of Zechariah, and Azariah, the commanders of the forces, heard of their brave deeds and of the heroic war they had fought. [57] So they said, "Let us also make a name for ourselves; let us go and make war on the Gentiles around us." [58] So they issued orders to the men of the forces that were with them and marched against Jamnia. [59] Gorgias and his men came out of the town to meet them

a   Other ancient authorities read *Alema*
b   Or *scribes*
c   Gk *his*

33–34: Cf. Gideon's tactics in Judg 7.19–20. 35: *Maapha*, both text and site intended are uncertain. 37: *Raphon*, er-Rafeh, 9 mi (15 km) west of Carnaim. 43–44: *Sacred precincts*, of the goddess Atargatis, consort of the Syrian god Hadad; see 2 Macc 12.26. 46: *Ephron*, et-Taiyibeh, 12 mi (20 km) south-southeast of Lake Gennesaret (the Sea of Galilee); see 2 Macc 12.27. 48: Judas follows Moses' example, Num 21.21–24. 52: *Beth-shan*, in Hellenistic times Scythopolis (2 Macc 12.29–30), in the Jordan Valley ca. 16 mi (26 km) south-southwest of Lake Gennesaret (the Sea of Galilee). 56: *Joseph* and *Azariah* envy Judas's success; for the author, only members of Judas's family

in battle. ⁶⁰ Then Joseph and Azariah were routed, and were pursued to the borders of Judea; as many as two thousand of the people of Israel fell that day. ⁶¹ Thus the people suffered a great rout because, thinking to do a brave deed, they did not listen to Judas and his brothers. ⁶² But they did not belong to the family of those men through whom deliverance was given to Israel.

⁶³ The man Judas and his brothers were greatly honored in all Israel and among all the Gentiles, wherever their name was heard. ⁶⁴ People gathered to them and praised them.

⁶⁵ Then Judas and his brothers went out and fought the descendants of Esau in the land to the south. He struck Hebron and its villages and tore down its strongholds and burned its towers on all sides. ⁶⁶ Then he marched off to go into the land of the Philistines, and passed through Marisa.^a ⁶⁷ On that day some priests, who wished to do a brave deed, fell in battle, for they went out to battle unwisely. ⁶⁸ But Judas turned aside to Azotus in the land of the Philistines; he tore down their altars, and the carved images of their gods he burned with fire; he plundered the towns and returned to the land of Judah.

6 King Antiochus was going through the upper provinces when he heard that Elymais in Persia was a city famed for its wealth in silver and gold. ² Its temple was very rich, containing golden shields, breastplates, and weapons left there by Alexander son of Philip, the Macedonian king who first reigned over the Greeks. ³ So he came and tried to take the city and plunder it, but he could not because his plan had become known to the citizens ⁴ and they withstood him in battle. So he fled and in great disappointment left there to return to Babylon.

⁵ Then someone came to him in Persia and reported that the armies that had gone into the land of Judah had been routed; ⁶ that Lysias had gone first with a strong force, but had turned and fled before the Jews;^b that the Jews^c had grown strong from the arms, supplies, and abundant spoils that they had taken from the armies they had cut down; ⁷ that they had torn down the abomination that he had erected on the altar in Jerusalem; and that they had surrounded the sanctuary with high walls as before, and also Beth-zur, his town.

⁸ When the king heard this news, he was astounded and badly shaken. He took to his bed and became sick from disappointment, because things had not turned out for him as he had planned. ⁹ He lay there for many days, because deep disappointment continually gripped him, and he realized that he was dying. ¹⁰ So he called all his Friends and said to them, "Sleep has departed from my eyes and I am downhearted with worry. ¹¹ I said to myself, 'To what distress I have come! And into what a great flood I now am plunged! For I was kind and beloved in my power.' ¹² But now I remember the wrong I did in Jerusalem. I seized all its vessels of silver and gold, and I sent to destroy the inhabitants of Judah without good reason. ¹³ I know that it is because of this that these misfortunes have come upon me; here I am, perishing of bitter disappointment in a strange land."

¹⁴ Then he called for Philip, one of his Friends, and made him ruler over all his

^a Other ancient authorities read *Samaria*
^b Gk *them*
^c Gk *they*

---

can claim to have saved Israel (v. 62). **58:** *Jamnia*, see 4.15. **65:** Hebron, where David ruled over Judah (1 Sam 5.5), now in Idumea; ca. 20 mi (31 km) south of Jerusalem. **66:** *Marisa*, 2 Macc 12.35, also in Idumea, ca. 12 mi (20 km) northwest of Hebron. **67:** The same point is made as in v. 62. **68:** *Azotus*, see 4.15. *Altars . . . images*, Judas, as at Carnaim (v. 44), destroys a pagan sanctuary, in accordance with Deuteronomy's command (Deut 7.5). Throughout the chapter 1 Macc presents Judas as a biblical hero.

6.1–17: Death of Antiochus IV and accession of Antiochus V. 1: *Upper provinces*, see 3.37n. *Elymais*, a region west of Persia, not a city. **2–3:** *Temple*, identified by 2 Macc 1.11–17 as the temple of the goddess Nanea (Gk Artemis), possibly located by 2 Macc 9.2 at Persepolis. **5–7:** *Reported*, these verses summarize 3.38–4.61, events from before Antiochus's death (see v. 16). **8–13:** The author's invention, suggesting (more charitably than 2 Macc 9) some remorse in Antiochus. **12:** See 1.20–23,30–31. **14–15:** Instead of Lysias, Antiochus appoints *Philip*, perhaps the "courtier" of 2 Macc 9.29 (cf. Manaen in Acts 13.1), as *ruler* and guardian of the child *Antiochus V*.

kingdom. [15] He gave him the crown and his robe and the signet, so that he might guide his son Antiochus and bring him up to be king. [16] Thus King Antiochus died there in the one hundred forty-ninth year.[a] [17] When Lysias learned that the king was dead, he set up Antiochus the king's[b] son to reign. Lysias[c] had brought him up from boyhood; he named him Eupator.

[18] Meanwhile the garrison in the citadel kept hemming Israel in around the sanctuary. They were trying in every way to harm them and strengthen the Gentiles. [19] Judas therefore resolved to destroy them, and assembled all the people to besiege them. [20] They gathered together and besieged the citadel[d] in the one hundred fiftieth year;[e] and he built siege towers and other engines of war. [21] But some of the garrison escaped from the siege and some of the ungodly Israelites joined them. [22] They went to the king and said, "How long will you fail to do justice and to avenge our kindred? [23] We were happy to serve your father, to live by what he said, and to follow his commands. [24] For this reason the sons of our people besieged the citadel[f] and became hostile to us; moreover, they have put to death as many of us as they have caught, and they have seized our inheritances. [25] It is not against us alone that they have stretched out their hands; they have also attacked all the lands on their borders. [26] And see, today they have encamped against the citadel in Jerusalem to take it; they have fortified both the sanctuary and Beth-zur; [27] unless you quickly prevent them, they will do still greater things, and you will not be able to stop them."

[28] The king was enraged when he heard this. He assembled all his Friends, the commanders of his forces and those in authority.[g] [29] Mercenary forces also came to him from other kingdoms and from islands of the seas. [30] The number of his forces was one hundred thousand foot soldiers, twenty thousand horsemen, and thirty-two elephants accustomed to war. [31] They came through Idumea and encamped against Beth-zur, and for many days they fought and built engines of war; but the Jews[h] sallied out and burned these with fire, and fought courageously.

[32] Then Judas marched away from the citadel and encamped at Beth-zechariah, opposite the camp of the king. [33] Early in the morning the king set out and took his army by a forced march along the road to Beth-zechariah, and his troops made ready for battle and sounded their trumpets. [34] They offered the elephants the juice of grapes and mulberries, to arouse them for battle. [35] They distributed the animals among the phalanxes; with each elephant they stationed a thousand men armed with coats of mail, and with brass helmets on their heads; and five hundred picked horsemen were assigned to each beast. [36] These took their position beforehand wherever the animal was; wherever it went, they went with it, and they never left it. [37] On the elephants[i] were wooden towers, strong and covered; they were fastened on each animal by special harness, and on each were four[j] armed men who fought from there,

a   163 B.C.
b   Gk *his*
c   Gk *He*
d   Gk *it*
e   162 B.C.
f   Meaning of Gk uncertain
g   Gk *those over the reins*
h   Gk *they*
i   Gk *them*
j   Cn: Some authorities read *thirty*; others *thirty-two*

Signet, the official seal, a symbol of authority together with the *crown* and the *robe*. **16:** *Died*, Antiochus's death is securely dated between 19/20 November and 18/19 December 164 BCE; *the one hundred forty-ninth year* began in spring or autumn 164 BCE. **17:** *Lysias* (see 3.32), in spite of Antiochus's wishes, remains regent for Antiochus V Eupator, "of a good father," and opposes Philip (see 6.55–56,63).

6.18–27: Judas attacks the citadel. 18: *Citadel*, see 1.33n. **20:** The *one hundred fiftieth year* began in spring or autumn 163 BCE; the event probably belongs to 163, not 162 BCE (cf. 2 Macc 13.1). *Siege towers* with other *engines* were commonly used in Hellenistic times; see 5.30; 6.51–52. **26:** *Fortified both the sanctuary and Beth-zur*, cf. 4.60–61.

6.28–63: Lysias's response. 31: *Beth–zur*, fortified by Judas (4.61). **32:** *Beth-zechariah*, ca. 7 mi (10 km) north of Beth-zur, between it and Jerusalem. Judas was blocking Lysias's approach to Jerusalem. **34:** The *elephants* are aroused by alcoholic *juice*; cf. 3 Macc 5.2. **35:** *Phalanxes*, infantry units in sixteen parallel columns sixteen ranks

and also its Indian driver. ³⁸ The rest of the cavalry were stationed on either side, on the two flanks of the army, to harass the enemy while being themselves protected by the phalanxes. ³⁹ When the sun shone on the shields of gold and brass, the hills were ablaze with them and gleamed like flaming torches.

⁴⁰ Now a part of the king's army was spread out on the high hills, and some troops were on the plain, and they advanced steadily and in good order. ⁴¹ All who heard the noise made by their multitude, by the marching of the multitude and the clanking of their arms, trembled, for the army was very large and strong. ⁴² But Judas and his army advanced to the battle, and six hundred of the king's army fell. ⁴³ Now Eleazar, called Avaran, saw that one of the animals was equipped with royal armor. It was taller than all the others, and he supposed that the king was on it. ⁴⁴ So he gave his life to save his people and to win for himself an everlasting name. ⁴⁵ He courageously ran into the midst of the phalanx to reach it; he killed men right and left, and they parted before him on both sides. ⁴⁶ He got under the elephant, stabbed it from beneath, and killed it; but it fell to the ground upon him and he died. ⁴⁷ When the Jews[a] saw the royal might and the fierce attack of the forces, they turned away in flight.

⁴⁸ The soldiers of the king's army went up to Jerusalem against them, and the king encamped in Judea and at Mount Zion. ⁴⁹ He made peace with the people of Beth-zur, and they evacuated the town because they had no provisions there to withstand a siege, since it was a sabbatical year for the land. ⁵⁰ So the king took Beth-zur and stationed a guard there to hold it. ⁵¹ Then he encamped before the sanctuary for many days. He set up siege towers, engines of war to throw fire and stones, machines to shoot arrows, and catapults. ⁵² The Jews[a] also made engines of war to match theirs, and fought for many days. ⁵³ But they had no food in storage,[b] because it was the seventh year; those who had found safety in Judea from the Gentiles had consumed the last of the stores. ⁵⁴ Only a few men were left in the sanctuary; the rest scattered to their own homes, for the famine proved too much for them.

⁵⁵ Then Lysias heard that Philip, whom King Antiochus while still living had appointed to bring up his son Antiochus to be king, ⁵⁶ had returned from Persia and Media with the forces that had gone with the king, and that he was trying to seize control of the government. ⁵⁷ So he quickly gave orders to withdraw, and said to the king, to the commanders of the forces, and to the troops, "Daily we grow weaker, our food supply is scant, the place against which we are fighting is strong, and the affairs of the kingdom press urgently on us. ⁵⁸ Now then let us come to terms with these people, and make peace with them and with all their nation. ⁵⁹ Let us agree to let them live by their laws as they did before; for it was on account of their laws that we abolished that they became angry and did all these things."

⁶⁰ The speech pleased the king and the commanders, and he sent to the Jews[c] an offer of peace, and they accepted it. ⁶¹ So the king and the commanders gave them their oath. On these conditions the Jews[a] evacuated the stronghold. ⁶² But when the king entered Mount Zion and saw what a strong fortress the place was, he broke the oath he had sworn and gave orders to tear down the wall all around. ⁶³ Then he set off in haste and returned to Antioch. He found Philip in control of the city, but he fought against him, and took the city by force.

7 In the one hundred fifty-first year[d] Demetrius son of Seleucus set out from Rome, sailed with a few men to a town by

---

[a] Gk *they*
[b] Other ancient authorities read *in the sanctuary*
[c] Gk *them*
[d] 161 B.C.

---

deep wielding long pikes. **43:** *Eleazar Avaran*, Judas's brother (2.5). **49–50:** *Beth-zur* had to be captured before the attack on Jerusalem. The *sabbatical year* (see Lev 25.2–7) began in autumn 164 BCE, with no harvesting in 163 BCE; cf. v. 53. **55:** *Philip*, see vv. 14–15. **57–59:** Threatened by Philip, isolated in Jerusalem, Lysias proposes *terms*, cancellation of the decree (1.51–60) for Jewish evacuation of Mount Zion (4.60). The letter of 2 Macc 11.22–27 probably reflects this situation. **62:** *Tear down the wall*, Lysias goes beyond the agreement.

the sea, and there began to reign. ² As he was entering the royal palace of his ancestors, the army seized Antiochus and Lysias to bring them to him. ³ But when this act became known to him, he said, "Do not let me see their faces!" ⁴ So the army killed them, and Demetrius took his seat on the throne of his kingdom.

⁵ Then there came to him all the renegade and godless men of Israel; they were led by Alcimus, who wanted to be high priest. ⁶ They brought to the king this accusation against the people: "Judas and his brothers have destroyed all your Friends, and have driven us out of our land. ⁷ Now then send a man whom you trust; let him go and see all the ruin that Judasᵃ has brought on us and on the land of the king, and let him punish them and all who help them."

⁸ So the king chose Bacchides, one of the king's Friends, governor of the province Beyond the River; he was a great man in the kingdom and was faithful to the king. ⁹ He sent him, and with him he sent the ungodly Alcimus, whom he made high priest; and he commanded him to take vengeance on the Israelites. ¹⁰ So they marched away and came with a large force into the land of Judah; and he sent messengers to Judas and his brothers with peaceable but treacherous words. ¹¹ But they paid no attention to their words, for they saw that they had come with a large force.

¹² Then a group of scribes appeared in a body before Alcimus and Bacchides to ask for just terms. ¹³ The Hasideans were first among the Israelites to seek peace from them, ¹⁴ for they said, "A priest of the line of Aaron has come with the army, and he will not harm us." ¹⁵ Alcimusᵇ spoke peaceable words to them and swore this oath to them, "We will not seek to injure you or your friends." ¹⁶ So they trusted him; but he seized sixty of them and killed them in one day, in accordance with the word that was written,

¹⁷ "The flesh of your faithful ones and their blood
    they poured out all around Jerusalem,
    and there was no one to bury them."

¹⁸ Then the fear and dread of them fell on all the people, for they said, "There is no truth or justice in them, for they have violated the agreement and the oath that they swore."

¹⁹ Then Bacchides withdrew from Jerusalem and encamped in Beth-zaith. And he sent and seized many of the men who had deserted to him,ᶜ and some of the people, and killed them and threw them into a great pit. ²⁰ He placed Alcimus in charge of the country and left with him a force to help him; then Bacchides went back to the king.

²¹ Alcimus struggled to maintain his high priesthood, ²² and all who were troubling their people joined him. They gained control of the land of Judah and did great damage in Israel. ²³ And Judas saw all the wrongs that Alcimus and those with him had done among the Israelites; it was more than the Gentiles had done. ²⁴ So Judasᵃ went out into all the surrounding parts of Judea, taking vengeance on those who had deserted and preventing those in the cityᵈ from going out into the country. ²⁵ When Alcimus saw that Judas and those with

ᵃ Gk *he*
ᵇ Gk *He*
ᶜ Or *many of his men who had deserted*
ᵈ Gk *and they were prevented*

7.1–4: Demetrius becomes king. 1: *One hundred fifty-first year,* beginning in spring or autumn 162 BCE. Demetrius I Soter (162–150 BCE), son of Seleucus IV (Antiochus IV's brother), was held hostage in Rome (175–162 BCE). Helped by the historian Polybius, he escaped. *A few men,* Polybius says sixteen. *Town by the sea*: Tripolis (2 Macc 14.1), in northern Lebanon. **2:** *Palace,* at Antioch.

7.5–25: Alcimus as high priest. 5: *Renegades,* Hellenizing opponents of the Maccabees, cf. 1.11. *High priest,* Alcimus's predecessor Menelaus, of dubious priestly descent (2 Macc 3.4; 4.23), had bought his office (2 Macc 4.23). Alcimus, of a genuine high-priestly family (7.14; 2 Macc 14.7), was compromised in Maccabean eyes as Hellenizing (7.9; 2 Macc 14.3). **8:** *Beyond the River,* i.e., west of the Euphrates (cf. 3.32; Ezra 4.11). **12:** *Scribes,* i.e., scholars of the Law. **13:** *The Hasideans* (see 2.42n.) apparently joined the scribes and trusted Alcimus, but he mistrusted the Hasideans. **17:** Ps 79.2–3. **19:** *Beth-zaith,* location uncertain; either 15 mi (24 km) south or 9 mi (15 km) north of Jerusalem.

him had grown strong, and realized that he could not withstand them, he returned to the king and brought malicious charges against them.

²⁶ Then the king sent Nicanor, one of his honored princes, who hated and detested Israel, and he commanded him to destroy the people. ²⁷ So Nicanor came to Jerusalem with a large force, and treacherously sent to Judas and his brothers this peaceable message, ²⁸ "Let there be no fighting between you and me; I shall come with a few men to see you face to face in peace."

²⁹ So he came to Judas, and they greeted one another peaceably; but the enemy were preparing to kidnap Judas. ³⁰ It became known to Judas that Nicanorᵃ had come to him with treacherous intent, and he was afraid of him and would not meet him again. ³¹ When Nicanor learned that his plan had been disclosed, he went out to meet Judas in battle near Caphar-salama. ³² About five hundred of the army of Nicanor fell, and the restᵇ fled into the city of David.

³³ After these events Nicanor went up to Mount Zion. Some of the priests from the sanctuary and some of the elders of the people came out to greet him peaceably and to show him the burnt offering that was being offered for the king. ³⁴ But he mocked them and derided them and defiled them and spoke arrogantly, ³⁵ and in anger he swore this oath, "Unless Judas and his army are delivered into my hands this time, then if I return safely I will burn up this house." And he went out in great anger. ³⁶ At this the priests went in and stood before the altar and the temple; they wept and said,

³⁷ "You chose this house to be called by
  your name,
  and to be for your people a house of
    prayer and supplication.

³⁸ Take vengeance on this man and on his
  army,
  and let them fall by the sword;
remember their blasphemies,
  and let them live no longer."

³⁹ Now Nicanor went out from Jerusalem and encamped in Beth-horon, and the Syrian army joined him. ⁴⁰ Judas encamped in Adasa with three thousand men. Then Judas prayed and said, ⁴¹ "When the messengers from the king spoke blasphemy, your angel went out and struck down one hundred eighty-five thousand of the Assyrians.ᶜ ⁴² So also crush this army before us today; let the rest learn that Nicanorᵃ has spoken wickedly against the sanctuary, and judge him according to this wickedness."

⁴³ So the armies met in battle on the thirteenth day of the month of Adar. The army of Nicanor was crushed, and he himself was the first to fall in the battle. ⁴⁴ When his army saw that Nicanor had fallen, they threw down their arms and fled. ⁴⁵ The Jewsᵇ pursued them a day's journey, from Adasa as far as Gazara, and as they followed they kept sounding the battle call on the trumpets. ⁴⁶ People came out of all the surrounding villages of Judea, and they outflanked the enemyᵈ and drove them back to their pursuers,ᵉ so that they all fell by the sword; not even one of them was left. ⁴⁷ Then the Jewsᵇ seized the spoils and the plunder; they cut off Nicanor's head and the right hand that he had so arrogantly stretched out, and brought them and displayed them just outside Jerusalem. ⁴⁸ The people rejoiced greatly and celebrated that day as a day of great gladness. ⁴⁹ They

ᵃ Gk *he*
ᵇ Gk *they*
ᶜ Gk *of them*
ᵈ Gk *them*
ᵉ Gk *these*

7.26–50: Judas and Nicanor. 26: *Nicanor*, possibly the Nicanor of 3.38 (in 2 Macc 14.12 an elephant commander and governor of Judea). 27,30: 1 Macc presents Nicanor as ever-treacherous, 2 Macc 14.18–25 as attempting friendly persuasion. 31: *Caphar-salama*, Khirbet Selma, ca. 7 mi (11 km) northwest of Jerusalem. 32: Nicanor lost men but remained in control; he demanded the surrender of Judas on pain of burning the Temple (v. 35, and replacing it with a temple to Dionysus, 2 Macc 14.33). 37: *Your name*, alluding to 1 Kings 8.29. 39: *Beth-horon*, see 3.16n. 40: *Adasa*, location uncertain, but somewhere between Beth-horon and Jerusalem. 41: Judas refers to 2 Kings 19.35. 43: *Adar*, i.e., March, probably 161 BCE. 45: The westward pursuit (cf. 1 Sam 14.31) to

decreed that this day should be celebrated each year on the thirteenth day of Adar. [50] So the land of Judah had rest for a few days.

8 Now Judas heard of the fame of the Romans, that they were very strong and were well-disposed toward all who made an alliance with them, that they pledged friendship to those who came to them, [2] and that they were very strong. He had been told of their wars and of the brave deeds that they were doing among the Gauls, how they had defeated them and forced them to pay tribute, [3] and what they had done in the land of Spain to get control of the silver and gold mines there, [4] and how they had gained control of the whole region by their planning and patience, even though the place was far distant from them. They also subdued the kings who came against them from the ends of the earth, until they crushed them and inflicted great disaster on them; the rest paid them tribute every year. [5] They had crushed in battle and conquered Philip, and King Perseus of the Macedonians,[a] and the others who rose up against them. [6] They also had defeated Antiochus the Great, king of Asia, who went to fight against them with one hundred twenty elephants and with cavalry and chariots and a very large army. He was crushed by them; [7] they took him alive and decreed that he and those who would reign after him should pay a heavy tribute and give hostages and surrender some of their best provinces, [8] the countries of India, Media, and Lydia. These they took from him and gave to King Eumenes. [9] The Greeks planned to come and destroy them, [10] but this became known to them, and they sent a general against the Greeks[b] and attacked them. Many of them were wounded and fell, and the Romans[c] took captive their wives and children; they plundered them, conquered the land, tore down their strongholds, and enslaved them to this day. [11] The remaining kingdoms and islands, as many as ever opposed them, they destroyed and enslaved; [12] but with their friends and those who rely on them they have kept friendship. They have subdued kings far and near, and as many as have heard of their fame have feared them. [13] Those whom they wish to help and to make kings, they make kings, and those whom they wish they depose; and they have been greatly exalted. [14] Yet for all this not one of them has put on a crown or worn purple as a mark of pride, [15] but they have built for themselves a senate chamber, and every day three hundred twenty senators constantly deliberate concerning the people, to govern them well. [16] They trust one man each year to rule over them and to control all their land; they all heed the one man, and there is no envy or jealousy among them.

---

a   Or *Kittim*
b   Gk *them*
c   Gk *they*

Gazara (see 4.15n.), the complete annihilation, and the decapitation (cf. 1 Sam 17.54) recall famous past victories. **49:** *Celebrated each year*, but dropped from the calendar after 70 CE. 1 Macc sees this event as introducing a short period of peace; in 2 Macc 15.28–37 it marks the Jewish permanent repossession of Jerusalem.

8.1–16: Eulogy of the Romans. 1 Macc lists Rome's achievements, presenting Rome as an ally against the Seleucids. Several of the details are inaccurate. **1:** *Friendship*, an official term indicating diplomatic relationship. **2:** Rome had conquered *Gauls* south of the Alps by 190 BCE. **3:** *Spain*, Roman exploitation began after Rome defeated Carthage (202 BCE). **4:** *Kings . . . of the earth*, identified in vv. 5–12. **5:** *Philip* V of Macedon was defeated at Cynoscephale in 197 BCE; his son *Perseus* was defeated at Pydna 168 BCE. **6:** The Seleucid *Antiochus* (III) *the Great* (223–187 BCE), who according to other sources had fifty-four, not *one hundred twenty elephants*, was *crushed* at Magnesia by Scipio Africanus (189 BCE). **7:** Antiochus remained free, but by the Treaty of Apamea (188 BCE) paid *tribute* of twelve thousand talents and gave *hostages* (including the future Antiochus IV). **8:** Rome transferred not *India* and *Media* but Asia Minor (including Lydia) to *King Eumenes* of Pergamum and to Rhodes. **9–10:** 1 Macc refers to the Achaean War of 146–145 BCE. *Strongholds*, particularly Corinth, mercilessly destroyed by L. Mummius. **11:** *Remaining kingdoms and islands*, including Carthage and Sicily. **14:** *Crown . . . purple*, the Roman republic banned kingship and its trappings, but magistrates wore togas with a purple hem. 1 Macc indirectly criticizes Jonathan (10.20,62,64) and Simon (14.43). **15:** The Roman *senate* numbered three hundred and did not meet daily. **16:** *One man each year*, i.e., a consul; in fact there were two.

So Judas chose Eupolemus son of John son of Accos, and Jason son of Eleazar, and sent them to Rome to establish friendship and alliance, [18] and to free themselves from the yoke; for they saw that the kingdom of the Greeks was enslaving Israel completely. [19] They went to Rome, a very long journey; and they entered the senate chamber and spoke as follows: [20] "Judas, who is also called Maccabeus, and his brothers and the people of the Jews have sent us to you to establish alliance and peace with you, so that we may be enrolled as your allies and friends." [21] The proposal pleased them, [22] and this is a copy of the letter that they wrote in reply, on bronze tablets, and sent to Jerusalem to remain with them there as a memorial of peace and alliance:

[23] "May all go well with the Romans and with the nation of the Jews at sea and on land forever, and may sword and enemy be far from them. [24] If war comes first to Rome or to any of their allies in all their dominion, [25] the nation of the Jews shall act as their allies wholeheartedly, as the occasion may indicate to them. [26] To the enemy that makes war they shall not give or supply grain, arms, money, or ships, just as Rome has decided; and they shall keep their obligations without receiving any return. [27] In the same way, if war comes first to the nation of the Jews, the Romans shall willingly act as their allies, as the occasion may indicate to them. [28] And to their enemies there shall not be given grain, arms, money, or ships, just as Rome has decided; and they shall keep these obligations and do so without deceit. [29] Thus on these terms the Romans make a treaty with the Jewish people. [30] If after these terms are in effect both parties shall determine to add or delete anything, they shall do so at their discretion, and any addition or deletion that they may make shall be valid.

[31] "Concerning the wrongs that King Demetrius is doing to them, we have written to him as follows, 'Why have you made your yoke heavy on our friends and allies the Jews? [32] If now they appeal again for help against you, we will defend their rights and fight you on sea and on land.'"

9 When Demetrius heard that Nicanor and his army had fallen in battle, he sent Bacchides and Alcimus into the land of Judah a second time, and with them the right wing of the army. [2] They went by the road that leads to Gilgal and encamped against Mesaloth in Arbela, and they took it and killed many people. [3] In the first month of the one hundred fifty-second year[a] they encamped against Jerusalem; [4] then they marched off and went to Berea with twenty thousand foot soldiers and two thousand cavalry.

[5] Now Judas was encamped in Elasa, and with him were three thousand picked men. [6] When they saw the huge number of the enemy forces, they were greatly frightened, and many slipped away from the camp, until no more than eight hundred of them were left.

[7] When Judas saw that his army had slipped away and the battle was imminent, he was crushed in spirit, for he had no time to assemble them. [8] He became faint, but he said to those who were left, "Let us get up and go against our enemies. We may have the strength to fight them." [9] But they tried to dissuade him, saying, "We do not have the strength. Let us rather save our own lives

---

a   160 B.C.

8.17–32: Alliance with Rome. 17: *Eupolemos*, grandson of *Accos*, of a priestly (Ezra 2.61) and diplomatic (2 Macc 4.11) family, may be the Jewish historian Eupolemus who wrote ca. 158 BCE. *Jason's* son Antipater also served on a mission to Rome (12.16; 14.22). These men had Greek names and presumably spoke Greek. **19:** *Long journey*, over a month, probably in 161 BCE. **20:** *Allies and friends*, Judas aims high; Judea was not even an independent state but subject to the Seleucid king. **22:** *Bronze tablets*, cf. 14.27. **23–30:** The format is standard, including mutual assistance in case of foreign aggression (vv. 24,27), prohibition of support for enemies (vv. 26,28), and provision for alterations (v. 30). **31–32:** An appended letter from Rome to Demetrius, probably inauthentic.

9.1–22: The death of Judas. This resumes the narrative from 7.50. **1:** *Bacchides and Alcimus*, see 7.19–20; *second time*, cf. 7.8–20. **2:** The topography requires close examination. *Gilgal* was near Jericho. *Mesaloth* perhaps transliterates a Heb word for "trails" and *in Arbela* the Heb for "Mount Bethel." **3:** The *one hundred fifty-second year* began in spring or autumn 161 BCE. **4:** *Berea*, possibly el-Bireh near Ramallah 10 mi (16 km) north of Je-

now, and let us come back with our kindred and fight them; we are too few." ¹⁰ But Judas said, "Far be it from us to do such a thing as to flee from them. If our time has come, let us die bravely for our kindred, and leave no cause to question our honor."

¹¹ Then the army of Bacchides[a] marched out from the camp and took its stand for the encounter. The cavalry was divided into two companies, and the slingers and the archers went ahead of the army, as did all the chief warriors. ¹² Bacchides was on the right wing. Flanked by the two companies, the phalanx advanced to the sound of the trumpets; and the men with Judas also blew their trumpets. ¹³ The earth was shaken by the noise of the armies, and the battle raged from morning until evening.

¹⁴ Judas saw that Bacchides and the strength of his army were on the right; then all the stouthearted men went with him, ¹⁵ and they crushed the right wing, and he pursued them as far as Mount Azotus. ¹⁶ When those on the left wing saw that the right wing was crushed, they turned and followed close behind Judas and his men. ¹⁷ The battle became desperate, and many on both sides were wounded and fell. ¹⁸ Judas also fell, and the rest fled.

¹⁹ Then Jonathan and Simon took their brother Judas and buried him in the tomb of their ancestors at Modein, ²⁰ and wept for him. All Israel made great lamentation for him; they mourned many days and said,

²¹ "How is the mighty fallen,
   the savior of Israel!"

²² Now the rest of the acts of Judas, and his wars and the brave deeds that he did, and his greatness, have not been recorded, but they were very many.

²³ After the death of Judas, the renegades emerged in all parts of Israel; all the wrongdoers reappeared. ²⁴ In those days a very great famine occurred, and the country went over to their side. ²⁵ Bacchides chose the godless and put them in charge of the country. ²⁶ They made inquiry and searched for the friends of Judas, and brought them to Bacchides, who took vengeance on them and made sport of them. ²⁷ So there was great distress in Israel, such as had not been since the time that prophets ceased to appear among them.

²⁸ Then all the friends of Judas assembled and said to Jonathan, ²⁹ "Since the death of your brother Judas there has been no one like him to go against our enemies and Bacchides, and to deal with those of our nation who hate us. ³⁰ Now therefore we have chosen you today to take his place as our ruler and leader, to fight our battle." ³¹ So Jonathan accepted the leadership at that time in place of his brother Judas.

³² When Bacchides learned of this, he tried to kill him. ³³ But Jonathan and his brother Simon and all who were with him heard of it, and they fled into the wilderness of Tekoa and camped by the water of the pool of Asphar. ³⁴ Bacchides found this out on the sabbath day, and he with all his army crossed the Jordan.

³⁵ So Jonathan[b] sent his brother as leader of the multitude and begged the Nabateans, who were his friends, for permission to store with them the great amount of baggage that they had. ³⁶ But the family of Jambri from Medeba came out and seized John and all that he had, and left with it.

a   Gk lacks *of Bacchides*
b   Gk *he*

rusalem. 5: *Elasa*, .6 mi (1 km) from el-Bireh. 15: *Mount Azotus*, perhaps a corruption of "to the slopes of the mountains." The whole campaign thus takes place in the central hill country north of Jerusalem. 19: *Modein*, see 2.1n. 21: *Mighty fallen*, quoting 2 Sam 1.19. 22: 1 Macc imitates the formulae used in the books of Kings (cf. 1 Kings 11.41; 1 Macc 16.23).

9.23–31: Jonathan succeeds Judas. 23: The author begins the second half of his history with the reappearance of the pro-Seleucid *renegades* (cf. 1.11,34), who assume control under Bacchides. 27: For 1 Macc, this is the nadir of the post-prophetic age (cf. 4.46n.). 28: *Jonathan*, apparently the youngest brother (2.5). 30: *Ruler and leader*, cf. Judg 11.4–11.

9.32–53: Jonathan and Bacchides. The topography of this section, which intertwines the accounts of Bacchides's pursuit of Jonathan (vv. 32–34,43–49) and a Nabatean-Maccabean vendetta (vv. 35–42), is confusing. 33: *Tekoa*, Amos's home (Am 1.1), 11 mi (18 km) south of Jerusalem. 34: Topographically difficult here; probably

[37] After these things it was reported to Jonathan and his brother Simon, "The family of Jambri are celebrating a great wedding, and are conducting the bride, a daughter of one of the great nobles of Canaan, from Nadabath with a large escort." [38] Remembering how their brother John had been killed, they went up and hid under cover of the mountain. [39] They looked out and saw a tumultuous procession with a great amount of baggage; and the bridegroom came out with his friends and his brothers to meet them with tambourines and musicians and many weapons. [40] Then they rushed on them from the ambush and began killing them. Many were wounded and fell, and the rest fled to the mountain; and the Jews[a] took all their goods. [41] So the wedding was turned into mourning and the voice of their musicians into a funeral dirge. [42] After they had fully avenged the blood of their brother, they returned to the marshes of the Jordan.

[43] When Bacchides heard of this, he came with a large force on the sabbath day to the banks of the Jordan. [44] And Jonathan said to those with him, "Let us get up now and fight for our lives, for today things are not as they were before. [45] For look! the battle is in front of us and behind us; the water of the Jordan is on this side and on that, with marsh and thicket; there is no place to turn. [46] Cry out now to Heaven that you may be delivered from the hands of our enemies." [47] So the battle began, and Jonathan stretched out his hand to strike Bacchides, but he eluded him and went to the rear. [48] Then Jonathan and the men with him leaped into the Jordan and swam across to the other side, and the enemy[a] did not cross the Jordan to attack them. [49] And about one thousand of Bacchides' men fell that day.

[50] Then Bacchides[b] returned to Jerusalem and built strong cities in Judea: the fortress in Jericho, and Emmaus, and Beth-horon, and Bethel, and Timnath, and[c] Pharathon, and Tephon, with high walls and gates and bars. [51] And he placed garrisons in them to harass Israel. [52] He also fortified the town of Beth-zur, and Gazara, and the citadel, and in them he put troops and stores of food. [53] And he took the sons of the leading men of the land as hostages and put them under guard in the citadel at Jerusalem.

[54] In the one hundred and fifty-third year,[d] in the second month, Alcimus gave orders to tear down the wall of the inner court of the sanctuary. He tore down the work of the prophets! [55] But he only began to tear it down, for at that time Alcimus was stricken and his work was hindered; his mouth was stopped and he was paralyzed, so that he could no longer say a word or give commands concerning his house. [56] And Alcimus died at that time in great agony. [57] When Bacchides saw that Alcimus was dead, he returned to the king, and the land of Judah had rest for two years.

[58] Then all the lawless plotted and said, "See! Jonathan and his men are living in quiet and confidence. So now let us bring Bacchides back, and he will capture them all in one night." [59] And they went and consulted with him. [60] He started to come with a large force, and secretly sent letters to all his al-

a Gk *they*
b Gk *he*
c Some authorities omit *and*
d 159 B.C.

a gloss from v. 43. **35:** *Nabateans*, see 5.25n. **36:** *Family of Jambri*, a local tribe. *Medeba*, ca. 20 mi (32 km) south-southwest of Philadelphia (Amman). *John*, see 2.1. **37:** *Nadabath*, perhaps a corruption of Medeba. **43:** Bacchides comes from the west. **45:** Jonathan is on the marshy west bank, with the Jordan curving round him on each side. **48:** Jonathan retreats back across the Jordan. **50–52:** Bacchides ensures control of the eastern (*Jericho*), northern/northwestern (*Emmaus, Beth-horon, Bethel, Timnath, Pharathon, Tephon*), western (*Gazara*) and southern (*Beth-zur*) approaches to Jerusalem; see maps on pp. 202, 205. **53:** *Citadel*, see 1.33n.

9.54–57: Death of Alcimus. 54: *The one hundred and fifty-third year* began in spring or autumn 160 BCE. *Wall*, probably that separating the outer, Gentile court from the inner courts reserved for Jews, perhaps with Hellenizing intentions. *Work of the prophets*: in what sense precisely is unclear. **57:** *Two years*, presumably ca. 159–158 BCE.

9.58–73: The continuing struggle. 62: *Bethbasi*, perhaps Khirbet Beit Bassi, ca. 7 mi (11 km) south of Jerusa-

lies in Judea, telling them to seize Jonathan and his men; but they were unable to do it, because their plan became known. [61] And Jonathan's men[a] seized about fifty of the men of the country who were leaders in this treachery, and killed them.

[62] Then Jonathan with his men, and Simon, withdrew to Bethbasi in the wilderness; he rebuilt the parts of it that had been demolished, and they fortified it. [63] When Bacchides learned of this, he assembled all his forces, and sent orders to the men of Judea. [64] Then he came and encamped against Bethbasi; he fought against it for many days and made machines of war.

[65] But Jonathan left his brother Simon in the town, while he went out into the country; and he went with only a few men. [66] He struck down Odomera and his kindred and the people of Phasiron in their tents. [67] Then he[b] began to attack and went into battle with his forces; and Simon and his men sallied out from the town and set fire to the machines of war. [68] They fought with Bacchides, and he was crushed by them. They pressed him very hard, for his plan and his expedition had been in vain. [69] So he was very angry at the renegades who had counseled him to come into the country, and he killed many of them. Then he decided to go back to his own land.

[70] When Jonathan learned of this, he sent ambassadors to him to make peace with him and obtain release of the captives. [71] He agreed, and did as he said; and he swore to Jonathan[c] that he would not try to harm him as long as he lived. [72] He restored to him the captives whom he had taken previously from the land of Judah; then he turned and went back to his own land, and did not come again into their territory. [73] Thus the sword ceased from Israel.

Jonathan settled in Michmash and began to judge the people; and he destroyed the godless out of Israel.

10 In the one hundred sixtieth year[d] Alexander Epiphanes, son of Antiochus, landed and occupied Ptolemais. They welcomed him, and there he began to reign. [2] When King Demetrius heard of it, he assembled a very large army and marched out to meet him in battle. [3] Demetrius sent Jonathan a letter in peaceable words to honor him; [4] for he said to himself, "Let us act first to make peace with him[e] before he makes peace with Alexander against us, [5] for he will remember all the wrongs that we did to him and to his brothers and his nation." [6] So Demetrius[f] gave him authority to recruit troops, to equip them with arms, and to become his ally; and he commanded that the hostages in the citadel should be released to him.

[7] Then Jonathan came to Jerusalem and read the letter in the hearing of all the people and of those in the citadel. [8] They were greatly alarmed when they heard that the king had given him authority to recruit troops. [9] But those in the citadel released the hostages to Jonathan, and he returned them to their parents.

[10] And Jonathan took up residence in Jerusalem and began to rebuild and restore the city. [11] He directed those who were doing the work to build the walls and encircle Mount Zion with squared stones, for better fortification; and they did so.

---

a   Gk *they*
b   Other ancient authorities read *they*
c   Gk *him*
d   152 B.C.
e   Gk *them*
f   Gk *he*

---

lem. **65–66:** Simon *struck down Odomera and . . . the people of Phasiron* (as local supporters of Bacchides?), or by a slight change "summoned" them, in which case the Greek "they" (v. 67; see textual note b) makes sense. **68:** Bacchides, besieging Bethbasi, was *crushed* between attacks from both town and surrounding country. **70–73:** Peace is agreed upon, and captives are returned. *Michmash*, ca. 9 mi (14 km) north-northeast of Jerusalem; cf. 1 Sam 13.23. *Judge the people*, Jonathan appears as a biblical hero (cf. 1 Sam 7.6), but has no political or priestly office.

10.1–50: Alexander Epiphanes and Demetrius I compete for Jonathan's support. 1: *The one hundred sixtieth year* probably began in spring or autumn 153, or possibly 152 BCE. *Alexander Epiphanes*, commonly called Balas, was an impostor who, helped by Eumenes of Pergamum (cf. 8.8), got Rome's support against Demetrius; he ruled until ca. 145. *Ptolemais*, see 5.15n. **6–8:** Hostages . . . released (cf. 9.53), an important concession. **10–11:**

¹² Then the foreigners who were in the strongholds that Bacchides had built fled; ¹³ all of them left their places and went back to their own lands. ¹⁴ Only in Beth-zur did some remain who had forsaken the law and the commandments, for it served as a place of refuge.

¹⁵ Now King Alexander heard of all the promises that Demetrius had sent to Jonathan, and he heard of the battles that Jonathan[a] and his brothers had fought, of the brave deeds that they had done, and of the troubles that they had endured. ¹⁶ So he said, "Shall we find another such man? Come now, we will make him our friend and ally." ¹⁷ And he wrote a letter and sent it to him, in the following words:

¹⁸ "King Alexander to his brother Jonathan, greetings. ¹⁹ We have heard about you, that you are a mighty warrior and worthy to be our friend. ²⁰ And so we have appointed you today to be the high priest of your nation; you are to be called the king's Friend and you are to take our side and keep friendship with us." He also sent him a purple robe and a golden crown.

²¹ So Jonathan put on the sacred vestments in the seventh month of the one hundred sixtieth year,[b] at the festival of booths,[c] and he recruited troops and equipped them with arms in abundance. ²² When Demetrius heard of these things he was distressed and said, ²³ "What is this that we have done? Alexander has gotten ahead of us in forming a friendship with the Jews to strengthen himself. ²⁴ I

also will write them words of encouragement and promise them honor and gifts, so that I may have their help." ²⁵ So he sent a message to them in the following words:

"King Demetrius to the nation of the Jews, greetings. ²⁶ Since you have kept your agreement with us and have continued your friendship with us, and have not sided with our enemies, we have heard of it and rejoiced. ²⁷ Now continue still to keep faith with us, and we will repay you with good for what you do for us. ²⁸ We will grant you many immunities and give you gifts.

²⁹ "I now free you and exempt all the Jews from payment of tribute and salt tax and crown levies, ³⁰ and instead of collecting the third of the grain and the half of the fruit of the trees that I should receive, I release them from this day and henceforth. I will not collect them from the land of Judah or from the three districts added to it from Samaria and Galilee, from this day and for all time. ³¹ Jerusalem and its environs, its tithes and its revenues, shall be holy and free from tax. ³² I release also my control of the citadel in Jerusalem and give it to the high priest, so that he may station in it men of his own choice to guard it. ³³ And everyone of the Jews taken as a captive from the land of Judah into any part of my kingdom, I set free without payment; and let all officials cancel also the taxes on their livestock.

a Gk *he*
b 152 B.C.
c Or *tabernacles*

Jonathan restores the defenses built by Judas (4.60) and destroyed by Lysias (6.62). **12:** *Strongholds*, cf. 9.50–53. **14:** *Beth-zur*, cf. 6.50. **20:** *We have appointed you . . . high priest*, Alexander had no right in Jewish law to do this. *King's Friend*, see 2.18n. *Purple robe*, appropriate both for a Friend and for the high priest (Ex 28.5). *Golden crown*, a gift: the high priest could wear a golden rosette and a "holy diadem" (Ex 28.36; 29.6) on the turban. **21:** *Vestments*, Ex 28.1–39; 39.1–26. *The one hundred sixtieth year* here began in spring, as the references to *the seventh month* and the autumn *festival of booths* (Lev 23.33–43) require, possibly in 153 but probably in 152 BCE. **22–45:** Demetrius offers new, remarkable concessions (vv. 29–45). Some major concessions reappear in Demetrius II's proposals (11.30–37: the exemption from *salt tax and crown levies* [v. 29; 11.35], from payments of *grain* and *fruit* [v. 30; 11.34]), and therefore were probably not part of Demetrius I's offer. Demetrius's astonishing offer of exemption from *tribute* (v. 29) is not granted until 13.39, as part of a peace agreement. Ceding *control of the citadel* (v. 32) (in fact never returned but captured by Simon, 13.50), the gift of *Ptolemais and* its *lands* (v. 39; cf. v. 1), the annual grant of *fifteen thousand shekels of silver* (v. 40), are also unlikely concessions at this stage. More realistically, Demetrius I may have conceded tax freedom and inviolability for *Jerusalem* (v. 31), *festivals* as *days of immunity and release* (v. 34), enrollment of Jews in the *king's forces* and administration with freedom to *live by their own laws* (vv. 36–37), the annexation to Judea of three Samarian districts (v. 38), various provisions for Temple finances and debtors taking sanctuary in the Temple (vv. 41–45), and the costs of *restoring the sanctuary* and

34 "All the festivals and sabbaths and new moons and appointed days, and the three days before a festival and the three after a festival—let them all be days of immunity and release for all the Jews who are in my kingdom. 35 No one shall have authority to exact anything from them or annoy any of them about any matter.

36 "Let Jews be enrolled in the king's forces to the number of thirty thousand men, and let the maintenance be given them that is due to all the forces of the king. 37 Let some of them be stationed in the great strongholds of the king, and let some of them be put in positions of trust in the kingdom. Let their officers and leaders be of their own number, and let them live by their own laws, just as the king has commanded in the land of Judah.

38 "As for the three districts that have been added to Judea from the country of Samaria, let them be annexed to Judea so that they may be considered to be under one ruler and obey no other authority than the high priest. 39 Ptolemais and the land adjoining it I have given as a gift to the sanctuary in Jerusalem, to meet the necessary expenses of the sanctuary. 40 I also grant fifteen thousand shekels of silver yearly out of the king's revenues from appropriate places. 41 And all the additional funds that the government officials have not paid as they did in the first years,[a] they shall give from now on for the service of the temple.[b] 42 Moreover, the five thousand shekels of silver that my officials[c] have received every year from the income of the services of the temple, this too is canceled, because it belongs to the priests who minister there. 43 And all who take refuge at the temple in Jerusalem, or in any of its precincts, because they owe money to the king or are in debt, let them be released and receive back all their property in my kingdom.

44 "Let the cost of rebuilding and restoring the structures of the sanctuary be paid from the revenues of the king. 45 And let the cost of rebuilding the walls of Jerusalem and fortifying it all around, and the cost of rebuilding the walls in Judea, also be paid from the revenues of the king."

46 When Jonathan and the people heard these words, they did not believe or accept them, because they remembered the great wrongs that Demetrius[d] had done in Israel and how much he had oppressed them. 47 They favored Alexander, because he had been the first to speak peaceable words to them, and they remained his allies all his days.

48 Now King Alexander assembled large forces and encamped opposite Demetrius. 49 The two kings met in battle, and the army of Demetrius fled, and Alexander[e] pursued him and defeated them. 50 He pressed the battle strongly until the sun set, and on that day Demetrius fell.

51 Then Alexander sent ambassadors to Ptolemy king of Egypt with the following message: 52 "Since I have returned to my kingdom and have taken my seat on the throne of my ancestors, and established my rule—for I crushed Demetrius and gained control of our country; 53 I met him in battle, and he and his army were crushed by us, and we have taken our seat on the throne of his kingdom— 54 now therefore let us establish friendship with one another; give me now your daughter as my wife, and I will become your son-in-law, and will make gifts to you and to her in keeping with your position."

55 Ptolemy the king replied and said, "Happy was the day on which you returned to the land of your ancestors and took your seat on the throne of their kingdom. 56 And now I will do for you as you wrote, but meet me at Ptolemais, so that we may see one another, and I will become your father-in-law, as you have said."

a Meaning of Gk uncertain
b Gk house
c Gk they
d Gk he
e Other ancient authorities read Alexander fled, and Demetrius

walls of Jerusalem and in Judea (vv. 44–45). 46: Great wrongs, cf. chs 7–9. 47: First to speak, in fact, Demetrius was (v. 3). The Greek perhaps means that Alexander provided the original opportunity for peace. 48–50: This follows from v. 2. The battleground is unknown; see Josephus, Ant. 13.58–61. The date is probably summer 150 BCE.
    10.51–66: Alexander, Ptolemy, and Jonathan. 51: Ptolemy VI Philometor (180–145 BCE), cf. 1.18. 54: Daughter, Cleopatra Thea (v. 57). 55: Ptolemy recognizes Alexander's legitimacy. 56: Ptolemais (cf. v. 1), a symbol of Egyp-

[57] So Ptolemy set out from Egypt, he and his daughter Cleopatra, and came to Ptolemais in the one hundred sixty-second year.[a] [58] King Alexander met him, and Ptolemy[b] gave him his daughter Cleopatra in marriage, and celebrated her wedding at Ptolemais with great pomp, as kings do.

[59] Then King Alexander wrote to Jonathan to come and meet him. [60] So he went with pomp to Ptolemais and met the two kings; he gave them and their Friends silver and gold and many gifts, and found favor with them. [61] A group of malcontents from Israel, renegades, gathered together against him to accuse him; but the king paid no attention to them. [62] The king gave orders to take off Jonathan's garments and to clothe him in purple, and they did so. [63] The king also seated him at his side; and he said to his officers, "Go out with him into the middle of the city and proclaim that no one is to bring charges against him about any matter, and let no one annoy him for any reason." [64] When his accusers saw the honor that was paid him, in accord with the proclamation, and saw him clothed in purple, they all fled. [65] Thus the king honored him and enrolled him among his chief[c] Friends, and made him general and governor of the province. [66] And Jonathan returned to Jerusalem in peace and gladness.

[67] In the one hundred sixty-fifth year[d] Demetrius son of Demetrius came from Crete to the land of his ancestors. [68] When King Alexander heard of it, he was greatly distressed and returned to Antioch. [69] And Demetrius appointed Apollonius the governor of Coelesyria, and he assembled a large force and encamped against Jamnia. Then he sent the following message to the high priest Jonathan:

[70] "You are the only one to rise up against us, and I have fallen into ridicule and disgrace because of you. Why do you assume authority against us in the hill country? [71] If you now have confidence in your forces, come down to the plain to meet us, and let us match strength with each other there, for I have with me the power of the cities. [72] Ask and learn who I am and who the others are that are helping us. People will tell you that you cannot stand before us, for your ancestors were twice put to flight in their own land. [73] And now you will not be able to withstand my cavalry and such an army in the plain, where there is no stone or pebble, or place to flee."

[74] When Jonathan heard the words of Apollonius, his spirit was aroused. He chose ten thousand men and set out from Jerusalem, and his brother Simon met him to help him. [75] He encamped before Joppa, but the people of the city closed its gates, for Apollonius had a garrison in Joppa. [76] So they fought against it, and the people of the city became afraid and opened the gates, and Jonathan gained possession of Joppa.

[77] When Apollonius heard of it, he mustered three thousand cavalry and a large army, and went to Azotus as though he were going farther. At the same time he advanced into the plain, for he had a large troop of cavalry and put confidence in it. [78] Jonathan[b] pursued him to Azotus, and the armies engaged in battle. [79] Now Apollonius had secretly left a thousand cavalry behind them. [80] Jonathan learned that there was an ambush

a   150 B.C.
b   Gk *he*
c   Gk *first*
d   147 B.C.

tian presence on the coast. **57:** *The one hundred sixty-second year*, probably summer-autumn 150 BCE. **60:** *He*, i.e., Jonathan; *two kings*, Alexander and Ptolemy. **65:** *Chief Friends*, promotion, cf. v. 20. *General and governor*, i.e., military and civil head of the *province*, i.e., Judea. Jonathan is now a Seleucid official.

10.67–89: Jonathan defeats Apollonius. 67: *The one hundred sixty-fifth year* probably began in autumn 148 BCE; *Demetrius* II Nicator *came from Crete* to Cilicia in spring 147 BCE with Cretan mercenaries led by Lasthenes (cf. 11.32). **68:** *Returned to Antioch*, the Seleucid capital. **69:** *Apollonius*, known from Polybius (*Hist.* 31.11.19). *Coelesyria*, originally "hollow Syria" between the Lebanon and Anti-Lebanon ranges, then with wider reference. *Jamnia*, see 4.15n. Demetrius has to control Jonathan before attacking Alexander. **72:** *Twice put to flight*, perhaps referring to Judas's defeats, 6.47; 9.6–19. **73:** *No stone or pebble*, i.e., for ammunition. **74:** *Simon* (2.3) appears in action for the first time. **75:** *Joppa* (cf. 2 Macc 3–9), on the coast north of Jamnia, Azotus, and As-

behind him, for they surrounded his army and shot arrows at his men from early morning until late afternoon. ⁸¹ But his men stood fast, as Jonathan had commanded, and the enemy's^a horses grew tired.

⁸² Then Simon brought forward his force and engaged the phalanx in battle (for the cavalry was exhausted); they were overwhelmed by him and fled, ⁸³ and the cavalry was dispersed in the plain. They fled to Azotus and entered Beth-dagon, the temple of their idol, for safety. ⁸⁴ But Jonathan burned Azotus and the surrounding towns and plundered them; and the temple of Dagon, and those who had taken refuge in it, he burned with fire. ⁸⁵ The number of those who fell by the sword, with those burned alive, came to eight thousand.

⁸⁶ Then Jonathan left there and encamped against Askalon, and the people of the city came out to meet him with great pomp.

⁸⁷ He and those with him then returned to Jerusalem with a large amount of booty. ⁸⁸ When King Alexander heard of these things, he honored Jonathan still more; ⁸⁹ and he sent to him a golden buckle, such as it is the custom to give to the King's Kinsmen. He also gave him Ekron and all its environs as his possession.

11 Then the king of Egypt gathered great forces, like the sand by the seashore, and many ships; and he tried to get possession of Alexander's kingdom by trickery and add it to his own kingdom. ² He set out for Syria with peaceable words, and the people of the towns opened their gates to him and went to meet him, for King Alexander had commanded them to meet him, since he was Alexander's^b father-in-law. ³ But when Ptole-

my entered the towns he stationed forces as a garrison in each town.

⁴ When he^c approached Azotus, they showed him the burnt-out temple of Dagon, and Azotus and its suburbs destroyed, and the corpses lying about, and the charred bodies of those whom Jonathan^d had burned in the war, for they had piled them in heaps along his route. ⁵ They also told the king what Jonathan had done, to throw blame on him; but the king kept silent. ⁶ Jonathan met the king at Joppa with pomp, and they greeted one another and spent the night there. ⁷ And Jonathan went with the king as far as the river called Eleutherus; then he returned to Jerusalem.

⁸ So King Ptolemy gained control of the coastal cities as far as Seleucia by the sea, and he kept devising wicked designs against Alexander. ⁹ He sent envoys to King Demetrius, saying, "Come, let us make a covenant with each other, and I will give you in marriage my daughter who was Alexander's wife, and you shall reign over your father's kingdom. ¹⁰ I now regret that I gave him my daughter, for he has tried to kill me." ¹¹ He threw blame on Alexander^e because he coveted his kingdom. ¹² So he took his daughter away from him and gave her to Demetrius. He was estranged from Alexander, and their enmity became manifest.

¹³ Then Ptolemy entered Antioch and put on the crown of Asia. Thus he put two crowns

---

^a Gk *their*
^b Gk *his*
^c Other ancient authorities read *they*
^d Gk *he*
^e Gk *him*

---

calon; Jonathan thus separates Apollonius from Demetrius. **82:** Simon's forces complete the rout. **83–84:** *Azotus,* see 4.15n. *Beth-dagon,* lit. "the house of Dagon" (a West Semitic and later a Philistine god) at Azotus/ Ashdod; see 1 Sam 5.1–5; cf. Judg 16.23. 1 Macc emphasizes Maccabean hostility to paganism. **86:** *Askalon,* earlier Ashkelon, about 10 mi (16 km) south of Azotus. **88–89:** *Buckle,* to fasten the cloak; cf. 11.58. *Kinsmen,* see 2.18. *Ekron,* Tel Miqne, a former Philistine city (Josh 14.3), important for olive oil production. Judea begins to extend her territory.

11.1–19: The end of Ptolemy VI and Alexander. 1: *By trickery,* Josephus (*Ant.* 13.106–8) claims that Ptolemy set out as Alexander's ally but changed his mind after Alexander plotted against his life. **4:** See 10.84. **5:** *The king kept silent,* needing Jonathan's support. **7:** *River called Eleutherus,* Nahr el-Kebir, north of Tripolis. **8:** *Seleucia,* Antioch's port at the mouth of the Orontes River, founded by Antiochus I. **9:** *Demetrius* II, see 10.67. *My daughter,* i.e., Cleopatra; see 10.57. **10:** *Tried to kill me,* a reference to the plot (v. 1). **12:** Ptolemy was supporting Demetrius to undermine *Alexander.* **13:** *Two crowns,* Antiochus IV had also wished (1.16) to "reign over both

on his head, the crown of Egypt and that of Asia. ¹⁴ Now King Alexander was in Cilicia at that time, because the people of that region were in revolt. ¹⁵ When Alexander heard of it, he came against him in battle. Ptolemy marched out and met him with a strong force, and put him to flight. ¹⁶ So Alexander fled into Arabia to find protection there, and King Ptolemy was triumphant. ¹⁷ Zabdiel the Arab cut off the head of Alexander and sent it to Ptolemy. ¹⁸ But King Ptolemy died three days later, and his troops in the strongholds were killed by the inhabitants of the strongholds. ¹⁹ So Demetrius became king in the one hundred sixty-seventh year.ᵃ

²⁰ In those days Jonathan assembled the Judeans to attack the citadel in Jerusalem, and he built many engines of war to use against it. ²¹ But certain renegades who hated their nation went to the king and reported to him that Jonathan was besieging the citadel. ²² When he heard this he was angry, and as soon as he heard it he set out and came to Ptolemais; and he wrote Jonathan not to continue the siege, but to meet him for a conference at Ptolemais as quickly as possible.

²³ When Jonathan heard this, he gave orders to continue the siege. He chose some of the elders of Israel and some of the priests, and put himself in danger, ²⁴ for he went to the king at Ptolemais, taking silver and gold and clothing and numerous other gifts. And

he won his favor. ²⁵ Although certain renegades of his nation kept making complaints against him, ²⁶ the king treated him as his predecessors had treated him; he exalted him in the presence of all his Friends. ²⁷ He confirmed him in the high priesthood and in as many other honors as he had formerly had, and caused him to be reckoned among his chiefᵇ Friends. ²⁸ Then Jonathan asked the king to free Judea and the three districts of Samariaᶜ from tribute, and promised him three hundred talents. ²⁹ The king consented, and wrote a letter to Jonathan about all these things; its contents were as follows:

³⁰ "King Demetrius to his brother Jonathan and to the nation of the Jews, greetings. ³¹ This copy of the letter that we wrote concerning you to our kinsman Lasthenes we have written to you also, so that you may know what it says. ³² 'King Demetrius to his father Lasthenes, greetings. ³³ We have determined to do good to the nation of the Jews, who are our friends and fulfill their obligations to us, because of the goodwill they show toward us. ³⁴ We have confirmed as their possession both the territory of Judea and the three districts of Aphairema and Lydda and Rathamin; the latter, with all

---

ᵃ   145 B.C.
ᵇ   Gk *first*
ᶜ   Cn: Gk *the three districts and Samaria*

kingdoms," the Ptolemaic and the Seleucid, but was prevented by Rome. **14**: *Cilicia*, on the southeast coast of Turkey. **15**: Strabo (*Geog.* 16.2.8) locates the *battle* on the river Oenoparus near Antioch. **16**: *Arabia*, the great desert east of Damascus and extending into southern Jordan; cf. Gal 1.17. **17**: *Zabdiel*; Diodorus 32.9,10 gives the name Diocles, blaming Alexander's death on two of his officers. **18**: Seriously wounded, *Ptolemy* died after surgery, having seen Alexander's severed head (Josephus, *Ant.* 13.118). *Strongholds*, cf. 11.3. **19**: *Demetrius* had arrived to claim his crown two years earlier (10.67), and took it in *the one hundred sixty-seventh year*, probably summer 145 BCE.

11.20–37: Jonathan's agreement with Demetrius II. 20: Jonathan's attack on the *citadel* shows that Demetrius's promise (10.32), if authentic, was not fulfilled. **23**: Jonathan negotiates from a position of strength. **26**: *Predecessors*, i.e., Demetrius I and Alexander. **27**: *High priesthood*, see 10.20n. *Other honors*, presumably his military and civil rule of Judea (10.65). *Chief Friends*, cf. Alexander's honors, 10.65. **28**: *To free . . . from tribute*, a major request; possession of the *three districts* (10.38) was confirmed, but *tribute* remission not granted (v. 34). *Three hundred talents*, in lieu of tribute; a talent weighed about 75 lb (34 kg). **32**: *Lasthenes*, not Demetrius's *father* but the general of his Cretan mercenaries. **34**: *Confirmed as their possession*, according to 10.38, specifically under the high priest's authority. *Aphairema* (Ephraim in Jn 11.54), *Lydda* (Lod, Ezra 2.2) and *Rathamin* (Arimathea in Lk 23.50) lie to the north and northwest of Judea; see maps on pp. 202, 205. *To all those who offer sacrifice in Jerusalem* (i.e., the priesthood), if taken with the preceding words, the revenues of the three districts benefit the priesthood (cf. 10.38); if with the following words (so NRSV), the priests are offered *release* from *taxes* on *crops* and *fruit, salt,* and *crown taxes* (v. 35; see 10.29–30). Demetrius is perhaps allowing that Jerusalem shall be "holy

the region bordering them, were added to Judea from Samaria. To all those who offer sacrifice in Jerusalem we have granted release from[a] the royal taxes that the king formerly received from them each year, from the crops of the land and the fruit of the trees. [35] And the other payments henceforth due to us of the tithes, and the taxes due to us, and the salt pits and the crown taxes due to us—from all these we shall grant them release. [36] And not one of these grants shall be canceled from this time on forever. [37] Now therefore take care to make a copy of this, and let it be given to Jonathan and put up in a conspicuous place on the holy mountain.'"

[38] When King Demetrius saw that the land was quiet before him and that there was no opposition to him, he dismissed all his troops, all of them to their own homes, except the foreign troops that he had recruited from the islands of the nations. So all the troops who had served under his predecessors hated him. [39] A certain Trypho had formerly been one of Alexander's supporters; he saw that all the troops were grumbling against Demetrius. So he went to Imalkue the Arab, who was bringing up Antiochus, the young son of Alexander, [40] and insistently urged him to hand Antiochus[b] over to him, to become king in place of his father. He also reported to Imalkue[b] what Demetrius had done and told of the hatred that the troops of Demetrius[c] had for him; and he stayed there many days.

[41] Now Jonathan sent to King Demetrius the request that he remove the troops of the citadel from Jerusalem, and the troops in the strongholds; for they kept fighting against Israel. [42] And Demetrius sent this message back to Jonathan: "Not only will I do these things for you and your nation, but I will confer great honor on you and your nation, if I find an opportunity. [43] Now then you will do well to send me men who will help me, for all my troops have revolted." [44] So Jonathan sent three thousand stalwart men to him at Antioch, and when they came to the king, the king rejoiced at their arrival.

[45] Then the people of the city assembled within the city, to the number of a hundred and twenty thousand, and they wanted to kill the king. [46] But the king fled into the palace. Then the people of the city seized the main streets of the city and began to fight. [47] So the king called the Jews to his aid, and they all rallied around him and then spread out through the city; and they killed on that day about one hundred thousand. [48] They set fire to the city and seized a large amount of spoil on that day, and saved the king. [49] When the people of the city saw that the Jews had gained control of the city as they pleased, their courage failed and they cried out to the king with this entreaty: [50] "Grant us peace, and make the Jews stop fighting against us and our city." [51] And they threw down their arms and made peace. So the Jews gained glory in the sight of the king and of all the people in his kingdom, and they returned to Jerusalem with a large amount of spoil.

[52] So King Demetrius sat on the throne of his kingdom, and the land was quiet before him. [53] But he broke his word about all that he had promised; he became estranged from Jonathan and did not repay the favors that Jonathan[d] had done him, but treated him very harshly.

[54] After this Trypho returned, and with him the young boy Antiochus who began to reign and put on the crown. [55] All the troops that Demetrius had discharged gathered

a   Or *Samaria, for all those who offer sacrifice in Jerusalem, in place of*

b   Gk *him*

c   Gk *his troops*

d   Gk *he*

and tax-free" (cf. 10.31), the taxes going to support the official rituals. **37:** *Copy*, cf. 8.22; *holy mountain*, Mount Zion. Note that Demetrius rejects cancellation of tribute, and retains control of the citadel.

11.38–59: The appearance of Trypho. 39: *Trypho*, "self-indulgent," the nickname of Diodotus, former officer of Demetrius I and Alexander. *Imalkue*, possibly son of Zabdiel (11.17). *Antiochus*, born ca. 150 BCE. **41:** *Remove the troops*, presumably Jonathan had withdrawn his attack (11.20) under the agreement. *Strongholds*, Beth-zur and Gazara (see 9.52). **42–44:** Demetrius agrees, in return for military assistance. *Antioch*, ca. 300 mi (500 km) north of Jerusalem. **46–48:** Josephus (*Ant.* 13.135–41) describes the fighting. **53:** Demetrius reneges and, according to

around him; they fought against Demetrius,[a] and he fled and was routed. [56] Trypho captured the elephants[b] and gained control of Antioch. [57] Then the young Antiochus wrote to Jonathan, saying, "I confirm you in the high priesthood and set you over the four districts and make you one of the king's Friends." [58] He also sent him gold plates and a table service, and granted him the right to drink from gold cups and dress in purple and wear a gold buckle. [59] He appointed Jonathan's[c] brother Simon governor from the Ladder of Tyre to the borders of Egypt.

[60] Then Jonathan set out and traveled beyond the river and among the towns, and all the army of Syria gathered to him as allies. When he came to Askalon, the people of the city met him and paid him honor. [61] From there he went to Gaza, but the people of Gaza shut him out. So he besieged it and burned its suburbs with fire and plundered them. [62] Then the people of Gaza pleaded with Jonathan, and he made peace with them, and took the sons of their rulers as hostages and sent them to Jerusalem. And he passed through the country as far as Damascus.

[63] Then Jonathan heard that the officers of Demetrius had come to Kadesh in Galilee with a large army, intending to remove him from office. [64] He went to meet them, but left his brother Simon in the country. [65] Simon encamped before Beth-zur and fought against it for many days and hemmed it in. [66] Then they asked him to grant them terms of peace, and he did so. He removed them from there,

took possession of the town, and set a garrison over it.

[67] Jonathan and his army encamped by the waters of Gennesaret. Early in the morning they marched to the plain of Hazor, [68] and there in the plain the army of the foreigners met him; they had set an ambush against him in the mountains, but they themselves met him face to face. [69] Then the men in ambush emerged from their places and joined battle. [70] All the men with Jonathan fled; not one of them was left except Mattathias son of Absalom and Judas son of Chalphi, commanders of the forces of the army. [71] Jonathan tore his clothes, put dust on his head, and prayed. [72] Then he turned back to the battle against the enemy[d] and routed them, and they fled. [73] When his men who were fleeing saw this, they returned to him and joined him in the pursuit as far as Kadesh, to their camp, and there they encamped. [74] As many as three thousand of the foreigners fell that day. And Jonathan returned to Jerusalem.

12 Now when Jonathan saw that the time was favorable for him, he chose men and sent them to Rome to confirm and renew the friendship with them. [2] He also sent letters to the same effect to the Spartans and to other places. [3] So they went to Rome and entered the senate chamber

a   Gk *him*
b   Gk *animals*
c   Gk *his*
d   Gk *them*

Josephus (*Ant.* 13.143), demands payment of back taxes. **54:** Trypho establishes *Antiochus VI*. **55:** *Discharged*, Gk "sent to the crows," suggesting contempt; this rebounded on Demetrius. **57:** The *four districts*, i.e., the three Samarian districts with Judea (11.34), or perhaps with Ekron (10.89). **58:** *Gold buckle*, cf. 10.89. **59:** Jonathan was already governor of Judea (10.65); *Simon* is now made Seleucid *governor* of the whole coastal region (with which he was familiar; see 10.74–85) from Ras en-Naqura, north of Ptolemais, to the Egyptian border (cf. Cendebaeus, 15.38).

   11.60–74: Campaigns of Jonathan and Simon. 60: *Beyond the river*, the Greek means that Jonathan toured the province west of the Euphrates. *Askalon* (see 10.86n.) welcomed Jonathan; *Gaza* (ca. 12 mi [20 km] south of Askalon) opposed him, as it had Alexander the Great. **63:** *Kadesh in Galilee*, Tell Qades (Josh 12.22). **65–66:** *Beth-zur*, cf. 9.52; 11.41. **67:** *The waters of Gennesaret*, the Sea of Galilee, to the north of which, in *the plain of Hazor*, Jonathan intended to counter Demetrius at Kadesh. **71:** Cf. Josh 7.6–9. **74:** This narrative continues in 12.24.

   12.1–23: Alliances with Rome and Sparta. 1: *The time was favorable*, the date is between Antiochus VI's accession (145 BCE) and Jonathan's death (142 BCE; 13.23), after Rome's destruction of the Achaean League in Greece (see 8.9–10n.). *Renew*, see 8.17–32. **2:** The *Spartans* (v. 2), a militaristic people, the rival of Athens in Greece, whose constitution, founded by the lawgiver Lycurgus, may have seemed to the Jews comparable to the Law of Moses. **3–4:** The renewal is assumed; the Romans sent *letters* to *people in every place* (compare the list in 15.22–23) requesting *safe conduct* for the envoys' return; Josephus preserves a similar letter (*Ant.* 14.233). **5–18:**

and said, "The high priest Jonathan and the Jewish nation have sent us to renew the former friendship and alliance with them." [4] And the Romans[a] gave them letters to the people in every place, asking them to provide for the envoys[b] safe conduct to the land of Judah.

[5] This is a copy of the letter that Jonathan wrote to the Spartans: [6] "The high priest Jonathan, the senate of the nation, the priests, and the rest of the Jewish people to their brothers the Spartans, greetings. [7] Already in time past a letter was sent to the high priest Onias from Arius,[c] who was king among you, stating that you are our brothers, as the appended copy shows. [8] Onias welcomed the envoy with honor, and received the letter, which contained a clear declaration of alliance and friendship. [9] Therefore, though we have no need of these things, since we have as encouragement the holy books that are in our hands, [10] we have undertaken to send to renew our family ties and friendship with you, so that we may not become estranged from you, for considerable time has passed since you sent your letter to us. [11] We therefore remember you constantly on every occasion, both at our festivals and on other appropriate days, at the sacrifices that we offer and in our prayers, as it is right and proper to remember brothers. [12] And we rejoice in your glory. [13] But as for ourselves, many trials and many wars have encircled us; the kings around us have waged war against us. [14] We were unwilling to annoy you and our other allies and friends with these wars, [15] for we have the help that comes from Heaven for our aid, and so we were delivered from our enemies, and our enemies were humbled. [16] We therefore have chosen Numenius son of Antiochus and Antipater son of Jason, and have sent them to Rome to renew our former friendship and alliance with them. [17] We have commanded them to go also to you and greet you and deliver to you this letter from us concerning the renewal of our family ties. [18] And now please send us a reply to this."

[19] This is a copy of the letter that they sent to Onias: [20] "King Arius of the Spartans, to the high priest Onias, greetings. [21] It has been found in writing concerning the Spartans and the Jews that they are brothers and are of the family of Abraham. [22] And now that we have learned this, please write us concerning your welfare; [23] we on our part write to you that your livestock and your property belong to us, and ours belong to you. We therefore command that our envoys[a] report to you accordingly."

[24] Now Jonathan heard that the commanders of Demetrius had returned, with a larger force than before, to wage war against him. [25] So he marched away from Jerusalem and met them in the region of Hamath, for he gave them no opportunity to invade his own country. [26] He sent spies to their camp, and they returned and reported to him that the enemy[a] were being drawn up in formation to attack the Jews[b] by night. [27] So when the

a Gk *they*
b Gk *them*
c Vg Compare verse 20: Gk *Darius*

This *letter* is a fiction concocted by the author; behind it lies the letter of vv. 19–21. **6:** Senate (Gk "gerousia"), elsewhere "elders" (cf. 7.33); later the Sanhedrin. *Brothers*, see vv. 6,11,21. **7:** *High priest Onias, Arius*, either Onias I (323–300 BCE) and Arius I (309–265), though the contact is most unlikely at this date; or Onias III (so Josephus, *Ant.* 12.225) murdered in 174 BCE (2 Macc 4.34), though there was no contemporary king *Arius* of Sparta (the author perhaps used the only Spartan royal name known to him). *Appended copy*, vv. 19–21. **9:** *Holy books*, "the Law and the Prophets and the other books of our ancestors" (Sir *Prologue*). **11–12:** Surely insincere. **13–15:** If authentic, tactless, with no reference to Spartan political difficulties. **16:** *Numenius, Antipater*, cf. 8.17n.; 14.22. **17:** The sending of ambassadors to Rome *also to you* is equally undiplomatic. **19–21:** This letter is probably inauthentic, though perhaps deriving from a source also known to Josephus (*Ant.* 12.225–27). **21:** *Brothers, of the family of Abraham*, an idea unlikely from a Spartan king. **23:** *Livestock* and *property*, most unlikely between Sparta and Judea. Although these letters were fictional, however, the diplomatic contacts they presuppose were real; the Spartan "kinship" is noted in 2 Macc 5.9.

12.24–38: Jonathan's war with Demetrius, continued. This narrative continues from 11.74. **25:** Reference to Jerusalem here and in 11.74 suggests that Jonathan returned south for the winter. **25:** *Hamath*, on the Orontes

sun had set, Jonathan commanded his troops to be alert and to keep their arms at hand so as to be ready all night for battle, and he stationed outposts around the camp. [28] When the enemy heard that Jonathan and his troops were prepared for battle, they were afraid and were terrified at heart; so they kindled fires in their camp and withdrew.[a] [29] But Jonathan and his troops did not know it until morning, for they saw the fires burning. [30] Then Jonathan pursued them, but he did not overtake them, for they had crossed the Eleutherus river. [31] So Jonathan turned aside against the Arabs who are called Zabadeans, and he crushed them and plundered them. [32] Then he broke camp and went to Damascus, and marched through all that region.

[33] Simon also went out and marched through the country as far as Askalon and the neighboring strongholds. He turned aside to Joppa and took it by surprise, [34] for he had heard that they were ready to hand over the stronghold to those whom Demetrius had sent. And he stationed a garrison there to guard it.

[35] When Jonathan returned he convened the elders of the people and planned with them to build strongholds in Judea, [36] to build the walls of Jerusalem still higher, and to erect a high barrier between the citadel and the city to separate it from the city, in order to isolate it so that its garrison[b] could neither buy nor sell. [37] So they gathered together to rebuild the city; part of the wall on the valley to the east had fallen, and he repaired the section called Chaphenatha. [38] Simon also built Adida in the Shephelah; he fortified it and installed gates with bolts.

[39] Then Trypho attempted to become king in Asia and put on the crown, and to raise his hand against King Antiochus. [40] He feared that Jonathan might not permit him to do so, but might make war on him, so he kept seeking to seize and kill him, and he marched out and came to Beth-shan. [41] Jonathan went out to meet him with forty thousand picked warriors, and he came to Beth-shan. [42] When Trypho saw that he had come with a large army, he was afraid to raise his hand against him. [43] So he received him with honor and commended him to all his Friends, and he gave him gifts and commanded his Friends and his troops to obey him as they would himself. [44] Then he said to Jonathan, "Why have you put all these people to so much trouble when we are not at war? [45] Dismiss them now to their homes and choose for yourself a few men to stay with you, and come with me to Ptolemais. I will hand it over to you as well as the other strongholds and the remaining troops and all the officials, and will turn around and go home. For that is why I am here."

[46] Jonathan[c] trusted him and did as he said; he sent away the troops, and they returned to the land of Judah. [47] He kept with himself three thousand men, two thousand of whom he left in Galilee, while one thousand accompanied him. [48] But when Jonathan entered Ptolemais, the people of Ptolemais closed the gates and seized him, and they killed with the sword all who had entered with him.

[49] Then Trypho sent troops and cavalry into Galilee and the Great Plain to destroy all Jonathan's soldiers. [50] But they realized that Jonathan had been seized and had perished

---

a Other ancient authorities omit *and withdrew*
b Gk *they*
c Gk *he*

River in northern Syria. **30**: *Crossed the Eleutherus river* (see 11.7n.), i.e., southwest toward the coast. **31**: *Zabadeans*, cf. Zabdiel (11.17), and modern Zebdani, north-northwest of *Damascus* (v. 32). **33–34**: Simon, in the south (11.64–65) surprises *Joppa* (previously taken by Jonathan, 10.76) and garrisons it. **35**: *Strongholds*, perhaps those built by Bacchides (9.50) and later deserted (10.12). **36**: *Still higher*, cf. 10.11. The *barrier* blockading the citadel and its garrison presaged its fall (13.49–52). **37**: *Valley to the east*, the Kidron. *Chaphenatha*, unidentified. **38**: *Adida*, Hadid (Ezra 2.33) near Lydda (11.34). *Shephelah*, foothills west of Judea.

12.39–53: Trypho captures Jonathan. 39: *King in Asia*, cf. 11.13. **40**: *Beth-shan* (see 5.52n.), at a strategic point in the Jordan Valley (5.52). **45**: *Ptolemais*, hostile to the Jews (5.15). Trypho repeats Demetrius's false promise (10.39). *Other strongholds*, apart from Beth-zur, Joppa, and Adida, already in Jewish hands. **48**: *Jonathan is seized*, but not yet killed (see 13.23). **49**: *Great Plain*, also called the Valley of Jezreel (Judg 6.33) and the plain of Es-

along with his men, and they encouraged one another and kept marching in close formation, ready for battle. ⁵¹ When their pursuers saw that they would fight for their lives, they turned back. ⁵² So they all reached the land of Judah safely, and they mourned for Jonathan and his companions and were in great fear; and all Israel mourned deeply. ⁵³ All the nations around them tried to destroy them, for they said, "They have no leader or helper. Now therefore let us make war on them and blot out the memory of them from humankind."

13 Simon heard that Trypho had assembled a large army to invade the land of Judah and destroy it, ² and he saw that the people were trembling with fear. So he went up to Jerusalem, and gathering the people together ³ he encouraged them, saying to them, "You yourselves know what great things my brothers and I and the house of my father have done for the laws and the sanctuary; you know also the wars and the difficulties that my brothers and I have seen. ⁴ By reason of this all my brothers have perished for the sake of Israel, and I alone am left. ⁵ And now, far be it from me to spare my life in any time of distress, for I am not better than my brothers. ⁶ But I will avenge my nation and the sanctuary and your wives and children, for all the nations have gathered together out of hatred to destroy us."

⁷ The spirit of the people was rekindled when they heard these words, ⁸ and they answered in a loud voice, "You are our leader in place of Judas and your brother Jonathan. ⁹ Fight our battles, and all that you say to us we will do." ¹⁰ So he assembled all the warriors and hurried to complete the walls of Jerusalem, and he fortified it on every side. ¹¹ He sent Jonathan son of Absalom to Joppa, and with him a considerable army; he drove out its occupants and remained there.

¹² Then Trypho left Ptolemais with a large army to invade the land of Judah, and Jonathan was with him under guard. ¹³ Simon encamped in Adida, facing the plain. ¹⁴ Trypho learned that Simon had risen up in place of his brother Jonathan, and that he was about to join battle with him, so he sent envoys to him and said, ¹⁵ "It is for the money that your brother Jonathan owed the royal treasury, in connection with the offices he held, that we are detaining him. ¹⁶ Send now one hundred talents of silver and two of his sons as hostages, so that when released he will not revolt against us, and we will release him."

¹⁷ Simon knew that they were speaking deceitfully to him, but he sent to get the money and the sons, so that he would not arouse great hostility among the people, who might say, ¹⁸ "It was because Simonᵃ did not send him the money and the sons, that Jonathanᵇ perished." ¹⁹ So he sent the sons and the hundred talents, but Tryphoᵇ broke his word and did not release Jonathan.

²⁰ After this Trypho came to invade the country and destroy it, and he circled around by the way to Adora. But Simon and his army kept marching along opposite him to every place he went. ²¹ Now the men in the citadel kept sending envoys to Trypho urging him to come to them by way of the wilderness and to send them food. ²² So Trypho got all his cavalry

ᵃ Gk *I*
ᵇ Gk *he*

---

draelon (Jdt 1.8), extending from Mount Carmel to the Jordan Valley. **52–53:** *Mourned*, though Jonathan was not dead; *blot out the memory*, dramatic exaggeration (cf. 3.35).

13.1–11: Simon becomes leader. The date is somewhere between the accession of Demetrius II in 145 BCE (11.19) and the regaining of independence in 143 or 142 BCE (13.41). If Jonathan's campaigns (11.63–74; 12.24–32) belong to 144 BCE, Simon perhaps took over in 143 BCE. **4:** *Brothers . . . perished*, Eleazar (6.46), Judas (9.18), John (9.38); *I alone am left*, cf. 1 Kings 18.22. Jonathan, however, was still alive (cf. 13.23). **7–8:** These verses echo 2.67–68 and 9.28–31. In 2.67–68 Mattathias commissions his sons; in 9.28 the "friends of Judas" appointed Jonathan; now the people appoint Simon, an indication of political development. **10:** Simon urgently completes Jonathan's fortification of Jerusalem (12.35–37). **11:** *Jonathan son of Absalom*, perhaps brother of Mattathias (11.70). Simon strengthens his control of *Joppa* (cf. 12.33–34). The capture of this harbor was "to crown all his honor" (14.5).

13.12–30: Trypho invades Judea; the death of Jonathan. 13: *Adida*, see 12.38n. **16:** *Talents*, see 11.28n. **20:** *Ado-*

ready to go, but that night a very heavy snow fell, and he did not go because of the snow. He marched off and went into the land of Gilead. [23] When he approached Baskama, he killed Jonathan, and he was buried there. [24] Then Trypho turned and went back to his own land.

[25] Simon sent and took the bones of his brother Jonathan, and buried him in Modein, the city of his ancestors. [26] All Israel bewailed him with great lamentation, and mourned for him many days. [27] And Simon built a monument over the tomb of his father and his brothers; he made it high so that it might be seen, with polished stone at the front and back. [28] He also erected seven pyramids, opposite one another, for his father and mother and four brothers. [29] For the pyramids[a] he devised an elaborate setting, erecting about them great columns, and on the columns he put suits of armor for a permanent memorial, and beside the suits of armor he carved ships, so that they could be seen by all who sail the sea. [30] This is the tomb that he built in Modein; it remains to this day.

[31] Trypho dealt treacherously with the young King Antiochus; he killed him [32] and became king in his place, putting on the crown of Asia; and he brought great calamity on the land. [33] But Simon built up the strongholds of Judea and walled them all around, with high towers and great walls and gates and bolts, and he stored food in the strongholds. [34] Simon also chose emissaries and sent them to King Demetrius with a request to grant relief to the country, for all that Trypho did was to plunder. [35] King Demetrius sent him a favorable reply to this request, and wrote him a letter as follows, [36] "King Demetrius to Simon, the high priest and friend of kings, and to the elders and nation of the Jews, greetings. [37] We have received the gold crown and the palm branch that you[b] sent, and we are ready to make a general peace with you and to write to our officials to grant you release from tribute. [38] All the grants that we have made to you remain valid, and let the strongholds that you have built be your possession. [39] We pardon any errors and offenses committed to this day, and cancel the crown tax that you owe; and whatever other tax has been collected in Jerusalem shall be collected no longer. [40] And if any of you are qualified to be enrolled in our bodyguard,[c] let them be enrolled, and let there be peace between us."

[41] In the one hundred seventieth year[d] the yoke of the Gentiles was removed from Israel, [42] and the people began to write in their documents and contracts, "In the first year of Simon the great high priest and commander and leader of the Jews."

[43] In those days Simon[e] encamped against Gazara[f] and surrounded it with troops. He

---

a Gk *For these*
b The word *you* in verses 37-40 is plural
c Or *court*
d 142 B.C.
e Gk *he*
f Cn: Gk *Gaza*

---

ra (Adoraim, 2 Chr 11.9), a Hellenistic town in Idumea, southwest of Beth-zur, held by Simon. **22:** *Gilead*, east of the River Jordan. **23:** *Baskama*, unidentified, perhaps near the Sea of Galilee. **25–29:** *Modein*, see 2.1. Simon builds above the family tomb a typically Hellenistic victory *monument*, with *pyramids, columns, armor* (trophies), and *carved ships*; Simon (perhaps emulating Solomon; see 1 Kings 9.26–28; 10.11–12,22) was signaling Jewish marine ambitions for which the capture of Joppa was important.

13.31–53. Simon regains independence for Judea. 31–32: *Trypho . . . became king*, killing Antiochus, probably late 143, or 142 BCE. The last known coins of Antiochus VI are dated year 171, i.e., 142–141 BCE. *Crown of Asia*, cf. 12.39. **33:** *Strongholds*, Simon continues the policy of 11.66; 12.35,38. **34:** *Plunder*: the underlying Heb word ("ṭerepah") puns on Trypho. **36:** *High priest*, see 14.38,41. *Friend of kings*, an irregular and suspect phrase. *Elders*, see 7.33; 12.6n.,35. *Nation*, 11.30. **37:** *Gold crown, palm branch*, diplomatic gifts, tokens of allegiance (cf. 2 Macc 14.4). *General peace, release from tribute*, the latter, long sought (cf. 11.28) meant independence. **38:** *Strongholds*, Beth-zur, Adida, Joppa. **39:** *Crown tax, other tax*, ceded already (11.35). **40:** *Enrolled in our bodyguard*, cf. 10.36, which merely allowed enrollment in the king's forces. **41:** *Yoke of the Gentiles*, i.e., Seleucid rule. *The one hundred seventieth year*, reckoned from 312 or 311 BCE, began in spring 143 or 142 BCE; the date is therefore 142 or 141 BCE. **42:** *Documents and contracts*, unfortunately none survive. The titles *high priest* (14.27,38,41), *commander* (11.59), and *leader of the Jews* (perhaps the "ethnarch" of 14.47) were conferred by the Seleucids. **43:** *Gazara*, a correction

made a siege engine, brought it up to the city, and battered and captured one tower. [44] The men in the siege engine leaped out into the city, and a great tumult arose in the city. [45] The men in the city, with their wives and children, went up on the wall with their clothes torn, and they cried out with a loud voice, asking Simon to make peace with them; [46] they said, "Do not treat us according to our wicked acts but according to your mercy." [47] So Simon reached an agreement with them and stopped fighting against them. But he expelled them from the city and cleansed the houses in which the idols were located, and then entered it with hymns and praise. [48] He removed all uncleanness from it, and settled in it those who observed the law. He also strengthened its fortifications and built in it a house for himself.

[49] Those who were in the citadel at Jerusalem were prevented from going in and out to buy and sell in the country. So they were very hungry, and many of them perished from famine. [50] Then they cried to Simon to make peace with them, and he did so. But he expelled them from there and cleansed the citadel from its pollutions. [51] On the twenty-third day of the second month, in the one hundred seventy-first year,[a] the Jews[b] entered it with praise and palm branches, and with harps and cymbals and stringed instruments, and with hymns and songs, because a great enemy had been crushed and removed from Israel. [52] Simon[c] decreed that every year they should celebrate this day with rejoicing. He strengthened the fortifications of the temple hill alongside the citadel, and he and his men lived there. [53] Simon saw that his son John

had reached manhood, and so he made him commander of all the forces; and he lived at Gazara.

14 In the one hundred seventy-second year[d] King Demetrius assembled his forces and marched into Media to obtain help, so that he could make war against Trypho. [2] When King Arsaces of Persia and Media heard that Demetrius had invaded his territory, he sent one of his generals to take him alive. [3] The general[c] went and defeated the army of Demetrius, and seized him and took him to Arsaces, who put him under guard.

[4] The land[e] had rest all the days of Simon.
   He sought the good of his nation;
his rule was pleasing to them,
   as was the honor shown him, all his
      days.
[5] To crown all his honors he took Joppa for
    a harbor,
   and opened a way to the isles of the sea.
[6] He extended the borders of his nation,
   and gained full control of the country.
[7] He gathered a host of captives;
   he ruled over Gazara and Beth-zur and
     the citadel,
and he removed its uncleanness from it;
   and there was none to oppose him.
[8] They tilled their land in peace;
   the ground gave its increase,
   and the trees of the plains their fruit.

---

a   141 B.C.
b   Gk *they*
c   Gk *He*
d   140 B.C.
e   Other ancient authorities add *of Judah*

for Gk "Gaza" (11.61), which remained independent until 96 BCE. Gazara, garrisoned by Bacchides (9.52), was an important capture. **47:** *Idols*, cf. the treatment of Azotus (5.68). **48:** *House*, an inscription found in Gazara calls for fire to descend on Simon's palace. **49–50:** The *citadel* (cf. 12.36) is finally starved out and ritually cleansed. **51:** *Twenty-third day of the second month* (Iyyar), a major event, dated precisely in late May/early June 142 or 141 BCE, and celebrated annually (mentioned in *Megillat Ta'anith*, "Scroll of Fasting"). *Harps*, etc: cf. 4.54. **52:** *Fortifications of the temple hill*, cf. 12.36. **53:** *John*, see 16.1–24.

14.1–3: Exile of Demetrius II. 1: The *one hundred and seventy-second year* began in autumn 141 BCE, and the campaign in spring 140 BCE. **2:** *Persia and Media*, formerly part of the Seleucid empire, were under Parthian control; *Arsaces* VI Mithradates I (171–138 BCE) occupied Seleucia on the Tigris. Demetrius attempted to recover Babylonia. **3:** Arsaces held Demetrius, but gave him his daughter as wife. Demetrius regained his throne and ruled 129–126 BCE.

14.4–15: Poetic eulogy of Simon. Compare the ode in praise of Judas, 3.3–9. **4:** *Had rest*, cf. Judg 3.30; 5.31; etc. **5:** *Joppa*, 13.11. **6:** *Extended the borders*, Jonathan had added three districts (11.34); Simon settled Jews in

⁹ Old men sat in the streets;
> they all talked together of good things,
> and the youths put on splendid military
> attire.

¹⁰ He supplied the towns with food,
> and furnished them with the means of
> defense,
> until his renown spread to the ends of
> the earth.

¹¹ He established peace in the land,
> and Israel rejoiced with great joy.

¹² All the people sat under their own vines
> and fig trees,
> and there was none to make them
> afraid.

¹³ No one was left in the land to fight them,
> and the kings were crushed in those
> days.

¹⁴ He gave help to all the humble among his
> people;
> he sought out the law,
> and did away with all the renegades and
> outlaws.

¹⁵ He made the sanctuary glorious,
> and added to the vessels of the
> sanctuary.

¹⁶ It was heard in Rome, and as far away as Sparta, that Jonathan had died, and they were deeply grieved. ¹⁷ When they heard that his brother Simon had become high priest in his stead, and that he was ruling over the country and the towns in it, ¹⁸ they wrote to him on bronze tablets to renew with him the friendship and alliance that they had established with his brothers Judas and Jonathan.

¹⁹ And these were read before the assembly in Jerusalem.

²⁰ This is a copy of the letter that the Spartans sent:

"The rulers and the city of the Spartans to the high priest Simon and to the elders and the priests and the rest of the Jewish people, our brothers, greetings. ²¹ The envoys who were sent to our people have told us about your glory and honor, and we rejoiced at their coming. ²² We have recorded what they said in our public decrees, as follows, 'Numenius son of Antiochus and Antipater son of Jason, envoys of the Jews, have come to us to renew their friendship with us. ²³ It has pleased our people to receive these men with honor and to put a copy of their words in the public archives, so that the people of the Spartans may have a record of them. And they have sent a copy of this to the high priest Simon.'"

²⁴ After this Simon sent Numenius to Rome with a large gold shield weighing one thousand minas, to confirm the alliance with the Romans.ᵃ

²⁵ When the people heard these things they said, "How shall we thank Simon and his sons? ²⁶ For he and his brothers and the house of his father have stood firm; they have fought and repulsed Israel's enemies and established its freedom." ²⁷ So they made a record on bronze tablets and put it on pillars on Mount Zion.

ᵃ Gk *them*

Joppa and Gazara. **7:** The capture of *Gazara, Beth-zur,* and the *citadel* were major achievements. **8–15:** Simon's Judea is pictured in idyllic and scriptural terms from Lev 26.4; 1 Kings 4.25; Ezek 36.33–36; Mic 4.4; Zech 8.4; and elsewhere. **15:** *Made the sanctuary glorious,* no details are known.

14.16–24: Diplomacy with Rome and Sparta. These verses, interweaving contacts with Rome and Sparta, must be connected with 12.1–23 and 15.15–24, and present many problems. **16:** *As far away as Sparta,* an editorial link between two separate accounts. **18:** The Romans *wrote,* a most unlikely initiative. Probably they were responding to Simon's initiative described in v. 24. *Bronze tablets* suggest memorial plaques, not letters. *Renew . . . established with . . . Judas and Jonathan,* cf. 8.21; 12.1. **20–23:** This *letter* is clearly linked with that of 12.5–18 and seems equally inauthentic. **24:** *Numenius,* cf. 12.16; 14.22; 15.15. His travels are incomprehensible in their present sequence; this visit to Rome *to confirm the alliance* belongs before the Roman response of 14.8. *Gold shield . . . one thousand minas,* an enormous gift (weighing more than 1,100 lb [500 kg]) for a small nation.

14.25–49: Decree in honor of Simon. Such decrees were common in the Hellenistic world. They usually record the honorand's achievements in "whereas" clauses (cf. "since," v. 29), ending with the decree ("it seemed good to . . . "; cf. "have resolved," v. 41). **27:** *A record on bronze tablets,* cf. 8.21; 14.18. *Mount Zion,* 4.37; cf. Ps 2.6. *Copy,* vv. 27–45 seem partly quotation, partly reportage by 1 Macc. *The eighteenth day of Elul, in the one hundred seventy-second year,* a Jewish date, 13 September 141 or 140 BCE. Simon's *third year,* his first was year 170; cf. 13.41.

This is a copy of what they wrote: "On the eighteenth day of Elul, in the one hundred seventy-second year,[a] which is the third year of the great high priest Simon, [28] in Asaramel,[b] in the great assembly of the priests and the people and the rulers of the nation and the elders of the country, the following was proclaimed to us:

[29] "Since wars often occurred in the country, Simon son of Mattathias, a priest of the sons[c] of Joarib, and his brothers, exposed themselves to danger and resisted the enemies of their nation, in order that their sanctuary and the law might be preserved; and they brought great glory to their nation. [30] Jonathan rallied the[d] nation, became their high priest, and was gathered to his people. [31] When their enemies decided to invade their country and lay hands on their sanctuary, [32] then Simon rose up and fought for his nation. He spent great sums of his own money; he armed the soldiers of his nation and paid them wages. [33] He fortified the towns of Judea, and Beth-zur on the borders of Judea, where formerly the arms of the enemy had been stored, and he placed there a garrison of Jews. [34] He also fortified Joppa, which is by the sea, and Gazara, which is on the borders of Azotus, where the enemy formerly lived. He settled Jews there, and provided in those towns[e] whatever was necessary for their restoration.

[35] "The people saw Simon's faithfulness[f] and the glory that he had resolved to win for his nation, and they made him their leader and high priest, because he had done all these things and because of the justice and loyalty that he had maintained toward his nation. He sought in every way to exalt his people. [36] In his days things prospered in his hands, so that the Gentiles were put out of the[d] country, as were also those in the city of David in Jerusalem, who had built themselves a citadel from which they used to sally forth and defile the environs of the sanctuary, doing great damage to its purity. [37] He settled Jews in it and fortified it for the safety of the country and of the city, and built the walls of Jerusalem higher.

[38] "In view of these things King Demetrius confirmed him in the high priesthood, [39] made him one of his Friends, and paid him high honors. [40] For he had heard that the Jews were addressed by the Romans as friends and allies and brothers, and that the Romans[g] had received the envoys of Simon with honor.

[41] "The Jews and their priests have resolved that Simon should be their leader and high priest forever, until a trustworthy prophet should arise, [42] and that he should be governor over them and that he should take charge of the sanctuary and appoint officials over its tasks and over the country and the weapons and the strongholds, and that he should take charge of the sanctuary, [43] and that he should be obeyed by all, and that all contracts in the

---

a   140 B.C.
b   This word resembles the Hebrew words for *the court of the people of God* or *the prince of the people of God*
c   Meaning of Gk uncertain
d   Gk *their*
e   Gk *them*
f   Other ancient authorities read *conduct*
g   Gk *they*

28: *Asaramel,* a corruption (see textual note *b*), possibly of the title "prince of God's people." **30:** *Became their high priest,* 10.20–21. This reference to Jonathan is intrusive in a decree honoring Simon. **31:** *Enemies . . . invade their country,* i.e., Trypho, 13.1. **32:** *His own money,* like other Hellenistic rulers, Simon paid for his army. **33–34:** *Fortified . . . Judea* (12.38; 13.33), *Beth-zur* (11.65–66), *Joppa* (12.33–34), *Gazara* (13.43–48), near *Azotus* (14.34). **35:** This verse, speaking of the people's actions, divides vv. 34 and 36, which belong together. **36:** *Gentiles . . . put out,* from Beth-zur (11.66), Joppa (13.1), Gazara (13.47), *citadel* (13.50). **37:** *Settled Jews in it and fortified it,* not mentioned in 13.50. *Built the walls of Jerusalem higher,* continuing Jonathan's work (12.36; 13.52). **38–39:** 1 Macc reports *Demetrius* II's action, not explicitly stated in 13.36–37, and motivation, clearly not original to the decree. **40:** The author similarly adds reference to Roman approval of Simon. **41–43:** The actual decree making Simon *leader* (Gk "hegoumenos," 13.8,42), *high priest* ("archiereus," 13.36,42), and *governor* ("strategos"; cf. 13.42), with civil, religious and military powers. *High priest forever,* i.e., for life, or to create a priestly dynasty. *Until a trustworthy prophet should arise,* i.e., to approve this high priesthood or reveal another. **42:** *Take charge of the sanctuary,* repeated later (v. 43) and additional here. **43:** *All contracts,* cf. 13.42. *Purple and . . . gold* (buckle): the insignia

country should be written in his name, and that he should be clothed in purple and wear gold.

⁴⁴ "None of the people or priests shall be permitted to nullify any of these decisions or to oppose what he says, or to convene an assembly in the country without his permission, or to be clothed in purple or put on a gold buckle. ⁴⁵ Whoever acts contrary to these decisions or rejects any of them shall be liable to punishment."

⁴⁶ All the people agreed to grant Simon the right to act in accordance with these decisions. ⁴⁷ So Simon accepted and agreed to be high priest, to be commander and ethnarch of the Jews and priests, and to be protector of them all.[a] ⁴⁸ And they gave orders to inscribe this decree on bronze tablets, to put them up in a conspicuous place in the precincts of the sanctuary, ⁴⁹ and to deposit copies of them in the treasury, so that Simon and his sons might have them.

15 Antiochus, son of King Demetrius, sent a letter from the islands of the sea to Simon, the priest and ethnarch of the Jews, and to all the nation; ² its contents were as follows: "King Antiochus to Simon the high priest and ethnarch and to the nation of the Jews, greetings. ³ Whereas certain scoundrels have gained control of the kingdom of our ancestors, and I intend to lay claim to the kingdom so that I may restore it as it formerly was, and have recruited a host of mercenary troops and have equipped warships, ⁴ and intend to make a landing in the country so that I may proceed against those who have destroyed our country and those who have devastated many cities in my kingdom, ⁵ now therefore I confirm to you all the tax remis-

sions that the kings before me have granted you, and a release from all the other payments from which they have released you. ⁶ I permit you to mint your own coinage as money for your country, ⁷ and I grant freedom to Jerusalem and the sanctuary. All the weapons that you have prepared and the strongholds that you have built and now hold shall remain yours. ⁸ Every debt you owe to the royal treasury and any such future debts shall be canceled for you from henceforth and for all time. ⁹ When we gain control of our kingdom, we will bestow great honor on you and your nation and the temple, so that your glory will become manifest in all the earth."

¹⁰ In the one hundred seventy-fourth year[b] Antiochus set out and invaded the land of his ancestors. All the troops rallied to him, so that there were only a few with Trypho. ¹¹ Antiochus pursued him, and Trypho[c] came in his flight to Dor, which is by the sea; ¹² for he knew that troubles had converged on him, and his troops had deserted him. ¹³ So Antiochus encamped against Dor, and with him were one hundred twenty thousand warriors and eight thousand cavalry. ¹⁴ He surrounded the town, and the ships joined battle from the sea; he pressed the town hard from land and sea, and permitted no one to leave or enter it.

¹⁵ Then Numenius and his companions arrived from Rome, with letters to the kings and countries, in which the following was written: ¹⁶ "Lucius, consul of the Romans, to King Ptolemy, greetings. ¹⁷ The envoys of the Jews have come to us as our friends and allies

---

a   Or *to preside over them all*
b   138 B.C.
c   Gk *he*

---

of kings' Friends and high priests (cf. 10.20,89; 14.44). **44–45:** Safeguarding Simon's position. **47:** Simon *agreed to be high priest . . . commander* (Gk "strategos"), *and ethnarch*, an alternate Greek title for "leader of the people." **48:** *Bronze tablets*, cf. v. 27.

15.1–41: Antiochus VII, Trypho, and Simon. 1: With Antiochus VI dead and Demetrius II captive in Parthia, Demetrius's brother *Antiochus* VII Sidetes (named after his home town Side in Pamphylia) acceded in 139 or 138 BCE. *Islands of the sea*, probably Rhodes in the Aegean off the coast of Asia Minor. **2:** *Priest, ethnarch*, cf. 14.47. **5:** *Remissions*, cf. 10.25–45; 11.30–37; 13.38–39. **6:** *Coinage*, a new privilege (but soon withdrawn, v. 27), of minting copper (not silver or gold) coins. No coins of Simon are known. **7:** *Freedom to Jerusalem and the sanctuary* (cf. 10.31; 11.34) may have meant that Jerusalem was to be sacred, with right of asylum, rather than tax exempt. **9:** Antiochus clearly assumes that Judea, though with some independence, remains part of his empire. **10:** *Trypho*, cf. 12.39. *The one hundred and seventy-fourth year* began in autumn 139 BCE; Antiochus set out the following spring. **11:** *Dor*, an ancient port south of Mount Carmel. **15–24:** These verses interrupt the account of Antio-

to renew our ancient friendship and alliance. They had been sent by the high priest Simon and by the Jewish people [18] and have brought a gold shield weighing one thousand minas. [19] We therefore have decided to write to the kings and countries that they should not seek their harm or make war against them and their cities and their country, or make alliance with those who war against them. [20] And it has seemed good to us to accept the shield from them. [21] Therefore if any scoundrels have fled to you from their country, hand them over to the high priest Simon, so that he may punish them according to their law."

[22] The consul[a] wrote the same thing to King Demetrius and to Attalus and Ariarathes and Arsaces, [23] and to all the countries, and to Sampsames,[b] and to the Spartans, and to Delos, and to Myndos, and to Sicyon, and to Caria, and to Samos, and to Pamphylia, and to Lycia, and to Halicarnassus, and to Rhodes, and to Phaselis, and to Cos, and to Side, and to Aradus and Gortyna and Cnidus and Cyprus and Cyrene. [24] They also sent a copy of these things to the high priest Simon.

[25] King Antiochus besieged Dor for the second time, continually throwing his forces against it and making engines of war; and he shut Trypho up and kept him from going out or in. [26] And Simon sent to Antiochus[c] two thousand picked troops, to fight for him, and silver and gold and a large amount of military equipment. [27] But he refused to receive them, and broke all the agreements he formerly had made with Simon, and became estranged from him. [28] He sent to him Athenobius, one of his Friends, to confer with him, saying, "You hold control of Joppa and Gazara and the citadel in Jerusalem; they are cities of my kingdom. [29] You have devastated their territory, you have done great damage in the land, and you have taken possession of many places in my kingdom. [30] Now then, hand over the cities that you have seized and the tribute money of the places that you have conquered outside the borders of Judea; [31] or else pay me five hundred talents of silver for the destruction that you have caused and five hundred talents more for the tribute money of the cities. Otherwise we will come and make war on you."

[32] So Athenobius, the king's Friend, came to Jerusalem, and when he saw the splendor of Simon, and the sideboard with its gold and silver plate, and his great magnificence, he was amazed. When he reported to him the king's message, [33] Simon said to him in reply: "We have neither taken foreign land nor seized foreign property, but only the inheritance of our ancestors, which at one time had been unjustly taken by our enemies. [34] Now that we have the opportunity, we are firmly holding the inheritance of our ancestors. [35] As for Joppa and Gazara, which you demand, they were causing great damage among the people and to our land; for them we will give you one hundred talents."

a   Gk *He*
b   The name is uncertain
c   Gk *him*

chus's pursuit of Trypho and clearly belong with 14.24. **16:** *Lucius*, possibly Lucius Caecilius Metellus, *consul* in Rome 142 BCE, or Lucius Valerius Flaccus, praetor 134 BCE and consul 131 BCE, with whom Josephus (*Ant.* 145–148) associates an almost identical Jewish mission (though dating it to Hyrcanus II's time [63–40 BCE]). Josephus has perhaps confused consuls and dating. **18:** *Weighing one thousand minas* (see 14,24n.), according to Josephus (*Ant.* 14.147), "worth fifty thousand gold pieces." **22:** *Demetrius* II, cf. 11.19; 14.1; *Attalus* II (159–38) of Pergamum; *Ariarathes* V (162–131) of Cappadocia; *Arsaces*, cf. 14.2. **23:** A list of independent cities and states: *Sampsames*, possibly Samsun on the Black Sea. In Greece: the *Spartans* (see 12.2), and *Sicyon*, on the Gulf of Corinth. Aegean islands: *Delos*, a free port, notorious for its slave trade, with a Jewish population and synagogue; *Samos*; *Rhodes* (cf. Acts 21.1); *Cos* (cf. Acts 21.1). Crete: *Gortyna*. On the southwest coast of modern Turkey: *Caria* and *Lycia*, states; *Myndos*; *Halicarnassus*, birthplace of the Greek historian Herodotus; *Cnidus*. On the south coast of Turkey: *Pamphylia* (cf. Acts 13.13); *Phaselis*; *Side* (cf.15.1n.), later notorious for piracy. Phoenician coast: *Aradus*. Eastern Mediterranean: *Cyprus*. North Africa: *Cyrene* (cf. Mark 15.21). Ptolemy VIII of Egypt claimed these last two for his empire. **25:** *For the second time*, an inaccurate gloss probably caused by the intrusion of vv. 15–24 into this narrative. **26:** Simon sends military aid to Antiochus, thus accepting his political allegiance. **27:** *Agreements*, cf. vv. 5–9. **28:** *Joppa, Gazara*, and the *citadel* were Seleucid possessions before Simon took them, and Antiochus's claims (vv. 30–31) had some justification. **31:** *Or else* suggests that Antiochus was open to negotiation. *Talents,*

Athenobius[a] did not answer him a word, [36] but returned in wrath to the king and reported to him these words, and also the splendor of Simon and all that he had seen. And the king was very angry.

[37] Meanwhile Trypho embarked on a ship and escaped to Orthosia. [38] Then the king made Cendebeus commander-in-chief of the coastal country, and gave him troops of infantry and cavalry. [39] He commanded him to encamp against Judea, to build up Kedron and fortify its gates, and to make war on the people; but the king pursued Trypho. [40] So Cendebeus came to Jamnia and began to provoke the people and invade Judea and take the people captive and kill them. [41] He built up Kedron and stationed horsemen and troops there, so that they might go out and make raids along the highways of Judea, as the king had ordered him.

16 John went up from Gazara and reported to his father Simon what Cendebeus had done. [2] And Simon called in his two eldest sons Judas and John, and said to them: "My brothers and I and my father's house have fought the wars of Israel from our youth until this day, and things have prospered in our hands so that we have delivered Israel many times. [3] But now I have grown old, and you by Heaven's[b] mercy are mature in years. Take my place and my brother's, and go out and fight for our nation, and may the help that comes from Heaven be with you."

[4] So John[c] chose out of the country twenty thousand warriors and cavalry, and they marched against Cendebeus and camped for the night in Modein. [5] Early in the morning they started out and marched into the plain, where a large force of infantry and cavalry was coming to meet them; and a stream lay between them. [6] Then he and his army lined up against them. He saw that the soldiers were afraid to cross the stream, so he crossed over first; and when his troops saw him, they crossed over after him. [7] Then he divided the army and placed the cavalry in the center of the infantry, for the cavalry of the enemy were very numerous. [8] They sounded the trumpets, and Cendebeus and his army were put to flight; many of them fell wounded and the rest fled into the stronghold. [9] At that time Judas the brother of John was wounded, but John pursued them until Cendebeus[d] reached Kedron, which he had built. [10] They also fled into the towers that were in the fields of Azotus, and John[d] burned it with fire, and about two thousand of them fell. He then returned to Judea safely.

[11] Now Ptolemy son of Abubus had been appointed governor over the plain of Jericho; he had a large store of silver and gold, [12] for he was son-in-law of the high priest. [13] His heart was lifted up; he determined to get control of the country, and made treacherous plans against Simon and his sons, to do away with them. [14] Now Simon was visiting the towns of the country and attending to their needs, and he went down to Jericho with his sons Mattathias and Judas, in the one hundred seventy-seventh year,[e] in the eleventh month, which is the month of Shebat. [15] The son of Abubus received them treacherously

a   Gk *He*
b   Gk *his*
c   Other ancient authorities read *he*
d   Gk *he*
e   134 B.C.

see 11.28n. **32:** *Gold and silver plate*, the gifts of Trypho (11.58), provocatively displayed. **35:** Simon is prepared to negotiate over *Joppa* and *Gazara*. **37:** *Orthosia*, a Phoenician city north of Tripolis. **38:** *Commander-in-chief of the coastal country*, Simon was governor ("strategos") of the coast south of the Ladder of Tyre (cf. 11.59); Antiochus apparently replaces him with the higher ranking ("epistrategos") Cendebaeus. **39:** *Kedron*, cf. 16.9, near Jamnia, perhaps the village of Qatra. **40:** *Jamnia*, cf. 4.15n.; 10.69.

   16.1–10: John defeats Cendebeus. 1: *Gazara*, John's home, cf.13.53. **2–3:** Cf. Mattathias's speech, 2.49–68. **4:** *Modein*, see 2.1n. **8:** *Stronghold*, i.e., Kedron, cf. v. 9; 15.39. **10:** *Azotus*, burned by Jonathan (10.84). These verses give a confusing picture.

   16.11–22: The deaths of Simon and his sons Mattathias and Judas, and the accession of John Hyrcanus. 11–12: *Ptolemy son of Abubus*, Hellenized Semitic names. His wealth came from his governorship of the rich plain of Jericho (cf. Gen 13.10) and his father-in-law's income. **14:** Though retired (v. 3) Simon is still active. *Mattathias* and *Judas*, probably named after Simon's father and uncle. *Shebat*, the date, cast in Jewish form, is

in the little stronghold called Dok, which he had built; he gave them a great banquet, and hid men there. [16] When Simon and his sons were drunk, Ptolemy and his men rose up, took their weapons, rushed in against Simon in the banquet hall and killed him and his two sons, as well as some of his servants. [17] So he committed an act of great treachery and returned evil for good.

[18] Then Ptolemy wrote a report about these things and sent it to the king, asking him to send troops to aid him and to turn over to him the towns and the country. [19] He sent other troops to Gazara to do away with John; he sent letters to the captains asking them to come to him so that he might give them silver and gold and gifts; [20] and he sent other troops to take possession of Jerusalem and the temple hill. [21] But someone ran ahead and reported to John at Gazara that his father and brothers had perished, and that "he has sent men to kill you also." [22] When he heard this, he was greatly shocked; he seized the men who came to destroy him and killed them, for he had found out that they were seeking to destroy him.

[23] The rest of the acts of John and his wars and the brave deeds that he did, and the building of the walls that he completed, and his achievements, [24] are written in the annals of his high priesthood, from the time that he became high priest after his father.

January/February 135 or 134 BCE. **15:** *Dok*, the fortress on the Mount of Temptation above the spring 'Ain Duk, overlooking Jericho. **19:** *Gazara*, John's home (cf. v. 1), ca. 34 mi (55 km) west of Jericho. **20:** Ptolemy's plot failed, information reaching John before Ptolemy could take control. Ptolemy retreated to Dok, where John besieged him, and then fled to Philadelphia (Amman); Josephus, *Ant.* 13.230–235.

16.23–24: Epilogue. Compare the epilogue to Judas's career, 9.22. These verses imitate summaries familiar from 1–2 Kings, e.g., 2 Kings 14.28–29. **23:** John is presented as a worthy successor, with his *brave deeds* and *building of the walls* (probably walls destroyed by Antiochus VII, [Josephus, *Ant.* 13.247], who invaded Judea in 134 BCE, cf. his threat, 15.31). **24:** The author prefers not to describe John's career, referring the reader to *annals*: any existing were probably lost when the Romans destroyed the Temple (70 CE). John's *high priesthood* (134–104 BCE) appears to be in the past. 1 Macc was perhaps written during his high priesthood and completed shortly after it.

2 MACCABEES

TITLE

The title Maccabees derives from Heb *maqqabi*, "hammer" (cf. Isa 44.12), the nickname given to Judas Maccabeus, the leader of the Jewish revolt that the story narrates. The original Greek title was "Book Recounting the Matters Pertaining to Maccabeus." The titles of the two main manuscripts of this work specifically refer to "the deeds of Judas Maccabeus" (terming it, respectively, an "epistle" or an "epitome" about those deeds). This title is especially appropriate for this work, in contrast to 1 Maccabees, which develops the history of several subsequent members of the Hasmonean dynasty after Judas.

CANONICAL STATUS

Second Maccabees is part of the Roman Catholic canon and Eastern Orthodox canons and the Protestant Apocrypha, but has no sacred status in Judaism. The text survived as part of the Septuagint (LXX), the Greek version of the Hebrew scriptures.

DATE, AUTHORSHIP, AND LITERARY HISTORY

In the introduction, the author tells us that the work is an abridgement of a longer work, now lost, written by Jason of Cyrene. Jason, otherwise unknown probably wrote in the mid-second century BCE, within a decade or so of the last events described in the work. The present abridgement was produced not long thereafter, around the same time as 1 Maccabees. Whereas 1 Maccabees was originally composed in Hebrew, 2 Maccabees was composed in Greek.

STRUCTURE AND CONTENTS

The body of the work (chs 4–15) deals with Judean history from King Antiochus IV Epiphanes' ascent to the Seleucid throne in 175 BCE to Judas Maccabeus's victory over the Seleucid general Nicanor in 161 BCE. It is prefaced (chs 1–2) by Palestinian letters urging the Jews of Egypt to celebrate the festival of Hanukkah, which commemorates Judas's purification and rededication of the Temple of Jerusalem in 164 BCE; by the abridger's introduction (2.19–32); and by a story (ch 3) about the way the Temple was miraculously preserved from desecration in the days of Antiochus's predecessor, an episode that in its present context serves as something of an idyllic prologue to the book's main story.

Chapter 4 begins that story with the introduction of Hellenized institutions into Jerusalem, which, according to the author, engendered sinful neglect of true Judaism. God, in response, "disregarded" (5.17) Jerusalem, i.e., suspended his providential care for it and thus allowed terrible things to happen, culminating in Antiochus's decrees against Judaism. These decrees then led to the noble martyrdom of those who refused to obey (chs 6–7).

Beginning in ch 8, however, God's anger changes to mercy (8.5; the pivotal verse of the book), and things go dramatically uphill: Judas Maccabeus wins battle after battle, Antiochus dies a terrible death (ch 9), Judas retakes Jerusalem and restores proper worship in the Temple (ch 10), and further victories bring about the repeal of Antiochus's decrees against Judaism (ch 11). More campaigns follow (chs 12–13) until the Seleucid army, commanded by Nicanor, is finally and decisively defeated. The book ends with the establishment of a holiday, "Nicanor's Day," to commemorate that event.

Accordingly, the main part of the book has two parts, in each of which, in the tradition of biblical dual causality, history and theology coincide. Chapters 4–7 present the problem: sin leads to persecution and Antiochus has the upper hand, while chs 8–15 present the solution: atonement makes for "reconciliation" (5.20; 7.33; 8.29) between the Jews and God, and Judas wins victory after victory until the circle is completed. The narrative opens in 3.1 with "the city" being once upon a time in ideal circumstances, and closes with the announcement in 15.37 that "the city" was restored to (other) ideal circumstances and so remained happily ever after.

INTERPRETATION

The book is a fascinating blend of Hellenism and Judaism. It was composed in the literary Greek of its day, comparable to that of the second-century BCE Greek historian Polybius, and has numerous allusions to Greek literature. For example, the author compares Antiochus's arrogance to that of the Persian king Xerxes (5.21; 9.8), portrays his heroes as complete Hellenistic gentlemen (4.37; 15.12,30), depicts his central martyr as a Jewish Socrates, and throughout the story, focuses upon Jerusalem as the Jews' *polis*, portraying Antiochus as a "barbarian" who tried to change the city's "constitution" and forbid Jews to "act as citizens" (6.1) according to Jewish law. But it is also a very Jewish book; its basic interpretative model is the Song of Moses (Deut 32), according to which God providentially cares for the Jews but hides his face when they sin, thus allowing foreigners to persecute them until the shedding of "his servants'" blood works atonement, so that God steps in, revenges himself upon their enemies, and restores his providential care for them. The author composes several substantial excurses (4.16–17; 5.17–20; 6.12–17), as well as various shorter remarks (e.g., 8.5; 9.13) to make sure readers understand his interpretation of events.

In addition to providing a parallel witness to the events reported in 1 Macc 1–7, this work (apart from the two introductory epistles) also bears witness to Judaism in the Hellenistic Diaspora. While those opening epistles have much in common with 1 Maccabees, the body of the book aligns more easily with such Diaspora works as 3 Maccabees, the Letter of Aristeas, and the works of Philo. This affinity is especially evident in the book's rosy picture of the Jews' usual relations with Gentiles (e.g. 4.35–36,49; contrast 1 Macc 5.1–2; 12.53), its assumption that Gentile rulers are usually benevolent (3.1–3; 5.16; contrast 1 Macc 1.9), its relative lack of interest in the Temple rituals (contrast 5.16 with the detail in 1 Macc 1.21–22 and note 2 Maccabees' emphasis upon God's residence in heaven in 3.39; 14.35), its high esteem for martyrs (see 6.11n.), and its insistence upon the priority of the people rather than the place (5.19; see also 5.6n).

Daniel R. Schwartz

1 The Jews in Jerusalem and those in the land of Judea,
To their Jewish kindred in Egypt,
Greetings and true peace.
² May God do good to you, and may he remember his covenant with Abraham and Isaac and Jacob, his faithful servants. ³ May he give you all a heart to worship him and to do his will with a strong heart and a willing spirit. ⁴ May he open your heart to his law and his commandments, and may he bring peace. ⁵ May he hear your prayers and be reconciled to you, and may he not forsake you in time of evil. ⁶ We are now praying for you here.
⁷ In the reign of Demetrius, in the one hundred sixty-ninth year,[a] we Jews wrote to you, in the critical distress that came upon us in those years after Jason and his company revolted from the holy land and the kingdom ⁸ and burned the gate and shed innocent blood. We prayed to the Lord and were heard, and we offered sacrifice and grain offering, and we lit the lamps and set out the loaves. ⁹ And now see that you keep the festival of booths in the month of Chislev, in the one hundred eighty-eighth year.[b]

a   143 B.C.
b   124 B.C.

1.1–9: Letter to the Jews in Egypt. This letter from Jerusalem invites the Jews of Egypt to observe the Hanukkah festival by referring to a previous letter written in the *one hundred sixty-ninth year* of the Seleucid era (v. 7), in the reign of Demetrius II, i.e., 143/142 BCE, which overlapped the first year of Hasmonean independence, according to 1 Macc 13.41. The letter portrays the Jews' troubles as having begun with Jason's revolt against the kingdom (v. 7), i.e., the kingdom of God; see ch 4. Thus, this epistle was written as something of a cover letter accompanying the body of the work, in an attempt to convince the Jews of Egypt to join in celebrating the Hasmoneans' victory. **2:** See Gen 15.18; 26.3; 35.12. **8:** *Lit the lamps and set out the loaves*, as mandated by Lev 24.1–9; see 10.3. **9:** *Festival of booths in the month of Chislev*, i.e., Hanukkah. The festival of booths (or tabernacles; Heb "Sukkoth") is celebrated in the autumn month of Tishri (September); Chislev (November/December) of 164 is when Judas retook the Temple, purified it, and rededicated it in a celebration reminiscent of that of the autumn festival (see 10.6–7). *In the one hundred eighty-eighth year*, if this date, ca. 124 BCE, is authentic, then this letter is quoting one of 143/142 BCE. But the date may be corrupt.

¹⁰ The people of Jerusalem and of Judea and the senate and Judas,

To Aristobulus, who is of the family of the anointed priests, teacher of King Ptolemy, and to the Jews in Egypt,

Greetings and good health.

¹¹ Having been saved by God out of grave dangers we thank him greatly for taking our side against the king,[a] ¹² for he drove out those who fought against the holy city. ¹³ When the leader reached Persia with a force that seemed irresistible, they were cut to pieces in the temple of Nanea by a deception employed by the priests of the goddess[b] Nanea. ¹⁴ On the pretext of intending to marry her, Antiochus came to the place together with his Friends, to secure most of its treasures as a dowry. ¹⁵ When the priests of the temple of Nanea had set out the treasures and Antiochus had come with a few men inside the wall of the sacred precinct, they closed the temple as soon as he entered it. ¹⁶ Opening a secret door in the ceiling, they threw stones and struck down the leader and his men; they dismembered them and cut off their heads and threw them to the people outside. ¹⁷ Blessed in every way be our God, who has brought judgment on those who have behaved impiously.

¹⁸ Since on the twenty-fifth day of Chislev we shall celebrate the purification of the temple, we thought it necessary to notify you, in order that you also may celebrate the festival of booths and the festival of the fire given when Nehemiah, who built the temple and the altar, offered sacrifices.

¹⁹ For when our ancestors were being led captive to Persia, the pious priests of that time took some of the fire of the altar and secretly hid it in the hollow of a dry cistern, where they took such precautions that the place was unknown to anyone. ²⁰ But after many years had passed, when it pleased God, Nehemiah, having been commissioned by the king of Persia, sent the descendants of the priests who had hidden the fire to get it. And when they reported to us that they had not found fire but only a thick liquid, he ordered them to dip it out and bring it. ²¹ When the materials for the sacrifices were presented, Nehemiah ordered the priests to sprinkle the liquid on the wood and on the things laid upon it. ²² When this had been done and some time had passed,

a Cn: Gk *as those who array themselves against a king*
b Gk lacks *the goddess*

1.10–2.18: Another letter to the Jews of Egypt. This letter focuses on the history of the fire on the altar of the Temple of Jerusalem, working backward from Nehemiah through Jeremiah to Solomon. It claims that the fire that descended from heaven in the days of Solomon (2.10; 2 Chr 7.3) was hidden by pious priests at the time of the destruction of the First Temple (1.19). At the time of the restoration, it was found by Nehemiah, after a metamorphosis into a viscous and combustible liquid (1.20–36). He used some of it to rekindle the fire on the altar of the Second Temple, while the rest of it was preserved in rocks (1.31–32), from which Judas would eventually extract it when rededicating the Temple (10.3). So the restored Temple still had the original fire that descended from heaven. Thus, this letter constitutes an extended argument for the legitimacy of the Second Temple by connecting Nehemiah's restoration and Judas's rededication to Solomon's original dedication. **10:** *The senate,* lit. "council of elders." *Judas* Maccabeus; this letter is presented as if it were written in contemplation of the first Hanukkah or perhaps its first anniversary. *Aristobulus* was an Alexandrian Jewish philosopher and biblical exegete in the days of *Ptolemy* VI Philometor, king of Egypt, 180–145 BCE. By naming him merely "Ptolemy" the Judean authors show how little they care about that foreign king; contrast the use of "Philometor" in the body of the book (4.21; 9.29).

1.11–16: Antiochus Epiphanes' death in Persia. For other versions of Antiochus's death during his eastern campaign, taken here to be part of God's rescue of the Jews, see ch 9 and 1 Macc 6.1–16. **14:** *His Friends,* courtiers of high rank; cf. 7.24; 14.11. This is not the only case of a fictive "sacred marriage" being used as a pretext to obtain money from a sanctuary. **18:** *The festival of booths,* cf. 1 Macc 10.21; 1 Kings 8.2; Neh 8.13–18.

1.19–36: The latest link: the preservation of the fire. This story assumes that Nehemiah rebuilt the Second Temple. In fact, he was active in the mid-fifth century BCE, several generations after the construction of the Second Temple. The mistake was common in Jewish tradition, which frequently remembered the Persian period as shorter than it really was. **19:** *Persia,* the exiles were actually led to Babylonia (cf. 2 Kings 24.14), which later became part of the Persian empire. **20:** *Nehemiah . . . commissioned,* Neh 2.7–8. **22:** *The sun . . . a great fire blazed*

and when the sun, which had been clouded over, shone out, a great fire blazed up, so that all marveled. ²³ And while the sacrifice was being consumed, the priests offered prayer— the priests and everyone. Jonathan led, and the rest responded, as did Nehemiah. ²⁴ The prayer was to this effect:

"O Lord, Lord God, Creator of all things, you are awe-inspiring and strong and just and merciful, you alone are king and are kind, ²⁵ you alone are bountiful, you alone are just and almighty and eternal. You rescue Israel from every evil; you chose the ancestors and consecrated them. ²⁶ Accept this sacrifice on behalf of all your people Israel and preserve your portion and make it holy. ²⁷ Gather together our scattered people, set free those who are slaves among the Gentiles, look on those who are rejected and despised, and let the Gentiles know that you are our God. ²⁸ Punish those who oppress and are insolent with pride. ²⁹ Plant your people in your holy place, as Moses promised."

³⁰ Then the priests sang the hymns. ³¹ After the materials of the sacrifice had been consumed, Nehemiah ordered that the liquid that was left should be poured on large stones. ³² When this was done, a flame blazed up; but when the light from the altar shone back, it went out. ³³ When this matter became known, and it was reported to the king of the Persians that, in the place where the exiled priests had hidden the fire, the liquid had appeared with which Nehemiah and his associates had burned the materials of the sacrifice, ³⁴ the king investigated the matter, and enclosed the place and made it sacred. ³⁵ And with those persons whom the king favored he exchanged many excellent gifts.

³⁶ Nehemiah and his associates called this "nephthar," which means purification, but by most people it is called naphtha.[a]

2 One finds in the records that the prophet Jeremiah ordered those who were being deported to take some of the fire, as has been mentioned, ² and that the prophet, after giving them the law, instructed those who were being deported not to forget the commandments of the Lord, or to be led astray in their thoughts on seeing the gold and silver statues and their adornment. ³ And with other similar words he exhorted them that the law should not depart from their hearts.

⁴ It was also in the same document that the prophet, having received an oracle, ordered that the tent and the ark should follow with him, and that he went out to the mountain where Moses had gone up and had seen the inheritance of God. ⁵ Jeremiah came and found a cave-dwelling, and he brought there the tent and the ark and the altar of incense; then he sealed up the entrance. ⁶ Some of those who followed him came up intending to mark the way, but could not find it. ⁷ When Jeremiah learned of it, he rebuked them and declared: "The place shall remain unknown until God gathers his people together again and shows his mercy. ⁸ Then the Lord will disclose these things, and the glory of the Lord and the cloud will appear, as they were shown in the case of Moses, and as Solomon asked that the place should be specially consecrated."

⁹ It was also made clear that being possessed of wisdom Solomon[b] offered sacrifice

---

[a] Gk *nephthai*
[b] Gk *he*

---

up, with no human involvement, as in the days of Solomon (2.10; 2 Chr 7.3). The story also echoes one about Elijah in 1 Kings 18.33–38. **23:** *Jonathan* is unknown, although it may refer to Mattaniah "who was the leader to begin the thanksgiving in prayer" (Neh 11.17) and whose name, like Jonathan, also means "God's gift" in Hebrew. **27:** *Gather . . . set free those who are slaves among the Gentiles,* this Judean attitude contrasts diametrically with that of the Diaspora author of the body of the book. **29:** *As Moses promised,* Ex 15.17; Deut 30.5. **34:** The Persians considered fire holy and sometimes *enclosed* sites of *sacred* fire. **36:** *"Nephthar," which means purification,* this etymology is obscure but Hanukkah is often seen as a purification; cf. 2.18; 10.3.

2.1–8: The penultimate link: Jeremiah. The tradition that Jeremiah saw to the hiding of various ritual objects at the time the First Temple was destroyed supplements the preceding one about what "pious priests" (1.19) did at the same time. For similar traditions, see *2 Baruch* 6. **2:** *Instructed those who were being deported,* see Letter of Jeremiah. **4:** *Mountain,* Nebo (Deut 32.49). *Inheritance of God* refers to the Holy Land in this Judean letter; elsewhere, notably in Deut 32.9, it often refers to the people (see 5.19n. and 6.16n.). **9–10:** *Solomon,* 1 Kings 8.62–64;

for the dedication and completion of the temple. [10] Just as Moses prayed to the Lord, and fire came down from heaven and consumed the sacrifices, so also Solomon prayed, and the fire came down and consumed the whole burnt offerings. [11] And Moses said, "They were consumed because the sin offering had not been eaten." [12] Likewise Solomon also kept the eight days.

[13] The same things are reported in the records and in the memoirs of Nehemiah, and also that he founded a library and collected the books about the kings and prophets, and the writings of David, and letters of kings about votive offerings. [14] In the same way Judas also collected all the books that had been lost on account of the war that had come upon us, and they are in our possession. [15] So if you have need of them, send people to get them for you.

[16] Since, therefore, we are about to celebrate the purification, we write to you. Will you therefore please keep the days? [17] It is God who has saved all his people, and has returned the inheritance to all, and the kingship and the priesthood and the consecration, [18] as he promised through the law. We have hope in God that he will soon have mercy on us and will gather us from everywhere under heaven into his holy place, for he has rescued us from great evils and has purified the place.

[19] The story of Judas Maccabeus and his brothers, and the purification of the great temple, and the dedication of the altar, [20] and further the wars against Antiochus Epiphanes and his son Eupator, [21] and the appearances that came from heaven to those who fought bravely for Judaism, so that though few in number they seized the whole land and pursued the barbarian hordes, [22] and regained possession of the temple famous throughout the world, and liberated the city, and re-established the laws that were about to be abolished, while the Lord with great kindness became gracious to them— [23] all this, which has been set forth by Jason of Cyrene in five volumes, we shall attempt to condense into a single book. [24] For considering the flood of statistics involved and the difficulty there is for those who wish to enter upon the narratives of history because of the mass of material, [25] we have aimed to please those who wish to read, to make it easy for those who are inclined to memorize, and to profit all readers. [26] For us who have undertaken the toil of abbreviating, it is no light matter but calls for sweat and loss of sleep, [27] just as it is not easy for one who prepares a banquet and seeks the benefit of others. Nevertheless, to secure the gratitude of many we will gladly endure the uncomfortable toil, [28] leaving the responsibility for exact details to the compiler, while devoting our effort to arriving at the outlines of the condensation. [29] For as the master builder of a new house must be concerned with the whole construction, while the one who undertakes

---

2 Chr 7.1. **10:** *Moses prayed*, Lev 9.24. **11:** *"They were consumed . . ."* does not appear in the Bible, but may refer to the story in Lev 10.16–19. **12:** *The eight days* of dedicatory celebrations by Moses (Lev 8.33–9.1) and Solomon (2 Chr 7.9) are cited as precedents for Hanukkah (10.6). **13–14:** *Memoirs of Nehemiah . . . Judas also collected*, the biblical book of Nehemiah does not contain these references. Cf. Ezra 3.1–6; 1 Esd 5.46–50. It is important for the author, however, to underline these parallels between the putative founder of the Second Temple and its restorer, so that his claims are documented and thus should be believed by his addressees. Although there is no other evidence for the claim that Nehemiah *founded a library*, the reference to *kings and prophets, and the writings of David* sounds like a way of referring to the latter two parts of the Hebrew canon; compare the prologue to Sir and Lk 24.44. *Votive offerings*, such as those mentioned in 3.2 and 5.16. **17:** *All . . . to all*, including the Jews of Egypt. *Kingship and the priesthood*, a usual Jewish way of reading the promise of Ex 19.6.

2.19–32: The author's preface. 19–23. An involved sentence, in which the author shows his control of Greek from the outset. **21:** *Appearances* (Gk "epiphaneiai") *. . . from heaven* are given significant attention in the ensuing narrative at 3.24–26; 5.2–4; 10.29; 11.8; 12.22; etc. These true "epiphanies" are contrasted with the arrogant villain's byname, "Epiphanes." *Judaism*, the first known use of this term for the religion. *Barbarian hordes* as a term referring to the Greeks is a calculated reversal, which allows the author to mobilize the sympathies of Greek readers; so too 5.22; 13.9; 15.2. **23:** The five-volume work of *Jason of Cyrene*, of which 2 Macc is an abridgement, is no longer extant. *Cyrene*, in Libya. **29:** The author compares his work to that of a decorator, in

its painting and decoration has to consider only what is suitable for its adornment, such in my judgment is the case with us. [30] It is the duty of the original historian to occupy the ground, to discuss matters from every side, and to take trouble with details, [31] but the one who recasts the narrative should be allowed to strive for brevity of expression and to forego exhaustive treatment. [32] At this point therefore let us begin our narrative, without adding any more to what has already been said; for it would be foolish to lengthen the preface while cutting short the history itself.

3 While the holy city was inhabited in unbroken peace and the laws were strictly observed because of the piety of the high priest Onias and his hatred of wickedness, [2] it came about that the kings themselves honored the place and glorified the temple with the finest presents, [3] even to the extent that King Seleucus of Asia defrayed from his own revenues all the expenses connected with the service of the sacrifices.

[4] But a man named Simon, of the tribe of Benjamin, who had been made captain of the temple, had a disagreement with the high priest about the administration of the city market. [5] Since he could not prevail over Onias, he went to Apollonius of Tarsus,[a] who

at that time was governor of Coelesyria and Phoenicia, [6] and reported to him that the treasury in Jerusalem was full of untold sums of money, so that the amount of the funds could not be reckoned, and that they did not belong to the account of the sacrifices, but that it was possible for them to fall under the control of the king. [7] When Apollonius met the king, he told him of the money about which he had been informed. The king[b] chose Heliodorus, who was in charge of his affairs, and sent him with commands to effect the removal of the reported wealth. [8] Heliodorus at once set out on his journey, ostensibly to make a tour of inspection of the cities of Coelesyria and Phoenicia, but in fact to carry out the king's purpose.

[9] When he had arrived at Jerusalem and had been kindly welcomed by the high priest of[c] the city, he told about the disclosure that had been made and stated why he had come, and he inquired whether this really was the situation. [10] The high priest explained that there were some deposits belonging to widows and orphans, [11] and also some money of Hyrcanus son of Tobias, a man of very promi-

---

a   Gk *Apollonius son of Tharseas*
b   Gk *He*
c   Other ancient authorities read *and*

relation to Jason's original construction; for another analogy, see 15.39.

3.1–3: **Prologue.** Once upon a time everything was fine. **1:** *The holy city*, this opening bracket announces the book's topic; for the closing bracket, see 15.37. In the next two verses, the author quickly moves, using the inclusive term "place" (v. 2, compare 13.23), to the Temple. *Onias* III, son of Simeon II (whose praises are sung in Sir 50). He turned against Syria and collaborated with Egypt, while his cousins, the family of Tobias, to which Simon (v. 4) belonged, were pro-Syrian. For the notion that his piety guaranteed the stability of the city, compare Sir 10.2. *Hatred of wickedness*, a universal moral quality that also characterizes good Gentiles (4.36,49) and God himself (8.4). **3:** *King Seleucus* IV ruled 187–175 BCE. *Asia* was frequently used of the Seleucid kingdom.

3.4–40: **Simon's plot against Onias. 4:** *But* signals the beginning of the story; compare 12.2 and 14.26. *A man named Simon*, just as Greek kings are generally represented as benevolent and the villainous Antiochus is an exception, so too concerning Jewish villains, our author prefers lone wolves and bad apples, not parties; see 4.7 (contrast 1 Macc 1.13–14),40; 14.3 (contrast 1 Macc 7.5, also 1.11; 2.46). That is, the author in general portrays his world as good, with only occasional problems; contrast the world according to 1 Maccabees, which needed serious revision by the Hasmoneans. *Of the tribe of Benjamin*, since 4.23 identifies Menelaus as Simon's brother, many scholars prefer to read, with Latin witnesses, "of Bilgah" (a priestly clan, 1 Chr 24.14). **5:** *Tarsus*, capital of Cilicia in southern Asia Minor (Acts 21.39), then part of the Seleucid empire. *Coelesyria*, lit. "hollow Syria" (see 1 Macc 10.69n.), here used of Palestine. **6:** Simon apparently claimed that the royal budgets, earmarked for sacrifices (as in v. 3), were in fact being accumulated. **7:** *Heliodorus*, the prime minister of Seleucus IV, is known from inscriptions and historical sources. **11:** *Hyrcanus son of Tobias*, a well-known aristocratic Jewish family in Transjordan; see also 12.17. Hyrcanus was pro-Egyptian. He fled east of the Jordan after 198 BCE and built the fortress now known as Araq el-Emir. He committed suicide on the accession of Antiochus IV in 175. A *talent*

nent position, and that it totaled in all four hundred talents of silver and two hundred of gold. To such an extent the impious Simon had misrepresented the facts. ¹² And he said that it was utterly impossible that wrong should be done to those people who had trusted in the holiness of the place and in the sanctity and inviolability of the temple that is honored throughout the whole world.

¹³ But Heliodorus, because of the orders he had from the king, said that this money must in any case be confiscated for the king's treasury. ¹⁴ So he set a day and went in to direct the inspection of these funds.

There was no little distress throughout the whole city. ¹⁵ The priests prostrated themselves before the altar in their priestly vestments and called toward heaven upon him who had given the law about deposits, that he should keep them safe for those who had deposited them. ¹⁶ To see the appearance of the high priest was to be wounded at heart, for his face and the change in his color disclosed the anguish of his soul. ¹⁷ For terror and bodily trembling had come over the man, which plainly showed to those who looked at him the pain lodged in his heart. ¹⁸ People also hurried out of their houses in crowds to make a general supplication because the holy place was about to be brought into dishonor. ¹⁹ Women, girded with sackcloth under their breasts, thronged the streets. Some of the young women who were kept indoors ran together to the gates, and some to the walls, while others peered out of the windows. ²⁰ And holding up their hands to heaven, they all made supplication. ²¹ There was something pitiable in the prostration of the whole populace and the anxiety of the high priest in his great anguish.

²² While they were calling upon the Almighty Lord that he would keep what had been entrusted safe and secure for those who had entrusted it, ²³ Heliodorus went on with what had been decided. ²⁴ But when he arrived at the treasury with his bodyguard, then and there the Sovereign of spirits and of all authority caused so great a manifestation that all who had been so bold as to accompany him were astounded by the power of God, and became faint with terror. ²⁵ For there appeared to them a magnificently caparisoned horse, with a rider of frightening mien; it rushed furiously at Heliodorus and struck at him with its front hoofs. Its rider was seen to have armor and weapons of gold. ²⁶ Two young men also appeared to him, remarkably strong, gloriously beautiful and splendidly dressed, who stood on either side of him and flogged him continuously, inflicting many blows on him. ²⁷ When he suddenly fell to the ground and deep darkness came over him, his men took him up, put him on a stretcher, ²⁸ and carried him away—this man who had just entered the aforesaid treasury with a great retinue and all his bodyguard but was now unable to help himself. They recognized clearly the sovereign power of God.

²⁹ While he lay prostrate, speechless because of the divine intervention and deprived of any hope of recovery, ³⁰ they praised the Lord who had acted marvelously for his own place. And the temple, which a little while before was full of fear and disturbance, was filled with joy and gladness, now that the Almighty Lord had appeared.

³¹ Some of Heliodorus's friends quickly begged Onias to call upon the Most High to grant life to one who was lying quite at his last breath. ³² So the high priest, fearing that the king might get the notion that some foul play had been perpetrated by the Jews with regard to Heliodorus, offered sacrifice for the man's recovery. ³³ While the high priest was making an atonement, the same young men appeared again to Heliodorus dressed in the same clothing, and they stood and said, "Be very grateful to the high priest Onias, since for his sake the Lord has granted you your life. ³⁴ And see that you, who have been

weighed ca. 75 lb (34 kg). **14–21:** A purple passage, typical of Hellenistic "pathetic" historiography meant to make readers share in the emotions of the characters depicted by vivid rhetoric, as if they were being watched on stage. **15:** *The law about deposits*, see Ex 22.7–13. **19:** *Sackcloth* was a common sign of self-humiliation or mourning, used to support appeals for divine aid; compare 10.25 and Esth 4.1. *Young women who were kept indoors*, cf. Sir 42.9–12. **22–23:** *They . . . Heliodorus*, the author often emphasizes the opposition of the two sides set for a showdown; cf. 10.28; 15.25–26. **26:** *Two young men*, angelic figures, as in 10.30 and 3 Macc 6.18. **34:**

flogged by heaven, report to all people the majestic power of God." Having said this they vanished.

35 Then Heliodorus offered sacrifice to the Lord and made very great vows to the Savior of his life, and having bidden Onias farewell, he marched off with his forces to the king. 36 He bore testimony to all concerning the deeds of the supreme God, which he had seen with his own eyes. 37 When the king asked Heliodorus what sort of person would be suitable to send on another mission to Jerusalem, he replied, 38 "If you have any enemy or plotter against your government, send him there, for you will get him back thoroughly flogged, if he survives at all; for there is certainly some power of God about the place. 39 For he who has his dwelling in heaven watches over that place himself and brings it aid, and he strikes and destroys those who come to do it injury." 40 This was the outcome of the episode of Heliodorus and the protection of the treasury.

4 The previously mentioned Simon, who had informed about the money against[a] his own country, slandered Onias, saying that it was he who had incited Heliodorus and had been the real cause of the misfortune. 2 He dared to designate as a plotter against the government the man who was the benefactor of the city, the protector of his compatriots, and a zealot for the laws. 3 When his hatred progressed to such a degree that even murders were committed by one of Simon's approved agents, 4 Onias recognized that the rivalry was serious and that Apollonius son of Menestheus,[b] and governor of Coelesyria and Phoenicia, was intensifying the malice of Simon. 5 So he appealed to the king, not accusing his compatriots but having in view the welfare, both public and private, of all the people. 6 For he saw that without the king's attention public affairs could not again reach a peaceful settlement, and that Simon would not stop his folly.

7 When Seleucus died and Antiochus, who was called Epiphanes, succeeded to the kingdom, Jason the brother of Onias obtained the high priesthood by corruption, 8 promising the king at an interview[c] three hundred sixty talents of silver, and from another source of revenue eighty talents. 9 In addition to this he promised to pay one hundred fifty more if permission were given to establish by his authority a gymnasium and a body of youth for it, and to enroll the people of Jerusalem as citizens of Antioch. 10 When the king assented and Jason[d] came to office, he at once shifted his compatriots over to the Greek way of life.

11 He set aside the existing royal concessions to the Jews, secured through John

---

a Gk *and*

b Vg Compare verse 21: Meaning of Gk uncertain

c Or *by a petition*

d Gk *he*

Flogged by heaven, in answer to prayers of vv. 15, 20; note esp. v. 39. **36:** *He bore testimony*, as do others in this book who learned the same lesson (8.36; 9.17; 11.13). **39:** *Dwelling in heaven*, an important belief for Diaspora Jews; compare 5.19 and Acts 7.47–50.

4.1–6: Simon plots against Onias again. See 3.4n. The hostility resumes between the two rival Jewish families, contrasting in good Diaspora fashion the Jewish troublemaker Simon to the providential monarch. **4–5:** *Coelesyria*, see 3.5n.

4.7–17: Jason's reforms; "Antioch in Jerusalem." **7:** *When Seleucus died*, 175 BCE. He was said to have been assassinated by Heliodorus (see 3.7). After the Roman defeat of Antiochus III at the battle of Magnesia (190 BCE) and Antiochus's capitulation to Rome in the subsequent Treaty of Apamea, one of his sons, *Antiochus IV*, was held hostage in Rome while another, *Seleucus IV*, reigned on the Syrian throne. With the death of *Seleucus*, Antiochus IV returned to Syria and ascended to the throne, being replaced in Rome by Demetrius I, Seleucus's young son; see 14.1n. **8:** *Talent*, see 3.11n. **9:** *Gymnasium*, a Greek school, the place not only of sport but also of political and cultural education, in short, the hallmark and bearer of Hellenism; cf. 1 Macc 1.14. *As citizens of Antioch*, that is, Jason received permission to establish a "polis", a Greek-style city-state in which citizenship status was essential to participation in political and economic life, called "Antioch in Jerusalem." **11:** *The existing royal concessions*, privileges recorded by Josephus granted by Antiochus III upon the establishment of Seleucid rule in Judea around 200 BCE, including the promise that Jewish law would be observed. The establishment of Antioch in Jerusalem is taken, by our pious author, to abrogate or undercut those privileges. *John the father of*

the father of Eupolemus, who went on the mission to establish friendship and alliance with the Romans; and he destroyed the lawful ways of living and introduced new customs contrary to the law. [12] He took delight in establishing a gymnasium right under the citadel, and he induced the noblest of the young men to wear the Greek hat. [13] There was such an extreme of Hellenization and increase in the adoption of foreign ways because of the surpassing wickedness of Jason, who was ungodly and no true[a] high priest, [14] that the priests were no longer intent upon their service at the altar. Despising the sanctuary and neglecting the sacrifices, they hurried to take part in the unlawful proceedings in the wrestling arena after the signal for the discus-throwing, [15] disdaining the honors prized by their ancestors and putting the highest value upon Greek forms of prestige. [16] For this reason heavy disaster overtook them, and those whose ways of living they admired and wished to imitate completely became their enemies and punished them. [17] It is no light thing to show irreverence to the divine laws—a fact that later events will make clear.

[18] When the quadrennial games were being held at Tyre and the king was present, [19] the vile Jason sent envoys, chosen as being Antiochian citizens from Jerusalem, to carry three hundred silver drachmas for the sacrifice to Hercules. Those who carried the money, however, thought best not to use it for sacrifice, because that was inappropriate, but to expend it for another purpose. [20] So this money was intended by the sender for the sacrifice to Hercules, but by the decision of its carriers it was applied to the construction of triremes.

[21] When Apollonius son of Menestheus was sent to Egypt for the coronation[b] of Philometor as king, Antiochus learned that Philometor[c] had become hostile to his government, and he took measures for his own security. Therefore upon arriving at Joppa he proceeded to Jerusalem. [22] He was welcomed magnificently by Jason and the city, and ushered in with a blaze of torches and with shouts. Then he marched his army into Phoenicia.

[23] After a period of three years Jason sent Menelaus, the brother of the previously mentioned Simon, to carry the money to the king and to complete the records of essential business. [24] But he, when presented to the king, extolled him with an air of authority, and secured the high priesthood for himself,

---

[a] Gk lacks true
[b] Meaning of Gk uncertain
[c] Gk he

Eupolemus is said, here, to have negotiated those privileges, just as his son, Eupolemus, was later to be a Jewish ambassador to Rome (1 Macc 8.17). The move from the father's Hebrew name to the son's Greek name illustrates the rise of Hellenism in contemporary Jerusalem, as does "Jason son of Eleazar," Eupolemus's partner (1 Macc 8.17). **12:** *The Greek hat* was broad-rimmed; symbolic of the acceptance of Greek culture, it also allows our author to show off here with an impressive pun (Gk "hypotasson . . . hypo petason," "induced . . . the hat"). **16–17:** An authorial excursus asserting that sin will not go unpunished.

4.18–22: Two pictures of life in Antioch in Jerusalem. The first story (vv. 18–20) shows that one may be a citizen of a "polis" and still avoid idolatry, and the second (vv. 21–22) shows the Jews were good subjects of the Seleucid king. **18:** *Tyre,* a major city north of Palestine. Regular games had been held there since the late fourth century BCE. **19:** *Envoys* were commonly sent by Greek cities to observe games and celebrations in others. A drachma was equivalent to a day's wages for a laborer. *Hercules,* the Greek name of the god Melkart of Tyre. **20:** *Triremes* were standard Phoenician, Greek, and Roman war ships, with three benches of rowers on each side. **21–22:** *Apollonius,* see v. 4. *Coronation,* or perhaps a coming-of-age ceremony. Ptolemy VI *Philometor* (ca. 180–145 BCE) became *hostile* to Syria, and claimed Palestine, which is why the Seleucid king travels east to secure his relationship with Jerusalem before proceeding to *Phoenicia,* the coastal plain. *Jason and the city,* as at 3.9, the high priest serves as something of a mayor; compare Sir 50.1–4.

4.23–50: Menelaus. The quality of the high priest now goes from bad to worse. If Jason, who supplanted Onias (4.7–8), was guilty of institutionalizing Hellenization in Jerusalem, Menelaus, who supplanted Jason (v. 26!), was a cruel (v. 25) and negligent (v. 27) governor who corruptly sought his own enrichment (v. 32) and did not shrink from murder (v. 34) and bribery (v. 45). He held onto his position, or tried to, until ca. 162 BCE

outbidding Jason by three hundred talents of silver. ²⁵ After receiving the king's orders he returned, possessing no qualification for the high priesthood, but having the hot temper of a cruel tyrant and the rage of a savage wild beast. ²⁶ So Jason, who after supplanting his own brother was supplanted by another man, was driven as a fugitive into the land of Ammon. ²⁷ Although Menelaus continued to hold the office, he did not pay regularly any of the money promised to the king. ²⁸ When Sostratus the captain of the citadel kept requesting payment—for the collection of the revenue was his responsibility—the two of them were summoned by the king on account of this issue. ²⁹ Menelaus left his own brother Lysimachus as deputy in the high priesthood, while Sostratus left Crates, the commander of the Cyprian troops.

³⁰ While such was the state of affairs, it happened that the people of Tarsus and of Mallus revolted because their cities had been given as a present to Antiochis, the king's concubine. ³¹ So the king went hurriedly to settle the trouble, leaving Andronicus, a man of high rank, to act as his deputy. ³² But Menelaus, thinking he had obtained a suitable opportunity, stole some of the gold vessels of the temple and gave them to Andronicus; other vessels, as it happened, he had sold to Tyre and the neighboring cities. ³³ When Onias became fully aware of these acts, he publicly exposed them, having first withdrawn to a place of sanctuary at Daphne near Antioch. ³⁴ Therefore Menelaus, taking Andronicus aside, urged him to kill Onias. Andronicus[a] came to Onias, and resorting to treachery, offered him sworn pledges and gave him his right hand; he persuaded him, though still suspicious, to come out from the place of sanctuary; then, with no regard for justice, he immediately put him out of the way.

³⁵ For this reason not only Jews, but many also of other nations, were grieved and displeased at the unjust murder of the man. ³⁶ When the king returned from the region of Cilicia, the Jews in the city[b] appealed to him with regard to the unreasonable murder of Onias, and the Greeks shared their hatred of the crime. ³⁷ Therefore Antiochus was grieved at heart and filled with pity, and wept because of the moderation and good conduct of the deceased. ³⁸ Inflamed with anger, he immediately stripped off the purple robe from Andronicus, tore off his clothes, and led him around the whole city to that very place where he had committed the outrage against Onias, and there he dispatched the bloodthirsty fellow. The Lord thus repaid him with the punishment he deserved.

³⁹ When many acts of sacrilege had been committed in the city by Lysimachus with the connivance of Menelaus, and when report of them had spread abroad, the populace gathered against Lysimachus, because many of the gold vessels had already been stolen. ⁴⁰ Since the crowds were becoming aroused and filled with anger, Lysimachus armed about three thousand men and launched an unjust attack, under the leadership of a certain Auranus, a man advanced in years and no less advanced in folly. ⁴¹ But when the Jews[c] became aware that Lysimachus was attacking them, some picked up stones, some blocks of wood, and others took handfuls of the ashes that were lying around, and threw them in wild confusion at Lysimachus and his men. ⁴² As a result, they wounded many of them, and killed some, and put all the rest to flight;

a   Gk *He*
b   Or *in each city*
c   Gk *they*

(see 13.3–8). **26:** *Land of Ammon*, east of the Jordan, near modern Amman. **30:** *Tarsus . . . Mallus* were cities in southeastern Asia Minor. Hellenistic kings often provided a wife or concubine with a regular income by giving her a city. Antiochus, being extravagant (see 1 Macc 3.30), was often in need of money. **31:** It is important for our author to claim that when injustice was done the king was absent, and that upon his return (v. 36) the king was enraged and meted out well-deserved punishment. **33:** *Sanctuary at Daphne*, of Apollo. Daphne is about 5 mi (8 km) from Antioch. Andronicus is thus shown to have violated the sanctity of a Greek temple in order to murder the Jewish high priest. **35–36:** *Not only Jews . . . other nations . . . Greeks*, the author insists on the basic unity of humanity and especially upon the Greeks' respect for Jews (see also v. 49 and 12.30–31); after all, Onias was a *man*. **37:** *Moderation and good conduct* were appropriate to a Hellenistic gentleman; cf. 15.12. **38:** *The Lord,*

the temple robber himself they killed close by the treasury.

⁴³ Charges were brought against Menelaus about this incident. ⁴⁴ When the king came to Tyre, three men sent by the senate presented the case before him. ⁴⁵ But Menelaus, already as good as beaten, promised a substantial bribe to Ptolemy son of Dorymenes to win over the king. ⁴⁶ Therefore Ptolemy, taking the king aside into a colonnade as if for refreshment, induced the king to change his mind. ⁴⁷ Menelaus, the cause of all the trouble, he acquitted of the charges against him, while he sentenced to death those unfortunate men, who would have been freed uncondemned if they had pleaded even before Scythians. ⁴⁸ And so those who had spoken for the city and the villagesᵃ and the holy vessels quickly suffered the unjust penalty. ⁴⁹ Therefore even the Tyrians, showing their hatred of the crime, provided magnificently for their funeral. ⁵⁰ But Menelaus, because of the greed of those in power, remained in office, growing in wickedness, having become the chief plotter against his compatriots.

5 About this time Antiochus made his second invasion of Egypt. ² And it happened that, for almost forty days, there appeared over all the city golden-clad cavalry charging through the air, in companies fully armed with lances and drawn swords— ³ troops of cavalry drawn up, attacks and counterattacks made on this side and on that, brandishing of shields, massing of spears, hurling of missiles, the flash of golden trappings, and armor of all kinds. ⁴ Therefore everyone prayed that the apparition might prove to have been a good omen.

⁵ When a false rumor arose that Antiochus was dead, Jason took no fewer than a thousand men and suddenly made an assault on the city. When the troops on the wall had been forced back and at last the city was being taken, Menelaus took refuge in the citadel. ⁶ But Jason kept relentlessly slaughtering his compatriots, not realizing that success at the cost of one's kindred is the greatest misfortune, but imagining that he was setting up trophies of victory over enemies and not over compatriots. ⁷ He did not, however, gain control of the government; in the end he got only disgrace from his conspiracy, and fled again into the country of the Ammonites. ⁸ Finally he met a miserable end. Accusedᵇ before Aretas the ruler of the Arabs, fleeing from city to city, pursued by everyone, hated as a rebel against the laws, and abhorred as the executioner of his country and his compatriots, he was cast ashore in Egypt. ⁹ There he who had driven many from their

---

ᵃ Other ancient authorities read *the people*

ᵇ Cn: Gk *Imprisoned*

---

an explicit statement of dual causality: Antiochus did the Lord's work. **39**: *The city*, Jerusalem. **42**: *Killed close by the treasury*, frequently the punishment fits the crime in 2 Maccabees, thus demonstrating God's equitable management of history; see also vv. 16,26,38. For Menelaus's own end, see 13.8. **45**: *Dorymenes* had fought for Ptolemy IV against Antiochus III; his son *Ptolemy* had been governor of Cyprus and had deserted to Antiochus IV (see 10.12–13). **47**: *Scythians*, a proverbially brutal people north of the Black Sea; see 7.4n. **48**: *The city and the villages and the holy vessels*, see textual note *a*. The reference first of all to the city, and only thereafter to the holy vessels, although the issue pertained to the latter, is typical for the orientation of this book; see 3.1n.

5.1–27: Antiochus IV desecrates the Temple. 1–4: Apparition over Jerusalem. **1:** *Antiochus made his second invasion of Egypt* in the spring of 168 BCE, the first having occurred in 170. The second was successful, although a Roman ultimatum forced him to withdraw (Dan 11.29–30). This humiliation may have created the "false rumor" of Antiochus's death (v. 5). **2–4:** *There appeared over all the city*, an apparition of a military nature. Because its meaning was ambiguous, all the Jerusalemites could do was pray that it be for the good; the rest of the chapter shows it was not. **5–10:** Jason attempts to take Jerusalem. Jason, who had been ousted by Menelaus and expelled from the city (4.26), now attempts a comeback. Because Jason had been forced out of the city (v. 7), although Menelaus had withdrawn to the *citadel* (the Temple mount, v. 5), there was probably a nationalist rebellion against Seleucid rule at the same time, as Antiochus inferred (v. 11). But our author prefers to ignore that; compare 3.4n. **6:** *Compatriots*, lit. "fellow citizens." *Trophies* commemorate victories over *enemies* (15.6), not *compatriots*, lit. "members of his people." In this sentence, the Diaspora author uses first a political (city-oriented) category and then two ethnic ones ("kindred," "members of his people"). **8:** *Aretas* I, king of Nabatean

own country into exile died in exile, having embarked to go to the Lacedaemonians in hope of finding protection because of their kinship. [10] He who had cast out many to lie unburied had no one to mourn for him; he had no funeral of any sort and no place in the tomb of his ancestors.

[11] When news of what had happened reached the king, he took it to mean that Judea was in revolt. So, raging inwardly, he left Egypt and took the city by storm. [12] He commanded his soldiers to cut down relentlessly everyone they met and to kill those who went into their houses. [13] Then there was massacre of young and old, destruction of boys, women, and children, and slaughter of young girls and infants. [14] Within the total of three days eighty thousand were destroyed, forty thousand in hand-to-hand fighting, and as many were sold into slavery as were killed.

[15] Not content with this, Antiochus[a] dared to enter the most holy temple in all the world, guided by Menelaus, who had become a traitor both to the laws and to his country. [16] He took the holy vessels with his polluted hands, and swept away with profane hands the votive offerings that other kings had made to enhance the glory and honor of the place. [17] Antiochus was elated in spirit, and did not perceive that the Lord was angered for a little while because of the sins of those who lived in the city, and that this was the reason he was disregarding the holy place. [18] But if it had not happened that they were involved in many sins, this man would have been flogged and turned back from his rash act as soon as he came forward, just as Heliodorus had been, whom King Seleucus sent to inspect the treasury. [19] But the Lord did not choose the nation for the sake of the holy place, but the place for the sake of the nation. [20] Therefore the place itself shared in the misfortunes that befell the nation and afterward participated in its benefits; and what was forsaken in the wrath of the Almighty was restored again in all its glory when the great Lord became reconciled.

[21] So Antiochus carried off eighteen hundred talents from the temple, and hurried away to Antioch, thinking in his arrogance that he could sail on the land and walk on the sea, because his mind was elated. [22] He left governors to oppress the people: at Jerusalem, Philip, by birth a Phrygian and in character more barbarous than the man who appointed him; [23] and at Gerizim, Andronicus; and besides these Menelaus, who lorded it over his compatriots worse than the others did. In his malice toward the Jewish citizens,[b] [24] Antiochus[a] sent Apollonius, the captain

[a] Gk he
[b] Or worse than the others did in his malice toward the Jewish citizens

Arabia, south and east of Palestine; his capital was at Petra. 9: Rejected in Egypt, Jason fled to the Lacedaemonians in Sparta; other Jewish sources (e.g., 1 Macc 12.7,21) allege a kinship between the Jews and Spartans. 10: Unburied . . . no funeral, a common theme in this book (9.15,28; 12.39; 13.7). 11–16: Antiochus attacks Jerusalem thinking that all Judea, not just the villain Jason, was in revolt. He was raging inwardly because the Romans had forced him out of Egypt (the Roman envoy, Popillius Laenas, had threatened him with war if he attempted to annex Egypt; see 1 Macc 1.20); both his foreign and his domestic programs were collapsing. 12–13: This account of murder of young and old, outside and inside, seems to allude to Deut 32.25. (On Deut 32 as the basic biblical subtext of this book, see the Introduction.) 15: Even Jews were forbidden to enter the most holy parts of the temple. That the high priest Menelaus would guide Antiochus further indicts him as unfit (4.25). 16: The relative lack of interest in ritual details (only "holy vessels"; contrast 1 Macc 1.21–23), and the need to underline that most Gentile kings are benevolent and respectful to Jews, are typically Diasporan.

5.17–20: Authorial excursus (cf. 4.16–17). The author explains that the Temple could suffer this profanation and robbery because it was secondary to the people; for a similar argument see Mk 2.27. 17: For a little while . . . disregarding is the author's Greek way of rendering the biblical notion of God's hiding his face (Deut 32.20), something which he does at times "for a little while" (Isa 54.7–8) due to the Jews' sins. 18: Heliodorus, see ch 3.

5.21–27: Further troubles. 21: Thinking in his arrogance that he could sail on the land and walk on the sea describes Antiochus according to the standard Greek topos of an arrogant oriental monarch. 22: Phrygia, a region of western Asia Minor. 22–23: The people: at Jerusalem . . . at Gerizim, the author considers Samaritans to be Jews, although they worshiped at a different temple. The author's evenhandedness reflects the situation of Diaspora

of the Mysians, with an army of twenty-two thousand, and commanded him to kill all the grown men and to sell the women and boys as slaves. 25 When this man arrived in Jerusalem, he pretended to be peaceably disposed and waited until the holy sabbath day; then, finding the Jews not at work, he ordered his troops to parade under arms. 26 He put to the sword all those who came out to see them, then rushed into the city with his armed warriors and killed great numbers of people.

27 But Judas Maccabeus, with about nine others, got away to the wilderness, and kept himself and his companions alive in the mountains as wild animals do; they continued to live on what grew wild, so that they might not share in the defilement.

6 Not long after this, the king sent an Athenian[a] senator[b] to compel the Jews to forsake the laws of their ancestors and no longer to live by the laws of God; 2 also to pollute the temple in Jerusalem and to call it the temple of Olympian Zeus, and to call the one in Gerizim the temple of Zeus-the-Friend-of-Strangers, as did the people who lived in that place.

3 Harsh and utterly grievous was the onslaught of evil. 4 For the temple was filled with debauchery and reveling by the Gentiles, who dallied with prostitutes and had intercourse with women within the sacred precincts, and besides brought in things

for sacrifice that were unfit. 5 The altar was covered with abominable offerings that were forbidden by the laws. 6 People could neither keep the sabbath, nor observe the festivals of their ancestors, nor so much as confess themselves to be Jews.

7 On the monthly celebration of the king's birthday, the Jews[c] were taken, under bitter constraint, to partake of the sacrifices; and when a festival of Dionysus was celebrated, they were compelled to wear wreaths of ivy and to walk in the procession in honor of Dionysus. 8 At the suggestion of the people of Ptolemais[d] a decree was issued to the neighboring Greek cities that they should adopt the same policy toward the Jews and make them partake of the sacrifices, 9 and should kill those who did not choose to change over to Greek customs. One could see, therefore, the misery that had come upon them. 10 For example, two women were brought in for having circumcised their children. They publicly paraded them around the city, with their babies hanging at their breasts, and then hurled them down headlong from the wall. 11 Others who had assembled in the caves nearby, in order to observe the seventh day secretly, were betrayed to Philip and were

[a] Other ancient authorities read *Antiochian*
[b] Or *Geron an Athenian*
[c] Gk *they*
[d] Cn: Gk *suggestion of the Ptolemies* (or *of Ptolemy*)

Jews who worshiped at neither; cf. Jn 4.21. **24:** *Captain of the Mysians*, lit. "Mysarch," commander of mercenary troops from Mysia, a region of Asia Minor. **25:** *Parade under arms* recalls the apparition in vv. 1–3 and clarifies its meaning. **27:** *Judas Maccabeus*, the third son of Mattathias, of the Hasmonean family (1 Macc 2.1–28). Mention of him here provides a ray of hope throughout the next two chapters of suffering. He will reappear, with a much larger force, at the beginning of ch 8. *Live on what grew wild*, in observance of Jewish dietary laws that prohibited the consumption of unclean animals; cf. 11.31; 1 Macc 1.62–63; Dan 1.8.

6.1–11: Decrees against Judaism. If Jason made Hellenization available in the social, political, and economic spheres, Antiochus now pollutes the Jews' Temple and attempts to force new rituals upon them which, however Semitic or syncretistic, were viewed by many Jews as Greek customs (v. 9), because a Greek king imposed them. **1:** *Athenian*, Antiochus's ties to Athens are well documented; compare 9.15. **2:** As at 5.22–23, the author has no problems about drawing a parallel between the Temple of Jerusalem and that of the Samaritans, which was considered illegitimate by some Jerusalemite Jews. **4:** *The temple* was polluted; see also 1 Macc 1.46–59 and Dan 11.31. **7:** Antiochus's *birthday* was celebrated on the twenty-fifth of each month (1 Macc 1.58–59). *Dionysus*, the Greek god of wine and harvest. **8:** *Ptolemais*, the Hellenistic city founded at Acco, north of Haifa. **10–11:** These first stories of martyrs are paralleled at 1 Macc 1.60–61 and 2.29–38. In contrast to 1 Maccabees, however, our "pathetic" work (see 3.14–21n.) refers (as at 3.19) to the mothers' breasts, not their necks; and as a Diaspora work it praises the martyrs in the caves who refused to fight on the sabbath, as opposed to 1 Macc 2, which uses them as foils for the Hasmoneans.

all burned together, because their piety kept them from defending themselves, in view of their regard for that most holy day.

[12] Now I urge those who read this book not to be depressed by such calamities, but to recognize that these punishments were designed not to destroy but to discipline our people. [13] In fact, it is a sign of great kindness not to let the impious alone for long, but to punish them immediately. [14] For in the case of the other nations the Lord waits patiently to punish them until they have reached the full measure of their sins; but he does not deal in this way with us, [15] in order that he may not take vengeance on us afterward when our sins have reached their height. [16] Therefore he never withdraws his mercy from us. Although he disciplines us with calamities, he does not forsake his own people. [17] Let what we have said serve as a reminder; we must go on briefly with the story.

[18] Eleazar, one of the scribes in high position, a man now advanced in age and of noble presence, was being forced to open his mouth to eat swine's flesh. [19] But he, welcoming death with honor rather than life with pollution, went up to the rack of his own accord, spitting out the flesh, [20] as all ought to go who have the courage to refuse things that it is not right to taste, even for the natural love of life. [21] Those who were in charge of that unlawful sacrifice took the man aside because of their long acquaintance with him, and privately urged him to bring meat of his own providing, proper for him to use, and to pretend that he was eating the flesh of the sacrificial meal that had been commanded by the king, [22] so that by doing this he might be saved from death, and be treated kindly on account of his old friendship with them. [23] But making a high resolve, worthy of his years and the dignity of his old age and the gray hairs that he had reached with distinction and his excellent life even from childhood, and moreover according to the holy God-given law, he declared himself quickly, telling them to send him to Hades.

[24] "Such pretense is not worthy of our time of life," he said, "for many of the young might suppose that Eleazar in his ninetieth year had gone over to an alien religion, [25] and through my pretense, for the sake of living a brief moment longer, they would be led astray because of me, while I defile and disgrace my old age. [26] Even if for the present I would avoid the punishment of mortals, yet whether I live or die I will not escape the hands of the Almighty. [27] Therefore, by bravely giving up my life now, I will show myself worthy of my old age [28] and leave to the young a noble example of how to die a good death willingly and nobly for the revered and holy laws."

When he had said this, he went[a] at once to the rack. [29] Those who a little before had acted toward him with goodwill now changed to ill will, because the words he had uttered were in their opinion sheer madness.[b] [30] When he was about to die under the blows, he groaned aloud and said: "It is clear to the Lord in his holy knowledge that, though I might have been saved from death, I am enduring terrible sufferings in my body under this beating, but in my soul I am glad to suffer these things because I fear him."

[31] So in this way he died, leaving in his death an example of nobility and a memorial of courage, not only to the young but to the great body of his nation.

---

a Other ancient authorities read *was dragged*
b Meaning of Gk uncertain

6.12–17: **Authorial excursus** (cf. 4.16–17; 5.17–20). The author explains to his readers that it is God's graciousness to his people that brings him to allow punishment for sins as they occur, thus enabling atonement and reconciliation. **12:** *To discipline*, as in Deut 8.5. **14:** *Full measure of their sins*, which would then bring upon them irrevocable punishment; Gen 15.16. **16:** *He does not forsake his own people*, Ps 94.14.

6.18–31 **Martyrdom of Eleazar. 18:** *Scribes* were scholars of the Torah; cf. 1 Macc 7.12. 4 Macc 5.4 adds, on unknown authority but not improbably, that Eleazar was a priest. *Swine's flesh* is the best known of biblically prohibited meats (Lev 11.7–8). In this case the problem is compounded because the meat was sacrificed in a pagan rite (v. 21). **23:** *Hades*, the Gk name of the underworld (Heb "Sheol"). **28:** *Leave to the young a noble example*, Eleazar is presented as a Jewish Socrates; his speech resembles Socrates's final speech in Plato's *Apology*. **30:** *Body . . . soul*, a distinction that reflects the influence of Greek anthropology on Jewish thought. *Fear*, revere. **31:** *Not only to the young*, as he said in v. 28; the next chapter, however, focuses on the young.

7 It happened also that seven brothers and their mother were arrested and were being compelled by the king, under torture with whips and thongs, to partake of unlawful swine's flesh. ² One of them, acting as their spokesman, said, "What do you intend to ask and learn from us? For we are ready to die rather than transgress the laws of our ancestors."

³ The king fell into a rage, and gave orders to have pans and caldrons heated. ⁴ These were heated immediately, and he commanded that the tongue of their spokesman be cut out and that they scalp him and cut off his hands and feet, while the rest of the brothers and the mother looked on. ⁵ When he was utterly helpless, the king[a] ordered them to take him to the fire, still breathing, and to fry him in a pan. The smoke from the pan spread widely, but the brothers[b] and their mother encouraged one another to die nobly, saying, ⁶ "The Lord God is watching over us and in truth has compassion on us, as Moses declared in his song that bore witness against the people to their faces, when he said, 'And he will have compassion on his servants.'"[c]

⁷ After the first brother had died in this way, they brought forward the second for their sport. They tore off the skin of his head with the hair, and asked him, "Will you eat rather than have your body punished limb by limb?" ⁸ He replied in the language of his ancestors and said to them, "No." Therefore he in turn underwent tortures as the first brother had done. ⁹ And when he was at his last breath, he said, "You accursed wretch, you dismiss us from this present life, but the King of the universe will raise us up to an everlasting renewal of life, because we have died for his laws."

¹⁰ After him, the third was the victim of their sport. When it was demanded, he quickly put out his tongue and courageously stretched forth his hands, ¹¹ and said nobly, "I got these from Heaven, and because of his laws I disdain them, and from him I hope to get them back again." ¹² As a result the king himself and those with him were astonished at the young man's spirit, for he regarded his sufferings as nothing.

¹³ After he too had died, they maltreated and tortured the fourth in the same way. ¹⁴ When he was near death, he said, "One cannot but choose to die at the hands of mortals and to cherish the hope God gives of being raised again by him. But for you there will be no resurrection to life!"

¹⁵ Next they brought forward the fifth and maltreated him. ¹⁶ But he looked at the king,[d] and said, "Because you have authority among mortals, though you also are mortal, you do what you please. But do not think that God has forsaken our people. ¹⁷ Keep on, and see how his mighty power will torture you and your descendants!"

¹⁸ After him they brought forward the sixth. And when he was about to die, he said, "Do not deceive yourself in vain. For we are suffering these things on our own account, because of our sins against our own God. Therefore[e] astounding things have happened. ¹⁹ But do not think that you will go unpunished for having tried to fight against God!"

---

a   Gk *he*
b   Gk *they*
c   Gk *slaves*
d   Gk *at him*
e   Lat: Other ancient authorities lack *Therefore*

7.1–42: Martyrdom of seven brothers and their mother. This story—which has a life of its own in Jewish literature, is the principal subject of 4 Maccabees, and may be inspired by Jer 15.9—may have been appropriated from an independent source, as is suggested by the king's presence and by the absence of political formulations so typical of this book. **1:** *The king* is Antiochus IV (v. 24), although he returned to Syria in ch 5 and imposed the decrees through his agents. **2:** *Ancestors*, lit. "fathers," who are thus made to compete with the king; compare "language of his ancestors" (i.e., Hebrew) in vv. 8,21,27. **4:** *Scalp*, lit. "cut him around the Scythian way"; see 4.47n. **6:** *As Moses declared*, Deut 32.36. On Deut 32, see Introduction. **9:** *Raise us up*, resurrection is a recurrent theme in this chapter; see also 12.43–45 and 14.46. This belief's only clear attestation in the Hebrew Bible, Dan 12.1–3, seems to be a response to the same persecutions. **11:** *Heaven*, a circumlocution for God; see v. 34. **18:** *Because of our sins*, as in v. 32 and throughout this book; "our" is both specific (as in 12.40) and collective,

²⁰ The mother was especially admirable and worthy of honorable memory. Although she saw her seven sons perish within a single day, she bore it with good courage because of her hope in the Lord. ²¹ She encouraged each of them in the language of their ancestors. Filled with a noble spirit, she reinforced her woman's reasoning with a man's courage, and said to them, ²² "I do not know how you came into being in my womb. It was not I who gave you life and breath, nor I who set in order the elements within each of you. ²³ Therefore the Creator of the world, who shaped the beginning of humankind and devised the origin of all things, will in his mercy give life and breath back to you again, since you now forget yourselves for the sake of his laws."

²⁴ Antiochus felt that he was being treated with contempt, and he was suspicious of her reproachful tone. The youngest brother being still alive, Antiochus[a] not only appealed to him in words, but promised with oaths that he would make him rich and enviable if he would turn from the ways of his ancestors, and that he would take him for his Friend and entrust him with public affairs. ²⁵ Since the young man would not listen to him at all, the king called the mother to him and urged her to advise the youth to save himself. ²⁶ After much urging on his part, she undertook to persuade her son. ²⁷ But, leaning close to him, she spoke in their native language as follows, deriding the cruel tyrant: "My son, have pity on me. I carried you nine months in my womb, and nursed you for three years, and have reared you and brought you up to this point in your life, and have taken care of you.[b] ²⁸ I beg you, my child, to look at the heaven and the earth and see everything that is in them, and recognize that God did not make them out of things that existed.[c] And

in the same way the human race came into being. ²⁹ Do not fear this butcher, but prove worthy of your brothers. Accept death, so that in God's mercy I may get you back again along with your brothers."

³⁰ While she was still speaking, the young man said, "What are you[d] waiting for? I will not obey the king's command, but I obey the command of the law that was given to our ancestors through Moses. ³¹ But you,[e] who have contrived all sorts of evil against the Hebrews, will certainly not escape the hands of God. ³² For we are suffering because of our own sins. ³³ And if our living Lord is angry for a little while, to rebuke and discipline us, he will again be reconciled with his own servants.[f] ³⁴ But you, unholy wretch, you most defiled of all mortals, do not be elated in vain and puffed up by uncertain hopes, when you raise your hand against the children of heaven. ³⁵ You have not yet escaped the judgment of the almighty, all-seeing God. ³⁶ For our brothers after enduring a brief suffering have drunk[g] of ever-flowing life, under God's covenant; but you, by the judgment of God, will receive just punishment for your arrogance. ³⁷ I, like my brothers, give up body and life for the laws of our ancestors, appealing to God to show mercy soon to our nation and by trials and plagues to make you confess that he alone is God, ³⁸ and through me and my brothers to bring to an end the wrath of the Almighty that has justly fallen on our whole nation."

a Gk *he*
b Or *have borne the burden of your education*
c Or *God made them out of things that did not exist*
d The Gk here for *you* is plural
e The Gk here for *you* is singular
f Gk *slaves*
g Cn: Gk *fallen*

as in the excurses (4.16–17; 5.18). *Astounding things have happened,* namely, your successes against the Jews. 22: *It was not I who gave you life,* The mother's speech appears to combine references to Sir 1.1–3, which it refutes, with technical vocabulary from Greek philosophy (*set in order the elements*; Plato, *Theaetetus* 210e; Aristotle, *Metaphysics* 998a.23). The author argues that resurrection is a mystery analogous to the creation of the world, or of a human being. Just as God caused something to exist that had not existed previously (see v. 28), so God can resurrect a person who has ceased to exist. 24: *His Friend,* see 1.14n. 28: *Did not make them out of things that existed,* this verse was understood by Origen (185–254 CE) and subsequent Christian authors to be a statement of the doctrine that God created the universe out of nothing. 33: *Angry for a little while,* see 5.17n. *Reconciled with his own servants,* alluding to Deut 32.36; see v. 6 above and 8.29. 34: *Children of heaven,* the Jews; see v.11n. 38: *Through me and my brothers to bring to an end the wrath,* their deaths are not in vain, but rather effective; con-

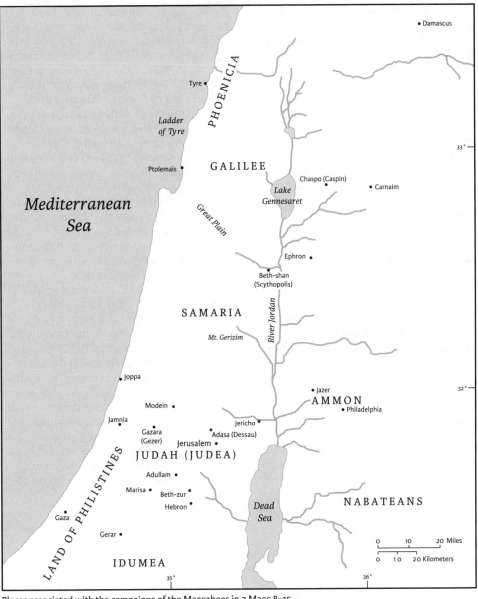

Places associated with the campaigns of the Maccabees in 2 Macc 8–15.

39 The king fell into a rage, and handled him worse than the others, being exasperated at his scorn. **40** So he died in his integrity, putting his whole trust in the Lord.

41 Last of all, the mother died, after her sons.

42 Let this be enough, then, about the eating of sacrifices and the extreme tortures.

8 Meanwhile Judas, who was also called Maccabeus, and his companions secretly entered the villages and summoned their kindred and enlisted those who had continued in the Jewish faith, and so they gathered about six thousand. **2** They implored the Lord to look upon the people who were oppressed by all; and to have pity on the temple that had been profaned by the godless; **3** to have mercy on the city that was being destroyed and about to be leveled to the ground; to hearken to the blood that cried out to him; **4** to remember also the lawless destruction of the innocent babies and the blasphemies committed against his name; and to show his hatred of evil.

5 As soon as Maccabeus got his army organized, the Gentiles could not withstand him, for the wrath of the Lord had turned to mercy. **6** Coming without warning, he would set fire to towns and villages. He captured strategic positions and put to flight not a few of the enemy. **7** He found the nights most advantageous for such attacks. And talk of his valor spread everywhere.

8 When Philip saw that the man was gaining ground little by little, and that he was pushing ahead with more frequent successes, he wrote to Ptolemy, the governor of Coelesyria and Phoenicia, to come to the aid of the king's government. **9** Then Ptolemy[a] promptly appointed Nicanor son of Patroclus, one of the king's chief[b] Friends, and sent him, in command of no fewer than twenty thousand Gentiles of all nations, to wipe out the whole race of Judea. He associated with him Gorgias, a general and a man of experience in military service. **10** Nicanor determined to make up for the king the tribute due to the Romans, two thousand talents, by selling captured Jews into slavery. **11** So he immediately sent to the towns on the seacoast, inviting them to buy Jewish slaves and promising to hand over ninety slaves for a talent, not expecting the judgment from the Almighty that was about to overtake him.

12 Word came to Judas concerning Nicanor's invasion; and when he told his companions of the arrival of the army, **13** those who were cowardly and distrustful of God's justice ran off and got away. **14** Others sold all their remaining property, and at the same time implored the Lord to rescue those who had been sold by the ungodly Nicanor before he ever met them, **15** if not for their own sake, then for the sake of the covenants made with their ancestors, and because he had called them by his holy and glorious name. **16** But Maccabeus gathered his forces together, to the number six thousand, and exhorted them

a Gk *he*

b Gk *one of the first*

---

trast 1 Macc 1.62–63; 2.29–41; 3.8. In 1 Macc it is not the death of the martyrs but Judas's valor that turns away the wrath. In 2 Macc the deaths increase the suffering of Israel to such a degree that God is moved to intervene for them; cf. Deut 32.36; Bar 4.

8.1–7: Judas begins the revolt. See 1 Macc 3.1–41. **2–4:** The troops' prayer summarizes the events narrated by the book so far. **3:** *The blood that cried out to him,* cf. Gen 4.10. **4:** *Innocent babies,* 6.10; in context, this also refers, with some exaggeration, to the seven sons of ch 7. **7:** *The nights,* see 10:28; 12:6,9; 13:15; and especially 1 Macc 4:1–25.

8.8–36: First victory over Nicanor. See 1 Macc 3.38–4.25. **8:** *Philip,* see 5.22. *Ptolemy* (see 10.12–13, 1 Macc 3.38). **9:** *Nicanor son of Patroclus,* according to 1 Macc 3–4, *Gorgias* was the main figure in this campaign, but 2 Macc makes Nicanor the principal villain. Chs 14–15 narrate Judas's further clashes with him, and the book ends with the establishment of a festival commemorating his final defeat. **10:** *The tribute due to the Romans* imposed by the Treaty of Apamea (188 BCE; see 4.7n.); the Seleucids were in arrears. *Talent,* see 3.11n. **11:** *Ninety slaves for a talent* was half or less of the usual price. **13:** *Ran off,* 1 Macc 3.55–56 portrays this as part of a ceremony mandated by Deut 20.5–8, but 2 Macc uses the occasion to emphasize the courage of those who remained. **15:** *Covenants,* see 1.2n. *Because he had called them by his . . . name,* a standard argument in prayers asking God to

not to be frightened by the enemy and not to fear the great multitude of Gentiles who were wickedly coming against them, but to fight nobly, ¹⁷ keeping before their eyes the lawless outrage that the Gentiles[a] had committed against the holy place, and the torture of the derided city, and besides, the overthrow of their ancestral way of life. ¹⁸ "For they trust to arms and acts of daring," he said, "but we trust in the Almighty God, who is able with a single nod to strike down those who are coming against us, and even, if necessary, the whole world."

¹⁹ Moreover, he told them of the occasions when help came to their ancestors; how, in the time of Sennacherib, when one hundred eighty-five thousand perished, ²⁰ and the time of the battle against the Galatians that took place in Babylonia, when eight thousand Jews[b] fought along with four thousand Macedonians; yet when the Macedonians were hard pressed, the eight thousand, by the help that came to them from heaven, destroyed one hundred twenty thousand Galatians[c] and took a great amount of booty.

²¹ With these words he filled them with courage and made them ready to die for their laws and their country; then he divided his army into four parts. ²² He appointed his brothers also, Simon and Joseph and Jonathan, each to command a division, putting fifteen hundred men under each. ²³ Besides, he appointed Eleazar to read aloud[d] from the holy book, and gave the watchword, "The help of God"; then, leading the first division himself, he joined battle with Nicanor.

²⁴ With the Almighty as their ally, they killed more than nine thousand of the enemy,

and wounded and disabled most of Nicanor's army, and forced them all to flee. ²⁵ They captured the money of those who had come to buy them as slaves. After pursuing them for some distance, they were obliged to return because the hour was late. ²⁶ It was the day before the sabbath, and for that reason they did not continue their pursuit. ²⁷ When they had collected the arms of the enemy and stripped them of their spoils, they kept the sabbath, giving great praise and thanks to the Lord, who had preserved them for that day and allotted it to them as the beginning of mercy. ²⁸ After the sabbath they gave some of the spoils to those who had been tortured and to the widows and orphans, and distributed the rest among themselves and their children. ²⁹ When they had done this, they made common supplication and implored the merciful Lord to be wholly reconciled with his servants.[e]

³⁰ In encounters with the forces of Timothy and Bacchides they killed more than twenty thousand of them and got possession of some exceedingly high strongholds, and they divided a very large amount of plunder, giving to those who had been tortured and to the orphans and widows, and also to the aged, shares equal to their own. ³¹ They collected the arms of the enemy,[f] and carefully stored all of them in strategic places; the

a   Gk *they*
b   Gk lacks *Jews*
c   Gk lacks *Galatians*
d   Meaning of Gk uncertain
e   Gk *slaves*
f   Gk *their arms*

intervene: God's own reputation was at stake; cf. Ex 32.12; Deut 32.27; 1 Macc 4.33. **19:** *Sennacherib*, king of Assyria; see Isa 37.36; 2 Kings 19.35; this miracle is also cited at 15.22 . **20:** *Galatians*, a people of Asia Minor, known for their invasions westward in the third century BCE and for their service as mercenaries; the battle mentioned here is otherwise unknown. If "Jews" is omitted (see textual note b), Judas would be citing a case in which God helps worthy people regardless of their identity; see 4.35–36n. **21:** *Four parts*, Judas commanded the first (v. 23). **22:** *His brothers*, see 1 Macc 2.2–5. Although they scarcely figure in 2 Macc, *Simon* was high priest from 142 to 134 BCE (see 1 Macc 13–16), and *Jonathan* from 160 to 143 or 142 (see 1 Macc 9.23–12.53). *Joseph*, perhaps John is meant; see 1 Macc 2.2; 9.35–36. **23:** *Eleazar*, another brother, was killed at Beth-zechariah (1 Macc 2.5; 6.43–46). **25:** *Captured the money of those who had come to buy them*, the punishment fitting the crime, as often in this book (4.42n.). **26:** *Day before the sabbath* required preparations; compare 12.38; Mk 15.42. 1 Macc 4.15–16 has no such religious explanation; rather, the Jews broke off the pursuit when it became too dangerous. **27–29:** *Beginning of mercy . . . wholly reconciled with his servants*, completes the process predicted at 7.33. **30–33:** This scene is located here, although out of place chronologically, to illustrate the pious practice of sharing spoils

rest of the spoils they carried to Jerusalem. [32] They killed the commander of Timothy's forces, a most wicked man, and one who had greatly troubled the Jews. [33] While they were celebrating the victory in the city of their ancestors, they burned those who had set fire to the sacred gates, Callisthenes and some others, who had fled into one little house; so these received the proper reward for their impiety.[a]

[34] The thrice-accursed Nicanor, who had brought the thousand merchants to buy the Jews, [35] having been humbled with the help of the Lord by opponents whom he regarded as of the least account, took off his splendid uniform and made his way alone like a runaway slave across the country until he reached Antioch, having succeeded chiefly in the destruction of his own army! [36] So he who had undertaken to secure tribute for the Romans by the capture of the people of Jerusalem proclaimed that the Jews had a Defender, and that therefore the Jews were invulnerable, because they followed the laws ordained by him.

9 About that time, as it happened, Antiochus had retreated in disorder from the region of Persia. [2] He had entered the city called Persepolis and attempted to rob the temples and control the city. Therefore the people rushed to the rescue with arms, and Antiochus and his army were defeated,[b] with the result that Antiochus was put to flight by the inhabitants and beat a shameful retreat. [3] While he was in Ecbatana, news came to him of what had happened to Nicanor and the forces of Timothy. [4] Transported with rage, he conceived the idea of turning upon the Jews the injury done by those who had put him to flight; so he ordered his charioteer to drive without stopping until he completed the journey. But the judgment of heaven rode with him! For in his arrogance he said, "When I get there I will make Jerusalem a cemetery of Jews."

[5] But the all-seeing Lord, the God of Israel, struck him with an incurable and invisible blow. As soon as he stopped speaking he was seized with a pain in his bowels, for which there was no relief, and with sharp internal tortures— [6] and that very justly, for he had tortured the bowels of others with many and strange inflictions. [7] Yet he did not in any way stop his insolence, but was even more filled with arrogance, breathing fire in his rage against the Jews, and giving orders to drive even faster. And so it came about that he fell out of his chariot as it was rushing along, and the fall was so hard as to torture every limb of his body. [8] Thus he who only a little while before had thought in his superhuman arrogance that he could command the waves of the sea, and had imagined that he could weigh the high mountains in a balance, was brought down to earth and carried in a litter, making the power of God manifest to all. [9] And so the ungodly man's body swarmed with worms, and while he was still living in anguish and pain, his flesh rotted away, and because of

---

[a] Meaning of Gk uncertain
[b] Gk *they were defeated*

---

with the needy (see Num 31.25–47; 1 Sam 30.21–25). **34**: *Thrice-accursed Nicanor*, as in 15.3. **35**: *Having succeeded chiefly in the destruction of his own army*, the author loves to gloat; compare e.g., v. 25; 3.28; 5.9–10; 9.8–10. **36**: *Proclaimed*, like Heliodorus (see 3.39n.), *that the Jews had a Defender*, i.e., God; compare 11.13.

    9.1–12: Antiochus's retreat and illness. See 1 Macc 6.1–16. Antiochus IV Epiphanes began his eastern campaign in 165 BCE, leaving behind his young son Antiochus Eupator with a guardian, Lysias (1 Macc 3.31). 2 Macc simplifies matters by first mentioning that pair only after recounting Antiochus IV's demise; see 10.10–11. For another version of the king's defeat and death, see 1.11–17. **1**: *Antiochus* went to *Persia* to strengthen his authority there and to get funds. **2**: *Persepolis*, the capital of Persia, near modern Shiraz, founded by Darius I. **3**: Antiochus was on his way to Babylon (1 Macc 6.4) but apparently went north by way of Ecbatana (modern Hamadan). **4**: *But the judgment of heaven rode with him*, as elsewhere in this chapter, the author employs irony: Antiochus thinks he will punish the Jews but does not even know his own nemesis is riding along with him. **5**: *Incurable*, as in Isa 14.6. That chapter, on the fall of the king of Babylon, informs other parts of this chapter as well. **6**: *Tortured the bowels*, both by inflicting pain and by forcing Jews to eat forbidden foods (chs 6–7). **8**: *Command the waves of the sea*, 5.21. *Weigh the high mountains in a balance* is something only God can do (Isa 40.12).

the stench the whole army felt revulsion at his decay. [10] Because of his intolerable stench no one was able to carry the man who a little while before had thought that he could touch the stars of heaven. [11] Then it was that, broken in spirit, he began to lose much of his arrogance and to come to his senses under the scourge of God, for he was tortured with pain every moment. [12] And when he could not endure his own stench, he uttered these words, "It is right to be subject to God; mortals should not think that they are equal to God."[a]

[13] Then the abominable fellow made a vow to the Lord, who would no longer have mercy on him, stating [14] that the holy city, which he was hurrying to level to the ground and to make a cemetery, he was now declaring to be free; [15] and the Jews, whom he had not considered worth burying but had planned to throw out with their children for the wild animals and for the birds to eat, he would make, all of them, equal to citizens of Athens; [16] and the holy sanctuary, which he had formerly plundered, he would adorn with the finest offerings; and all the holy vessels he would give back, many times over; and the expenses incurred for the sacrifices he would provide from his own revenues; [17] and in addition to all this he also would become a Jew and would visit every inhabited place to proclaim the power of God. [18] But when his sufferings did not in any way abate, for the judgment of God had justly come upon him, he gave up all

hope for himself and wrote to the Jews the following letter, in the form of a supplication. This was its content:

[19] "To his worthy Jewish citizens, Antiochus their king and general sends hearty greetings and good wishes for their health and prosperity. [20] If you and your children are well and your affairs are as you wish, I am glad. As my hope is in heaven, [21] I remember with affection your esteem and goodwill. On my way back from the region of Persia I suffered an annoying illness, and I have deemed it necessary to take thought for the general security of all. [22] I do not despair of my condition, for I have good hope of recovering from my illness, [23] but I observed that my father, on the occasions when he made expeditions into the upper country, appointed his successor, [24] so that, if anything unexpected happened or any unwelcome news came, the people throughout the realm would not be troubled, for they would know to whom the government was left. [25] Moreover, I understand how the princes along the borders and the neighbors of my kingdom keep watching for opportunities and waiting to see what will happen. So I have appointed my son Antiochus to be king, whom I have often entrusted and commended to most of you when I hurried off to the upper provinces; and I have written to him what is written here. [26] I therefore urge and beg you to remember the public

---

[a] Or *not think thoughts proper only to God*

9: *Worms,* a common motif in narratives about the death of tyrants, e.g., Jdt 16.17; Acts 12.23. *Stench,* from Joel 2.20, of "the northerner," who was easily identified as Antiochus Epiphanes (the "king of the north" of Dan 11). **10:** *Touch the stars of heaven,* Isa 14.13.

9.13–27: Antiochus's vow and letter to the Jews. The author enjoys himself, concocting promises and self-humiliation by the desperate king. **14:** *Free,* of taxes; perhaps also having asylum status. **15:** *Not considered worth burying,* see 5.10n. **16:** Cf. 3.3; 5.16. Antiochus's promises conform to his brother's practice (3.3). **17:** *To proclaim the power of God,* as did Heliodorus (3.37–39) and Nicanor (8.36). **17–18:** *Would visit . . . had justly come upon him,* the Greek verbs are identical, ironically underlining the contrast between Antiochus's confident promise and his inability to fulfill it. **19–27:** The letter is no supplication (v. 18). Some scholars consider this to be an authentic letter, but one that was addressed only to Jews loyal to the king, bidding them to support his *son Antiochus* V (vv. 25–27); cf. the authentic letters in 11.16,22,27,34. If it is authentic, it does not fit the context. Alternatively, it may be an ironic composition by the author, designed to make Antiochus appear ridiculous. **19:** *Citizens* means fellow-citizens (as in 5.6, "compatriots"), reflecting Antiochus's promise to become a Jew. By naming the addressees first Antiochus ascribes them greater importance, another example of the author's humor; contrast the authentic letters in ch 11. **23:** *My father,* Antiochus III, who appointed Seleucus IV as his successor. *The upper country,* i.e., Babylonia and Persia, the inlands of Asia, as in 1 Macc 3.37; 6.1. **25:** *What is written here,* lit. "What is written below," as if the letter had an appendix: more spoofing of official letters (such as 1 Macc 11.31; 12.7).

and private services rendered to you and to maintain your present goodwill, each of you, toward me and my son. ²⁷ For I am sure that he will follow my policy and will treat you with moderation and kindness."

²⁸ So the murderer and blasphemer, having endured the more intense suffering, such as he had inflicted on others, came to the end of his life by a most pitiable fate, among the mountains in a strange land. ²⁹ And Philip, one of his courtiers, took his body home; then, fearing the son of Antiochus, he withdrew to Ptolemy Philometor in Egypt.

10 Now Maccabeus and his followers, the Lord leading them on, recovered the temple and the city; ² they tore down the altars that had been built in the public square by the foreigners, and also destroyed the sacred precincts. ³ They purified the sanctuary, and made another altar of sacrifice; then, striking fire out of flint, they offered sacrifices, after a lapse of two years, and they offered incense and lighted lamps and set out the bread of the Presence. ⁴ When they had done this, they fell prostrate and implored the Lord that they might never again fall into such misfortunes, but that, if they should ever sin, they might be disciplined by him with forbearance and not be handed over to blasphemous and barbarous nations. ⁵ It happened that on the same day on which the sanctuary had been profaned by the foreigners, the purification of the sanctuary took place, that is, on the twenty-fifth day of the same month, which was Chislev. ⁶ They celebrated it for eight days with rejoicing, in the manner of the festival of booths, remembering how not long before, during the festival of booths, they had been wandering in the mountains and caves like wild animals. ⁷ Therefore, carrying ivy-wreathed wands and beautiful branches and also fronds of palm, they offered hymns of thanksgiving to him who had given success to the purifying of his own holy place. ⁸ They decreed by public edict, ratified by vote, that the whole nation of the Jews should observe these days every year.

⁹ Such then was the end of Antiochus, who was called Epiphanes.

¹⁰ Now we will tell what took place under Antiochus Eupator, who was the son of that ungodly man, and will give a brief summary of the principal calamities of the wars. ¹¹ This man, when he succeeded to the kingdom, appointed one Lysias to have charge of the government and to be chief governor of Coelesyria and Phoenicia. ¹² Ptolemy, who was called Macron, took the lead in showing justice to the Jews because of the wrong that had been done to them, and attempted to maintain peaceful relations with them. ¹³ As a result he was accused before Eupator by the king's Friends.

Cf. 11.17n. **26:** *Your present goodwill*, the way this contradicts the facts so blatantly again constitutes authorial humor.

9.28–29: Antiochus's death. *Philip* apparently tried to seize the Seleucid government (1 Macc 6.55–56) without success and so went over to their enemy, Ptolemy VI (see 4.21). As cuneiform evidence attests, Antiochus died late in 164 BCE, around the same time as the rededication of the Temple.

10.1–8: Rededication of the Temple (cf. 1 Macc 4.36–61). This passage, needed to support the invitation in the letters prefaced to the book, seems to have been inserted by the Judean authors of those letters. It interrupts the preceding account, which continues in 10.9, and in contrast to the book as a whole displays an interest in the Temple and an antipathy for Gentiles. **1:** *The temple and the city*, historical order reversed; contrast 3.1–3; 4.48; 15.17. **3:** *Striking fire out of flint*, lit. "igniting rocks and extracting fire from them"; see 1.10–2.18n. The *incense, lamps,* and *bread of the Presence*, prescribed by Ex 30.7–8; 25.30. **4:** *Disciplined*, see 6.12n. **5–6:** *Chislev . . . festival of booths*, (December 164 BCE); see 1.9,18. The Hanukkah festival, celebrated *for eight days* like Solomon's dedication of the first Temple (1 Kings 8.65–66) and Hezekiah's reconsecration (2 Chr 29.17), commemorates this event. See also 1 Macc 4.52–59. *In the mountains and caves like wild animals*, see 5.27. **7:** *Ivy-wreathed wands*, contrast 6.7. *Fronds of palm*, cf. 1 Macc 13.51; Jn 12.13.

10.9–13: Antiochus V Eupator ascends to throne. See 9.1–12n. *Antiochus V*, son of Antiochus IV Epiphanes, ruled 164–162 BCE, when he was murdered by order of Demetrius I at the age of eleven. **10:** *Eupator, who was the son of that ungodly man* is ironic, since "Eupator" means "who has a good father." **11:** *Lysias*, see 1 Macc 3.32–33. **12:** *Ptolemy Macron*, see 4.45. We know no more about his fair policy toward the Jews. **13:** *Philometor*, see 1.10n.

He heard himself called a traitor at every turn, because he had abandoned Cyprus, which Philometor had entrusted to him, and had gone over to Antiochus Epiphanes. Unable to command the respect due his office,[a] he took poison and ended his life.

[14] When Gorgias became governor of the region, he maintained a force of mercenaries, and at every turn kept attacking the Jews. [15] Besides this, the Idumeans, who had control of important strongholds, were harassing the Jews; they received those who were banished from Jerusalem, and endeavored to keep up the war. [16] But Maccabeus and his forces, after making solemn supplication and imploring God to fight on their side, rushed to the strongholds of the Idumeans. [17] Attacking them vigorously, they gained possession of the places, and beat off all who fought upon the wall, and slaughtered those whom they encountered, killing no fewer than twenty thousand.

[18] When at least nine thousand took refuge in two very strong towers well equipped to withstand a siege, [19] Maccabeus left Simon and Joseph, and also Zacchaeus and his troops, a force sufficient to besiege them; and he himself set off for places where he was more urgently needed. [20] But those with Simon, who were money-hungry, were bribed by some of those who were in the towers, and on receiving seventy thousand drachmas let some of them slip away. [21] When word of what had happened came to Maccabeus, he gathered the leaders of the people, and accused these men of having sold their kindred for money by setting their enemies free to fight against them. [22] Then he killed these men who had turned traitor, and immediately captured the two towers. [23] Having

success at arms in everything he undertook, he destroyed more than twenty thousand in the two strongholds.

[24] Now Timothy, who had been defeated by the Jews before, gathered a tremendous force of mercenaries and collected the cavalry from Asia in no small number. He came on, intending to take Judea by storm. [25] As he drew near, Maccabeus and his men sprinkled dust on their heads and girded their loins with sackcloth, in supplication to God. [26] Falling upon the steps before the altar, they implored him to be gracious to them and to be an enemy to their enemies and an adversary to their adversaries, as the law declares. [27] And rising from their prayer they took up their arms and advanced a considerable distance from the city; and when they came near the enemy they halted. [28] Just as dawn was breaking, the two armies joined battle, the one having as pledge of success and victory not only their valor but also their reliance on the Lord, while the other made rage their leader in the fight.

[29] When the battle became fierce, there appeared to the enemy from heaven five resplendent men on horses with golden bridles, and they were leading the Jews. [30] Two of them took Maccabeus between them, and shielding him with their own armor and weapons, they kept him from being wounded. They showered arrows and thunderbolts on the enemy, so that, confused and blinded, they were thrown into disorder and cut to pieces. [31] Twenty thousand five hundred were slaughtered, besides six hundred cavalry.

[32] Timothy himself fled to a stronghold called Gazara, especially well garrisoned,

---

[a] Cn: Meaning of Gk uncertain

In claiming that Seleucid courtiers condemned Ptolemy Macron for moving his loyalty to the Seleucids, our author is condemning them, as usual; cf. 14.11.

    10.14–23: Fighting the Idumeans. Cf. 1 Macc 5.3–5. **14:** *The region,* of Idumea (southern Palestine) according to 12.32, which explains the link to the next verse. **15:** *Those who were banished from Jerusalem,* apparently by Judas when he retook the city. **17:** *Twenty thousand,* a favorite number (see also v. 23; 8.9,30). **20:** *Drachma,* see 4.19n.

    10.24–38: Fighting Timothy. 24: *Timothy, who had been defeated by the Jews before,* this might be a secondary gloss (see 8.30–33n.). *To take Judea,* but according to 1 Macc 5.6–8,11 this warfare was in Transjordan; see v. 32n. **25:** *Sprinkled dust,* or possibly "ashes," as in Esth 4.1; cf. 14.15 and Josh 7.6. **26:** *The steps before the altar,* compare Joel 2.17 and see 9.9n. *As the law declares,* at Ex 23.22. The very next verse there promises that God's angel will go before the Jews; see below, v. 29. **28:** *The one . . . the other,* cf. 3:22–23n. **29:** *Horses with golden bridles,* as at 3.25. **32:**

where Chaereas was commander. [33] Then Maccabeus and his men were glad, and they besieged the fort for four days. [34] The men within, relying on the strength of the place, kept blaspheming terribly and uttering wicked words. [35] But at dawn of the fifth day, twenty young men in the army of Maccabeus, fired with anger because of the blasphemies, bravely stormed the wall and with savage fury cut down everyone they met. [36] Others who came up in the same way wheeled around against the defenders and set fire to the towers; they kindled fires and burned the blasphemers alive. Others broke open the gates and let in the rest of the force, and they occupied the city. [37] They killed Timothy, who was hiding in a cistern, and his brother Chaereas, and Apollophanes. [38] When they had accomplished these things, with hymns and thanksgivings they blessed the Lord who shows great kindness to Israel and gives them the victory.

11 Very soon after this, Lysias, the king's guardian and kinsman, who was in charge of the government, being vexed at what had happened, [2] gathered about eighty thousand infantry and all his cavalry and came against the Jews. He intended to make the city a home for Greeks, [3] and to levy tribute on the temple as he did on the sacred places of the other nations, and to put up the high priesthood for sale every year. [4] He took no account whatever of the power of God, but was elated with his ten thousands of infantry, and his thousands of cavalry, and his eighty

elephants. [5] Invading Judea, he approached Beth-zur, which was a fortified place about five stadia[a] from Jerusalem, and pressed it hard.

[6] When Maccabeus and his men got word that Lysias[b] was besieging the strongholds, they and all the people, with lamentations and tears, prayed the Lord to send a good angel to save Israel. [7] Maccabeus himself was the first to take up arms, and he urged the others to risk their lives with him to aid their kindred. Then they eagerly rushed off together. [8] And there, while they were still near Jerusalem, a horseman appeared at their head, clothed in white and brandishing weapons of gold. [9] And together they all praised the merciful God, and were strengthened in heart, ready to assail not only humans but the wildest animals or walls of iron. [10] They advanced in battle order, having their heavenly ally, for the Lord had mercy on them. [11] They hurled themselves like lions against the enemy, and laid low eleven thousand of them and sixteen hundred cavalry, and forced all the rest to flee. [12] Most of them got away stripped and wounded, and Lysias himself escaped by disgraceful flight.

[13] As he was not without intelligence, he pondered over the defeat that had befallen him, and realized that the Hebrews were invincible because the mighty God fought

[a] Meaning of Gk uncertain
[b] Gk *he*

Gazara (Gezer) was conquered by the Hasmoneans only decades later (1 Macc 13.43–48); here we should probably read (as in 1 Macc 5.8) "Jazer," a town in Transjordan, west of Amman. *Chaereas*, Timothy's brother, according to v. 37. **37**: *Timothy, who was hiding in a cistern*. A *cistern* was a large pit with plaster walls that stored water. The author often denies his enemies honorable death in battle; compare 8.34–35; 9.1–2; 11.12; 12.35.

11.1–15: Beth-zur campaign. Compare 1 Macc 4.26–35 and 6.31. Beth-zur was a fortress 16 mi (25 km) southsoutheast of Jerusalem. **1**: *Lysias*, see 9.1–12n. *Kinsman*, honorific usage, as at 1 Macc 11.31; compare v. 22, "brother." **2**: *He intended*, lit. "thinking"; see v. 4n. **3**: *High priesthood for sale every year*, which would demean it greatly, for traditionally, until Jason (4.7; cf. 4.24), it had been held for life and passed from father to son. **4**: *He took no account whatever*, lit. "not thinking more," responding to the verb in v. 2: i.e., Lysias depended upon his own thoughts, and did not give more consideration to the power of God. He will learn: see v. 13. *Elephants*, often used to force openings in opposing ranks of soldiers (cf. 1 Macc 1.17; 3.34; 6.34–35). **5**: *Five stadia*, lit. "five schoinoi"; a "schoinos" was a Persian measure popular in Egypt, equivalent to ca. thirty stadia (see 12.10–28n.), so the distance here is approximately 18 mi (29 km), which is close to the actual distance of 16 mi (26 km). **6**: *A good angel*, as at 15.23; see 10.26n. **12**: *Lysias himself escaped by disgraceful flight*, see 10.37n. **13–15**: According to 1 Macc 4.35 no peace was made, but Lysias returned to Antioch for reinforcements. He may have heard of Antiochus's death and hastened home to take control. **13**: *God fought on their side*, as at 8.36.

on their side. So he sent to them [14] and persuaded them to settle everything on just terms, promising that he would persuade the king, constraining him to be their friend.[a] [15] Maccabeus, having regard for the common good, agreed to all that Lysias urged. For the king granted every request in behalf of the Jews which Maccabeus delivered to Lysias in writing.

[16] The letter written to the Jews by Lysias was to this effect:

"Lysias to the people of the Jews, greetings. [17] John and Absalom, who were sent by you, have delivered your signed communication and have asked about the matters indicated in it. [18] I have informed the king of everything that needed to be brought before him, and he has agreed to what was possible. [19] If you will maintain your goodwill toward the government, I will endeavor in the future to help promote your welfare. [20] And concerning such matters and their details, I have ordered these men and my representatives to confer with you. [21] Farewell. The one hundred forty-eighth year,[b] Dioscorinthius twenty-fourth."

[22] The king's letter ran thus:

"King Antiochus to his brother Lysias, greetings. [23] Now that our father has gone on to the gods, we desire that the subjects of the kingdom be undisturbed in caring for their own affairs. [24] We have heard that the Jews do not consent to our father's change to Greek customs, but prefer their own way of living and ask that their own customs be allowed them. [25] Accordingly, since we choose that this nation also should be free from disturbance, our decision is that their temple be restored to them and that they shall live according to the customs of their ancestors. [26] You will do well, therefore, to send word to them and give them pledges of friendship, so that they may know our policy and be of good cheer and go on happily in the conduct of their own affairs."

[27] To the nation the king's letter was as follows:

"King Antiochus to the senate of the Jews and to the other Jews, greetings. [28] If you are well, it is as we desire. We also are in good health. [29] Menelaus has informed us that you wish to return home and look after your own affairs. [30] Therefore those who go home by the thirtieth of Xanthicus will have our pledge of friendship and full permission [31] for the Jews to enjoy their own food and laws, just as formerly, and none of them shall be molested in any way for what may have been done in ignorance. [32] And I have also sent Menelaus to encourage you.

---

[a] Meaning of Gk uncertain
[b] 164 B.C.

11.16–38: Four official letters. These are usually assumed to be authentic, but their location here, after the death of Antiochus IV (ch 9) and ascent of Eupator to the throne (ch 10), is problematic. True, the second letter is definitely by Antiochus Eupator, who refers to his father's death in v. 23. But the other three bear dates in 164 BCE, when Antiochus IV Epiphanes was still alive and ruling, although campaigning in the east; see 9.28–29n. The author's mistaken assumption that all four letters are from the period after that king's death caused problems in the narrative; see 12.1n., 12.10n., and 13.23n.

11.16–21: Lysias's letter to the Jews. 17: *John*, perhaps Judas's brother (1 Macc 2.2); for *Absalom*, see 1 Macc 11.70; 13.11. *Your signed communication*, read "your communication attached below"; the reference is to the document mentioned in v. 15, which was unfortunately not preserved. **18:** *And he has agreed*, read "and I have agreed" (see vv. 35–36); Lysias distinguishes between decisions he is authorized to take and others that require the king's attention. **19:** *Maintain your goodwill*, Lysias diplomatically ignores the warfare. **21:** *The one hundred forty-eighth year* of the Seleucid era ran from autumn 165 to autumn 164; the name of the month is corrupt. The date is before Judas rededicated the Temple.

11.22–26: The king's letter to Lysias. 24: *We have heard that the Jews do not consent*, more diplomatic understatement. **25:** *Temple be restored . . . live according to the customs of their ancestors*, Antiochus rescinds his father's decrees against Judaism (ch 6), ignoring the fact that the Temple was already in Jewish hands.

11.27–33: The king's letter to the Jews. 29: *Menelaus* as late as spring 164 BCE was attempting to mediate between Antiochus and the Jews. **30:** *Thirtieth of Xanthicus*, equivalent to Heb Nisan (March/April). **31:** *Their own food and laws*, the special emphasis upon food corresponds to that focus of the decrees (chs 6–7; 1 Macc 1.62–63). **33:** *Xanthicus fifteenth*, the amnesty's deadline was only two weeks later (v. 30), which is unlikely. Given

33 Farewell. The one hundred forty-eighth year,[a] Xanthicus fifteenth."

34 The Romans also sent them a letter, which read thus:

"Quintus Memmius and Titus Manius, envoys of the Romans, to the people of the Jews, greetings. 35 With regard to what Lysias the kinsman of the king has granted you, we also give consent. 36 But as to the matters that he decided are to be referred to the king, as soon as you have considered them, send some one promptly so that we may make proposals appropriate for you. For we are on our way to Antioch. 37 Therefore make haste and send messengers so that we may have your judgment. 38 Farewell. The one hundred forty-eighth year,[a] Xanthicus fifteenth."

12 When this agreement had been reached, Lysias returned to the king, and the Jews went about their farming.

2 But some of the governors in various places, Timothy and Apollonius son of Gennaeus, as well as Hieronymus and Demophon, and in addition to these Nicanor the governor of Cyprus, would not let them live quietly and in peace. 3 And the people of Joppa did so ungodly a deed as this: they invited the Jews who lived among them to embark, with their wives and children, on boats that they had provided, as though there were no ill will to the Jews;[b] 4 and this was done by public vote of the city. When they accepted, because they wished to live peaceably and suspected nothing, the people of Joppa[c] took them out to sea and drowned them, at least two hundred. 5 When Judas heard of the cruelty visited on his compatriots, he gave orders to his men 6 and, calling upon God, the righteous judge, attacked the murderers of his kindred. He set fire to the harbor by night, burned the boats, and massacred those who had taken refuge there. 7 Then, because the city's gates were closed, he withdrew, intending to come again and root out the whole community of Joppa. 8 But learning that the people in Jamnia meant in the same way to wipe out the Jews who were living among them, 9 he attacked the Jamnites by night and set fire to the harbor and the fleet, so that the glow of the light was seen in Jerusalem, thirty miles[d] distant.

10 When they had gone more than a mile[e] from there, on their march against Timothy, at least five thousand Arabs with five

---

a 164 B.C.
b Gk to them
c Gk they
d Gk two hundred forty stadia
e Gk nine stadia

---

the identity of the date in v. 38, which too is suspicious, it is likely that this date is corrupt.

11.34–38: Letter of the Romans to the Jews. 34: *The Romans* in this period were periodically sending embassies to the East. Judas apparently asked them to use their influence with the Seleucids, just as a few years later he would establish a mutual defense pact with them (1 Macc 8). **35–36:** *What Lysias . . . has granted . . . referred to the king,* see v. 18n.

12.1–9: Clashes in coastal towns. 1: *This agreement,* lit. "these covenants." But the documents in ch 11 are not covenants; they are one–sided decisions. Chapter 13, in contrast, does end with "covenants" (13.25, same term in Greek). Given the author's difficulties coordinating ch 13 with earlier material (see 13.1–26n.), perhaps it originally preceded ch 12. *The Jews went about their farming,* a pastoral image of returning "to their own affairs" (11.23,26,29). **2:** *Timothy,* 8.30–33; 10.24–37. *Governor of Cyprus,* read "Cypriarch," i.e., commander of mercenaries from Cyprus (cf. 5.24n.). **3:** *Joppa,* Jaffa, next to modern Tel Aviv; a major port on the Mediterranean, later conquered by the Hasmoneans (1 Macc 12.33–34). **8:** *Jamnia,* ca. 14 mi (22 km) south of Joppa; compare v. 40 and 1 Macc 5.58.

12.10–28: Fighting in Transjordan. This section parallels much of 1 Macc 5, which contains a fuller account. The order is confused here, for "one mile" (v. 10, lit. "nine stadia"; a stadion was ca. 625 ft [190 m]) would not take Judas's forces from the Mediterranean coast to Transjordan; "ninety–five miles" (v. 17) could. Perhaps the two stories have been erroneously exchanged. **10:** *Timothy,* some confusion is present here too, as he had been killed at 10.37; see 11.16–38n. **10–11:** *Arabs . . . nomads,* the author often varies his terminology; compare "no light matter . . . not easy" in 2.26–27 and "festival of weeks . . . Pentecost" in 12.31–32. 1 Macc 5.25 identifies these Arabs as Nabateans and claims they were peaceable from the outset; 2 Macc first allows Judas another heroic

hundred cavalry attacked them. [11] After a hard fight, Judas and his companions, with God's help, were victorious. The defeated nomads begged Judas to grant them pledges of friendship, promising to give him livestock and to help his people[a] in all other ways. [12] Judas, realizing that they might indeed be useful in many ways, agreed to make peace with them; and after receiving his pledges they went back to their tents.

[13] He also attacked a certain town that was strongly fortified with earthworks[b] and walls, and inhabited by all sorts of Gentiles. Its name was Caspin. [14] Those who were within, relying on the strength of the walls and on their supply of provisions, behaved most insolently toward Judas and his men, railing at them and even blaspheming and saying unholy things. [15] But Judas and his men, calling upon the great Sovereign of the world, who without battering rams or engines of war overthrew Jericho in the days of Joshua, rushed furiously upon the walls. [16] They took the town by the will of God, and slaughtered untold numbers, so that the adjoining lake, a quarter of a mile[c] wide, appeared to be running over with blood.

[17] When they had gone ninety-five miles[d] from there, they came to Charax, to the Jews who are called Toubiani. [18] They did not find Timothy in that region, for he had by then left there without accomplishing anything, though in one place he had left a very strong garrison. [19] Dositheus and Sosipater, who were captains under Maccabeus, marched out and destroyed those whom Timothy had left in the stronghold, more than ten thousand men. [20] But Maccabeus arranged his army in divisions, set men[a] in command of the divisions, and hurried after Timothy, who had with him one hundred twenty thousand infantry and two thousand five hundred cavalry. [21] When Timothy learned of the approach of Judas, he sent off the women and the children and also the baggage to a place called Carnaim; for that place was hard to besiege and difficult of access because of the narrowness of all the approaches. [22] But when Judas's first division appeared, terror and fear came over the enemy at the manifestation to them of him who sees all things. In their flight they rushed headlong in every direction, so that often they were injured by their own men and pierced by the points of their own swords. [23] Judas pressed the pursuit with the utmost vigor, putting the sinners to the sword, and destroyed as many as thirty thousand.

[24] Timothy himself fell into the hands of Dositheus and Sosipater and their men. With great guile he begged them to let him go in safety, because he held the parents of most of them, and the brothers of some, to whom no consideration would be shown. [25] And when with many words he had confirmed his solemn promise to restore them unharmed, they let him go, for the sake of saving their kindred.

[26] Then Judas[e] marched against Carnaim and the temple of Atargatis, and slaughtered twenty-five thousand people. [27] After the rout and destruction of these, he marched also against Ephron, a fortified town where Lysias lived with multitudes of people of all nationalities.[b] Stalwart young men took their stand before the walls and made a vigorous defense; and great stores of war engines and missiles were there. [28] But the Jews[f] called upon the Sovereign who with power shatters

a Gk *them*
b Meaning of Gk uncertain
c Gk *two stadia*
d Gk *seven hundred fifty stadia*
e Gk *he*
f Gk *they*

victory before they make peace. **13:** *All sorts of Gentiles* is pejorative, as in v. 27. *Caspin,* ca. 10 mi (16 km) east of Lake Gennesaret (the Sea of Galilee). **15:** *Overthrew Jericho,* Josh 6.1–21. **16:** *Adjoining lake,* perhaps a swamp. **17:** *Charax,* "fortified camp"; location unknown. *Toubiani,* Jews associated with the Tobiad family (3.11n.); cf. 1 Macc 5.13. **21:** *Women . . . children . . . baggage,* lit. "women, children, and other baggage," reflecting patriarchal values. *Carnaim,* farther east in Transjordan (1 Macc 5.26–27). **22:** *Manifestation,* epiphany; see 2.21n. *Injured by their own men,* a literary convention in battle scenes. **26:** *Carnaim,* see v. 21n. *Atargatis* was a Syrian goddess, corresponding to the Canaanite Ashtoreth; cf. "Ashteroth-karnaim" in Gen 14.5. **27:** *Ephron,* ca. 8 mi (13 km) east of the Jordan River, opposite Scythopolis (v. 29; 1 Macc 5.46–51). *War engines,* large catapults.

the might of his enemies, and they got the town into their hands, and killed as many as twenty-five thousand of those who were in it.

²⁹ Setting out from there, they hastened to Scythopolis, which is seventy-five miles[a] from Jerusalem. ³⁰ But when the Jews who lived there bore witness to the goodwill that the people of Scythopolis had shown them and their kind treatment of them in times of misfortune, ³¹ they thanked them and exhorted them to be well disposed to their race in the future also. Then they went up to Jerusalem, as the festival of weeks was close at hand.

³² After the festival called Pentecost, they hurried against Gorgias, the governor of Idumea, ³³ who came out with three thousand infantry and four hundred cavalry. ³⁴ When they joined battle, it happened that a few of the Jews fell. ³⁵ But a certain Dositheus, one of Bacenor's men, who was on horseback and was a strong man, caught hold of Gorgias, and grasping his cloak was dragging him off by main strength, wishing to take the accursed man alive, when one of the Thracian cavalry bore down on him and cut off his arm; so Gorgias escaped and reached Marisa.

³⁶ As Esdris and his men had been fighting for a long time and were weary, Judas called upon the Lord to show himself their ally and leader in the battle. ³⁷ In the language of their ancestors he raised the battle cry, with hymns; then he charged against Gorgias's troops when they were not expecting it, and put them to flight.

³⁸ Then Judas assembled his army and went to the city of Adullam. As the seventh day was coming on, they purified themselves according to the custom, and kept the sabbath there.

³⁹ On the next day, as had now become necessary, Judas and his men went to take up the bodies of the fallen and to bring them back to lie with their kindred in the sepulchres of their ancestors. ⁴⁰ Then under the tunic of each one of the dead they found sacred tokens of the idols of Jamnia, which the law forbids the Jews to wear. And it became clear to all that this was the reason these men had fallen. ⁴¹ So they all blessed the ways of the Lord, the righteous judge, who reveals the things that are hidden; ⁴² and they turned to supplication, praying that the sin that had been committed might be wholly blotted out. The noble Judas exhorted the people to keep themselves free from sin, for they had seen with their own eyes what had happened as the result of the sin of those who had fallen. ⁴³ He also took up a collection, man by man, to the amount of two thousand drachmas of silver, and sent it to Jerusalem to provide for a sin offering. In doing this he acted very well and honorably, taking account of the resurrection. ⁴⁴ For if he were not expecting that those who had fallen would rise again, it would have been superfluous and foolish to pray for the dead. ⁴⁵ But if he was looking to the splendid reward that is laid up for those who fall asleep in godliness, it was a holy and pious thought. Therefore he made atonement for the dead, so that they might be delivered from their sin.

13 In the one hundred forty-ninth year[b] word came to Judas and his men that Antiochus Eupator was coming with a great

---

[a] Gk *six hundred stadia*
[b] 163 B.C.

12.29–31: Return to Jerusalem. 29: *Scythopolis* (Hellenistic Beth-shan), a major city west of the Jordan River, ca. 16 mi (26 km) south of the Sea of Galilee (Judg 1.27; 1 Kings 4.12). 31: *Went up*, the usual verb for pilgrimage to Jerusalem; e.g. 1 Sam 1.3; Acts 21.15. 31–32: *Festival of weeks . . . Pentecost*, this holiday comes seven weeks ("Pentecost" = fifty [days]) after Passover (Lev 23.15–16; Acts 2.1). 35: *Thracians* were well-known mercenaries in the Hellenistic period. *Marisa* was a major Idumean town, 20 mi (32 km) southwest of Jerusalem. 37: *Language of their ancestors*, i.e., Hebrew. 38: *Adullam*, ca. 10 mi (16 km) southeast of Marisa. 40: Although only "a few" Jews had died (v. 34), it is important for the author that it is sin, not the chances of war, that caused their death. *Sacred tokens of the idols of Jamnia*, probably taken as booty. *Which the law forbids*, see Num 33.52; Deut 7.25–26. 43–45: The author expounds upon Judas's care for the dead as evidence of his belief that their lives did not end with death; see 7.9n. 45: *Fall asleep*, a common metaphor for death.

13.1–26: A new invasion. This chapter, which makes no allusion to ch 11, reports yet another campaign by Lysias and Antiochus Eupator that focuses on Beth-zur (vv. 18–22). This is problematic, both because no at-

army against Judea, ² and with him Lysias, his guardian, who had charge of the government. Each of them had a Greek force of one hundred ten thousand infantry, five thousand three hundred cavalry, twenty-two elephants, and three hundred chariots armed with scythes.

³ Menelaus also joined them and with utter hypocrisy urged Antiochus on, not for the sake of his country's welfare, but because he thought that he would be established in office. ⁴ But the King of kings aroused the anger of Antiochus against the scoundrel; and when Lysias informed him that this man was to blame for all the trouble, he ordered them to take him to Beroea and to put him to death by the method that is customary in that place. ⁵ For there is a tower there, fifty cubits high, full of ashes, and it has a rim running around it that on all sides inclines precipitously into the ashes. ⁶ There they all push to destruction anyone guilty of sacrilege or notorious for other crimes. ⁷ By such a fate it came about that Menelaus the lawbreaker died, without even burial in the earth. ⁸ And this was eminently just; because he had committed many sins against the altar whose fire and ashes were holy, he met his death in ashes.

⁹ The king with barbarous arrogance was coming to show the Jews things far worse than those that had been done[a] in his father's time. ¹⁰ But when Judas heard of this, he ordered the people to call upon the Lord day and night, now if ever to help those who were on the point of being deprived of the law and their country and the holy temple, ¹¹ and not to let the people who had just begun to revive fall into the hands of the blasphemous Gentiles. ¹² When they had all joined in the same petition and had implored the merciful Lord with weeping and fasting and lying prostrate for three days without ceasing, Judas exhorted them and ordered them to stand ready.

¹³ After consulting privately with the elders, he determined to march out and decide the matter by the help of God before the king's army could enter Judea and get possession of the city. ¹⁴ So, committing the decision to the Creator of the world and exhorting his troops to fight bravely to the death for the laws, temple, city, country, and commonwealth, he pitched his camp near Modein. ¹⁵ He gave his troops the watchword, "God's victory," and with a picked force of the bravest young men, he attacked the king's pavilion at night and killed as many as two thousand men in the camp. He stabbed[b] the leading elephant and its rider. ¹⁶ In the end they filled the camp with terror and confusion and withdrew in triumph. ¹⁷ This happened, just as day was dawning, because the Lord's help protected him.

¹⁸ The king, having had a taste of the daring of the Jews, tried strategy in attacking their positions. ¹⁹ He advanced against Beth-

---

[a] Or *the worst of the things that had been done*
[b] Meaning of Gk uncertain

---

tempt is made to coordinate this narrative with that of ch 11, and because according to the parallel narrative in 1 Maccabees this second campaign began around Beth-zur (1 Macc 6.31) but quickly moved north to Beth-zechariah (1 Macc 6.32–47), which is not mentioned here. Similarly, Philip's role is puzzling; see 13.23n. It appears that the author was confused. **3–8:** Death of Menelaus. This interruptive interlude takes care of a loose end. **3:** *Menelaus*, see 4.23–50n. **4:** *King of kings*, a typical Persian epithet. Here it refers to God. *Beroea*, Aleppo in northern Syria. **5:** *Fifty cubits high*, cf. Esth 7.9; a cubit was ca. 18 in (45 cm). This method was Persian; we are not told here whether the ashes were hot, so that Menelaus died by burning, or cold, and so by suffocating. **7:** *Without even burial*, see 5.10n. **8:** The apparent artificiality of this explanation of poetic justice shows how important the notion is for 2 Macc; see 4.42n. **9:** To explain why the invasion continued although the real troublemaker had been recognized and executed, the author can only claim that the king's attitude toward the Jews changed for the worse; no reason is given. **11:** *Just begun to revive*, so relapse would be all the worse; cf. 14.36. **12:** *Fasting . . . for three days*, as in Esth 4.16. **14:** *Modein*, ca. 20 mi (32 km) northwest of Jerusalem, the hometown of the Hasmoneans (1 Macc 2.1). **15:** *Watchword*, as in 8.23. *Leading elephant and its rider*, cf. 1 Macc 6.43–46, where Eleazar dies after heroically killing the lead elephant. **16:** According to 1 Macc 6.47, the Jews fled. **19:** *Beth-zur*,

zur, a strong fortress of the Jews, was turned back, attacked again,[a] and was defeated. [20] Judas sent in to the garrison whatever was necessary. [21] But Rhodocus, a man from the ranks of the Jews, gave secret information to the enemy; he was sought for, caught, and put in prison. [22] The king negotiated a second time with the people in Beth-zur, gave pledges, received theirs, withdrew, attacked Judas and his men, was defeated; [23] he got word that Philip, who had been left in charge of the government, had revolted in Antioch; he was dismayed, called in the Jews, yielded and swore to observe all their rights, settled with them and offered sacrifice, honored the sanctuary and showed generosity to the holy place. [24] He received Maccabeus, left Hegemonides as governor from Ptolemais to Gerar, [25] and went to Ptolemais. The people of Ptolemais were indignant over the treaty; in fact they were so angry that they wanted to annul its terms.[b] [26] Lysias took the public platform, made the best possible defense, convinced them, appeased them, gained their goodwill, and set out for Antioch. This is how the king's attack and withdrawal turned out.

14 Three years later, word came to Judas and his men that Demetrius son of

Seleucus had sailed into the harbor of Tripolis with a strong army and a fleet, [2] and had taken possession of the country, having made away with Antiochus and his guardian Lysias.

[3] Now a certain Alcimus, who had formerly been high priest but had willfully defiled himself in the times of separation,[c] realized that there was no way for him to be safe or to have access again to the holy altar, [4] and went to King Demetrius in about the one hundred fifty-first year,[d] presenting to him a crown of gold and a palm, and besides these some of the customary olive branches from the temple. During that day he kept quiet. [5] But he found an opportunity that furthered his mad purpose when he was invited by Demetrius to a meeting of the council and was asked about the attitude and intentions of the Jews. He answered:

[6] "Those of the Jews who are called Hasideans, whose leader is Judas Maccabeus, are keeping up war and stirring up sedition, and will not let the kingdom attain tranquility. [7] Therefore I have laid aside my ancestral glory—I mean the high priesthood—and have

[a] Or *faltered*
[b] Meaning of Gk uncertain
[c] Other ancient authorities read *of mixing*
[d] 161 B.C.

see 11.1–15n. **23:** *Philip, who had been left in charge of the government, had revolted*, this comment is confusing, since 9.29 reported that Philip had fled to Egypt out of fear of Eupator; see 11.16–38n. **24:** *Received Maccabeus*, formally taking leave of him, as at 3.35. *Hegemonides*, like Heliodorus (3.7) and Ptolemy Macron (10:12), this Seleucid official is known from inscriptions. *From Ptolemais to Gerar*, the Palestinian coastal region from Acco down to below Gaza; for this administrative district, see also 1 Macc 11.59 and 15.38. **25:** *The treaty*, see 12.1n.

14.1–25: Alcimus and Nicanor. Enter a new villain, Alcimus, said to have formerly been high priest, which is possible if Antiochus V appointed him after the death of Menelaus. He incites the new Seleucid king against Judas, and a royal expedition is sent out, commanded by Nicanor, who is taken by the author, perhaps mistakenly, to be identical with the "thrice-accursed" (8.34; 15.3) villain of ch 8. According to 1 Macc 7.12–25 the first campaign incited by Alcimus was commanded by Bacchides; 2 Macc assigns it to Nicanor in light of its general focus upon him, culminating in his defeat in ch 15 and the festival established to celebrate it (15.36); cf. 8.9n. **1:** *Three years later*, about 162 or 161 BCE. *Demetrius I, son of Seleucus* IV (reigned 162–150), had been sent to Rome to replace Antiochus IV Epiphanes as a hostage. When Seleucus IV died in 175 BCE, Demetrius was still a child, and Antiochus assumed the throne (see 4.7n.). After the death of Antiochus IV, Demetrius viewed his cousin Antiochus V Eupator as a usurper (see 4.7n.). Demetrius escaped from Rome in the late summer of 162 BCE and quickly established himself upon the Seleucid throne. *Tripolis*, in northern Lebanon. **2:** See 1 Macc 7.3–4. **3:** *A certain Alcimus*, alone; compare 1 Macc 7.5, where he leads a delegation; see 3.4n. *Times of separation* refers to the days of Antiochus's decrees. **4:** *Crown of gold and a palm*, customary gifts to kings; compare 1 Macc 13.37. **6–11:** Alcimus's speech is meant to be understood as self-serving. His concern for the commonweal is a parody serving to contrast him with Onias (4.1–6) **6:** *Hasideans*, meaning "pious ones"; see also 1 Macc 7.13 where they are a party separate from the Maccabees, and Judas is not their leader. In 1 Macc their pious peace-seeking is represented as naïve, and many of them are killed, making them, in 1 Macc 1.62–63 and 2.29–38, foils for the

now come here, [8] first because I am genuinely concerned for the interests of the king, and second because I have regard also for my compatriots. For through the folly of those whom I have mentioned our whole nation is now in no small misfortune. [9] Since you are acquainted, O king, with the details of this matter, may it please you to take thought for our country and our hard-pressed nation with the gracious kindness that you show to all. [10] For as long as Judas lives, it is impossible for the government to find peace." [11] When he had said this, the rest of the king's Friends,[a] who were hostile to Judas, quickly inflamed Demetrius still more. [12] He immediately chose Nicanor, who had been in command of the elephants, appointed him governor of Judea, and sent him off [13] with orders to kill Judas and scatter his troops, and to install Alcimus as high priest of the great[b] temple. [14] And the Gentiles throughout Judea, who had fled before[c] Judas, flocked to join Nicanor, thinking that the misfortunes and calamities of the Jews would mean prosperity for themselves.

[15] When the Jews[d] heard of Nicanor's coming and the gathering of the Gentiles, they sprinkled dust on their heads and prayed to him who established his own people forever and always upholds his own heritage by manifesting himself. [16] At the command of the leader, they[e] set out from there immediately and engaged them in battle at a village called Dessau.[c] [17] Simon, the brother of Judas, had encountered Nicanor, but had been temporarily[f] checked because of the sudden consternation created by the enemy.

[18] Nevertheless Nicanor, hearing of the valor of Judas and his troops and their courage in battle for their country, shrank from deciding the issue by bloodshed. [19] Therefore he sent Posidonius, Theodotus, and Mattathias to give and receive pledges of friendship. [20] When the terms had been fully considered,

and the leader had informed the people, and it had appeared that they were of one mind, they agreed to the covenant. [21] The leaders[d] set a day on which to meet by themselves. A chariot came forward from each army; seats of honor were set in place; [22] Judas posted armed men in readiness at key places to prevent sudden treachery on the part of the enemy; so they duly held the consultation.

[23] Nicanor stayed on in Jerusalem and did nothing out of the way, but dismissed the flocks of people that had gathered. [24] And he kept Judas always in his presence; he was warmly attached to the man. [25] He urged him to marry and have children; so Judas[e] married, settled down, and shared the common life.

[26] But when Alcimus noticed their goodwill for one another, he took the covenant that had been made and went to Demetrius. He told him that Nicanor was disloyal to the government, since he had appointed that conspirator against the kingdom, Judas, to be his successor. [27] The king became excited and, provoked by the false accusations of that depraved man, wrote to Nicanor, stating that he was displeased with the covenant and commanding him to send Maccabeus to Antioch as a prisoner without delay.

[28] When this message came to Nicanor, he was troubled and grieved that he had to annul their agreement when the man had done no wrong. [29] Since it was not possible to oppose the king, he watched for an opportunity to accomplish this by a stratagem. [30] But Maccabeus, noticing that Nicanor was more aus-

---

a Gk *of the Friends*
b Gk *greatest*
c Meaning of Gk uncertain
d Gk *they*
e Gk *he*
f Other ancient authorities read *slowly*

---

smarter, more violent, Hasmoneans. Cf. 15.27n. **11:** *Friends*, see 1.14n. **14:** Cf. 8.11. **15:** *Dust*, see 10.25n. **16:** *Dessau*, precise location uncertain. **17:** As at 10.20, Simon is something of a foil for Judas, although not condemned. **18:** *Country*, lit. "fatherland"; see 7.2n. **23–25:** Idyllic relations between Nicanor and Judas. The author again portrays mutual respect between Jew and Gentile, as long as troublemakers do not interfere; see 4.35–36n.

14.26–15.36: Alcimus and Nicanor, continued. As elsewhere (3.4; 12.2), the idyll is destroyed, and so the story resumes, with a heavy "But." Alcimus again misrepresents the good relations between Nicanor and Judas to Demetrius, and the king responds by renewing his orders to Nicanor to assert royal rule and arrest Judas.

tere in his dealings with him and was meeting him more rudely than had been his custom, concluded that this austerity did not spring from the best motives. So he gathered not a few of his men, and went into hiding from Nicanor. ³¹ When the latter became aware that he had been cleverly outwitted by the man, he went to the great[a] and holy temple while the priests were offering the customary sacrifices, and commanded them to hand the man over. ³² When they declared on oath that they did not know where the man was whom he wanted, ³³ he stretched out his right hand toward the sanctuary, and swore this oath: "If you do not hand Judas over to me as a prisoner, I will level this shrine of God to the ground and tear down the altar, and build here a splendid temple to Dionysus."

³⁴ Having said this, he went away. Then the priests stretched out their hands toward heaven and called upon the constant Defender of our nation, in these words: ³⁵ "O Lord of all, though you have need of nothing, you were pleased that there should be a temple for your habitation among us; ³⁶ so now, O holy One, Lord of all holiness, keep undefiled forever this house that has been so recently purified."

³⁷ A certain Razis, one of the elders of Jerusalem, was denounced to Nicanor as a man who loved his compatriots and was very well thought of and for his goodwill was called father of the Jews. ³⁸ In former times, when there was no mingling with the Gentiles, he had been accused of Judaism, and he had most zealously risked body and life for Judaism. ³⁹ Nicanor, wishing to exhibit the enmity that he had for the Jews, sent more than five hundred soldiers to arrest him; ⁴⁰ for he thought

that by arresting[b] him he would do them an injury. ⁴¹ When the troops were about to capture the tower and were forcing the door of the courtyard, they ordered that fire be brought and the doors burned. Being surrounded, Razis[c] fell upon his own sword, ⁴² preferring to die nobly rather than to fall into the hands of sinners and suffer outrages unworthy of his noble birth. ⁴³ But in the heat of the struggle he did not hit exactly, and the crowd was now rushing in through the doors. He courageously ran up on the wall, and bravely threw himself down into the crowd. ⁴⁴ But as they quickly drew back, a space opened and he fell in the middle of the empty space. ⁴⁵ Still alive and aflame with anger, he rose, and though his blood gushed forth and his wounds were severe he ran through the crowd; and standing upon a steep rock, ⁴⁶ with his blood now completely drained from him, he tore out his entrails, took them in both hands and hurled them at the crowd, calling upon the Lord of life and spirit to give them back to him again. This was the manner of his death.

15 When Nicanor heard that Judas and his troops were in the region of Samaria, he made plans to attack them with complete safety on the day of rest. ² When the Jews who were compelled to follow him said, "Do not destroy so savagely and barbarously, but show respect for the day that he who sees all things has honored and hallowed above other

---

a   Gk *greatest*
b   Meaning of Gk uncertain
c   Gk *he*

Nicanor has no choice but to obey, and so the way is paved for a new clash. **28–33:** Cf. 1 Macc 7.30–38. **30:** Cf. Gen 31.2. **33:** *Stretched out his right hand*, usually a gesture of prayer (3.20; 15.12), but here it is a threat, apparently modeled on Isa 10.32, where it is ascribed to an Assyrian king leading an army against Jerusalem. The threatening gesture is answered first in the next verse and then, conclusively, at 15.32. **34:** *Toward heaven*, to protect the Temple, as in 3.39. **35:** In contrast to the parallel in 1 Macc 7.36–38, the Diaspora theology of 2 Macc emphasizes that God resides in heaven, not in what the Bible calls "the house of God." **36:** *Been so recently purified*, see 10.1–8; 13.11.

14.37–46: Martyrdom of Razis. This account of martyrdom functions similarly to those in chs 6–7. It is the premise of the victory over Nicanor depicted in the next chapter. **37:** *Father of the Jews*, honorifically; compare 11.1n. **38:** *Risked body and life for Judaism*, the reference to Judaism shows that Razis fought, in his way, for the same cause as did Judas and his men in theirs (2.21; 8.1). **42:** *Die nobly*, like Eleazar (6.28). **43–44:** *Courageously . . . bravely*: the Diaspora author emphasizes that martyrs share the same qualities as heroic soldiers. **46:** See 7.9n.

15.1–36: Death of Nicanor. 1: *Attack . . . on the day of rest*, cf. 5.25; 8.26. **3:** *Thrice-accursed* Nicanor, as 8.34.

days," [3] the thrice-accursed wretch asked if there were a sovereign in heaven who had commanded the keeping of the sabbath day. [4] When they declared, "It is the living Lord himself, the Sovereign in heaven, who ordered us to observe the seventh day," [5] he replied, "But I am a sovereign also, on earth, and I command you to take up arms and finish the king's business." Nevertheless, he did not succeed in carrying out his abominable design.

[6] This Nicanor in his utter boastfulness and arrogance had determined to erect a public monument of victory over Judas and his forces. [7] But Maccabeus did not cease to trust with all confidence that he would get help from the Lord. [8] He exhorted his troops not to fear the attack of the Gentiles, but to keep in mind the former times when help had come to them from heaven, and so to look for the victory that the Almighty would give them. [9] Encouraging them from the law and the prophets, and reminding them also of the struggles they had won, he made them the more eager. [10] When he had aroused their courage, he issued his orders, at the same time pointing out the perfidy of the Gentiles and their violation of oaths. [11] He armed each of them not so much with confidence in shields and spears as with the inspiration of brave words, and he cheered them all by relating a dream, a sort of vision,[a] which was worthy of belief.

[12] What he saw was this: Onias, who had been high priest, a noble and good man, of modest bearing and gentle manner, one who spoke fittingly and had been trained from childhood in all that belongs to excellence, was praying with outstretched hands for the whole body of the Jews. [13] Then in the same fashion another appeared, distinguished by his gray hair and dignity, and of marvelous majesty and authority. [14] And Onias spoke, saying, "This is a man who loves the family of Israel and prays much for the people and the holy city—Jeremiah, the prophet of God."

[15] Jeremiah stretched out his right hand and gave to Judas a golden sword, and as he gave it he addressed him thus: [16] "Take this holy sword, a gift from God, with which you will strike down your adversaries."

[17] Encouraged by the words of Judas, so noble and so effective in arousing valor and awaking courage in the souls of the young, they determined not to carry on a campaign[b] but to attack bravely, and to decide the matter by fighting hand to hand with all courage, because the city and the sanctuary and the temple were in danger. [18] Their concern for wives and children, and also for brothers and sisters[c] and relatives, lay upon them less heavily; their greatest and first fear was for the consecrated sanctuary. [19] And those who had to remain in the city were in no little distress, being anxious over the encounter in the open country.

[20] When all were now looking forward to the coming issue, and the enemy was already close at hand with their army drawn up for battle, the elephants[d] strategically stationed and the cavalry deployed on the flanks, [21] Maccabeus, observing the masses that were in front of him and the varied supply of arms and the savagery of the elephants, stretched out his hands toward heaven and called upon the Lord who works wonders; for he knew that it is not by arms, but as the Lord[e] decides, that he gains the victory for those who deserve it. [22] He called upon him in these words: "O Lord, you sent your angel in the time of King Hezekiah of Judea, and he killed fully one hundred eighty-five thousand in the camp of Sennacherib. [23] So now, O Sovereign of the heavens, send a good angel to spread terror and trembling before us. [24] By the

---

[a]   Meaning of Gk uncertain
[b]   Or *to remain in camp*
[c]   Gk *for brothers*
[d]   Gk *animals*
[e]   Gk *he*

4–5: *Sovereign in heaven . . . sovereign also, on earth*, see 3.22–23n. **8–9:** Cf. v. 22 and 8.19. **9:** *The law and the prophets*, the Torah (Pentateuch) and the prophetic books were now regarded as scripture (see Prologue to Sirach). **10:** *Violation of oaths*, 11.27–32; 14.18–29. **12–16:** Judas receives the support of both priest (Onias) and prophet (Jeremiah) to defend the Jews on the Sabbath; compare the treatment of the sabbath question in 1 Macc 2.39–41. **12:** On *Onias's* qualities, see 4.37n. *Was praying*, as a priest invoking God's blessing upon a congregation; see Lev 9.22 and Sir 50.20. **20:** *Elephants . . . cavalry*, compare 1 Macc 6.34–38. **22:** See 8.19n. **23:** *Good angel*, as at

might of your arm may these blasphemers who come against your holy people be struck down." With these words he ended his prayer.

²⁵ Nicanor and his troops advanced with trumpets and battle songs, ²⁶ but Judas and his troops met the enemy in battle with invocations to God and prayers. ²⁷ So, fighting with their hands and praying to God in their hearts, they laid low at least thirty-five thousand, and were greatly gladdened by God's manifestation.

²⁸ When the action was over and they were returning with joy, they recognized Nicanor, lying dead, in full armor. ²⁹ Then there was shouting and tumult, and they blessed the Sovereign Lord in the language of their ancestors. ³⁰ Then the man who was ever in body and soul the defender of his people, the man who maintained his youthful goodwill toward his compatriots, ordered them to cut off Nicanor's head and arm and carry them to Jerusalem. ³¹ When he arrived there and had called his compatriots together and stationed the priests before the altar, he sent for those who were in the citadel. ³² He showed them the vile Nicanor's head and that profane man's arm, which had been boastfully stretched out against the holy house of the Almighty. ³³ He cut out the tongue of the ungodly Nicanor and said that he would feed it piecemeal to the birds and would hang up these rewards of his folly opposite the sanctuary. ³⁴ And they all, looking to heaven, blessed the Lord who had manifested himself, saying, "Blessed is he who has kept his own place undefiled!" ³⁵ Judasª hung Nicanor's head from the citadel, a clear and conspicuous sign to everyone of the help of the Lord. ³⁶ And they all decree by public vote never to let this day go unobserved, but to celebrate the thirteenth day of the twelfth month—which is called Adar in the Aramaic language—the day before Mordecai's day.

³⁷ This, then, is how matters turned out with Nicanor, and from that time the city has been in the possession of the Hebrews. So I will here end my story.

³⁸ If it is well told and to the point, that is what I myself desired; if it is poorly done and mediocre, that was the best I could do. ³⁹ For just as it is harmful to drink wine alone, or, again, to drink water alone, while wine mixed with water is sweet and delicious and enhances one's enjoyment, so also the style of the story delights the ears of those who read the work. And here will be the end.

ª   Gk *He*

11.6. **24:** *Might of your arm,* Ex 15.16. **27:** *Fighting with their hands and praying,* Ps 149.6. **29:** *Shouting and tumult,* words that usually bespeak fear; see 3.30; 10.30; 11.25; 12.37; 13.16. Indeed, some fear is expected among those who witness divine intervention, even on their behalf; compare Ex 14.30–31; Ps 52.6; Mk 4.41; Lk 1.65. *Language of their ancestors,* i.e., Hebrew; Palestinian Jews spoke Aramaic, but formal prayer, using the language of scripture, was typically in Hebrew. **30–36:** Disposition of Nicanor's corpse; cf. 1 Macc 7.47–49. **31:** *The citadel,* the garrison north of the Temple was still held by the Syrians (1 Macc 1.33; 6.18), but the Jews had built another fort (1 Macc 4.60). **32:** See 14.33. **34:** *Who has kept his own place undefiled,* answering, verbatim, the prayer of 14.36. **35:** 1 Sam 31.9; Jdt 14.1; 1 Macc 7.47. **36:** *Decreed by public vote,* as at 10.8. Compare 1 Macc 7.48–49. *Adar,* February/March. *Aramaic,* the contemporary vernacular, as opposed to Hebrew, "the language of their ancestors" (12.37; 15.29; cf. 7.8,21,27). *Mordecai's day,* the festival of Purim, celebrated on the fourteenth day of Adar (Esth 9.21). There is evidence for the celebration of Nicanor's Day even centuries later.

15.37–39: Conclusion. 37: *So I will here end,* by using the first person the author reintroduces himself and thus announces the conclusion of his work, clearly explaining that it is the restoration of Jerusalem that ends his story, thus closing the circle that began with the idyllic Jerusalem of 3.1–3. The fact that the city was under Seleucid rule in ch 3 and now it was *in the possession of the Hebrews* does not interest the Diaspora author. For the history of Jerusalem, and the revolt, from this point on, see 1 Macc 8ff. **39:** *Harmful to drink wine alone,* in the Greco-Roman world it was usual to drink wine mixed with water; only barbarians, famously the Scythians (see 4.47n.), drank it undiluted. As at 2.29, the author emphasizes that his job was only to beautify Jason of Cyrene's work, making it more palatable and enjoyable.

(b) The books from 1 Esdras through 3 Maccabees are recognized as Deuterocanonical Scripture by the Greek and the Russian Orthodox Churches. They are not so recognized by the Roman Catholic Chruch, but 1 Esdras and the Prayer of Manasseh (together with 2 Esdras) are placed in an appendix to the Latin Vulgate Bible.

1 ESDRAS

NAME AND CANONICAL STATUS

First Esdras (the Greek form of Ezra) is one of several books bearing the name of Ezra. It is included in the canon by Greek and Russian Orthodox churches. Known in the early Greek mss as Esdras Apocrypha or 1 Esdras; the book is called 3 Esdras in the Latin Vulgate Bible, where it was often placed in an appendix after the New Testament.

DATE OF COMPOSITION AND LITERARY HISTORY

The book has been preserved in Greek and reflects Hellenistic values and vocabulary. Although the latest events it narrates are from the mid-fifth century, it probably dates in its current form to the second century BCE. It is unclear whether the book is a translation of an earlier Hebrew or Aramaic version (possibly as ancient as Ezra-Nehemiah) or a late adaptation of 2 Chronicles and Ezra-Nehemiah composed originally in Greek. The work in Greek was used by the late first-century CE historian Josephus for his account of the return from the exile.

With one significant exception, the book repeats, with minor (yet often significant) variations, sections from the books of 2 Chronicles and Ezra-Nehemiah. First Esdras begins with King Josiah's Passover celebration in Jerusalem in 622 BCE, reproducing the substance of 2 Chr 35.1–36.21. It continues directly with all of the canonical book of Ezra (with a few changes), which describes the return to Judea beginning in 538 BCE, followed by Nehemiah 8, which describes events that ostensibly (in 1 Esdras) transpired in 458–457 BCE in which Ezra participated. The only material unique to 1 Esdras is the story of the three young bodyguards in the court of King Darius (3.1–5.6).

STRUCTURE AND CONTENTS

Although the book largely overlaps other biblical books, its compositional pattern offers a distinct perspective on the history it recounts. It traces a trajectory between Josiah's Passover (1.1–24) and an unnamed holy day in the time of Ezra (9.49–55 || Neh 8:1–13). The destruction of Jerusalem, exile, and rebuilding that it narrates are framed by celebrations, which imply complete restoration and a return to the "good old days." It thereby depicts a more positive historical development than the longer report in Ezra-Nehemiah, which begins and concludes with challenges rather than festivities. The main divisions of the book are:

1.1–24	An ideal state of affairs: Josiah's Passover celebration (=2 Chr 35.1–27)
1.25–58	Decline and destruction (=2 Chr 36.1–21)
2.1–9.55 [except 3.1-5.6]	Stages of return and restoration (=Ezra 1–10 and Neh 8):
2.1–30	Initial preparations for a return and rebuilding (||Ezra 1 and 4.7–24)
3.1–5.6	The three bodyguards and the commissioning of Zerubbabel
5.7–7.15	Zerubbabel leads the rebuilding of the altar and the temple (||Ezra 2:1–4:6 and 5.1–6.22)
8.1–9.55	Ezra leads the reforms and introduces the law (||Ezra 7–9; Neh 8.1–13a)

INTERPRETATION AND GUIDE TO READING

The book begins and concludes with a ceremony in Jerusalem in front of the Temple—highlighting the unquestioned centrality of the Temple. The troubled time between the ceremonies—namely, the destruction of the Temple and Jerusalem, and the exile to Babylon—is treated as a brief period, followed immediately by a gradual but effective restoration of the altar, the Temple, and the community. Whereas the book of Ezra-Nehemiah contrasts the preexilic period with that of the return from exile, 1 Esdras, like Chronicles, underscores continuities between them. First Esdras also contrasts with the accounts in Ezra-Nehemiah in glorifying leaders, especially King David's descendant Zerubbabel, whose role it expands significantly. In particular, the lengthy story (unique to 1 Esdras) of the three bodyguards in Darius's court focuses on Zerubbabel's achievements. This story portrays

Zerubbabel as the wise hero who wins Darius's support for the reconstruction of the Temple and successfully accomplishes his goal. Ezra the priest also rises to a higher level than in Ezra-Nehemiah, explicitly called a chief priest (but see Ezra 7.5n.). Ezra's prominence is further increased by the absence of collaboration with Nehemiah (who is portrayed in Nehemiah 1–13 as a governor responsible for rebuilding Jerusalem's walls). In First Esdras, Ezra is the dominant figure in the final stages of the restoration and the climax of the entire story (8.1–9.55).

Tamara Cohn Eskenazi

1 Josiah kept the passover to his Lord in Jerusalem; he killed the passover lamb on the fourteenth day of the first month, ² having placed the priests according to their divisions, arrayed in their vestments, in the temple of the Lord. ³ He told the Levites, the temple servants of Israel, that they should sanctify themselves to the Lord and put the holy ark of the Lord in the house that King Solomon, son of David, had built; ⁴ and he said, "You need no longer carry it on your shoulders. Now worship the Lord your God and serve his people Israel; prepare yourselves by your families and kindred, ⁵ in accordance with the directions of King David of Israel and the magnificence of his son Solomon. Stand in order in the temple according to the groupings of the ancestral houses of you Levites, who minister before your kindred the people of Israel, ⁶ and kill the passover lamb and prepare the sacrifices for your kindred, and keep the passover according to the commandment of the Lord that was given to Moses."

⁷ To the people who were present Josiah gave thirty thousand lambs and kids, and three thousand calves; these were given from the king's possessions, as he promised, to the people and the priests and Levites. ⁸ Hilkiah, Zechariah, and Jehiel,[a] the chief officers of the temple, gave to the priests for the passover two thousand six hundred sheep and three hundred calves. ⁹ And Jeconiah and Shemaiah and his brother Nethanel, and Hashabiah and Ochiel and Joram, captains over thousands, gave the Levites for the passover five thousand sheep and seven hundred calves.

¹⁰ This is what took place. The priests and the Levites, having the unleavened bread, stood in proper order according to kindred ¹¹ and the grouping of the ancestral houses, before the people, to make the offering to the Lord as it is written in the book of Moses; this they did in the morning. ¹² They roasted the passover lamb with fire, as required; and they boiled the sacrifices in bronze pots and caldrons, with a pleasing odor, ¹³ and carried them to all the people. Afterward they prepared the passover for themselves and for their kindred the priests, the sons of Aaron, ¹⁴ because the priests were offering the fat until nightfall; so the Levites prepared it for themselves and for their kindred the priests, the sons of Aaron. ¹⁵ The temple singers, the sons of Asaph, were in their place according to the arrangement made by David, and also Asaph, Zechariah, and Eddinus, who represented the king. ¹⁶ The gatekeepers were at each gate; no one needed to interrupt his

---

[a] Gk *Esyelus*

1.1–24: An ideal state of affairs: Josiah's Passover celebration (2 Chr 35.1–19). This event constitutes a high point just prior to the destruction of Jerusalem and its Temple. According to 2 Kings 23.21–23 and 2 Chr 34.14–33, the Passover celebration of 622 BCE was the culmination of the religious reforms of Josiah, king of Judah (640–609 BCE). First Esdras does not include an account of the reforms. The author of 1 Esdras is interested in the continuity between the First and Second Temples, and thus shapes its narrative as a movement from one high point (Passover celebration under Josiah) to another, at the time of Ezra (1 Esdras 9), with the destruction and exile but a brief interlude (1 Esdras 1.25–58), followed directly by return and restoration. **3:** *The Levites* were religious functionaries; the priests (v.2) were a subgroup of Levites who, according to tradition, were descended from Aaron, the first priest (see Ex 28.1) with unique responsibilities for the sanctuary. For rules concerning Levites, see 1 Chr 3.1–5.1. **5:** For an understanding of David's role, see 1 Chr 23; 28.13,21; 2 Chr 8.14. **6:** For Passover rules, see Ex 12.1–13; Deut 16.1–8. **7–9:** The list of offerings differs slightly from that in 2 Chr 35.7–9.

daily duties, for their kindred the Levites prepared the passover for them.

17 So the things that had to do with the sacrifices to the Lord were accomplished that day: the passover was kept 18 and the sacrifices were offered on the altar of the Lord, according to the command of King Josiah. 19 And the people of Israel who were present at that time kept the passover and the festival of unleavened bread seven days. 20 No passover like it had been kept in Israel since the times of the prophet Samuel; 21 none of the kings of Israel had kept such a passover as was kept by Josiah and the priests and Levites and the people of Judah and all of Israel who were living in Jerusalem. 22 In the eighteenth year of the reign of Josiah this passover was kept.

23 And the deeds of Josiah were upright in the sight of the Lord, for his heart was full of godliness. 24 In ancient times the events of his reign have been recorded—concerning those who sinned and acted wickedly toward the Lord beyond any other people or kingdom, and how they grieved the Lord[a] deeply, so that the words of the Lord fell upon Israel.

25 After all these acts of Josiah, it happened that Pharaoh, king of Egypt, went to make war at Carchemish on the Euphrates, and Josiah went out against him. 26 And the king of Egypt sent word to him saying, "What have we to do with each other, O king of Judea? 27 I was not sent against you by the Lord God, for my war is at the Euphrates. And now the Lord is with me! The Lord is with me, urging me on! Stand aside, and do not oppose the Lord."

28 Josiah, however, did not turn back to his chariot, but tried to fight with him, and did not heed the words of the prophet Jeremiah from the mouth of the Lord. 29 He joined battle with him in the plain of Megiddo, and the commanders came down against King Josiah. 30 The king said to his servants, "Take me away from the battle, for I am very weak." And immediately his servants took him out of the line of battle. 31 He got into his second chariot; and after he was brought back to Jerusalem he died, and was buried in the tomb of his ancestors.

32 In all Judea they mourned for Josiah. The prophet Jeremiah lamented for Josiah, and the principal men, with the women,[b] have made lamentation for him to this day; it was ordained that this should always be done throughout the whole nation of Israel. 33 These things are written in the book of the histories of the kings of Judea; and every one of the acts of Josiah, and his splendor, and his understanding of the law of the Lord, and the things that he had done before, and these that are now told, are recorded in the book of the kings of Israel and Judah.

34 The men of the nation took Jeconiah[c] son of Josiah, who was twenty-three years old, and made him king in succession to his father Josiah. 35 He reigned three months in Judah and Jerusalem. Then the king of Egypt deposed him from reigning in Jerusalem, 36 and fined the nation one hundred talents of silver and one talent of gold. 37 The king of Egypt made his brother Jehoiakim king of Judea and Jerusalem. 38 Jehoiakim put the nobles in prison, and seized his brother Zarius and brought him back from Egypt.

a Gk *him*
b Or *their wives*
c 2 Kings 23.30; 2 Chr 36.1 *Jehoahaz*

12: See 2 Chr 35.13n. 20: Cf. 2 Kings 23.22. 22: *The eighteenth year,* 622 BCE. 23–24: The evaluation of Josiah in 1 Esdras elaborates on Chronicles.

1.25–58: Decline and destruction. 25–33: Josiah's death and the beginning of decline in 1 Esdras largely follow the account in 2 Chr 35.20–27, omitting the report that Josiah disguised himself, and that he was struck by an arrow. 28: The author of 1 Esdras probably found the Chronicler's account difficult because it depicts the Pharaoh as a prophet, and revised it to suggest that Josiah's death resulted from ignoring the warning of Jeremiah, though no passage in the book of Jeremiah explicitly relates to the battle in which Josiah died. 33: Josiah is the last good king in the books of Kings and Chronicles, and his death in 609 BCE marks the end of an era.

1.34–49: The last kings of Judah (2 Chr 36.1–14). The good king Josiah is followed by evil kings. 34: *Jeconiah* as successor to Josiah does not appear in 2 Chr or 2 Kings, and is probably an error for Jehoahaz (ruled briefly in 609 BCE; see 2 Kings 23.30–31; 2 Chr 36.1–2). Jeconiah is an alternate form of the name of Jehoiachin (see v. 43); see Jer 28.4; cf. Jer 22.24. *Men of the nation,* this corresponds to "the people of the land" of 2 Chr 36.1; in preexilic times these were probably landowners who often came to the support of reforming kings or who themselves

³⁹ Jehoiakim was twenty-five years old when he began to reign in Judea and Jerusalem; he did what was evil in the sight of the Lord. ⁴⁰ King Nebuchadnezzar of Babylon came up against him; he bound him with a chain of bronze and took him away to Babylon. ⁴¹ Nebuchadnezzar also took some holy vessels of the Lord, and carried them away, and stored them in his temple in Babylon. ⁴² But the things that are reported about Jehoiakim,^a and his uncleanness and impiety, are written in the annals of the kings.

⁴³ His son Jehoiachin^b became king in his place; when he was made king he was eighteen years old, ⁴⁴ and he reigned three months and ten days in Jerusalem. He did what was evil in the sight of the Lord. ⁴⁵ A year later Nebuchadnezzar sent and removed him to Babylon, with the holy vessels of the Lord, ⁴⁶ and made Zedekiah king of Judea and Jerusalem.

Zedekiah was twenty-one years old, and he reigned eleven years. ⁴⁷ He also did what was evil in the sight of the Lord, and did not heed the words that were spoken by the prophet Jeremiah from the mouth of the Lord. ⁴⁸ Although King Nebuchadnezzar had made him swear by the name of the Lord, he broke his oath and rebelled; he stiffened his neck and hardened his heart and transgressed the laws of the Lord, the God of Israel. ⁴⁹ Even the leaders of the people and of the priests committed many acts of sacrilege and lawlessness beyond all the unclean deeds of all the nations, and polluted the temple of the Lord in Jerusalem—the temple that God had made holy. ⁵⁰ The God of their ancestors sent his messenger to call them back, because he would have spared them and his dwelling place. ⁵¹ But they mocked his messengers, and whenever the Lord spoke, they scoffed at his prophets, ⁵² until in his anger against his people because of their ungodly acts he gave command to bring against them the kings of the Chaldeans. ⁵³ These killed their young men with the sword around their holy temple, and did not spare young man or young woman,^c old man or child, for he gave them all into their hands. ⁵⁴ They took all the holy vessels of the Lord, great and small, the treasure chests of the Lord, and the royal stores, and carried them away to Babylon. ⁵⁵ They burned the house of the Lord, broke down the walls of Jerusalem, burned their towers with fire, ⁵⁶ and utterly destroyed all its glorious things. The survivors he led away to Babylon with the sword, ⁵⁷ and they were servants to him and to his sons until the Persians began to reign, in fulfillment of the word of the Lord by the mouth of Jeremiah, ⁵⁸ saying, "Until the land has enjoyed its sabbaths, it shall keep sabbath all the time of its desolation until the completion of seventy years."

2 In the first year of Cyrus as king of the Persians, so that the word of the Lord by the mouth of Jeremiah might be accomplished— ² the Lord stirred up the spirit of

a   Gk *him*
b   Gk *Jehoiakim*
c   Gk *virgin*

instituted reforms (2 Kings 12.18,20; 21.24; 23.30). **36:** A talent weighed about 75 lb (34 kg). **38:** The author recasts 2 Chr 36.4, in which Neco of Egypt removed Jehoahaz from the throne and installed Josiah's elder son Eliakim as king, changing his name to Jehoiakim. Jehoahaz was taken to Egypt, where presumably he died (Jer 22.10–12). In 1 Esdras, Jehoiakim brings up his brother Zarius from Egypt; the name Zarius may be a corruption of Jehoahaz or of Zedekiah, both of whom were brothers of Jehoiakim (2 Kings 24.17; 2 Chr 36.4,10). **39:** According to 2 Chr 36.5, Jehoiakim reigned eleven years (608–598). **43:** 1 Esdras (in contrast to 2 Chr and 2 Kings) gives the name Jehoiakim rather than Jehoiachin to this king's son and successor; but the king's age at the beginning of his reign is more credible (eighteen years; not eight, as in 2 Chr 36.9; cf. 2 Kings 24.8); he ruled in 597. **46:** *Zedekiah*, the last king of Judah, ruled 597–586.

1.50–58: Jerusalem falls to the Babylonians (2 Chr 36.15–21). **52:** *Chaldeans*, a late biblical name for the Babylonians. **58:** To keep sabbath means here that the land is to lie untended, as in the seventh or sabbatical years, until the exiles return (Jer 25.11–12; 29.10; cf. Lev 25.1–7; 26.27–39,43). Like Chronicles, 1 Esdras stresses the temporary nature of exile, in contrast to 2 Kings 25 and Jer 52, which present it as a tragedy with only a glimmer of hope.

2.1–9.55: Stages of return and restoration. Except for the new material in 3.1–5.6, from here on 1 Esdras

King Cyrus of the Persians, and he made a proclamation throughout all his kingdom and also put it in writing:

³ "Thus says Cyrus king of the Persians: The Lord of Israel, the Lord Most High, has made me king of the world, ⁴ and he has commanded me to build him a house at Jerusalem, which is in Judea. ⁵ If any of you, therefore, are of his people, may your Lord be with you; go up to Jerusalem, which is in Judea, and build the house of the Lord of Israel—he is the Lord who dwells in Jerusalem— ⁶ and let each of you, wherever you may live, be helped by the people of your place with gold and silver, ⁷ with gifts and with horses and cattle, besides the other things added as votive offerings for the temple of the Lord that is in Jerusalem."

⁸ Then arose the heads of families of the tribes of Judah and Benjamin, and the priests and the Levites, and all whose spirit the Lord had stirred to go up to build the house in Jerusalem for the Lord; ⁹ their neighbors helped them with everything, with silver and gold, with horses and cattle, and with a very great number of votive offerings from many whose hearts were stirred.

¹⁰ King Cyrus also brought out the holy vessels of the Lord that Nebuchadnezzar had carried away from Jerusalem and stored in his temple of idols. ¹¹ When King Cyrus of the Persians brought these out, he gave them to Mithridates, his treasurer, ¹² and by him they were given to Sheshbazzar,ᵃ the governor of Judea. ¹³ The number of these was: one thousand gold cups, one thousand silver cups, twenty-nine silver censers, thirty gold bowls, two thousand four hundred ten silver bowls, and one thousand other vessels. ¹⁴ All the vessels were handed over, gold and silver, five thousand four hundred sixty-nine, ¹⁵ and they were carried back by Sheshbazzar with the returning exiles from Babylon to Jerusalem.

¹⁶ In the time of King Artaxerxes of the Persians, Bishlam, Mithridates, Tabeel, Rehum,

---

ᵃ Gk *Sanabassaros*

---

follows Ezra 1–10 and Neh 8, reshaping the material through artful composition that shifts the emphases from the community to exceptional leaders, mostly Zerubbabel the governor and Ezra the priest and scribe. Some changes in sequence highlight these emphases (see 2.16–30).

2.1–15: Cyrus, king of Persia permits the exiles to return (Ezra 1.1–11). The text is almost identical with the end of 2 Chr and the beginning of Ezra, which are also nearly identical. **1:** *First year of Cyrus,* 538 BCE; the year after he conquered Babylon. **3–7:** The substance of the decree is consistent with Persian religious and political policy; ancient inscriptions depict Cyrus as the restorer of several temples. *Jeremiah* lived through the destruction of Judah and repeatedly promised a restoration; see, e.g., Jer 29.10. **8–9:** These verses sum up the enthusiastic response by the people to the decree, a response that leads to the reconstruction described in 5.47–7.15. **8:** *Judah and Benjamin,* these tribes had constituted the Southern Kingdom of Judah. They now represent the sole remnant of the twelve tribes of ancient Israel. According to 2 Kings 17, the other tribes were deported, and their land was repopulated by foreigners. **10–15:** The return of the sacred vessels symbolizes continuity with the destroyed Temple, whose looting is described in 1.54. The inventory of the sacred vessels is smoother in 1 Esdras than in Ezra. **12:** *Sheshbazzar,* a Jewish leader and the first governor of the province of Yehud (Judea) appointed by the Persians. He may have been a descendant of David.

2.16–30: Opposition to the rebuilding of the Temple and the city walls (Ezra 4.7–24). This account in Ezra 4 represents a later stage in the process of return and reconstruction, describing opposition to rebuilding the walls of Jerusalem in the time of Artaxerxes I (465–424 BCE), after the Temple had been founded (Ezra 3). Its location in the Ezra narrative is out of chronological order and seeks to explain why Zerubbabel and Joshua were unable to finish rebuilding the Temple. Here it serves to explain why nothing was accomplished until the hero Zerubbabel took charge. The sequence is still out of chronological order because it presents Artaxerxes (who ruled after Darius I) as preceding Darius. The fact that the Persian Empire had several kings with the same names may have facilitated this error. As in Ezra 4, adversaries led by Samarians (from the former Northern Kingdom of Israel) allege seditious activities by the returnees and successfully halt the rebuilding of Jerusalem. Historical records show that Cyrus was followed by Cambyses (530–522) and after him by Darius I (522–486). Josephus (*Ant.* 11.2.1–3), who typically follows 1 Esdras, substitutes Cambyses for Artaxerxes, thus providing the correct sequence of Persian kings. **16–20:** The opponents' letter claims that rebuilding the Temple and city

Beltethmus, the scribe Shimshai, and the rest of their associates, living in Samaria and other places, wrote him the following letter, against those who were living in Judea and Jerusalem:

[17] "To King Artaxerxes our lord, your servants the recorder Rehum and the scribe Shimshai and the other members of their council, and the judges in Coelesyria and Phoenicia: [18] Let it now be known to our lord the king that the Jews who came up from you to us have gone to Jerusalem and are building that rebellious and wicked city, repairing its market places and walls and laying the foundations for a temple. [19] Now if this city is built and the walls finished, they will not only refuse to pay tribute but will even resist kings. [20] Since the building of the temple is now going on, we think it best not to neglect such a matter, [21] but to speak to our lord the king, in order that, if it seems good to you, search may be made in the records of your ancestors. [22] You will find in the annals what has been written about them, and will learn that this city was rebellious, troubling both kings and other cities, [23] and that the Jews were rebels and kept setting up blockades in it from of old. That is why this city was laid waste. [24] Therefore we now make known to you, O lord and king, that if this city is built

and its walls finished, you will no longer have access to Coelesyria and Phoenicia."

[25] Then the king, in reply to the recorder Rehum, Beltethmus, the scribe Shimshai, and the others associated with them and living in Samaria and Syria and Phoenicia, wrote as follows:

[26] "I have read the letter that you sent me. So I ordered search to be made, and it has been found that this city from of old has fought against kings, [27] that the people in it were given to rebellion and war, and that mighty and cruel kings ruled in Jerusalem and exacted tribute from Coelesyria and Phoenicia. [28] Therefore I have now issued orders to prevent these people from building the city and to take care that nothing more be done [29] and that such wicked proceedings go no further to the annoyance of kings."

[30] Then, when the letter from King Artaxerxes was read, Rehum and the scribe Shimshai and their associates went quickly to Jerusalem, with cavalry and a large number of armed troops, and began to hinder the builders. And the building of the temple in Jerusalem stopped until the second year of the reign of King Darius of the Persians.

3 Now King Darius gave a great banquet for all that were under him, all that were born in his house, and all the nobles of Media

walls will lead to rebellion. **16:** The name *Beltethmus* is an awkward Greek transliteration of the Aramaic title ("be'el te'em") of the office ("royal deputy") held by Rehum. **17:** *Rehum*, designated "the royal deputy" in Ezra 4.8; the title is supported by Josephus. The persons named are officials of the region called "Beyond the River" (Ezra 4.10), which included the lands of (Coele-) Syria, Phoenicia, Samaria, and Judah. **20:** The account differs from that in Ezra 4.14, which contains no reference to the rebuilding of the Temple at this point. However, Ezra 4.24 states that work on the Temple stopped. This revision and reworking of material is consistent with the focus of 1 Esdras on the Temple. **21:** *Records of your ancestors*, the Assyrians and Babylonians kept careful records, and the Persians inherited and enlarged their bureaucracy. Here, as in ch 8, written records play a crucial role in establishing authority. **24:** Revolt in Jerusalem will endanger Persian rule throughout the western region of the empire. **25–30:** The king's investigation confirms the danger inherent in the rebuilding of the city, and he issues an order to stop it. **29:** Ezra 4.21 includes "until I make a decree," setting the stage for a reversal at a later date. **30:** *Until the second year of . . . Darius*, King Darius I (522–486), the ruler in the subsequent narrative, is identified also in Haggai and Zechariah as the Persian king during whose reign the Temple was rebuilt. 1 Esdras (like Ezra 1–6) does not allow for the prospect that work on the Temple stopped because of Judean inertia (as Haggai and Zechariah indicate) but rather attributes the neglect to external opposition.

3.1–7.15: Zerubbabel leads the return and restoration. In 1 Esdras, Samarian opponents successfully stop rebuilding before any restoration takes place (in contrast to Ezra 3–6, where Zerubbabel and Joshua lead in laying the Temple's foundation before being stopped). This arrangement of the narrative magnifies the accomplishments of Zerubbabel, making him responsible for the very first successful return. Here, then, Zerubbabel wins King Darius's favor and as a result receives permission to go and restore the Temple.

3.1–5.6: The three young bodyguards in the court of Darius. This lively story, unique to 1 Esdras, describes

and Persia, [2] and all the satraps and generals and governors that were under him in the hundred twenty-seven satrapies from India to Ethiopia. [3] They ate and drank, and when they were satisfied they went away, and King Darius went to his bedroom; he went to sleep, but woke up again.

[4] Then the three young men of the bodyguard, who kept guard over the person of the king, said to one another, [5] "Let each of us state what one thing is strongest; and to the one whose statement seems wisest, King Darius will give rich gifts and great honors of victory. [6] He shall be clothed in purple, and drink from gold cups, and sleep on a gold bed,[a] and have a chariot with gold bridles, and a turban of fine linen, and a necklace around his neck; [7] and because of his wisdom he shall sit next to Darius and shall be called Kinsman of Darius."

[8] Then each wrote his own statement, and they sealed them and put them under the pillow of King Darius, [9] and said, "When the king wakes, they will give him the writing; and to the one whose statement the king and the three nobles of Persia judge to be wisest the victory shall be given according to what is written." [10] The first wrote, "Wine is strongest." [11] The second wrote, "The king is strong-est." [12] The third wrote, "Women are strong-est, but above all things truth is victor."[b]

[13] When the king awoke, they took the writing and gave it to him, and he read it. [14] Then he sent and summoned all the nobles of Persia and Media and the satraps and generals and governors and prefects, [15] and he took his seat in the council chamber, and the writing was read in their presence. [16] He said, "Call the young men, and they shall explain their statements." So they were summoned, and came in. [17] They said to them, "Explain to us what you have written."

Then the first, who had spoken of the strength of wine, began and said: [18] "Gentlemen, how is wine the strongest? It leads astray the minds of all who drink it. [19] It makes equal the mind of the king and the orphan, of the slave and the free, of the poor and the rich. [20] It turns every thought to feasting and mirth, and forgets all sorrow and debt. [21] It makes all hearts feel rich, forgets kings and satraps, and makes everyone talk in millions.[c] [22] When people drink they forget to be friendly with friends and kindred, and

---

a   Gk *on gold*

b   Or *but truth is victor over all things*

c   Gk *talents*

---

how Zerubbabel found favor in King Darius's eyes. It magnifies the role of Zerubbabel, the last Davidic heir to have political power, making him the first great hero of the restoration. In Ezra-Nehemiah, Zerubbabel is no more prominent than his co-worker, Jeshua the priest. Although Zerubbabel the governor is a key figure in Haggai and Zechariah, along with the high priest Joshua (Jeshua in Ezra-Nehemiah and 1 Esdras), no other text suggests direct contact between him and the king. The story probably originated as a secular tale praising the relative strength of kings, wine, and women, to which praise of truth was added (4.33–41); it has close parallels in Greek literature. The author of 1 Esdras adopted the story, identified the third, wisest youth with Zerubbabel (4.13), and added a sequel to the tale, relating how Darius rewarded Zerubbabel by supporting the rebuilding of Jerusalem and its Temple (4.42–5.6). Josephus, who includes this story (*Ant.* 11.3.2–9), has a slightly different version of it.

3.1–17a: The three royal bodyguards plan a contest. The royal banquet scene is a favorite Hellenistic motif, though this case is unusual in that the bodyguards, not the king, choose the entertainment. **1–3:** Although the location is not explicitly mentioned, the Persian capital Susa may be implied (cf. Esth 1.2–3). *Media,* one of the two main original kingdoms of the Persian Empire, in northern Iran. **2:** *Satraps,* high officials in the Persian government, usually provincial governors. There were only about twenty provinces (satrapies) during Darius's reign (522–486 BCE); this number was later increased, and the total one hundred twenty-seven became conventional in later Jewish literature (Esth 1.1; Josephus, *Ant.* 11.3.2). **4–12:** The three bodyguards decide of their own initiative to entertain the king, thereby bringing riches and honor to one of them. In Josephus (*Ant.* 11.3.2), the king proposes the contest. **13–17a:** The entire court is assembled to hear the three men defend their respective answers; the scene accurately depicts court practices in the ancient world.

3.17b–24: The first guard praises the strength of wine. As the great equalizer of society, wine takes away the capacity for discernment and remembrance, overpowering king and commoner alike.

before long they draw their swords. [23] And when they recover from the wine, they do not remember what they have done. [24] Gentlemen, is not wine the strongest, since it forces people to do these things?" When he had said this, he stopped speaking.

4 Then the second, who had spoken of the strength of the king, began to speak: [2] "Gentlemen, are not men strongest, who rule over land and sea and all that is in them? [3] But the king is stronger; he is their lord and master, and whatever he says to them they obey. [4] If he tells them to make war on one another, they do it; and if he sends them out against the enemy, they go, and conquer mountains, walls, and towers. [5] They kill and are killed, and do not disobey the king's command; if they win the victory, they bring everything to the king—whatever spoil they take and everything else. [6] Likewise those who do not serve in the army or make war but till the soil; whenever they sow and reap, they bring some to the king; and they compel one another to pay taxes to the king. [7] And yet he is only one man! If he tells them to kill, they kill; if he tells them to release, they release; [8] if he tells them to attack, they attack; if he tells them to lay waste, they lay waste; if he tells them to build, they build; [9] if he tells them to cut down, they cut down; if he tells them to plant, they plant. [10] All his people and his armies obey him. Furthermore, he reclines, he eats and drinks and sleeps, [11] but they keep watch around him, and no one may go away to attend to his own affairs, nor do they disobey him. [12] Gentlemen, why is not the king the strongest, since he is to be obeyed in this fashion?" And he stopped speaking.

[13] Then the third, who had spoken of women and truth (and this was Zerubbabel), began to speak: [14] "Gentlemen, is not the king great, and are not men many, and is not wine strong? Who is it, then, that rules them, or has the mastery over them? Is it not women? [15] Women gave birth to the king and to every people that rules over sea and land. [16] From women they came; and women brought up the very men who plant the vineyards from which comes wine. [17] Women make men's clothes; they bring men glory; men cannot exist without women. [18] If men gather gold and silver or any other beautiful thing, and then see a woman lovely in appearance and beauty, [19] they let all those things go, and gape at her, and with open mouths stare at her, and all prefer her to gold or silver or any other beautiful thing. [20] A man leaves his own father, who brought him up, and his own country, and clings to his wife. [21] With his wife he ends his days, with no thought of his father or his mother or his country. [22] Therefore you must realize that women rule over you!

"Do you not labor and toil, and bring everything and give it to women? [23] A man takes his sword, and goes out to travel and rob and steal and to sail the sea and rivers; [24] he faces lions, and he walks in darkness, and when he steals and robs and plunders, he brings it back to the woman he loves. [25] A man loves his wife more than his father or his mother. [26] Many men have lost their minds because of women, and have become slaves because of them. [27] Many have perished, or stumbled, or sinned because of women. [28] And now do you not believe me?

"Is not the king great in his power? Do not all lands fear to touch him? [29] Yet I have seen him with Apame, the king's concubine, the daughter of the illustrious Bartacus; she would sit at the king's right hand [30] and take the crown from the king's head and put it on her own, and slap the king with her left hand. [31] At this the king would gaze at her with mouth agape. If she smiles at him, he laughs; if she loses her temper with him, he flatters

---

4.1–12: The second guard praises the strength of kings. The unchecked power of ancient kings is accurately portrayed here, but this passage should not be viewed as a polemic against kingship.

4.13–32: The third guard praises the strength of women as well as wisdom. He first depicts women as those who give birth to kings, who receive from men the treasures won in warfare through heroic deeds, who can humiliate their masters, including kings, and yet are sought after and fawned upon even by those whom they humiliate. **13:** *The third . . . (and this was Zerubbabel),* according to 1 Chr 3.19, Zerubbabel is a descendant of David. His name is added here as the traditional tale is incorporated into 1 Esdras (see 3.1–5.6n.). **20:** *Clings to his wife,* see Gen 2.24. **29:** *Apame, the king's concubine,* is not mentioned in other ancient sources.

her, so that she may be reconciled to him. ³²Gentlemen, why are not women strong, since they do such things?"

³³Then the king and the nobles looked at one another; and he began to speak about truth: ³⁴"Gentlemen, are not women strong? The earth is vast, and heaven is high, and the sun is swift in its course, for it makes the circuit of the heavens and returns to its place in one day. ³⁵Is not the one who does these things great? But truth is great, and stronger than all things. ³⁶The whole earth calls upon truth, and heaven blesses it. All God's works[a] quake and tremble, and with him there is nothing unrighteous. ³⁷Wine is unrighteous, the king is unrighteous, women are unrighteous, all human beings are unrighteous, all their works are unrighteous, and all such things. There is no truth in them and in their unrighteousness they will perish. ³⁸But truth endures and is strong forever, and lives and prevails forever and ever. ³⁹With it there is no partiality or preference, but it does what is righteous instead of anything that is unrighteous or wicked. Everyone approves its deeds, ⁴⁰and there is nothing unrighteous in its judgment. To it belongs the strength and the kingship and the power and the majesty of all the ages. Blessed be the God of truth!" ⁴¹When he stopped speaking, all the people shouted and said, "Great is truth, and strongest of all!"

⁴²Then the king said to him, "Ask what you wish, even beyond what is written, and we will give it to you, for you have been found to be the wisest. You shall sit next to me, and be called my Kinsman." ⁴³Then he said to the king, "Remember the vow that you made on the day when you became king, to build Jerusalem, ⁴⁴and to send back all the vessels that were taken from Jerusalem, which Cyrus set apart when he began[b] to destroy Babylon, and vowed to send them back there. ⁴⁵You also vowed to build the temple, which the Edomites burned when Judea was laid waste by the Chaldeans. ⁴⁶And now, O lord the king, this is what I ask and request of you, and this befits your greatness. I pray therefore that you fulfill the vow whose fulfillment you vowed to the King of heaven with your own lips."

⁴⁷Then King Darius got up and kissed him, and wrote letters for him to all the treasurers and governors and generals and satraps, that they should give safe conduct to him and to all who were going up with him to build Jerusalem. ⁴⁸And he wrote letters to all the governors in Coelesyria and Phoenicia and to those in Lebanon, to bring cedar timber from Lebanon to Jerusalem, and to help him build the city. ⁴⁹He wrote in behalf of all the Jews who were going up from his kingdom to Judea, in the interest of their freedom, that no officer or satrap or governor or treasurer should forcibly enter their doors; ⁵⁰that all the country that they would occupy should be theirs without tribute; that the Idumeans should give up the villages of the Jews that they held; ⁵¹that twenty talents a year should

---

[a] Gk *All the works*
[b] Cn: Gk *vowed*

4.33–41: Zerubbabel adds praise of truth. This addition to the original story was probably made prior to the story's adaptation to the Jewish author's purpose. Truth is portrayed in imagery familiar in Greek literature, although the Jewish adapter of the story may have modified the original to conform to the meaning of the Hebrew word for truth, which conveys firmness and reliability. **40:** A clever maneuver by a Jewish adapter of the story to suggest that truth is virtually equivalent to the will of God. **41:** The Latin Vulgate translation of the people's response, "Magna est veritas et praevalet," became a famous proverb.

4.42–57: Zerubbabel's reward. At Zerubbabel's request, Darius agrees to authorize Zerubbabel to return to Jerusalem and rebuild the Temple, with generous support from the Persian treasury. **43:** This improbable vow of Darius to rebuild Jerusalem and its Temple upon his accession to kingship is not otherwise attested and is likely the creation of the author. **45:** *Edomites,* this group is not mentioned in 1.55 as having burned the Temple, but see Ob 11–14 and Ps 137.7. **48–57:** Darius magnificently supports the program outlined by Zerubbabel. The extravagant royal support depicted here is improbable. A more plausible version is found in the decree Darius issues later after receiving a report about building activities (Ezra 6.1–13; 1 Esd 6.23–34). **50:** *Idumeans,* a later designation of the Edomites. The demand that they give back their villages to the returning exiles implies that Edomites encroached upon Judean land during the exile.

be given for the building of the temple until it was completed, [52] and an additional ten talents a year for burnt offerings to be offered on the altar every day, in accordance with the commandment to make seventeen offerings; [53] and that all who came from Babylonia to build the city should have their freedom, they and their children and all the priests who came. [54] He wrote also concerning their support and the priests' vestments in which[a] they were to minister. [55] He wrote that the support for the Levites should be provided until the day when the temple would be finished and Jerusalem built. [56] He wrote that land and wages should be provided for all who guarded the city. [57] And he sent back from Babylon all the vessels that Cyrus had set apart; everything that Cyrus had ordered to be done, he also commanded to be done and to be sent to Jerusalem.

[58] When the young man went out, he lifted up his face to heaven toward Jerusalem, and praised the King of heaven, saying, [59] "From you comes the victory; from you comes wisdom, and yours is the glory. I am your servant. [60] Blessed are you, who have given me wisdom; I give you thanks, O Lord of our ancestors."

[61] So he took the letters, and went to Babylon and told this to all his kindred. [62] And they praised the God of their ancestors, because he had given them release and permission [63] to go up and build Jerusalem and the temple that is called by his name; and they feasted, with music and rejoicing, for seven days.

5 After this the heads of ancestral houses were chosen to go up, according to their tribes, with their wives and sons and daughters, and their male and female servants, and their livestock. [2] And Darius sent with them a thousand cavalry to take them back to Jerusalem in safety, with the music of drums and flutes; [3] all their kindred were making merry. And he made them go up with them.

[4] These are the names of the men who went up, according to their ancestral houses in the tribes, over their groups: [5] the priests, the descendants of Phinehas son of Aaron; Jeshua son of Jozadak son of Seraiah and Joakim son of Zerubbabel son of Shealtiel, of the house of David, of the lineage of Phares, of the tribe of Judah, [6] who spoke wise words before King Darius of the Persians, in the second year of his reign, in the month of Nisan, the first month.

[7] These are the Judeans who came up out of their sojourn in exile, whom King Nebuchadnezzar of Babylon had carried away to Babylon [8] and who returned to Jerusalem and the rest of Judea, each to his own town. They came with Zerubbabel and Jeshua, Nehemiah, Seraiah, Resaiah, Eneneus, Mordecai, Beelsarus, Aspharasus, Reeliah, Rehum, and Baanah, their leaders.

[9] The number of those of the nation and their leaders: the descendants of Parosh, two thousand one hundred seventy-two. The descendants of Shephatiah, four hundred seventy-two. [10] The descendants of Arah, seven hundred fifty-six. [11] The descendants of Pahath-moab, of the descendants of Jeshua and Joab, two thousand eight hundred twelve. [12] The descendants of Elam, one thousand two hundred fifty-four. The descendants of Zattu, nine hundred forty-five. The descendants of Chorbe, seven hundred five. The descendants of Bani, six hundred forty-eight. [13] The descendants of Bebai, six hundred twenty-three. The descendants of

---

a   Gk *in what priestly vestments*

4.58–60: Zerubbabel's prayer. The language of this prayer resembles a prayer of Daniel (Dan 2.20–23) and may be dependent upon it.

4.61–5.6: Preparations for the return to Judah. Zerubbabel journeys (perhaps from Susa) to Babylon and there recruits leaders from the priestly and royal families for the returning exiles (5.4–6). The genealogies of the leaders are hopelessly confused. The material unique to 1 Esdras concludes here, with the rest of the book paralleling Ezra 2–10 and Neh 8.

5.7–46: A list of the returning exiles (Ezra 2.1–70 and Neh 7.6–73a). The list in 1 Esdras differs somewhat from that in Ezra 2 and Nehemiah 7, both in the names and numbers listed. The totals, however, are identical, and the numbers of the priests and Levites are almost identical in the three lists, an indication that priestly and levitical genealogies were more carefully preserved than others. **6:** *Nisan,* March–April. **9–23:** Lay Israelites are

Azgad, one thousand three hundred twenty-two. ¹⁴ The descendants of Adonikam, six hundred sixty-seven. The descendants of Bigvai, two thousand sixty-six. The descendants of Adin, four hundred fifty-four. ¹⁵ The descendants of Ater, namely of Hezekiah, ninety-two. The descendants of Kilan and Azetas, sixty-seven. The descendants of Azaru, four hundred thirty-two. ¹⁶ The descendants of Annias, one hundred one. The descendants of Arom. The descendants of Bezai, three hundred twenty-three. The descendants of Arsiphurith, one hundred twelve. ¹⁷ The descendants of Baiterus, three thousand five. The descendants of Bethlomon, one hundred twenty-three. ¹⁸ Those from Netophah, fifty-five. Those from Anathoth, one hundred fifty-eight. Those from Bethasmoth, forty-two. ¹⁹ Those from Kiriatharim, twenty-five. Those from Chephirah and Beeroth, seven hundred forty-three. ²⁰ The Chadiasans and Ammidians, four hundred twenty-two. Those from Kirama and Geba, six hundred twenty-one. ²¹ Those from Macalon, one hundred twenty-two. Those from Betolio, fifty-two. The descendants of Niphish, one hundred fifty-six. ²² The descendants of the other Calamolalus and Ono, seven hundred twenty-five. The descendants of Jerechus, three hundred forty-five. ²³ The descendants of Senaah, three thousand three hundred thirty.

²⁴ The priests: the descendants of Jedaiah son of Jeshua, of the descendants of Anasib, nine hundred seventy-two. The descendants of Immer, one thousand and fifty-two. ²⁵ The descendants of Pashhur, one thousand two hundred forty-seven. The descendants of Charme, one thousand seventeen.

²⁶ The Levites: the descendants of Jeshua and Kadmiel and Bannas and Sudias, seventy-four. ²⁷ The temple singers: the descendants of Asaph, one hundred twenty-eight. ²⁸ The gatekeepers: the descendants of Shallum, the descendants of Ater, the descendants of Talmon, the descendants of Akkub, the descendants of Hatita, the descendants of Shobai, in all one hundred thirty-nine.

²⁹ The temple servants: the descendants of Esau, the descendants of Hasupha, the descendants of Tabbaoth, the descendants of Keros, the descendants of Sua, the descendants of Padon, the descendants of Lebanah, the descendants of Hagabah, ³⁰ the descendants of Akkub, the descendants of Uthai, the descendants of Ketab, the descendants of Hagab, the descendants of Subai, the descendants of Hana, the descendants of Cathua, the descendants of Geddur, ³¹ the descendants of Jairus, the descendants of Daisan, the descendants of Noeba, the descendants of Chezib, the descendants of Gazera, the descendants of Uzza, the descendants of Phinoe, the descendants of Hasrah, the descendants of Basthai, the descendants of Asnah, the descendants of Maani, the descendants of Nephisim, the descendants of Acuph,ᵃ the descendants of Hakupha, the descendants of Asur, the descendants of Pharakim, the descendants of Bazluth, ³² the descendants of Mehida, the descendants of Cutha, the descendants of Charea, the descendants of Barkos, the descendants of Serar, the descendants of Temah, the descendants of Neziah, the descendants of Hatipha.

³³ The descendants of Solomon's servants: the descendants of Assaphioth, the descendants of Peruda, the descendants of Jaalah, the descendants of Lozon, the descendants of Isdael, the descendants of Shephatiah, ³⁴ the descendants of Agia, the descendants of Pochereth-hazzebaim, the descendants of Sarothie, the descendants of Masiah, the descendants of Gas, the descendants of Addus, the descendants of Subas, the descendants of Apherra, the descendants of Barodis, the descendants of Shaphat, the descendants of Allon.

³⁵ All the temple servants and the descendants of Solomon's servants were three hundred seventy-two.

³⁶ The following are those who came up from Tel-melah and Tel-harsha, under the leadership of Cherub, Addan, and Immer,

---

ᵃ Other ancient authorities read *Acub* or *Acum*

---

listed by family ancestral names (vv. 9–17, 21b–23) and towns of origin (vv. 18–21a). **24–25:** *Priests* include four families claiming descent from Aaron (cf. 1 Chr 24). **26–27:** *Levites* are listed according to their Temple functions in the postexilic period. **29–35:** Other Temple personnel and miscellaneous groups. **36–37:** The inability of some

[37] though they could not prove by their ancestral houses or lineage that they belonged to Israel: the descendants of Delaiah son of Tobiah, and the descendants of Nekoda, six hundred fifty-two.

[38] Of the priests the following had assumed the priesthood but were not found registered: the descendants of Habaiah, the descendants of Hakkoz, and the descendants of Jaddus who had married Agia, one of the daughters of Barzillai, and was called by his name. [39] When a search was made in the register and the genealogy of these men was not found, they were excluded from serving as priests. [40] And Nehemiah and Attharias[a] told them not to share in the holy things until a high priest should appear wearing Urim and Thummim.[b]

[41] All those of Israel, twelve or more years of age, besides male and female servants, were forty-two thousand three hundred sixty; [42] their male and female servants were seven thousand three hundred thirty-seven; there were two hundred forty-five musicians and singers. [43] There were four hundred thirty-five camels, and seven thousand thirty-six horses, two hundred forty-five mules, and five thousand five hundred twenty-five donkeys.

[44] Some of the heads of families, when they came to the temple of God that is in Jerusalem, vowed that, to the best of their ability, they would erect the house on its site, [45] and that they would give to the sacred treasury for the work a thousand minas of gold, five thousand minas of silver, and one hundred priests' vestments.

[46] The priests, the Levites, and some of the people[c] settled in Jerusalem and its vicinity; and the temple singers, the gatekeepers, and all Israel in their towns.

[47] When the seventh month came, and the Israelites were all in their own homes,

a   Or *the governor*
b   Gk *Manifestation and Truth*
c   Or *those who were of the people*

returnees to prove their Israelite ancestry is recorded, but without mention of any repercussions. **38–40:** Proof of legitimate priestly genealogies is needed for any who may serve in the Temple in order to preserve the holiness of the Temple and protect the community from danger. Priests whose credentials are in question cannot serve until a mechanism for verification becomes available. **38:** *Barzillai,* see 2 Sam 17.27; 19.31. The adoption of the father-in-law's name suggests that Barzillai did not have a male heir. **40:** The name *Nehemiah,* not found in the parallel in Ezra-Nehemiah, is added here to compensate for the fact that 1 Esdras omits the story of Nehemiah (who, according to Neh 5.14 and 8.9 was the governor at the time of Ezra) in order to focus on Zerubbabel as governor and Ezra as high priest. *Attharias,* in Neh 8:9 a similar word, understood as the title "governor," describes Nehemiah. *Urim and Thummim* are the sacred lots used by the priests to receive oracular decisions (Ex 28.30; Lev 8.8; Deut 33.8; 1 Sam 14.41). This type of divine communication was a means of verification in the absence of other sources. **41:** The total of 42,360 returnees exceeds the sum total of the several groups listed but is identical with that in Ezra 2.66 and Neh 7.64. This larger number may include women and older children. *Twelve or more years,* this detail, which marks a boy's entry into formal standing in the community. is unique to 1 Esdras (see Luke 2:42 for a later allusion to this life stage). **45:** The precise monetary value of this contribution to the Temple (for which different amounts are given in Ezra 2.69) is uncertain because the value of the mina fluctuated. Nevertheless, the passage suggests that the community invested a great deal in restoring its Temple. The *priests' vestments* are specialized garments for official service.

5.47–73: Work on the Temple commences and is interrupted (Ezra 3.1–4.5; cf. Josephus, *Ant.* 11.4.1–3). Ezra 3–6 places the building of the Temple in both the reign of Cyrus (539–530 BCE) and that of Darius (522–486), merging several returns of exiles in a chronologically confusing fashion. First Esdras offers a more coherent and historically credible sequence, with Sheshbazzar beginning the work under Cyrus, and Zerubbabel working only under Darius. The likely sequence of events is that Sheshbazzar returned to Yehud shortly after 538, restored the sacrificial altar, reestablished public worship and perhaps even attempted to start building the Temple by laying its foundation, but with little success. The work on the Temple only resumed around 520 with Zerubbabel and Jeshua (during King Darius's reign). The prophets Haggai and Zechariah encouraged the community to complete the Temple, and the Temple was finally dedicated in 515.

5.47–55: Building the altar and resumption of sacrifices. The restoration of the altar and a functioning

they gathered with a single purpose in the square before the first gate toward the east. ⁴⁸ Then Jeshua son of Jozadak, with his fellow priests, and Zerubbabel son of Shealtiel, with his kinsmen, took their places and prepared the altar of the God of Israel, ⁴⁹ to offer burnt offerings upon it, in accordance with the directions in the book of Moses the man of God. ⁵⁰ And some joined them from the other peoples of the land. And they erected the altar in its place, for all the peoples of the land were hostile to them and were stronger than they; and they offered sacrifices at the proper times and burnt offerings to the Lord morning and evening. ⁵¹ They kept the festival of booths, as it is commanded in the law, and offered the proper sacrifices every day, ⁵² and thereafter the regular offerings and sacrifices on sabbaths and at new moons and at all the consecrated feasts. ⁵³ And all who had made any vow to God began to offer sacrifices to God, from the new moon of the seventh month, though the temple of God was not yet built. ⁵⁴ They gave money to the masons and the carpenters, and food and drink ⁵⁵ and carts[a] to the Sidonians and the Tyrians, to bring cedar logs from Lebanon and convey them in rafts to the harbor of Joppa, according to the decree that they had in writing from King Cyrus of the Persians.

⁵⁶ In the second year after their coming to the temple of God in Jerusalem, in the second month, Zerubbabel son of Shealtiel and Jeshua son of Jozadak made a beginning, together with their kindred and the levitical priests and all who had come back to Jerusalem from exile; ⁵⁷ and they laid the foundation of the temple of God on the new moon of the second month in the second year after they came to Judea and Jerusalem. ⁵⁸ They appointed the Levites who were twenty or more years of age to have charge of the work of the Lord. And Jeshua arose, and his sons and kindred and his brother Kadmiel and the sons of Jeshua Emadabun and the sons of Joda son of Iliadun, with their sons and kindred, all the Levites, pressing forward the work on the house of God with a single purpose.

So the builders built the temple of the Lord. ⁵⁹ And the priests stood arrayed in their vestments, with musical instruments and trumpets, and the Levites, the sons of Asaph, with cymbals, ⁶⁰ praising the Lord and blessing him, according to the directions of King David of Israel; ⁶¹ they sang hymns, giving thanks to the Lord, "For his goodness and his glory are forever upon all Israel." ⁶² And all the people sounded trumpets and shouted with a great shout, praising the Lord for the erection of the house of the Lord. ⁶³ Some of the levitical priests and heads of ancestral houses, old men who had seen the former house, came to the building of this one with outcries and loud weeping, ⁶⁴ while many

[a] Meaning of Gk uncertain

priesthood indicates the resumption of sacrificial worship, a central means of religious expression in the ancient world. Here 1 Esdras credits Zerubbabel and Jeshua (v. 48) with the successful rebuilding, beginning with the altar itself, now during the reign of Darius. Ezra 3 places this event earlier, still at the time of Cyrus. **47:** *The seventh month,* Tishri (September-October). **49:** *The book of Moses,* the Torah. Conformity to God's teachings embodied in the Torah plays a major role in accounts of the restoration period. **50:** Although the returnees elsewhere oppose marriages with peoples of the land, they do allow persons to join the community under certain conditions that are not specified in this text. This phrase does not appear in the parallel in Ezra 3, but the idea appears in Ezra 6.21. **51:** *The festival of booths* is celebrated in autumn, beginning on the fifteenth day of the seventh month (Lev 23.34). **52:** *New moons,* see Num 29.6. **55:** Sidon and Tyre helped build Solomon's Temple (1 Kings 5–7).

5.56–65: The Temple's foundation is laid (Ezra 3.8–13). **56:** Ezra 3 implies the second year of Cyrus, but 1 Esdras implies the second year of Darius (520 BCE), a date which more closely conforms to material in Haggai and Zechariah. **59–62:** Celebration of temple-foundings is a common ancient Near Eastern practice. **61:** The quoted words paraphrase a frequently occurring refrain in late Psalms (e.g., 106.1; 107.1; 118.1, 136.1). **63:** *The former house,* Solomon's Temple, destroyed in 586. *Loud weeping,* the founding of the Temple is an emotionally charged event. It is unclear whether the tears of the old result from sorrow about what had been lost (since the new Temple is presumably smaller than the one they remember) or from joy at seeing the beginning of restoration and the fulfillment of earlier hopes.

came with trumpets and a joyful noise, [65] so that the people could not hear the trumpets because of the weeping of the people.

For the multitude sounded the trumpets loudly, so that the sound was heard far away; [66] and when the enemies of the tribe of Judah and Benjamin heard it, they came to find out what the sound of the trumpets meant. [67] They learned that those who had returned from exile were building the temple for the Lord God of Israel. [68] So they approached Zerubbabel and Jeshua and the heads of the ancestral houses and said to them, "We will build with you. [69] For we obey your Lord just as you do and we have been sacrificing to him ever since the days of King Esar-haddon[a] of the Assyrians, who brought us here." [70] But Zerubbabel and Jeshua and the heads of the ancestral houses in Israel said to them, "You have nothing to do with us in building the house for the Lord our God, [71] for we alone will build it for the Lord of Israel, as Cyrus, the king of the Persians, has commanded us." [72] But the peoples of the land pressed hard[b] upon those in Judea, cut off their supplies, and hindered their building; [73] and by plots and demagoguery and uprisings they prevented the completion of the building as long as King Cyrus lived. They were kept from building for two years, until the reign of Darius.

6 Now in the second year of the reign of Darius, the prophets Haggai and Zechariah son of Iddo prophesied to the Jews who were in Judea and Jerusalem; they prophesied to them in the name of the Lord God of Israel. [2] Then Zerubbabel son of Shealtiel and Jeshua son of Jozadak began to build the house of the Lord that is in Jerusalem, with the help of the prophets of the Lord who were with them.

[3] At the same time Sisinnes the governor of Syria and Phoenicia and Sathrabuzanes and their associates came to them and said, [4] "By whose order are you building this house and this roof and finishing all the other things? And who are the builders that are finishing these things?" [5] Yet the elders of the Jews were dealt with kindly, for the providence of the Lord was over the captives; [6] they were not prevented from building until word could be sent to Darius concerning them and a report made.

[7] A copy of the letter that Sisinnes the governor of Syria and Phoenicia, and Sathrabuzanes, and their associates the local rulers in Syria and Phoenicia, wrote and sent to Darius:

[8] "To King Darius, greetings. Let it be fully known to our lord the king that, when we went to the country of Judea and entered the city of Jerusalem, we found the elders of the Jews, who had been in exile, [9] building in the city of Jerusalem a great new house for the Lord, of hewn stone, with costly timber laid in the walls. [10] These operations are going on rapidly, and the work is prospering in their hands and being completed with all splendor and care. [11] Then we asked these elders, 'At whose command are you build-

---

[a] Gk *Asbasareth*

[b] Meaning of Gk uncertain

5.66–73: Enemies interrupt the work of the returned exiles (Ezra 4.1–5). The returnees refuse to rebuild the Temple with outsiders who by their own admission did not belong to the Israelite community. 2 Kings 17 describes the resettling of non-Israelites in the territory of Samaria after its destruction by Assyria in 722 BCE. **69:** Instead of *Esar-haddon*, the Assyrian king who ruled 681–669 BCE, Josephus (*Ant.* 11.4.3) has Shalmaneser (727–722) as in 2 Kings 17.3; 18.9. **73:** This verse smoothes over the more problematic sequence in Ezra 3–6 (which inserts material from the reign of later kings, Xerxes and Artaxerxes, at this point; see Ezra 4.6–24).

6.1–34: Temple work resumes (Ezra 5.1–6.12). The prophets Haggai and Zechariah encourage the resumption of work on the Temple and succeed in gaining support for Zerubbabel and Jeshua (Joshua; cf. Hag 1.1–4; 2.1–4; Zech 4.9; 6.15). Although investigated by the governor of the entire Persian province Beyond the River (west of Babylon and encompassing Judah as well as Lebanon and Syria), the Judeans nonetheless are able to work with no interruption. **3:** *Sisinnes the governor of Syria and Phoenicia* is Tattenai in Ezra 5.3, and governor of the province Beyond the River, namely the Persian province west of Babylon, including Judah; *Phoenicia* corresponds to modern Lebanon. *Sathrabuzanes* is Shethar-bozenai in Ezra 5.3.

6.7–22: The governor's report and request. In this letter, the provincial governor seeks to find out whether King Darius will confirm and authorize the permission to build the Temple first granted by Cyrus. The report is

ing this house and laying the foundations of this structure?' ¹² In order that we might inform you in writing who the leaders are, we questioned them and asked them for a list of the names of those who are at their head. ¹³ They answered us, 'We are the servants of the Lord who created the heaven and the earth. ¹⁴ The house was built many years ago by a king of Israel who was great and strong, and it was finished. ¹⁵ But when our ancestors sinned against the Lord of Israel who is in heaven, and provoked him, he gave them over into the hands of King Nebuchadnezzar of Babylon, king of the Chaldeans; ¹⁶ and they pulled down the house, and burned it, and carried the people away captive to Babylon. ¹⁷ But in the first year that Cyrus reigned over the country of Babylonia, King Cyrus wrote that this house should be rebuilt. ¹⁸ And the holy vessels of gold and of silver, which Nebuchadnezzar had taken out of the house in Jerusalem and stored in his own temple, these King Cyrus took out again from the temple in Babylon, and they were delivered to Zerubbabel and Sheshbazzarᵃ the governor ¹⁹ with the command that he should take all these vessels back and put them in the temple at Jerusalem, and that this temple of the Lord should be rebuilt on its site. ²⁰ Then this Sheshbazzar, after coming here, laid the foundations of the house of the Lord that is in Jerusalem. Although it has been in process of construction from that time until now, it has not yet reached completion.' ²¹ Now therefore, O king, if it seems wise to do so, let search be made in the royal archives of our lordᵇ the king that are in Babylon; ²² if it is found that the building of the house of the Lord in Jerusalem was done with the consent of King Cyrus, and if it is approved by our lord the king, let him send us directions concerning these things."

²³ Then Darius commanded that search be made in the royal archives that were deposited in Babylon. And in Ecbatana, the fortress that is in the country of Media, a scrollᶜ was found in which this was recorded: ²⁴ "In the first year of the reign of King Cyrus, he ordered the building of the house of the Lord in Jerusalem, where they sacrifice with perpetual fire; ²⁵ its height to be sixty cubits and its width sixty cubits, with three courses of hewn stone and one course of new native timber; the cost to be paid from the treasury of King Cyrus; ²⁶ and that the holy vessels of the house of the Lord, both of gold and of silver, which Nebuchadnezzar took out of the house in Jerusalem and carried away to Babylon, should be restored to the house in Jerusalem, to be placed where they had been."

²⁷ So Dariusᵈ commanded Sisinnes the governor of Syria and Phoenicia, and Sathrabuzanes, and their associates, and those who were appointed as local rulers in Syria and Phoenicia, to keep away from the place, and to permit Zerubbabel, the servant of the Lord and governor of Judea, and the elders of the Jews to build this house of the Lord on its site. ²⁸ "And I command that it be built completely, and that full effort be made to help those who have returned from the exile of Judea, until the house of the Lord is finished; ²⁹ and that out of the tribute of Coelesyria and Phoenicia a portion be scrupulously given to these men, that is, to Zerubbabel the governor, for sacrifices to the Lord, for bulls and rams and lambs, ³⁰ and likewise wheat and salt and wine and oil, regularly every

ᵃ Gk *Sanabassarus*
ᵇ Other ancient authorities read *of Cyrus*
ᶜ Other authorities read *passage*
ᵈ Gk *he*

neutral in tone. **14**: *A king of Israel*, namely Solomon (1 Kings 6). **15**: *Chaldeans*, the Babylonians; see 1.52n. **18**: *Zerubbabel*, who is more prominent in 1 Esdras than in Ezra 3–6, is added here and in vv. 27, 29; only *Sheshbazzar* is mentioned in Ezra 5.14 and in Josephus (*Ant.* 11.4.4).

6.23–34: Darius's authorization of rebuilding and generous support for the Temple. The king's investigation recovers a copy of Cyrus's memorandum, which King Darius then confirms, thus adding his support to the Judeans' rebuilding efforts. In following the account in Ezra 5–6, 1 Esdras ignores the earlier report (1 Esd 5.42–57) in which Darius authorizes the bodyguard Zerubbabel to build the Temple; this reflects the complicated history of composition of 1 Esdras. **23**: *Ecbatana* was the summer residence of Persian kings, now Hamadan in Iran. **24–26**: The discovered copy of Cyrus's authorization confirms the claims of the Judean builders. See

you as necessary for the temple of your God, you may provide out of the royal treasury. ¹⁹ "I, King Artaxerxes, have commanded the treasurers of Syria and Phoenicia that whatever Ezra the priest and reader of the law of the Most High God sends for, they shall take care to give him, ²⁰ up to a hundred talents of silver, and likewise up to a hundred cors of wheat, a hundred baths of wine, and salt in abundance. ²¹ Let all things prescribed in the law of God be scrupulously fulfilled for the Most High God, so that wrath may not come upon the kingdom of the king and his sons. ²² You are also informed that no tribute or any other tax is to be laid on any of the priests or Levites or temple singers or gatekeepers or temple servants or persons employed in this temple, and that no one has authority to impose any tax on them.

²³ "And you, Ezra, according to the wisdom of God, appoint judges and justices to judge all those who know the law of your God, throughout all Syria and Phoenicia; and you shall teach it to those who do not know it. ²⁴ All who transgress the law of your God or the law of the kingdom shall be strictly punished, whether by death or some other punishment, either fine or imprisonment."

²⁵ Then Ezra the scribe said,^a "Blessed be the Lord alone, who put this into the heart of the king, to glorify his house that is in Jerusalem, ²⁶ and who honored me in the sight of the king and his counselors and all his Friends and nobles. ²⁷ I was encouraged by the help of the Lord my God, and I gathered men from Israel to go up with me."

²⁸ These are the leaders, according to their ancestral houses and their groups, who went up with me from Babylon, in the reign of King Artaxerxes: ²⁹ Of the descendants of Phineas, Gershom. Of the descendants of Ithamar, Gamael. Of the descendants of David, Hattush son of Shecaniah. ³⁰ Of the descendants of Parosh, Zechariah, and with him a hundred fifty men enrolled. ³¹ Of the descendants of Pahath-moab, Eliehoenai son of Zerahiah, and with him two hundred men. ³² Of the descendants of Zattu, Shecaniah son of Jahaziel, and with him three hundred men. Of the descendants of Adin, Obed son of Jonathan, and with him two hundred fifty men. ³³ Of the descendants of Elam, Jeshaiah son of Gotholiah, and with him seventy men. ³⁴ Of the descendants of Shephatiah, Zeraiah son of Michael, and with him seventy men. ³⁵ Of the descendants of Joab, Obadiah son of Jehiel, and with him two hundred twelve men. ³⁶ Of the descendants of Bani, Shelomith son of Josiphiah, and with him a hundred sixty men. ³⁷ Of the descendants of Bebai, Zechariah son of Bebai, and with him twenty-eight men. ³⁸ Of the descendants of Azgad, Johanan son of Hakkatan, and with him a hundred ten men. ³⁹ Of the descendants of Adonikam, the last ones, their names being Eliphelet, Jeuel, and Shemaiah, and with them seventy men. ⁴⁰ Of the descendants of Bigvai, Uthai son of Istalcurus, and with him seventy men.

⁴¹ I assembled them at the river called Theras, and we encamped there three days,

---

^a Other ancient authorities lack *Then Ezra the scribe said*

---

plus. **18:** Artaxerxes virtually gives Ezra a blank check, showing great trust in Ezra. **19–22:** Artaxerxes assures a generous year's supply of provisions for the Temple. **19:** Additional support is to come from local officials. **20:** A *talent* was 75 lb (34 kg); a *cor* 6.5 bu (230 L); and a *bath* about 6 gal (23 L). **22:** Temple personnel are exempt from all taxes. **23–24:** Ezra is given authority to appoint judges throughout the entire province in order to maintain Jewish law. **24:** *The law of your God or the law of the kingdom,* the imperial authorization of the specific Jewish Law is important in that it grants the Jewish community the ability to preserve its distinctive religious heritage. The king's letter presents royal law and Jewish law as equally binding.

8.25–60: Ezra's report: leading the exiles to Jerusalem (Ezra 7.27–8.30). In a first-person account (sometimes called "the Ezra memoir"), Ezra describes his response to the royal letter, his prayer of thanks, and preparations for the journey to Jerusalem. **25–27:** Ezra's first words are a prayer of thanksgiving. **28–40:** Having thanked God, Ezra lists the names of exiles who went to Jerusalem with him. The list differs only slightly from the parallel in Ezra, although the numbers are higher, with a total of about 1,700 males. **29:** *Hattush,* several persons with this name appear in the Hebrew Bible but here and in the parallel in Ezra 8.2 only this Hattush is identified as a descendant of David.

8.41–60: Communal preparations (Ezra 8.15–30) include surveying the company, fasting, and commis-

and I inspected them. ⁴²When I found there none of the descendants of the priests or of the Levites, ⁴³I sent word to Eliezar, Iduel, Maasmas, ⁴⁴Elnathan, Shemaiah, Jarib, Nathan, Elnathan, Zechariah, and Meshullam, who were leaders and men of understanding; ⁴⁵I told them to go to Iddo, who was the leading man at the place of the treasury, ⁴⁶and ordered them to tell Iddo and his kindred and the treasurers at that place to send us men to serve as priests in the house of our Lord. ⁴⁷And by the mighty hand of our Lord they brought us competent men of the descendants of Mahli son of Levi, son of Israel, namely Sherebiahᵃ with his descendants and kinsmen, eighteen; ⁴⁸also Hashabiah and Annunus and his brother Jeshaiah, of the descendants of Hananiah, and their descendants, twenty men; ⁴⁹and of the temple servants, whom David and the leaders had given for the service of the Levites, two hundred twenty temple servants; the list of all their names was reported.

⁵⁰There I proclaimed a fast for the young men before our Lord, to seek from him a prosperous journey for ourselves and for our children and the livestock that were with us. ⁵¹For I was ashamed to ask the king for foot soldiers and cavalry and an escort to keep us safe from our adversaries; ⁵²for we had said to the king, "The power of our Lord will be with those who seek him, and will support them in every way." ⁵³And again we prayed to our Lord about these things, and we found him very merciful.

⁵⁴Then I set apart twelve of the leaders of the priests, Sherebiah and Hashabiah, and ten of their kinsmen with them; ⁵⁵and I weighed out to them the silver and the gold and the holy vessels of the house of our Lord, which the king himself and his counselors and the nobles and all Israel had given. ⁵⁶I weighed and gave to them six hundred fifty talents of silver, and silver vessels worth a hundred talents, and a hundred talents of gold, ⁵⁷and twenty golden bowls, and twelve bronze vessels of fine bronze that glittered like gold. ⁵⁸And I said to them, "You are holy to the Lord, and the vessels are holy, and the silver and the gold are vowed to the Lord, the Lord of our ancestors. ⁵⁹Be watchful and on guard until you deliver them to the leaders of the priests and the Levites, and to the heads of the ancestral houses of Israel, in Jerusalem, in the chambers of the house of our Lord." ⁶⁰So the priests and the Levites who took the silver and the gold and the vessels that had been in Jerusalem carried them to the temple of the Lord.

⁶¹We left the river Theras on the twelfth day of the first month; and we arrived in Jerusalem by the mighty hand of our Lord, which was upon us; he delivered us from every enemy on the way, and so we came to Jerusalem. ⁶²When we had been there three days, the silver and the gold were weighed and delivered in the house of our Lord to the priest Meremoth son of Uriah; ⁶³with him was Eleazar son of Phinehas, and with them were Jozabad son of Jeshua and Moeth son of Binnui,ᵇ the Levites. ⁶⁴The whole was counted and weighed, and the weight of everything was recorded at that very time. ⁶⁵And those

ᵃ Gk *Asbebias*
ᵇ Gk *Sabannus*

sioning cult personnel as conveyers of vessels for the Temple. **41:** *The river . . . Theras* is probably a tributary of the Euphrates. **42–49:** Because neither priests nor Levites were among the group first assembled by Ezra, special measures had to be taken to secure the required number of both (Ezra 8 mentions only missing Levites). **45:** *The treasury,* Ezra 8.17 mentions a place name, Casiphia, of unknown location. The treasure may be derived from interpretation of Casiphia, a word related to silver (Heb "kesep"). **50:** Fasting prior to an important undertaking was common, especially in the postexilic period (2 Chr 20.3; Esth 4.16). **56:** *Talents* weighed about 34 kg (75 lb) each. **58:** Holy objects could be entrusted only to those who were holy themselves.

8.61–67: Arrival in Jerusalem (Ezra 8.31–36). Upon arriving, Ezra ensured that the treasures were turned over to the Jerusalem Temple personnel. This is followed by sacrifices to God and delivering the king's orders to the provincial officers, who are given no choice but to respect Ezra's mission. **61:** *Twelfth day of the first month* (Nisan [March-April]), two days before the Passover commemorating the Exodus. A new Exodus may be implicit; however, for reasons of weather, spring was the season for expeditions (see 2 Sam 11.1).

who had returned from exile offered sacrific-es to the Lord, the God of Israel, twelve bulls for all Israel, ninety-six rams, [66] seventy-two lambs, and as a thank offering twelve male goats—all as a sacrifice to the Lord. [67] They delivered the king's orders to the royal stew-ards and to the governors of Coelesyria and Phoenicia; and these officials[a] honored the people and the temple of the Lord.

[68] After these things had been done, the leaders came to me and said, [69] "The people of Israel and the rulers and the priests and the Levites have not put away from themselves the alien peoples of the land and their pollutions, the Canaanites, the Hittites, the Perizzites, the Jebusites, the Moabites, the Egyptians, and the Edomites. [70] For they and their descendants have married the daughters of these people,[b] and the holy race has been mixed with the alien peoples of the land; and from the begin-ning of this matter the leaders and the nobles have been sharing in this iniquity."

[71] As soon as I heard these things I tore my garments and my holy mantle, and pulled out hair from my head and beard, and sat down in anxiety and grief. [72] And all who were ever moved at[c] the word of the Lord of Israel gathered around me, as I mourned over this iniquity, and I sat grief-stricken until the evening sacrifice. [73] Then I rose from my fast, with my garments and my holy mantle torn, and kneeling down and stretching out my hands to the Lord [74] I said,

"O Lord, I am ashamed and confused before your face. [75] For our sins have risen higher than our heads, and our mistakes have mounted up to heaven [76] from the times of our ancestors, and we are in great sin to this day. [77] Because of our sins and the sins of our ancestors, we with our kindred and our kings and our priests were given over to the kings of the earth, to the sword and exile and plun-dering, in shame until this day. [78] And now in some measure mercy has come to us from you, O Lord, to leave to us a root and a name in your holy place, [79] and to uncover a light for us in the house of the Lord our God, and to give us food in the time of our servitude. [80] Even in our bondage we were not forsaken by our Lord, but he brought us into favor with the kings of the Persians, so that they have given us food [81] and glorified the temple of our Lord, and raised Zion from desolation, to give us a stronghold in Judea and Jerusalem.

[82] "And now, O Lord, what shall we say, when we have these things? For we have transgressed your commandments, which you gave by your servants the prophets, saying, [83] 'The land that you are entering to take pos-session of is a land polluted with the pollution of the aliens of the land, and they have filled it with their uncleanness. [84] Therefore do not give your daughters in marriage to their de-

[a] Gk they
[b] Gk their daughters
[c] Or zealous for

8.68–9.36: The crisis of mixed marriages in Judah (Ezra 9.1–10.44). Ezra records that he was told about mar-riages of Judeans and "alien people of the land," which he viewed as violation of God's commandments. It appears that Ezra and his supporters considered the ethnic and religious cohesiveness of the returned exiles to be in danger when living as a minority in the land, among more numerous ethnicities and groups. This best explains the harsh, separatist measures that Ezra and his supporters take to protect communal boundaries. 1 Esdras follows the parallel in Ezra 9–10 with but a few, albeit important, differences.

8.68–70: The nature of the crisis (Ezra 9.1–2). Some members of the community, including leaders, have married women from the residents of the land, who are described as "alien." The parallel in Ezra 9.1–2 charges that the objectionable people's practices were like the ancient Canaanites, Moabites, and other groups men-tioned in Deuteronomy as proscribed (see Deut 7.1–5 and 23.4–7). 1 Esdras gives the impression that the peo-ples of the land are in fact these earlier proscribed groups. 70: Holy, that is dedicated to God. Race, lit. "seed" (offspring).

8.71–90: Ezra's response to the crisis: mourning and prayer (Ezra 9.3–15). Ezra interprets for the community the significance of mixed marriages, noting that they may again cause an exile. 71: Holy, Ezra 9.3 does not ascribe holiness to Ezra's mantle; the addition in 1 Esdras stresses Ezra's significant position as high priest (see note on 9.39). 82–85: The prophetic books contain no such statement; the author may have in mind such pas-sages as Lev 18.24–30 and Deut 7.3–4, attributed to Moses as a prophet.

scendants, and do not take their daughters for your descendants; [85] do not seek ever to have peace with them, so that you may be strong and eat the good things of the land and leave it for an inheritance to your children forever.' [86] And all that has happened to us has come about because of our evil deeds and our great sins. For you, O Lord, lifted the burden of our sins [87] and gave us such a root as this; but we turned back again to transgress your law by mixing with the uncleanness of the peoples of the land. [88] Were you not angry enough with us to destroy us without leaving a root or seed or name? [89] O Lord of Israel, you are faithful; for we are left as a root to this day. [90] See, we are now before you in our iniquities; for we can no longer stand in your presence because of these things."

[91] While Ezra was praying and making his confession, weeping and lying on the ground before the temple, there gathered around him a very great crowd of men and women and youths from Jerusalem; for there was great weeping among the multitude. [92] Then Shecaniah son of Jehiel, one of the men of Israel, called out, and said to Ezra, "We have sinned against the Lord, and have married foreign women from the peoples of the land; but even now there is hope for Israel. [93] Let us take an oath to the Lord about this, that we will put away all our foreign wives, with their children, [94] as seems good to you and to all who obey the law of the Lord. [95] Rise up[a] and take action, for it is your task, and we are with you to take strong measures." [96] Then Ezra rose up and made the leaders of the priests and Levites of all Israel swear that they would do this. And they swore to it.

9 Then Ezra set out and went from the court of the temple to the chamber of Jehohanan son of Eliashib, [2] and spent the night there; and he did not eat bread or drink water, for he was mourning over the great iniquities of the multitude. [3] And a proclamation was made throughout Judea and Jerusalem to all who had returned from exile that they should assemble at Jerusalem, [4] and that if any did not meet there within two or three days, in accordance with the decision of the ruling elders, their livestock would be seized for sacrifice and the men themselves[b] expelled from the multitude of those who had returned from the captivity.

[5] Then the men of the tribe of Judah and Benjamin assembled at Jerusalem within three days; this was the ninth month, on the twentieth day of the month. [6] All the multitude sat in the open square before the temple, shivering because of the bad weather that prevailed. [7] Then Ezra stood up and said to them, "You have broken the law and married foreign women, and so have increased the sin of Israel. [8] Now then make confession and give glory to the Lord the God of our ancestors, [9] and do his will; separate yourselves from the peoples of the land and from your foreign wives."

[10] Then all the multitude shouted and said with a loud voice, "We will do as you have said. [11] But the multitude is great and it is winter, and we are not able to stand in the open air. This is not a work we can do in one day or two, for we have sinned too much in these things. [12] So let the leaders of the multitude stay, and let all those in our settlements who have foreign wives come at the time appointed, [13] with the elders and judges of each place,

a Other ancient authorities read *as seems good to you." And all who obeyed the law of the Lord rose and said to Ezra,* [95]*"Rise up*

b Gk *he himself*

8.91–9.36: The people repent and dismiss their foreign wives (Ezra 10.1–44). As in Ezra 10, the account switches from a first-person report ("the Ezra Memoirs") to a third-person report about Ezra's reforms. **8.91–96:** A proposal to remove foreign wives is made. **93:** The children of such marriages are to be sent away as well, thereby not being separated from their mothers. **9.1–17:** Ezra leads the communal process toward dismissing foreign wives. **1:** *The chamber,* an office within the Temple complex that as a priest, Ezra may use. **4:** The ruling elders issue orders for the entire community to assemble; Ezra exercises religious, not political, authority in the land. **7:** *The law,* an allusion to Deut 7.3. **8:** *To give glory to the Lord* is to acknowledge themselves to be in the wrong (cf. Josh 7.19). **5–6:** Cold weather and heavy rains are typical of the *ninth month,* Chislev (November–December). **11–13:** Because of the severe winter weather and the complexity of the task, it is agreed that the separation should be handled by a committee, with the help of leaders from various districts. The multitude

until we are freed from the wrath of the Lord over this matter."

¹⁴ Jonathan son of Asahel and Jahzeiah son of Tikvahᵃ undertook the matter on these terms, and Meshullam and Levi and Shabbethai served with them as judges. ¹⁵ And those who had returned from exile acted in accordance with all this.

¹⁶ Ezra the priest chose for himself the leading men of their ancestral houses, all of them by name; and on the new moon of the tenth month they began their sessions to investigate the matter. ¹⁷ And the cases of the men who had foreign wives were brought to an end by the new moon of the first month.

¹⁸ Of the priests, those who were brought in and found to have foreign wives were: ¹⁹ of the descendants of Jeshua son of Jozadak and his kindred, Maaseiah, Eliezer, Jarib, and Jodan. ²⁰ They pledged themselves to put away their wives, and to offer rams in expiation of their error. ²¹ Of the descendants of Immer: Hanani and Zebadiah and Maaseiah and Shemaiah and Jehiel and Azariah. ²² Of the descendants of Pashhur: Elioenai, Maaseiah, Ishmael, and Nathanael, and Gedaliah, and Salthas.

²³ And of the Levites: Jozabad and Shimei and Kelaiah, who was Kelita, and Pethahiah and Judah and Jonah. ²⁴ Of the temple singers: Eliashib and Zaccur.ᵇ ²⁵ Of the gatekeepers: Shallum and Telem.ᶜ

²⁶ Of Israel: of the descendants of Parosh: Ramiah, Izziah, Malchijah, Mijamin, and Eleazar, and Asibias, and Benaiah. ²⁷ Of the descendants of Elam: Mattaniah and Zechariah, Jezrielus and Abdi, and Jeremoth and Elijah. ²⁸ Of the descendants of Zamoth: Eliadas, Eliashib, Othoniah, Jeremoth, and Zabad and Zerdaiah. ²⁹ Of the descendants of Bebai: Jehohanan and Hananiah and Zabbai and Emathis. ³⁰ Of the descendants of Mani: Olamus, Mamuchus, Adaiah, Jashub, and Sheal and Jeremoth. ³¹ Of the descendants of Addi: Naathus and Moossias, Laccunus and Naidus, and Bescaspasmys and Sesthel, and Belnuus and Manasseas. ³² Of the descendants of Annan, Elionas and Asaias and Melchias and Sabbaias and Simon Chosamaeus. ³³ Of the descendants of Hashum: Mattenai and Mattattah and Zabad and Eliphelet and Manasseh and Shimei. ³⁴ Of the descendants of Bani: Jeremai, Momdius, Maerus, Joel, Mamdai and Bedeiah and Vaniah, Carabasion and Eliashib and Mamitanemus, Eliasis, Binnui, Elialis, Shimei, Shelemiah, Nethaniah. Of the descendants of Ezora: Shashai, Azarel, Azael, Samatus, Zambris, Joseph. ³⁵ Of the descendants of Nooma: Mazitias, Zabad, Iddo, Joel, Benaiah. ³⁶ All these had married foreign women, and they put them away together with their children.

³⁷ The priests and the Levites and the Israelites settled in Jerusalem and in the

ᵃ Gk *Thocanos*
ᵇ Gk *Bacchurus*
ᶜ Gk *Tolbanes*

is dismissed. **16–17:** Investigating the cases of intermarriage takes three months, from the first of the tenth month, Tebet (December-January) to the first of the first month, Nisan (March-April). **18–36:** Ezra 10.18–44. The list of those who put away foreign wives, which includes priests, Levites, and the laity, may have been preserved in the Temple archives. **20:** The priests, whose violation of genealogical purity endangers the sanctity of the Temple, are required to make a guilt offering in expiation of the sin. **36:** *They put them away*, only 1 Esdras specifies that the women and children were expelled. The parallel in Ezra 10.44 does not; verses 18–44 only indicate that priests put away their wives. Many translators, however, append 1 Esd 9.36 to Ezra 10.44.

9.37–55: The restoration is complete with Ezra's public reading of the law (Neh 7.73–8.12). First Esdras concludes with a grand celebration, reminiscent of the Passover celebration with which the book began (see ch 1), thereby rendering the destruction and exile as a temporary crisis that has been fully overcome by the end of the book; 1 Esdras departs markedly from Ezra-Nehemiah at this juncture. In Ezra-Nehemiah the reading of the Torah (NRSV "law"; see 8.7n.) follows the rebuilding of Jerusalem's walls under Nehemiah's leadership (Neh 1–6). For the author of 1 Esdras, the only important leaders are David's descendant Zerubbabel and Ezra the priest, who together restore (rather than transform) Israel's institutions and communal life. The celebrative, public reading of the book constitutes the completion of the restoration. Thus the ceremony recalls Sinai as the receiving of God's teachings by the entire people, transforming them into "the people of the Book." **37:** *The new moon* or first day of the seventh month, Tishri (September-October), was a day of holy convocation (Lev 23.23–

country. On the new moon of the seventh month, when the people of Israel were in their settlements, ³⁸ the whole multitude gathered with one accord in the open square before the east gate of the temple; ³⁹ they told Ezra the chief priest and reader to bring the law of Moses that had been given by the Lord God of Israel. ⁴⁰ So Ezra the chief priest brought the law, for all the multitude, men and women, and all the priests to hear the law, on the new moon of the seventh month. ⁴¹ He read aloud in the open square before the gate of the temple from early morning until midday, in the presence of both men and women; and all the multitude gave attention to the law. ⁴² Ezra the priest and reader of the law stood on the wooden platform that had been prepared; ⁴³ and beside him stood Mattathiah, Shema, Ananias, Azariah, Uriah, Hezekiah, and Baalsamus on his right, ⁴⁴ and on his left Pedaiah, Mishael, Malchijah, Lothasubus, Nabariah, and Zechariah. ⁴⁵ Then Ezra took up the book of the law in the sight of the multitude, for he had the place of honor in the presence of all. ⁴⁶ When he opened the law, they all stood erect. And Ezra blessed the Lord God Most High, the God of hosts, the Almighty, ⁴⁷ and the multitude answered, "Amen." They lifted up their hands, and fell to the ground and worshiped the Lord. ⁴⁸ Jeshua and Anniuth and Sherebiah, Jadinus, Akkub, Shabbethai, Hodiah, Maiannas and Kelita, Azariah and Jozabad, Hanan, Pelaiah, the Levites, taught the law of the Lord,ᵃ at the same time explaining what was read.

⁴⁹ Then Attharatesᵇ said to Ezra the chief priest and reader, and to the Levites who were teaching the multitude, and to all, ⁵⁰ "This day is holy to the Lord"—now they were all weeping as they heard the law— ⁵¹ "so go your way, eat the fat and drink the sweet, and send portions to those who have none; ⁵² for the day is holy to the Lord; and do not be sorrowful, for the Lord will exalt you." ⁵³ The Levites commanded all the people, saying, "This day is holy; do not be sorrowful." ⁵⁴ Then they all went their way, to eat and drink and enjoy themselves, and to give portions to those who had none, and to make great rejoicing; ⁵⁵ because they were inspired by the words which they had been taught. And they came together.ᶜ

ᵃ Other ancient authorities add *and read the law of the Lord to the multitude*

ᵇ Or *the governor*

ᶜ The Greek text ends abruptly: compare Neh 8.13

24; Num 29.1). The date for the ceremony is September 444 (or perhaps 443). **38:** *The east gate of the temple,* Neh 8 does not mention the Temple and includes no other priests except Ezra in this ceremony of reading. **39:** *They told Ezra,* the people, not Ezra, initiate the ceremony. Ezra is not identified elsewhere as *the chief priest. The law of Moses,* i.e., the Torah. From the people's reaction and other details in Ezra-Nehemiah, scholars conclude that some form of today's Pentateuch, especially Deuteronomy, is being used. **40–41:** Both men and women participate in this ceremony of hearing and receiving the Torah (see Deut 31.12). **42:** The *platform* erected for Ezra probably continued the tradition whereby kings would appear before the people to reaffirm the covenant law on the festal occasion (cf. 2 Chr 20.5; 23.13; 29.4). It also served a practical need: to make the book of the Torah visible and audible to all. **43:** *Beside him stood . . .* Ezra's assistants include laity, as well as Levites, who are elsewhere connected to the study of the law. Their participation expresses broadened access to the authoritative teachings, a move away from exclusive control by priests (see Jer 18.18). **48:** The *Levites* explained the law to the people or possibly translated it into Aramaic for those who may not have been familiar with Hebrew.

9.49–55: The concluding celebration. 49: *Attharates* (see also 5.40) is a corruption of "tirshatha" (governor) in Neh 8.9. The author of 1 Esdras does not intend to indicate that Nehemiah, the named governor in Neh 8.9, was a participant in the festivity. **50–55:** The people are to rejoice even though the words of the law cause them to recognize their sin, because the law is associated with joy. **55:** *They came together,* some consider the ending abrupt, with the continuation in the parallel in Neh 8 (a second gathering and the feast of booths in Neh 8.13–18) a more fitting conclusion. Nevertheless, coming together as a community around the law and celebrating in the Temple in Jerusalem constitute an appropriate ending for a book that began with a celebration under Josiah in the same location.

THE PRAYER OF MANASSEH

NAME AND DATE

Manasseh, the idolatrous seventh-century BCE king of Judah, uttered a prayer, according to 2 Chr 33, while lying in shackles as a captive of Babylon. The Chronicler suggests that he had before him a text containing the king's actual words; the Prayer of Manasseh purports to be that very source. In reality, this composition was most likely written around the turn of the Common Era, perhaps even in Greek rather than in Hebrew.

CANONICAL STATUS AND LOCATION

Evidence for the Prayer of Manasseh is first found in a Syriac translation of a third-century CE Greek work, the *Didascalia Apostolorum*, and in the fourth-century Greek work *The Apostolic Constitutions*. It is appended to the Psalter in a few manuscripts of the Septuagint, and though beloved by many Christian communities, became canonical only in the Eastern Orthodox churches.

STRUCTURE, CONTENTS, AND INTERPRETATION

This prayer for forgiveness follows a typical structure: praise of God (vv. 1–8), lament (vv. 9–10), petition (vv. 11–13), and vow of additional praise (vv. 14–15). Like other late biblical prayers (Ezra 9.1–15; Neh 1.4–11; 9.6–37; Dan 9.4–19; Bar 1.15–3.8), it dwells on sin in order to emphasize the extent of the need for divine intervention. Such sin must be removed for the petitioner to be released from suffering. The way the prayer uses an emergent doctrine of repentance is novel. With his power, God has "made heaven and earth with all their order" (v. 2), and, in his mercy, he has "appointed repentance for sinners" (v. 7). Manasseh praises God for his creation of the world and thereby gains an opportunity to remind him that he also "created" repentance at that time. He establishes the basis, as a penitent, on which he can expect, even demand, to have his petition favorably received.

 The distinctive theology of repentance found in the prayer may be profitably compared to a variety of late Hebrew and Greek texts. Nehemiah 1.8–9 and Bar 3.5–7 allude to a divine promise based on the book of Deuteronomy to redeem those who turn away from sin, but the focus of these texts is on the nation, not individuals. With its interest in the individual sinner, the Prayer of Manasseh resembles rabbinic texts with their interpretation of Deuteronomy's promise as applying to individuals and their view that repentance was established at the time of creation. The notion that repentance is a grant ("promised," v. 7; "appointed," vv. 8–9) probably comes from Greek military terminology; amnesty is granted to those who repent of their rebellion. The sense of repentance as having an established existence is also found in such Greek texts as the pagan *Tabula of Cebes*, the Hellenistic Jewish *Joseph and Aseneth* and the Christian *Shepherd of Hermas*.

David Lambert

¹O Lord Almighty,
God of our ancestors,
of Abraham and Isaac and Jacob
and of their righteous offspring;
²you who made heaven and earth
with all their order;
³who shackled the sea by your word of
     command,
who confined the deep
and sealed it with your terrible and
     glorious name;
⁴at whom all things shudder,
and tremble before your power,
⁵for your glorious splendor cannot be
     borne,
and the wrath of your threat to sinners is
     unendurable;
⁶yet immeasurable and unsearchable

 1–8: Praise of the creator. 1: *God of our ancestors*, Ex 3.15–16; Dan 2.23; cf. Acts 3.13. *Their righteous offspring*, an unusual phrase, which may indicate that the prayer was meant to be uttered by a convert. **3:** The restraining of the sea by the creator is a common poetic theme of the Bible (Pss 29.10; 104.7–9; 148.5–6; Job 38.8–11). **5:** God's power, exemplified by creation and his mastery over the deep, naturally leads to the utter destruction of

is your promised mercy,
[7] for you are the Lord Most High,
of great compassion, long-suffering, and
    very merciful,
and you relent at human suffering.
O Lord, according to your great goodness
you have promised repentance and
    forgiveness
to those who have sinned against you,
and in the multitude of your mercies
you have appointed repentance for
    sinners,
so that they may be saved.[a]
[8] Therefore you, O Lord, God of the
    righteous,
have not appointed repentance for the
    righteous,
for Abraham and Isaac and Jacob, who did
    not sin against you,
but you have appointed repentance for me,
    who am a sinner.
[9] For the sins I have committed are more in
    number than the sand of the sea;
my transgressions are multiplied, O Lord,
    they are multiplied!
I am not worthy to look up and see the
    height of heaven
because of the multitude of my iniquities.
[10] I am weighted down with many an iron
    fetter,
so that I am rejected[b] because of my sins,
and I have no relief;

for I have provoked your wrath
and have done what is evil in your sight,
setting up abominations and multiplying
    offenses.
[11] And now I bend the knee of my heart,
imploring you for your kindness.
[12] I have sinned, O Lord, I have sinned,
and I acknowledge my transgressions.
[13] I earnestly implore you,
forgive me, O Lord, forgive me!
Do not destroy me with my transgressions!
Do not be angry with me forever or store
    up evil for me;
do not condemn me to the depths of the
    earth.
For you, O Lord, are the God of those who
    repent,
[14] and in me you will manifest your
    goodness;
for, unworthy as I am, you will save me
    according to your great mercy,
[15] and I will praise you continually all the
    days of my life.
For all the host of heaven sings your
    praise,
and yours is the glory forever. Amen.

---

[a] Other ancient authorities lack *O Lord, according…*
be saved

[b] Other ancient authorities read *so that I cannot lift
up my head*

---

sinners. **6–7**: His power is tempered by equally boundless mercy. In late biblical texts (e.g. 2 Chr 30.9), the "turn away from sin" enables divine mercy to operate. In the Prayer, God's establishment of repentance as a perennial opportunity is itself an expression of his mercy. **7**: Cf. Ex 34.6–7; the Greek is very close to the LXX translation of Joel 2.13 and Jon 4.21.

    9–10: **Lament**. A presentation of the central problem: the petitioner's sin has ruined him. **10**: *An iron fetter*, cf. 2 Chr 33.11. *I … have done what is evil in your sight*, Ps 51.4 (LXX 50.6).

    11–13: **Petition**. **11**: *And now*, the dramatic climax. *I bend the knee*, usually an act of supplication. *Of my heart* probably serves as an indication of the supplicant's inner sincerity. That Manasseh is bound in fetters (v. 10), makes "bending the knee of the heart" ironically the only method of prostration available.

    14–15: **Vow of praise**. Reminder of how heeding the petitioner's request will benefit God. Such a vow is often found at the end of laments in the Psalms (e.g., 22.22–31; 80.18). **15**: *Host of heaven*, the multitude of angelic beings (Job 38.7; Neh 9.6; cf. Lk 2.13).

PSALM 151

CANONICAL STATUS, ANCIENT VERSIONS, AND DATE OF COMPOSITION

Although Psalm 151 does not appear in the Masoretic Text, it is the final psalm in the book of Psalms in the Greek Septuagint (LXX). One manuscript of the Septuagint contains a postscript to Psalm 151 that reads "the 151 Psalms of David," thus attributing the entire collection to King David. Other Septuagint manuscripts, however, contain a superscription to the psalm that indicates it is "outside the number" (of 150 psalms). A more expansive version of Psalm 151 was discovered among the Dead Sea Scrolls toward the end of the long psalms scroll from Cave 11 (11QPsa). This version comprises two distinct psalms, referred to as Psalm 151A (roughly LXX Ps 151) and 151B (fragmentary), each with its own superscription. The psalm also appears in somewhat expanded form as the first of five additional psalms in the Syriac translation. Psalm 151 is part of the canon of Orthodox churches and is included in the Apocrypha.

Psalm 151 was likely composed no later than the third century BCE when the exact content and ordering of the book of Psalms was not yet fixed. Such fluidity in form and content suggests that the psalms were used, memorized, and transmitted orally.

CONTENTS

In contrast to the final psalms of the canonical Psalter (146–150), which all offer praise to the LORD, Psalm 151 focuses on David, making explicit reference to incidents from David's life as described in 1 Samuel 16–17.

Verses 1 and 4b–5 of the psalm form a unit (with framed references to "brothers," "father's sheep") before the transition in vv. 6–7 to David's conflict with Goliath.

Judith H. Newman

This psalm is ascribed to David as his own composition (though it is outside the number[a]), after he had fought in single combat with Goliath.

[1] I was small among my brothers,
    and the youngest in my father's house;
I tended my father's sheep.

[2] My hands made a harp;
    my fingers fashioned a lyre.

[3] And who will tell my Lord?
    The Lord himself; it is he who hears.[b]

[4] It was he who sent his messenger[c]
    and took me from my father's sheep,
    and anointed me with his
        anointing oil.

[5] My brothers were handsome and tall,
    but the Lord was not pleased with them.

[6] I went out to meet the Philistine,[d]
    and he cursed me by his idols.

[7] But I drew his own sword;
    I beheaded him, and took away disgrace
        from the people of Israel.

---

a   Other ancient authorities add *of the one hundred fifty* (psalms)
b   Other ancient authorities add *everything*; others add *me*; others read *who will hear me*
c   Or *angel*
d   Or *foreigner*

1: *The youngest*, cf. 1 Sam 16.11; 17.14. 2: David's ability to play the *lyre* allowed him to soothe Saul's "evil spirit" (1 Sam 16.14–23; 18.10). Such musical ability was closely associated with the gift of poetry in antiquity and likely contributed to David's reputation as the author of the psalms. 4: *His messenger*, specified in 11QPsa as the prophet Samuel; see 1 Sam 16.1–13. 6–7: The focus of the psalm shifts to David's feat of slaying "the Philistine" Goliath (1 Sam 17). *Idols*, see 1 Sam 17.43. On Israel's subjugation by Goliath as a "disgrace" see Sir 47.4.

3 MACCABEES

NAME AND CANONICAL STATUS

The title of the book known as 3 Maccabees is a misnomer, for it is not a historical account of the Maccabees but a fictional story about Egyptian Jews under Ptolemy IV Philopator (221–204 BCE), half a century before the Maccabean period. The book is preserved in the Greek Septuagint (LXX) and the Syriac Peshitta, as well as in most manuscripts of the Armenian Bible. It is not, however, included in the Latin Vulgate. This may explain why it was not included in the canon of the Roman Catholic Church or in the traditional Protestant Apocrypha. It is included in the canon of the Eastern Orthodox churches.

CONTENTS

Third Maccabees begins with a brief account of how Ptolemy was saved from assassination at the battle of Raphia by the intervention of a Jew (1.1–5). This brief story of Jewish loyalty provides a foil against which the king's hostility to the Jews must be seen. The second episode (1.6–2.24) tells of the king's unsuccessful attempt to enter the holy of holies in the Jerusalem Temple. The desecration is averted by divine intervention in response to the prayer of the high priest Simon. The third episode, which takes up most of the book, describes the persecution of the Jews in Egypt. Upon his return there, the king determines to take vengeance upon the Jews for his humiliation in Jerusalem. He radically alters their legal status and attempts to force them to worship the Greek god Dionysus, promising to those who comply full citizenship in Alexandria (2.25–33). The vast majority of Jews resist, and with great cruelty they are herded together to be registered, tortured, and put to death. Again divine intervention averts disaster; after forty days the writing materials have been exhausted, and the registration cannot be completed (3.1–4.21). Finally, the king decrees that drugged elephants be turned upon the Jews, who have been detained in the city's arena. Twice this is providentially delayed, and the third miracle occurs in answer to the prayer of the aged priest Eleazar, paralleling the prayer of the high priest in the second episode. The elephants turn on the king's forces, and he repents, allowing the Jews to return to their homes (5.1–6.21). The book ends with a royal letter decreeing protection for the Jews, who punish those of their number who had apostatized, and rejoice at the providential deliverance (ch 7).

DATE AND HISTORICAL CONTEXT

The work was originally written in Greek by an unknown Egyptian Jew. The date of composition is disputed. Some scholars argue that the language of the book and its familiarity with the terminology of the Ptolemaic court argue for a date about 100 BCE. Others hold that the threatened change in the status of the Jews, and the promise of Alexandrian citizenship to those who abandoned their religion, reflect the situation of the Alexandrian Jews after Rome conquered Egypt in 30 BCE. Non-Jews were subjected to a new tax, called the "laographia" (the word used in connection with the change of status in 3 Macc 2.28). Citizenship normally required the worship of other gods, and so was unacceptable to most Jews, but some Jews who abandoned their religion rose to prominence in Roman service (most notably Tiberius Julius Alexander, nephew of the philosopher Philo). The book is not a historical account, although it does depict some earlier historical events, such as the battle of Raphia, known from other sources.

Although the book is written in a bombastic style, it provides a colorful drama of danger and deliverance. It also conveys a strict message of the need for solidarity in the Jewish community.

GUIDE TO READING

Third Maccabees belongs to a narrative genre that was especially popular among Jews who lived in the Diaspora, outside the land of Israel. Other examples are found in the book of Esther and in Daniel 2–6. These stories tell of some great danger that threatens the Jewish community, which is then averted, either through heroic action (Esther) or, more typically, through divine intervention. Such stories provided both entertainment and edification, allowing the Jewish readers to confront their fears of destruction and then allaying those fears by the happy ending.

John J. Collins

1 When Philopator learned from those who returned that the regions that he had controlled had been seized by Antiochus, he gave orders to all his forces, both infantry and cavalry, took with him his sister Arsinoë, and marched out to the region near Raphia, where the army of Antiochus was encamped. ² But a certain Theodotus, determined to carry out the plot he had devised, took with him the best of the Ptolemaic arms that had been previously issued to him,ᵃ and crossed over by night to the tent of Ptolemy, intending single-handed to kill him and thereby end the war. ³ But Dositheus, known as the son of Drimylus, a Jew by birth who later changed his religion and apostatized from the ancestral traditions, had led the king away and arranged that a certain insignificant man should sleep in the tent; and so it turned out that this man incurred the vengeance meant for the king.ᵇ ⁴ When a bitter fight resulted, and matters were turning out rather in favor of Antiochus, Arsinoë went to the troops with wailing and tears, her locks all disheveled, and exhorted them to defend themselves and their children and wives bravely, promising to give them each two minas of gold if they won the battle. ⁵ And so it came about that the enemy was

routed in the action, and many captives also were taken. ⁶ Now that he had foiled the plot, Ptolemyᶜ decided to visit the neighboring cities and encourage them. ⁷ By doing this, and by endowing their sacred enclosures with gifts, he strengthened the morale of his subjects.

⁸ Since the Jews had sent some of their council and elders to greet him, to bring him gifts of welcome, and to congratulate him on what had happened, he was all the more eager to visit them as soon as possible. ⁹ After he had arrived in Jerusalem, he offered sacrifice to the supreme Godᵈ and made thank offerings and did what was fitting for the holy place.ᵉ Then, upon entering the place and being impressed by its excellence and its beauty, ¹⁰ he marveled at the good order of the temple, and conceived a desire to enter the sanctuary. ¹¹ When they said that this was not permitted, because not even members of their own nation were allowed to enter,

ᵃ Or *the best of the Ptolemaic soldiers previously put under his command*
ᵇ Gk *that one*
ᶜ Gk *he*
ᵈ Gk *the greatest God*
ᵉ Gk *the place*

1.1–7: The battle of Raphia (217 BCE). The abruptness with which the book opens and the use of the Greek conjunctive particle "de" may indicate that the introduction to 3 Maccabees has not survived (see also 2.25n.). Alternatively, the account of the battle may have been excerpted from a historical source. It resembles the account given by the second-century BCE historian Polybius (book 5), who also reports a plot to kill the king, but not the role of Dositheus in foiling it. **1:** Ptolemy IV [Philopator] was king of Egypt 221–204. *From those who returned,* fugitives who had escaped. *Antiochus* III, later called the Great, was king of Syria 223–187. *Raphia,* a city of Palestine, three miles from Gaza and not far from the Egyptian frontier. *Arsinoë,* Ptolemy's sister, who became his wife, was later put to death at the instigation of her husband. **2:** *Theodotus* had been chief commander of the Egyptian forces in Syria, but subsequently became disaffected and deserted to Antiochus III (Polybius, 5.40). **3:** *Dositheus* is mentioned in Hibeh papyrus 90 as priest of Alexander in 222 BCE, a very exalted position, and he is also mentioned in earlier papyri as a Ptolemaic administrator. The papyri, however, do not identify him as Jewish. *A certain insignificant* man, Polybius identifies the man as Andreas, the king's physician. **4:** *Two minas,* ca. 2.5 lb (1.1 kg). **5:** According to Polybius (5.86.5–6), Antiochus lost nearly 10,000 infantry, 300 cavalry, and 4,000 prisoners; Ptolemy lost 1,500 infantry and 700 cavalry.

1.8–15: Ptolemy attempts to enter the sanctuary at Jerusalem. 9: Reference to *the supreme God,* Greek "megistos theos," occurs frequently in 3 Maccabees (1.9,16; 3.11; 4.16; 5.25; 7.22) as well as in 2 Maccabees (3.36). The God of the Jews was often known as The Most High God in antiquity. It was customary for kings to show respect to local deities. According to Josephus (*Ant.* 11.336), Alexander the Great had offered sacrifice in the Jerusalem Temple. *The holy place,* an alternative term for "the Temple" in 3 Maccabees and other Jewish literature. **10:** No attempt by a Ptolemy to enter the holy of holies is otherwise known. The Roman general Pompey did enter it in 63 BCE, but the closest parallel to 3 Maccabees on this point is found in the story of Heliodorus in 2 Macc 3, although the details of the stories are different (Heliodorus was attempting to seize the Temple treasure). **11:** *High priest . . . once a year,* Lev 16.2,34.

not even all of the priests, but only the high priest who was pre-eminent over all—and he only once a year—the king was by no means persuaded. [12] Even after the law had been read to him, he did not cease to maintain that he ought to enter, saying, "Even if those men are deprived of this honor, I ought not to be." [13] And he inquired why, when he entered every other temple,[a] no one there had stopped him. [14] And someone answered thoughtlessly that it was wrong to take that as a portent.[b] [15] "But since this has happened," the king[c] said, "why should not I at least enter, whether they wish it or not?"

[16] Then the priests in all their vestments prostrated themselves and entreated the supreme God[d] to aid in the present situation and to avert the violence of this evil design, and they filled the temple with cries and tears; [17] those who remained behind in the city were agitated and hurried out, supposing that something mysterious was occurring. [18] Young women who had been secluded in their chambers rushed out with their mothers, sprinkled their hair with dust,[e] and filled the streets with groans and lamentations. [19] Those women who had recently been arrayed for marriage abandoned the bridal chambers[f] prepared for wedded union, and, neglecting proper modesty, in a disorderly rush flocked together in the city. [20] Mothers and nurses abandoned even newborn children here and there, some in houses and some in the streets, and without a backward look they crowded together at the most high temple. [21] Various were the supplications of those gathered there because of what the king was profanely plotting. [22] In addition, the bolder of the citizens would not tolerate the completion of his plans or the fulfillment of his intended purpose.

[23] They shouted to their compatriots to take arms and die courageously for the ancestral law, and created a considerable disturbance in the holy place;[g] and being barely restrained by the old men and the elders,[h] they resorted to the same posture of supplication as the others. [24] Meanwhile the crowd, as before, was engaged in prayer, [25] while the elders near the king tried in various ways to change his arrogant mind from the plan that he had conceived. [26] But he, in his arrogance, took heed of nothing, and began now to approach, determined to bring the aforesaid plan to a conclusion. [27] When those who were around him observed this, they turned, together with our people, to call upon him who has all power to defend them in the present trouble and not to overlook this unlawful and haughty deed. [28] The continuous, vehement, and concerted cry of the crowds[i] resulted in an immense uproar; [29] for it seemed that not only the people but also the walls and the whole earth around echoed, because indeed all at that time[j] preferred death to the profanation of the place.

2 Then the high priest Simon, facing the sanctuary, bending his knees and extending his hands with calm dignity, prayed as

---

[a] Or *entered the temple precincts*
[b] Or *to boast of this*
[c] Gk *he*
[d] Gk *the greatest God*
[e] Other ancient authorities add *and ashes*
[f] Or *the canopies*
[g] Gk *the place*
[h] Other ancient authorities read *priests*
[i] Other ancient authorities read *vehement cry of the assembled crowds*
[j] Other ancient authorities lack *at that time*

1.16–29: Jewish reaction to Ptolemy's determination to enter the sanctuary. Compare the reaction to the attempt of Heliodorus in 2 Macc 3.14–21, and also the historical episodes when Pontius Pilate introduced the sacrilegious Roman standards into Jerusalem (Josephus, *War* 1.169–74; *Ant.* 18.55–59) and when Caligula attempted to have his statue installed in the Temple (*War* 2.184–203; *Ant.* 18.269–72). **18:** *Young women* were not permitted to appear in public before marriage; cf. 2 Macc 3.19. **19:** For other references to bridal chambers see Joel 2.16; 2 Esd 16.33–34; Bar 2.23. **23:** *Die courageously for the ancestral law,* 1 Macc 2.40; 3.21; 13.3–4; 2 Macc 8.21. It is noteworthy that the militants are restrained by the elders here, in contrast to the Maccabean rebellion and to the later Jewish revolt against Rome.

2.1–20: The prayer of Simon, the high priest. Simon II, son of Onias II and called "the Just," was high priest about 219–196 BCE (see Sir 50.1n.). The prayer is in a classic Jewish form that, like Eleazar's prayer in 6.1–15, follows the pattern of Ps 105 and 106 in confessing the sins of the people but calling on God to deliver them as he

more bitterly hostile toward those in the countryside; and he ordered that all should promptly be gathered into one place, and put to death by the most cruel means. ²While these matters were being arranged, a hostile rumor was circulated against the Jewish nation by some who conspired to do them ill, a pretext being given by a report that they hindered others[a] from the observance of their customs. ³The Jews, however, continued to maintain goodwill and unswerving loyalty toward the dynasty; ⁴but because they worshiped God and conducted themselves by his law, they kept their separateness with respect to foods. For this reason they appeared hateful to some; ⁵but since they adorned their style of life with the good deeds of upright people, they were established in good repute with everyone. ⁶Nevertheless those of other races paid no heed to their good service to their nation, which was common talk among all; ⁷instead they gossiped about the differences in worship and foods, alleging that these people were loyal neither to the king nor to his authorities, but were hostile and greatly opposed to his government. So they attached no ordinary reproach to them.

⁸The Greeks in the city, though wronged in no way, when they saw an unexpected tumult around these people and the crowds that suddenly were forming, were not strong enough to help them, for they lived under tyranny. They did try to console them, being grieved at the situation, and expected that matters would change; ⁹for such a great community ought not be left to its fate when it had committed no offense. ¹⁰And already some of their neighbors and friends and business associates had taken some of them aside privately and were pledging to protect them and to exert more earnest efforts for their assistance.

¹¹Then the king, boastful of his present good fortune, and not considering the might of the supreme God,[b] but assuming that he would persevere constantly in his same purpose, wrote this letter against them:

¹²"King Ptolemy Philopator to his generals and soldiers in Egypt and all its districts, greetings and good health:

¹³"I myself and our government are faring well. ¹⁴When our expedition took place in Asia, as you yourselves know, it was brought to conclusion, according to plan, by the gods' deliberate alliance with us in battle, ¹⁵and we considered that we should not rule the nations inhabiting Coelesyria and Phoenicia by the power of the spear, but should cherish them with clemency and great benevolence, gladly treating them well. ¹⁶And when we had granted very great revenues to the temples in the cities, we came on to Jerusalem also, and went up to honor the temple of those wicked people, who never cease from their folly. ¹⁷They accepted our presence by word, but insincerely by deed, because when we proposed to enter their inner temple and honor it with magnificent and most beautiful offerings, ¹⁸they were carried away by their traditional arrogance, and excluded us from entering; but they were spared the exercise of

a Gk *them*
b Gk *the greatest God*

attempt by Ptolemy to take a census of the Jews in rural areas. **2:** The *rumor* maliciously represents the Jews as hostile to the best interests of the state (cf. Esth 3.8), whereas the author insists on their loyalty. Some scholars think 3 Maccabees was written by a Jew from the countryside. His Greek is less sophisticated than that of Alexandrian Jews, such as Philo. **4:** *Separateness with respect to foods* was one of the barriers between Jew and Gentile, cf. 1 Macc 1.62–63; 2 Macc 11.30–31. Many Hellenistic Jewish writings avoid the subject. For a defense of the observance of Jewish dietary rules, by explaining them allegorically, see the *Letter of Aristeas,* 128–66. **5:** Deut 4.5–6. **7:** For similar charges see Esth 3.8; Add Esth 13.4–5. **8:** *The Greeks,* the elite, cultivated class, in distinction from *those of other races* (v. 6). The Alexandrian Greeks were bitter enemies of the Jews in the Roman period, but the author portrays a relationship of support and respect between the two groups, even though the king and his friends were obviously Greek.

3.11–30: Ptolemy orders the arrest of all Jews in his kingdom. **11:** The king is *boastful,* and therefore guilty of "hubris," the sin that leads to disaster in Greek tragedy. *Assuming that he would persevere,* an anticipatory reference to the calamity that came upon him by which he forgot his own previous commands (5.27–28). **15:** *Coelesyria,* western Syria. *Phoenicia,* modern Lebanon. *Benevolence,* Greek "philanthropia" (see vv. 18,20), was

our power because of the benevolence that we have toward all. ¹⁹ By maintaining their manifest ill-will toward us, they become the only people among all nations who hold their heads high in defiance of kings and their own benefactors, and are unwilling to regard any action as sincere.

²⁰ "But we, when we arrived in Egypt victorious, accommodated ourselves to their folly and did as was proper, since we treat all nations with benevolence. ²¹ Among other things, we made known to all our amnesty toward their compatriots here, both because of their alliance with us and the myriad affairs liberally entrusted to them from the beginning; and we ventured to make a change, by deciding both to deem them worthy of Alexandrian citizenship and to make them participants in our regular religious rites.ª ²² But in their innate malice they took this in a contrary spirit, and disdained what is good. Since they incline constantly to evil, ²³ they not only spurn the priceless citizenship, but also both by speech and by silence they abominate those few among them who are sincerely disposed toward us; in every situation, in accordance with their infamous way of life, they secretly suspect that we may soon alter our policy. ²⁴ Therefore, fully convinced by these indications that they are ill-disposed toward us in every way, we have taken precautions so that, if a sudden disorder later arises against us, we shall not have these impious people behind our backs as traitors and barbarous enemies. ²⁵ Therefore we have given orders that, as soon as this letter arrives, you are to send to us those who live among you, together with their wives and children, with insulting and harsh treatment, and bound securely with iron fetters, to suffer the sure and shameful death that befits enemies. ²⁶ For when all of these have been punished, we are sure that for the remaining time the government will be established for ourselves in good order and in the best state. ²⁷ But those who shelter any of the Jews, whether old people or children or even infants, will be tortured to death with the most hateful torments, together with their families. ²⁸ Any who are willing to give information will receive the property of those who incur the punishment, and also two thousand drachmas from the royal treasury, and will be awarded their freedom.ᵇ ²⁹ Every place detected sheltering a Jew is to be made unapproachable and burned with fire, and shall become useless for all time to any mortal creature." ³⁰ The letter was written in the above form.

4 In every place, then, where this decree arrived, a feast at public expense was arranged for the Gentiles with shouts and gladness, for the inveterate enmity that had long ago been in their minds was now made evident and outspoken. ² But among the Jews there was incessant mourning, lamentation, and tearful cries; everywhere their hearts were burning, and they groaned because of the unexpected destruction that had suddenly been decreed for them. ³ What district or city, or what habitable place at all, or what streets were not filled with mourning and wailing for them? ⁴ For with such a harsh and ruthless spirit were they being sent off, all together, by the generals in the several cities, that at the sight of their unusual punishments, even some of their enemies, perceiving the common object of pity before their eyes, reflected

ª Other ancient authorities read *partners of our regular priests*

ᵇ Gk *crowned with freedom*

regarded as a major political virtue during the Hellenistic period. **21:** For the confidence placed in Jews, see 6.25 and Josephus, *Ag. Ap.* 2.49, who says that Ptolemy VI Philometor gave two Jewish generals, Onias and Dositheus, command of his whole army. Jews were often employed in Egypt as mercenaries. *Alexandrian citizenship* normally entailed participation in Greek religious ceremonies. Alexandrian Greeks, such as the first-century CE scholar Apion, complained that the Jews wanted the privileges of citizenship but were unwilling to fulfill the religious obligations that it usually entailed. **24:** *Behind our backs,* cf. Ex 1.10. **28:** *Awarded their freedom,* another rendering is "crowned at the Eleutheria" (a festival of Dionysus; see 2.29n.). **29:** *Useless for all time,* cf. Add Esth 16.24.

4.1–21: The Jews brought to Alexandria and imprisoned. 1: *Enmity* on the part of native-born Egyptians for the Jews is assumed in 3 Maccabees; contrast the depiction of the Greeks in 3.8. **2:** *Mourning, lamentation, and*

on the uncertainty of life and shed tears at the most miserable expulsion of these people. [5] For a multitude of gray-headed old men, sluggish and bent with age, was being led away, forced to march at a swift pace by the violence with which they were driven in such a shameful manner. [6] And young women who had just entered the bridal chamber[a] to share married life exchanged joy for wailing, their myrrh-perfumed hair sprinkled with ashes, and were carried away unveiled, all together raising a lament instead of a wedding song, as they were torn by the harsh treatment of the heathen.[b] [7] In bonds and in public view they were violently dragged along as far as the place of embarkation. [8] Their husbands, in the prime of youth, their necks encircled with ropes instead of garlands, spent the remaining days of their marriage festival in lamentations instead of good cheer and youthful revelry, seeing death immediately before them.[c] [9] They were brought on board like wild animals, driven under the constraint of iron bonds; some were fastened by the neck to the benches of the boats, others had their feet secured by unbreakable fetters, [10] and in addition they were confined under a solid deck, so that, with their eyes in total darkness, they would undergo treatment befitting traitors during the whole voyage.

[11] When these people had been brought to the place called Schedia, and the voyage was concluded as the king had decreed, he commanded that they should be enclosed in the hippodrome that had been built with a monstrous perimeter wall in front of the city, and that was well suited to make them an obvious spectacle to all coming back into the city and to those from the city[d] going out into the country, so that they could neither communicate with the king's forces nor in any way claim to be inside the circuit of the city.[e] [12] And when this had happened, the king, hearing that the Jews' compatriots

from the city frequently went out in secret to lament bitterly the ignoble misfortune of their kindred, [13] ordered in his rage that these people be dealt with in precisely the same fashion as the others, not omitting any detail of their punishment. [14] The entire race was to be registered individually, not for the hard labor that has been briefly mentioned before, but to be tortured with the outrages that he had ordered, and at the end to be destroyed in the space of a single day. [15] The registration of these people was therefore conducted with bitter haste and zealous intensity from the rising of the sun until its setting, coming to an end after forty days but still uncompleted.

[16] The king was greatly and continually filled with joy, organizing feasts in honor of all his idols, with a mind alienated from truth and with a profane mouth, praising speechless things that are not able even to communicate or to come to one's help, and uttering improper words against the supreme God.[f] [17] But after the previously mentioned interval of time the scribes declared to the king that they were no longer able to take the census of the Jews because of their immense number, [18] though most of them were still in the country, some still residing in their homes, and some at the place;[g] the task was impossible for all the generals in Egypt. [19] After he had threatened them severely, charging that they had been bribed to contrive a means of escape, he was clearly convinced about the matter [20] when they said and proved that

a   Or the canopy
b   Other ancient authorities read as though torn by heathen whelps
c   Gk seeing Hades already lying at their feet
d   Gk those of them
e   Or claim protection of the walls; meaning of Gk uncertain
f   Gk the greatest God
g   Other ancient authorities read on the way

tearful cries, cf. Esth 4.3. **11:** *Schedia,* a promontory about three miles from Alexandria. *The hippodrome* (arena) was situated at the east or Canobic gate of Alexandria; according to Strabo (17.1.10,16) a canal joined Schedia and the Canobic gate. *Inside . . . the city,* implies that Jews living in Alexandria (see v. 12, *compatriots from the city*) had been thus far unmolested (but cf. 3.1). **14:** *Mentioned before,* see 2.28. The registration for poll tax and slave status is transformed into an instrument for the execution of *the entire race* of Jews. **16:** *Speechless things,* see Ps 115.3–7; Jer 10.5; Hab 2.18; Bar 6.7. *Supreme God,* see 1.9n. **17:** *Their immense number,* an obvious hyperbole. **19:** *Bribed,* see 2.32.

both the paper[a] and the pens they used for writing had already given out. [21] But this was an act of the invincible providence of him who was aiding the Jews from heaven.

5 Then the king, completely inflexible, was filled with overpowering anger and wrath; so he summoned Hermon, keeper of the elephants, [2] and ordered him on the following day to drug all the elephants—five hundred in number—with large handfuls of frankincense and plenty of unmixed wine, and to drive them in, maddened by the lavish abundance of drink, so that the Jews might meet their doom. [3] When he had given these orders he returned to his feasting, together with those of his Friends and of the army who were especially hostile toward the Jews. [4] And Hermon, keeper of the elephants, proceeded faithfully to carry out the orders. [5] The servants in charge of the Jews[b] went out in the evening and bound the hands of the wretched people and arranged for their continued custody through the night, convinced that the whole nation would experience its final destruction. [6] For to the Gentiles it appeared that the Jews were left without any aid, [7] because in their bonds they were forcibly confined on every side. But with tears and a voice hard to silence they all called upon the Almighty Lord and Ruler of all power, their merciful God and Father, praying [8] that he avert with vengeance the evil plot against them and in a glorious manifestation rescue them from the fate now prepared for them. [9] So their entreaty ascended fervently to heaven.

[10] Hermon, however, when he had drugged the pitiless elephants until they had been filled with a great abundance of wine and satiated with frankincense, presented himself at the courtyard early in the morning to report to the king about these preparations. [11] But the Lord[c] sent upon the king a portion of sleep, that beneficence that from the beginning, night and day, is bestowed by him who grants it to whomever he wishes. [12] And by the action of the Lord he was overcome by so pleasant and deep a sleep[d] that he quite failed in his lawless purpose and was completely frustrated in his inflexible plan. [13] Then the Jews, since they had escaped the appointed hour, praised their holy God and again implored him who is easily reconciled to show the might of his all-powerful hand to the arrogant Gentiles.

[14] But now, since it was nearly the middle of the tenth hour, the person who was in charge of the invitations, seeing that the guests were assembled, approached the king and nudged him. [15] And when he had with difficulty roused him, he pointed out that the hour of the banquet was already slipping by, and he gave him an account of the situation. [16] The king, after considering this, returned to his drinking, and ordered those present for the banquet to recline opposite him. [17] When this was done he urged them to give themselves over to revelry and to make the present[e] portion of the banquet joyful by celebrating all the more. [18] After the party had been going on for some time, the king summoned Hermon and with sharp threats demanded to know why the Jews had been allowed to remain alive through the present day. [19] But when he, with the corroboration of the king's[f] Friends, pointed out that while it was still night he had carried out completely the order given him, [20] the king,[c] possessed by a savagery

a Or *paper factory*
b Gk *them*
c Gk *he*
d Other ancient authorities add *from evening until the ninth hour*
e Other ancient authorities read *delayed* (Gk *untimely*)
f Gk *his*

5.1–51: Ptolemy orders the execution of the Jews, but is thwarted. A variant of this story is told in Josephus, *Ag. Ap.* 2.53–55, but there the Ptolemy is Ptolemy VIII Euergetes II Physcon (144–117 BCE). **1:** *Hermon,* the name of the keeper of the elephants, recalls the figure of Haman in Esther. **2:** *Elephants—five hundred* is an exaggeration; according to Polybius, Ptolemy had seventy-three elephants at the battle of Raphia. After Alexander the Great encountered them in India, war-*elephants* were often a component of Hellenistic armies; see 1 Macc 1.17. Similar stimulation of war-elephants is reported in 1 Macc 6.34. **3:** *Returned to his feasting,* 4.16. **7:** *Father,* see Isa 63.16; Mal 2.10; Tob 13.4; Wis 11.10. **11:** The divine gift of *sleep* is extolled by Roman poets (e.g., Seneca, *Hercules Furens* 1065–78; Statius, *Silvae* 5.4); see Ps 127.2. **14:** *Middle of the tenth hour,* 3:30 pm. **19:** *Friends,* see 2.23n. **20:** *Phalaris,*

worse than that of Phalaris, said that the Jews[a] were benefited by today's sleep, "but," he added, "tomorrow without delay prepare the elephants in the same way for the destruction of the lawless Jews!" [21] When the king had spoken, all those present readily and joyfully with one accord gave their approval, and all went to their own homes. [22] But they did not so much employ the duration of the night in sleep as in devising all sorts of insults for those they thought to be doomed.

[23] Then, as soon as the cock had crowed in the early morning, Hermon, having equipped[b] the animals, began to move them along in the great colonnade. [24] The crowds of the city had been assembled for this most pitiful spectacle and they were eagerly waiting for daybreak. [25] But the Jews, at their last gasp—since the time had run out—stretched their hands toward heaven and with most tearful supplication and mournful dirges implored the supreme God[c] to help them again at once. [26] The rays of the sun were not yet shed abroad, and while the king was receiving his Friends, Hermon arrived and invited him to come out, indicating that what the king desired was ready for action. [27] But he, on receiving the report and being struck by the unusual invitation to come out—since he had been completely overcome by incomprehension—inquired what the matter was for which this had been so zealously completed for him. [28] This was the act of God who rules over all things, for he had implanted in the king's mind a forgetfulness of the things he had previously devised. [29] Then Hermon and all the king's Friends[d] pointed out that the animals and the armed forces were ready, "O king, according to your eager purpose."[e] [30] But at these words he was filled with an overpowering wrath, because by the providence of God his whole mind had been deranged concerning these matters; and with a threatening look he said, [31] "If your parents or children were present, I would have prepared them to be a rich feast for the savage animals instead of the Jews, who give me no ground for complaint and have exhibited to an extraordinary degree a full and firm loyalty to my ancestors. [32] In fact you would have been deprived of life instead of these, if it were not for an affection arising from our nurture in common and your usefulness." [33] So Hermon suffered an unexpected and dangerous threat, and his eyes wavered and his face fell. [34] The king's Friends one by one sullenly slipped away and dismissed[f] the assembled people to their own occupations. [35] Then the Jews, on hearing what the king had said, praised the manifest Lord God, King of kings, since this also was his aid that they had received.

[36] The king, however, reconvened the party in the same manner and urged the guests to return to their celebrating. [37] After summoning Hermon he said in a threatening tone, "How many times, you poor wretch, must I give you orders about these things? [38] Equip[g] the elephants now once more for the destruction of the Jews tomorrow!" [39] But the officials who were at table with him, wondering at his instability of mind, remonstrated as follows: [40] "O king, how long will you put us to the test, as though we are idiots, ordering now for a third time that they be destroyed, and again revoking your decree in the matter?[h] [41] As a result the city is in a tumult because of its expectation; it is crowded with masses of people, and also in constant danger of being plundered."

[42] At this the king, a Phalaris in everything and filled with madness, took no account of the changes of mind that had come about within him for the protection of the Jews, and he firmly swore an irrevocable oath that he would send them to death[i] without

---

a Gk *they*
b Or *armed*
c Gk *the greatest God*
d Gk *all the Friends*
e Other ancient authorities read *pointed to the beasts and the armed forces, saying, "They are ready, O king, according to your eager purpose."*
f Other ancient authorities read *he dismissed*
g Or *Arm*
h Other ancient authorities read *when the matter is in hand*
i Gk *Hades*

tyrant of Agrigentum in Sicily (ca. 570–554 BCE) whose cruelty was proverbial (Polybius 12.25). **28**: *The act of God,* cf. Prov 21.1. **29**: An addition in several Greek manuscripts indicates that though Ptolemy was moved by compassion and determined to release the Jews, Hermon influenced him to proceed with his plans to destroy

delay, mangled by the knees and feet of the animals, ⁴³ and would also march against Judea and rapidly level it to the ground with fire and spear, and by burning to the ground the temple inaccessible to himᵃ would quickly render it forever empty of those who offered sacrifices there. ⁴⁴ Then the Friends and officers departed with great joy, and they confidently posted the armed forces at the places in the city most favorable for keeping guard.

⁴⁵ Now when the animals had been brought virtually to a state of madness, so to speak, by the very fragrant draughts of wine mixed with frankincense and had been equipped with frightful devices, the elephant keeper ⁴⁶ entered at about dawn into the courtyard—the city now being filled with countless masses of people crowding their way into the hippodrome—and urged the king on to the matter at hand. ⁴⁷ So he, when he had filled his impious mind with a deep rage, rushed out in full force along with the animals, wishing to witness, with invulnerable heart and with his own eyes, the grievous and pitiful destruction of the aforementioned people.

⁴⁸ When the Jews saw the dust raised by the elephants going out at the gate and by the following armed forces, as well as by the trampling of the crowd, and heard the loud and tumultuous noise, ⁴⁹ they thought that this was their last moment of life, the end of their most miserable suspense, and giving way to lamentation and groans they kissed each other, embracing relatives and falling into one another's armsᵇ—parents and children, mothers and daughters, and others with babies at their breasts who were drawing their last milk.

⁵⁰ Not only this, but when they considered the help that they had received before from heaven, they prostrated themselves with one accord on the ground, removing the babies from their breasts, ⁵¹ and cried out in a very loud voice, imploring the Ruler over every power to manifest himself and be merciful to them, as they stood now at the gates of death.ᶜ

6 Then a certain Eleazar, famous among the priests of the country, who had attained a ripe old age and throughout his life had been adorned with every virtue, directed the elders around him to stop calling upon the holy God, and he prayed as follows: ² "King of great power, Almighty God Most High, governing all creation with mercy, ³ look upon the descendants of Abraham, O Father, upon the children of the sainted Jacob, a people of your consecrated portion who are perishing as foreigners in a foreign land. ⁴ Pharaoh with his abundance of chariots, the former ruler of this Egypt, exalted with lawless insolence and boastful tongue, you destroyed together with his arrogant army by drowning them in the sea, manifesting the light of your mercy on the nation of Israel. ⁵ Sennacherib exulting in his countless forces, oppressive king of the Assyrians, who had already gained control of the whole world by the spear and was lifted up against your holy city, speaking grievous words with boasting and insolence, you, O Lord, broke in pieces, showing your power to many nations. ⁶ The three companions in Babylon who had

---

ᵃ   Gk *us*
ᵇ   Gk *falling upon their necks*
ᶜ   Gk *Hades*

them. **42:** *Phalaris,* see v. 20n. **45:** The *frightful devices* were probably scythes, knives, and other military equipment attached to different parts of the bodies of the elephants. **49:** *Embracing,* but according to 6.27 they are still bound. **50–51:** The author continues to build up his thesis that God was the only resort for the captives, and that their hope would not be frustrated. **51:** *Gates of death,* Pss 9.13; 107.18.

6.1–15: The prayer of Eleazar. Like Simon's prayer in 2.1–20, it is plainly Jewish in form and style, containing doxology, thanksgiving for God's earlier interventions in Israel's history, and petition for a new miracle. The emphasis is on the exclusiveness and separate standing of Israel before God (v. 3). Eleazar expects God's intervention, not on account of Israel's virtues or merits, but because of divine mercy. Unlike many Jewish prayers from this period, however, there is little confession of sin (but see v. 10). **1:** *Eleazar,* the name of one of Aaron's sons (Ex 6.23), of a martyr in 2 Macc 6 and 4 Macc 5–6, and of a high priest in the *Letter of Aristeas. Priests* were always numerous in the Jewish community. There was a Jewish temple at Leontopolis in Egypt, erected by an exiled high priest (Onias IV) in the second century BCE, in defiance of Deuteronomistic law (Deut 12). **4:** *Pharaoh,* Ex 14.28. **5:** *Sennacherib,* 2 Kings 18.13; 19.35–37. **6:** *Three companions in Babylon,* Dan 3.22,27; Song of Thr 22–27.

with barbarous penalties as traitors; [4] for they declared that our government would never be firmly established until this was accomplished, because of the ill-will that these people had toward all nations. [5] They also led them out with harsh treatment as slaves, or rather as traitors, and, girding themselves with a cruelty more savage than that of Scythian custom, they tried without any inquiry or examination to put them to death. [6] But we very severely threatened them for these acts, and in accordance with the clemency that we have toward all people we barely spared their lives. Since we have come to realize that the God of heaven surely defends the Jews, always taking their part as a father does for his children, [7] and since we have taken into account the friendly and firm goodwill that they had toward us and our ancestors, we justly have acquitted them of every charge of whatever kind. [8] We also have ordered all people to return to their own homes, with no one in any place[a] doing them harm at all or reproaching them for the irrational things that have happened. [9] For you should know that if we devise any evil against them or cause them any grief at all, we always shall have not a mortal but the Ruler over every power, the Most High God, in everything and inescapably as an antagonist to avenge such acts. Farewell."

[10] On receiving this letter the Jews[b] did not immediately hurry to make their departure, but they requested of the king that at their own hands those of the Jewish nation who had willfully transgressed against the holy God and the law of God should receive the punishment they deserved. [11] They declared that those who for the belly's sake had transgressed the divine commandments would never be favorably disposed toward the king's government. [12] The king[c]

then, admitting and approving the truth of what they said, granted them a general license so that freely, and without royal authority or supervision, they might destroy those everywhere in his kingdom who had transgressed the law of God. [13] When they had applauded him in fitting manner, their priests and the whole multitude shouted the Hallelujah and joyfully departed. [14] And so on their way they punished and put to a public and shameful death any whom they met of their compatriots who had become defiled. [15] In that day they put to death more than three hundred men; and they kept the day as a joyful festival, since they had destroyed the profaners. [16] But those who had held fast to God even to death and had received the full enjoyment of deliverance began their departure from the city, crowned with all sorts of very fragrant flowers, joyfully and loudly giving thanks to the one God of their ancestors, the eternal Savior[d] of Israel, in words of praise and all kinds of melodious songs.

[17] When they had arrived at Ptolemais, called "rose-bearing" because of a characteristic of the place, the fleet waited for them, in accordance with the common desire, for seven days. [18] There they celebrated their deliverance,[e] for the king had generously provided all things to them for their journey until all of them arrived at their own houses. [19] And when they had all landed in peace with appropriate thanksgiving, there too in

---

a   Other ancient authorities read *way*
b   Gk *they*
c   Gk *He*
d   Other ancient authorities read *the holy Savior*; others, *the holy one*
e   Gk *they made a cup of deliverance*

king seeks to exonerate himself, blaming others (see 6.24). **4**: *Ill-will*, 3.2,7. **5**: *Scythian custom*, see 2 Macc 4.47n.; 4 Macc 10.7n. The Scythians were known for barbarism. **6**: *Threatened them*, that is, the enemies of the Jews. *Father*, 5.7n.; Ps 103.13. **8**: *In any place* through which the Jews might pass on their return.

7.10–23: The Jews punish the renegades and return home. 10: *They requested of the king*, in the Hellenistic and Roman periods the Jews were often obliged to seek permission from their foreign rulers to carry out their own laws pertaining to capital punishment (Deut 13.6–18; Esth 8.8–11). **13**: *Hallelujah*, see Ps 105n.; Tob 13.18. **17**: This *Ptolemais* was probably not the city of this name near Thebes in Upper Egypt, but "Ptolemais at the harbor" in the Arsinoite nome (province), about twelve miles from present-day Cairo. *Rose-bearing* is not elsewhere applied to Ptolemais. **22–23**: The book closes with a benediction to the *supreme God*; cf. 4 Macc 18.24.

like manner they decided to observe these days as a joyous festival during the time of their stay. [20] Then, after inscribing them as holy on a pillar and dedicating a place of prayer at the site of the festival, they departed unharmed, free, and overjoyed, since at the king's command they had all of them been brought safely by land and sea and river to their own homes. [21] They also possessed greater prestige among their enemies, being held in honor and awe; and they were not subject at all to confiscation of their belongings by anyone. [22] Besides, they all recovered all of their property, in accordance with the registration, so that those who held any of it restored it to them with extreme fear.[a] So the supreme God perfectly performed great deeds for their deliverance. [23] Blessed be the Deliverer of Israel through all times! Amen.

[a] Other ancient authorities read *with a very large supplement*

section of the book receives two further mystical visions (the fifth and sixth), both indicating that the true solution to the problem of God's justice is an apocalyptic one: The suffering righteous will receive their reward at the end of the world. Finally, in the climactic seventh vision, the inspired Ezra is granted permission by God to rewrite the scriptures that had been burned by the "Babylonians," but with one variation: In addition to the traditional books of the Hebrew canon, he writes seventy secret books meant for the "wise" among his people. Fourth Ezra's author thus displays his penchant for mystical, esoteric, and apocalyptic modes of thinking, and his conviction that these hold the answers to the ethical and theological dilemmas of Israel, and indeed of all humankind.

Fifth Ezra reflects the growing tension between Christian and Jewish communities. It indicts the people of Israel for their sins and "predicts" the coming of a new people (the Christians) who will inherit the promises originally made to Israel. One is best advised to read the book as a pseudonymous effort by an anonymous Christian author to place a "prophecy" of the coming of Christianity in the mouth of a respected Jewish figure of the fifth century BCE. The "prophecy" is made more convincing by the fact that the author strives to be historically authentic, never referring to "Christianity" explicitly and never mentioning Jesus by name.

In 6 Ezra, an anonymous prophet predicts terrible catastrophes that will afflict the whole earth as a result of human iniquity and warns God's "elect" to abstain from sin if they wish to escape the calamities. The book reflects a situation in which its Christian community was experiencing persecution and strives to convince its audience to stand firm. The author seeks to make sense of the severe persecution threatening the Christian community, and, as in the case of 4 Ezra, 6 Ezra's eschatology is presented as a solution to a situation of extreme social and religious challenge.

INTERPRETATION

Because of its position on the margins of the canon, 2 Esdras has not received a great deal of interpretive attention. Traditional exegetes have generally interpreted 2 Esdras as a genuine prophecy of future events by the biblical figure Ezra. Modern scholars, however, tend to regard it as prophecy formulated after the fact, or as inspired by historical exigencies of the periods in which the book's components were written.

Theodore A. Bergren

COMPRISING WHAT IS SOMETIMES CALLED 5 EZRA (CHAPTERS 1–2), 4 EZRA (CHAPTERS 3–14), AND 6 EZRA (CHAPTERS 15–16)

1 The book[a] of the prophet Ezra son of Seraiah, son of Azariah, son of Hilkiah, son of Shallum, son of Zadok, son of Ahitub, [2] son of Ahijah, son of Phinehas, son of Eli, son of Amariah, son of Azariah, son of Meraimoth, son of Arna, son of Uzzi, son of Borith, son of Abishua, son of Phinehas, son of Eleazar, [3] son of Aaron, of the tribe of Levi, who was a captive in the country of the Medes in the reign of Artaxerxes, king of the Persians.[b]

[4] The word of the Lord came to me, saying, [5] "Go, declare to my people their evil deeds, and to their children the iniquities that they have committed against me, so that they may tell[c] their children's children [6] that the sins of their parents have increased in them, for they have forgotten me and have offered sacrifices to strange gods. [7] Was it not I who brought them out of the land of Egypt, out of the house of bondage? But they have angered me and despised my counsels. [8] Now you,

---

a   Other ancient authorities read *The second book*
b   Other ancient authorities, which place chapters 1 and 2 after 16.78, lack verses 1-3 and begin the chapter: *The word of the Lord that came to Ezra son of Chusi in the days of King Nebuchadnezzar, saying, "Go,*
c   Other ancient authorities read *nourish*

Chapters 1–2 comprise a separate literary composition also known as 5 Ezra (see Introduction).

1.1–3: **Ascription.** Ezra is given a high-priestly genealogy similar to Ezra 7.1–5 and 1 Esd 8.1–2, but with several differences (cf. 1 Sam 14.3). **1:** *Prophet* is unusual; Ezra is usually called "priest" or "scribe" (Ezra 7.6,11; see 2 Esd 12.42n.). **3:** Probably *Artaxerxes I* (465–424 BCE).

1.4–2.9: **A prophetic indictment against Israel. 1.4–23: Prophetic historical recital of God's benefits during the Exodus** (cf. Pss 78; 106; Neh 9). **4:** *The word of the Lord came . . .* , a typical expression in narratives about prophets. **5:** Isa 58.1; Ezek 23.36; Joel 1.3. **6:** *Strange gods,* cf. Deut 32.16. **7:** *Was it not I . . . ?,* the Exodus was God's

pull out the hair of your head and hurl[a] all evils upon them, for they have not obeyed my law—they are a rebellious people. [9] How long shall I endure them, on whom I have bestowed such great benefits? [10] For their sake I have overthrown many kings; I struck down Pharaoh with his servants and all his army. [11] I destroyed all nations before them, and scattered in the east the peoples of two provinces,[b] Tyre and Sidon; I killed all their enemies.

[12] "But speak to them and say, Thus says the Lord: [13] Surely it was I who brought you through the sea, and made safe highways for you where there was no road; I gave you Moses as leader and Aaron as priest; [14] I provided light for you from a pillar of fire, and did great wonders among you. Yet you have forgotten me, says the Lord.

[15] "Thus says the Lord Almighty:[c] The quails were a sign to you; I gave you camps for your protection, and in them you complained. [16] You have not exulted in my name at the destruction of your enemies, but to this day you still complain.[d] [17] Where are the benefits that I bestowed on you? When you were hungry and thirsty in the wilderness, did you not cry out to me, [18] saying, 'Why have you led us into this wilderness to kill us? It would have been better for us to serve the Egyptians than to die in this wilderness.' [19] I pitied your groanings and gave you manna for food; you ate the bread of angels. [20] When you were thirsty, did I not split the rock so that waters flowed in abundance? Because of the heat I clothed you with the leaves of trees.[e] [21] I divided fertile lands among you; I drove out the Canaanites, the Perizzites, and the Philistines[f] before you. What more can I do

for you? says the Lord. [22] Thus says the Lord Almighty:[c] When you were in the wilderness, at the bitter stream, thirsty and blaspheming my name, [23] I did not send fire on you for your blasphemies, but threw a tree into the water and made the stream sweet.

[24] "What shall I do to you, O Jacob? You, Judah, would not obey me. I will turn to other nations and will give them my name, so that they may keep my statutes. [25] Because you have forsaken me, I also will forsake you. When you beg mercy of me, I will show you no mercy. [26] When you call to me, I will not listen to you; for you have defiled your hands with blood, and your feet are swift to commit murder. [27] It is not as though you had forsaken me; you have forsaken yourselves, says the Lord.

[28] "Thus says the Lord Almighty: Have I not entreated you as a father entreats his sons or a mother her daughters or a nurse her children, [29] so that you should be my people and I should be your God, and that you should be my children and I should be your father? [30] I gathered you as a hen gath-

[a] Other ancient authorities read *and shake out*
[b] Other ancient authorities read *Did I not destroy the city of Bethsaida because of you, and to the south burn two cities…?*
[c] Other ancient authorities lack *Almighty*
[d] Other ancient authorities read verse 16, *Your pursuer with his army I sank in the sea, but still the people complain also concerning their own destruction.*
[e] Other ancient authorities read *I made for you trees with leaves*
[f] Other ancient authorities read *Perizzites and their children*

paradigmatic mighty act for Israel. **8:** Ezra is to *pull out* his *hair* as a prophetic sign signaling his disgust with the people (see Ezra 9.3; Neh 13.25; Jer 6.19). *Rebellious people*, see Deut 28.50; Isa 30.9. **9:** *How long shall I endure them…?* Frequent rhetorical questions like this highlight God's exasperation (see Num 14.27). **10:** Ex 14.28; Pss 135.9–11; 136.17. **11:** The scattering of the peoples of *Tyre and Sidon* is not recorded in other Exodus traditions. **13:** Ex 14.21–22,29; Num 33.1; Pss 77.20; 78.13. **14:** Ex 13.21. *You have forgotten me*, God indicts the people. **15:** Ex 16.13; Num 11.1,31–34; Deut 1.27; Ps 105.40; Wis 15.2–3. **17–18:** Num 14.3; Ps 77.11. **19:** *The bread of angels*, manna; Ps 78.24–25; Ex 16.13–16; Num 11.4–9; Wis 16.20. **20:** *Split the rock*, Num 20.11; Wis 11.4. *I clothed you with the leaves*, this is not mentioned in other Exodus traditions; protection from the heat is sometimes attributed to the pillar of cloud (Ex 13.21). **22–23:** Ex 15.22–25; Sir 38.5.

1.24–34: Pronouncement of judgment against Israel. 24: Isa 43.22. *I will turn to other nations*, the pivotal point of 5 Ezra, in which God decisively rejects the former nation (see Mt 21.43). See also Ex 32.10; Num 14.12. **25:** Jer 13.14. **26:** Prov 1.28; Isa 1.15; 59.3,7; Jer 7.16. **29:** Lev 26.12; Jer 7.23 24.7; 2 Cor 6.16–18; Heb 8.10. **30–33:** Compare

ers her chicks under her wings. But now, what shall I do to you? I will cast you out from my presence. [31] When you offer oblations to me, I will turn my face from you; for I have rejected your[a] festal days, and new moons, and circumcisions of the flesh.[b] [32] I sent you my servants the prophets, but you have taken and killed them and torn their bodies[c] in pieces; I will require their blood of you, says the Lord.[d]

[33] "Thus says the Lord Almighty: Your house is desolate; I will drive you out as the wind drives straw; [34] and your sons will have no children, because with you[e] they have neglected my commandment and have done what is evil in my sight. [35] I will give your houses to a people that will come, who without having heard me will believe. Those to whom I have shown no signs will do what I have commanded. [36] They have seen no prophets, yet will recall their former state.[f] [37] I call to witness the gratitude of the people that is to come, whose children rejoice with gladness;[g] though they do not see me with bodily eyes, yet with the spirit they will believe the things I have said.

[38] "And now, father,[h] look with pride and see the people coming from the east; [39] to them I will give as leaders Abraham, Isaac, and Jacob, and Hosea and Amos and Micah and Joel and Obadiah and Jonah [40] and Nahum and Habakkuk, Zephaniah, Haggai, Zechariah and Malachi, who is also called the messenger of the Lord.[i]

2 "Thus says the Lord: I brought this people out of bondage, and I gave them commandments through my servants the prophets; but they would not listen to them, and made my counsels void. [2] The mother who bore them[j] says to them, 'Go, my children, be-

cause I am a widow and forsaken. [3] I brought you up with gladness; but with mourning and sorrow I have lost you, because you have sinned before the Lord God and have done what is evil in my sight.[k] [4] But now what can I do for you? For I am a widow and forsaken. Go, my children, and ask for mercy from the Lord.' [5] Now I call upon you, father, as a witness in addition to the mother of the

a Other ancient authorities read *I have not commanded for you*
b Other ancient authorities lack *of the flesh*
c Other ancient authorities read *the bodies of the apostles*
d Other ancient authorities add *Thus says the Lord Almighty: Recently you also laid hands on me, crying out before the judge's seat for him to deliver me to you. You took me as a sinner, not as a father who freed you from slavery, and you delivered me to death by hanging me on the tree; these are the things you have done. Therefore, says the Lord, let my Father and his angels return and judge between you and me; if I have not kept the commandment of the Father, if I have not nourished you, if I have not done the things my Father commanded, I will contend in judgment with you, says the Lord.*
e Other ancient authorities lack *with you*
f Other ancient authorities read *their iniquities*
g Other ancient authorities read *The apostles bear witness to the coming people with joy*
h Other ancient authorities read *brother*
i Other ancient authorities read *and Jacob, Elijah and Enoch, Zechariah and Hosea, Amos, Joel, Micah, Obadiah, Zephaniah, [40]Nahum, Jonah, Mattia (or Mattathias), Habakkuk, and twelve angels with flowers*
j Other ancient authorities read *They begat for themselves a mother who*
k Other ancient authorities read *in his sight*

Mt 23.30–38. This is the closest New Testament parallel in 5 Ezra, and it suggests Christian authorship. See also Lk 11.49–51; 13.34–35. **31**: Isa 1.11–15. The rejection of circumcision also reveals the Christian identity of the author. **32**: Jer 7.25; 25.4. **33**: Job 21.18; Ps 1.4; Jer 13.24.

1.35–40: Description and vision of the coming people. Emphasis is placed on the untutored goodness of the *people that will come*. **35**: *A people that will come*, that is, the Gentile Christians. *Signs*, cf. Num 14.11. **36–37**: Heb 2.3–4; 1 Pet 1.8–12. *With bodily eyes*, Jn 20.29. **38**: God addresses Ezra as *father*, a term of respect. The people coming *from the east* suggests a return from exile (see Bar 4.36–37; 5.5). **39–40**: The three patriarchs, and the twelve minor prophets arranged in the order of the Septuagint (see Mt 8.11–12; Lk 13.28–29).

2.1–9: Further pronouncement of judgment. The "mother" of the old people is consigned to destruction. **1**: Jer 7.25–26; Ezra 9.10–11; Dan 9.10. **2**: *The mother who bore them*, Jerusalem (Isa 49.21; 54.1). **2–4**: This section, like 1.38, draws on the last chapters of the book of Baruch (Bar 4.8–23). **5**: This time it is God who is invoked as

children, because they would not keep my covenant, ⁶ so that you may bring confusion on them and bring their mother to ruin, so that they may have no offspring. ⁷ Let them be scattered among the nations; let their names be blotted out from the earth, because they have despised my covenant.

⁸ "Woe to you, Assyria, who conceal the unrighteous within you! O wicked nation, remember what I did to Sodom and Gomorrah, ⁹ whose land lies in lumps of pitch and heaps of ashes.ᵃ That is what I will do to those who have not listened to me, says the Lord Almighty."

¹⁰ Thus says the Lord to Ezra: "Tell my people that I will give them the kingdom of Jerusalem, which I was going to give to Israel. ¹¹ Moreover, I will take back to myself their glory, and will give to these others the everlasting habitations, which I had prepared for Israel.ᵇ ¹² The tree of life shall give them fragrant perfume, and they shall neither toil nor become weary. ¹³ Goᶜ and you will receive; pray that your days may be few, that they may be shortened. The kingdom is already prepared for you; be on the watch! ¹⁴ Call, O call heaven and earth to witness: I set aside evil and created good; for I am the Living One, says the Lord.

¹⁵ "Mother, embrace your children; bring them up with gladness, as does a dove; strengthen their feet, because I have chosen you, says the Lord. ¹⁶ And I will raise up the dead from their places, and bring them out from their tombs, because I recognize my name in them. ¹⁷ Do not fear, mother of children, for I have chosen you, says the Lord. ¹⁸ I will send you help, my servants Isaiah and Jeremiah. According to their counsel I have consecrated and prepared for you twelve trees loaded with various fruits, ¹⁹ and the same number of springs flowing with milk and honey, and seven mighty mountains on which roses and lilies grow; by these I will fill your children with joy.

²⁰ "Guard the rights of the widow, secure justice for the ward, give to the needy, defend the orphan, clothe the naked, ²¹ care for the injured and the weak, do not ridicule the lame, protect the maimed, and let the blind have a vision of my splendor. ²² Protect the old and the young within your walls. ²³ When you find any who are dead, commit them to the grave and mark it,ᵈ and I will give you the first place in my resurrection. ²⁴ Pause and be quiet, my people, because your rest will come.

²⁵ "Good nurse, nourish your children; strengthen their feet. ²⁶ Not one of the servantsᵉ whom I have given you will perish, for I will require them from among your number. ²⁷ Do not be anxious, for when the day of tribulation and anguish comes, others

ᵃ Other ancient authorities read *Gomorrah, whose land descends to hell*
ᵇ Lat *for those*
ᶜ Other ancient authorities read *Seek*
ᵈ Or *seal it*; or *mark them and commit them to the grave*
ᵉ Or *slaves*

father, in conjunction with Jerusalem as *mother* (cf. 1.38). **6:** *Bring their mother to ruin*, a reference to the fall of Jerusalem in 70 or 135 CE (cf. Mt 22.1–14). **7:** *Let them be scattered*, as punishment, see Lev 26.33; Deut 4.27; Ps 44.11; Jer 9.16. The endurance of *names* is a form of immortality (see Sir 41:11–13). **8–9:** Woe against Assyria. The exact significance of this reference is uncertain; some scholars view *Assyria* as a reference to Rome. Here Assyria is cursed for concealing the Jews (cf. Zeph 2.13-3.5). *Sodom and Gomorrah*, Gen 19.

2.10–41: Prophetic exhortation of the new people. 10–14: Blessing and instruction; listing of eschatological delights. **10:** *My people*, the newly chosen Christians. See Mt 21.43. **11:** *Everlasting habitations*, dwelling places in the world to come; see Lk 16.9; Jn 14.2–3; 2 Cor 5.1,4; Rev 21.3. **12:** *Tree of life*, Gen 2.9; 3.17–19,22; Rev 2.7; 22.2,14; 1 *Enoch* 24.4–25.7. **13:** Mt 7.7–8; 13.20,33–37; 14.34–38; 24.22; 25.34; Mk 13.37; Jn 16.24. **14:** *Heaven and earth*, Deut 4.26; Isa 1.2. *Living One*, Rev 1.18.

2.15–32: Exhortation of the mother. In distinction to 2.2–6, it is now the church, not Jerusalem, that is addressed as *mother*. **15:** *Dove*, Song 2.13–14. *Chosen*, Isa 44.1–2; 49.7; **16:** Resurrection is promised; see Isa 26.19; Ezek 37.12; Rev 3.12; 14.1; 22.4. **18–19:** 1 *Enoch* 24–25; 31–32; 48; Hermas *Sim.* 9. **18:** *Twelve trees*, Rev 22.2. **19:** *Springs . . . mountains*, 1 *Enoch* 18.6; 24.2–3; 32.1; 48.1. **20–23:** A recital of the traditional "works of mercy" of the church (see Isa 58.6–10; Tob 1.17–19; Mt 25.35–45; Hermas *Mand.* 8.10). **22:** *The old and the young*, Joel 2.16. **23:** Concern for proper burial, cf. Ezek 39.15; Sir 38.16. **24:** *Rest*, an eschatological reward; cf. Dan 12.13; Heb 3.18–19.

shall weep and be sorrowful, but you shall rejoice and have abundance. [28] The nations shall envy you, but they shall not be able to do anything against you, says the Lord. [29] My power will protect[a] you, so that your children may not see hell.[b]

[30] "Rejoice, O mother, with your children, because I will deliver you, says the Lord. [31] Remember your children that sleep, because I will bring them out of the hiding places of the earth, and will show mercy to them; for I am merciful, says the Lord Almighty. [32] Embrace your children until I come, and proclaim mercy to them; because my springs run over, and my grace will not fail."

[33] I, Ezra, received a command from the Lord on Mount Horeb to go to Israel. When I came to them they rejected me and refused the Lord's commandment. [34] Therefore I say to you, O nations that hear and understand, "Wait for your shepherd; he will give you everlasting rest, because he who will come at the end of the age is close at hand. [35] Be ready for the rewards of the kingdom, because perpetual light will shine on you forevermore. [36] Flee from the shadow of this age, receive the joy of your glory; I publicly call on my savior to witness.[c] [37] Receive what the Lord has entrusted to you and be joyful, giving thanks to him who has called you to the celestial kingdoms. [38] Rise, stand erect and see the number of those who have been sealed at the feast of the Lord. [39] Those who have departed from the shadow of this age have received glorious garments from the Lord. [40] Take again your full number, O Zion, and close the list of your people who are clothed in white,

who have fulfilled the law of the Lord. [41] The number of your children, whom you desired, is now complete; implore the Lord's authority that your people, who have been called from the beginning, may be made holy."

[42] I, Ezra, saw on Mount Zion a great multitude that I could not number, and they all were praising the Lord with songs. [43] In their midst was a young man of great stature, taller than any of the others, and on the head of each of them he placed a crown, but he was more exalted than they. And I was held spellbound. [44] Then I asked an angel, "Who are these, my lord?" [45] He answered and said to me, "These are they who have put off mortal clothing and have put on the immortal, and have confessed the name of God. Now they are being crowned, and receive palms." [46] Then I said to the angel, "Who is that young man who is placing crowns on them and putting palms in their hands?" [47] He answered and said to me, "He is the Son of God, whom they confessed in the world." So I began to praise those who had stood valiantly for the name of the Lord.[d] [48] Then the angel said to me, "Go, tell my people how great and how many are the wonders of the Lord God that you have seen."

---

3 In the thirtieth year after the destruction of the city, I was in Babylon—I, Salathiel, who am also called Ezra. I was troubled as I

---

a   Lat *hands will cover*
b   Lat *Gehenna*
c   Other ancient authorities read *I testify that my savior has been commissioned by the Lord*
d   Other ancient authorities read *to praise and glorify the Lord*

25: *Nurse*, the church; cf. 2.15; Num 11.12. **26:** Jn 17.12; 18.9. **27–32:** The author emphasizes eschatology and resurrection. **31:** *Sleep*, i.e., death; Dan 12.2. *Hiding places*, cf. 1 *Enoch* 22. **32:** See 2.15n.

2.33–41: Description of the glorified state to be enjoyed by God's newly chosen people. **33:** *On Mount Horeb*, depicting Ezra as a second Moses; see 14.1–4,30,37–38; Ex 3.1. *Rejected me*, Acts 13.46. **34:** *Nations*, Gentiles; *Shepherd*, Christ; cf. 1 Pet 5.4. **35:** *Light will shine*, cf. Isa 9.2; 60.19–20; Rev 21.23–25; 22.5. **38:** *Sealed*, Rev 7.4. **39:** *Glorious garments*, 1 *Enoch* 62.15–16. See also Bar 5.1–3; Rev 3.4–5. **40:** *Full number*, see 4.36–37; Rev 6.11; *Clothed in white*, Rev 3.4; 6.11; 7.14; 1 *Enoch* 71.1. **41:** 1 *Enoch* 47.4.

2.42–48: Ezra's vision of a great multitude (cf. Rev 7.9–17). **42:** *Mount Zion*, contrasted here with the *Mount Horeb* of 2.33. *Great multitude*, 13.5,12,35; Rev 7.9; 14.1; 2 Bar 40; 1 *Enoch* 39.12–40.1. *Songs*, Rev 14.1–5; 15.2–4. **43:** *Young man*, a messianic figure, here referring to Jesus. See 13.5,35; Rev 14.1; *Gospel of Peter* 40; Hermas *Sim.* 9.6.1. *Crown*, 2 Tim 4.8; 1 Pet 5.4; Rev 2.10; 3.11. *Spellbound*, 13.11; Rev 17.6–7. **44–47:** Rev 7.13–14. **45:** *Put off mortal clothing*, 1 Cor 15.53–54; 2 Cor 5.2–4. *Palms*, Rev 7.9. **47:** *Son of God*, here a Christian designation, can also be Jewish (see 7.28–29; 13.32,37,52). *Confessed in the world*, signifying Christian martyrs.

lay on my bed, and my thoughts welled up in my heart, ² because I saw the desolation of Zion and the wealth of those who lived in Babylon. ³ My spirit was greatly agitated, and I began to speak anxious words to the Most High, and said, ⁴ "O sovereign Lord, did you not speak at the beginning when you plantedᵃ the earth—and that without help—and commanded the dustᵇ ⁵ and it gave you Adam, a lifeless body? Yet he was the creation of your hands, and you breathed into him the breath of life, and he was made alive in your presence. ⁶ And you led him into the garden that your right hand had planted before the earth appeared. ⁷ And you laid upon him one commandment of yours; but he transgressed it, and immediately you appointed death for him and for his descendants. From him there sprang nations and tribes, peoples and clans without number. ⁸ And every nation walked after its own will; they did ungodly things in your sight and rejected your commands, and you did not hinder them. ⁹ But again, in its time you brought the flood upon the inhabitants of the world and destroyed them. ¹⁰ And the same fate befell all of them: just as death came upon Adam, so the flood upon them. ¹¹ But you left one of them, Noah with his household, and all the righteous who have descended from him.

¹² "When those who lived on earth began to multiply, they produced children and peoples and many nations, and again they began to be more ungodly than were their ancestors. ¹³ And when they were committing iniquity in your sight, you chose for yourself one of them, whose name was Abraham; ¹⁴ you loved him, and to him alone you revealed the end of the times, secretly by night. ¹⁵ You made an everlasting covenant with him, and promised him that you would never forsake his descendants; and you gave him Isaac, and to Isaac you gave Jacob and Esau. ¹⁶ You set apart Jacob for yourself, but Esau you rejected; and Jacob became a great multitude. ¹⁷ And when you led his descendants out of Egypt, you brought them to Mount Sinai. ¹⁸ You bent down the heavens and shookᶜ the earth, and moved the world, and caused the depths to tremble, and troubled the times. ¹⁹ Your glory passed through the four gates of fire and earthquake and wind and ice, to give

---

ᵃ Other ancient authorities read *formed*
ᵇ Syr Ethiop: Lat *people* or *world*
ᶜ Syr Ethiop Arab 1 Georg: Lat *set fast*

Chapters 3–14 comprise a separate literary composition also known as 4 Ezra (see Introduction).

3.1–5.20: The first vision. 3.1–3: Introduction. 1: *The thirtieth year after the destruction* of Jerusalem by Nebuchadnezzar in 586 BCE (2 Kings 25.1–21) would be 556. The date specified may imply that the author was writing about 100 CE (i.e., thirty years after the fall of Jerusalem in 70 CE). The historical Ezra lived almost a century after the claimed setting of the book. *Babylon*, the historical Ezra was born in Babylon, then led a group of exiled Jews returning to Jerusalem about 458 BCE; see Ezra 7.7n. *Salathiel* is the Greek form of "Shealtiel" (Ezra 3.2; 5.2; Neh 12.1), appropriately meaning in Hebrew, "I asked God." The identification of Salathiel with Ezra has never been adequately explained. *On my bed*, cf. Dan 7.1. 2: *Zion*, Jerusalem. 3: *My spirit was greatly agitated*, the author immediately signals Ezra's emotional sensitivity.

3.4–36: Addressing God, the author raises perplexing questions. What is the origin of sin with its consequent misery? How can Israel's continuing affliction be reconciled with God's justice? Each of the first four visions opens with a long, reflective prayer of Ezra addressed to God (see 5.23–30; 6.38–59; 9.29–37). Here Ezra presents a historical review of God's interactions with humanity and with Israel. 4–5: The creation of *Adam*, based on Gen 2.7, draws on the concept of creation by divine speech in Gen 1. 6–8: Adam's disobedience (see Gen 2.16–17; 3.1–13) gives rise to sin and death for all humans. 7: The words *immediately you appointed death* imply that Adam was not originally intended to be mortal (see Gen 3.22; cf. Wis 1.13–14; 2.23–24). *Death for him and his descendants*, see also 3.21,26; 4.30; 7.116–118. Similar ideas are expressed by Paul in Rom 5.12–21; 1 Cor 15.21–22. 8: Gen 6.12. 9–11: *The flood* (Gen 6.11–8.22). 12–15: The choice of and covenant with Abraham (Gen 12.1; 17.5). 14: *The end of the times* is not the topic of Gen 15. See, however, *The Apocalypse of Abraham*, roughly contemporary with chs 3–14. *By night*, Gen 15.5,12,17. 15–16: *Jacob and Esau*, Gen 25.19–26. 17–19: The Exodus and the giving of the law. 18: Compare Ex 19.16–18; Ps 68.7–8. 19: *Four gates*, according to certain early Jewish cosmological models, meteorological phenomena passed from heaven to earth through *gates* in the heavenly firmament, here enumerated as *four*. See 1 Enoch 36.1,76; cf. Ps 78.23; 1 Kings 19.11–12. Here God's

the law to the descendants of Jacob, and your commandment to the posterity of Israel.

20 "Yet you did not take away their evil heart from them, so that your law might produce fruit in them. 21 For the first Adam, burdened with an evil heart, transgressed and was overcome, as were also all who were descended from him. 22 Thus the disease became permanent; the law was in the hearts of the people along with the evil root; but what was good departed, and the evil remained. 23 So the times passed and the years were completed, and you raised up for yourself a servant, named David. 24 You commanded him to build a city for your name, and there to offer you oblations from what is yours. 25 This was done for many years; but the inhabitants of the city transgressed, 26 in everything doing just as Adam and all his descendants had done, for they also had the evil heart. 27 So you handed over your city to your enemies.

28 "Then I said in my heart, Are the deeds of those who inhabit Babylon any better? Is that why it has gained dominion over Zion? 29 For when I came here I saw ungodly deeds without number, and my soul has seen many sinners during these thirty years.ᵃ And my heart failed me, 30 because I have seen how you endure those who sin, and have spared those who act wickedly, and have destroyed your people, and protected your enemies, 31 and have not shown to anyone how your way may be comprehended.ᵇ Are the deeds of Babylon better than those of Zion? 32 Or has another nation known you besides Israel? Or what tribes have so believed the covenants as these tribes of Jacob? 33 Yet their reward has not appeared and their labor has borne no fruit. For I have traveled widely among the nations and have seen that they abound in wealth, though they are unmindful of your commandments. 34 Now therefore weigh in a balance our iniquities and those of the inhabitants of the world; and it will be found which way the turn of the scale will incline. 35 When have the inhabitants of the earth not sinned in your sight? Or what nation has kept your commandments so well? 36 You may indeed find individuals who have kept your commandments, but nations you will not find."

4 Then the angel that had been sent to me, whose name was Uriel, answered 2 and said to me, "Your understanding has utterly failed regarding this world, and do you think you can comprehend the way of the Most High?" 3 Then I said, "Yes, my lord." And he replied to me, "I have been sent to show you three ways, and to put before you three problems. 4 If you can solve one of them for me, then I will show you the way you desire to see, and will teach you why the heart is evil."

5 I said, "Speak, my lord."

ᵃ Ethiop Arab 1 Arm: Lat Syr *in this thirtieth year*
ᵇ Syr; compare Ethiop: Lat *how this way should be forsaken*

glory descends through these *gates* to *give the law* on Mount Sinai. **20–27:** The tendency to sin is universal and permanent. **20:** *You did not take away*, here, as in 3.8 (*you did not hinder them*), Ezra implies that God bears some responsibility for human sinfulness. *Evil heart*, possibly, in the Hebrew (now lost), the evil "yetser," an inclination or tendency to sin (Gen 6.5; 2 Esd 4.30–31). The "yetser" can also be an inclination to good (Isa 26.3; 1 Chr 29.18). *Fruit*, see 8.6. **22:** Contrast 9.34–37. *Evil root*, cf. 8.53. **23–27:** *David*, see 1 Sam 16.1–13; 2 Sam 7.1–17; Ps 89.19–29. The *city* is Jerusalem. **27:** *Handed over your city*, the Babylonian conquest of Jerusalem in 586 BCE (2 Kings 25.1–21). **28–36:** Ezra questions whether the deeds of Babylon are any better than those of Israel. **28:** *Babylon*, here, as regularly in the book, stands for Rome (compare Rev 14.8). **30–31:** Here the author expresses the essence of the problem: God permits evildoers to continue in their wickedness, does not spare the suffering people of God, and does not let anyone understand why this should be so. **33–36:** Ezra claims that God's judgment regarding the present world order has been faulty. **34:** *Scale*, see Job 31.6; Dan 5.27; 1 Enoch 4.1; 61.8. **36:** *Individuals* among the Gentiles.

4.1–25: Dialogic dispute between Ezra and the angel Uriel. The message is that God's ways are beyond human understanding. **1–12:** Three riddles illustrate the limitations of human knowledge. **1:** *Angel*, representing the viewpoint of God. The name *Uriel* in Hebrew means "God is my fire" (or "my light"). According to *1 Enoch* 20.2, Uriel is a watcher over both the world and Tartaros, the lowest part of hell (cf. 2 Pet 2.4, textual note *e*). **5:** The angel's method of instructing Ezra regularly employs analogies drawn from nature;

And he said to me, "Go, weigh for me the weight of fire, or measure for me a blast[a] of wind, or call back for me the day that is past."

[6] I answered and said, "Who of those that have been born can do that, that you should ask me about such things?"

[7] And he said to me, "If I had asked you, 'How many dwellings are in the heart of the sea, or how many streams are at the source of the deep, or how many streams are above the firmament, or which are the exits of Hades, or which are the entrances[b] of paradise?' [8] perhaps you would have said to me, 'I never went down into the deep, nor as yet into Hades, neither did I ever ascend into heaven.' [9] But now I have asked you only about fire and wind and the day—things that you have experienced and from which you cannot be separated, and you have given me no answer about them." [10] He said to me, "You cannot understand the things with which you have grown up; [11] how then can your mind comprehend the way of the Most High? And how can one who is already worn out[c] by the corrupt world understand incorruption?"[d] When I heard this, I fell on my face[e] [12] and said to him, "It would have been better for us not to be here than to come here and live in ungodliness, and to suffer and not understand why."

[13] He answered me and said, "I went into a forest of trees of the plain, and they made a plan [14] and said, 'Come, let us go and make war against the sea, so that it may recede before us and so that we may make for ourselves more forests.' [15] In like manner the waves of the sea also made a plan and said, 'Come, let us go up and subdue the forest of the plain so that there also we may gain more territory for ourselves.' [16] But the plan of the forest was in vain, for the fire came and consumed it; [17] likewise also the plan of the waves of the sea was in vain,[f] for the sand stood firm and blocked it. [18] If now you were a judge between them, which would you undertake to justify, and which to condemn?"

[19] I answered and said, "Each made a foolish plan, for the land has been assigned to the forest, and the locale of the sea a place to carry its waves."

[20] He answered me and said, "You have judged rightly, but why have you not judged so in your own case? [21] For as the land has been assigned to the forest and the sea to its waves, so also those who inhabit the earth can understand only what is on the earth, and he who is[g] above the heavens can understand what is above the height of the heavens."

[22] Then I answered and said, "I implore you, my lord, why[h] have I been endowed with the power of understanding? [23] For I did not wish to inquire about the ways above, but about those things that we daily experience: why Israel has been given over to the Gentiles in disgrace; why the people whom you loved has been given over to godless tribes, and the law of our ancestors has been brought to destruction and the written covenants no longer exist. [24] We pass from the world like locusts, and our life is like a mist,[i] and we are not worthy to obtain mercy. [25] But what will he do for his[j] name that is invoked over us? It is about these things that I have asked."

---

[a] Syr Ethiop Arab 1 Arab 2 Georg *a measure*
[b] Syr Compare Ethiop Arab 2 Arm: Lat lacks *of Hades, or which are the entrances*
[c] Meaning of Lat uncertain
[d] Syr Ethiop *the way of the incorruptible?*
[e] Syr Ethiop Arab 1: Meaning of Lat uncertain
[f] Lat lacks *was in vain*
[g] Or *those who are*
[h] Syr Ethiop Arm: Meaning of Lat uncertain
[i] Syr Ethiop Arab Georg: Lat *a trembling*
[j] Ethiop adds *holy*

---

see 4.13–21,28–32,40–42,48–50; 5.36–37,46–55. **7**: *How many dwellings . . . ?* In many apocalypses, these types of questions are in fact issues of proper concern. **8**: See Deut 30.11–13. *Hades*, the underworld. **10–11**: See Job 38–41; Jn 3.12. **12**: For the seer, to live without understanding of life's meaning is intolerable. **13–21**: Parable of the conflict between the forest and the sea. **18–19**: As a skillful teacher, the angel leads Ezra to answer his own question; see also 5.36–40, 46–47; 7.52–58. **21**: Isa 55.8–9. **22–25**: Ezra protests that he is inquiring only about the meaning of earthly, historical happenings, not about cosmic events. **24**: Ps 109.23; Wis 2.4.

4.26–52: Dialogic prediction regarding the future. 26–32: The angel's concern shifts to the end of the present, evil age and the distinction between this age and the next. This section marks the beginning of the

²⁶ He answered me and said, "If you are alive, you will see, and if you live long,[a] you will often marvel, because the age is hurrying swiftly to its end. ²⁷ It will not be able to bring the things that have been promised to the righteous in their appointed times, because this age is full of sadness and infirmities. ²⁸ For the evil about which[b] you ask me has been sown, but the harvest of it has not yet come. ²⁹ If therefore that which has been sown is not reaped, and if the place where the evil has been sown does not pass away, the field where the good has been sown will not come. ³⁰ For a grain of evil seed was sown in Adam's heart from the beginning, and how much ungodliness it has produced until now—and will produce until the time of threshing comes! ³¹ Consider now for yourself how much fruit of ungodliness a grain of evil seed has produced. ³² When heads of grain without number are sown, how great a threshing floor they will fill!"

³³ Then I answered and said, "How long?[b] When will these things be? Why are our years few and evil?" ³⁴ He answered me and said, "Do not be in a greater hurry than the Most High. You, indeed, are in a hurry for yourself,[c] but the Highest is in a hurry on behalf of many. ³⁵ Did not the souls of the righteous in their chambers ask about these matters, saying, 'How long are we to remain here?[d] And when will the harvest of our reward come?' ³⁶ And the archangel Jeremiel answered and said, 'When the number of those like yourselves is completed;[e] for he has weighed the age in the balance, ³⁷ and measured the times by measure, and numbered the times by number; and he will not move or arouse them until that measure is fulfilled.'"

³⁸ Then I answered and said, "But, O sovereign Lord, all of us also are full of ungodliness. ³⁹ It is perhaps on account of us that the time of threshing is delayed for the righteous—on account of the sins of those who inhabit the earth."

⁴⁰ He answered me and said, "Go and ask a pregnant woman whether, when her nine months have been completed, her womb can keep the fetus within her any longer."

⁴¹ And I said, "No, lord, it cannot."

He said to me, "In Hades the chambers of the souls are like the womb. ⁴² For just as a woman who is in labor makes haste to escape the pangs of birth, so also do these places hasten to give back those things that were committed to them from the beginning. ⁴³ Then the things that you desire to see will be disclosed to you."

⁴⁴ I answered and said, "If I have found favor in your sight, and if it is possible, and if I am worthy, ⁴⁵ show me this also: whether more time is to come than has passed, or whether for us the greater part has gone by. ⁴⁶ For I know what has gone by, but I do not know what is to come."

⁴⁷ And he said to me, "Stand at my right side, and I will show you the interpretation of a parable."

⁴⁸ So I stood and looked, and lo, a flaming furnace passed by before me, and when the

a   Syr: Lat *live*
b   Syr Ethiop: Meaning of Lat uncertain
c   Syr Ethiop Arab Arm: Meaning of Lat uncertain
d   Syr Ethiop Arab 2 Georg: Lat *How long do I hope thus?*
e   Syr Ethiop Arab 2: Lat *number of seeds is completed for you*

angel's esoteric eschatological teaching, the main focus of 4 Ezra. **28–32:** *Harvest*, the time of judgment. Cf. Mt 3.12; 13.24–30. **29:** Cf. the fourth vision, 9.26–10.59. **30:** The *grain of evil seed*, or evil "yetser" (see 3.20n.) *sown in Adam's heart*, introduced in 3.7–27, must ripen and be harvested before the coming, righteous age can appear. **33–52:** Ezra's questions concerning the time of the end. **33:** *How long?*, the question is a prophetic and apocalyptic commonplace; see 4.35; 6.59; Isa 6.11; Dan 8.13; 12.6; Zech 1.12; Rev 6.10. Ezra's concerns, like the angel's, also move to the end of the age. **34:** An exhortation to patience in the face of coming judgment. **35–37:** This passage is similar to Rev 6.9–11. **35:** *Souls of the righteous in their chambers*, according to Jewish thought of the time, the souls of the righteous dead are placed in "chambers," or "treasuries," to await the last judgment (see 2.31; 4.41; 7.32,80,95,101; 1 Enoch 22; 2 Apoc. Bar. 21.23). **36:** *Archangel Jeremiel*, see 1 Enoch 20.8, Apoc. Zeph. 6.11–17; 2 Bar. 53–74. In 1 Enoch 20.8 the angel, called Remiel, is "in charge of those who rise." *When the number . . . is completed*, cf. 2.40–41; Rev 6.11. **36–37:** *Weighed . . . measured . . . numbered*, God has determined the times and periods of history (see Sir 36.10). **40–43:** The analogy of *a woman who is in labor* explains the inevitability of the end (cf. 5.46–55; 16.38–39; 1 Thess 5.3). **41:** *Hades*, the underworld. *Chambers*, see v. 35n. **44–50:** The seer

flame had gone by I looked, and lo, the smoke remained. [49] And after this a cloud full of water passed before me and poured down a heavy and violent rain, and when the violent rainstorm had passed, drops still remained in the cloud.[a]

[50] He said to me, "Consider it for yourself; for just as the rain is more than the drops, and the fire is greater than the smoke, so the quantity that passed was far greater; but drops and smoke remained."

[51] Then I prayed and said, "Do you think that I shall live until those days? Or who will be alive in those days?"

[52] He answered me and said, "Concerning the signs about which you ask me, I can tell you in part; but I was not sent to tell you concerning your life, for I do not know.

5 "Now concerning the signs: lo, the days are coming when those who inhabit the earth shall be seized with great terror,[b] and the way of truth shall be hidden, and the land shall be barren of faith. [2] Unrighteousness shall be increased beyond what you yourself see, and beyond what you heard of formerly. [3] And the land that you now see ruling shall be a trackless waste, and people shall see it desolate. [4] But if the Most High grants that you live, you shall see it thrown into confusion after the third period;[c]

and the sun shall suddenly begin to shine
    at night,
    and the moon during the day.
[5] Blood shall drip from wood,
    and the stone shall utter its voice;
the peoples shall be troubled,
    and the stars shall fall.[d]
[6] And one shall reign whom those who inhabit the earth do not expect, and the birds shall fly

away together; [7] and the Dead Sea[e] shall cast up fish; and one whom the many do not know shall make his voice heard by night, and all shall hear his voice.[f] [8] There shall be chaos also in many places, fire shall often break out, the wild animals shall roam beyond their haunts, and menstruous women shall bring forth monsters. [9] Salt waters shall be found in the sweet, and all friends shall conquer one another; then shall reason hide itself, and wisdom shall withdraw into its chamber, [10] and it shall be sought by many but shall not be found, and unrighteousness and unrestraint shall increase on earth. [11] One country shall ask its neighbor, 'Has righteousness, or anyone who does right, passed through you?' And it will answer, 'No.' [12] At that time people shall hope but not obtain; they shall labor, but their ways shall not prosper. [13] These are the signs that I am permitted to tell you, and if you pray again, and weep as you do now, and fast for seven days, you shall hear yet greater things than these."

[14] Then I woke up, and my body shuddered violently, and my soul was so troubled that it fainted. [15] But the angel who had come and talked with me held me and strengthened me and set me on my feet.

---

a   Lat *in it*
b   Syr Ethiop: Meaning of Lat uncertain
c   Literally *after the third*; Ethiop *after three months*; Arm *after the third vision*; Georg *after the third day*
d   Ethiop Compare Syr and Arab: Meaning of Lat uncertain
e   Lat *Sea of Sodom*
f   Cn: Lat *fish; and it shall make its voice heard by night, which the many have not known, but all shall hear its voice.*

---

asks what proportion of time remains; he is told by a parable that the end is near (see 5.50–55; 14.10–12). **48:** *Flaming furnace . . . smoke*, see also Gen 15.17; Zech 12.6.

5.1–13: Direct prediction of the future by the angel, who uses classical apocalyptic "signs" to describe the end of this age (cf. the "synoptic apocalypse" in Mt 24.4–31; Mk 13.5–27; Lk 21.8–28). Each of the first three visions contains similar lists of apocalyptic signs (see 6.11–29; 7.26–44; 8.63–9.13). **2:** Mt 24.12. **3:** Rome will be destroyed. **4–9:** The natural order, mirroring the moral order, will be confused and overturned (cf. Joel 2.10; Mt 24.3–35; Mk 13.3–31; Lk 21.7–28). **4:** The reference to the *third period* is cryptic (cf. 14.10–12). **5:** *The stone shall utter its voice*, Hab 2.11; Lk 19.40. **7:** Cf. Ezek 47.8–10. **8a:** Syriac, "There shall be chasms also in many places" (cf. Zech 14.4). **8:** *Menstruous women*, cf. 6.21; Mt 24.19; Mk 13.17. **9–11:** *Wisdom*, personified as in the wisdom literature, *shall withdraw*, another classic apocalyptic theme (cf. Isa 59.14–15; 2 *Apoc. Bar.* 48.36). **13:** For the author, fasting, prayer, and mourning prepared one to receive a divine revelation; he refers to four such preparatory periods of seven days (5.20; 6.35; 9.23–25; 12.51).

5.14–20: Transition to the second vision. 14: *Then I woke up*, from the dream vision. *My soul . . . fainted*, cf.

¹⁶ Now on the second night Phaltiel, a chief of the people, came to me and said, "Where have you been? And why is your face sad? ¹⁷ Or do you not know that Israel has been entrusted to you in the land of their exile? ¹⁸ Rise therefore and eat some bread, and do not forsake us, like a shepherd who leaves the flock in the power of savage wolves."

¹⁹ Then I said to him, "Go away from me and do not come near me for seven days; then you may come to me."

He heard what I said and left me. ²⁰ So I fasted seven days, mourning and weeping, as the angel Uriel had commanded me.

²¹ After seven days the thoughts of my heart were very grievous to me again. ²² Then my soul recovered the spirit of understanding, and I began once more to speak words in the presence of the Most High. ²³ I said, "O sovereign Lord, from every forest of the earth and from all its trees you have chosen one vine, ²⁴ and from all the lands of the world you have chosen for yourself one region,ᵃ and from all the flowers of the world you have chosen for yourself one lily, ²⁵ and from all the depths of the sea you have filled for yourself one river, and from all the cities that have been built you have consecrated Zion for yourself, ²⁶ and from all the birds that have been created you have named for yourself one dove, and from all the flocks that have been made you have provided for yourself one sheep, ²⁷ and from all the multitude of peoples you have gotten for yourself one people; and to this people, whom you have loved, you have given the law that is approved by all. ²⁸ And now, O Lord, why have you handed the one over to the many, and dishonoredᵇ the one root beyond the others, and scattered your only one among the many? ²⁹ And those who opposed your promises have trampled on those who believed your covenants. ³⁰ If you really hate your people, they should be punished at your own hands."

³¹ When I had spoken these words, the angel who had come to me on a previous night was sent to me. ³² He said to me, "Listen to me, and I will instruct you; pay attention to me, and I will tell you more."

³³ Then I said, "Speak, my lord." And he said to me, "Are you greatly disturbed in mind over Israel? Or do you love him more than his Maker does?"

³⁴ I said, "No, my lord, but because of my grief I have spoken; for every hour I suffer agonies of heart, while I strive to understand the way of the Most High and to search out some part of his judgment."

³⁵ He said to me, "You cannot." And I said, "Why not, my lord? Why then was I born? Or why did not my mother's womb become my grave, so that I would not see the travail of Jacob and the exhaustion of the people of Israel?"

³⁶ He said to me, "Count up for me those who have not yet come, and gather for me the scattered raindrops, and make the withered flowers bloom again for me; ³⁷ open for me the closed chambers, and bring out for me the winds shut up in them, or show me the picture of a voice; and then I will explain to you the travail that you ask to understand."ᶜ

ᵃ Ethiop: Lat *pit*
ᵇ Syr Ethiop Arab: Lat *prepared*
ᶜ Lat *see*

Dan 7.28; 8.27; 10.9–10,17b–19. **16–19:** *Phaltiel, a chief of the people*, named only here, tries unsuccessfully to dissuade Ezra from his solitary visionary quest. See also 12.40–51.

5.21–6.34: The second vision. **5.21–22:** Introduction; cf. 3.1–3.

5.23–30: Addressing God, the seer reiterates his complaints of divine injustice in dealing with Israel. **23–28:** In this series of comparisons, most of the *chosen* elements are biblical figures representing Israel: the *vine* (v. 23), Ps 80.8–15; Jer 2.21; the *lily* (v. 24), Song 2.2 (interpreted allegorically); Hos 14.5; the *river* (v. 25), Isa 8.6; the city of *Zion* (v. 25), Ps 132.13; the *dove* (v. 26), Ps 74.19; the *sheep* (v. 26), Ps 79.13; Isa 53.7; the *root* (v. 28), 1 *Enoch* 93.8. The author has a penchant for compiling similar, long lists of synonymous or analogous elements (see 5.36–37; 6.1–5; 8.52–54; 10.21–23). **27:** The claim that God has *loved* Israel (see Deut 7.8) is contrasted with the idea of *hate* in v. 30. **30:** Ezra wishes that punishment would come directly from God, not human agents; see also 2 Sam 24.14; Sir 2.18.

5.31–40: Dialogic dispute with the angel. The issue of contention is the same as in the first vision. **31:** *The angel who had come to me*, see 4.1n. **33:** The angel answers Ezra's concern for God's *love* for Israel. **35:** Job 3.11;

38 I said, "O sovereign Lord, who is able to know these things except him whose dwelling is not with mortals? 39 As for me, I am without wisdom, and how can I speak concerning the things that you have asked me?"

40 He said to me, "Just as you cannot do one of the things that were mentioned, so you cannot discover my judgment, or the goal of the love that I have promised to my people."

41 I said, "Yet, O Lord, you have charge of those who are alive at the end, but what will those do who lived before me, or we, ourselves, or those who come after us?"

42 He said to me, "I shall liken my judgment to a circle;[a] just as for those who are last there is no slowness, so for those who are first there is no haste."

43 Then I answered and said, "Could you not have created at one time those who have been and those who are and those who will be, so that you might show your judgment the sooner?"

44 He replied to me and said, "The creation cannot move faster than the Creator, nor can the world hold at one time those who have been created in it."

45 I said, "How have you said to your servant that you[b] will certainly give life at one time to your creation? If therefore all creatures will live at one time[c] and the creation will sustain them, it might even now be able to support all of them present at one time."

46 He said to me, "Ask a woman's womb, and say to it, 'If you bear ten[d] children, why one after another?' Request it therefore to produce ten at one time."

47 I said, "Of course it cannot, but only each in its own time."

48 He said to me, "Even so I have given the womb of the earth to those who from time to time are sown in it. 49 For as an infant does not bring forth, and a woman who has become old does not bring forth any longer, so I have made the same rule for the world that I created."

50 Then I inquired and said, "Since you have now given me the opportunity, let me speak before you. Is our mother, of whom you have told me, still young? Or is she now approaching old age?"

51 He replied to me, "Ask a woman who bears children, and she will tell you. 52 Say to her, 'Why are those whom you have borne recently not like those whom you bore before, but smaller in stature?' 53 And she herself will answer you, 'Those born in the strength of youth are different from those born during the time of old age, when the womb is failing.' 54 Therefore you also should consider that you and your contemporaries are smaller in stature than those who were before you, 55 and those who come after you will be smaller than you, as born of a creation that already is aging and passing the strength of youth."

56 I said, "I implore you, O Lord, if I have found favor in your sight, show your servant through whom you will visit your creation."

6 He said to me, "At the beginning of the circle of the earth, before[e] the portals of the world were in place, and before the

---

a Or *crown*

b Syr Ethiop Arab 1: Meaning of Lat uncertain

c Lat lacks *If . . . one time*

d Syr Ethiop Arab 2 Arm: Meaning of Lat uncertain

e Meaning of Lat uncertain: Compare Syr *The beginning by the hand of humankind, but the end by my own hands. For as before the land of the world existed there, and before*; Ethiop: *At first by the Son of Man, and afterwards I myself. For before the earth and the lands were created, and before*

10.18–19; Jer 20.17. **36–40:** As in the first vision (4.5), the angel poses unanswerable riddles from nature. **40:** *My . . . I,* the angel speaks in God's name.

5.41–6.10: Dialogic prediction concerning the future. 5.41–49: Ezra's concern is for fair treatment of all at the judgment. **41:** *You have charge,* Ezra immediately resumes his questioning about the details of the end. The problem of the faithful who die before the end time was also an issue in early Christianity (1 Thess 4.13–15). **45:** *How have you said . . . ?* Ezra points out an apparent contradiction in the logic: *All . . . will live at one time,* namely at the resurrection. **48:** *The womb of the earth,* see Job 1.21. **50–55:** As in the first vision (4.44–46), Ezra asks about the timing of the end. **54:** Ezra's generation being *smaller in stature* shows that the end is near. Various traditions refer to an ancient race of giants (Gen 6.4; Num 13.33; Deut 3.11; 1 Enoch 6–11). **5.56–6.6:** To Ezra's question concerning an eschatological agent, the angel responds that God alone will act. **6.1:** *Portals of the*

assembled winds blew, ² and before the rumblings of thunder sounded, and before the flashes of lightning shone, and before the foundations of paradise were laid, ³ and before the beautiful flowers were seen, and before the powers of movementsᵃ were established, and before the innumerable hosts of angels were gathered together, ⁴ and before the heights of the air were lifted up, and before the measures of the firmaments were named, and before the footstool of Zion was established, ⁵ and before the present years were reckoned and before the imaginations of those who now sin were estranged, and before those who stored up treasures of faith were sealed— ⁶ then I planned these things, and they were made through me alone and not through another; just as the end shall come through me alone and not through another."

⁷ I answered and said, "What will be the dividing of the times? Or when will be the end of the first age and the beginning of the age that follows?"

⁸ He said to me, "From Abraham to Isaac,ᵇ because from him were born Jacob and Esau, for Jacob's hand held Esau's heel from the beginning. ⁹ Now Esau is the end of this age, and Jacob is the beginning of the age that follows. ¹⁰ The beginning of a person is the hand, and the end of a person is the heel;ᶜ seek for nothing else, Ezra, between the heel and the hand, Ezra!"

¹¹ I answered and said, "O sovereign Lord, if I have found favor in your sight, ¹² show your servant the last of your signs of which you showed me a part on a previous night."

¹³ He answered and said to me, "Rise to your feet and you will hear a full, resounding voice. ¹⁴ And if the place where you are

standing is greatly shaken ¹⁵ while the voice is speaking, do not be terrified; because the word concerns the end, and the foundations of the earth will understand ¹⁶ that the speech concerns them. They will tremble and be shaken, for they know that their end must be changed."

¹⁷ When I heard this, I got to my feet and listened; a voice was speaking, and its sound was like the sound of mightyᵈ waters. ¹⁸ It said, "The days are coming when I draw near to visit the inhabitants of the earth, ¹⁹ and when I require from the doers of iniquity the penalty of their iniquity, and when the humiliation of Zion is complete. ²⁰ When the seal is placed upon the age that is about to pass away, then I will show these signs: the books shall be opened before the face of the firmament, and all shall see my judgmentᵉ together. ²¹ Children a year old shall speak with their voices, and pregnant women shall give birth to premature children at three and four months, and these shall live and leap about. ²² Sown places shall suddenly appear unsown, and full storehouses shall suddenly be found to be empty; ²³ the trumpet shall sound aloud, and when all hear it, they shall suddenly be terrified. ²⁴ At that time friends shall make war on friends like enemies, the earth and those who inhabit it shall be terrified, and the springs of the fountains shall stand still, so that for three hours they shall not flow.

²⁵ "It shall be that whoever remains after all that I have foretold to you shall be saved

ᵃ Or *earthquakes*
ᵇ Other ancient authorities read *to Abraham*
ᶜ Syr: Meaning of Lat uncertain
ᵈ Lat *many*
ᵉ Syr: Lat lacks *my judgment*

world, here, as elsewhere, the author shows a fascination with natural phenomena and their origins (vv. 1–5). **4:** *Footstool*, see Pss 99.5; 132.7. **7–10:** The division of the ages. In allegorical language the seer is told that the present corrupt age (symbolized by *Esau*) will be followed immediately, without a break, by the glorious age to come (symbolized by *Jacob*). **8:** *Heel*, see Gen 25.26.

6.11–29: Direct prediction of the future, this time in response to Ezra's query (6.11–12). As in 5.1–13, the author uses classical apocalyptic signs. **14–16:** God's appearance causes the very foundations of the earth to shake; see Joel 3.16. **17:** *A voice . . . like the sound of mighty waters* signifies direct address by God. The image is developed from the vision of Ezekiel (Ezek 1.24–25). Compare Rev 1.15; 14.2; 19.6. **18:** *Visit*, bring judgment. **20:** *The books shall be opened*, the heavenly books in which are written the deeds of humankind (Dan 7.10; 12.1; Mal 3.16; cf. Ex 32.32; Ps 69.28). The motif is also common in Christian writings roughly contemporary with chs 3–14 (Lk 10.20; Heb 12.23; Rev 20.12). **23:** *The trumpet shall sound*, a common eschatological motif (1 Cor 15.52; 1 Thess

and shall see my salvation and the end of my world. 26 And they shall see those who were taken up, who from their birth have not tasted death; and the heart of the earth'sᵃ inhabitants shall be changed and converted to a different spirit. 27 For evil shall be blotted out, and deceit shall be quenched; 28 faithfulness shall flourish, and corruption shall be overcome, and the truth, which has been so long without fruit, shall be revealed."

29 While he spoke to me, little by little the place where I was standing began to rock to and fro.ᵇ 30 And he said to me, "I have come to show you these things this night.ᶜ 31 If therefore you will pray again and fast again for seven days, I will again declare to you greater things than these,ᵈ 32 because your voice has surely been heard by the Most High; for the Mighty One has seen your uprightness and has also observed the purity that you have maintained from your youth. 33 Therefore he sent me to show you all these things, and to say to you: 'Believe and do not be afraid! 34 Do not be quick to think vain thoughts concerning the former times; then you will not act hastily in the last times.'"

35 Now after this I wept again and fasted seven days in the same way as before, in order to complete the three weeks that had been prescribed for me. 36 Then on the eighth night my heart was troubled within me again, and I began to speak in the presence of the Most High. 37 My spirit was greatly aroused, and my soul was in distress.

38 I said, "O Lord, you spoke at the beginning of creation, and said on the first day, 'Let heaven and earth be made,' and your word accomplished the work. 39 Then the spirit was blowing, and darkness and silence embraced everything; the sound of human voices was not yet there.ᵉ 40 Then you commanded a ray of light to be brought out from your storechambers, so that your works could be seen.

41 "Again, on the second day, you created the spirit of the firmament, and commanded it to divide and separate the waters, so that one part might move upward and the other part remain beneath.

42 "On the third day you commanded the waters to be gathered together in a seventh part of the earth; six parts you dried up and kept so that some of them might be planted and cultivated and be of service before you. 43 For your word went forth, and at once the work was done. 44 Immediately fruit came forth in endless abundance and of varied appeal to the taste, and flowers of inimitable color, and odors of inexpressible fragrance. These were made on the third day.

45 "On the fourth day you commanded the brightness of the sun, the light of the moon, and the arrangement of the stars to come into being; 46 and you commanded them to serve humankind, about to be formed.

47 "On the fifth day you commanded the seventh part, where the water had been gathered together, to bring forth living creatures, birds, and fishes; and so it was done. 48 The dumb and lifeless water produced living creatures, as it was commanded, so that therefore the nations might declare your wondrous works.

ᵃ Syr Compare Ethiop Arab 1 Arm: Lat lacks *earth's*
ᵇ Syr Ethiop Compare Arab Arm: Meaning of Lat uncertain
ᶜ Syr Compare Ethiop: Meaning of Lat uncertain
ᵈ Syr Ethiop Arab 1 Arm: Lat adds *by day*
ᵉ Syr Ethiop: Lat *was not yet from you*

4.16). **25:** *See my salvation*, see 7.27; 9.8; 13.48,50; Ps 98.3; Isa 52.10; Lk 2.30. **26:** *Those who were taken up*, such as Enoch (Gen 5.24; Sir 44.16) and Elijah (2 Kings 2.11–12); cf. 8.19; 14.9. **26–28:** The transition from evil to truth.

6.30–34: The conclusion of the vision (compare 5.14–20). **34:** The seer is cautioned against being presumptuous.

6.35–9.25: The third vision. 6.35–7.44: The first section of the third vision. 6.35–37: Introduction (cf. 3.1–3 and 5.21–22). **35:** *I . . . fasted seven days*, see 5.13n. *The three weeks* (cf. Dan 10.2–3), so far only two fasts of seven days have been mentioned (here and at 5.20). The author may be referring to this as Ezra's third vision.

6.38–59: Addressing God, the seer recounts God's work in six days of creation. If the world was created for Israel (v. 55), why has the nation not possessed its inheritance? This is similar in theme and content to the addresses in 3.4–36 and 5.23–30. **38–54:** A summary of creation, roughly following Gen 1. **42:** *A seventh part . . . six parts*, although there is no exact parallel to this division in Genesis or other literature, explorers like Christopher

⁴⁹ "Then you kept in existence two living creatures;ᵃ the one you called Behemothᵇ and the name of the other Leviathan. ⁵⁰ And you separated one from the other, for the seventh part where the water had been gathered together could not hold them both. ⁵¹ And you gave Behemothᵇ one of the parts that had been dried up on the third day, to live in it, where there are a thousand mountains; ⁵² but to Leviathan you gave the seventh part, the watery part; and you have kept them to be eaten by whom you wish, and when you wish.

⁵³ "On the sixth day you commanded the earth to bring forth before you cattle, wild animals, and creeping things; ⁵⁴ and over these you placed Adam, as ruler over all the works that you had made; and from him we have all come, the people whom you have chosen.

⁵⁵ "All this I have spoken before you, O Lord, because you have said that it was for us that you created this world.ᶜ ⁵⁶ As for the other nations that have descended from Adam, you have said that they are nothing, and that they are like spittle, and you have compared their abundance to a drop from a bucket. ⁵⁷ And now, O Lord, these nations, which are reputed to be as nothing, domineer over us and devour us. ⁵⁸ But we your people, whom you have called your firstborn, only begotten, zealous for you,ᵈ and most dear, have been given into their hands. ⁵⁹ If the world has indeed been created for us, why do we not possess our world as an inheritance? How long will this be so?"

7 When I had finished speaking these words, the angel who had been sent to me on the former nights was sent to me again. ² He said to me, "Rise, Ezra, and listen to the words that I have come to speak to you."

³ I said, "Speak, my lord." And he said to me, "There is a sea set in a wide expanse so that it is deep and vast, ⁴ but it has an entrance set in a narrow place, so that it is like a river. ⁵ If there are those who wish to reach the sea, to look at it or to navigate it, how can they come to the broad part unless they pass through the narrow part? ⁶ Another example: There is a city built and set on a plain, and it is full of all good things; ⁷ but the entrance to it is narrow and set in a precipitous place, so that there is fire on the right hand and deep water on the left. ⁸ There is only one path lying between them, that is, between the fire and the water, so that only one person can walk on the path. ⁹ If now the city is given to someone as an inheritance, how will the heir receive the inheritance unless by passing through the appointed danger?"

¹⁰ I said, "That is right, lord." He said to me, "So also is Israel's portion. ¹¹ For I made the world for their sake, and when Adam transgressed my statutes, what had been made was judged. ¹² And so the entrances of this world were made narrow and sorrowful and toilsome; they are few and evil, full of dangers and involved in great hardships. ¹³ But the entrances of the greater world are broad and safe, and yield the fruit of immortality. ¹⁴ Therefore unless the living pass through the difficult and futile experiences, they can never receive those things that have been reserved for them. ¹⁵ Now therefore why are you disturbed, seeing that you are to perish? Why are you moved, seeing that you are mortal? ¹⁶ Why have you not considered in your mind what is to come, rather than what is now present?"

ᵃ Syr Ethiop: Lat *two souls*
ᵇ Other Lat authorities read *Enoch*
ᶜ Syr Ethiop Arab 2: Lat *the firstborn world* Compare Arab 1 *first world*
ᵈ Meaning of Lat uncertain

Columbus took this verse as an indicator of the world's layout. **49–52:** The land creature *Behemoth* and the sea creature *Leviathan* are two primeval monsters frequently found in Israelite mythology (see Job 7.12; 26.12–13; Pss 74.12–15; 89.10–11; Isa 30.7; 51.9–10). Their eschatological function is to serve as food for the elect (2 *Apoc. Bar.* 29.4; 1 *Enoch* 60.7–10). **55:** *For us* (Israel) *that you created this world*, a notion developed from such passages as Ex 4.22; Deut 10.15; 14.2. See 7.11. **56:** *A drop from a bucket*, Isa 40.15 (note especially the Septuagint version).

7.1–25: Dispute between Ezra and the angel. It is necessary first to undergo the trials of this world before one can receive the rewards of the next. **1:** *The former nights*, 4.1; 5.31. **3–9:** The angel tells two parables, of a sea and a city, to illustrate his point. **3:** *Sea*, the world to come. **4:** *Narrow place*, see also Mt 7.13–14; Lk 13.24. **11:** By implication, the *world* was created entirely good for Israel's *sake, and when Adam transgressed*, that inheritance

[17] Then I answered and said, "O sovereign Lord, you have ordained in your law that the righteous shall inherit these things, but that the ungodly shall perish. [18] The righteous, therefore, can endure difficult circumstances while hoping for easier ones; but those who have done wickedly have suffered the difficult circumstances and will never see the easier ones."

[19] He said to me, "You are not a better judge than the Lord,[a] or wiser than the Most High! [20] Let many perish who are now living, rather than that the law of God that is set before them be disregarded! [21] For the Lord[b] strictly commanded those who came into the world, when they came, what they should do to live, and what they should observe to avoid punishment. [22] Nevertheless they were not obedient, and spoke against him;

they devised for themselves vain thoughts,
  [23] and proposed to themselves wicked
      frauds;
they even declared that the Most High
      does not exist,
  and they ignored his ways.
[24] They scorned his law,
  and denied his covenants;
they have been unfaithful to his statutes,
  and have not performed his works.
[25] That is the reason, Ezra, that empty things are for the empty, and full things are for the full.

[26] "For indeed the time will come, when the signs that I have foretold to you will come to pass, that the city that now is not seen shall appear,[c] and the land that now is hidden shall be disclosed. [27] Everyone who has been delivered from the evils that I have foretold shall see my wonders. [28] For my son the Messiah[d] shall be revealed with those who are with him, and those who remain shall rejoice four hundred years. [29] After those years my son the Messiah shall die, and all who draw human breath.[e] [30] Then the world shall be turned back to primeval silence for seven days, as it was at the first beginnings, so that no one shall be left. [31] After seven days the world that is not yet awake shall be roused, and that which is corruptible shall perish. [32] The earth shall give up those who are asleep in it, and the dust those who rest there in silence; and the chambers shall give up the souls that have been committed to them. [33] The Most High shall be revealed on the seat of judgment, and compassion shall pass away, and patience shall be withdrawn.[f] [34] Only judgment shall remain, truth shall stand, and faithfulness shall grow strong. [35] Recompense shall follow, and the reward shall be manifested; righteous deeds shall awake, and unrighteous deeds shall not sleep.[g] [36] The pit[h] of torment shall appear,

---

[a] Other ancient authorities read God; Ethiop Georg the only One

[b] Other ancient authorities read God

[c] Arm: Lat Syr that the bride shall appear, even the city appearing

[d] Syr Arab 1: Ethiop my Messiah; Arab 2 the Messiah; Arm the Messiah of God; Lat my son Jesus

[e] Arm all who have continued in faith and in patience

[f] Lat shall gather together

[g] The passage from verse 36 to verse 105, formerly missing, has been restored to the text

[h] Syr Ethiop: Lat place

---

was despoiled (see 3.7,21). **12–13:** This world . . . evil is contrasted with the greater world to come. **17:** Cf. Deut 8.1; Ps 37.9. **17–18:** The seer exhibits a heartfelt, characteristic concern for the ungodly but is told that their punishment is deserved (vv. 19–25). **21:** Commanded, Deut 30:15–19.

7.26–44: Direct prediction of the future by the angel, again using classical apocalyptic signs (cf. 5.1–13; 6.11–29). In this section the focus is on God's judgment (cf. Mt 25.31–46). **26:** The city, the heavenly Jerusalem; see 10.25–54. **28:** My son the Messiah, a term used often in this book (see 13.32,37,52; 14.9). The precise connection between this term and Christian notions of Jesus "the Messiah" as "son of God" is uncertain, and in any event is indirect. Those who are with him, 13.52; 14.9. **29:** My son the Messiah shall die, this idea is unparalleled in Jewish sources. **30:** Primeval silence, as before creation. See 6.39. **32:** Dan 12.2. Chambers, see 4.35n. Resurrection precedes the day of judgment. **33–34:** On the day of judgment, only judgment shall remain; mercy is put aside (see 7.104–5). **36–105:** These verses are lacking from the standard editions of the Latin Vulgate, and from the King James Version. They are present in the Syriac, Ethiopic, Arabic, and Armenian versions, and in seven Latin manuscripts. The section was probably deliberately cut out of an ancestor of most surviving Latin manuscripts for dogmatic reasons, because the passage contains an emphatic denial of the value of prayers for the dead (v. 105). **36–38:** There exist only two possible destinations for those who are judged: a place of reward and a place

and opposite it shall be the place of rest; and the furnace of hell[a] shall be disclosed, and opposite it the paradise of delight. [37]Then the Most High will say to the nations that have been raised from the dead, 'Look now, and understand whom you have denied, whom you have not served, whose commandments you have despised. [38]Look on this side and on that; here are delight and rest, and there are fire and torments.' Thus he will[b] speak to them on the day of judgment— [39]a day that has no sun or moon or stars, [40]or cloud or thunder or lightning, or wind or water or air, or darkness or evening or morning, [41]or summer or spring or heat or winter[c] or frost or cold, or hail or rain or dew, [42]or noon or night, or dawn or shining or brightness or light, but only the splendor of the glory of the Most High, by which all shall see what has been destined. [43]It will last as though for a week of years. [44]This is my judgment and its prescribed order; and to you alone I have shown these things."

[45] I answered and said, "O sovereign Lord, I said then and[d] I say now: Blessed are those who are alive and keep your commandments! [46]But what of those for whom I prayed? For who among the living is there that has not sinned, or who is there among mortals that has not transgressed your covenant? [47]And now I see that the world to come will bring delight to few, but torments to many. [48]For an evil heart has grown up in us, which has alienated us from God,[e] and has brought us into corruption and the ways of death, and has shown us the paths of perdition and removed us far from life—and that not merely for a few but for almost all who have been created."

[49] He answered me and said, "Listen to me, Ezra,[f] and I will instruct you, and will admonish you once more. [50]For this reason the Most High has made not one world but two. [51]Inasmuch as you have said that the righteous are not many but few, while the ungodly abound, hear the explanation for this.

[52] "If you have just a few precious stones, will you add to them lead and clay?"[g] [53]I said, "Lord, how could that be?" [54]And he said to me, "Not only that, but ask the earth and she will tell you; defer to her, and she will declare it to you. [55]Say to her, 'You produce gold and silver and bronze, and also iron and lead and clay; [56]but silver is more abundant than gold, and bronze than silver, and iron than bronze, and lead than iron, and clay than lead.' [57]Judge therefore which things are precious and desirable, those that are abundant or those that are rare?"

[58] I said, "O sovereign Lord, what is plentiful is of less worth, for what is more rare is more precious."

[59] He answered me and said, "Consider within yourself[h] what you have thought, for the person who has what is hard to get rejoices more than the person who has what is plentiful. [60]So also will be the judgment[i] that I have promised; for I will rejoice over the few who shall be saved, because it is they who have made my glory to prevail now, and through them my name has now been honored. [61]I will not grieve over the great number of those who perish; for it is they who are now like a mist, and are similar to a flame and

---

a   Lat Syr Ethiop *Gehenna*
b   Syr Ethiop Arab 1: Lat *you shall*
c   Or *storm*
d   Syr: Lat *And I answered, "I said then, O Lord, and*
e   Cn: Lat Syr Ethiop *from these*
f   Syr Arab 1 Georg: Lat Ethiop lack *Ezra*
g   Arab 1: Meaning of Lat Syr Ethiop uncertain
h   Syr Ethiop Arab 1: Meaning of Lat uncertain
i   Syr Arab 1: Lat *creation*

---

of punishment. See also 7.79–99. **36:** *Pit*, Isa 38.17–18; Rev 9.2. **39–43:** A description of the day of judgment; cf. Gen 8.22; Zech 14.6–7. **42:** Isa 60.19–20; Rev 21.23. **42:** *The glory of the Most High* is the revelation of God's appearance, see 3.19; 7.60,112,122. **43:** *A week of years*, seven years; cf. Dan 9.24,26.

    7.45–8.3: The second section of the third vision. **45–74:** Dispute between Ezra and the angel. God rejoices over the few who will be saved and does not lament the many wicked who perish. **45–48:** Ezra again bemoans the fate of sinners. **46:** Cf. 1 Kings 8.46; Prov 20.9. **48:** *An evil heart*, see 3.20n. *The ways of death* affect nearly all; see 3.7–11. **52–57:** *Precious*, that is, the righteous, as opposed to common metals and substances; see the

smoke—they are set on fire and burn hotly, and are extinguished."

⁶² I replied and said, "O earth, what have you brought forth, if the mind is made out of the dust like the other created things? ⁶³ For it would have been better if the dust itself had not been born, so that the mind might not have been made from it. ⁶⁴ But now the mind grows with us, and therefore we are tormented, because we perish and we know it. ⁶⁵ Let the human race lament, but let the wild animals of the field be glad; let all who have been born lament, but let the cattle and the flocks rejoice. ⁶⁶ It is much better with them than with us; for they do not look for a judgment, and they do not know of any torment or salvation promised to them after death. ⁶⁷ What does it profit us that we shall be preserved alive but cruelly tormented? ⁶⁸ For all who have been born are entangled inᵃ iniquities, and are full of sins and burdened with transgressions. ⁶⁹ And if after death we were not to come into judgment, perhaps it would have been better for us."

⁷⁰ He answered me and said, "When the Most High made the world and Adam and all who have come from him, he first prepared the judgment and the things that pertain to the judgment. ⁷¹ But now, understand from your own words—for you have said that the mind grows with us. 72 For this reason, therefore, those who live on earth shall be tormented, because though they had understanding, they committed iniquity; and though they received the commandments, they did not keep them; and though they obtained the law, they dealt unfaithfully with what they received. ⁷³ What, then, will they have to say in the judgment, or how will they answer in the last times? ⁷⁴ How long the Most High has been patient with those who

inhabit the world!—and not for their sake, but because of the times that he has foreordained."

⁷⁵ I answered and said, "If I have found favor in your sight, O Lord, show this also to your servant: whether after death, as soon as everyone of us yields up the soul, we shall be kept in rest until those times come when you will renew the creation, or whether we shall be tormented at once?"

⁷⁶ He answered me and said, "I will show you that also, but do not include yourself with those who have shown scorn, or number yourself among those who are tormented. ⁷⁷ For you have a treasure of works stored up with the Most High, but it will not be shown to you until the last times. ⁷⁸ Now concerning death, the teaching is: When the decisive decree has gone out from the Most High that a person shall die, as the spirit leaves the body to return again to him who gave it, first of all it adores the glory of the Most High. ⁷⁹ If it is one of those who have shown scorn and have not kept the way of the Most High, who have despised his law and hated those who fear God— ⁸⁰ such spirits shall not enter into habitations, but shall immediately wander about in torments, always grieving and sad, in seven ways. ⁸¹ The first way, because they have scorned the law of the Most High. ⁸² The second way, because they cannot now make a good repentance so that they may live. ⁸³ The third way, they shall see the reward laid up for those who have trusted the covenants of the Most High. ⁸⁴ The fourth way, they shall consider the torment laid up for themselves in the last days. ⁸⁵ The fifth way, they shall see how the habitations of the others are guarded by angels in profound quiet. ⁸⁶ The sixth way, they shall see how some of them will cross

---

ᵃ Syr *defiled with*

---

similar arguments in 8.1–3. *62–69*: Ezra's heated lament (*better if . . . had not been born*) is typical of his reactions to the angel's arguments (see 4.12; 5.35). *64–68*: The *human race*, aware of their sins and their fate, are worse off than the blissfully ignorant *wild animals*. Knowledge has adverse effects; cf. Gen 3.7. *72*: Humans who are sinful deserve their fate.

   7.75–101: **Dialogic prediction of the future.** The state of souls after death and before the judgment. *76–77*: *Do not include yourself*, the angel repeatedly asserts that Ezra is specially favored by God (see 6.32–33; 7.44; 8.19,47–54; 13.53–56; 14.9). *77*: *A treasure of works*, 8.33,36. Cf. Mt 6.20; Mk 10.21; Lk 12.33. *79–99*: The fates of two different types of souls, good and evil, are laid out in parallel fashion. *80–87*: Seven kinds of torment for the wicked; cf. Lk 16.19–31. *80*: *Habitations*, elsewhere called "chambers," see 4.35n. *85*: *Guarded by angels*, see v.

over[a] into torments. [87] The seventh way, which is worse[b] than all the ways that have been mentioned, because they shall utterly waste away in confusion and be consumed with shame,[c] and shall wither with fear at seeing the glory of the Most High in whose presence they sinned while they were alive, and in whose presence they are to be judged in the last times.

[88] "Now this is the order of those who have kept the ways of the Most High, when they shall be separated from their mortal body.[d] [89] During the time that they lived in it,[c] they laboriously served the Most High, and withstood danger every hour so that they might keep the law of the Lawgiver perfectly. [90] Therefore this is the teaching concerning them: [91] First of all, they shall see with great joy the glory of him who receives them, for they shall have rest in seven orders. [92] The first order, because they have striven with great effort to overcome the evil thought that was formed with them, so that it might not lead them astray from life into death. [93] The second order, because they see the perplexity in which the souls of the ungodly wander and the punishment that awaits them. [94] The third order, they see the witness that he who formed them bears concerning them, that throughout their life they kept the law with which they were entrusted. [95] The fourth order, they understand the rest that they now enjoy, being gathered into their chambers and guarded by angels in profound quiet, and the glory waiting for them in the last days. [96] The fifth order, they rejoice that they have now escaped what is corruptible and shall inherit what is to come; and besides they see the straits and toil[e] from which they have been delivered, and the spacious liberty that they are to receive and enjoy in immortality. [97] The sixth order, when it is shown them how their face is to shine like the sun, and how they are to be made like the light of the stars, being incor-

ruptible from then on. [98] The seventh order, which is greater than all that have been mentioned, because they shall rejoice with boldness, and shall be confident without confusion, and shall be glad without fear, for they press forward to see the face of him whom they served in life and from whom they are to receive their reward when glorified. [99] This is the order of the souls of the righteous, as henceforth is announced;[f] and the previously mentioned are the ways of torment that those who would not give heed shall suffer hereafter."

[100] Then I answered and said, "Will time therefore be given to the souls, after they have been separated from the bodies, to see what you have described to me?"

[101] He said to me, "They shall have freedom for seven days, so that during these seven days they may see the things of which you have been told, and afterwards they shall be gathered in their habitations."

[102] I answered and said, "If I have found favor in your sight, show further to me, your servant, whether on the day of judgment the righteous will be able to intercede for the ungodly or to entreat the Most High for them— [103] fathers for sons or sons for parents, brothers for brothers, relatives for their kindred, or friends for those who are most dear."

[104] He answered me and said, "Since you have found favor in my sight, I will show you this also. The day of judgment is decisive[g] and displays to all the seal of truth. Just as now a father does not send his son, or a son his father, or a master his servant, or a friend his dearest friend, to be ill[a] or sleep or eat or

a   Cn: Meaning of Lat uncertain
b   Lat Syr Ethiop *greater*
c   Syr Ethiop: Meaning of Lat uncertain
d   Lat *the corruptible vessel*
e   Syr Ethiop: Lat *fullness*
f   Syr: Meaning of Lat uncertain
g   Lat *bold*

95; 1 *Enoch* 100.5. **87:** *Glory,* see 6.14–16; 7.42n. **88–99:** Seven kinds of joyous rest for the righteous. Compare the teaching regarding death in Dan 12.2–3; Wis 3–5. **92:** *The evil thought,* the evil "yetser" (see 3.20n.). **95:** *Chambers,* see 4.35n. **97:** *Sun . . . stars,* v. 125; Dan 12.3; Mt 13.43; 2 *Bar.* 51. **98:** *To see the face* of God (Ex 33.20; 1 Jn 3.2; Rev 22.4). *Reward,* cf. Rev 22.12. **99–101:** *The souls of the righteous* are gathered in their *habitations* (see 4.35n.), while the souls of the unjust wander aimlessly.

7.102–115: Dispute between Ezra and the angel, mainly concerning the idea that there will be no interces-

be healed in his place, [105] so no one shall ever pray for another on that day, neither shall anyone lay a burden on another;[b] for then all shall bear their own righteousness and unrighteousness."

36 [106] I answered and said, "How then do we find that first Abraham prayed for the people of Sodom, and Moses for our ancestors who sinned in the desert, 37 [107] and Joshua after him for Israel in the days of Achan, 38 [108] and Samuel in the days of Saul,[c] and David for the plague, and Solomon for those at the dedication, 39 [109] and Elijah for those who received the rain, and for the one who was dead, that he might live, 40 [110] and Hezekiah for the people in the days of Sennacherib, and many others prayed for many? 41 [111] So if now, when corruption has increased and unrighteousness has multiplied, the righteous have prayed for the ungodly, why will it not be so then as well?"

42 [112] He answered me and said, "This present world is not the end; the full glory does not[d] remain in it;[e] therefore those who were strong prayed for the weak. 43 [113] But the day of judgment will be the end of this age and the beginning[f] of the immortal age to come, in which corruption has passed away, 44 [114] sinful indulgence has come to an end, unbelief has been cut off, and righteousness has increased and truth has appeared. 45 [115] Therefore no one will then be able to have mercy on someone who has been condemned in the judgment, or to harm[g] someone who is victorious."

46 [116] I answered and said, "This is my first and last comment: it would have been better if the earth had not produced Adam, or else, when it had produced him, had restrained him from sinning. 47 [117] For what good is it to all that they live in sorrow now and expect punishment after death? 48 [118] O Adam, what have you done? For though it was you who sinned, the fall was not yours alone, but ours also who are your descendants. 49 [119] For what good is it to us, if an immortal time has been promised to us, but we have done deeds that bring death? 50 [120] And what good is it that an everlasting hope has been promised to us, but we have miserably failed? 51 [121] Or that safe and healthful habitations have been reserved for us, but we have lived wickedly? 52 [122] Or that the glory of the Most High will defend those who have led a pure life, but we have walked in the most wicked ways? 53 [123] Or that a paradise shall be revealed, whose fruit remains unspoiled and in which are abundance and healing, but we shall not enter it 54 [124] because we have lived in perverse ways?[h] 55 [125] Or that the faces of those who practiced self-control shall shine more than the stars, but our faces shall be blacker than darkness? 56 [126] For while we lived and committed iniquity we did not consider what we should suffer after death."

57 [127] He answered and said, "This is the significance of the contest that all who are born on earth shall wage: 58 [128] if they are defeated they shall suffer what you have said, but if they are victorious they shall receive what I have said.[i] 59 [129] For this is the way of which Moses, while he was alive, spoke to the peo-

a   Syr Ethiop Arm: Lat *to understand*
b   Syr Ethiop: Lat lacks *on that … another*
c   Syr Ethiop Arab 1: Lat Arab 2 Arm lack *in the days of Saul*
d   Lat lacks *not*
e   Or *the glory does not continuously abide in it*
f   Syr Ethiop: Lat lacks *the beginning*
g   Syr Ethiop: Lat *overwhelm*
h   Cn: Lat Syr *places*
i   Syr Ethiop Arab 1: Lat *what I say*

sion for the evil on the day of judgment (cf. Deut 24.16; Jer 31.30; Ezek 18.1–32). *104:* Decisive, 7.33–34. *106:* At v. 106 we come to the continuation of ch 7 as preserved in the standard editions of the Latin Vulgate (see. vv. *36–105n.*); NRSV resumes the Latin numbering here, designating verses *106–140* as *36–70*, but with the numbers *106–140* in italics added as well. *106: Abraham*, Gen 18.23; *Moses*, Ex 32.11. *107: Joshua*, Josh 7.6–7. *108: Samuel*, 1 Sam 7.9; 12.23. *David*, 2 Sam 24.17. *Solomon*, 1 Kings 8.22–23,30. *109: Elijah*, 1 Kings 18.42,45; 17.20–21. *110: Hezekiah*, 2 Kings 19.15–19. *112–115:* The angel again contrasts the present and future ages. *7.116–8.3:* Further dispute between Ezra and the angel, returning to the issue of the seeming unfairness of the human condition. *7.116–126:* Ezra again laments the fate of humans (cf. 4.12,22–24; 5.35; 7.62–69). *116: My first . . . comment*, 3.5–7. See also Job 3. *118:* 3.7–10; 4.30–31. *123: Fruit*, cf. Ezek 47.12; Rev 22.2. *125: Shine more than the stars*, see 7.97n. *Darkness*, 1 Enoch 62.10. *127–131:* The idea of life as a *contest*, in which one can be *defeated* or *victorious*. *129: Moses*, Deut 30.19. *130: Prophets*, 2 Chr 36.15–16; cf. Mt 5.17; 23.31–37. *132–140:* As the angel had quoted scripture

ple, saying, 'Choose life for yourself, so that you may live!' [60] [130] But they did not believe him or the prophets after him, or even myself who have spoken to them. [61] [131] Therefore there shall not be[a] grief at their destruction, so much as joy over those to whom salvation is assured."

[62] [132] I answered and said, "I know, O Lord, that the Most High is now called merciful, because he has mercy on those who have not yet come into the world; [63] [133] and gracious, because he is gracious to those who turn in repentance to his law; [64] [134] and patient, because he shows patience toward those who have sinned, since they are his own creatures; [65] [135] and bountiful, because he would rather give than take away;[b] [66] [136] and abundant in compassion, because he makes his compassions abound more and more to those now living and to those who are gone and to those yet to come— [67] [137] for if he did not make them abound, the world with those who inhabit it would not have life— [68] [138] and he is called the giver, because if he did not give out of his goodness so that those who have committed iniquities might be relieved of them, not one ten-thousandth of humankind could have life; [69] [139] and the judge, because if he did not pardon those who were created by his word and blot out the multitude of their sins,[c] [70] [140] there would probably be left only very few of the innumerable multitude."

8 He answered me and said, "The Most High made this world for the sake of many, but the world to come for the sake of only a few. [2] But I tell you a parable, Ezra. Just as, when you ask the earth, it will tell you that it provides a large amount of clay from which earthenware is made, but only a little dust from which gold comes, so is the course of the present world. [3] Many have been created, but only a few shall be saved."

[4] I answered and said, "Then drink your fill of understanding,[d] O my soul, and drink wisdom, O my heart. [5] For not of your own will did you come into the world,[e] and against your will you depart, for you have been given only a short time to live. [6] O Lord above us, grant to your servant that we may pray before you, and give us a seed for our heart and cultivation of our understanding so that fruit may be produced, by which every mortal who bears the likeness[f] of a human being may be able to live. [7] For you alone exist, and we are a work of your hands, as you have declared. [8] And because you give life to the body that is now fashioned in the womb, and furnish it with members, what you have created is preserved amid fire and water, and for nine months the womb[g] endures your creature that has been created in it. [9] But that which keeps and that which is kept shall both be kept by your keeping.[e] And when the womb gives up again what has been created in it, [10] you have commanded that from the members themselves (that is, from the breasts) milk, the fruit of the breasts, should be supplied, [11] so that what has been fashioned may be nourished for a time; and afterwards you will still guide it in your mercy. [12] You have nurtured it in your righteousness, and instructed it in your law, and reproved it in your wisdom. [13] You put it to death as your creation, and make it live as your work. [14] If then you will suddenly and quickly[h] destroy what with so great labor was fashioned by your command, to what purpose was it made? [15] And now I will speak

---

a Syr: Lat *there was not*
b Or *he is ready to give according to requests*
c Lat *contempts*
d Syr: Lat *Then release understanding*
e Syr: Meaning of Lat uncertain
f Syr: Lat *place*
g Lat *what you have formed*
h Syr: Lat *will with a light command*

(Deut 30.19), the seer responds with a rabbinic-like exegesis, or "midrash," of Ex 34.6–7. He pleads that God *is now called merciful . . . and gracious . . . and patient. 138: Life,* eternal life. **8.1–3:** The angel repeats the arguments and parable used in 7.52–61. **3:** Cf. Mt 22.14.

8.4–9.25: The third section of the third vision. 8.4–19a: Monologue of Ezra: Why should God wonderfully fashion and sustain all humankind, only to destroy a great majority? **6:** Ezra seeks *a seed . . . so that fruit may be produced* that will counteract the effect of the *evil seed . . . sown in Adam's heart* (4.30). **7:** *You alone* exist, a confession of God's sovereignty, see Deut 4.35; 6.4; Isa 44.6; 45.11; 60.21. **8–14:** The enigma of God's creative activity

out: About all humankind you know best; but I will speak about your people, for whom I am grieved, ¹⁶ and about your inheritance, for whom I lament, and about Israel, for whom I am sad, and about the seed of Jacob, for whom I am troubled. ¹⁷ Therefore I will pray before you for myself and for them, for I see the failings of us who inhabit the earth; ¹⁸ and now alsoª I have heard of the swiftness of the judgment that is to come. ¹⁹ Therefore hear my voice and understand my words, and I will speak before you."

The beginning of the words of Ezra's prayer,ᵇ before he was taken up. He said: ²⁰ "O Lord, you who inhabit eternity,ᶜ whose eyes are exalted ᵈ and whose upper chambers are in the air, ²¹ whose throne is beyond measure and whose glory is beyond comprehension, before whom the hosts of angels stand trembling ²² and at whose command they are changed to wind and fire,ᵉ whose word is sure and whose utterances are certain, whose command is strong and whose ordinance is terrible, ²³ whose look dries up the depths and whose indignation makes the mountains melt away, and whose truth is establishedᶠ forever— ²⁴ hear, O Lord, the prayer of your servant, and give ear to the petition of your creature; attend to my words. ²⁵ For as long as I live I will speak, and as long as I have understanding I will answer. ²⁶ O do not look on the sins of your people, but on those who serve you in truth. ²⁷ Do not take note of the endeavors of those who act wickedly, but of the endeavors of those who have kept your covenants amid afflictions. ²⁸ Do not think of those who have

lived wickedly in your sight, but remember those who have willingly acknowledged that you are to be feared. ²⁹ Do not will the destruction of those who have the ways of cattle, but regard those who have gloriously taught your law.ᵍ ³⁰ Do not be angry with those who are deemed worse than wild animals, but love those who have always put their trust in your glory. ³¹ For we and our ancestors have passed our lives in ways that bring death;ʰ but it is because of us sinners that you are called merciful. ³² For if you have desired to have pity on us, who have no works of righteousness, then you will be called merciful. ³³ For the righteous, who have many works laid up with you, shall receive their reward in consequence of their own deeds. ³⁴ But what are mortals, that you are angry with them; or what is a corruptible race, that you are so bitter against it? ³⁵ For in truth there is no one among those who have been born who has not acted wickedly; among those who have existedⁱ there is no one who has not done wrong. ³⁶ For in this, O Lord, your righteousness and goodness will

a Syr: Lat *but*
b Syr Ethiop; Lat *beginning of Ezra's words*
c Or *you who abide forever*
d Another Lat text reads *whose are the highest heavens*
e Syr: Lat *they whose service takes the form of wind and fire*
f Arab 2: Other authorities read *truth bears witness*
g Syr *have received the brightness of your law*
h Syr Ethiop: Meaning of Lat uncertain
i Syr: Meaning of Lat uncertain

and providential care followed by destruction recalls Job 10.8–13. **15–16:** The seer leaves the fate of *humankind* in God's hands, and speaks particularly about Israel, God's *inheritance* (Ps 28.9). **17:** *I will pray*, in 8.19b–36.

8.19b–36: Ezra's prayer, a beautiful and liturgically structured piece (invocation to God, whose attributes are recalled, vv. 20–23; petitions, interspersed with confession and intercessions, vv. 24–35; concluding ascription of praise, v. 36). This prayer also occurs separately, with the title "Confessio Esdrae," in the section of canticles and hymns contained in many manuscripts of the Latin Vulgate Bible. This circumstance probably accounts for the presence (in v. 19b) of a superscription in the third person. **19b:** The words *before he was taken up* point to the belief that Ezra, like Enoch and Elijah, was taken up to heaven without dying (see 6.26n.). **20:** *Upper chambers*, see Ps 104.3; Amos 9.6. **21:** *Hosts of angels* are a traditional element in the description of the heavenly throne room; see 1 Kings 22.19; Isa 6.2–3; Dan 7.9–10; Rev 5.11–12; 7.11–12. **22:** *Wind and fire*, Ps 104.4; Heb 1.7. **23:** *Dries up*, Isa 50.2; 51.10. *Mountains melt*, Mic 1.4; Sir 16.18–19. **26–36:** A strikingly developed series of rhetorical contrasts between sinners and the righteous introduces an appeal to the mercy of God, the quality highlighted in the influential liturgical formula found in Ex 34.6–7. See also 7.132–140n. **33–36:** Ezra is concerned not for those who have *many works laid up* with God (see 7.77), but for those who have *no store of good works* (v. 36). **34:** Cf. Ps 8.4.

be declared, when you are merciful to those who have no store of good works."

[37] He answered me and said, "Some things you have spoken rightly, and it will turn out according to your words. [38] For indeed I will not concern myself about the fashioning of those who have sinned, or about their death, their judgment, or their destruction; [39] but I will rejoice over the creation of the righteous, over their pilgrimage also, and their salvation, and their receiving their reward. [40] As I have spoken, therefore, so it shall be.

[41] "For just as the farmer sows many seeds in the ground and plants a multitude of seedlings, and yet not all that have been sown will come up[a] in due season, and not all that were planted will take root; so also those who have been sown in the world will not all be saved."

[42] I answered and said, "If I have found favor in your sight, let me speak. [43] If the farmer's seed does not come up, because it has not received your rain in due season, or if it has been ruined by too much rain, it perishes.[b] [44] But people, who have been formed by your hands and are called your own image because they are made like you, and for whose sake you have formed all things—have you also made them like the farmer's seed? [45] Surely not, O Lord[c] above! But spare your people and have mercy on your inheritance, for you have mercy on your own creation."

[46] He answered me and said, "Things that are present are for those who live now, and things that are future are for those who will live hereafter. [47] For you come far short of being able to love my creation more than I love it. But you have often compared yourself[d] to the unrighteous. Never do so! [48] But even in this respect you will be praiseworthy before the Most High, [49] because you have humbled yourself, as is becoming for you, and have not considered yourself to be among the righteous. You will

receive the greatest glory, [50] for many miseries will affect those who inhabit the world in the last times, because they have walked in great pride. [51] But think of your own case, and inquire concerning the glory of those who are like yourself, [52] because it is for you that paradise is opened, the tree of life is planted, the age to come is prepared, plenty is provided, a city is built, rest is appointed,[e] goodness is established and wisdom perfected beforehand. [53] The root of evil[f] is sealed up from you, illness is banished from you, and death[g] is hidden; Hades has fled and corruption has been forgotten;[h] [54] sorrows have passed away, and in the end the treasure of immortality is made manifest. [55] Therefore do not ask any more questions about the great number of those who perish. [56] For when they had opportunity to choose, they despised the Most High, and were contemptuous of his law, and abandoned his ways. [57] Moreover, they have even trampled on his righteous ones, [58] and said in their hearts that there is no God—though they knew well that they must die. [59] For just as the things that I have predicted await[i] you, so the thirst and torment that are prepared await them. For the Most High did not intend that anyone should be destroyed; [60] but those who were created have themselves defiled the name of him who made them, and have been ungrateful to him

---

a   Syr Ethiop *will live*; Lat *will be saved*
b   Cn: Compare Syr Arab 1 Arm Georg 2: Meaning of Lat uncertain
c   Ethiop Arab Compare Syr: Lat lacks *O Lord*
d   Syr Ethiop: Lat *brought yourself near*
e   Syr Ethiop: Lat *allowed*
f   Lat lacks *of evil*
g   Syr Ethiop Arm: Lat lacks *death*
h   Syr: Lat *Hades and corruption have fled into oblivion*; or *corruption has fled into Hades to be forgotten*
i   Syr: Lat *will receive*

8.37–62a: Dispute between Ezra and the angel. 37–40: God's reply to Ezra's prayer is characteristic (see 7.60–61; 7.127–131). As after 7.132–140, Ezra's plea for mercy goes unacknowledged. In stating that God will *not concern* himself with sinners but will *rejoice over . . . the righteous*, the angel playfully admits that Ezra has ironically *spoken rightly* about *some things*, namely, in Ezra's plea (vv. 26–36) that God ignore the wicked and pay attention only to the righteous. **41–45:** To God's analogy of *seeds* (cf. Mt 13.3–9), Ezra protests that surely humans are more valuable than plants. **46–62a:** The final divine reply: The seer is assured that his lot is with the blessed and is advised to think no more about sinners, who deserve their doom because they have *despised the Most High* (v. 56). **46:** 7.14–18,25. **47:** See 5.33; 7.76–77n. **48–54:** The angel praises Ezra's character and offers a list of delights awaiting *those who are like* him (see 14.9). **52:** *Paradise*, 7.123; *tree of life*, Gen 2.9; Rev 2.7; 22.2. *City*, the

who prepared life for them now. [61] Therefore my judgment is now drawing near; [62] I have not shown this to all people, but only to you and a few like you."

Then I answered and said, [63] "O Lord, you have already shown me a great number of the signs that you will do in the last times, but you have not shown me when you will do them."

9 He answered me and said, "Measure carefully in your mind, and when you see that some of the predicted signs have occurred, [2] then you will know that it is the very time when the Most High is about to visit the world that he has made. [3] So when there shall appear in the world earthquakes, tumult of peoples, intrigues of nations, wavering of leaders, confusion of princes, [4] then you will know that it was of these that the Most High spoke from the days that were of old, from the beginning. [5] For just as with everything that has occurred in the world, the beginning is evident,[a] and the end manifest; [6] so also are the times of the Most High: the beginnings are manifest in wonders and mighty works, and the end in penalties[b] and in signs.

[7] "It shall be that all who will be saved and will be able to escape on account of their works, or on account of the faith by which they have believed, [8] will survive the dangers that have been predicted, and will see my salvation in my land and within my borders, which I have sanctified for myself from the beginning. [9] Then those who have now abused my ways shall be amazed, and those who have rejected them with contempt shall live in torments. [10] For as many as did not acknowledge me in their lifetime, though they received my benefits, [11] and as many as scorned my law while they still had freedom, and did not understand but despised it[c] while an opportunity of repentance was

still open to them, [12] these must in torment acknowledge it[c] after death. [13] Therefore, do not continue to be curious about how the ungodly will be punished; but inquire how the righteous will be saved, those to whom the age belongs and for whose sake the age was made."[d]

[14] I answered and said, [15] "I said before, and I say now, and will say it again: there are more who perish than those who will be saved, [16] as a wave is greater than a drop of water."

[17] He answered me and said, "As is the field, so is the seed; and as are the flowers, so are the colors; and as is the work, so is the product; and as is the farmer, so is the threshing floor. [18] For there was a time in this age when I was preparing for those who now exist, before the world was made for them to live in, and no one opposed me then, for no one existed; [19] but now those who have been created in this world, which is supplied both with an unfailing table and an inexhaustible pasture,[e] have become corrupt in their ways. [20] So I considered my world, and saw that it was lost. I saw that my earth was in peril because of the devices of those who[f] had come into it. [21] And I saw and spared some[g] with great difficulty, and saved for myself one grape out of a cluster, and one plant out of a great forest.[h] [22] So let the multitude perish that has been born in vain, but let my grape

---

a   Syr: Ethiop *is in the word*; Meaning of Lat uncertain
b   Syr: Lat Ethiop *in effects*
c   Or *me*
d   Syr: Lat *saved, and whose is the age and for whose sake the age was made and when*
e   Cn: Lat *law*
f   Cn: Lat *devices that*
g   Lat *them*
h   Syr Ethiop Arab 1: Lat *tribe*

---

heavenly Jerusalem; see 7.26; 10.27,44,54. **53:** *Hades*, the realm of the dead. **58:** Cf. Pss 14.1; 53.1. **59:** *Torment*, 7.80–87. **61:** *Drawing near*, see 4.50; 5.55. **62:** *Only to you*, see 7.44. *A few like you*, see 8.51; 14.9,46.

8.62b–9.22: Direct prediction of the future by the angel, now in response to Ezra's request, and again using the key word *signs* (v. 63) (cf. 5.1–13; 6.11–29; 7.26–44). **8.63:** *When*, see 4.33; Mk 13.4. **9.1–4:** The author uses classical apocalyptic signs (see Mk 13.7–8,29). **7:** *Able to escape*, cf. 13.23; Mk 13.14–16. The author counts both *works* and *faith* as valid criteria for salvation. **8:** *See my salvation*, cf. Mk 13.13. *Within my borders*, 12.34; 13.48. **9:** *Torments*, 7.79–87. **11:** *Scorned . . . despised*, 7.22–24,37,72,79–81; 8.56–60. **13:** 8.38–39,55. *For whose sake*, 6.59; 7.11. **14–22:** The final explanation of why so few are saved: The many *have become corrupt in their ways*. Cf. Gen 6.5, where the corruption of humankind provokes the flood, which kills all but Noah and his family. **22:** *Let the multitude perish*, God disclaims responsibility for the fates of the mass of humanity.

and my plant be saved, because with much labor I have perfected them.

²³ "Now, if you will let seven days more pass—do not, however, fast during them, ²⁴ but go into a field of flowers where no house has been built, and eat only of the flowers of the field, and taste no meat and drink no wine, but eat only flowers— ²⁵ and pray to the Most High continually, then I will come and talk with you."

²⁶ So I went, as he directed me, into the field that is called Ardat;ᵃ there I sat among the flowers and ate of the plants of the field, and the nourishment they afforded satisfied me. ²⁷ After seven days, while I lay on the grass, my heart was troubled again as it was before. ²⁸ Then my mouth was opened, and I began to speak before the Most High, and said, ²⁹ "O Lord, you showed yourself among us, to our ancestors in the wilderness when they came out from Egypt and when they came into the untrodden and unfruitful wilderness; ³⁰ and you said, 'Hear me, O Israel, and give heed to my words, O descendants of Jacob. ³¹ For I sow my law in you, and it shall bring forth fruit in you, and you shall be glorified through it forever.' ³² But though our ancestors received the law, they did not keep it and did not observe theᵇ statutes; yet the fruit of the law did not perish—for it could not, because it was yours. ³³ Yet those who received it perished, because they did not keep what had been sown in them. ³⁴ Now this is the general rule that, when the ground has received seed, or the sea a ship, or any dish food or drink, and when it comes about that

what was sown or what was launched or what was put in is destroyed, ³⁵ they are destroyed, but the things that held them remain; yet with us it has not been so. ³⁶ For we who have received the law and sinned will perish, as well as our hearts that received it; ³⁷ the law, however, does not perish but survives in its glory."

³⁸ When I said these things in my heart, I looked around,ᶜ and on my right I saw a woman; she was mourning and weeping with a loud voice, and was deeply grieved at heart; her clothes were torn, and there were ashes on her head. ³⁹ Then I dismissed the thoughts with which I had been engaged, and turned to her ⁴⁰ and said to her, "Why are you weeping, and why are you grieved at heart?"

⁴¹ She said to me, "Let me alone, my lord, so that I may weep for myself and continue to mourn, for I am greatly embittered in spirit and deeply distressed."

⁴² I said to her, "What has happened to you? Tell me."

⁴³ And she said to me, "Your servant was barren and had no child, though I lived with my husband for thirty years. ⁴⁴ Every hour and every day during those thirty years I prayed to the Most High, night and day. ⁴⁵ And after thirty years God heard your servant, and looked upon my low estate, and considered my distress, and gave me a son. I rejoiced greatly over him, I and my husband

---

ᵃ   Syr Ethiop *Arpad*; Arm *Ardab*
ᵇ   Lat *my*
ᶜ   Syr Arab Arm: Lat *I looked about me with my eyes*

9.23–25: **Conclusion and injunctions.** Ezra's prescribed diet of *flowers* recalls Dan 1.8–16 (cf. 2 Macc 5.27). **24:** *Where no house has been built,* see 10.51–54.

9.26–10.59: **The fourth vision.** 9.26–28: **Introduction.** **26:** *Ardat,* an unknown location. **27:** *As it was before,* before each of the first three visions.

9.29–37: **Ezra's address.** Instead of challenging God, as he had done in the first three visions, Ezra praises the *law,* which *survives in its glory* despite the perishing of humankind, its vessel. **29:** An allusion to the theophany at Mount Sinai, Ex 19.9; 24.10; Deut 4.12. **30–37:** Unlike the normal case, where the container outlasts what is placed in it, with humankind it is just the opposite: We perish, while God's law, implanted within us, survives intact. **30:** *Hear me, O Israel,* Deut 6.4. **31:** See 3.20.

9.38–10.4: **The first part of the vision.** Ezra converses with a disconsolate woman. The sudden departure from the pattern of the first three visions, wherein the angel had appeared, signals a shift in tone. **9.38:** *Clothes were torn, ashes,* signs of mourning; Josh 7.6; Job 2.12–13. **39:** *I dismissed the thoughts,* for the first time in the book, Ezra turns his attention from his own concerns to those of another (see also 10.5). **40:** Now it is the woman who is *weeping* and *grieved,* as Ezra had been during the first three visions. **45:** *After thirty years,* see 3.1. Like Sarah (Gen 18.11–14), Hannah (1 Sam 1.20), and Elizabeth (Lk 1.24), the woman conceives a child in her old

and all my neighbors;[a] and we gave great glory to the Mighty One. [46] And I brought him up with much care. [47] So when he grew up and I came to take a wife for him, I set a day for the marriage feast.

10 "But it happened that when my son entered his wedding chamber, he fell down and died. [2] So all of us put out our lamps, and all my neighbors[a] attempted to console me; I remained quiet until the evening of the second day. [3] But when all of them had stopped consoling me, encouraging me to be quiet, I got up in the night and fled, and I came to this field, as you see. [4] And now I intend not to return to the town, but to stay here; I will neither eat nor drink, but will mourn and fast continually until I die."

[5] Then I broke off the reflections with which I was still engaged, and answered her in anger and said, [6] "You most foolish of women, do you not see our mourning, and what has happened to us? [7] For Zion, the mother of us all, is in deep grief and great distress. [8] It is most appropriate to mourn now, because we are all mourning, and to be sorrowful, because we are all sorrowing; you are sorrowing for one son, but we, the whole world, for our mother.[b] [9] Now ask the earth, and she will tell you that it is she who ought to mourn over so many who have come into being upon her. [10] From the beginning all have been born of her, and others will come; and, lo, almost all go[c] to perdition, and a multitude of them will come to doom. [11] Who then ought to mourn the more, she who lost so great a multitude, or you who are griev-

ing for one alone? [12] But if you say to me, 'My lamentation is not like the earth's, for I have lost the fruit of my womb, which I brought forth in pain and bore in sorrow; [13] but it is with the earth according to the way of the earth—the multitude that is now in it goes as it came'; [14] then I say to you, 'Just as you brought forth in sorrow, so the earth also has from the beginning given her fruit, that is, humankind, to him who made her.' [15] Now, therefore, keep your sorrow to yourself, and bear bravely the troubles that have come upon you. [16] For if you acknowledge the decree of God to be just, you will receive your son back in due time, and will be praised among women. [17] Therefore go into the town to your husband."

[18] She said to me, "I will not do so; I will not go into the city, but I will die here."

[19] So I spoke again to her, and said, [20] "Do not do that, but let yourself be persuaded— for how many are the adversities of Zion?— and be consoled because of the sorrow of Jerusalem. [21] For you see how our sanctuary has been laid waste, our altar thrown down, our temple destroyed; [22] our harp has been laid low, our song has been silenced, and our rejoicing has been ended; the light of our lampstand has been put out, the ark of our covenant has been plundered, our holy things have been polluted, and the name by which we are called has been almost profaned; our

---

[a] Literally *all my citizens*
[b] Compare Syr: Meaning of Lat uncertain
[c] Literally *walk*

---

age. **10.1:** Cf. Tob 7.11; 8.10. **4:** *Mourn and fast*, as Ezra had done previously.

10.5–24: The second part of the vision. Ezra tries to convince the woman of the relative insignificance of her own sorrows in relation to the broader concerns of *the whole world* (v. 8), just as the angel had done with Ezra in the earlier visions. **5:** *Broke off the reflections*, as before (*dismissed the thoughts*, 9.39), Ezra is forced to leave aside his prior concerns. **5–6:** *In anger . . . you most foolish*, Ezra's highly emotional disposition, evident in the first three visions, continues here, but is redirected. **7:** *Zion, the mother of us all*, Isa 50.1; Jer 50.12; Bar 4.8–5.9; Gal 4.26. For *Zion in deep grief*, see Lam 1.12–22. **9–10:** Ezra's arguments recall those of the angel in the first three visions. **9:** *Ask the earth*, who is also the mother of all humankind (v. 10). Thus, the figure of the mother functions on three levels: Ezra's interlocutor, Zion (Jerusalem), and the whole earth. **10:** This is the perspective Ezra refused to accept in the third vision. **16:** *If you acknowledge*, as the angel had earlier encouraged Ezra to do. *You will receive your son back in due time*, perhaps in the resurrection; Heb 11.35; 2 Macc 7.23,29. **18:** *I will not*, the woman's stubbornness recalls Ezra's earlier attitude. **21–23:** Ezra sadly recalls the desolation of Jerusalem (cf. Lam 1.10; 2.7; 1 Macc 1.36–40; 2.7–13); ultimately, this refers to the destruction of the city in 70 CE. **22:** *Harp* symbolizes the service of praise. The extinction of the perpetually burning lamp marked the cessation of Temple services. *Our holy things* are enumerated in 1 Macc 4.49–51. *The name* "Israel" was bestowed by God (Gen 32.28).

children[a] have suffered abuse, our priests have been burned to death, our Levites have gone into exile, our virgins have been defiled, and our wives have been ravished; our righteous men[b] have been carried off, our little ones have been cast out, our young men have been enslaved and our strong men made powerless. [23] And, worst of all, the seal of Zion has been deprived of its glory, and given over into the hands of those that hate us. [24] Therefore shake off your great sadness and lay aside your many sorrows, so that the Mighty One may be merciful to you again, and the Most High may give you rest, a respite from your troubles."

[25] While I was talking to her, her face suddenly began to shine exceedingly; her countenance flashed like lightning, so that I was too frightened to approach her, and my heart was terrified. While[c] I was wondering what this meant, [26] she suddenly uttered a loud and fearful cry, so that the earth shook at the sound. [27] When I looked up, the woman was no longer visible to me, but a city was being built,[d] and a place of huge foundations showed itself. I was afraid, and cried with a loud voice and said, [28] "Where is the angel Uriel, who came to me at first? For it was he who brought me into this overpowering bewilderment; my end has become corruption, and my prayer a reproach."

[29] While I was speaking these words, the angel who had come to me at first came to me, and when he saw me [30] lying there like a corpse, deprived of my understanding, he grasped my right hand and strengthened me and set me on my feet, and said to me, [31] "What is the matter with you? And why are you troubled? And why are your understanding and the thoughts of your mind troubled?"

[32] I said, "It was because you abandoned me. I did as you directed, and went out into the field, and lo, what I have seen and can still see, I am unable to explain."

[33] He said to me, "Stand up like a man, and I will instruct you."

[34] I said, "Speak, my lord; only do not forsake me, so that I may not die before my time.[e] [35] For I have seen what I did not know, and I hear[f] what I do not understand [36]—or is my mind deceived, and my soul dreaming? [37] Now therefore I beg you to give your servant an explanation of this bewildering vision."

[38] He answered me and said, "Listen to me, and I will teach you, and tell you about the things that you fear; for the Most High has revealed many secrets to you. [39] He has seen your righteous conduct, and that you have sorrowed continually for your people and mourned greatly over Zion. [40] This therefore is the meaning of the vision. [41] The woman who appeared to you a little while ago, whom you saw mourning and whom you began to console [42] (you do not now see the form of a woman, but there appeared to you a city being built)[g] [43] and who

---

a   Ethiop *free men*
b   Syr *our seers*
c   Syr Ethiop Arab 1: Lat lacks *I was too… terrified. While*
d   Lat: Syr Ethiop Arab 1 Arab 2 Arm *but there was an established city*
e   Syr Ethiop Arab: Lat *die to no purpose*
f   Other ancient authorities read *have heard*
g   Lat: Syr Ethiop Arab 1 Arab 2 Arm *an established city*

23: *The seal … has been deprived of its glory*, i.e., the city is under enemy control. 24: In Ezra's final words to the woman, he has fully become a consoler to her, just as the angel earlier had been to him.

10.25–27a: **A vision of the transformed Jerusalem. 25:** *Suddenly began to shine*, the figure of the woman had only been a foil for the inner transformation of Ezra, who is now worthy to receive the vision. **27:** *A city was being built*, Zech 2.1–5; Rev 21.9–21. Jerusalem, whose destruction was movingly described in vv. 21–23, is being transformed or rebuilt in a way open only to visionary experience.

10.27b–37: **The appearance of the angel. 28:** *At first*, 4.1. Although the angel (Uriel; 4.1) has had no part in this vision, it is he upon whom Ezra immediately calls for guidance. **30:** *Like a corpse*, cf. Dan 8.18; 10.9; Rev 1.17. **32:** *And can still see*, the vision is still before the seer's eyes. The seer is *unable to explain* the vision, much as he had earlier been unable to come to terms with the angel's more rational explanations. **33:** Cf. Job 38.3; 40.7; see 5.15; 6.13,17; 7.2. **34–37:** Cf. 12.3b–9; 13.13b–15. **34:** *Do not forsake me*, Ezra's plea is ironic. See 5.18 and 12.41, where Ezra's compatriots beg him not to "forsake" them.

10.38–54: **Interpretation of the vision. 38–39:** See 7.76–77n. **44:** *Zion*, the transformed Jerusalem. **45:** *Three*

told you about the misfortune of her son—this is the interpretation: [44] The woman whom you saw is Zion, which you now behold as a city being built.[a] [45] And as for her telling you that she was barren for thirty years, the reason is that there were three thousand[b] years in the world before any offering was offered in it.[c] [46] And after three thousand[d] years Solomon built the city, and offered offerings; then it was that the barren woman bore a son. [47] And as for her telling you that she brought him up with much care, that was the period of residence in Jerusalem. [48] And as for her saying to you, 'My son died as he entered his wedding chamber,' and that misfortune had overtaken her,[e] this was the destruction that befell Jerusalem. [49] So you saw her likeness, how she mourned for her son, and you began to console her for what had happened.[f] [50] For now the Most High, seeing that you are sincerely grieved and profoundly distressed for her, has shown you the brilliance of her glory, and the loveliness of her beauty. [51] Therefore I told you to remain in the field where no house had been built, [52] for I knew that the Most High would reveal these things to you. [53] Therefore I told you to go into the field where there was no foundation of any building, [54] because no work of human construction could endure in a place where the city of the Most High was to be revealed.

[55] "Therefore do not be afraid, and do not let your heart be terrified; but go in and see the splendor or[g] the vastness of the building, as far as it is possible for your eyes to see it, [56] and afterward you will hear as much as your ears can hear. [57] For you are more blessed than many, and you have been called to be with[h] the Most High as few have been.

[58] But tomorrow night you shall remain here, [59] and the Most High will show you in those dream visions what the Most High will do to those who inhabit the earth in the last days."

So I slept that night and the following one, as he had told me.

11 On the second night I had a dream: I saw rising from the sea an eagle that had twelve feathered wings and three heads. [2] I saw it spread its wings over[i] the whole earth, and all the winds of heaven blew upon it, and the clouds were gathered around it.[j] [3] I saw that out of its wings there grew opposing wings; but they became little, puny wings. [4] But its heads were at rest; the middle head was larger than the other heads, but it too was at rest with them. [5] Then I saw that the eagle flew with its wings, and it reigned over the earth and over those who inhabit it. [6] And I saw how all things under heaven were subjected to it, and no one spoke against it—not a single creature that was on the earth. [7] Then I saw the eagle rise upon its talons, and it uttered a cry to its wings, saying, [8] "Do not all watch at the same time; let each sleep in its

a Cn: Lat *an established city*
b Most Lat Mss read *three*
c Cn: Lat Syr Arab Arm *her*
d Syr Ethiop Arab Arm: Lat *three*
e Or *him*
f Most Lat Mss and Arab 1 add *These were the things to be opened to you*
g Other ancient authorities read *and*
h Or *been named by*
i Arab 2 Arm: Lat Syr Ethiop *in*
j Syr: Compare Ethiop Arab: Lat lacks *the clouds* and *around it*

thousand years, the time between the creation of the world and construction of the Temple. **46**: *A son*, the historical Jerusalem. *Solomon*, although David established Jerusalem as an Israelite city, Solomon built the Temple (1 Kings 5–6). **48**: *The destruction*, see 10.21–23 and note. In its context, this passage refers to the destruction of Jerusalem in 586 BCE. **49**: Zion, in the universal sense, *mourned for* the destruction of her physical manifestation, the earthly city. **49–50**: Ezra's vision is a direct reward for his sincere consolation of the mourning woman (see 10.41).

10.55–59: Conclusion and injunctions. 55–56: *Go in and see*, the city is conceived as still present to Ezra (see vv. 32,42,44). **59:** The remainder of the book will consist of *dream visions* rather than argumentation.

11.1–12.51: The fifth vision (the eagle vision). **11.1–12.3a: Description of the vision. 11.1:** The interpretation of the fifth vision that is set forth in the notes to 11.1–12.3a anticipates that given in the text of 2 Esdras itself in 12.10–36. *From the sea*, Dan 7.3; Rev 13.1. *An eagle*, symbol of the Roman Empire, used on the standards of Roman legions. **2:** *Spread its wings*, asserted its dominion. *The winds*, 13.2; Dan 7.2. At the time of 4 Ezra's composition, the Romans ruled almost the *whole* inhabited *earth*. **3:** *Opposing wings*, symbolizing usurpers who revolted

own place, and watch in its turn; ⁹ but let the heads be reserved for the last."

¹⁰ I looked again and saw that the voice did not come from its heads, but from the middle of its body. ¹¹ I counted its rival wings, and there were eight of them. ¹² As I watched, one wing on the right side rose up, and it reigned over all the earth. ¹³ And after a time its reign came to an end, and it disappeared, so that even its place was no longer visible. Then the next wing rose up and reigned, and it continued to reign a long time. ¹⁴ While it was reigning its end came also, so that it disappeared like the first. ¹⁵ And a voice sounded, saying to it, ¹⁶ "Listen to me, you who have ruled the earth all this time; I announce this to you before you disappear. ¹⁷ After you no one shall rule as long as you have ruled, not even half as long."

¹⁸ Then the third wing raised itself up, and held the rule as the earlier ones had done, and it also disappeared. ¹⁹ And so it went with all the wings; they wielded power one after another and then were never seen again. ²⁰ I kept looking, and in due time the wings that followedᵃ also rose up on the rightᵇ side, in order to rule. There were some of them that ruled, yet disappeared suddenly; ²¹ and others of them rose up, but did not hold the rule.

²² And after this I looked and saw that the twelve wings and the two little wings had disappeared, ²³ and nothing remained on the eagle's body except the three heads that were at rest and six little wings.

²⁴ As I kept looking I saw that two little wings separated from the six and remained under the head that was on the right side; but four remained in their place. ²⁵ Then I saw that these little wingsᶜ planned to set themselves up and hold the rule. ²⁶ As I kept looking, one was set up, but suddenly disappeared; ²⁷ a second also, and this disappeared more quickly than the first. ²⁸ While I continued to look the two that remained were planning between themselves to reign together; ²⁹ and while they were planning, one of the heads that were at rest (the one that was in the middle) suddenly awoke; it was greater than the other two heads. ³⁰ And I saw how it allied the two heads with itself, ³¹ and how the head turned with those that were with it and devoured the two little wingsᶜ that were planning to reign. ³² Moreover this head gained control of the whole earth, and with much oppression dominated its inhabitants; it had greater power over the world than all the wings that had gone before.

³³ After this I looked again and saw the head in the middle suddenly disappear, just as the wings had done. ³⁴ But the two heads remained, which also in like manner ruled over the earth and its inhabitants. ³⁵ And while I looked, I saw the head on the right side devour the one on the left.

³⁶ Then I heard a voice saying to me, "Look in front of you and consider what you see." ³⁷ When I looked, I saw what seemed to be a lion roused from the forest, roaring; and I heard how it uttered a human voice to the eagle, and spoke, saying, ³⁸ "Listen and I will speak to you. The Most High says to you, ³⁹ 'Are you not the one that remains of the four beasts that I had made to reign in my world, so that the end of my times might come through them? ⁴⁰ You, the fourth that has come, have conquered all the beasts that have gone before; and you have held sway over the world with great terror, and over all the earth with grievous oppression; and for so long you have lived on the earth with deceit.ᵈ ⁴¹ You have judged the earth, but not with truth, ⁴² for you have oppressed the meek and injured the peaceable; you have hated those who tell the truth, and have loved liars; you have destroyed the homes of those who brought forth fruit, and have laid low the walls of those who did you no harm.

ᵃ Syr Arab 2 *the little wings*
ᵇ Some Ethiop Mss read *left*
ᶜ Syr: Lat *underwings*
ᵈ Syr Arab Arm: Lat Ethiop *The fourth came, however, and conquered … and held sway … and for so long lived*

against the Roman emperors. *But they became little*, they were subdued. **11**: *Rival wings*, the "opposing wings" of v. 3. **13**: *Its reign came to an end*, the ruler symbolized by the wing perished. **35**: At this point, only the *head on the right* and the two little wings under it remain. **37**: The *lion* is a symbol of the messiah; cf. Rev 5.5. **39**: *Four beasts*, Dan 7. In Daniel, however, the fourth beast is not an eagle but a horned monster. **40**: *With grievous oppression*, at this time in history, after the Romans had destroyed Jerusalem and its Temple, they were considered evil op-

[43] Your insolence has come up before the Most High, and your pride to the Mighty One. [44] The Most High has looked at his times; now they have ended, and his ages have reached completion. [45] Therefore you, eagle, will surely disappear, you and your terrifying wings, your most evil little wings, your malicious heads, your most evil talons, and your whole worthless body, [46] so that the whole earth, freed from your violence, may be refreshed and relieved, and may hope for the judgment and mercy of him who made it.'"

12 While the lion was saying these words to the eagle, I looked [2] and saw that the remaining head had disappeared. The two wings that had gone over to it rose up and[a] set themselves up to reign, and their reign was brief and full of tumult. [3] When I looked again, they were already vanishing. The whole body of the eagle was burned, and the earth was exceedingly terrified.

Then I woke up in great perplexity of mind and great fear, and I said to my spirit, [4] "You have brought this upon me, because you search out the ways of the Most High. [5] I am still weary in mind and very weak in my spirit, and not even a little strength is left in me, because of the great fear with which I have been terrified tonight. [6] Therefore I will now entreat the Most High that he may strengthen me to the end."

[7] Then I said, "O sovereign Lord, if I have found favor in your sight, and if I have been accounted righteous before you beyond many others, and if my prayer has indeed come up before your face, [8] strengthen me and show me, your servant, the interpretation and meaning of this terrifying vision so that you may fully comfort my soul. [9] For you have judged me worthy to be shown the end of the times and the last events of the times."

[10] He said to me, "This is the interpretation of this vision that you have seen: [11] The eagle that you saw coming up from the sea is the fourth kingdom that appeared in a vision to your brother Daniel. [12] But it was not explained to him as I now explain to you or have explained it. [13] The days are coming when a kingdom shall rise on earth, and it shall be more terrifying than all the kingdoms that have been before it. [14] And twelve kings shall reign in it, one after another. [15] But the second that is to reign shall hold sway for a longer time than any other one of the twelve. [16] This is the interpretation of the twelve wings that you saw.

[17] "As for your hearing a voice that spoke, coming not from the eagle's[b] heads but from the midst of its body, this is the interpretation: [18] In the midst of[c] the time of that kingdom great struggles shall arise, and it shall be in danger of falling; nevertheless it shall not fall then, but shall regain its former power.[d] [19] As for your seeing eight little wings[e] clinging to its wings, this is the interpretation: [20] Eight kings shall arise in it, whose times shall be short and their years swift; [21] two of them shall perish when the middle of its time draws near; and four shall be kept for the time when its end approaches, but two shall be kept until the end.

[22] "As for your seeing three heads at rest, this is the interpretation: [23] In its last days the Most High will raise up three kings,[f] and

---

a   Ethiop: Lat lacks *rose up and*
b   Lat *his*
c   Syr Arm: Lat *After*
d   Ethiop Arab 1 Arm: Lat Syr *its beginning*
e   Syr: Lat *underwings*
f   Syr Ethiop Arab Arm: Lat *kingdoms*

---

pressors by the Jews. **44:** God's judgment of the fourth beast is a sign that the *ages have reached completion* (see 11.39). **12.3a:** This is the beginning of the end times.

12.3b–9: The seer's response. Ezra, terrified, seeks an explanation of the vision (cf. 10.27–37; 13.13b–20).

12.10–36: The interpretation. 11: *The fourth kingdom* in Daniel's vision (Dan 7.7) symbolized the Greek or Macedonian Empire; here, however, it is reinterpreted (cf. v. 12) to refer to the Roman Empire (see 11.1n.; 11.39n.). **13:** *The days are coming*, since the seer is represented as prophesying during the exile, the rise of the Roman Empire is depicted as a future event. **14:** *Kings*, the Roman emperors. **15:** *The second* king is Augustus (ruled 27 BCE–14 CE); cf. 11.17. **18:** There is nothing in the vision that corresponds to what is said in this verse. The author may refer to *the time of . . . great struggles* for power that followed the death of Nero in 68 CE. **19:** *Little wings*, 11.3,11. **20–21:** These apparently represent imperial usurpers or pretenders; they cannot be identified precisely.

they[a] shall renew many things in it, and shall rule the earth [24] and its inhabitants more oppressively than all who were before them. Therefore they are called the heads of the eagle, [25] because it is they who shall sum up his wickedness and perform his last actions. [26] As for your seeing that the large head disappeared, one of the kings[b] shall die in his bed, but in agonies. [27] But as for the two who remained, the sword shall devour them. [28] For the sword of one shall devour him who was with him; but he also shall fall by the sword in the last days.

[29] "As for your seeing two little wings[c] passing over to[d] the head which was on the right side, [30] this is the interpretation: It is these whom the Most High has kept for the eagle's[e] end; this was the reign which was brief and full of tumult, as you have seen.

[31] "And as for the lion whom you saw rousing up out of the forest and roaring and speaking to the eagle and reproving him for his unrighteousness, and as for all his words that you have heard, [32] this is the Messiah[f] whom the Most High has kept until the end of days, who will arise from the offspring of David, and will come and speak[g] with them. He will denounce them for their ungodliness and for their wickedness, and will display before them their contemptuous dealings. [33] For first he will bring them alive before his judgment seat, and when he has reproved them, then he will destroy them. [34] But in mercy he will set free the remnant of my people, those who have been saved throughout my borders, and he will make them joyful until the end comes, the day of judgment, of which I spoke to you at the beginning. [35] This is the dream that you saw, and this is its interpretation. [36] And you alone were worthy to learn this secret of the

Most High. [37] Therefore write all these things that you have seen in a book, put it[h] in a hidden place; [38] and you shall teach them to the wise among your people, whose hearts you know are able to comprehend and keep these secrets. [39] But as for you, wait here seven days more, so that you may be shown whatever it pleases the Most High to show you." Then he left me.

[40] When all the people heard that the seven days were past and I had not returned to the city, they all gathered together, from the least to the greatest, and came to me and spoke to me, saying, [41] "How have we offended you, and what harm have we done you, that you have forsaken us and sit in this place? [42] For of all the prophets you alone are left to us, like a cluster of grapes from the vintage, and like a lamp in a dark place, and like a haven for a ship saved from a storm. [43] Are not the disasters that have befallen us enough? [44] Therefore if you forsake us, how much better it would have been for us if we also had been consumed in the burning of Zion. [45] For we are no better than those who died there." And they wept with a loud voice.

Then I answered them and said, [46] "Take courage, O Israel; and do not be sorrowful, O house of Jacob; [47] for the Most High has you in remembrance, and the Mighty One has not forgotten you in your struggle. [48] As for me, I have neither forsaken you nor withdrawn

---

a   Syr Ethiop Arm: Lat *he*
b   Lat *them*
c   Arab 1: Lat *underwings*
d   Syr Ethiop: Lat lacks *to*
e   Lat *his*
f   Literally *anointed one*
g   Syr: Lat lacks *of days … and speak*
h   Ethiop Arab 1 Arab 2 Arm: Lat Syr *them*

22: *Three heads,* the Flavian emperors (Vespasian, 69–79 CE; Titus, 79–81; and Domitian, 81–96). **23–25:** 11.30–32. **26:** The *large head,* Vespasian. Vespasian did *die in his bed,* perhaps a rarity for Roman emperors, but the attendant *agonies* are otherwise unattested. **30:** *As you have seen,* vv. 2–3. **32:** *Messiah,* 7.28–29n.; *1 Enoch* 62.7. **33–34:** See *2 Bar.* 40. **33:** Here, unlike earlier in the book (6.6; 7.28–44), the Messiah functions as eschatological judge. **34:** *Throughout my borders,* 9.8; 13.48. *He will make them joyful,* 7.28. This verse envisions a second *day of judgment* after that described in v. 33.

12.37–39: Conclusion and injunctions. 37–38: The angel's command to *write* a secret *book* for the *wise* anticipates 14.23–26,37–48 (cf. Isa 8.16; Dan 12.3–4; Rev 1.11; 22.10).

12.40–51: The seer comforts those who were grieved because of his absence (cf. 5.16–19). **40:** *The seven days,* 9.23,27. **42:** Only here and in 1.1 in biblical and apocryphal literature is Ezra called a prophet. *Cluster of grapes,* see 9.21. **44–45:** The people's lament recalls Ezra's earlier words (4.12; 5.35; 7.63). **46–47:** Ezra's reply in

from you; but I have come to this place to pray on account of the desolation of Zion, and to seek mercy on account of the humiliation of our[a] sanctuary. [49] Now go to your homes, every one of you, and after these days I will come to you." [50] So the people went into the city, as I told them to do. [51] But I sat in the field seven days, as the angel[b] had commanded me; and I ate only of the flowers of the field, and my food was of plants during those days.

13 After seven days I dreamed a dream in the night. [2] And lo, a wind arose from the sea and stirred up[c] all its waves. [3] As I kept looking the wind made something like the figure of a man come up out of the heart of the sea. And I saw[d] that this man flew[e] with the clouds of heaven; and wherever he turned his face to look, everything under his gaze trembled, [4] and whenever his voice issued from his mouth, all who heard his voice melted as wax melts[f] when it feels the fire.

[5] After this I looked and saw that an innumerable multitude of people were gathered together from the four winds of heaven to make war against the man who came up out of the sea. [6] And I looked and saw that he carved out for himself a great mountain, and flew up on to it. [7] And I tried to see the region or place from which the mountain was carved, but I could not.

[8] After this I looked and saw that all who had gathered together against him, to wage war with him, were filled with fear, and yet they dared to fight. [9] When he saw the onrush of the approaching multitude, he neither lifted his hand nor held a spear or any weapon of war; [10] but I saw only how he sent forth from his mouth something like a stream of fire, and from his lips a flaming breath, and from his tongue he shot forth a storm of sparks.[g] [11] All these were mingled together, the stream of fire and the

flaming breath and the great storm, and fell on the onrushing multitude that was prepared to fight, and burned up all of them, so that suddenly nothing was seen of the innumerable multitude but only the dust of ashes and the smell of smoke. When I saw it, I was amazed.

[12] After this I saw the same man come down from the mountain and call to himself another multitude that was peaceable. [13] Then many people[h] came to him, some of whom were joyful and some sorrowful; some of them were bound, and some were bringing others as offerings.

Then I woke up in great terror, and prayed to the Most High, and said, [14] "From the beginning you have shown your servant these wonders, and have deemed me worthy to have my prayer heard by you; [15] now show me the interpretation of this dream also. [16] For as I consider it in my mind, alas for those who will be left in those days! And still more, alas for those who are not left! [17] For those who are not left will be sad [18] because they understand the things that are reserved for the last days, but cannot attain them. [19] But alas for those also who are left, and for that very reason! For they shall see great dangers and much distress, as these dreams show. [20] Yet it is better[i] to come into these things,[j] though

---

a   Syr Ethiop: Lat *your*
b   Literally *he*
c   Other ancient authorities read *I saw a wind arise from the sea and stir up*
d   Syr: Lat lacks *the wind ... I saw*
e   Syr Ethiop Arab Arm: Lat *grew strong*
f   Syr: Lat *burned as the earth rests*
g   Meaning of Lat uncertain
h   Lat Syr Arab 2 literally *the faces of many people*
i   Ethiop Compare Arab 2: Lat *easier*
j   Syr: Lat *this*

---

turn recalls the earlier encouragement of the angel. **51:** 9.24–26. Ezra's vegetarian diet is clearly linked to the onset of his dream visions.

13.1–58: The sixth vision (the man from the sea). **1–13a:** Description of the vision. **2:** *A wind ... from the sea,* 11.1–2; Dan 7.2. **3:** *Something like the figure of a man,* a messianic figure (cf. Dan 7.13), later in the vision called God's *Son* (13.32; Ezek 1.26). *Flew with the clouds,* Isa 19.1; Dan 7.13; Mk 13.26; Rev 1.7. **4:** *As wax melts,* Mic 1.4; Jdt 16.15. **5:** *Innumerable multitude,* see 13.33–34n. *Four winds of heaven,* Dan 7.2. **6:** *Carved out,* Dan 2.45. **10:** Cf. Isa 11.4; 2 Thess 2.8. **11:** *Burned up,* 12.3; cf. Rev 20.9. **12:** See 2 *Bar.* 40.2. **13a:** *Some ... were bound,* Jews who came from captivity. *Others as offerings,* cf. Isa 66.20.

13.13b–20a: The seer prays that God will interpret the vision to him. See 7.116–126n.; 10.34–37n. **14:** *My prayer,* 9.25–37. **20:** Contrast 4.12.

incurring peril, than to pass from the world like a cloud, and not to see what will happen in the last days."

He answered me and said, [21] "I will tell you the interpretation of the vision, and I will also explain to you the things that you have mentioned. [22] As for what you said about those who survive, and concerning those who do not survive,[a] this is the interpretation: [23] The one who brings the peril at that time will protect those who fall into peril, who have works and faith toward the Almighty. [24] Understand therefore that those who are left are more blessed than those who have died.

[25] "This is the interpretation of the vision: As for your seeing a man come up from the heart of the sea, [26] this is he whom the Most High has been keeping for many ages, who will himself deliver his creation; and he will direct those who are left. [27] And as for your seeing wind and fire and a storm coming out of his mouth, [28] and as for his not holding a spear or weapon of war, yet destroying the onrushing multitude that came to conquer him, this is the interpretation: [29] The days are coming when the Most High will deliver those who are on the earth. [30] And bewilderment of mind shall come over those who inhabit the earth. [31] They shall plan to make war against one another, city against city, place against place, people against people, and kingdom against kingdom. [32] When these things take place and the signs occur that I showed you before, then my Son will be revealed, whom you saw as a man coming up from the sea.[b]

[33] "Then, when all the nations hear his voice, all the nations shall leave their own lands and the warfare that they have against one another; [34] and an innumerable multitude shall be gathered together, as you saw, wishing to come and conquer him. [35] But he shall stand on the top of Mount Zion. [36] And Zion shall come and be made manifest to all

people, prepared and built, as you saw the mountain carved out without hands. [37] Then he, my Son, will reprove the assembled nations for their ungodliness (this was symbolized by the storm), [38] and will reproach them to their face with their evil thoughts and the torments with which they are to be tortured (which were symbolized by the flames), and will destroy them without effort by means of the law[c] (which was symbolized by the fire).

[39] "And as for your seeing him gather to himself another multitude that was peaceable, [40] these are the nine[d] tribes that were taken away from their own land into exile in the days of King Hoshea, whom Shalmaneser, king of the Assyrians, made captives; he took them across the river, and they were taken into another land. [41] But they formed this plan for themselves, that they would leave the multitude of the nations and go to a more distant region, where no human beings had ever lived, [42] so that there at least they might keep their statutes that they had not kept in their own land. [43] And they went in by the narrow passages of the Euphrates river. [44] For at that time the Most High performed signs for them, and stopped the channels of the river until they had crossed over. [45] Through that region there was a long way to go, a journey of a year and a half; and that country is called Arzareth.[e]

[46] "Then they lived there until the last times; and now, when they are about to come again, [47] the Most High will stop[f] the channels of the river again, so that they may be able to cross over. Therefore you saw the multitude

[a] Syr Arab 1: Lat lacks *and . . . not survive*
[b] Syr and most Lat Mss lack *from the sea*
[c] Syr: Lat *effort and the law*
[d] Other Lat Mss *ten*; Syr Ethiop Arab 1 Arm *nine and a half*
[e] That is *Another Land*
[f] Syr: Lat *stops*

13.20b–55: The interpretation. 21: *Things . . . mentioned*, in vv. 16–20. 23: *The one who brings the peril*, the Messiah; vv. 3–13a. *Works and faith*, see 9.7n. 24: Contrast 5.41–42. 26: *He whom the Most High has been keeping for many ages*, the Messiah, v. 52; 12.32. 31: Cf. Isa 19.2; Mt 24.7. 32: Cf. 6.20; 7.26–28; 9.1–2; Mk 13.29. 33–34: Cf. Rev 16.14–16; 19.19; 20.7–9. 35: Cf. Heb 12.22–24; Rev 14.1; 2 Bar. 40. 36: *Zion shall come and be made manifest*, 7.26; 10.25–54; Rev 21.2,9–14. *Without hands*, Dan 2.34,45. 37–38: *Reprove . . . reproach . . . destroy*, as in 11.37–46; 12.31–33. 40: 2 Kings 17.1–6. *The nine tribes*, the northern kingdom of Israel (usually "ten tribes"; see textual note d). *The river*, the Euphrates. 44: *Stopped . . . the river*, cf. Josh 3.14–16. 45: *Arzareth*, Heb for "Another Land" (cf.

gathered together in peace. [48] But those who are left of your people, who are found within my holy borders, shall be saved.[a] [49] Therefore when he destroys the multitude of the nations that are gathered together, he will defend the people who remain. [50] And then he will show them very many wonders."

[51] I said, "O sovereign Lord, explain this to me: Why did I see the man coming up from the heart of the sea?"

[52] He said to me, "Just as no one can explore or know what is in the depths of the sea, so no one on earth can see my Son or those who are with him, except in the time of his day.[b] [53] This is the interpretation of the dream that you saw. And you alone have been enlightened about this, [54] because you have forsaken your own ways and have applied yourself to mine, and have searched out my law; [55] for you have devoted your life to wisdom, and called understanding your mother. [56] Therefore I have shown you these things; for there is a reward laid up with the Most High. For it will be that after three more days I will tell you other things, and explain weighty and wondrous matters to you."

[57] Then I got up and walked in the field, giving great glory and praise to the Most High for the wonders that he does[c] from time to time, [58] and because he governs the times and whatever things come to pass in their seasons. And I stayed there three days.

14 On the third day, while I was sitting under an oak, suddenly a voice came out of a bush opposite me and said, "Ezra, Ezra!" [2] And I answered, "Here I am, Lord," and I rose to my feet. [3] Then he said to me, "I revealed myself in a bush and spoke to Moses when my people were in bondage in Egypt; [4] and I sent him and led[d] my people out of Egypt; and I led

him up on Mount Sinai, where I kept him with me many days. [5] I told him many wondrous things, and showed him the secrets of the times and declared to him[e] the end of the times. Then I commanded him, saying, [6] 'These words you shall publish openly, and these you shall keep secret.' [7] And now I say to you: [8] Lay up in your heart the signs that I have shown you, the dreams that you have seen, and the interpretations that you have heard; [9] for you shall be taken up from among humankind, and henceforth you shall live with my Son and with those who are like you, until the times are ended. [10] The age has lost its youth, and the times begin to grow old. [11] For the age is divided into twelve parts, and nine[f] of its parts have already passed, [12] as well as half of the tenth part; so two of its parts remain, besides half of the tenth part.[g] [13] Now therefore, set your house in order, and reprove your people; comfort the lowly among them, and instruct those that are wise.[h] And now renounce the life that is corruptible, [14] and put away from you mortal thoughts; cast away from you the burdens of humankind, and divest yourself now of your weak nature; [15] lay to one side the thoughts that are most grievous to you, and hurry to escape from these times. [16] For evils worse than those that you have now seen

---

a   Syr: Lat lacks *shall be saved*
b   Syr: Ethiop *except when his time and his day have come.* Lat lacks *his*
c   Lat *did*
d   Syr Arab 1 Arab 2 *he led*
e   Syr Ethiop Arab Arm: Lat lacks *declared to him*
f   Cn: Lat Ethiop *ten*
g   Syr lacks verses 11, 12: Ethiop *For the world is divided into ten parts, and has come to the tenth, and half of the tenth remains. Now...*
h   Lat lacks *and... wise*

Deut 29.28). **47:** *Will stop ... the river*, cf. Isa 11.15–16. **48:** *Within my ... borders*, presumably the borders of Israel (cf. 9.8; 12.34). This answers the seer's previous questions about the fate of Israel. **52:** *Those who are with him*, perhaps "those who were taken up," 6.26. Cf. 8.51; 14.9. **53–55:** See 7.76–77n.

13.56–58: Conclusion and injunctions. Ezra's giving *great glory and praise* to God shows the change in attitude that he has experienced since his earlier petulance.

14.1–48: The seventh vision (the legend of Ezra and the holy scriptures). **1–18: God speaks to Ezra. 1–2:** A *bush ... "Here I am,"* cf. Ex 3.4. **2:** *I rose*, in contrast to previous occasions, when Ezra was asked to rise (6.13; 7.2; 10.33). **3:** This chapter explicitly draws a parallel between Ezra and *Moses*. **4:** Cf. Ex 34.28. **5–6:** The biblical Moses was never instructed to *keep* some teachings *secret*. Further, see 12.37–38; 14.26,45–47. **5:** *Secrets ... the end of the times*, see 3.14n. **9:** *You shall be taken up*, see 6.26n. *My Son*, the Messiah (7.28–29; 13.32,37,52). *Those who are like you*, 8.51; cf. 13.52. **10:** 4.44–50n.; 5.50–55. **11:** See *2 Bar.* 53–70 for a similar division of world history into

happen shall take place hereafter. [17] For the weaker the world becomes through old age, the more shall evils be increased upon its inhabitants. [18] Truth shall go farther away, and falsehood shall come near. For the eagle[a] that you saw in the vision is already hurrying to come."

[19] Then I answered and said, "Let me speak[b] in your presence, Lord. [20] For I will go, as you have commanded me, and I will reprove the people who are now living; but who will warn those who will be born hereafter? For the world lies in darkness, and its inhabitants are without light. [21] For your law has been burned, and so no one knows the things which have been done or will be done by you. [22] If then I have found favor with you, send the holy spirit into me, and I will write everything that has happened in the world from the beginning, the things that were written in your law, so that people may be able to find the path, and that those who want to live in the last days may do so."

[23] He answered me and said, "Go and gather the people, and tell them not to seek you for forty days. [24] But prepare for yourself many writing tablets, and take with you Sarea, Dabria, Selemia, Ethanus, and Asiel—these five, who are trained to write rapidly; [25] and you shall come here, and I will light in your heart the lamp of understanding, which shall not be put out until what you are about to write is finished. [26] And when you have finished, some things you shall make public, and some you shall deliver in secret to the wise; tomorrow at this hour you shall begin to write."

[27] Then I went as he commanded me, and I gathered all the people together, and said, [28] "Hear these words, O Israel. [29] At first our ancestors lived as aliens in Egypt,

and they were liberated from there [30] and received the law of life, which they did not keep, which you also have transgressed after them. [31] Then land was given to you for a possession in the land of Zion; but you and your ancestors committed iniquity and did not keep the ways that the Most High commanded you. [32] And since he is a righteous judge, in due time he took from you what he had given. [33] And now you are here, and your people[c] are farther in the interior.[d] [34] If you, then, will rule over your minds and discipline your hearts, you shall be kept alive, and after death you shall obtain mercy. [35] For after death the judgment will come, when we shall live again; and then the names of the righteous shall become manifest, and the deeds of the ungodly shall be disclosed. [36] But let no one come to me now, and let no one seek me for forty days."

[37] So I took the five men, as he commanded me, and we proceeded to the field, and remained there. [38] And on the next day a voice called me, saying, "Ezra, open your mouth and drink what I give you to drink." [39] So I opened my mouth, and a full cup was offered to me; it was full of something like water, but its color was like fire. [40] I took it and drank; and when I had drunk it, my heart poured forth understanding, and wisdom increased in my breast, for my spirit retained its memory, [41] and my mouth was opened and was no longer closed. [42] Moreover, the Most High gave understanding to the five men, and

---

a   Syr Ethiop Arab Arm: Meaning of Lat uncertain
b   Most Lat Mss lack *Let me speak*
c   Lat *brothers*
d   Syr Ethiop Arm: Lat *are among you*

---

twelve parts. **16–18:** Mk 13.7–8. **18:** 5.9–11. *The eagle*, chs 11–12.

14.19–26: Ezra's prayer for inspiration to restore the holy scriptures is granted. **20:** *Who will warn?*, Ezra's characteristic concern for his fellow Jews finally bears fruit in his desire to rewrite the scriptures. *Without light*, without the light of God's law (cf. Ps 19.8b). **21:** According to one tradition, the *law* had *been burned* by the Babylonians when they destroyed Jerusalem in 586 BCE (4.23). **22:** *The holy spirit* will guide Ezra in rewriting the law. **23:** *Forty days*, cf. Ex 24.18; 34.28; Deut 9.9,18. **26:** *Some things . . . make public*, namely, the rewritten books of the Jewish scriptures. *Some . . . deliver in secret*, namely, some extracanonical books (see 12.37–38; 14.5–6,45–47).

14.27–36: Ezra reproves the people (14.13,20), reminding them of the reasons for their state of exile. **28:** See 9.30; Deut 6.4. **33:** *Farther*, apparently referring to the ten northern tribes (13.39–45).

14.37–48: The revelation of scriptures. **37:** *The five men*, v. 24. *The field*, the same one in which Ezra has received the fourth through the seventh visions (see 9.24). **39:** *A full cup* of inspiration, containing the fire of the spirit (v. 22). **42:** *Using characters that they did not know*, in a new script for Hebrew, the Aramaic square

by turns they wrote what was dictated, using characters that they did not know.[a] They sat forty days; they wrote during the daytime, and ate their bread at night. [43] But as for me, I spoke in the daytime and was not silent at night. [44] So during the forty days, ninety-four[b] books were written. [45] And when the forty days were ended, the Most High spoke to me, saying, "Make public the twenty-four[c] books that you wrote first, and let the worthy and the unworthy read them; [46] but keep the seventy that were written last, in order to give them to the wise among your people. [47] For in them is the spring of understanding, the fountain of wisdom, and the river of knowledge." [48] And I did so.[d]

15[e] Speak in the ears of my people the words of the prophecy that I will put in your mouth, says the Lord, [2] and cause them to be written on paper; for they are trustworthy and true. [3] Do not fear the plots against you, and do not be troubled by the unbelief of those who oppose you. [4] For all unbelievers shall die in their unbelief.[f]

[5] Beware, says the Lord, I am bringing evils upon the world, the sword and famine, death and destruction, [6] because iniquity has spread throughout every land, and their harmful doings have reached their limit. [7] Therefore, says the Lord, [8] I will be silent no longer concerning their ungodly acts that they impiously commit, neither will I tolerate their wicked practices. Innocent and righteous blood cries out to me, and the souls of the righteous cry out continually. [9] I will surely avenge them,

says the Lord, and will receive to myself all the innocent blood from among them. [10] See, my people are being led like a flock to the slaughter; I will not allow them to live any longer in the land of Egypt, [11] but I will bring them out with a mighty hand and with an uplifted arm, and will strike Egypt with plagues, as before, and will destroy all its land.

[12] Let Egypt mourn, and its foundations, because of the plague of chastisement and castigation that the Lord will bring upon it. [13] Let the farmers that till the ground mourn, because their seed shall fail to grow[g] and their trees shall be ruined by blight and hail and by a terrible tempest. [14] Alas for the world and for those who live in it! [15] For the sword and misery draw near them, and nation shall rise up to fight against nation, with swords in their

---

[a] Syr Compare Ethiop Arab 2 Arm: Meaning of Lat uncertain

[b] Syr Ethiop Arab 1 Arm: Meaning of Lat uncertain

[c] Syr Arab 1: Lat lacks *twenty-four*

[d] Syr adds *in the seventh year of the sixth week, five thousand years and three months and twelve days after creation. At that time Ezra was caught up, and taken to the place of those who are like him, after he had written all these things. And he was called the scribe of the knowledge of the Most High for ever and ever.* Ethiop Arab 1 Arm have a similar ending

[e] Chapters 15 and 16 (except 15.57-59, which has been found in Greek) are extant only in Lat

[f] Other ancient authorities add *and all who believe shall be saved by their faith*

[g] Lat lacks *to grow*

---

characters. **45:** *Twenty-four books* is one traditional reckoning of the Hebrew canon: the five books of the Law (Gen, Ex, Lev, Num, Deut), eight books of the Prophets (the former prophets: Josh; Judg; 1 and 2 Sam [as one book]; 1 and 2 Kings [as one book]; the latter prophets: Isa; Jer; Ezek; and the Twelve [as one book]), and eleven books of the Writings (Ps; Prov; Job; Song; Ruth; Lam; Eccl; Esth; Dan; Ezra-Neh [as one book]; 1 and 2 Chr [as one book]). **46:** *The seventy* are esoteric, apocryphal books (see 12.37–38; 14.26). **48:** The original version of 4 Ezra probably ended with an account of Ezra's being taken up into heaven and functioning as a heavenly scribe (see textual note *d*; cf. 8.19bn.; 14.9). This ending was apparently dropped from the Latin version to make way for the prophecies of chs 15–16 when they were added at a later time.

Chapters 15–16 comprise a separate literary composition also known as 6 Ezra (see Introduction).

15.1–4: The commissioning of the prophet, who in this context is not named. See Jer 1.7–9; 26.2; Hab 2.2. **2:** Cf. Rev 21.5,22b. **3:** Cf. Jer 18.20–23.

15.5–16.34: Prediction of worldwide catastrophes. 15.5–27: God will destroy the world because of human sinfulness. 8: *Innocent and righteous blood cries out,* cf. Gen 4.10; Rev 6.9–10. **9:** Cf. Deut 32.43. **10–11:** *Egypt* and the *plagues* are probably symbols for the author's own situation of crisis. Cf. Ps 44.22; Isa 53.7. See also Deut 4.34; 26.8; Jer 51.40. **13:** Joel 1.11. **14:** The destruction will be universal. **15–17:** Cf. 2 Chr 15.5–6. **15:** *Nation . . .*

hands. [16] For there shall be unrest among people; growing strong against one another, they shall in their might have no respect for their king or the chief of their leaders. [17] For a person will desire to go into a city, and shall not be able to do so. [18] Because of their pride the cities shall be in confusion, the houses shall be destroyed, and people shall be afraid. [19] People shall have no pity for their neighbors, but shall make an assault upon[a] their houses with the sword, and plunder their goods, because of hunger for bread and because of great tribulation.

[20] See how I am calling together all the kings of the earth to turn to me, says God, from the rising sun and from the south, from the east and from Lebanon; to turn and repay what they have given them. [21] Just as they have done to my elect until this day, so I will do, and will repay into their bosom. Thus says the Lord God: [22] My right hand will not spare the sinners, and my sword will not cease from those who shed innocent blood on earth. [23] And a fire went forth from his wrath, and consumed the foundations of the earth and the sinners, like burnt straw. [24] Alas for those who sin and do not observe my commandments, says the Lord;[b] [25] I will not spare them. Depart, you faithless children! Do not pollute my sanctuary. [26] For God[c] knows all who sin against him; therefore he will hand them over to death and slaughter. [27] Already calamities have come upon the whole earth, and you shall remain in them; God[c] will not deliver you, because you have sinned against him.

[28] What a terrifying sight, appearing from the east! [29] The nations of the dragons of Arabia shall come out with many chariots, and from the day that they set out, their hissing shall spread over the earth, so that all who hear them will fear and tremble. [30] Also the Carmonians, raging in wrath, shall go forth like wild boars[d] from the forest, and

with great power they shall come and engage them in battle, and with their tusks they shall devastate a portion of the land of the Assyrians with their teeth. [31] And then the dragons,[e] remembering their origin, shall become still stronger; and if they combine in great power and turn to pursue them, [32] then these shall be disorganized and silenced by their power, and shall turn and flee.[f] [33] And from the land of the Assyrians an enemy in ambush shall attack them and destroy one of them, and fear and trembling shall come upon their army, and indecision upon their kings.

[34] See the clouds from the east, and from the north to the south! Their appearance is exceedingly threatening, full of wrath and storm. [35] They shall clash against one another and shall pour out a heavy tempest on the earth, and their own tempest;[g] and there shall be blood from the sword as high as a horse's belly [36] and a man's thigh and a camel's hock. [37] And there shall be fear and great trembling on the earth; those who see that wrath shall be horror-stricken, and they shall be seized with trembling. [38] After that, heavy storm clouds shall be stirred up from the south, and from the north, and another part from the west. [39] But the winds from the east shall prevail over the cloud that was[h] raised in wrath, and shall dispel it; and the tempest[g] that was to cause destruction by the east wind shall be driven violently toward the south and west. [40] Great and mighty

---

a   Cn: Lat *shall empty*
b   Other ancient authorities read *God*
c   Other ancient authorities read *the Lord*
d   Other ancient authorities lack *like wild boars*
e   Cn: Lat *dragon*
f   Other ancient authorities read *turn their face to the north*
g   Meaning of Lat uncertain
h   Literally *that he*

---

against nation, cf. Mk 13.8. **18:** Cf. Lk 21.26. *Confusion* and social unrest is the result of pride; cf. Gen 11.7–8. **20:** Ps 72.11. **21:** Isa 65.6. **22–27:** Woes against *sinners.* **23:** Cf. Jer 4.4.

15.28–33: A vision of warfare in the east. This section may reflect conflicts between Odenathus of Palmyra (*dragons of Arabia*) and Shapur I of Persia (*Carmonians*) that took place on the eastern borders of the Roman Empire between 261 and 267 CE. **30:** *The Carmonians,* from Carmania (Kerman in modern Iran), a southern province of the Parthian Empire.

15.34–63: A vision of destructive storm clouds. The exact historical referents of this section, if any, are un-

clouds, full of wrath and tempest, shall rise and destroy all the earth and its inhabitants, and shall pour out upon every high and lofty place[a] a terrible tempest, [41] fire and hail and flying swords and floods of water, so that all the fields and all the streams shall be filled with the abundance of those waters. [42] They shall destroy cities and walls, mountains and hills, trees of the forests, and grass of the meadows, and their grain. [43] They shall go on steadily to Babylon and blot it out. [44] They shall come to it and surround it; they shall pour out on it the tempest[b] and all its fury;[c] then the dust and smoke shall reach the sky, and all who are around it shall mourn for it. [45] And those who survive shall serve those who have destroyed it.

[46] And you, Asia, who share in the splendor of Babylon and the glory of her person— [47] woe to you, miserable wretch! For you have made yourself like her; you have decked out your daughters for prostitution to please and glory in your lovers, who have always lusted after you. [48] You have imitated that hateful one in all her deeds and devices.[d] Therefore God[e] says, [49] I will send evils upon you: widowhood, poverty, famine, sword, and pestilence, bringing ruin to your houses, bringing destruction and death. [50] And the glory of your strength shall wither like a flower when the heat shall rise that is sent upon you. [51] You shall be weakened like a wretched woman who is beaten and wounded, so that you cannot receive your mighty lovers. [52] Would I have dealt with you so violently, says the Lord, [53] if you had not killed my chosen people continually, exulting and clapping your hands and talking about their death when you were drunk?

[54] Beautify your face! [55] The reward of a prostitute is in your lap; therefore you shall receive your recompense. [56] As you will do to my chosen people, says the Lord, so God will do to you, and will hand you over to adversities. [57] Your children shall die of hunger, and you shall fall by the sword; your cities shall be wiped out, and all your people who are in the open country shall fall by the sword. [58] Those who are in the mountains and highlands[f] shall perish of hunger, and they shall eat their own flesh in hunger for bread and drink their own blood in thirst for water. [59] Unhappy above all others, you shall come and suffer fresh miseries. [60] As they pass by they shall crush the hateful[g] city, and shall destroy a part of your land and abolish a portion of your glory, when they return from devastated Babylon. [61] You shall be broken down by them like stubble,[h] and they shall be like fire to you. [62] They shall devour you and your cities, your land and your mountains; they shall burn with fire all your forests and your fruitful trees. [63] They shall carry your children away captive, plunder your wealth, and mar the glory of your countenance.

16 Woe to you, Babylon and Asia! Woe to you, Egypt and Syria! [2] Bind on sackcloth and cloth of goats' hair,[i] and wail for your children, and lament for them; for your destruction is at hand. [3] The sword has been sent upon you, and who is there to turn it back? [4] A fire has been sent upon you, and who is there to quench it? [5] Calamities have been sent upon you, and who is there to drive

---

a Or *eminent person*
b Meaning of Lat uncertain
c Other ancient authorities add *until they destroy it to its foundations*
d Other ancient authorities read *devices, and you have followed after that one about to gratify her magnates and leaders so that you may be made proud and be pleased by her fornications*
e Other ancient authorities read *the Lord*
f Gk: Lat omits *and highlands*
g Another reading is *idle* or *unprofitable*
h Other ancient authorities read *like dry straw*
i Other ancient authorities lack *cloth of goats' hair*

---

clear. **35:** *As high as . . .* , cf. Rev 14.20. **43:** *Babylon*, Rome. **43–44:** Cf. Rev 18.9–10,15; 19.3. **46–63:** Polemic against *Asia*, imitator of the corrupt *splendor of Babylon* (Rome). *Asia*, here and in 16.1, probably designates the whole of Asia Minor. **47–48:** Cf. Ezek 16.33; Rev 14.8; 17.2–5; 18.3. **49:** Cf. Rev 18.7–8. **50:** Cf. Rev 17.16. **51:** Cf. Jer 3.1; etc.; Rev 18.9–10. **52–53:** Cf. Rev 17.6; 18.24. **56:** Cf. Rev 19.2. **57–59:** This section survives in Greek in a parchment fragment from Oxyrhynchus, Egypt. **57:** Cf. Jer 18.21. **60:** Cf. Rev 18.21. *The hateful city*, Babylon/Rome. **63:** Cf. Rev 18.14.

16.1–17: The inevitability of God's judgment (cf. Am 3.3–8). **1–2:** A reprise of ch 15. **2:** *Sackcloth and cloth of*

them away? [6] Can one drive off a hungry lion in the forest, or quench a fire in the stubble once it has started to burn?[a] [7] Can one turn back an arrow shot by a strong archer? [8] The Lord God sends calamities, and who will drive them away? [9] Fire will go forth from his wrath, and who is there to quench it? [10] He will flash lightning, and who will not be afraid? He will thunder, and who will not be terrified? [11] The Lord will threaten, and who will not be utterly shattered at his presence? [12] The earth and its foundations quake, the sea is churned up from the depths, and its waves and the fish with them shall be troubled at the presence of the Lord and the glory of his power. [13] For his right hand that bends the bow is strong, and his arrows that he shoots are sharp and when they are shot to the ends of the world will not miss once. [14] Calamities are sent forth and shall not return until they come over the earth. [15] The fire is kindled, and shall not be put out until it consumes the foundations of the earth. [16] Just as an arrow shot by a mighty archer does not return, so the calamities that are sent upon the earth shall not return. [17] Alas for me! Alas for me! Who will deliver me in those days?

[18] The beginning of sorrows, when there shall be much lamentation; the beginning of famine, when many shall perish; the beginning of wars, when the powers shall be terrified; the beginning of calamities, when all shall tremble. What shall they do, when the calamities come? [19] Famine and plague, tribulation and anguish are sent as scourges for the correction of humankind. [20] Yet for all this they will not turn from their iniquities, or ever be mindful of the scourges. [21] Indeed, provisions will be so cheap upon earth that people will imagine that peace is assured for them, and then calamities shall spring up on the earth—the sword, famine, and great confusion. [22] For many of those who live on the earth shall perish by famine; and those who survive the famine shall die by the sword. [23] And the dead shall be thrown out like dung, and there shall be no one to console

them; for the earth shall be left desolate, and its cities shall be demolished. [24] No one shall be left to cultivate the earth or to sow it. [25] The trees shall bear fruit, but who will gather it? [26] The grapes shall ripen, but who will tread them? For in all places there shall be great solitude; [27] a person will long to see another human being, or even to hear a human voice. [28] For ten shall be left out of a city; and two, out of the field, those who have hidden themselves in thick groves and clefts in the rocks. [29] Just as in an olive orchard three or four olives may be left on every tree, [30] or just as, when a vineyard is gathered, some clusters may be left[b] by those who search carefully through the vineyard, [31] so in those days three or four shall be left by those who search their houses with the sword. [32] The earth shall be left desolate, and its fields shall be plowed up,[c] and its roads and all its paths shall bring forth thorns, because no sheep will go along them. [33] Virgins shall mourn because they have no bridegrooms; women shall mourn because they have no husbands; their daughters shall mourn, because they have no help. [34] Their bridegrooms shall be killed in war, and their husbands shall perish of famine.

[35] Listen now to these things, and understand them, you who are servants of the Lord. [36] This is the word of the Lord; receive it and do not disbelieve what the Lord says.[d] [37] The calamities draw near, and are not delayed. [38] Just as a pregnant woman, in the ninth month when the time of her delivery draws near, has great pains around her womb for two or three hours beforehand, but when the child comes forth from the womb, there will not be a moment's delay, [39] so the calamities will not

---

a Other ancient authorities read *fire when dry straw has been set on fire*
b Other ancient authorities read *a cluster may remain exposed*
c Other ancient authorities read *be for briers*
d Cn: Lat *do not believe the gods of whom the Lord speaks*

---

goats' hair, signs of mourning. **9:** Cf. Jer 4.4. **12–13:** 6.14–16n.; 2 Sam 22.8,16; Pss 7.3; 18.7,14–15; Isa 51.15; Sir 16.19. **14:** Cf. Jer 30.23–24. **15:** Cf. Deut 32.22; 2 Pet 3.10. **17:** A plaintive, personal interlude by the prophet.

 16.18–34: Prediction of desolation on the earth. 19: Calamity is for the *correction of humankind*, see Amos 4.6–12. **20:** Cf. Hag 2.17; Rev 9.20–21. **23:** Cf. Jer 9.22. **28:** Cf. Am 5.3. **29–31:** Cf. Isa 17.6. **30:** *Clusters*, see 9.21; 12.42. **32:** Cf. Isa 7.23–25. **33:** Cf. Isa 33.8. **34:** Cf. Joel 1.8.

 16.35–78: Exhortation of God's people. 35–52: Advice and instruction. **38–39:** 4.40–42; cf. 1 Thess 5.3. **40–**

delay in coming upon the earth, and the world will groan, and pains will seize it on every side.

⁴⁰ Hear my words, O my people; prepare for battle, and in the midst of the calamities be like strangers on the earth. ⁴¹ Let the one who sells be like one who will flee; let the one who buys be like one who will lose; ⁴² let the one who does business be like one who will not make a profit; and let the one who builds a house be like one who will not live in it; ⁴³ let the one who sows be like one who will not reap; so also the one who prunes the vines, like one who will not gather the grapes; ⁴⁴ those who marry, like those who will have no children; and those who do not marry, like those who are widowed. ⁴⁵ Because of this, those who labor, labor in vain; ⁴⁶ for strangers shall gather their fruits, and plunder their goods, overthrow their houses, and take their children captive; for in captivity and famine they will produce their children.ᵃ ⁴⁷ Those who conduct business, do so only to have it plundered; the more they adorn their cities, their houses and possessions, and their persons, ⁴⁸ the more angry I will be with them for their sins, says the Lord. ⁴⁹ Just as a respectable and virtuous woman abhors a prostitute, ⁵⁰ so righteousness shall abhor iniquity, when she decks herself out, and shall accuse her to her face when he comes who will defend the one who searches out every sin on earth.

⁵¹ Therefore do not be like her or her works. ⁵² For in a very short time iniquity will be removed from the earth, and righteousness will reign over us. ⁵³ Sinners must not say that they have not sinned;ᵇ for Godᶜ will burn coals of fire on the head of everyone who says, "I have not sinned before God and his glory." ⁵⁴ The Lordᵈ certainly knows everything that people do; he knows their imaginations and their thoughts and their hearts. ⁵⁵ He said, "Let the earth be made," and it was made, and "Let the heaven be made," and it was made. ⁵⁶ At his word the stars were fixed in their places, and he knows the number of the stars. ⁵⁷ He

searches the abyss and its treasures; he has measured the sea and its contents; ⁵⁸ he has confined the sea in the midst of the waters;ᵉ and by his word he has suspended the earth over the water. ⁵⁹ He has spread out the heaven like a dome and made it secure upon the waters; ⁶⁰ he has put springs of water in the desert, and pools on the tops of the mountains, so as to send rivers from the heights to water the earth. ⁶¹ He formed human beings and put a heart in the midst of each body, and gave each person breath and life and understanding ⁶² and the spiritᶠ of Almighty God,ᵍ who surely made all things and searches out hidden things in hidden places. ⁶³ He knows your imaginations and what you think in your hearts! Woe to those who sin and want to hide their sins! ⁶⁴ The Lord will strictly examine all their works, and will make a public spectacle of all of you. ⁶⁵ You shall be put to shame when your sins come out before others, and your own iniquities shall stand as your accusers on that day. ⁶⁶ What will you do? Or how will you hide your sins before the Lord and his glory? ⁶⁷ Indeed, Godʰ is the judge; fear him! Cease from your sins, and forget your iniquities, never to commit them again; so Godʰ will lead you forth and deliver you from all tribulation.

⁶⁸ The burning wrath of a great multitude is kindled over you; they shall drag some of you away and force you to eat what was sacri-

ᵃ Other ancient authorities read *therefore those who are married may know that they will produce children for captivity and famine*
ᵇ Other ancient authorities add *or the unjust done injustice*
ᶜ Lat *for he*
ᵈ Other ancient authorities read *Lord God*
ᵉ Other ancient authorities read *confined the world between the waters and the waters*
ᶠ Or *breath*
ᵍ Other ancient authorities read *of the Lord Almighty*
ʰ Other ancient authorities read *the Lord*

47: Every form of worldly activity is useless. See Deut 28.30–33,38–42; 1 Cor 7.29–31. **46:** Cf. Lev 26.16; Deut 28.33.

16.53–67: The impossibility of hiding sins from God. 53: Cf. Prov 25.22. **54:** Cf. Ps 33.15; Sir 15.18–19; 39.19. **55–62:** This recital of God's acts of creation underscores God's omniscience; cf. Job 38; Sir 43. **55:** See Gen 1.6,9. **56:** Cf. Ps 147.4. **58–59:** Cf. Ps 136.6; Prov 8.29; Isa 44.24. **59:** Cf. Isa 40.22; Ps 104.2. **60:** Cf. Ps 107.35; Isa 41.18. **61-62:** Cf. Job 32.8; 33.4. **62:** Cf. Rev 2.23.

16.68–73: Prediction of persecutions. These descriptions have close parallels with third- and early fourth-

ficed to idols. [69] And those who consent to eat shall be held in derision and contempt, and shall be trampled under foot. [70] For in many places[a] and in neighboring cities there shall be a great uprising against those who fear the Lord. [71] They shall[b] be like maniacs, sparing no one, but plundering and destroying those who continue to fear the Lord.[c] [72] For they shall destroy and plunder their goods, and drive them out of house and home. [73] Then the tested quality of my elect shall be manifest, like gold that is tested by fire.

[74] Listen, my elect ones, says the Lord; the days of tribulation are at hand, but I will deliver you from them. [75] Do not fear or doubt, for God[d] is your guide. [76] You who keep my commandments and precepts, says the Lord God, must not let your sins weigh you down, or your iniquities prevail over you. [77] Woe to those who are choked by their sins and overwhelmed by their iniquities! They are like a field choked with underbrush and its path[e] overwhelmed with thorns, so that no one can pass through. [78] It is shut off and given up to be consumed by fire.

a Meaning of Lat uncertain
b Other ancient authorities read *For people, because of their misfortunes, shall*
c Other ancient authorities read *fear God*
d Other ancient authorities read *the Lord*
e Other ancient authorities read *seed*

century Roman persecutions of Christians. **68:** Eating food *sacrificed to idols* was forbidden for many Jewish and early Christian groups. See Ex 34.15; Acts 15.20,29; 1 Cor 8.1–13; 10.14–22; Rev 2.14,20; 4 Macc 5.2. **73:** Cf. Zech 13.9; 1 Pet 1.7. **74:** Cf. Dan 12.1.

16.74–78: Concluding instructions to the elect. 77–78: Cf. 2 Sam 23.6–7; Heb 6.8. **77:** Cf. Prov 5.22.

(d) The following book appears in an appendix to the Greek Bible.

4 MACCABEES

NAME

This book is linked with 1 and 2 Maccabees on the basis of its focus on the events also related in them, the conflict between Jewish factions that eventually precipitated the persecution by the Seleucid king Antiochus IV Epiphanes (reigned 175–164 BCE) and the Jewish revolt led by Judas Maccabeus. In 4 Maccabees, however, the family of Judas Maccabeus and its exploits are never mentioned. The focus is rather on the torture and death of the martyrs (see 2 Macc 7). The work was also known as *On the Supremacy of Reason* in the early church (Eusebius, *Hist. eccl.* 3.10.6; Jerome, *De vir. ill.* 13).

CANONICAL STATUS

No modern religious community regards the work as strictly canonical, although it is included in two important copies of the Bible from the fourth and fifth century Christian Church.

AUTHORSHIP

The anonymous author is a Torah-observant Jew who exhibits a greater mastery of Greek language, philosophy, literature, and rhetoric than any canonical author. The church fathers Eusebius and Jerome both attributed the work to Josephus, the first-century CE Jewish historian, though it does not suit his style, greater historical accuracy, and more indulgent attitude toward assimilation.

DATE AND HISTORICAL CONTEXT

Plausible arguments have been made for a date of composition anywhere between 20 and 130 CE, with a date later in that range more likely. Many earlier scholars thought that 4 Maccabees was written in Alexandria in Egypt, the generally assumed place of origin for Hellenistic Jewish literature. But the interest in these martyrs in Antioch (in northern Syria), and the fact that the literary epitaph in 17.9–10 reflects the wording of actual Jewish epitaphs in Cilicia (in southeast Turkey), point to an origin in the northeast Mediterranean basin. The author does not write in response to any known crisis affecting the Jewish community, but instead addresses the everyday challenge of maintaining pride in, and commitment to, the Jewish way of life in an often hostile environment.

LITERARY HISTORY

4 Maccabees is a thoroughly original composition rather than the product of editing various sources. The author has read 2 Macc 3–7, but completely recasts the story in keeping with his own interests and goals. The work appears to have been written, in Greek, for oral delivery on a particular occasion (1.10; 3.20), perhaps during a celebration of Hanukkah, which celebrates the reconsecration of the Temple in 164 BCE, or a festival connected with the giving of the Torah (e.g., the Feast of Weeks).

STRUCTURE AND CONTENTS

The author presents the work as a philosophical demonstration of the popular maxim that reason is able to master the passions, with the added dimension that Torah observance provides the most effective training to achieve this goal. The work has two main parts: a more deductive development of the thesis (1.13–3.18), and a narrative demonstration of the thesis focused on the historical example of nine martyrs (3.19–17.6). The combination of logical argumentation and extended examples is found in other Greek and Roman ethical works. The author prepares the hearers for this two-part structure (1.1,7–8,12), and the two parts of the work are thoroughly integrated, as its outline shows:

1:1–12	**Introduction**
1:13–3:18	**Development of the thesis**
1:13–30a	Definitions of terms and relationships
1:30b–3:18	Evidence from the scriptures
3:19–17:24	**Narrative demonstration of the thesis**
3:19–4:26	Historical background
5:1–6:30	The example of Eleazar
6:31–7:23	Reflection on Eleazar's example
8:1–12:19	The example of the seven brothers
13:1–14:10	Reflection on the seven brothers' example
14:11–17:6	The example of the mother and reflection
17:7–18:24	**Epilogue**
17:7–18:5	Summary of the martyrs' accomplishments and exhortation
18:6–19	The mother's testimony to feminine virtue and additional exhortation
18:20–24	Conclusion

INTERPRETATION

Fourth Maccabees is one of several texts from the Second Temple period interpreting the Jewish law and way of life in terms of Greco-Roman philosophy. Rather than using an allegorical approach, as did Philo of Alexandria, this author casts the Torah as a training program in the right exercise of reason and the cultivation of the cardinal virtues of justice, courage, self-control, and wisdom. It belongs thus to a larger literary movement promoting the Jewish way of life in close dialogue with the Greek cultural milieu.

As with other Jewish writings composed in Greek, it was not influential in the rabbinic Judaism that emerged in the wake of the disastrous revolts against Rome (66–70 and 132–35 CE). While early Christian authors recognized its philosophical dimensions, 4 Maccabees exercised its most enduring influence in the development of Christian martyrology during the second through fourth centuries.

GUIDE TO READING

The author gives several cues concerning how the work is to be read. He uses the language of "demonstration" (1.1; 3.19), suggesting that it can be read as an essay marshaling evidence for an ethical thesis: reason can rise above the passions and choose the path of virtue. He uses the language of praise or eulogy (1.10), suggesting that it can also be read as a celebration of the achievement of particular individuals, whose virtue is therefore to be imitated by all who strive for a praiseworthy remembrance. His exhortations to the audience (1.1, 18.1) and his interest in demonstrating that the Jewish law provides the surest path to ethical virtue add a third dimension, that of the "protreptic speech" that promotes a particular philosophy or way of life as worth following. Finally, the work can be read as resistance literature, both within the frame of the story of the martyrdoms and from the vantage point of an author who has mastered the dominant culture's tools as resources for promoting a minority culture's way of life.

David A. deSilva

1 The subject that I am about to discuss is most philosophical, that is, whether devout reason is sovereign over the emotions. So it is right for me to advise you to pay earnest attention to philosophy. ² For the subject is essential to everyone who is seeking knowledge, and in addition it includes the praise of the highest virtue—I mean, of course, rational judgment. ³ If, then, it is evident that reason rules over those emotions that hinder self-control, namely, gluttony and lust, ⁴ it is also clear that it masters the emotions that hinder one from justice, such as malice, and those that stand in the way of courage, namely anger, fear, and pain. ⁵ Some might perhaps ask, "If reason rules the emotions, why is it not sovereign over forgetfulness and ignorance?" Their attempt at argument is ridiculous!ᵃ ⁶ For reason does not rule its own emotions, but those that are opposed to justice, courage, and self-control;ᵇ and it is not for the purpose of destroying them, but so that one may not give way to them.

⁷ I could prove to you from many and various examples that reasonᶜ is dominant over the emotions, ⁸ but I can demonstrate it best from the noble bravery of those who died for the sake of virtue, Eleazar and the seven brothers and their mother. ⁹ All of these, by

despising sufferings that bring death, demonstrated that reason controls the emotions. ¹⁰ On this anniversaryᵈ it is fitting for me to praise for their virtues those who, with their mother, died for the sake of nobility and goodness, but I would also call them blessed for the honor in which they are held. ¹¹ All people, even their torturers, marveled at their courage and endurance, and they became the cause of the downfall of tyranny over their nation. By their endurance they conquered the tyrant, and thus their native land was purified through them. ¹² I shall shortly have an opportunity to speak of this; but, as my custom is, I shall begin by stating my main principle, and then I shall turn to their story, giving glory to the all-wise God.

¹³ Our inquiry, accordingly, is whether reason is sovereign over the emotions. ¹⁴ We shall decide just what reason is and what emotion is, how many kinds of emotions there are, and whether reason rules over all these.

ᵃ Or *They are attempting to make my argument ridiculous!*
ᵇ Other ancient authorities add *and rational judgment*
ᶜ Other ancient authorities read *devout reason*
ᵈ Gk *At this time*

1.1–12: Introduction. 1: *Reason . . . emotions*, the Greek word translated "emotions" includes desires and drives, emotional responses, and physical sensations. Greco-Roman philosophical writers regularly promoted mastery of these experiences, or self-mastery, as the path to lead a consistently virtuous life. *Devout reason*, the mind shaped by training in and obedience to the Jewish Torah (2.21–23; 5.19–26; 18.1–2). The author will claim for Judaism the status of a *philosophy* (as do the first-century CE Jewish writers Josephus and Philo), and argue for its superiority for achieving the Greek ideal of virtue. **3–4:** These topics are covered sequentially in 1.30–2.6a, 2.6b–3.18, and 5.1–17.6. **4:** *Anger* is more properly an obstacle to justice, not to courage, and is so treated in 2.6b,16–20. **5–6a:** The first-century CE Roman writer Cicero (*Fin.* 5.1.3.36), as well as Philo (*Migr.* 206), made similar distinctions between voluntary and involuntary defects or passions, holding the individual morally responsible only for the former. **6b:** The author, aware of this larger debate, aligns himself with philosophers promoting mastery and moderation of the emotions, drives, and sensations rather than with hardline Stoics who sought to eliminate such experiences; see also 3.2–18. **7:** *Examples* function here, as in Greek rhetoric generally, as a form of inductive proof. The extreme case of the martyrs will prove the general rule. **8:** See 2 Macc 6.18–7.42. **10:** Those who are most committed to the Jewish law thus achieve *nobility and goodness*, the highest Greek ideal. **11:** The author avoids all mention of the Maccabean revolutionaries throughout the speech and locates the cause for Judea's liberation squarely in the martyrs' effective, nonviolent resistance to imperialism.

1.13–3.18: Development of the thesis. 1.13–30a: Definitions of terms. 13: The author is not, strictly speaking, concerned with *whether*, but rather what enables reason to achieve such mastery. **16–17:** The author shares this definition of *wisdom* with Greco-Roman philosophers but reveals his particular allegiance to the Jewish "philosophy" by naming the Torah, *the law*, as the path to this *wisdom* (Sir 1:26; 19:20; Wis 6:17–20). *Education* (Gk "paideia") was what distinguished the civilized Greeks from the barbarians; the author claims for Torah-

¹⁵ Now reason is the mind that with sound logic prefers the life of wisdom. ¹⁶ Wisdom, next, is the knowledge of divine and human matters and the causes of these. ¹⁷ This, in turn, is education in the law, by which we learn divine matters reverently and human affairs to our advantage. ¹⁸ Now the kinds of wisdom are rational judgment, justice, courage, and self-control. ¹⁹ Rational judgment is supreme over all of these, since by means of it reason rules over the emotions. ²⁰ The two most comprehensive types[a] of the emotions are pleasure and pain; and each of these is by nature concerned with both body and soul. ²¹ The emotions of both pleasure and pain have many consequences. ²² Thus desire precedes pleasure and delight follows it. ²³ Fear precedes pain and sorrow comes after. ²⁴ Anger, as a person will see by reflecting on this experience, is an emotion embracing pleasure and pain. ²⁵ In pleasure there exists even a malevolent tendency, which is the most complex of all the emotions. ²⁶ In the soul it is boastfulness, covetousness, thirst for honor, rivalry, and malice; ²⁷ in the body, indiscriminate eating, gluttony, and solitary gormandizing.

²⁸ Just as pleasure and pain are two plants growing from the body and the soul, so there are many offshoots of these plants,[b] ²⁹ each of which the master cultivator, reason, weeds and prunes and ties up and waters and thoroughly irrigates, and so tames the jungle of habits and emotions. ³⁰ For reason is the guide of the virtues, but over the emotions it is sovereign.

Observe now, first of all, that rational judgment is sovereign over the emotions by virtue of the restraining power of self-control. ³¹ Self-control, then, is dominance over the desires. ³² Some desires are mental, others are physical, and reason obviously rules over both. ³³ Otherwise, how is it that when we are attracted to forbidden foods we abstain from the pleasure to be had from them? Is it not because reason is able to rule over appetites? I for one think so. ³⁴ Therefore when we crave seafood and fowl and animals and all sorts of foods that are forbidden to us by the law, we abstain because of domination by reason. ³⁵ For the emotions of the appetites are restrained, checked by the temperate mind, and all the impulses of the body are bridled by reason.

2 And why is it amazing that the desires of the mind for the enjoyment of beauty are rendered powerless? ² It is for this reason, certainly, that the temperate Joseph is praised, because by mental effort[c] he overcame sexual desire. ³ For when he was young and in his prime for intercourse, by his reason he nullified the frenzy[d] of the passions. ⁴ Not only is reason proved to rule over the frenzied urge of sexual desire, but also over every desire.[e] ⁵ Thus the law says, "You shall not covet your neighbor's wife or

---

a   Or *sources*
b   Other ancient authorities read *these emotions*
c   Other ancient authorities add *in reasoning*
d   Or *gadfly*
e   Or *all covetousness*

observance the status and fruits of such education. **18–19:** The four cardinal virtues of Platonic and Stoic ethics. The elevation of *rational judgment* as supreme emerges from the focus on the contest between reason and the emotions. **20:** The author follows Aristotle's twofold classification of the emotions based on *pleasure* and *pain* (*Rh.* 2.1–11) rather than the fourfold Stoic classification of desire, pain, pleasure, and fear; but see 1.22–23. **24:** The definition of anger as a mixture of pleasure and pain is particularly Aristotelian (*Rh.* 2.2.1–2). **28–29:** The author employs common agricultural analogies for the cultivation of the soul. *Habits*, predispositions particularly associated with the stages of life like youth, adulthood, and old age. The author treats the mastery of these challenges specifically in 2.3; 7.13–14.

1.30b–3.18: Evidence from the scriptures. 1.33–34: The author offers the ability of Jews to observe the dietary restrictions of the Torah (here, Lev 11.4–23,41–42; Deut 14.4–21) as proof of the power of self-control over desire. The commandments, however, also provide the training necessary to develop self-control (2.6b–9; 5.22–26). This represents a significant defense against Gentile ridicule of the Torah's restrictions as barbaric or superstitious (Josephus, *Ag. Ap.* 2.137; Tacitus, *Hist.* 5.4.3; Juvenal, *Sat.* 14.98–99; Plutarch, *Mor.* 169C). **2.2:** *Joseph* (Gen 39.7–12) is a model of temperance also in *T. Jos.* 2.7–10.4. **3:** *Young*, see 1.29n. **5:** Ex 20.17; Deut 5.21. **6a:** Contrast Paul's claim that the commandment awakens sin, rather than proves that sin can be mastered (Rom 7.7–24). **6b:** *Justice* involves giving to each person his or her due, which includes giving

anything that is your neighbor's." [6] In fact, since the law has told us not to covet, I could prove to you all the more that reason is able to control desires.

Just so it is with the emotions that hinder one from justice. [7] Otherwise how could it be that someone who is habitually a solitary gormandizer, a glutton, or even a drunkard can learn a better way, unless reason is clearly lord of the emotions? [8] Thus, as soon as one adopts a way of life in accordance with the law, even though a lover of money, one is forced to act contrary to natural ways and to lend without interest to the needy and to cancel the debt when the seventh year arrives. [9] If one is greedy, one is ruled by the law through reason so that one neither gleans the harvest nor gathers the last grapes from the vineyard.

In all other matters we can recognize that reason rules the emotions. [10] For the law prevails even over affection for parents, so that virtue is not abandoned for their sakes. [11] It is superior to love for one's wife, so that one rebukes her when she breaks the law. [12] It takes precedence over love for children, so that one punishes them for misdeeds. [13] It is sovereign over the relationship of friends, so that one rebukes friends when they act wickedly. [14] Do not consider it paradoxical when reason, through the law, can prevail even over

enmity. The fruit trees of the enemy are not cut down, but one preserves the property of enemies from marauders and helps raise up what has fallen.[a]

[15] It is evident that reason rules even[b] the more violent emotions: lust for power, vainglory, boasting, arrogance, and malice. [16] For the temperate mind repels all these malicious emotions, just as it repels anger—for it is sovereign over even this. [17] When Moses was angry with Dathan and Abiram, he did nothing against them in anger, but controlled his anger by reason. [18] For, as I have said, the temperate mind is able to get the better of the emotions, to correct some, and to render others powerless. [19] Why else did Jacob, our most wise father, censure the households of Simeon and Levi for their irrational slaughter of the entire tribe of the Shechemites, saying, "Cursed be their anger"? [20] For if reason could not control anger, he would not have spoken thus. [21] Now when God fashioned human beings, he planted in them emotions and inclinations, [22] but at the same time he enthroned the mind among the senses as a sacred governor over them all. [23] To the mind he gave the law; and one who lives subject to this will rule a kingdom that is temperate, just, good, and courageous.

---

[a] Or *the beasts that have fallen*

[b] Other ancient authorities read *through*

God God's due by honoring God's right thus to regulate human relationships. **8–9:** *Lend without interest,* Ex 22:25; Deut 23:19–20; *the seventh year,* Deut 15:1–2,9; *neither gleans,* so as to leave something for the poor, Ex 23:10–11; Lev 19:9–10. Specific commandments of the Torah provide ways to remedy specific vices. **10–13:** Commitment to virtue must outweigh even positive emotions like love for one's family and friends (cf. Deut 13.6–11). The author will return to this topic at length (13.19–14.1; 14.13–20; 15.4–23). **12:** See Prov 13.24; 19.18; 23.13–14; 29.15,17. **14:** Ex 23.4–5; Deut 20.19–20,24. Far from being a law that promotes hatred of foreigners (a frequent criticism; Diod. Sic. 34/35.1.1–4; Tacitus, *Hist.* 5.5; Josephus, *Ag. Ap.* 2.121), the Torah teaches kindness and humaneness toward one's enemies. **17:** When challenged by Dathan and Abiram, Moses acted justly by submitting the matter to God's adjudication (Num 16.1–35). **19–20:** Jacob's deathbed censure of Simeon and Levi (Gen 49:7) for their refusal to reconcile with the inhabitants of Shechem after the seduction of their sister Dinah (see Gen 34:1–31) indicates that reason should be expected to master anger. Other Jewish authors praise Simeon and Levi for this act, suggesting that Jacob was at fault (Jdt 8.2–4; *T. Levi* 5–6). **21–23:** The author regards inclinations and emotions to be part of God's design of the human being, and therefore aligns with the schools that seek to master rather than eliminate them. Diligent observance of the Torah promises the enjoyment of the "kingship" familiar from Stoic discourse, the exercise of perfect rule over the passions and enjoyment of the fruits of virtuous self-governance. **2.24–3.2:** See 1.5–6a n. 3.2–5: See 1.6b n. **6–18:** The story of David's thirst (2 Sam 23.13–17; 1 Chr 11.15–19) provides a proof from example of the position taken in 3.2. David regards the water as *blood* (v. 15) because the soldiers risked their lives. Although he still experiences thirst at the close (hence does not eliminate his craving), David does not allow it to lead him

24 How is it then, one might say, that if reason is master of the emotions, it does not control forgetfulness and ignorance?

3 **1** But this argument is entirely ridiculous; for it is evident that reason rules not over its own emotions, but over those of the body. **2** No one of us[a] can eradicate that kind of desire, but reason can provide a way for us not to be enslaved by desire. **3** No one of us can eradicate anger from the mind, but reason can help to deal with anger. **4** No one of us can eradicate malice, but reason can fight at our side so that we are not overcome by malice. **5** For reason does not uproot the emotions but is their antagonist.

6 Now this can be explained more clearly by the story of King David's thirst. **7** David had been attacking the Philistines all day long, and together with the soldiers of his nation had killed many of them. **8** Then when evening fell, he[b] came, sweating and quite exhausted, to the royal tent, around which the whole army of our ancestors had encamped. **9** Now all the rest were at supper, **10** but the king was extremely thirsty, and though springs were plentiful there, he could not satisfy his thirst from them. **11** But a certain irrational desire for the water in the enemy's territory tormented and inflamed him, undid and consumed him. **12** When his guards complained bitterly because of the king's craving, two staunch young soldiers, respecting[c] the king's desire, armed themselves fully, and taking a pitcher climbed over the enemy's ramparts. **13** Eluding the sentinels at the gates, they went searching throughout the enemy camp **14** and found the spring, and from it boldly brought the king a drink. **15** But David,[d] though he was burning with thirst, considered it an altogether fearful danger to his soul to drink what was regarded as equivalent to blood. **16** Therefore, opposing reason to desire, he poured out the drink as an offering to God. **17** For the temperate mind can conquer the drives of the emotions and quench the flames of frenzied desires; **18** it can overthrow bodily agonies even when they are extreme, and by nobility of reason spurn all domination by the emotions.

19 The present occasion now invites us to a narrative demonstration of temperate reason. **20** At a time when our ancestors were enjoying profound peace because of their observance of the law and were prospering, so that even Seleucus Nicanor, king of Asia, had both appropriated money to them for the temple service and recognized their commonwealth— **21** just at that time certain persons attempted a revolution against the public harmony and caused many and various disasters.

4 Now there was a certain Simon, a political opponent of the noble and good man, Onias, who then held the high priesthood for life. When despite all manner of slander he was unable to injure Onias in the eyes of the nation, he fled the country with the purpose of betraying it. **2** So he came to Apollonius, governor of Syria, Phoenicia, and Cilicia, and said, **3** "I have come here because I am loyal to the king's government, to report that in the Jerusalem treasuries there are deposited tens of thousands in private funds, which are not the property of the temple but belong to

---

a   Gk *you*
b   Other ancient authorities read *he hurried and*
c   Or *embarrassed because of*
d   Gk *he*

---

into an act of pride (hence he masters his craving). The author modifies the story to underscore the severity of David's thirst and the irrational element of his desire for water beyond his reach (3.10 has no parallel in the biblical narratives).

3.19–17.24: Narrative demonstration of the thesis. 3.19–4.26: Historical background. A highly condensed version of 2 Macc 3:1–6:11. **3.19:** The martyrdoms provide the primary proof from historical example for the author's thesis, a connection made explicit in 6.31–35; 13.1–5; 16.1–2. **20–21:** *Seleucus Nicanor,* Seleucus IV Philopator (king of Syria, 187–175 BCE), not Seleucus I Nicator (305–281). Jerusalem is portrayed as the ideal Greek city-state, exhibiting *peace,* lawful *observance,* and *public harmony* through observing its native way of life; ironically, the Hellenization of the city will destroy this ideal. **4.1:** *Simon,* see 2 Macc 3.4; 4.1–6. *Onias* III was the legitimate high priest (son of the Simon celebrated in Sir 50.1–21). **3:** *Private funds* were deposited in temples for safekeeping. **5:** In 2 Macc 3.7–8 Heliodorus, not Apollonius, is put in command. **7:** Burdensome tribute imposed by Rome led the Seleucid kings to raid several temple treasur-

King Seleucus." [4] When Apollonius learned the details of these things, he praised Simon for his service to the king and went up to Seleucus to inform him of the rich treasure. [5] On receiving authority to deal with this matter, he proceeded quickly to our country accompanied by the accursed Simon and a very strong military force. [6] He said that he had come with the king's authority to seize the private funds in the treasury. [7] The people indignantly protested his words, considering it outrageous that those who had committed deposits to the sacred treasury should be deprived of them, and did all that they could to prevent it. [8] But, uttering threats, Apollonius went on to the temple. [9] While the priests together with women and children were imploring God in the temple to shield the holy place that was being treated so contemptuously, [10] and while Apollonius was going up with his armed forces to seize the money, angels on horseback with lightning flashing from their weapons appeared from heaven, instilling in them great fear and trembling. [11] Then Apollonius fell down half dead in the temple area that was open to all, stretched out his hands toward heaven, and with tears begged the Hebrews to pray for him and propitiate the wrath of the heavenly army. [12] For he said that he had committed a sin deserving of death, and that if he were spared he would praise the blessedness of the holy place before all people. [13] Moved by these words, the high priest Onias, although otherwise he had scruples about doing so, prayed for him so that King Seleucus would not suppose that Apollonius had been overcome by human treachery and not by divine justice. [14] So Apollonius,[a] having been saved beyond all expectations, went away to report to the king what had happened to him.

[15] When King Seleucus died, his son Antiochus Epiphanes succeeded to the throne, an arrogant and terrible man, [16] who removed Onias from the priesthood and appointed Onias's[b] brother Jason as high priest. [17] Jason[c] agreed that if the office were conferred on him he would pay the king three thousand six hundred sixty talents annually. [18] So the king appointed him high priest and ruler of the nation. [19] Jason[c] changed the nation's way of life and altered its form of government in complete violation of the law, [20] so that not only was a gymnasium constructed at the very citadel[d] of our native land, but also the temple service was abolished. [21] The divine justice was angered by these acts and caused Antiochus himself to make war on them. [22] For when he was warring against Ptolemy in Egypt, he heard that a rumor of his death had spread and that the people of Jerusalem

a   Gk *he*
b   Gk *his*
c   Gk *He*
d   Or *high place*

ies (see 1 Macc 6.9–13; 2 Macc 1.11–17; 9.1–2,13–16), despite the taboos against sacrilege. **9–12:** As long as the people adhere to the Torah, they enjoy God's patronage and protection from their enemies (compare 3 Macc 1.8–2.24). **13:** Perhaps better, "Moved by these words, although in other respects concerned so that King Seleucus would not suppose that Apollonius had been overcome . . . , the high priest Onias prayed for him." Onias is not scrupulous about offering prayers for Apollonius. **15:** *Antiochus* IV *Epiphanes* (reigned 175–164 BCE) was in fact the son of Antiochus III (the Great) and the brother of *Seleucus* IV. **16–17:** *Jason*, Onias's younger brother and an avid reformer. The (exaggerated) sum he offers as a bribe signals the breadth of his support among Jerusalem's elite. **19–20:** Like many cities following Alexander the Great's conquests in the late fourth century BCE, Jerusalem's plan is now altered to conform to the pattern of the Greek city. *Gymnasium*, a center for Greek education and enculturation as well as athletic contests. According to 2 Macc 4.10–15, *the temple service* was not abolished under Jason, only neglected. **21:** God uses the Gentile king Antiochus IV to punish the people who turned from the covenant (see Deut 28.49–50), as for example he had used Nebuchadnezzar in 586 BCE. The author affirms Deuteronomy's theology of history, encouraging the hearers to follow the Torah as the means to advance the peace and prosperity of the Jewish community. **22–23:** *Ptolemy* VI Philometor (180–145 BCE). 2 Macc 5.5–12 cites rumors of an insurrection in Jerusalem as the reason for Antiochus's response. This author, by contrast, portrays Antiochus's persecution of the Jews as an irrational, heated response to their joy at the rumor of his death; cf. 8.2; 9.10–11.

had rejoiced greatly. He speedily marched against them, [23] and after he had plundered them he issued a decree that if any of them were found observing the ancestral law they should die. [24] When, by means of his decrees, he had not been able in any way to put an end to the people's observance of the law, but saw that all his threats and punishments were being disregarded [25] —even to the extent that women, because they had circumcised their sons, were thrown headlong from heights along with their infants, though they had known beforehand that they would suffer this— [26] when, I say, his decrees were despised by the people, he himself tried through torture to compel everyone in the nation to eat defiling foods and to renounce Judaism.

5 The tyrant Antiochus, sitting in state with his counselors on a certain high place, and with his armed soldiers standing around him, [2] ordered the guards to seize each and every Hebrew and to compel them to eat pork and food sacrificed to idols. [3] If any were not willing to eat defiling food, they were to be broken on the wheel and killed. [4] When many persons had been rounded up, one man, Eleazar by name, leader of the flock, was brought[a] before the king. He was a man of priestly family, learned in the law, advanced in age, and known to many in the tyrant's court because of his philosophy.[b]

[5] When Antiochus saw him he said, [6] "Before I begin to torture you, old man, I would advise you to save yourself by eating pork, [7] for I respect your age and your gray hairs. Although you have had them for so long a time, it does not seem to me that you are a philosopher when you observe the religion of the Jews. [8] When nature has granted it to us, why should you abhor eating the very excellent meat of this animal? [9] It is senseless not to enjoy delicious things that are not shameful, and wrong to spurn the gifts of nature. [10] It seems to me that you will do something even more senseless if, by holding a vain opinion concerning the truth, you continue to despise me to your own hurt. [11] Will you not awaken from your foolish philosophy, dispel your futile reasonings, adopt a mind appropriate to your years, philosophize according to the truth of what is beneficial, [12] and have compassion on your old age by honoring my humane advice? [13] For consider this: if there is some power watching over this religion of yours, it will excuse you from any transgression that arises out of compulsion."

[14] When the tyrant urged him in this fashion to eat meat unlawfully, Eleazar asked to have a word. [15] When he had received permission to speak, he began to address the people as follows: [16] "We, O Antiochus, who have been persuaded to govern our lives by the divine law, think that there is no compulsion more powerful than our obedience to the law. [17] Therefore we consider that we should not transgress it in any respect. [18] Even if, as you suppose, our law were not truly divine and we had wrongly held it to be divine, not even so would it be right for us to invalidate our reputation for piety. [19] Therefore do not suppose that it would be a petty sin if we were to eat defiling food; [20] to transgress the law in

---

[a] Or *was the first of the flock to be brought*
[b] Other ancient authorities read *his advanced age*

5.1–6.30: The example of Eleazar. 5.1–4: Antiochus is presented throughout the book as a stereotypical *tyrant*, inventing cruel torments, displaying arrogance, and suppressing time-honored, local laws. The scene of the tyrant confronting the sage is familiar in Greco-Roman philosophical texts, except that here an aged Jewish priest is cast in the role of the sage. **5–38:** The "speech duel" between Antiochus and Eleazar gives the author an opportunity to state and refute the dominant culture's case against Judaism. **7–8:** Philosophers claimed that the universal law of *nature* trumped the imperfect, particularistic laws of any one people. The prohibition of pork (see Lev 11.7; Deut 14.8) was frequently targeted for ridicule as a barbaric peculiarity that flew in the face of nature. **9:** Antiochus critiques the avoidance of pork as unjust, as it shows ingratitude toward *the gifts of nature*, and a sign of ignorance concerning what is truly permissible and what is truly shameful. **13:** Transgression of a law under compulsion was excusable according to Greek philosophers. **15:** Eleazar addresses not only the tyrant, but also the audience, which includes the other Jewish captives. He seeks as much to encourage the latter as to answer the former. **19–21:** Like the Stoics, Eleazar considers all sins to be *of equal seriousness* since all show

matters either small or great is of equal seriousness, ²¹ for in either case the law is equally despised. ²² You scoff at our philosophy as though living by it were irrational, ²³ but it teaches us self-control, so that we master all pleasures and desires, and it also trains us in courage, so that we endure any suffering willingly; ²⁴ it instructs us in justice, so that in all our dealings we act impartially,ᵃ and it teaches us piety, so that with proper reverence we worship the only living God.

²⁵ "Therefore we do not eat defiling food; for since we believe that the law was established by God, we know that in the nature of things the Creator of the world in giving us the law has shown sympathy toward us. ²⁶ He has permitted us to eat what will be most suitable for our lives,ᵇ but he has forbidden us to eat meats that would be contrary to this. ²⁷ It would be tyrannical for you to compel us not only to transgress the law, but also to eat in such a way that you may deride us for eating defiling foods, which are most hateful to us. ²⁸ But you shall have no such occasion to laugh at me, ²⁹ nor will I transgress the sacred oaths of my ancestors concerning the keeping of the law, ³⁰ not even if you gouge out my eyes and burn my entrails. ³¹ I am not so old and cowardly as not to be young in reason on behalf of piety. ³² Therefore get your torture wheels ready and fan the fire more vehemently! ³³ I do not so pity my old age as to break the ancestral law by my own act. ³⁴ I will not play false to you, O law that trained me, nor will I renounce you, beloved self-control. ³⁵ I will not put you to shame, philosophical reason, nor will I reject you, honored priesthood and knowledge of the law. ³⁶ You, O king,ᶜ shall not defile the honorable mouth of my old age, nor my long life lived lawfully. ³⁷ My ancestors will receive me as pure, as one who does not fear your violence even to death. ³⁸ You may tyrannize the ungodly, but you shall not dominate my religious principles, either by words or through deeds."

6 When Eleazar in this manner had made eloquent response to the exhortations of the tyrant, the guards who were standing by dragged him violently to the instruments of torture. ² First they stripped the old man, though he remained adorned with the gracefulness of his piety. ³ After they had tied his arms on each side they flogged him, ⁴ while a herald who faced him cried out, "Obey the king's commands!" ⁵ But the courageous and noble man, like a true Eleazar, was unmoved, as though being tortured in a dream; ⁶ yet while the old man's eyes were raised to heaven, his flesh was being torn by scourges, his blood flowing, and his sides were being cut to pieces. ⁷ Although he fell to the ground because his body could not endure the agonies, he kept his reason upright and unswerving. ⁸ One of the cruel guards rushed at him and began to kick him in the side to make him get up again after he fell. ⁹ But he bore the pains and scorned the punishment and endured the tortures. ¹⁰ Like a noble athlete the old man, while being beaten, was victorious over his torturers; ¹¹ in fact, with his face bathed in sweat, and gasping heavily for breath, he amazed even his torturers by his courageous spirit.

ᵃ Or *so that we hold in balance all our habitual inclinations*
ᵇ Or *souls*
ᶜ Gk lacks *O king*

---

equal affront to God, whether or not an outsider like Antiochus considers the particular issue weighty. **22–24:** Eleazar counters Antiochus's challenge to Judaism's status as a worthy philosophy (5.7,11) with the functional proof that obedience to the Torah nurtures the cardinal virtues prized by Platonic and Stoic philosophers (*piety* replaces "rational judgment" here; see 1.18). **25–26:** *In the nature of things*, lit., "according to nature." Stoics sought to live in accordance with the divine order inherent in creation. Eleazar counters Antiochus's criticism that the Torah contradicts nature (5.8–9) by affirming the Torah's origin in the mind of the *Creator* of nature, thus providing an even more reliable guide to virtue. **29:** *Sacred oaths*, Ex 24.3,7; Josh 24.18,21,24. **38:** Eleazar exhibits the freedom of the sage prized by Stoic philosophy. **6.2:** Eleazar's honor was not diminished by the degrading treatment he received. **5:** *Like a true Eleazar*, "Eleazar" means "God has helped," hence, "like someone truly helped by God." **7:** Keeping *reason upright* is the goal of the sage, even as it is for Eleazar. **10:** The victim becomes the victor by being able to endure, without capitulation, more than the torturers can inflict. Comparing Eleazar to *a noble athlete* reflects widespread philosophical usage of athletic imagery to transform passive

[12] At that point, partly out of pity for his old age, [13] partly out of sympathy from their acquaintance with him, partly out of admiration for his endurance, some of the king's retinue came to him and said, [14] "Eleazar, why are you so irrationally destroying yourself through these evil things? [15] We will set before you some cooked meat; save yourself by pretending to eat pork."

[16] But Eleazar, as though more bitterly tormented by this counsel, cried out: [17] "Never may we, the children of Abraham,[a] think so basely that out of cowardice we feign a role unbecoming to us! [18] For it would be irrational if having lived in accordance with truth up to old age and having maintained in accordance with law the reputation of such a life, we should now change our course [19] and ourselves become a pattern of impiety to the young by setting them an example in the eating of defiling food. [20] It would be shameful if we should survive for a little while and during that time be a laughingstock to all for our cowardice, [21] and be despised by the tyrant as unmanly by not contending even to death for our divine law. [22] Therefore, O children of Abraham, die nobly for your religion! [23] And you, guards of the tyrant, why do you delay?"

[24] When they saw that he was so courageous in the face of the afflictions, and that he had not been changed by their compassion, the guards brought him to the fire. [25] There they burned him with maliciously contrived instruments, threw him down, and poured stinking liquids into his nostrils. [26] When he was now burned to his very bones and about to expire, he lifted up his eyes to God and said, [27] "You know, O God, that though I might have saved myself, I am dying in burning torments for the sake of the law. [28] Be merciful to your people, and let our punishment suffice for them. [29] Make my blood their purification, and take my life in exchange for theirs." [30] After he said this, the holy man died nobly in his tortures; even in the tortures of death he resisted, by virtue of reason, for the sake of the law.

[31] Admittedly, then, devout reason is sovereign over the emotions. [32] For if the emotions had prevailed over reason, we would have testified to their domination. [33] But now that reason has conquered the emotions, we properly attribute to it the power to govern. [34] It is right for us to acknowledge the dominance of reason when it masters even external agonies. It would be ridiculous to deny it.[b] [35] I have proved not only that reason has mastered agonies, but also that it masters pleasures and in no respect yields to them.

7 For like a most skillful pilot, the reason of our father Eleazar steered the ship of religion over the sea of the emotions, [2] and though buffeted by the stormings of the tyrant and overwhelmed by the mighty waves of tortures, [3] in no way did he turn the rudder of religion until he sailed into the haven of immortal victory. [4] No city besieged with many ingenious war machines has ever held out as did that most holy man. Although his sacred life was consumed by tortures and racks, he conquered the besiegers with the shield of his devout reason. [5] For in setting his mind firm like a jutting cliff, our father Eleazar broke the maddening waves of the emotions. [6] O priest, worthy of the priesthood, you neither defiled your sacred teeth

a   Or *O children of Abraham*
b   Syr: Meaning of Gk uncertain

endurance into active resistance. This imagery recurs in 9.23; 11.20; 12.11,14; 13.13,15; 16.16; 17.11–16. **12–23:** See 2 Macc 6.21–22. Eleazar's rejection of the ruse recalls Socrates' rejection of the escape planned by his friends. Neither consented to purchasing a few more years of life at the cost of preserving the virtue of that life unblemished (5.36; 6.18–21; Plato, *Cri.* 52A–54C). Eleazar cannot maintain his private integrity without also preserving his public witness and example. **28–29:** The author combines the belief that a display of covenant obedience would bring an end to God's wrath upon the disobedient nation (Deut 30.1–5) with the sacrificial practice of using a victim's blood to atone for a life (Lev 17.11) to interpret the significance of the martyrdoms (cf. 17.21–22). This is an instructive parallel development to early Christian reflection on the death of Jesus as an act of atonement for the unrighteous. Greek drama also frequently features voluntary deaths as sacrifices that allow others to live or a nation to survive.

6.31–7.23: Reflection on Eleazar's example. 6.31–35: See 3.19n. **7.1–5:** The author uses a series of images familiar from popular ethical philosophy to praise Eleazar's achievement of mastery over emotions and sensa-

nor profaned your stomach, which had room only for reverence and purity, by eating defiling foods. [7] O man in harmony with the law and philosopher of divine life! [8] Such should be those who are administrators of the law, shielding it with their own blood and noble sweat in sufferings even to death. [9] You, father, strengthened our loyalty to the law through your glorious endurance, and you did not abandon the holiness that you praised, but by your deeds you made your words of divine[a] philosophy credible. [10] O aged man, more powerful than tortures; O elder, fiercer than fire; O supreme king over the passions, Eleazar! [11] For just as our father Aaron, armed with the censer, ran through the multitude of the people and conquered the fiery[b] angel, [12] so the descendant of Aaron, Eleazar, though being consumed by the fire, remained unmoved in his reason. [13] Most amazing, indeed, though he was an old man, his body no longer tense and firm,[c] his muscles flabby, his sinews feeble, he became young again [14] in spirit through reason; and by reason like that of Isaac he rendered the many-headed rack ineffective. [15] O man of blessed age and of venerable gray hair and of law-abiding life, whom the faithful seal of death has perfected!

[16] If, therefore, because of piety an aged man despised tortures even to death, most certainly devout reason is governor of the emotions. [17] Some perhaps might say, "Not all have full command of their emotions, because not all have prudent reason." [18] But as many as attend to religion with a whole heart, these alone are able to control the passions of the flesh, [19] since they believe that they, like our patriarchs Abraham and Isaac and Jacob, do not die to God, but live to God. [20] No contradiction therefore arises when some persons appear to be dominated by their emotions because of the weakness of their reason. [21] What person who lives as a philosopher by the whole rule of philosophy, and trusts in God, [22] and knows that it is blessed to endure any suffering for the sake of virtue, would not be able to overcome the emotions through godliness? [23] For only the wise and courageous are masters of their emotions.

8 For this is why even the very young, by following a philosophy in accordance with devout reason, have prevailed over the most painful instruments of torture. [2] For when the tyrant was conspicuously defeated in his first attempt, being unable to compel an aged man to eat defiling foods, then in violent rage he commanded that others of the Hebrew captives be brought, and that any who ate defiling food would be freed after eating, but if any were to refuse, they would be tortured even more cruelly.

[3] When the tyrant had given these orders, seven brothers—handsome, modest, noble, and accomplished in every way—were brought before him along with their aged mother. [4] When the tyrant saw them, grouped about their mother as though a chorus, he was pleased with them. And struck by

---

[a] Other ancient authorities lack *divine*
[b] Other ancient authorities lack *fiery*
[c] Gk *the tautness of the body already loosed*

---

tions. **6:** Far from devaluing his body, Eleazar honors it in his choice of endurance over capitulation. **9:** Consistency in word and speech is the test of the value of one's *philosophy*, or way of life. **11–12:** *Aaron*, see Num 16.41–50; Wis 18.20–25. Both priests courageously took a stand in a place of great danger for the sake of the nation in order to perform an act of expiation. **14:** *Isaac*, see Gen 22.1–19. **15:** *The faithful seal of death . . . perfected*, because Eleazar preserved his honor and virtue intact to the end, and they are now unassailable forever. **18:** *Religion*, specifically Judaism, is here affirmed as essential to achieving the ethical goal of the Greco-Roman philosophers. **19:** Freedom from the fear of death is essential if one is to be free to make the sacrifices that virtue sometimes demands.

8.1–12.19: The example of the seven brothers. 8.2: *Conspicuously defeated*, Antiochus is aware that the martyrs' effective resistance unto death publicly shames him. *In violent rage*, Antiochus fails to master his own emotions, giving them instead the upper hand. The Greco-Syrian king falls short of the Greek ideal so fully embodied by the non-Greek martyrs (see 9.10–11), and is indeed unfit to rule others (Plato, *Gorg.* 491D; Dio Chrys., *Or.* 62.1). **3–5:** Embodying the Greek ideal of male beauty and skill, the brothers do not lack the potential for success in the Greek world. **4:** *Chorus*, an image from the Greek stage, often speaking in unison and represent-

their appearance and nobility, he smiled at them, and summoned them nearer and said, [5] "Young men, with favorable feelings I admire each and every one of you, and greatly respect the beauty and the number of such brothers. Not only do I advise you not to display the same madness as that of the old man who has just been tortured, but I also exhort you to yield to me and enjoy my friendship. [6] Just as I am able to punish those who disobey my orders, so I can be a benefactor to those who obey me. [7] Trust me, then, and you will have positions of authority in my government if you will renounce the ancestral tradition of your national life. [8] Enjoy your youth by adopting the Greek way of life and by changing your manner of living. [9] But if by disobedience you rouse my anger, you will compel me to destroy each and every one of you with dreadful punishments through tortures. [10] Therefore take pity on yourselves. Even I, your enemy, have compassion for your youth and handsome appearance. [11] Will you not consider this, that if you disobey, nothing remains for you but to die on the rack?"

[12] When he had said these things, he ordered the instruments of torture to be brought forward so as to persuade them out of fear to eat the defiling food. [13] When the guards had placed before them wheels and joint-dislocators, rack and hooks[a] and catapults[b] and caldrons, braziers and thumbscrews and iron claws and wedges and bellows, the tyrant resumed speaking: [14] "Be afraid, young fellows; whatever justice you revere will be merciful to you when you transgress under compulsion."

[15] But when they had heard the inducements and saw the dreadful devices, not only were they not afraid, but they also opposed the tyrant with their own philosophy, and by their right reasoning nullified his tyranny. [16] Let us consider, on the other hand, what arguments might have been used if some

of them had been cowardly and unmanly. Would they not have been the following? [17] "O wretches that we are and so senseless! Since the king has summoned and exhorted us to accept kind treatment if we obey him, [18] why do we take pleasure in vain resolves and venture upon a disobedience that brings death? [19] O men and brothers, should we not fear the instruments of torture and consider the threats of torments, and give up this vain opinion and this arrogance that threatens to destroy us? [20] Let us take pity on our youth and have compassion on our mother's age; [21] and let us seriously consider that if we disobey we are dead! [22] Also, divine justice will excuse us for fearing the king when we are under compulsion. [23] Why do we banish ourselves from this most pleasant life and deprive ourselves of this delightful world? [24] Let us not struggle against compulsion[c] or take hollow pride in being put to the rack. [25] Not even the law itself would arbitrarily put us to death for fearing the instruments of torture. [26] Why does such contentiousness excite us and such a fatal stubbornness please us, when we can live in peace if we obey the king?"

[27] But the youths, though about to be tortured, neither said any of these things nor even seriously considered them. [28] For they were contemptuous of the emotions and sovereign over agonies, [29] so that as soon as the tyrant had ceased counseling them to eat defiling food, all with one voice together, as from one mind, said:

9 "Why do you delay, O tyrant? For we are ready to die rather than transgress our ancestral commandments; [2] we are obviously putting our forebears to shame unless we should practice ready obedience to the

---

[a] Meaning of Gk uncertain
[b] Here and elsewhere in 4 Macc an instrument of torture
[c] Or *fate*

ing a single role. The image underscores their harmonious agreement (see 8.29–9.9; 13.8–18; 17.23). **5:** *Friendship* here indicates personal patronage and the promise of holding offices in the king's government (see 8.7). **9:** *You will compel me*, the king is less free than his victims, who cannot be compelled by his most coercive tortures. **14:** See 5.13n. **16–26:** The author creates a hypothetical response to throw the brothers' actual resolve into sharper relief. While it may seem reasonable enough, it is also laced with expressions of cowardice found elsewhere (e.g., Aristotle, *Virt.* 6.5–6; Sophocles, *Ant.* 58–68). If members of the audience have similarly rationalized the loosening of adherence to the Torah's commandments, the effect will be to shame and challenge them. **29:**

law and to Moses[a] our counselor. [3] Tyrant and counselor of lawlessness, in your hatred for us do not pity us more than we pity ourselves.[b] [4] For we consider this pity of yours, which insures our safety through transgression of the law, to be more grievous than death itself. [5] You are trying to terrify us by threatening us with death by torture, as though a short time ago you learned nothing from Eleazar. [6] And if the aged men of the Hebrews because of their religion lived piously[c] while enduring torture, it would be even more fitting that we young men should die despising your coercive tortures, which our aged instructor also overcame. [7] Therefore, tyrant, put us to the test; and if you take our lives because of our religion, do not suppose that you can injure us by torturing us. [8] For we, through this severe suffering and endurance, shall have the prize of virtue and shall be with God, on whose account we suffer; [9] but you, because of your bloodthirstiness toward us, will deservedly undergo from the divine justice eternal torment by fire."

[10] When they had said these things, the tyrant was not only indignant, as at those who are disobedient, but also infuriated, as at those who are ungrateful. [11] Then at his command the guards brought forward the eldest, and having torn off his tunic, they bound his hands and arms with thongs on each side. [12] When they had worn themselves out beating him with scourges, without accomplishing anything, they placed him upon the wheel. [13] When the noble youth was stretched out around this, his limbs were dislocated, [14] and with every member disjointed he denounced the tyrant, saying, [15] "Most abominable tyrant, enemy of heavenly justice, savage of mind, you are mangling me in this manner, not because I am a murderer, or as one who acts impiously, but because I protect the divine law." [16] And when the guards said, "Agree to eat so that you may be released from the tortures," [17] he replied, "You abominable lackeys, your wheel is not so powerful as to strangle my reason. Cut my limbs, burn my flesh, and twist my joints; [18] through all these tortures I will convince you that children of the Hebrews alone are invincible where virtue is concerned." [19] While he was saying these things, they spread fire under him, and while fanning the flames[b] they tightened the wheel further. [20] The wheel was completely smeared with blood, and the heap of coals was being quenched by the drippings of gore, and pieces of flesh were falling off the axles of the machine. [21] Although the ligaments joining his bones were already severed, the courageous youth, worthy of Abraham, did not groan, [22] but as though transformed by fire into immortality, he nobly endured the rackings. [23] "Imitate me, brothers," he said. "Do not leave your post in my struggle[d] or renounce our courageous family ties. [24] Fight the sacred and noble battle for religion. Thereby the just Providence of our ancestors may become merciful to our nation and take vengeance on the accursed tyrant." [25] When he had said this, the saintly youth broke the thread of life.

[26] While all were marveling at his courageous spirit, the guards brought in the next eldest, and after fitting themselves with iron gauntlets having sharp hooks, they bound

---

a   Other ancient authorities read *knowledge*
b   Meaning of Gk uncertain
c   Other ancient authorities read *died*
d   Other ancient authorities read *post forever*

With one voice, see 8.4n. **9.6:** *More fitting*, because the young were deemed stronger and more courageous than the elderly. **7:** The ideal sage acknowledges no injury from outside, but fears only self-inflicted injury to his or her moral determination. **8–9:** Expectation of reward or punishment after death underlies the martyrs' commitment to the Law throughout the work. **10–11:** See 8.2n. **12:** See 6.10n. **15:** The first brother refuses to accept the deviant status that the tortures are meant to inscribe on him: he is in the right, and the imperial power is acting unjustly. **17–18:** The sage refuses to allow physical maltreatment to give an enemy leverage against his or her will, thus remaining *invincible* (also 11.21,27). The claim that *children of the Hebrews alone* achieve the Greek philosophical ideal encourages the audience to prize their own distinctive heritage in the context of Greek cultural imperialism (see 7.18–19). **21:** *Did not groan*, a familiar topic of fortitude (e.g., Plutarch, *Mor.* 234A, 498E). **23–24:** Military imagery transforms the endurance of degrading torture into the battle line against the enemy that must be held at all costs, hence an opportunity to display courage. **25:** *Thread of life*, an image from Greek

him to the torture machine and catapult. [27] Before torturing him, they inquired if he were willing to eat, and they heard his noble decision.[a] [28] These leopard-like beasts tore out his sinews with the iron hands, flayed all his flesh up to his chin, and tore away his scalp. But he steadfastly endured this agony and said, [29] "How sweet is any kind of death for the religion of our ancestors!" [30] To the tyrant he said, "Do you not think, you most savage tyrant, that you are being tortured more than I, as you see the arrogant design of your tyranny being defeated by our endurance for the sake of religion? [31] I lighten my pain by the joys that come from virtue, [32] but you suffer torture by the threats that come from impiety. You will not escape, you most abominable tyrant, the judgments of the divine wrath."

10 When he too had endured a glorious death, the third was led in, and many repeatedly urged him to save himself by tasting the meat. [2] But he shouted, "Do you not know that the same father begot me as well as those who died, and the same mother bore me, and that I was brought up on the same teachings? [3] I do not renounce the noble kinship that binds me to my brothers."[b] [5] Enraged by the man's boldness, they disjointed his hands and feet with their instruments, dismembering him by prying his limbs from their sockets, [6] and breaking his fingers and arms and legs and elbows. [7] Since they were not able in any way to break his spirit,[c] they abandoned the instruments[d] and scalped him with their fingernails in a Scythian fashion. [8] They immediately brought him to the wheel, and while his vertebrae were being dislocated by this, he saw his own flesh torn all around and drops of blood flowing from his entrails. [9] When he was about to die, he said, [10] "We, most abominable tyrant, are suffering be-

cause of our godly training and virtue, [11] but you, because of your impiety and bloodthirstiness, will undergo unceasing torments."

[12] When he too had died in a manner worthy of his brothers, they dragged in the fourth, saying, [13] "As for you, do not give way to the same insanity as your brothers, but obey the king and save yourself." [14] But he said to them, "You do not have a fire hot enough to make me play the coward. [15] No—by the blessed death of my brothers, by the eternal destruction of the tyrant, and by the everlasting life of the pious, I will not renounce our noble family ties. [16] Contrive tortures, tyrant, so that you may learn from them that I am a brother to those who have just now been tortured." [17] When he heard this, the bloodthirsty, murderous, and utterly abominable Antiochus gave orders to cut out his tongue. [18] But he said, "Even if you remove my organ of speech, God hears also those who are mute. [19] See, here is my tongue; cut it off, for in spite of this you will not make our reason speechless. [20] Gladly, for the sake of God, we let our bodily members be mutilated. [21] God will visit you swiftly, for you are cutting out a tongue that has been melodious with divine hymns."

11 When he too died, after being cruelly tortured, the fifth leaped up, saying, [2] "I will not refuse, tyrant, to be tortured for the sake of virtue. [3] I have come of my own accord, so that by murdering me you will incur punishment from the heavenly justice for even

---

a Other ancient authorities read *having heard his noble decision, they tore him to shreds*

b Other ancient authorities add verse 4, *So if you have any instrument of torture, apply it to my body; for you cannot touch my soul, even if you wish."*

c Gk *to strangle him*

d Other ancient authorities read *they tore off his skin*

---

mythology. **28:** The representatives of Greek civilization become more and more like barbarians and *beasts* as the speech progresses. **29:** Compare Horace, *Odes* 3.2.13: "Sweet and fitting it is to die for one's country." **31–32:** Plato taught that virtue brought its own sweetness, and vice its own punishment (*Gorg.* 470E-471A; 507B; also Plutarch, *Mor.* 498C-E). **10.5:** *Boldness* was an ideal of Greek democracy, especially important as a means of critique where democracy was threatened or replaced by tyranny or monarchy. *Enraged*, Antiochus's lackeys share in the king's failure to master their own passions (8.2; 9.10–11). **7:** The representatives of Greek culture show themselves to be the true barbarians; the Scythians, in the vicinity of the Black Sea, had a reputation for cruelty (2 Macc 4.47; 3 Macc 7.5). **15:** The fourth brother rejects the torturers' assessment of his brothers' conduct as "madness" (Gk "manian," 10.13), asserting instead that they died a *blessed* (Gk "makarion") death because they maintained their integrity to the end. **11.1, 3:** *Of my own accord*, by seizing what little initiative is available, the

more crimes. [4] Hater of virtue, hater of humankind, for what act of ours are you destroying us in this way? [5] Is it because[a] we revere the Creator of all things and live according to his virtuous law? [6] But these deeds deserve honors, not tortures."[b] [9] While he was saying these things, the guards bound him and dragged him to the catapult; [10] they tied him to it on his knees, and fitting iron clamps on them, they twisted his back[c] around the wedge on the wheel,[d] so that he was completely curled back like a scorpion, and all his members were disjointed. [11] In this condition, gasping for breath and in anguish of body, [12] he said, "Tyrant, they are splendid favors that you grant us against your will, because through these noble sufferings you give us an opportunity to show our endurance for the law."

[13] When he too had died, the sixth, a mere boy, was led in. When the tyrant inquired whether he was willing to eat and be released, he said, [14] "I am younger in age than my brothers, but I am their equal in mind. [15] Since to this end we were born and bred, we ought likewise to die for the same principles. [16] So if you intend to torture me for not eating defiling foods, go on torturing!" [17] When he had said this, they led him to the wheel. [18] He was carefully stretched tight upon it, his back was broken, and he was roasted[e] from underneath. [19] To his back they applied sharp spits that had been heated in the fire, and pierced his ribs so that his entrails were burned through. [20] While being tortured he said, "O contest befitting holiness, in which so many of us brothers have been summoned to an arena of sufferings for religion, and in which we have not been defeated! [21] For religious knowledge, O tyrant, is invincible. [22] I also, equipped with nobility, will die with my brothers, [23] and I my-

self will bring a great avenger upon you, you inventor of tortures and enemy of those who are truly devout. [24] We six boys have paralyzed your tyranny. [25] Since you have not been able to persuade us to change our mind or to force us to eat defiling foods, is not this your downfall? [26] Your fire is cold to us, and the catapults painless, and your violence powerless. [27] For it is not the guards of the tyrant but those of the divine law that are set over us; therefore, unconquered, we hold fast to reason."

12 When he too, thrown into the caldron, had died a blessed death, the seventh and youngest of all came forward. [2] Even though the tyrant had been vehemently reproached by the brothers, he felt strong compassion for this child when he saw that he was already in fetters. He summoned him to come nearer and tried to persuade him, saying, [3] "You see the result of your brothers' stupidity, for they died in torments because of their disobedience. [4] You too, if you do not obey, will be miserably tortured and die before your time, [5] but if you yield to persuasion you will be my friend and a leader in the government of the kingdom." [6] When he had thus appealed to him, he sent for the boy's mother to show compassion on her who had been bereaved of so many sons and to influence her to persuade the surviving son to obey and save himself.

---

[a] Other ancient authorities read *Or does it seem evil to you that*

[b] Other authorities add verses 7 and 8, [7]*If you but understood human feelings and had hope of salvation from God—* [8]*but, as it is, you are a stranger to God and persecute those who serve him."*

[c] Gk *loins*

[d] Meaning of Gk uncertain

[e] Other ancient authorities add *by fire*

---

fifth brother comes forward as a contender rather than a victim. **4:** The charge of hatred of humanity, frequently leveled against the Jews by those who held the Jewish law to be xenophobic (see 2.14n.), is turned back upon those who would persecute the Jews on account of their different religion and way of life. **6:** See 9.15n. **12:** The ideal sage engages hardships as a means of demonstrating commitment to virtue. These are the only *favors* the pious Jews will accept from Antiochus (contrast 8.6–7). **20:** *Contest . . . arena*, see 6.10n. *Not been defeated*, since their wills could not be corrupted. **24–25:** Antiochus has failed in his primary goal of forcing assimilation. **26:** *Fire is cold*, in the sense of powerless or ineffective to subvert the Judeans' will. The martyrs have not, however, extinguished the awareness of pain, as a Stoic might strive to do (11.11; 14.9–10). **12.2:** *Vehemently reproached*, better, "frightfully abused." With skillful irony, the author suggests that Antiochus is the one who has been beaten down here. **6:** Although the author presents Antiochus as acting out of *compassion* here, persuading the last brother to surrender would also effectively cancel his previous seven defeats. **7:** The use of the *Hebrew*

[7] But when his mother had exhorted him in the Hebrew language, as we shall tell a little later, [8] he said, "Let me loose, let me speak to the king and to all his friends that are with him." [9] Extremely pleased by the boy's declaration, they freed him at once. [10] Running to the nearest of the braziers, [11] he said, "You profane tyrant, most impious of all the wicked, since you have received good things and also your kingdom from God, were you not ashamed to murder his servants and torture on the wheel those who practice religion? [12] Because of this, justice has laid up for you intense and eternal fire and tortures, and these throughout all time[a] will never let you go. [13] As a man, were you not ashamed, you most savage beast, to cut out the tongues of men who have feelings like yours and are made of the same elements as you, and to maltreat and torture them in this way? [14] Surely they by dying nobly fulfilled their service to God, but you will wail bitterly for having killed without cause the contestants for virtue." [15] Then because he too was about to die, he said, [16] "I do not desert the excellent example[b] of my brothers, [17] and I call on the God of our ancestors to be merciful to our nation;[c] [18] but on you he will take vengeance both in this present life and when you are dead." [19] After he had uttered these imprecations, he flung himself into the braziers and so ended his life.[d]

13 Since, then, the seven brothers despised sufferings even unto death, everyone must concede that devout reason is sovereign over the emotions. [2] For if they had been slaves to their emotions and had eaten defiling food, we would say that they had

been conquered by these emotions. [3] But in fact it was not so. Instead, by reason, which is praised before God, they prevailed over their emotions. [4] The supremacy of the mind over these cannot be overlooked, for the brothers[e] mastered both emotions and pains. [5] How then can one fail to confess the sovereignty of right reason over emotion in those who were not turned back by fiery agonies? [6] For just as towers jutting out over harbors hold back the threatening waves and make it calm for those who sail into the inner basin, [7] so the seven-towered right reason of the youths, by fortifying the harbor of religion, conquered the tempest of the emotions. [8] For they constituted a holy chorus of religion and encouraged one another, saying, [9] "Brothers, let us die like brothers for the sake of the law; let us imitate the three youths in Assyria who despised the same ordeal of the furnace. [10] Let us not be cowardly in the demonstration of our piety." [11] While one said, "Courage, brother," another said, "Bear up nobly," [12] and another reminded them, "Remember whence you came, and the father by whose hand Isaac would have submitted to being slain for the sake of religion." [13] Each of them and all of them together looking at one another, cheerful and undaunted, said, "Let us with all our hearts consecrate

a   Gk *throughout the whole age*
b   Other ancient authorities read *the witness*
c   Other ancient authorities read *my race*
d   Gk *and so gave up*; other ancient authorities read *gave up his spirit* or *his soul*
e   Gk *they*

language here both hides the meaning of her speech from the king and is an act of resistance to Greek imperialism. When the speech is actually recounted *a little later*, however, the mother speaks to all her sons during Eleazar's ordeal (16.15–25). **11, 13:** The last brother charges Antiochus with injustice against the God who gave him his authority (cf. Dan 4:25), since he has used that power to harm God's loyal clients rather than benefit them and serve God's cause. He also condemns Antiochus for violating the universal bond of humanity that unites all people by brutally torturing fellow human beings. The charges that Jews do not give the gods their due and violate the universal bond of humanity are thus again turned back upon the dominant culture. **19:** The youngest brother seizes what little control he can by committing suicide; see 17.1n. Contrast 2 Macc 7.39–40.

   13.1–14.10: Reflection on the seven brothers' example. 13.1–5: See 3.19n. **8:** The brothers' harmony in their collective commitment to the Torah helps each individually to remain steadfast. Such harmony (see 8.4n.) was considered a valuable civic virtue, since it enhanced social reinforcement of the group's norms. **9:** Dan 3 (esp. 3.17–18). The *three youths*, together with Daniel himself (Dan 6), were prototypes of resistance against a tyrant's coercive threats and laws for the sake of maintaining their piety; see also 16.21; 18.12–13. **12:** Gen 22.1–19. The mother will also be compared to Abraham, with whom she shared a willingness to put obedience to God's command above the life of her children (14.20; 15.28). **13:** The brothers regard obedience to God to the point of death

ourselves to God, who gave us our lives,[a] and let us use our bodies as a bulwark for the law. [14] Let us not fear him who thinks he is killing us, [15] for great is the struggle of the soul and the danger of eternal torment lying before those who transgress the commandment of God. [16] Therefore let us put on the full armor of self-control, which is divine reason. [17] For if we so die,[b] Abraham and Isaac and Jacob will welcome us, and all the fathers will praise us." [18] Those who were left behind said to each of the brothers who were being dragged away, "Do not put us to shame, brother, or betray the brothers who have died before us."

[19] You are not ignorant of the affection of family ties, which the divine and all-wise Providence has bequeathed through the fathers to their descendants and which was implanted in the mother's womb. [20] There each of the brothers spent the same length of time and was shaped during the same period of time; and growing from the same blood and through the same life, they were brought to the light of day. [21] When they were born after an equal time of gestation, they drank milk from the same fountains. From such embraces brotherly-loving souls are nourished; [22] and they grow stronger from this common nurture and daily companionship, and from both general education and our discipline in the law of God.

[23] Therefore, when sympathy and brotherly affection had been so established, the brothers were the more sympathetic to one another. [24] Since they had been educated by the same law and trained in the same virtues and brought up in right living, they loved one another all the more. [25] A common zeal for nobility strengthened their goodwill toward one another, and their concord, [26] because they could make their brotherly love more fervent with the aid of their religion. [27] But although nature and companionship and virtuous habits had augmented the affection of family ties, those who were left endured for the sake of religion, while watching their brothers being maltreated and tortured to death.

14 Furthermore, they encouraged them to face the torture, so that they not only despised their agonies, but also mastered the emotions of brotherly love.

[2] O reason,[c] more royal than kings and freer than the free! [3] O sacred and harmonious concord of the seven brothers on behalf of religion! [4] None of the seven youths proved coward or shrank from death, [5] but all of them, as though running the course toward immortality, hastened to death by torture. [6] Just as the hands and feet are moved in harmony with the guidance of the mind, so those holy youths, as though moved by an immortal spirit of devotion, agreed to go to death for its sake. [7] O most holy seven, brothers in harmony! For just as the seven days of creation move in choral dance around religion, [8] so these youths, forming a chorus, encircled the sevenfold fear of tortures and dissolved it. [9] Even now, we ourselves shudder as we hear of the suffering of these young men; they not only saw what was happening, not only heard the direct word of threat, but also bore the sufferings patiently, and in agonies of fire at that. [10] What could

---

a   Or *souls*
b   Other ancient authorities read *suffer*
c   Or *O minds*

---

a fitting return of gratitude for the gift of life itself; see also 16.18–19. **14:** *Who thinks he is killing*, see 9.7n.; cf. Mt 10.28. **19–26:** Almost every detail in the author's discussion of the love between siblings has a counterpart in Greco-Roman philosophical discussions of this topic, another indication of how immersed the author was in Greek culture and learning while remaining fully committed to the Jewish way of life. **13.27–14.1:** Because of their training in the Torah, the brothers are able to strengthen rather than weaken each other's resolve, enabling one another to walk in line with virtue, thus fulfilling the Aristotelian ideal of friendship. **14.2:** The sage cannot be compelled to sacrifice virtue, bowing to any external pressure, and so remains *free* and exercises *royal* self-governance. **7:** *Seven* was mystically associated with the harmony of God's creation and created order (Philo, *Opif.* 90–128). **8:** *Chorus*, see 8.4n. and 13.8n. **9:** The author has justifiable confidence in his power of vivid description to make his audience squirm. He has used this rhetorical technique in order to heighten the audience's appreciation of the sensations the martyrs withstood, so as to embolden them to remain steadfast in their commitment to the Jewish way of life in the face of far less daunting difficulties.

be more excruciatingly painful than this? For the power of fire is intense and swift, and it consumed their bodies quickly.

[11] Do not consider it amazing that reason had full command over these men in their tortures, since the mind of woman despised even more diverse agonies, [12] for the mother of the seven young men bore up under the rackings of each one of her children.

[13] Observe how complex is a mother's love for her children, which draws everything toward an emotion felt in her inmost parts. [14] Even unreasoning animals, as well as human beings, have a sympathy and parental love for their offspring. [15] For example, among birds, the ones that are tame protect their young by building on the housetops, [16] and the others, by building at the tops of mountains and the depths of chasms, in holes of trees, and on tree-tops, hatch the nestlings and ward off the intruder. [17] If they are not able to keep the intruder[a] away, they do what they can to help their young by flying in circles around them in the anguish of love, warning them with their own calls. [18] And why is it necessary to demonstrate sympathy for children by the example of unreasoning animals, [19] since even bees at the time for making honeycombs defend themselves against intruders and, as though with an iron dart, sting those who approach their hive and defend it even to the death? [20] But sympathy for her children did not sway the mother of the young men; she was of the same mind as Abraham.

15 O reason of the children, tyrant over the emotions! O religion, more desirable to the mother than her children! [2] Two courses were open to this mother, that of religion, and that of preserving her seven sons for a time, as the tyrant had promised. [3] She loved religion more, the religion that preserves them for eternal life according to God's promise.[b]

[4] In what manner might I express the emotions of parents who love their children? We impress upon the character of a small child a wondrous likeness both of mind and of form. Especially is this true of mothers, who because of their birth pangs have a deeper sympathy toward their offspring than do the fathers. [5] Considering that mothers are the weaker sex and give birth to many, they are more devoted to their children.[c] [6] The mother of the seven boys, more than any other mother, loved her children. In seven pregnancies she had implanted in herself tender love toward them, [7] and because of the many pains she suffered with each of them she had sympathy for them; [8] yet because of the fear of God she disdained the temporary safety of her children. [9] Not only so, but also because of the nobility of her sons and their ready obedience to the law, she felt a greater tenderness toward them. [10] For they were righteous and self-controlled and brave and magnanimous, and loved their brothers and their mother, so that they obeyed her even to death in keeping the ordinances.

[11] Nevertheless, though so many factors influenced the mother to suffer with them out of love for her children, in the case of none of them were the various tortures strong enough to pervert her reason. [12] But each child separately and all of them together the mother urged on to death for religion's sake. [13] O sacred nature and affection of parental love, yearning of parents toward offspring, nurture and indomitable suffering by mothers! [14] This mother, who saw them tortured and burned one by one, because of religion

---

a Gk *it*
b Gk *according to God*
c Or *For to the degree that mothers are weaker and the more children they bear, the more they are devoted to their children.*

14.11–17.6: The example of the mother and reflection. The climactic example of the Torah's ability to empower the mind for mastery of the emotions is the mother of the seven brothers. **14.11:** *Since the mind of woman,* perhaps more accurately, "since even the mind of a woman." Women were generally held to be more prone to yield to the emotions and sensations than men (Aristotle, *Pol.* 1.13; Philo, *Leg. all.* 2.44–50), with the result that a female's mastery of such overwhelming experiences proves the efficacy of the Torah as a philosophical way of life beyond contradiction. **13–20:** The author's description of love for offspring once again shares many details with Greco-Roman writings on the topic; see 13.19–26n. **20:** See 13.12n. **15.1:** *O reason . . . O religion . . .!* The author makes extensive use of "apostrophe" (direct address to some ideal or person not physically present) throughout his oration in order to heighten its emotionally evocative power. **2–3:** *For a time . . . for eternal*

did not change her attitude. [15] She watched the flesh of her children being consumed by fire, their toes and fingers scattered[a] on the ground, and the flesh of the head to the chin exposed like masks.

[16] O mother, tried now by more bitter pains than even the birth pangs you suffered for them! [17] O woman, who alone gave birth to such complete devotion! [18] When the firstborn breathed his last, it did not turn you aside, nor when the second in torments looked at you piteously nor when the third expired; [19] nor did you weep when you looked at the eyes of each one in his tortures gazing boldly at the same agonies, and saw in their nostrils the signs of the approach of death. [20] When you saw the flesh of children burned upon the flesh of other children, severed hands upon hands, scalped heads upon heads, and corpses fallen on other corpses, and when you saw the place filled with many spectators of the torturings, you did not shed tears. [21] Neither the melodies of sirens nor the songs of swans attract the attention of their hearers as did the voices of the children in torture calling to their mother. [22] How great and how many torments the mother then suffered as her sons were tortured on the wheel and with the hot irons! [23] But devout reason, giving her heart a man's courage in the very midst of her emotions, strengthened her to disregard, for the time, her parental love.

[24] Although she witnessed the destruction of seven children and the ingenious and various rackings, this noble mother disregarded all these[b] because of faith in God. [25] For as in the council chamber of her own soul she saw mighty advocates—nature, family, parental love, and the rackings of her children— [26] this

mother held two ballots, one bearing death and the other deliverance for her children. [27] She did not approve the deliverance that would preserve the seven sons for a short time, [28] but as the daughter of God-fearing Abraham she remembered his fortitude.

[29] O mother of the nation, vindicator of the law and champion of religion, who carried away the prize of the contest in your heart! [30] O more noble than males in steadfastness, and more courageous than men in endurance! [31] Just as Noah's ark, carrying the world in the universal flood, stoutly endured the waves, [32] so you, O guardian of the law, overwhelmed from every side by the flood of your emotions and the violent winds, the torture of your sons, endured nobly and withstood the wintry storms that assail religion.

16 If, then, a woman, advanced in years and mother of seven sons, endured seeing her children tortured to death, it must be admitted that devout reason is sovereign over the emotions. [2] Thus I have demonstrated not only that men have ruled over the emotions, but also that a woman has despised the fiercest tortures. [3] The lions surrounding Daniel were not so savage, nor was the raging fiery furnace of Mishael so intensely hot, as was her innate parental love, inflamed as she saw her seven sons tortured in such varied ways. [4] But the mother quenched so many and such great emotions by devout reason.

[5] Consider this also: If this woman, though a mother, had been fainthearted, she would

---

a Or *quivering*

b Other ancient authorities read *having bidden them farewell, surrendered them*

---

life, see 9.8–9n. **4–7:** See 14.11n.; 14.13–20n. **8:** See 9.8–9n. **16–17:** *O mother . . . O woman*, see 15.1n. **18–22:** The author provides a concentrated summary of the brothers' sufferings to sharpen the audience's impression of the assaults that tortured the mother, pressing upon her to cry out and beg her sons to save themselves (see 12.6; 16.12). **19:** *Gazing boldly*, literally, "gazing bull-like," a classical Greek expression (Aristophanes, *Ran.* 804; Plato, *Phaed.* 1176). **21:** *The melodies of sirens* were so irresistible they lured sailors to their death (Homer, *Od.* 12.44–52), and *swans* (which do not sing) were believed to sing a beautiful song just before they died. **26:** *Two ballots*, a judicial image, one for acquittal, one for condemnation. **28:** See 13.12n. **30:** *More courageous than men*, an especially poignant pun in Greek where "courageous" ("andreia") is derived from the noun for "male human being" ("aner, andros"), like English "manly." See also 15.23; 16.14. Plutarch celebrates the stories of women who exemplified courage greater than or equal to men ("On the Bravery of Women," *Mor.* 242E–263C), with whose stories the mother's story shares several traits. **31–32:** See 7.1–3n. Philo gives a similar interpretation of Noah's ark (*Quaest. in Gen.* 2.18). **16.1–4:** See 3.19n. **2:** *Not only that men . . . but also that a woman*, see 14.11n. **3:**

have mourned over them and perhaps spoken as follows: [6] "O how wretched am I and many times unhappy! After bearing seven children, I am now the mother of none! [7] O seven childbirths all in vain, seven profitless pregnancies, fruitless nurturings and wretched nursings! [8] In vain, my sons, I endured many birth pangs for you, and the more grievous anxieties of your upbringing. [9] Alas for my children, some unmarried, others married and without offspring.[a] I shall not see your children or have the happiness of being called grandmother. [10] Alas, I who had so many and beautiful children am a widow and alone, with many sorrows.[b] [11] And when I die, I shall have none of my sons to bury me."

[12] Yet that holy and God-fearing mother did not wail with such a lament for any of them, nor did she dissuade any of them from dying, nor did she grieve as they were dying. [13] On the contrary, as though having a mind like adamant and giving rebirth for immortality to the whole number of her sons, she implored them and urged them on to death for the sake of religion. [14] O mother, soldier of God in the cause of religion, elder and woman! By steadfastness you have conquered even a tyrant, and in word and deed you have proved more powerful than a man. [15] For when you and your sons were arrested together, you stood and watched Eleazar being tortured, and said to your sons in the Hebrew language, [16] "My sons, noble is the contest to which you are called to bear witness for the nation. Fight zealously for our ancestral law. [17] For it would be shameful if, while an aged man endures such agonies for the sake of religion, you young men were to be terrified by tortures. [18] Remember that it is through God that you have had a share in the world and have enjoyed life, [19] and therefore you ought to endure any suffering for the sake of God. [20] For his sake also our father Abraham was zealous to sacrifice his son Isaac, the ancestor of our nation; and when Isaac saw his father's hand wielding a knife[c] and descending upon him, he did not cower. [21] Daniel the righteous was thrown to the lions, and Hananiah, Azariah, and Mishael were hurled into the fiery furnace and endured it for the sake of God. [22] You too must have the same faith in God and not be grieved. [23] It is unreasonable for people who have religious knowledge not to withstand pain."

[24] By these words the mother of the seven encouraged and persuaded each of her sons to die rather than violate God's commandment. [25] They knew also that those who die for the sake of God live to God, as do Abraham and Isaac and Jacob and all the patriarchs.

17 Some of the guards said that when she also was about to be seized and put to death she threw herself into the flames so that no one might touch her body.

[2] O mother, who with your seven sons nullified the violence of the tyrant, frustrated his evil designs, and showed the courage of your faith! [3] Nobly set like a roof on the pillars of your sons, you held firm and unswerving against the earthquake of the tortures. [4] Take courage, therefore, O holy-minded mother,

a Gk *without benefit*
b Or *much to be pitied*
c Gk *sword*

Daniel, Dan 6.1–24. *Mishael,* also called Meshach, Dan 1.7; 3.1–30. **5–11:** As for the brothers (8.16–26), the author provides a speech reflective of the mind-set that the mother refused to adopt. Almost every element in the hypothetical lament composed for the mother reflects the laments of bereaved mothers in the tragedies of Euripides (see especially *Tro.* 380–82, 473–88, 503–505, 758–60). Having raised many children only to lose them in a single struggle, the mother is worthy of comparison with Queen Hecuba of Troy. **12–13:** The author stresses, however, that despite similar loss she did not grieve like Hecuba, since she considered the faithful deaths of her sons the best course for them and for her. Her pregnancies were not profitless (v. 7) since she gave *rebirth for immortality* to all her sons. *Dissuade,* see 12.6–7. *Adamant,* here a hard metal or diamond. **15:** *Hebrew,* see 12.7n. **16:** *Noble . . . contest,* see 6.10n. The martyrs *bear witness* in this public arena to the value of the Jewish way of life and the nation's character. *Fight zealously,* again turning the passive experience of victimization into active resistance. **18–19:** See 13.12–13n. **20:** *Abraham . . . Isaac,* Gen 22.1–19. **21:** *Daniel . . . Mishael,* see 13.9n.; 16.3n. **22:** *Have the same faith,* or "show the same loyalty toward God." **25:** See 7.19n.; 9.8–9n. **17.1:** The mother commits suicide rather than allow herself to be inappropriately handled by other men. Suicide under such circumstances

maintaining firm an enduring hope in God. [5] The moon in heaven, with the stars, does not stand so august as you, who, after lighting the way of your star-like seven sons to piety, stand in honor before God and are firmly set in heaven with them. [6] For your children were true descendants of father Abraham.[a]

[7] If it were possible for us to paint the history of your religion as an artist might, would not those who first beheld it have shuddered as they saw the mother of the seven children enduring their varied tortures to death for the sake of religion? [8] Indeed it would be proper to inscribe on their tomb these words as a reminder to the people of our nation:[b]

[9] "Here lie buried an aged priest and an aged woman and seven sons, because of the violence of the tyrant who wished to destroy the way of life of the Hebrews. [10] They vindicated their nation, looking to God and enduring torture even to death."

[11] Truly the contest in which they were engaged was divine, [12] for on that day virtue gave the awards and tested them for their endurance. The prize was immortality in endless life. [13] Eleazar was the first contestant, the mother of the seven sons entered the competition, and the brothers contended. [14] The tyrant was the antagonist, and the world and the human race were the spectators. [15] Reverence for God was victor and gave the crown to its own athletes. [16] Who did not admire the athletes of the divine[c] legislation? Who were not amazed? [17] The tyrant himself and all his council marveled at their[d] endurance, [18] because

of which they now stand before the divine throne and live the life of eternal blessedness. [19] For Moses says, "All who are consecrated are under your hands." [20] These, then, who have been consecrated for the sake of God,[e] are honored, not only with this honor, but also by the fact that because of them our enemies did not rule over our nation, [21] the tyrant was punished, and the homeland purified—they having become, as it were, a ransom for the sin of our nation. [22] And through the blood of those devout ones and their death as an atoning sacrifice, divine Providence preserved Israel that previously had been mistreated.

[23] For the tyrant Antiochus, when he saw the courage of their virtue and their endurance under the tortures, proclaimed them to his soldiers as an example for their own endurance, [24] and this made them brave and courageous for infantry battle and siege, and he ravaged and conquered all his enemies.

18 O Israelite children, offspring of the seed of Abraham, obey this law and exercise piety in every way, [2] knowing that devout reason is master of all emotions, not only of sufferings from within, but also of those from without.

---

[a] Gk For your childbearing was from Abraham the father; other ancient authorities read For … Abraham the servant
[b] Or as a memorial to the heroes of our people
[c] Other ancient authorities read true
[d] Other ancient authorities add virtue and
[e] Other ancient authorities lack for the sake of God

(see also 12.19) was considered noble (1 Sam 31.1–6; 2 Macc 14.41–46; Josephus, J.W. 7.324–34, 377; Plutarch, Mor. 253D-E). **5:** The hearers are invited to imagine the martyrs enjoying their eternal reward, confirming their hope.

17.7–18.24: Epilogue. 17.7–18.5: Summary of the martyrs' accomplishments and exhortation. 17.7: Jurists were known to bring a painting of the crime into a courtroom to sway a jury's emotions (Quintilian, Inst. 6.1.32), although the author does not regard this as possible here, whether because of scruples about images (Ex 20.4) or good taste. Religion, better "piety." **8–10:** Literary epitaphs often appear in Greek speeches about the dead. **11–16:** See 6.10n. **20–22:** The martyrs' deaths are ennobled further by stressing the benefit they brought to their nation (see also 1.11; 18.4). **19:** Deut 33.3. **21–22:** Atoning sacrifice translates the Greek "hilasterion" (perhaps better "propitiation"), a term also used in Rom 3.25 to interpret the significance of a violent death in obedience to God's covenant. See 6.28–29n. **23–24:** The idea of becoming an example that even one's enemies would recognize and admire appears elsewhere; while historically improbable in this case, it is nevertheless rhetorically effective. Ravaged and conquered, a rhetorical flourish meant to underscore the power of the martyrs' example of courage. In fact, Antiochus suffered crushing defeat in the East shortly after leaving Jerusalem (see 1 Macc 6.1–4; 2 Macc 9.1), as 18.5 implies. **18.1–2:** The philosophical demonstration (18.2) ultimately serves a protreptic goal, namely promoting continued or intensified commitment to the Jewish way of life, particular the commandments of the Torah. An exhortation to imitate the virtuous conduct of the fallen is common in eulogistic speeches.

[3] Therefore those who gave over their bodies in suffering for the sake of religion were not only admired by mortals, but also were deemed worthy to share in a divine inheritance. [4] Because of them the nation gained peace, and by reviving observance of the law in the homeland they ravaged the enemy. [5] The tyrant Antiochus was both punished on earth and is being chastised after his death. Since in no way whatever was he able to compel the Israelites to become pagans and to abandon their ancestral customs, he left Jerusalem and marched against the Persians.

[6] The mother of seven sons expressed also these principles to her children: [7] "I was a pure virgin and did not go outside my father's house; but I guarded the rib from which woman was made.[a] [8] No seducer corrupted me on a desert plain, nor did the destroyer, the deceitful serpent, defile the purity of my virginity. [9] In the time of my maturity I remained with my husband, and when these sons had grown up their father died. A happy man was he, who lived out his life with good children, and did not have the grief of bereavement. [10] While he was still with you, he taught you the law and the prophets. [11] He read to you about Abel slain by Cain, and Isaac who was offered as a burnt offering, and about Joseph in prison. [12] He told you of the zeal of Phinehas, and he taught you about Hananiah, Azariah, and Mishael in the fire.

[13] He praised Daniel in the den of the lions and blessed him. [14] He reminded you of the scripture of Isaiah, which says, 'Even though you go through the fire, the flame shall not consume you.' [15] He sang to you songs of the psalmist David, who said, 'Many are the afflictions of the righteous.' [16] He recounted to you Solomon's proverb, 'There is a tree of life for those who do his will.' [17] He confirmed the query of Ezekiel, 'Shall these dry bones live?' [18] For he did not forget to teach you the song that Moses taught, which says, [19] 'I kill and I make alive: this is your life and the length of your days.'"

[20] O bitter was that day—and yet not bitter—when that bitter tyrant of the Greeks quenched fire with fire in his cruel caldrons, and in his burning rage brought those seven sons of the daughter of Abraham to the catapult and back again to more[b] tortures, [21] pierced the pupils of their eyes and cut out their tongues, and put them to death with various tortures. [22] For these crimes divine justice pursued and will pursue the accursed tyrant. [23] But the sons of Abraham with their victorious mother are gathered together into the chorus of the fathers, and have received pure and immortal[c] souls from God, [24] to whom be glory forever and ever. Amen.

---

a   Gk *the rib that was built*
b   Other ancient authorities read *to all his*
c   Other ancient authorities read *victorious*

18.6–19: The mother's testimony to feminine virtue and additional exhortation. This second speech of the mother is possibly a later addition, but nevertheless one well crafted to suit the larger text. 7–9a: Though celebrated mainly for her courage, the mother here reflects on her careful preservation throughout her life of her modesty and chastity, quintessential female virtues in the ancient world. 7: *Rib*, Gen 2.22. 8: *Desert plain*, Deut 22.25–27. *Serpent*, Gen 3.13; cf. 2 Cor 11.2–3. 10: The father laudably fulfilled the obligations to teach his children (Deut 4.9; 6.7; 11.19) the scriptures (*the law and the prophets*). 11: As *Abel* was attacked by *Cain* (Gen 4.8), so the ungodly continue to assault the pious. *Isaac*, Gen 22.1–19. *Joseph* endured prison rather than transgress virtue (Gen 39.1–23). 12a: *Phinehas* exemplified zeal for the Torah and watchfulness against assimilation (Num 25.1–9; Sir 45.23–24; 1 Macc 2.26, 54). 12b: *Hananiah . . . Daniel*, see 13.9n. 14–19: The quotations from scripture encourage perseverance in hardship for the sake of covenant loyalty. 14: Isa 43.2. The firm conviction in an afterlife allows the promise to remain true in an ultimate sense. 15: Ps 34.19. The context may be important and assumed, as the constant refrain of this psalm speaks of God's deliverance of the righteous from every trial (Ps 34.4, 6, 7, 17, 19). 16: Prov 3.18, slightly altered. 17: Ezek 37.2–3, as appropriate a question in Ezekiel's valley as in the courtyard where the tortures occurred. Even those who were "burned to the very bones" (6.26) will not fail to enjoy God's reward. 18: *Song*, Deut 31.30–32.44. 19: Deut 32.39; 30.20. The word order is crucial and climactic: God will *make alive* those righteous whom he has permitted to be killed. *Length of your days* is now transferred to eternity.

18.20–24: Conclusion. 18.20: Speaking of a *tyrant of the Greeks* is a bitterly ironic criticism of the imperialism of Alexander the Great and his successors, since the Greeks prized themselves on perfecting democracy. 22–24: The fates after death of martyrs and tyrant, foundational to the martyrs' resistance, are here confirmed in the author's closing sentences. Now the *chorus* (see 8.4n.) is in heaven.